Teaching Science for All Children

Teaching Science for All Children
An Inquiry Approach

fifth edition

Ralph Martin
Ohio University

Colleen Sexton
Governors State University

Teresa Franklin
Ohio University

with

Jack Gerlovich
Drake University

and

Dennis McElroy
Graceland University

PEARSON

Boston • New York • San Francisco
Mexico City • Montreal • Toronto • London • Madrid • Munich • Paris
Hong Kong • Singapore • Tokyo • Cape Town • Sydney

Series Editor: Kelly Villella Canton
Editorial Assistant: Christine Swayne
Marketing Manager: Darcy Betts
Production Editor: Janet Domingo
Editorial Production Service: Nesbitt Graphics, Inc.
Composition Buyer: Linda Cox
Manufacturing Buyer: Megan Cochran
Electronic Composition: Nesbitt Graphics, Inc.
Interior Design: Denise Hoffman
Photo Researcher: Annie Pickert
Cover Administrator: Joel Gendron

For related titles and support materials, visit our online catalog at www.pearsonhighered.com

Between the time website information is gathered and then published, it is not unusual for some sites to have closed. Also, the transcription of URLs can result in typographical errors. The publisher would appreciate notification where these errors occur so that they may be corrected in subsequent editions.

Library of Congress Cataloging-in-Publication Data
Teaching science for all children : an inquiry approach.-- 5th ed. / Ralph
Martin ... [et al.].
     p. cm.
  ISBN 0-205-59491-3
  1. Science--Study and teaching. 2. Science--Study and teaching
(Elementary) 3. Activity programs in education. I. Martin, Ralph E., 1951-
  Q181.T3534 2008
  372.35'044--dc22

                                                                                    2008004891

Printed in the United States of America

10 9 8 7 6 5 4 3 2 [RRD-MO] 12 11 10 09

Credits appear on page C-1, which constitutes an extension of the copyright page.

Allyn and Bacon
is an imprint of

www.pearsonhighered.com

ISBN-13: 978-0-205-59491-7
ISBN-10: 0-205-59491-3

For Jon and all things mechanical, may his future be bright. For Jen and her passion for No Child Left Inside. For Jess and her progress along a pathway of becoming a remarkable teacher. —R. M.

My work on this book is dedicated to Al Pogge from Quincy College for sharing his passion for science, to Leon Zalewski from Governors State University for sharing his passion for good science teaching, and to Ralph Martin from Ohio University for showing me how to put both together into a career I love. Thanks to all of you. Special thanks to Sarah, Celeste, and Jimmy for their love and understanding as I worked on this edition. —C. S.

To the men in my life, Doug and Matt, who constantly remind me that life is indeed an adventure! —T. F.

To the elementary science methods and science safety students at Drake University, for their tolerance and their inspiration. —J. G.

To the students who will soon be teachers and to their students who will benefit from these experiences. To Jack for reigniting my passion for science. —D. M.

About the Authors

Dr. Ralph Martin is Professor of Science Education at Ohio University, Athens, OH. During his 35 years as an educator, he has taught science lessons and led projects spanning K–16. His research and scholarship has produced more than 15 books and manuals (various editions) and netted millions in funding for teacher professional development in science and math. He has received numerous Ohio and national awards in recognition of his teaching and leadership and has coordinated, directed, and chaired many university programs and faculty units. Presently he serves as Chair of the Science Review Board for the *Ohio Resource Center for Mathematics, Science and Reading* (www.ohiorc.org) and is Co-Director of the *South East Ohio Center for Excellence in Mathematics and Science* (www.seocems.org), which conducts research, provides professional development programs, and supports educational improvement efforts focused on Appalachia Ohio.

Dr. Teresa Franklin is an Associate Professor in Instructional Technology at Ohio University, Athens, OH. Her love of teaching and learning through the integration of technology in the K–12 and higher education curriculum spans thirty years. As a science teacher in 1979, she began to use computers in her middle school Life Science and Earth Science lessons to help students gather data and solve problems. Teresa has served on the Ohio Technology Academic Content Standards Committee and the International Society for Technology in Education–National Educational Technology Standards for Teachers writing committee. Research interests include the integration of technology within the science curriculum, virtual environments for learning, handheld technologies in the classroom, and online course development.

Dr. Colleen Sexton is an Associate Professor of Science Education at Governors State University, University Park, IL. She is the Academic Director of the South Suburban Consortium for Grow Your Own Illinois Teachers. This initiative is designed to provide a college degree to teacher candidates committed to teaching in traditionally hard-to-staff school districts. She has a special interest in Environmental Education and effective Integration of Educational Technology in the classroom. She has traveled to Turkey and Cyprus to deliver professional development in science education to K–8 teachers and to present keynote addresses at International Technology Conferences on the effective use of educational technology tools in science classrooms. Prior to GSU she was an Associate Professor and Secondary Education Coordinator at Ohio University in Athens, OH. Dr. Sexton also served for four years as the Program Manager for the Ohio SchoolNet Plus Initiative. This $495M initiative was designed to provide one interactive workstation in the classroom for every five

children throughout Ohio's K–5 classrooms. While with Ohio SchoolNet she was also directly responsible for the professional development opportunities for the interactive video projects. From 1988–1996 Dr. Sexton served as instructor and then as an Assistant Professor for the College of Education at Ohio University, serving as Curriculum Director for the Appalachian Distance Learning Project — a 3rd grade interactive video pilot. Her K–12 experience includes eight years of high school science teaching in the Chicago area and one year of teaching introductory biology at the community college level. Her research areas include the use of handhelds in higher education, the integration of educational technology into the science curriculum, and teacher dispositions in an online learning environment.

Authors of Chapter 10:
How Can You Design and Manage a Safe Inquiry-Based Science Classroom?

Dr. Jack A. Gerlovich is Levvitt Distinguished Professor of science/education/safety at Drake University. A Levvitt Professor must exemplify the qualities of "effective consulting, research, teaching, mentoring, and relationship-building." He is the author or coauthor of seven books, thirty state and national journal articles, and two national and fifteen customized state software/CD-ROM programs on science safety. During his thirty-plus years in education, he has served as the State Science Supervisor for the Iowa Department of Education and as a science teacher at all levels of education. At Drake University, he teaches classes in Issues in Foundations of American Education (elementary, secondary, and graduate levels), Elementary Science Methods, and Science Safety. He has conducted nearly 200 science safety workshops throughout the nation; served as an expert witness in court cases involving science safety issues; assisted industry, government, and education as a safety consultant; and developed training programs and software/CD-ROM packages customized to individual state needs. He was also certified by the U.S. Department of Transportation, Safety Institute and the Iowa Office of Disaster Services, for successful completion of the Hazardous Materials Emergency Services Workshop. He also completed the National Institute for Occupational Safety and Health (NIOSH) and the Council of State Science Supervisors (CSSS) 16-hour Occupational Safety & Health course in Safety in the School Science Laboratory. Having been a commercially licensed, multiengine rated pilot for several years, he is also conscious of being safe and prepared.

Dr. Dennis McElroy is an Assistant Professor of Education at Graceland University and does science safety consulting with JaKel, Inc. He has also served as Graceland's Vice-President for Information Services, Educational Technologist at Drake University's School of Education, and Technology Consultant for the Iowa Department of Education. Dennis is on the National Science Teacher's Association Safety Board. He previously taught science at the high school level in Kansas, Arizona, and Iowa.

Contents

chapter 3 How Can You Improve Science Learning for Diverse Learners? 62

chapter 6 How Can You Use Questions to Foster Scientific Inquiry? 160

chapter 11   What Materials and Resources Promote Inquiry-Based Science?   314

part two
Learning Cycle Inquiry Lessons for Teaching Science   345

Lessons and Activities to Meet the NSE Standards for Elementary and Middle School Science

section 1 Life Science Lessons   346

section II   Physical Science Lessons   406

section III Earth and Space Science Lessons 466

Preface

How do children learn most effectively, and what can you do to extend their learning? The answer to these questions does not necessarily reside in how you would answer the same question about yourself. However, the answers are provided by a rich and abundant base of research that is used to guide the choices made while preparing the fifth edition of *Teaching Science for All Children: An Inquiry Approach.*

Our mission is to help you understand the importance of teaching in ways that learners prefer to learn and to help you use the National Science Education Standards (NSES) and National Education Technology Standards (NETS) in effective and natural ways so that you can help all of your learners excel in learning science and benefiting from it. This textbook will help you to do this in a seamless way, with interactive pedagogy and multimedia features. Each chapter contains a number of learning tools to help you access the relevant research, see classroom teaching examples, learn from the voices of experienced teachers, and think deeply about your chosen profession—all within the context of modern science and standards.

We feature many teaching skills and methods, but most important is our robust learning cycle model for planning, teaching, and learning, which is featured in each chapter. While there are many effective ways to teach and learn science, one of the most effective and enduring is a learning cycle. Our learning cycle lessons feature an **engaging question** to draw learners into a cyclic inquiry. **Exploration** activities are carefully planned to draw out the full nature of science, which blends seamlessly into **explanation**, a phase that uses thoughtful interaction to guide learners toward concept construction. Every lesson contains **expansion** activities, which help to overcome potential misconceptions that may linger and to address seriously the challenging new dimensions of the science content standards. **Evaluation** supports each phase of the cycle, which develops positive attitudes toward science, skillful uses of science processes, and clear conceptual understandings. As verified by numerous sources of science education and brain research, experience is an important foundation for the processes of inquiry if a learner is to be successful in making meaning out of the unique experiences that science can provide. Our learning cycle is rooted in a history of substantial research, which supports that using the learning cycle approach has improved student science achievement and development of process skills.

The text provides, in short, an opportunity to experience the nature of science by applying the methods and techniques described in Part One, "Inquiry Methods for Teaching Science," to the standards-based lessons offered in Part Two, "Learning Cycle Inquiry Lessons for Teaching Science."

New to This Edition

Organization

Part One consists of Chapters 1–11, the sequence being organized to fit the flow of most courses, beginning with the nature of science, children and learning, special needs, planning, teaching, assessment, questioning, integrated learning, uses of technology, safety, and resources for best practice. Part Two consists of learning cycle lessons and is organized into three science disciplines: *Life, Physical,* and *Earth and Space*. Each lesson integrates the additional National Science Education Standards disciplines of *Science in Personal and Social Perspective, Science and Technology, Science as Inquiry,* and *History and Nature of Science*. Icons are placed in the margins throughout the book to reveal clear alignment with science and technology standards. Lessons and chapters are written to stand independently and may be used in any sequence.

Pedagogy

Each chapter is titled in a question form and begins with *Focus Questions. What Research Says* features highlight the research base for each chapter, and *Teachers on Science Teaching* features illuminate the ways in which research is put into practice. One or more *Learning Cycle Featured Lessons* are placed in each chapter to help learners build a deeper understanding of inquiry as neophytes grow through its special challenges and benefits. At the end of each chapter, *Reflect and Respond* questions afford numerous opportunities for extending campus inquiry efforts. *MyEducationLab* is an interactive multimedia feature that extends the inquiry processes from campus into schools. All features are found in each chapter. All features support inquiry processes as learners experience the text.

Chapters

- Chapter 1, "What Is the Nature of Science?," expands its coverage of this topic, which affords learners a clear understanding of the importance of standards and serves as a foundation for the entire text. Children's perceptions of science and their achievement provide an urgent rationale for thinking carefully about what should be taught in schools.

- Chapter 2, "How Do Children Learn Science?," uses a cognitive constructivist process to guide readers toward understandings about the roles of brain research, cognition, theory, and social interaction. The work of Lev Vygotsky is new to this chapter, and learners are exposed to a learning cycle model that is used consistently throughout the chapters.

- Chapter 3, "How Can You Improve Science Learning for Diverse Learners?," examines the benefits, liabilities, processes, and accommodations for helping all learners to make meaning from essential experiences. The chapter is rich with tips for celebrating and including diversity in instruction.

- Chapter 4, "How Do You Plan for the Inquiry-Based Classroom?," helps readers to develop skills for making and using concept maps to make decisions for planning. The emphasis on lesson planning is focused on addressing the issues of inquiry through a learning cycle.

- Chapter 5, "What Inquiry Methods Help Learners to Construct Understanding?," provides an array of teaching methods for using inquiry. Methods may be used independently or in combination.

- Chapter 6, "How Can You Use Questions to Foster Scientific Inquiry?," helps readers to understand and compose better questions and use them more effectively as well to as embrace children's questions and help students to ask better questions as they learn to inquire.

- Chapter 7, "How Do You Develop and Use Authentic Assessment?," aligns a variety of evaluation tools to inquiry and provides numerous examples to help readers develop and use more effective assessments.

- Chapter 8, "How Do You Integrate Technology That Enriches Science Learning?," draws on national technology standards to focus on using digital technologies to improve science process skills and provides tools for selecting the most appropriate resources.

- Chapter 9, "How Do You Plan for and Integrate Science with Other Disciplines?," provides two clear models for achieving effective integrated teaching and learning.

- Chapter 10, "How Can You Design and Manage a Safe Inquiry-Based Classroom?," is rich in ways to address the legal demands of science teaching. Ranging from early grades through middle school, readers will find many tools for practicing science safely, including physical science, animals and plants, field trips, and classroom safety audits.

- Chapter 11, "What Materials and Resources Promote Inquiry-Based Science?," focuses on identifying and using resources for best practice in science, including web-based, community, and human resources.

Lessons

Part Two provides more than sixty complete lessons distributed across the Life, Physical, and Earth and Space disciplines. Each lesson has been redesigned and edited for easier use, with more emphasis on materials and classroom management. Each lesson is a complete learning cycle and begins its inquiry with an engaging question. All activity within a lesson is focused on helping learners to discover a central concept of science and expanding their understanding of it. All lessons have clear correlations with the National Science Education Content Standards.

Features of this Edition

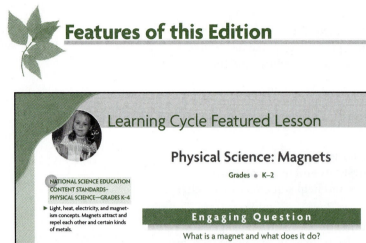

Learning Cycle Featured Lessons appear throughout each chapter in Part I, illustrating the 5-E method of teaching. Each lesson describes a hands-on, classroom-tested activity and includes images and student artifacts.

Teachers on Science Teaching

features authentic voices of practicing award winning teachers.

teachers on Science Teaching

How Can You Teach Science for All Children?

by Joan M. Yospin
Grade 5, Franklin Elementary School, Newton, Massachusetts

Science, more than any other subject, allows children to connect to their own lives, something that is essential to involvement, interest, and motivation. Beginning the school year with a study of some aspect of our planet—climate regions, topographical features, oceans, rivers, ponds, or forests—lets children connect their own lives to the greater environment. Some have visited   to the city

students copy words from the board and discuss the vocabulary at home with their parents. All students keep an "interactive notebook," or science journal, where they record ideas and vocabulary that are discussed in class. The left side of the page is for the student's own use of symbols, drawings, or words that will help them to remember the vo-   itten on the right si

what Research Says

Teaching Students Who Have Exceptionalities

Who has the wisdom and ability to predict which of our students will succeed and which will not? People who have disabilities are often erroneously thought to be mentally deficient, but the prevailing social attitude has slowly changed. Thanks to federal laws, inclusion, and local school efforts to service better   of children are

The lack of development of a basic science curriculum from kindergarten to the twelfth grade is a national disgrace and one that puts the deaf child at a disadvantage in comparison to the nonhandicapped child. Furthermore, these students are still being pushed into stereotyped job roles and dead-   male students it is even worse

What Research Says boxes offer brief accounts of the latest research on the most current topics in the field.

Reflect and Respond are

questions located at the end of each chapter to help you to think critically about the concepts you have just learned.

reflect and respond

1. What arguments support using inquiry science teaching methods? What barriers seem to limit the acceptance and use of inquiry in elementary classrooms? Will you use some of the methods described in this chapter? Why or why not?

2. What are the similarities and differences in the approaches described in this chapter? Under what circumstances would you favor any one approach over the others?

4. Inquiry methods tend to promote greater independence among learners. What are several things you can do to help students become more independent learners?

5. Inquiry teaching strives to accommodate individual student differences. Individual differences do, however, tend to complicate teaching. What are some things you could

Chapter Summaries concisely review the major concepts in the chapter for a quick recap or to help you study.

MyEducationLab boxes, organized around the learning cycle framework, direct students to access classroom video and weblinks to complete activities and better apply what they learn to practice.

NSES and ISTE-NETS Marginal Icons

indicate when text discussion relates to important National Science Education Standards and National Educational Technology Standards.

For the purpose of this text the icons use the following abbreviations in the icon references to reflect the various types of standards.

NSES
TS-D

ISTE-NETS
1, 2, 4

NSES Assessment Standards A-E	AS-A, AS-B, AS-C, AS-D, AS-E
NSES Content Standards A-G	CS-A, CS-B, etc.
NSES Professional Development Standards A-D	PD-A, PD-B, PD-C, PD-D
NSES Teaching Standards A-F	TS-A, TS-B, etc.
NSES Program Standards A-F	PR-A, PR-B, etc.
NSES System Standards A-G	SS-A, SS-B, etc.
ISTE-NETS 1-6	ISTE-NETS 1, ISTE-NETS 2, etc.

Supplements

Instructor's Manual and Test Bank

Prepared by the authors and available for download by logging into the Instructor Resource Center (IRC) at www.pearsonhighered.com, this manual contains six parts:

- *Teaching Suggestions:* A model syllabus with assignment guides and grading rubrics for field experience, draw-a-scientist, concept mapping, learning cycle lesson planning, peer-taught demonstration lessons, self-analysis of teaching papers

- *Chapter Outlines:* Capsule descriptions of the material and concepts for each chapter; useful for lecture preparation

- *Test Item Bank:* Hundreds of test items allow instructors to customize quizzes and examinations.

- *Concept Maps:* Multiple uses as exemplars for each chapter, study guides, and presentation graphics

- *Transparency Masters:* PowerPoint files are included to print and use as handouts.

- *Powerpoint ® Slides:* Prepared by the authors, these presentation slides for each chapter include select figures and tables from this edition of the text. These slides are available for download by logging into the IRC.

Contact your local sales representative if you need assistance accessing supplements on IRC.

Your Class. Your Career. Everyone's Future.

PEARSON
myeducationlab
Where the Classroom Comes to Life

MyEducationLab at www.myeducationlab.com is a research-based learning tool that brings teaching to life. Through authentic in-class video footage, interactive simulations, rich case studies, examples of authentic teacher and student work, and more, MyEducationLab prepares you for your teaching career by showing what quality instruction looks like.

MyEducationLab is easy to use! At the end of every chapter in the textbook, you will find the MyEducationLab logo adjacent to activities and exercises that correlate material you've just read in the chapter to your reading/viewing of multimedia assets on the MyEducationLab site. These assets include:

- *Video:* The authentic classroom videos in MyEducationLab show how real teachers handle actual classroom situations.

- *Case Studies:* A diverse set of robust cases illustrate the realities of teaching and offer valuable perspectives on common issues and challenges in education.

- *Simulations:* Created by the IRIS Center at Vanderbilt University, these interactive simulations give you hands-on practice at adapting instruction for a full spectrum of learners.

- *Readings:* Specially selected, topically relevant articles from ASCD's renowned *Educational Leadership* journal expand and enrich your perspectives on key issues and topics.

- *Student & Teacher Artifacts:* Authentic preK-12 student and teacher classroom artifacts are tied to course topics and offer you practice in working with the actual types of materials you will encounter daily as teachers.

  Other Resources:

- *Lesson & Portfolio Builders:* With this effective and easy-to-use tool, you can create, update, and share standards-based lesson plans and portfolios.

Other Versions of This Text

For maximum flexibility, *Teaching Science for All Children: An Inquiry Approach* is also available in a compact, paperback volume including only the eleven methods chapters.

Teaching Science for All Children: Inquiry Methods for Constructing Understanding, Fourth Edition, provides methods for future teachers to foster awareness among their students of the nature of science; to implement skills in the classroom using science inquiry processes; and to develop in their students an understanding of the interactions among science, technology, and society. ISBN: 0-205-59351-8

Acknowledgments

In addition to our author team, many important people supported the project and turned our dreams and ideas into a reality. Indeed, it is an understatement to say we are grateful to these talented people.

We are indebted to Kelly Canton Villella, Allyn and Bacon's education editor, whose vision shaped the project into a comprehensive product, her able assistant Christine Swayne, who ensured first-class support at every stage of the publishing process, and production editor Janet Domingo.

Other support was provided by Al Coté. It is through some interesting conversations with him that we have come to think of science instruction differently.

Our special thanks go to the reviewers who offered substantial suggestions that helped shape the fifth edition. They are Lars J. Helgeson, University of North Dakota, Grand Forks; Ann Holliman-Krueger, Kansas State University; and Pamela Kramer, East Stroudsburg University.

Finally, we are grateful to our spouses, children, and parents for their encouragement, support, and understanding, especially during the tense moments that always accompany the deadlines for such a project. Knowing that we could help our children's teachers gave inspiration and helped to shape our mission. There will always be a special place in our hearts for Marilyn, Jennifer, Jessica, Jonathan, Sarah, Celeste, Doug, Matthew, Pat, Jacque, Kelly, Bill, and Doris.

Teaching Science for All Children

part one

Inquiry Methods for Teaching Science

What Is the Nature of Science?

focus questions

- How do children's perceptions of scientists influence the children's attitudes toward learning science?

- How do your school experiences match with the nature of science?

- How does the nature of science define the roles of teachers and learners?

- What new challenges and opportunities do the "new dimensions" of science provide teachers and learners? How may those opportunities be used to nurture scientific literacy for children?

One of Jessica's first assignments was to observe two different age levels of children. Her science methods course was designed to immerse her into teaching so that she could form several snapshots of science teaching and impressions about the factors that affect learning, then use these experiences as a platform for constructing the main concepts of the course. Jessica selected Dawn from the kindergarten class and Jorge from the fourth-grade class. She decided to shadow the two students and to record her observations about the types of things each child did while learning science. She also had discussions with the children and used her field notes to write a summary for her methods course portfolio. Here is her account:

Today Dawn's teacher asked why it is that some things float and other things sink. She encouraged the children to explore and discuss their ideas. Dawn played with a small plastic boat at the water table. I observed her push the boat down into the water until it filled and sank. Dawn did this several times, and then the teacher suggested that Dawn try some investigations with marbles and wooden buttons of a uniform size. Dawn spent about five minutes putting the marbles and buttons into the water and watched the marbles sink immediately and the buttons float. She pushed the buttons down into the water, released them, noting that they popped back to the surface each time. I suggested that she put the objects into the boat to see what would happen. Dawn put six buttons and six marbles into the boat, and the boat slowly began to take on water until it sank to the bottom with the buttons floating to the surface.

Dawn persisted by piling six marbles into the dry boat. The boat began to take on water, and Dawn quickly added the buttons. The marbles went down with the boat, and the buttons floated to the top. "Pop!" exclaimed Dawn for each button that jetted to the surface: "Pop! Pop! Pop! Pop! Pop!" Dawn continued to investigate the boat's sinking and floating with different numbers of marbles and buttons, and she returned to the water table after snack time to try different objects in the boat. Dawn mentioned that heavy things always sink, and she was pretty certain.

Jorge had missed some school because of illness, and the teacher asked me to "tutor" him in electricity so that he could catch up with the rest of the class. My heart raced because I knew nothing about electricity, but having observed earlier lessons on electricity, I gave it a try and asked Jorge what he thought it took to make a bulb light up. Jorge remembered the concept of "circuit" from a prior class. Today's challenge was to use a variety of materials to construct a flashlight: a cardboard tube, a bottle cap, metal paper fasteners, a metal paper clip, batteries, a couple of short wires, and a flashlight bulb. Jorge had to construct the flashlight using these materials and what he knew about circuits and make it work at least one time. He dove right in, but I felt the pressure. To me, the minutes turned into hours, and I wondered whether we would succeed. The task had become our project because Jorge was teaching me about conductors, insulators, and a series circuit. Jorge needed help putting the bulb in place and was a little frustrated because the parts and connectors kept slipping and loosening. Finally, when all was hooked up, Jorge turned the paper clip switch, and the bulb lit. "You did it!" I shouted, attracting the attention of the whole class. I was immediately embarrassed, but I couldn't help myself. The shouting came as a natural release for me and a nice reinforcement for Jorge. He beamed. The teacher didn't frown or scold us as I expected. Instead, she winked as if this type of reaction happened all the time in her class.

Before this field experience, I dreaded having to take a science teaching course. Science was not one of my favorite subjects, but I think I can already see that it is important, and the children seem to like it. I am aware now that asking a pertinent question can help children to explore, find evidence, and offer explanations for the questions. Thinking seems to improve when children are encouraged to communicate and justify their answers. I wonder, though, what kind of difference I can make. I don't feel confident or competent in science. What kinds of things should I do or teach to help children have a better impression of science than I had before I started this course?

Jessica's prior experience in science (or lack of experience) influenced her perspective, attitude, and self-confidence. Our perceptions, attitudes, and confidence influence our teaching decisions and what we expect from our students. Our expectations also influence how students will perform. Jessica's two questions are very fair. What kind of difference can one teacher make in a science program? What things should be emphasized in science classes? We suggest adding another question: What factors help to make effective lessons?

From Jessica's notes, we see that Dawn's and Jorge's teachers made a difference. Each child demonstrated interest and persisted with the task by reaching meaningful conclusions. Five-year-old Dawn explored the concepts of floating and sinking—at her own pace—and she demonstrated several important skills such as observing, comparing, and investigating. These skills helped her to form rudimentary conceptions of cause and effect as she began to accumulate some factual knowledge through play. Jorge appeared more systematic, had a firmer grasp on cause-and-effect relationships, and had a repertoire of scientific attitudes to help him persist with thorny problems. Most likely, Jorge had acquired and developed his attitudes and skills from an early science program and from teachers who had a clear vision of what students should know and be able to do in science. Both children benefited from teacher expectations and programs that were built upon a strong foundation of science teaching.

Both teachers followed five key actions to make their lessons effective. The teachers:

1. *engaged students* in the content with purposeful interaction,
2. *created conducive environments* that provided respectful and rigorous learning opportunities,
3. *ensured access* for all learners by adjusting instruction,
4. *used questioning* skillfully to promote and assess understanding,
5. *helped students to make sense* of their experiences by making intellectual connections among important science ideas (Weiss et al., 2003).

What is science? In this chapter, we explore answers to this crucial question and develop a strong foundation for understanding the challenges of teaching modern science by introducing you to:

1. children's perceptions of science and scientists as well as children's science achievement,
2. the real nature of science,
3. the essential characteristics of science that will help your lessons to become more investigative and interactive, and
4. the aims of standards and research-based reform in science education.

How Do Children Perceive Science?

Jessica's professor assigned her to interview children in the next school on her field experience rotation. She was to find out what they thought about science and scientists. The professor suggested that the insights that Jessica gained would help her to understand the children's readiness and needs and prepare her for the challenges that lay ahead.

Science Is . . .

Jessica obtained permission to interview children of different ages. She used the question "What is science?" Some children simply shrugged off the question or chose to talk about something else. Jessica presumed that was because they were unfamiliar with "real" science, given that little time, she had observed, was devoted to it. She reported to her professor a sample of her findings*:

> "Real hard. Harder than reading. We aren't allowed to have it in kindergarten." (Antonio—kindergarten)

> "The weatherman. He gets to choose the weather each day and he gets to color on the wall." (Mary Beth—kindergarten)

> "It [science] is what brainy people who know a lot do." (first grader)

---

*These replies are direct quotations from a sample of children (distributed across race and socioeconomic status) in urban and suburban settings when asked the question "What is science?" (Wagner, 1988) and from children interviewed by the authors' preservice teachers through 2007.

"After lunch sometimes when there is nothing else to do." (Shawna—grade 1)

"I don't think we have science yet. I'm not a good reader." (Jeremy—grade 1)

"Mostly rocks and leaves. We put them on a table." (Lyn—grade 1)

"Computers and moving things with buttons you push. Also, anything with batteries or that plugs in. Rockets are my favorite part of science." (Carl—grade 1)

"When you smoke cigarettes and get cancer it is because of science." (Nancy—grade 1)

"Children can't be scientists until they are older." (first grader)

"On TV sometimes. *NOVA* is my favorite." (Alex—grade 2)

"When you go up in the space shuttle and you are an astronaut. Girls can be astronauts too, you know. I'm going to be in science when I grow up. The only thing is—I don't know if I will have enough money to buy a space shuttle. You have to be rich to be an astronaut." (Andrea—grade 3)

"The opposite of social studies." (Luanne—grade 3)

"Children can be scientists, and *really* good ones, too!" (third grader)

"We just read a book. I think you get it [science] in middle school. My brother is in middle school, and he has science." (William—grade 3)

"The same old stuff. I've seen the same video on erosion three years in a row." (Joshua—grade 4)

"It depends on what grade you're in and who your teacher is. If a teacher doesn't like science, then you don't get it very much. Once when the principal was coming, Mrs.— did this experiment with a can and a candle and a balloon—but that was the only time." (Greg—grade 5)

"Supposed to be about learning how we learn about the world and how to use the scientific method in thinking. I know because my dad is a scientist and he keeps asking me when we're going to learn that in science. I just tell him that we haven't gotten to it yet." (Doreen—grade 6)

Jessica pored over the messages and wrote a summary to report back to her methods class. Jessica was not certain how much she could generalize from the interviews. The children described science as something that usually was not given much time in the primary grades and was reserved for the more advanced grades or when children could read well. Children also had several misconceptions about what science is and isn't; for example, one child opined that science is responsible for causing disease or illness. Overall, the children did not seem to value science or perceive it as useful. Some thought it was repetitive or something to be watched and implied that teachers used it as a time filler or might not have felt comfortable or prepared to teach it adequately. On the positive side, Jessica noted that some children viewed science as a career opportunity for women, though access to science careers was believed to be limited, and some parents expected the science curriculum to help the children develop important cognitive skills.

Scientists Are . . .

When Jessica's professor urged her to probe a bit more into the values and stereotypes the children revealed, she decided to try the Draw-A-Scientist Test (Barman, 1996), which she had read about in several articles. This test was simple; it required only that she ask students to draw a picture of a scientist without prompting the students to do the drawing in any particular way. Jessica selected a new sample of students and hoped to get a fresh, unbiased perception. She collected dozens of drawings and compared them to find similarities. Then she selected two to put into her science methods class portfolio.

The first drawing (Figure 1.1) illustrates a composite view and was a common perception among several drawings. Jessica wrote in her summary: "Children think that scientists are middle-aged, white males who wear lab coats and glasses. Their facial features are indicative of their generally deranged behavior. They work indoors, alone, perhaps underground, surrounded by smoking test tubes and other pieces of technology. An air of secrecy and danger surrounds their work" (Flick, 1989, p. 8; Barman and Ostlund, 1996).

Jessica based her summary on the fact that most scientists were depicted as white males (Barman, 1997; Finson, 2002). Overall, only about 8 percent of the scientists were drawn as female—not close to the reality of the 24 percent of women in the engineering and scientific workforce (AIP, 2002). Only 1 percent of the students drew minority scientists, mostly African Americans; actually, 11% of scientists and engineers are Asian, and as a group, African Americans, Hispanics, and Native Americans, constituted 7% of the science and engineering workforce in 1999 (AIP, 2002). When they drew the scientists, the children reached back into their own experiences. Some drew the scientist by race and gender as a self-image (though this was rare); some took their images from television and movies; some were honoring a significant person who had affected them; and, of course, some knew only the general stereotype that is perceived to fit the look of most scientists (Sumrall, 1995). However, only a small number were drawn as fictional characters (Barman, 1997).

FIGURE 1.1 ● Children's Perception of a Scientist

After more than 50 years of studying drawings of scientists, we know from Kevin Finson's (2002) review of the literature that children of both genders overwhelmingly draw pictures depicting male scientists; the images of scientists (as middle-aged white males) have remained consistent across racial groups; the barrage of media (mostly in the form of television and children's literature) reinforces stereotypical images of scientists; stereotyped images extend across age groups, grade levels, and decades of time; early childhood and elementary education majors typically fail to recognize the problem of stereotyped scientists and do not have an understanding of "what a scientist is"; and teachers can make a positive impact on children's perceptions by connecting children with scientists through classroom visitations, field trips, careful selection of media and images of scientists, strategic discussions about who scientists are and what they do, and examples illustrating how science is helpful.

Jessica was now curious about why the children held these particular attitudes and beliefs about science and scientists and how the children's perceptions might reflect the beliefs of others, such as teachers. As she reflected on her findings, she decided to try to see a snapshot of the field of science teaching. Given all of the research and attention placed on improving science programs and teaching over the past several years, Jessica was motivated to ask what changes have occurred in elementary science.

What Changes Have Occurred in Elementary Science?

For more than thirty five years the National Assessment of Educational Progress (NAEP) has been the only continuing assessment of U.S. children's achievement in grades K–12. This test was mandated by the U.S. Congress and attempted to measure what students know and how they perform against agreed on expectations in science and other subject areas. NAEP scores denote three levels of student performance: (1) *Basic*—partial mastery of knowledge and skills that are fundamental for performing proficient work at each grade; (2) *Proficient*—solid academic performance over challenging subject matter, application to real-world situations, and ability to use appropriate analytical skills, and (3) *Advanced*—superior performance. NAEP science tests use multiple-choice and constructed-response questions and hands-on tasks to measure knowledge and performance of three science themes: systems, models, and patterns of

NSES
AS-E

change. For a simple way to locate and examine NAEP items, go to www.ohiorc.org. Enter "NAEP" into the Search Resources tool.

The test has changed over time, and longitudinal comparisons across 25 years of test scores are not possible. Comparisons of prior tests using the "old forms" revealed substantial increases in achievement during times of active experimentation with science curricula and decreases in scores during the "back to basics" era of the late 1970s and early 1980s. The following list shows the changes in science according to *The Nation's Report Card: Science 2005* (National Center for Education Statistics, 2006):

Fourth Grade Results Since 1996:

- Most states showed no significant improvement; however, five of the thirty-seven participating states did improve.
- Average achievement scores increased for all groups: white, black, and Hispanic.
- The percentage of student performing at or above the Basic achievement level increased from 63% in 1996 to 68% in 2005.
- Students who scored below the Basic level were 32% white, 30% black, 32% Hispanic, 3% Asian/Pacific Islander, 2% American Indian/Alaska Native; 67% eligible for free/reduced price lunch; 42% central city schools.
- Students who scored above the Proficient level were 91% white, 4% black, 7% Hispanic, 6% Asian/Pacific Islanders, 1% American Indian/Alaska Native; 17% eligible for free/reduced price lunch; 25% central city schools.
- The average scores for males and females have increased since 2000.
- The lowest-performing students and low-income students made the largest gains.
- Achievement gaps between whites and blacks have decreased steadily since 1996.
- Achievement gaps between whites and Hispanics have decreased since 2000.

Eighth Grade Results Since 1996:

- Most states showed no significant improvement; however, five of the thirty-seven participating states did improve.
- Scores in Physical Science declined.
- Overall, for eighth grade, there was no improvement for whites and Hispanics since 1996 and no improvement since 2000 for blacks.
- 59% of the students scored at or above Basic level.
- Achievement gaps between whites, blacks, and Hispanics have remained unchanged since 1996.
- Students from lower-income families gained in average achievement, gaining over the losses shown in 2000.
- Students who scored below the Basic level were 39% white, 29% black, 25% Hispanic, 4% Asian/Pacific Islander, 2% American Indian/Alaska Native; 56% eligible for free/reduced price lunch; 20% report always speaking a language other than English in the home.
- Students who scored above the Proficient level were 83% white, 4% black, 6% Hispanic, 5% Asian/Pacific Islanders, 1% American Indian/Alaska Native; 16% eligible for free/reduced price lunch; 7% report always speaking a language other than English in the home.

Teaching and Learning

The Center on Education Policy (Dillon, 2007) reports disturbing trends that may depress achievement scores even more. In the wake of No Child Left Behind (NCLB) and mandatory testing in reading and mathematics, nearly half of the nation's school districts report less teaching time for science—75 fewer minutes per week—while reading time was increased to 140 minutes per week, and math received 87 additional minutes. Besides decreased time for instruction, declining science scores are affected by additional factors.

An independent national study of K–12 science education in the United States offers insight that may help to explain why more children do not score higher on the national assessment. This study also may help us to understand better the key factors necessary to improve teaching and learning.

Led by Iris Weiss and colleagues (2003) of Horizon Research, numerous teams of researchers observed more than 360 lessons in mathematics and science. On the basis of findings from this national sample, only 15 percent of the observed lessons were judged to be of high quality and 27 percent of medium quality; 59 percent were low quality. Low-quality lessons are unlikely to help students understand important science concepts or to develop essential skills in doing science. High-quality lessons are planned with structure, taught in a manner that engage children with important concepts, and strive to help learners construct meaning and connect their understandings in ways that develop their capacity to do science successfully. High-quality teaching will stimulate powerful learning over time. High-quality lessons will

NSES
TS-E

- include content that is significant and worthwhile (standards-based),
- be taught with confidence and accuracy,
- require strong intellectual rigor,
- use skillful teacher questioning to enhance conceptual understanding, and
- emphasize sense-making that is appropriate for the learners and the purposes of the lesson.

The second drawing of a scientist that Jessica put in her portfolio appealed to her for its special message (Figure 1.2). A female student who had drawn a picture of her younger brother explained: "This is my brother and I think he is a scientist. He is very curious, like this time when he threw our cat down the stairs. He always wants to know why things work and what will happen when he tries a new idea." Jessica doubted that the sister was advocating violence or cruelty toward animals. Rather, her remarks seem to suggest that the brother was following his natural curiosity. This caused Jessica to ponder what science is and what it means to "do" science.

FIGURE 1.2 ● **Children as Scientists** Children are great examples of scientists. Their curiosity motivates them to act on their ideas. With appropriate guidance, children "make discoveries."

The Nature of Science

NSES
CS-G

The word *science* originates from the Latin word *scientia,* meaning "knowledge," as in possessing knowledge instead of misunderstanding or being ignorant. In fact, one of the authors distinctly remembers having to memorize a definition from a junior high textbook (long since forgotten, along with almost everything else in it!) that defined science as an "organized body of knowledge." Following that were the steps of the scientific method, also to be memorized: (1) identify the problem, (2) examine the data, (3) form a hypothesis, (4) experiment, and (5) make a conclusion. Textbook definitions and memory exercises are helpful only to a point in learning *about* how some of the ideas of science were developed, a process that was often the subject of large posters adorning walls in science classrooms.

Eventually, most science classrooms abandoned the posters and the scientific method as something to be memorized, perhaps because the mechanistic certainty of the steps did not reveal the true nature of science, its history, and its implications for society. For example, George deMestral did not set out to invent Velcro. However, he was curious about why some burrs stuck so tightly to his clothing (Roberts, 1989). By recognizing that the commonplace provided an important insight, deMestral developed a product that has a wide range of uses. Charles Townes too saw the commonplace in a special way, and his vision helped him to invent the laser. He said: "The laser was born one beautiful spring morning on a park bench in Washington, D.C. As I sat in Franklin Square, musing and admiring the azaleas, an idea came to me for a practical way to obtain a very pure form of electromagnetic waves from molecules" (Roberts, 1989, p. 82). Who among us does not use Velcro in some way? And consider how much the laser has changed whole fields: medicine, electronics, merchandising, and defense among many others. These examples of serendipities—accidental discoveries made possible by a mind receptive to scientific thinking—are typical of many sudden breakthroughs in science and help us to understand that not all of what is learned through science is orderly and predictable. Robert Hazen and James Trefil help us to see this a bit more clearly:

> There is a temptation, when presenting a subject as complex as the natural sciences, to present topics in a rigid, mathematical outline. . . . In the first place, it does not reflect the way science is actually performed. Real science, like any human activity, tends to be a little messy around the edges. More important, the things you need to know to be scientifically literate tend to be a somewhat mixed bag. You need to know some facts, to be familiar with some general concepts, to know a little about how science works and how it comes to conclusions, and to know a little about scientists as people. All of these things may affect how you interpret the news of the day. . . . Finally, . . . [science] is just plain fun—not just "good for you" like some foul-tasting medicine. It grew out of observations of everyday experience by thousands of our ancestors, most of whom actually enjoyed what they were doing. (Hazen & Trefil, 1992, p. xix)

Science naturally stimulates positive attitudes, enhances inquiry skills, and elevates understanding of our natural world.

A definition or a description does not always give a sufficient impression of what science is and how science should be taught for maximum effect. Consider Jessica's recollections of her classroom experiences with science and its effects on her. It seems fair to assume that Jessica's teachers carried an image and feeling about science that contributed to their beliefs and affected their teaching of science. This teaching then influenced Jessica's beliefs. And when Jessica teaches, she will continue the cycle by influencing her own students' beliefs. Perhaps this is not a desirable picture when you consider the influence Jessica could have on children—that is, *before* she acquired new impressions about science.

How does a child receive information, construct knowledge, and gain meaning from what is experienced and in a way that reveals the true nature of science? Hazen and Trefil's view of science offers some useful clues for answering this question. From their description, we may infer that human curiosity is important and that certain types of mental and physical skills are needed for learning: skills for acquiring useful information that has practical value and carries real meaning for learners, meaning that is constructed from the learners' experiences. This description of science is amplified by *Project 2061*'s careful description of the nature of science through the scientific worldview, scientific inquiry, and scientific enterprise (http://www.project2061.org/publications/sfaa/online/chap1.htm). Very succinctly, the nature of science consists of the following:

The Scientific Worldview

- **The world is understandable,** and its patterns can be discovered.
- **Scientific ideas are subject to change,** and science consists of processes for producing knowledge.
- **Scientific knowledge is durable,** rejects the notion of absolute truth, and accepts some uncertainty as the scientific enterprise grows in its ability to uncover how the natural world functions.
- **Science cannot provide complete answers to all questions,** especially for instances when beliefs prevail; beliefs by their nature cannot be proved or disproved.

Scientific Inquiry

- **Science demands evidence** from accurate data but does not follow a recipe of steps, since inquiry cannot be described apart from the unique context of an investigation.
- **Science is a blend of logic and imagination;** scientists are human and use tools of logic, and they embrace flashes of insight and inspiration to help them investigate.
- **Science explains and predicts** and deals with "how?" rather than "why?"; scientists try to make sense of careful observations to form explanations for how things function.
- **Scientists try to identify and avoid bias** by asking what evidence supports explanations to ensure that they themselves and other scientists are not misguided by personal preference.
- **Science is not authoritarian;** although scientists do defer to credible sources of information, conclusions and theories are judged by results, not by the reputation of advocates.

The Scientific Enterprise

- **Science is a complex social activity,** not an isolated enterprise, and men and women of all racial, ethnic, and national origins work to share information and create uses for scientific ideas while being conscious of social values and culture.
- **Science is organized into content disciplines and is conducted in various institutions;** dozens of disciplines exist, more are created as time passes, and many have coalesced into new dimensions of science for today's school curricula.
- **There are generally accepted ethical principles in the conduct of science;** strongly held traditions advocate ethical norms, limit harm that could come from experimentation and applications of research, and help scientists to maintain professional behavior through careful and accurate record keeping, openness, replication of research, and critical peer review.

- **Scientists participate in public affairs both as specialists and as citizens;** citizen-scientists play a crucial role in helping the public policymakers to understand potential causes of events and possible long-term effects of proposed policy.

(See *Science for All Americans Online* at http://www.project2061.org/publications/sfaa/online/chap1.htm, and check *myeducationlab* for additional resources, including a short-course on the nature of science.)

Considering all that science is and includes, how can a teacher ensure that children receive an authentic experience that conveys the true nature of science? The three typical science disciplines—earth/space science, life science, and physical science—just do not seem to cover the range. The National Science Education Standards (National Research Council, 1996) provide four new dimensions for science content standards and outcomes. These dimensions, listed in Table 1.1, provide a worldview of science and help learners to understand the scientific enterprise through inquiry by focusing on understanding the relationships of science and technology, using personal and social perspectives to understand science, and comprehending the nature of science throughout its history.

Children are naturally curious (remember the youngster who threw the cat down the stairs?), and that curiosity can be channeled into a wholesome science experience. Children's curiosity motivates them to discover new ways to unlock the mysteries of their world, make meaning from direct experiences, and find personal fulfillment and value from the "discoveries" they make. With thoughtful, gentle guidance, children develop impressions that their world is knowable, learn to blend imagination with logic, and acquire a sense that they, too, can be like scientists. If we globally reduce all of the big ideas about the nature of science into some simple components, we find three characteristics that help us to decide what to teach and how to involve children:

1. *Attitudes* are essential predispositions that help learners to channel natural curiosity into positive ways of knowing their world.
2. *Skills* are the mental tools for inquiry that scientists use to construct new ways of investigating and understanding.
3. *Knowledge* consists of what scientists (and young learners) discover and share with others, which can be used for developing new inventions with practical benefits.

The new things that children learn tend to stimulate curiosity and motivate them to investigate further. When children are given a complete experience with all that science is—whole science—a cycle of *knowing* very similar to the scientific enterprise is established that continues to build under its own momentum. Whole science thus consists of three parts: development of children's *attitudes* and *skills* and children's construction of useful ideas—*knowledge*. Children's experiences can stimulate their curiosity (*attitudes*), which can motivate them to develop new ways of processing ideas or solving problems (*skills*); these are used to construct the *knowledge* of science. Successful learning enriches the experience universe of children and stimulates further inquiry. Teachers provide children with a whole science experience when they are immersed in all of science's essential features.

Three Essential Characteristics of Science

Three characteristics of science are necessary for a wholesome, productive learning experience: development of children's attitudes, development of their thinking and kinesthetic skills (gross, fine motor, and eye–hand coordination, as well as training of the senses), and development of knowledge that is constructed from experiences in natural settings.

TABLE 1.1 ● Four New Dimensions of Science Content Standards and Outcomes

Dimension 1. Science as Inquiry Standard

The students will

NSES
CS-A

1.1 Develop abilities necessary to do scientific inquiry.
   - Ask questions about objects, organisms, and events in their natural environment.
   - Plan and conduct simple science investigations.
   - Use simple science equipment and other appropriate tools that extend their senses in order to gather, analyze, and interpret data.
   - Use data to construct descriptions, explanations, predictions, and models.
   - Identify relationships between evidence and explanations.
   - Communicate, critique, and analyze the work of other students and recognize and analyze alternative explanations and predictions.

1.2 Understand about scientific inquiry.
   - Ask and answer questions and compare answers to what scientists already know about the world.
   - Select the kind of investigation that fits the questions they are trying to answer.
   - Realize the instruments provide more information than a scientist can obtain only by using his or her senses, and enhance the accuracy of that information.
   - Develop explanations that are based on observation, evidence, and scientific concepts.
   - Describe investigations in ways that make it possible for others to repeat the same investigation.
   - Review and ask questions about the results of others' work and realize that science advances through legitimate skepticism.

Dimension 2. Science and Technology Standard

The students will

NSES
CS-E

2.1 Develop an ability to distinguish between natural objects and objects made by humans.
   - Realize that some objects occur in nature and that other objects have been designed by people to solve human problems.
   - Categorize objects into two groups, natural and designed.

2.2 Develop an ability to understand and produce a technological design.
   - Identify an age-appropriate problem for technological design, propose a solution, and design it, perhaps by collaborating with others.
   - Evaluate a product or design and communicate the results to others by describing the process of technological design.

2.3 Understand about science and technology.
   - Realize that science and technological design often have similarities and differences that make it necessary for scientists and engineers to work together, often in teams with other professionals, in order to solve problems.
   - Understand that science and technology provide opportunities to women and men of all ages, groups, backgrounds, races, religions, and abilities to do various scientific and technological work and that a person's appearance, gender, race, or national origin should not influence acceptance or rejection of his or her contributions to science or technology.
   - Understand that tools help scientists to make better observations, measurements, and equipment for investigations and that science helps drive technology.

(continued)

TABLE 1.1 ● Continued

- Understand that people have always had questions about the natural world and that scientists have invented tools and techniques to help answer those questions.
- Understand that technological designs have constraints and that the technological solutions may have intended benefits and unintended consequences, some of which may not be predictable.

Dimension 3. Science in Personal and Social Perspectives Standard

NSES
CS-F

The students will

3.1 Develop an understanding of personal health.
- Understand that safety and security are basic needs of humans.
- Demonstrate responsibility for their own health through regular exercise routines.
- Understand that good nutrition is essential to health, develop nutritious eating habits, and recognize that nutritional needs vary with age, sex, weight, activity, and body functions.
- Recognize and avoid substances that can damage the human body, including environmental hazards (e.g., lead, radon), and recognize that prescription drugs can be beneficial if taken as directed.
- Recognize the potential for accidents, identify safety hazards, and take precautions for safe living.
- Understand that the sex drive is a natural human instinct; the consequences of new life and disease must be understood.

3.2 Identify characteristics and describe changes in populations.
- Understand that human populations include groups of persons who live in a particular location.
- Understand that density refers to the number of individuals of a population who can live in a particular amount of space.
- Realize that the size of a human and animal population can increase or decrease and that populations will increase unless factors such as disease, insufficient food, or disasters limit them. Overpopulation increases the consumption of resources.

3.3 Identify types of resources.
- Understand resources are materials we get from the living and nonliving environment to meet the needs of a population.
- Identify examples of resources such as air, water, soil, food, fuel, building materials, and the nonmaterial such as quiet places, beauty, security, and safety.
- Understand that the supply of resources is limited but that recycling and reduced use can extend the length of time that resources are available; overconsumption and overpopulation deplete resources.

3.4 Identify environments and changes.
- Understand that the concept of environment includes the space, conditions, and factors that affect an individual's or an entire population's quality of life and ability to survive.
- Realize that environmental changes can be caused by natural or human causes and that some changes are good, some bad, others neither good nor bad.
- Understand that internal and external changes in the earth's system cause natural hazards and destruction of life.
- Understand that pollution is a change in the environment that can influence health and survival or limit the activities of organisms, including humans; pollution can be caused by natural occurrences and human activity.

TABLE 1.1 ● Continued

- Comprehend that some environmental changes occur slowly and others rapidly and describe examples of each (e.g., weather, climate, erosion, movements of large geologic masses).

3.5. Recognize the benefits and challenges of science and technology.
- Understand that inventions and problem solutions can affect other people in helpful and harmful ways.
- Recognize that science influences society through its knowledge and worldview and that technology influences society through its products and processes.
- Identify risks and analyze the potential benefits and consequences and understand that risks and benefits relate directly to personal and social decisions.
- Describe how science and technology have improved transportation, health, sanitation, and communication and realize that the benefits of science and technology are not always available to all people.
- Understand that science and technology have advanced through the contributions of many different people, different cultures, and at different times throughout history.
- Realize that scientists and engineers have codes of ethics that require humans who are part of their research to be fully informed about the risks and benefits associated with the research.
- Understand that science cannot answer all questions and that technology cannot solve all human problems or meet all human needs.

Dimension 4. History and Nature of Science Standard

The students will

NSES
CS-G

4.1 Understand that science is a human endeavor.
- Realize that science and technology have been used for a long time.
- Understand that women and men have made important contributions to science and technology throughout history.
- Understand that there is still much to learn about science.
- Understand that doing science requires persons of different abilities and talents.

4.2 Understand the nature of science.
- Realize that scientists use consistent procedures to test explanations and to form ideas.
- Understand that scientists do not always agree, particularly when active research is pursued in new experimental areas, but that science ideas are supported by considerable observation and confirmation, even though the nature of science is tentative.
- Understand that scientists expect their ideas and research to be evaluated by other scientists and that while scientists may disagree over conclusions, they agree that skepticism, questioning, and open communication are essential to progress in science.

4.3 Understand the importance of history to science.
- Realize that studying the lives and times of important scientists provides further understanding about the nature of scientific inquiry and the relationships between science and society.
- Realize that the history of science reveals that the scientists and engineers of high achievement are considered to be among the most valued contributors of any culture.
- Trace the history of science to understand how difficult it was for innovators to break through the dominant scientific preconceptions of their times and to reach conclusions that seem obvious today.

Source: Adapted from National Research Council, *National Science Education Standards* (Washington, DC: National Academy Press, 1996), pp. 121–171.

Science Attitudes

What Are Attitudes? Attitudes are mental predispositions toward people, objects, subjects, events, and so on. In science, attitudes are important because of three primary factors (Martin, 1984, pp. 13–14). First, a child's attitude carries a mental state of readiness with it. With a positive attitude, a child will perceive science objects, topics, activities, and people positively. A child who is unready or hesitant, for whatever reason, will be less willing to interact with people and things associated with science. This readiness factor occurs unconsciously in a child, without prior thought or overt consent.

Second, attitudes are not innate or inborn. Contemporary psychologists maintain that attitudes are learned and are organized through experiences as children develop (Halloran, 1970; Oskamp, 1977). Furthermore, a child's attitude can be changed through experience. Teachers and parents have the greatest influence on science attitudes (George & Kaplan, 1998).

Third, attitudes are dynamic results of experiences that act as directive factors when a child enters into new experiences. As a result, attitudes carry an emotional and an intellectual tone, both of which lead to making decisions and forming evaluations. These decisions and evaluations can cause a child to set priorities and hold different preferences. In the scenario, Jessica's attitude toward science and the way she values it shifts from a negative to a neutral and to even a positive viewpoint. In time, with continued positive experiences and adjustments in her attitude, Jessica may become more open to science, think differently about it, and accumulate more useful ideas and skills—all products of her learning. But all of this begins with her attitude.

Emotional Attitudes. Young children's attitudes often are more emotional than intellectual. Curiosity, the natural start of it all, may be accompanied by perseverance, a positive approach to failure (or acceptance of not getting one's own way all the time), and openness to new experiences and even other people's points of view (tolerance for other children's ways of playing a favorite game). These are fundamental attitudes that are useful for building specific scientific attitudes that are necessary for success and the continuation of the science cycle.

Intellectual Attitudes. Attitudes based on intellect or rational thought develop simultaneously with science process skill development (a second feature of science) and with the discovery or construction of useful science ideas (the third feature of science). Teacher guidance, learning materials that can be manipulated, and interactive teaching methods help encourage formation of intellectual attitudes. Examples include skepticism and the development of a desire to follow procedures that increase objectivity. (See Table 1.2.)

Importance of Attitudes. Younger children tend to have positive attitudes toward science and display many of these attitudes as they explore and interact with classmates. However, over time, these initial positive attitudes may decline.

Science Process Skills

Perhaps you remember hearing about the *scientific method* in your science classes. At one time, people believed that scientists used a specific, step-by-step method in their research. But when scientists were questioned about how they actually went about their work, it soon became clear that there were numerous ways to approach problems (Moreno, 2007). It was also obvious that several processes are common to most forms of inquiry, and these became known as the *science process skills*. These processes also apply to other subjects of study as well as to science, and you probably have been using some of them most of your life. What sets professional scientists apart from you might be little more than the skill to use these processes to solve problems. We think you will recognize the process skills as you review them and realize how important it is that children learn to use them to solve their own problems.

TABLE 1.2 ● Attitudes of Young Scientists

Emotional	Intellectual
From children's natural curiosity for learning and acquiring new experiences, we can encourage them to develop • more curiosity • perseverance • a positive approach to failure • open-mindedness • cooperation with others	From children's positive learning experiences, we can encourage them to develop • a desire for reliable sources of information • skepticism; a desire to be shown or to have alternative points of view proven • avoidance of broad generalizations when evidence is limited • tolerance for other opinions, explanations, or points of view • willingness to withhold judgment until all evidence or information is found or examined • refusal to believe in superstitions or to accept claims without proof • openness to changing their minds when evidence for change is given and openness to questions about their own ideas

The mission of elementary and middle school science is not to persuade all children to become scientists. The mission is to help make science more accessible to *all* children. One way this can be done is to help children discover how science can be important to them. Therefore, consider the process skills rooted in science that young children must develop and the ways children can use these skills to solve problems of learning and life.

Learning How to Learn. Some people refer to developing process skills as "learning how to learn." Children learn how to learn by thinking critically and using information creatively. Children continue to learn how to learn

> when making discriminating observations, when organizing and analyzing facts and concepts, when giving reasons for expecting particular outcomes, when evaluating and interpreting the results of experiments, and when drawing justifiable conclusions. [Also, children] . . . should be able to predict what will happen when the conditions of a phenomenon in nature are changed. (Victor, 1985, p. 47)

Types of Process Skills. In science, the ways of thinking, measuring, solving problems, and using thoughts are called *processes. Process skills* describe types of thinking and reasoning and may be divided into two types: basic skills and integrated skills (Arena, 1996). Table 1.3 on page 18 suggests the grade levels at which these skills are appropriate.

Basic Skills.   If children show they can observe, classify, communicate, measure, estimate, predict, and infer, they are showing understanding of basic science processes.

Observation is the primary way in which children obtain information. This does not mean that children benefit solely from watching someone else and listening to what others think. Children observe by using all their senses. For example, how do you observe a concert? Can you close your eyes and recreate it by recalling how your senses were stimulated? Can you see the lights and special effects? Can you smell the odors unique to the crowd and those special effects? Can you feel the vibrations of the bass and drums? Can you hear the music and vocals—really hear them with all of their rhythm? Can you taste the

Children's natural curiosity for learning will lead them to scientific discoveries.

Attitudes and the Nature of Science

Attitudes' role and influence on science teaching and learning have been recognized for more than fifty years. Attitudes influence nearly every aspect of teaching and learning. Typically, an attitude is regarded as a predisposition to respond to people, places, events, and objects in positive or negative ways or as the favorableness of a person's feeling about a task. A meta-analysis of research conducted over a span of twenty years reveals that boys typically have more positive attitudes toward science than girls do at a general level, high-performing girls have more positive attitudes than boys, and positive attitudes result in higher achievement in science.

The *National Science Education Standards* craft an image of attitudes bearing influence at an emotional and intellectual level, resulting in valuing inquiry and investigation. Teachers must model, and children are expected to examine, science-related attitudes in order for learners to acquire inquiry-rich values. This means that the social and cultural aspects of learning are used to help children understand their personal values and to learn to express their feelings in constructive ways. These actions can result in children developing more positive attitudes about science and more positive communication and interpersonal skills.

These values can help us in our quest toward an important standard from the *National Science Education Standards:* the History and Nature of Science, which is best learned through experiences that arise from activity rather than only

popcorn or the Junior Mints? Teachers stimulate useful observation through the five senses when they ask children questions that cause them to identify properties of objects, changes, and similarities and differences; and to determine the difference between an observation and an inference. Example: *The object is hard, gray, round, and*

TABLE 1.3 ● Science Process Skills

NSES
CS-A

Basic skills can be emphasized at the primary grades and then serve as a foundation for using integrated skills at the intermediate and higher grades.										
					Grades					
Basic Skills	PreK	K	1	2	3	4	5	6	7	8
Observation	X	X	X	X	X	X	X	X	X	X
Classification	X	X	X	X	X	X	X	X	X	X
Communication	X	X	X	X	X	X	X	X	X	X
Measurement	X	X	X	X	X	X	X	X	X	X
Estimation	X	X	X	X	X	X	X	X	X	X
Prediction	X	X	X	X	X	X	X	X	X	X
Inference		X	X	X	X	X	X	X	X	X
Integrated Skills										
Identifying variables					X	X	X	X	X	X
Controlling variables					X	X	X	X	X	X
Defining operationally					X	X	X	X	X	X
Forming hypotheses					X	X	X	X	X	X
Experimenting					X	X	X	X	X	X
Graphing					X	X	X	X	X	X
Interpreting data					X	X	X	X	X	X
Modeling					X	X	X	X	X	X
Investigating					X	X	X	X	X	X

superficially on an intellectual level. The idea that scientific knowledge is always subject to change may be difficult for children to grasp. However, the standard for grades K–4 and 5–8 requires that as a result of activities, all students should develop understanding of science as a human endeavor, the nature of science, and the importance of history to science.

The challenge for us is to create an educational system, beginning with our own classrooms, that exploits the natural curiosity of learners. Curiosity is the motivation and inspiration for doing science in pursuit of this standard and motivates learning during school years and later life. Curiosity is a fundamental emotional attitude and the sci-ence teacher is the key person for successful promotion of positive attitudes and affective attributes in children. Convince fellow teachers and parents that children's "why?" questions are important. Science teachers must have good knowledge of the nature of science and must be good role models so that children will emulate these valued attitudes. Demonstrate question-asking, hypothesizing, prediction-making, record-keeping, and making conclusions based on results. Enable children to perform experiments and solve problems that require use of the thinking skills involved in scientific inquiry so that they rise to the proficiency levels demanded by modern reform.

Source: Compiled from Molly Weinburgh, "Gender Differences in Student Attitudes toward Science: A Meta-Analysis of the Literature from 1970–1991." *Journal of Research in Science Teaching,* Vol. 32, No. 4, pp. 387–398, 1995; Lawrence Lowery (Ed.), *NSTA Pathways to the Science Standards,* Elementary School Edition (Arlington, VA: National Science Teachers Association, 2000), p. 103; and *National Research Council, Inquiry and the National Science Education Standards* (Washington, DC: National Academy Press, 2000). M. Gail Jones & Glenda Carter, "Science Teacher Attitudes and Beliefs," in Sandra K. Abell & Norman G. Lederman (Eds.), *Handbook of Research on Science Education* (Mahwah, NJ: Lawrence Erlbaum Associates, 2007), pp. 1967–1104; Kenneth P. King, *Integrating the National Science Education Standards into Classroom Practice* (Columbus, OH: Merrill Prentice Hall, 2007).

the size of a baseball. Instruments such as thermometers, balances, computers, and probes help to add precision to observations.

Classification requires organizing observations in ways that carry special meaning. Teachers can encourage children to classify when they ask them to group objects by their observed properties and/or to arrange objects or events in a particular order. An example is: *Group the buttons from your cup, and tell me why you made those groups.* Or: *Place all rocks of the same size, color, and hardness into the same group.*

When *communication* is emphasized, children use language (spoken, written, and symbolic in many forms) to express their thoughts in ways that others can understand. Development of useful communication skills is encouraged when you ask children to define words and terms operationally (based on what they did); to describe objects and events as they are perceived; and to record information and make pictures, charts, data tables, graphs, and models to show what they have found. Example: *Describe observed changes in the playground water puddles over time through speaking, writing, or making a graph or data table.*

Measurement adds precision to observations, classifications, and communications. Children can be encouraged to measure by using standard tools like rulers, meter sticks, balances, graduated cylinders, calibrated liquid containers, clocks, calculators, computers, electrical instruments, and even arbitrary units such as marbles, paper clips, and tongue depressors to measure quantity or distance. Example: *Use a meter stick to describe the height of a child.* (Note: The metric system is *the* measurement system in science.)

Estimation involves judging an approximate amount or value. The estimate is based on knowledge of measurement but is not a direct measure.

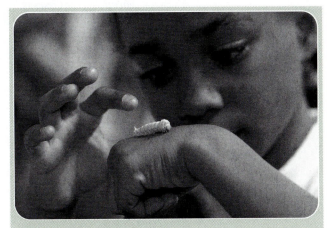

Observation is a basic science process.

Estimation is useful for quick observations for which precision is not necessary. Example: *I think the chair is about 1 meter high.* Or: *The glass looks as if it contains about 300 milliliters of water.*

Predictions are best guesses based on available information. Meteorologists, for example, predict the weather. Their predictions are made in advance of the weather's actual occurrence and are based on accumulated observations, analysis of information, and prior experience. Similarly, children can be encouraged to make predictions before they carry out an act, such as grouping different objects into classifications based on a prediction concerning whether the objects will float when placed in water. A teacher can stimulate predictive thinking by asking children to review the observed properties of objects or events and asking the children to tell what they think will happen when a change of some sort is made, such as our sink-or-float example. Example: *Predict the size and shape of an ice cube in a cup after letting it sit on the class window ledge for 20 minutes.*

Inferences are conclusions about the cause of an observation. Consider the sink-or-float example again. Children may observe that all lightweight objects from their collections float in water and infer that the light weight was the cause of floating. Of course, this could be disproved by items not included in the children's limited collection of objects. Therefore, it is necessary to help children make better inferences by guiding their thinking in ways that help them make conclusions about an observation based on the prior knowledge they have. Example: *A person is happy because she smiles and hums a song.*

Integrated Skills.   Integrated science process skills rely on the students' capabilities to think at a higher level and to consider more than one thought at a time. As the word *integrated* implies, several basic process skills are combined for greater power to form the tools to solve problems. The basic skills are prerequisites for integrated skills—those necessary to do science experiments. These integrated processes include identifying and controlling variables, defining operationally, forming hypotheses, experimenting, making graphs, interpreting data, forming models, and investigating.

Identifying and controlling variables requires students to identify aspects of an experiment that can affect its outcome and to keep as many aspects constant as possible, while manipulating only the aspects or factors (variables) that are independent. Example: *Vary only the amount of fertilizer used on similar plants while keeping soil type, amount of sunlight, water, and temperature the same.*

Defining operationally occurs when using observations and other information gained through experience to describe or label an object or event. Example: *An acid, like vinegar, is a substance that causes baking soda to fizz.*

Forming hypotheses is important for designed investigations and is similar to prediction, but more controlled and formal. Hypothesizing is using information to make a best educated guess about the expected outcome of an experiment. Example: *The more fertilizer is added to plants, the greater their growth.*

Experimenting requires using many thinking skills to design and conduct a controlled scientific test. This consists of asking a researchable question, forming a hypothesis, identifying and controlling variables, using operational definitions, conducting the experiment, and interpreting the data. Example: *The entire operational process is investigating the effects of amounts of fertilizer added to plants of the same type.*

Graphing is converting measurements into a diagram to show the relationships among and between the measures. Example: *Construct a graph (or pictogram) to show the heights of the plants, experimental and control, for each day (or week) of the experiment.*

Interpreting data consists of collecting observations and measurements (data) in an organized way and drawing conclusions from the information obtained by reading tables, graphs and diagrams. Example: *Read information in a table or graph about the growth of plants in the experiment described above and form conclusions based on the interpretation of the data.* The interpretation could help to "prove" that *more fertilizer added to plants causes greater growth.*

Forming models requires creating an abstract (mental) or concrete (physical) illustration of an object or event. Example: *A model shows the best amount of fertilizer to use on a plant and the consequences of using too little or too much.*

Investigating is a complex process skill that requires using observations, collecting and analyzing data, and drawing conclusions to solve a problem. Example: *Complete an investigation to evaluate the fertilizer dosage model as a way of deciding on a plant feeding routine for the class's garden.*

Importance of Process Skills. Basic science skills expand children's learning through experience. Beginning with simple ideas, these ideas compound and form new, more complex ideas. An accumulation of ideas is valuable because of assisting children to become decision makers and problem solvers. Emphasizing science process skills helps students to discover meaningful information and accumulate knowledge by constructing understanding within and beyond the science classroom.

Scientific knowledge consists of concepts, principles, and theories.

Science process skills are remarkably similar to those skills used in reading comprehension (Table 1.4 on pages 22–23). When children are doing science, following scientific procedures, and thinking as scientists, they are developing skills that are necessary for effective reading and understanding (Padilla, Muth, & Lund Padilla, 1991). A creative teacher can plan lessons that have students working on science and developing the skills that are useful to other subjects simultaneously. Science experiences can help preschool children to develop their intellect and get an early start on fundamental reading and thinking skills. Primary school students can become motivated through science activities and their natural interests to work on vocabulary development, word discrimination, and comprehension. Intermediate and middle school youths develop their communication abilities to identify and control variables, make meaningful conclusions, and express ideas clearly.

Science Knowledge

Importance of Science Knowledge. Children construct important ideas and discover much about the nature of science for themselves when they use science process skills. They gain knowledge by accumulating and processing information and by forming concepts about their natural world, humans' use of natural resources, and the impact of this use on society. Children also discover, in time, that knowledge provides power and carries with it a responsibility for its proper use. Perhaps most important, children can understand that much of science is tentative, changes over time, and is subject to future change. The content of science is not absolute, and research findings may be interpreted differently by different people, depending on their values and experiences.

NSES
CS-G

Examples of Science Knowledge. The knowledge base of science is often referred to as *products*. New discoveries that add to the base of scientific information are the

TABLE 1.4 ● Relationship of Science and Reading Skills

Science Skills	Reading Skills	Examples
Observation	Discriminating shapes, sounds, syllables, and word accents	Break words into syllables and list on chalkboard. Class pronounces new words aloud. Teacher mispronounces some words and rewards students who make corrections.
Identification	Recognizing letters, words, prefixes, suffixes, and base words	Select a common science prefix, suffix, or base word, define it, and list several words in which it may be used. Example: *kilo* (1,000): *kilometer, kilogram, kiloliter.*
Description	Isolating important attributes and characteristics Enumerating ideas Using appropriate terminology and synonyms	Ask students to state the purpose of an activity. Construct keys for student rock collections, etc. Play vocabulary games. Use characteristics to identify an object or animal.
Classification	Comparing and contrasting characteristics Arranging ideas and ordering and sequencing information Considering multiple attributes	List in order the steps of a mealworm's metamorphosis. Construct charts that compare and contrast characteristics. Put concepts in order.
Investigation design	Question asking Investigating possible relationships Following organized procedures	Use library resources and design an experiment from an outline. Write original lab reports. Outline facts and concepts.
Data collection	Note taking Using reference materials Using different parts of a book Recording information in an organized way Being precise and accurate	Prepare bibliographies from library information. Use tables of contents, indexes, and organizational features of chapters. Have students compare and discuss notes. Use quantitative skills in lab activities.
Interpretation of data	Recognizing cause-and-effect relationships Varying reading rate Organizing facts Summarizing new information Thinking inductively and deductively	Discuss matters that could affect the health of an animal. Teach students to preview and scan printed text. Have students organize notes in an outline. Have students construct concept maps, flowcharts, and new arrangements of facts.
Communication of results	Arranging information logically Sequencing ideas Using graphs Describing clearly	List discoveries through a time line. Ask for conclusions from graphed data or tables and figures. Describe chronological events.
Conclusion formation	Generalizing Critically analyzing Identifying main ideas Establishing relationships Using information in other situations	Ask "What if?" questions. Have students scrutinize conclusions for errors. Use case studies to develop conclusions through critical thinking.

Source: The comparisons are drawn from Glenda S. Carter and Ronald D. Simpson's "Science and Reading: A Basic Duo," *Science Teacher* (March 1978): 20, and from Ronald Simpson and Norman Anderson's *Science, Students and Schools: A Guide for the Middle and Secondary School Teacher* (New York: Wiley, 1980). M. Padilla, D. Muth, and R. Lund Padilla (1991) continue to clarify the similarities between science process skills and reading comprehension skills.

products of curiosity and experimentation. An interesting thing about science knowledge is that new discoveries often lead to more questions, more experiments, and more new discoveries. Indeed, the solutions to scientific problems can create new problems. Science cycles move under their own momentum, propelled initially and again later sustained by human curiosity and a desire to explain natural phenomena. The effect is an exploding accumulation of new information that is added to the knowledge base. Scientific knowledge consists primarily of facts, concepts, principles, and theories.

Facts are specific, verifiable pieces of information obtained through observation and measurement. For example, during a class project, Jessica observes over the course of two weeks that she produces an average of 1 kilogram of solid waste each day: cans, bottles, paper, plastic, and so on—a fact of her living habits.

Concepts are abstract ideas that are generalized from facts or specific relevant experiences. Jessica's class project may help her form the concept that her habits of consumption yield considerable solid waste over time. She believes her habits are typical of other young adults and she forms a concept about the amount of solid waste some people generate within a specific amount of time. Concepts are single ideas that may become linked to form more complex ideas.

Principles are complex ideas based on several related concepts. Jessica's example: "The reason people recycle solids is because they create a lot of waste." Jessica's principle is based on three concepts: creation, waste, and recycling.

Theories consist of broadly related principles that provide an explanation for a phenomenon. The purpose of a theory is to provide the best explanation based on evidence and not based on opinion or personal preference. Theories are used to explain, relate, and predict. After some added observation and consideration, Jessica may theorize that commercial marketing practices and convenience packaging are responsible for much of the eastern United States' landfill problems. She may use her theory to urge lawmakers to develop regulations and to persuade city leaders to establish recycling programs to ease the pressures on their landfills.

Throughout history, scientific thinkers have found that the accepted hierarchy of facts and ideas cannot answer certain important questions. As scientists struggle to refine the theories and principles in an effort to answer these questions, they sometimes generate a radical new idea that seems to solve the problem better. If the new idea answers the questions at least as well as the old ways of thinking did, the scientific community will eventually throw out the old ideas in favor of what Thomas Kuhn (1970) called a *new paradigm*. The work of Copernicus is a good example of what Kuhn called a *scientific revolution*. Copernicus was trying to explain the orbit of Mars using Ptolemy's geocentric theory of the structure of the universe, but he was having no success. As he tried to refine Ptolemy's system, it occurred to him that it would be a much simpler problem to solve if the sun, rather than the earth, were in the center of the universe. He came up with an idea that, on further examination, explained the orbits of the other planets as well as Ptolemy's theory did, and a new paradigm was born. It was many years before Copernicus's heliocentric theory was widely accepted by the scientific community as the basis for a new hierarchy of theories about the relationship of the earth to the sun and the other planets (Prather, 1991).

It is important for science teachers to help learners realize that scientific theories are based on the best information that scientists have been able to collect but that many theories have been discarded as the result of new ideas that provide greater problem-solving power. Therefore, many of the theories and principles that scientists believe today may be discarded by the discovery of new and better ideas. At first, this concept may seem confusing to learners. They may ask why they should bother to learn about such things as Newton's laws or the theory of evolution if it might be imperfect and

Learning Cycle Featured Lesson

CONCEPTS TO BE CONSTRUCTED:

▶ The physical properties of matter are used to distinguish one kind of matter from another.

▶ A cooked egg will spin freely, whereas a raw egg will be difficult to spin. It will have a slight wobble.

SCIENCE ATTITUDES TO NURTURE:

▶ Curiosity

▶ Cooperating with others

▶ Tolerating other opinions, explanations, or points of view

Physical Science: Physical Properties of Matter

Grades ● K–4

Engaging Question

How can objects be described?

Materials Needed:

For Exploration Phase • conducted whole class

- 1 egg for each student; make 1/2 of the eggs hard-boiled and 1/2 uncooked
- A bowl to place all of the eggs in at the beginning of the lesson
- Two cans of chicken broth and two cans of dog food
- Paper towels

For Expansion Phase • conducted in small teams with whole-class conclusions

- 3–4 packages of different brands of chocolate chip cookies
- Paper towels
- 1 ruler per student team
- 5–10 toothpicks per student team

One piece of paper per student team for recording data

Safety: Students will use all senses except taste to make observations. Strongly discourage them from licking the egg's shell. Remind students to wash their hands after the Exploration activity and before they begin the Expansion activity.

Exploration

PROCESS SKILLS USED:

▶ Observing

▶ Manipulating materials

▶ Collecting and recording data

▶ Communicating

Assessing Prerequisite Knowledge—Setting Up the Exploration.

The teacher will:

- Place a colorful beach ball on a table in front of the class. Ask them to describe the colors and the shape of the ball to

check for knowledge of colors and shapes to describe an object.

- Use a driving question to engage the students in the exploration phase. This question is "Do you think you can help me determine which are the cooked eggs and which are raw eggs among all of the eggs in this bowl?" Then ask, "How might I go about this task?" As you listen to their suggestions check for the extent to which their suggestions are consistent with a sound understanding of the lesson's concept or if this lesson will really teach the science behind how this problem can be solved. Make note of the individual student responses during this initial encounter so that you can check for growth later.

••Ask students to describe what a raw egg looks like and what a hard-boiled egg looks like. If many of the students cannot share memories of these two, you will have to have a raw egg and a hard-boiled egg available to show them the differences between the two.

Student-Centered Exploration Activity

Enter the classroom with a bowl full of eggs, telling the students that you have a problem, "My bowl contains both raw and cooked eggs, and I can't tell which are which." Ask the students whether they can help to determine which are raw and which are cooked. Solicit their responses to that question, and then challenge them to make as many observations as possible about an egg given to them, without breaking the egg. Ask them to record their observations, to share their observations with a partner, and even to compare their observations to those of other students in the class. Remind them to be careful not to break their egg, and that if one is broken, to send the materials manager from their group up to the front to get a paper towel to clean up any mess. Also remind them to safely make observations—no LICKING the egg shell—as they don't know which eggs are

cooked and which are raw. Allow sufficient time for all of the students to make and record as many observations as possible. Walk around the room to check on students' progress. This will help you to determine when it is time to move to the Explanation phase of the lesson. If the Explanation phase is to be done on Day Two, ask all of the students to use a marker to label or mark their egg in such a way that they will remember which egg they had during Day One's activity. They will need to have their egg back for Day Two's activity.

Students making "egg-citing" observations

Explanation

Ask students to share their observations from the "Day One" activity. Once each of the students has had an opportunity to share an observation, then ask:

1. Which of these observations describe the outward appearance of the egg? (Possible answers may include: the egg is oval, the egg is white, the egg has bumps.)

2. Which of these observations used a sense other than sight to describe the egg? (Possible answers include: The observation that I could hear something when I shook it meant I used the sense of hearing; or, when I held the egg it felt smooth which meant I used the sense of touch.)

3. Which of these observations described the way in which the egg behaved when you moved it around? (Possible answers include: When I tried to stand the egg on one end, I couldn't do it; or, I was able to get my egg to spin.)

4. Which of these observations will help me to determine which eggs are raw and which are cooked?

5. How will I know whether it is the cooked or the raw egg that behaves a certain way without breaking the egg

open? Allow the children to struggle with this question, then provide them with an analogy to help answer this question. Bring in two cans of dog food and two cans of chicken broth. Open up the can of chicken broth, asking the children to pay careful attention to the content of the can. Ask the children whether they think I can easily pour the contents of the can of chicken broth into a bowl. Solicit their ideas, and then pour out the chicken broth. Ask them if they had to compare the chicken broth to a raw or cooked egg, which egg do they think the chicken broth would be more like? Then do the same, this time using a can of dog food.

6. Ask a student to try to spin the other can of chicken broth, asking all of the students to observe what happens and to share their observations. Do the same with the can of dog food. Then go back to the comparison of the broth and dog food to the eggs. Lead the students to draw the conclusion that the chicken broth that pours out easily and hardly spins is more like a raw egg in its shell, whereas the dog food that keeps the shape of the can when pushed out of the can and that will easily spin when in the can is more like the hard-boiled egg. Ask the children to again look at the original egg observation data they shared and see which "physical properties" they recorded best helped in determining whether they had a raw or cooked egg.

7. Ask the children then, on the basis of the physical properties of the egg they had, to use those observations and the analogy shared between the chicken broth and dog food, to make a prediction as to the type of egg they have: cooked or raw. Ask them to share the prediction asking them to state which physical properties of the egg led them to that prediction. After all students have had an opportunity to share their predictions, tell them they can now check their predictions by cracking their egg open. In the interest of safety, have the children do this over a bucket set at each work station or over the garbage can.

With each question, make sure that you allow sufficient wait time both between asking the question and soliciting responses and between the time the student responds and the time you react to the response.

Allow sufficient time for this Explanation Phase of the lesson so that you do not rush your line of questioning; allow time to clean up the eggs and to write out on the board the concept statement that the students helped to create by their activities: *Objects have many observable properties, such as size, weight, color, and shape. These are known as the physical properties of the object. They can be used to describe the object.*

Expansion

During this phase, first check for student's understanding of the concept by placing several objects on the desk in front of the students. Ask them to choose an object, write the name of the object on the paper, and list three physical properties of that object. This can be used as a quick, simple expansion activity or as a form of evaluation.

To develop the concept further, you can perform this expansion activity. First check to be sure the students do not have any food allergies to the ingredients in chocolate chip cookies.

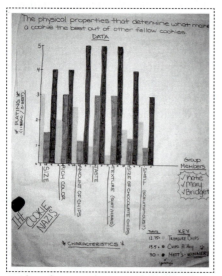

Student data on "The Best" Chocolate Chip Cookie

• Put out three or four different brands of chocolate chip cookies. Challenge the students to first design an experiment that uses physical properties to determine which brand of chocolate chip cookies is "best."

• Ask students to share the criteria—in this case, the physical properties—they are going to look at to determine which brand of cookies is "best."

• Ask them how they are going to go about determining whether the cookie meets their criteria, and remind them that if they do something like count the chocolate chips in one cookie, they need to count the chocolate chips in all of the cookies.

• Once the teams of students have demonstrated that the criteria they are using to judge their cookies are "physical properties" and you are reasonably sure that they will not do anything to harm themselves or other students while they inspect their cookies, then have them take a cookie from each brand and perform their experiment.

• This will be treated as an informal experiment, so do not identify a formal way to record their data. In fact, when student teams come up with different ways to collect and record their data you can use the differences to teach about the importance of performing *reproducible experiments.* This can lead into a later lesson about the importance of keeping accurate data. With this expansion activity, you are really interested in their ability to apply their understanding of using physical properties to describe an object in a new context.

• Walk around the room and make sure all students in the group are working, asking to see how they're recording the data, encouraging them, etc. Once you see that they are finished collecting their data to determine the best cookie, ask the student teams to share the results of their data collection.

• As the students share the data, check to make sure that they used only "physical properties" as their criteria. Because this concept was already made concrete, make sure that you continue to use the term "physical properties," almost stressing that term so that the students don't leave your class saying, "All we did was play with eggs and cookies." You want them to leave with an understanding that physical properties are observable.

A discussion about the "best cookie" will occur at this time. If the teams tasted the cookies, you could ask, "Did your response to how it tasted rely solely on the physical properties of the cookie?" This can lead to a new lesson on chemical properties.

If time permits, link the science concept to their personal perspectives by asking, "If you had to describe your best friend to another student, how would you do that? Would a description, such as 'He or she is really nice and cute,' be enough? Why or why not?" Also, try to link this concept to Science and Technology by asking the students, "Why has the auto industry gone from metal bumpers to plastic bumpers? What do the physical properties of matter have to do with that decision?"

Link an understanding of this concept to the History and Nature of Science by asking something like "Pretend you want a new sidewalk in front of your house. You need to hire a cement contractor to do the work. One contractor you interviewed said that it didn't matter what kind of material he or she used to pour your sidewalk. Does this person know much about distinguishing physical properties of matter? Would you be willing to hire that contractor? Why or why not?"

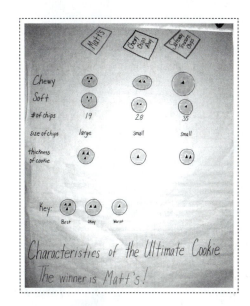

Evaluation

Hands-on Assessment

Provide the students with three different objects in their original store wrapping (e.g. a video game or CD; a small toy; a package of crackers). Ask them to choose one of the objects and describe the physical characteristics of the packaging of the object.

Reflective Assessment

Ask the students to write a statement about that object's packaging by answering this question: "Are the physical properties of the package that you described the only physical properties you would take into account when packaging this object? Why or why not?"

Pictorial Assessment

Ask the students to draw a picture of the kind of packaging they might use to mail a glass bowl to a friend. Ask them to label three physical properties of that package that make it a "good" package to send that bowl in.

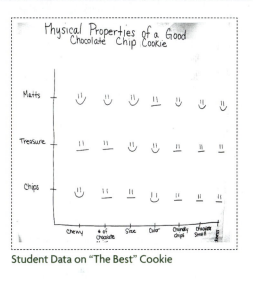

Student Data on "The Best" Cookie

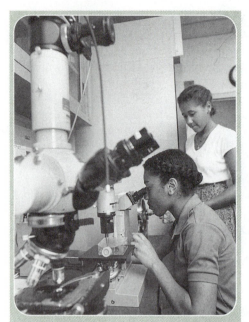

Children construct science knowledge for themselves.

replaced by another view. At this point, a teacher can use the history of science to help learners gain an appreciation of the nature of science and its worth. For example, Ptolemy's system was used for navigation for centuries, and Arab camel drivers used it with confidence to navigate the otherwise intolerably hot deserts in the cool of night. Also, it was Ptolemy's astronomy that Magellan's sailors used to sail safely around the earth—nearly a quarter of a century before Copernicus published his new astronomical theory (Prather, 1991).

Scientists are very aware of the limitations of their discoveries, but they are also aware that, based on the strength of evidence, it represents the best information available to them at the time. Therefore, it is useful to learn about the theories of science, even if they might be replaced later. Theories are the best explanations that scientists have. Scientists possess a holistic view of science. They use scientific attitudes to identify and define problems and scientific skills to inquire, and they contribute what they learn to the knowledge base of science, which makes it possible for the scientific community to attempt solutions to many important problems that can benefit us all.

The Aims of Standards and Research-Based Reform in Science Education

The nature of science is much more than remembering the three characteristics that we used as a focal point in this chapter. When children acquire consistent experiences with science, they accumulate an array of discoveries by developing and using the dispositions (attitudes) and processes (thinking skills) like scientists. Children also develop expanded worldviews and a greater appreciation for what science can and cannot do.

The nature of science has been promoted by numerous standard-setting organizations with a desire to help learners to achieve *scientific literacy*. A person who is scientifically literate is one who

> is aware that science, mathematics, and technology are interdependent human enterprises with strengths and limitations; understands key concepts and principles of science; is familiar with the natural world and recognizes both its diversity and unity; and uses scientific knowledge and scientific ways of thinking for individual and social purposes. (Rutherford & Ahlgren, 1990, p. ix)

NSES
TS-C

National legislation in the form of the *No Child Left Behind* (NCLB) act requires states to set and achieve research-based science content standards and then to measure accountability at the state level beginning in the 2007–08 school year. These requirements intend to ensure that children become scientifically literate. Annual tests of science achievement are required for three "grade bands": the early/intermediate grades, middle grades, and high school. States are bracing for poor results in science, since reading and mathematics received most of the early attention in meeting NCLB (Hovey, 2005). The federal law mandates that all learners must achieve proficiency in science by 2014–15.

Science teacher preparation programs look to the *National Science Teachers Association* (NSTA, http://www.nsta.org/ncate) or the *National Association for the Education of Young Children* (NAEYC, http://www.naeyc.org/accreditation/) for descriptions of standards to be met. States and school systems look to the *National Science Education*

How Do Science and Real Life Connect?

by Phyllis Frysinger, Retired

Grades 7 and 8, Miami View Elementary, South Charleston, Ohio

NSES

PD-C

Remember the first time you learned that spiders have book lungs, sponges have spicules, oak trees have inadequate abscission layers, and two round bacteria existing together are called diplococci? I thought that was really interesting, too, and I couldn't wait to tell kids all of this neat stuff. I found myself presenting discovery lessons on the value of spiders, natural carnivores, as possible pest controllers in soybean fields; on how strong sponge spicules would wreak havoc on populated beaches; how oak trees that keep their leaves longer would also lose more water in the fall; and I didn't teach that diplococcus business but rather demonstrated the subtlety of bacterial contamination.

Today's students are much more demanding that you as a teacher justify why you are teaching what you are. Be prepared: If you are using a text, don't try to cover all of Chapter 2 by Friday. Instead, sit down, read Chapter 2, and pretend that there is a student sitting beside you asking, "Why do we have to know this?" If you can't come up with an answer, then leave it out. Develop a list of outcomes or test objectives that you want to obtain from material to be studied. Give this list to the students at the beginning, develop a way to teach each of your objectives, and show them how you plan to present each of these goals. If you cannot come up with a way to teach a particular goal or objective without standing in front of the class and telling them about it, then leave it out.

Once you have decided what is important and how you are going to teach it, sit down and write the evaluation for the chapter. Yes, right now, not the night before so that you only have time to reproduce it. This way you can justify in your own mind how you will evaluate an objective or your evaluation technique. Newer evaluation techniques are being proposed, and I have used all sorts of things through the years. You will, too, if you keep up with the times.

Oh yes, keeping up with the times. This does not mean rapping the latest hit while you are dissecting a frog, but developing viable alternatives to dissection in general. I used dissecting for a long time and even developed anatomy lessons to use with my eighth-grade earth science classes.

By promoting science as an important part of the life of students, you will promote a positive attitude toward science and encourage students to develop science skills they will use for the rest of their lives.

To be more specific, I taught in a multidisciplinary situation with a pod scheduled time in which three teachers had all of the seventh-grade students in the morning and all of the eighth-grade students in the afternoon. During this time, we taught science, English, and literature.

We presented a lesson in which the science classes had been working on chemical reactions. We had mixed together several chemicals, including starch, sucrose, ovalbumin, ethyl buterate, and triglycerides, to note a chemical reaction. The product was a cake. In literature class, the students were reading *A Christmas Carol*, by Charles Dickens. In a combined class, we mixed the ingredients for a traditional plum pudding, noting the chemical ingredients and the importance of accurate measurement, as in the science class. The English teacher made the point that there were no plums in the plum pudding and discussed the origin of the word. The literature teacher reflected Mrs. Cratchit's anxiety over the preparation.

After the concoction was properly steamed and the traditions closely followed, including the stirring and wish making by each student, the pudding was flamed with orange extract, and we all enjoyed the feast.

With this approach, the students were presented the opportunity of learning the importance and the interrelationship of each of the disciplines involved. There really was an answer to "Why do we have to know this?" We write journals each day, and it was certainly rewarding to note the number of times that we read, "I'm going to take this recipe home and make plum pudding for my family." When the students want to take your lesson home and share it with others, then you know that you have taught science.

One more thing: Don't forget to join all the professional organizations that are available, and participate in them. You will not only learn the latest that is available in your field, but also have a great deal of support in your professional years. That's how I ended up taking physics almost thirty years after I entered the classroom when I didn't even teach physical science.

Standards (NSES by the National Research Council, 1996, *http://books.nap.edu/ readingroom/books/nses/*). As a teacher of science, you are affected by two levels of standards when learning how to help your learners become scientifically literate. As an aid, Krueger and Sutton (2001, p. 47) digested the far-reaching standards into some simple strategies for helping children to understand the nature of science:

NSES
TS-A

- Place *less emphasis* on knowing scientific facts and information, studying separate subject matter disciplines (earth, life, physical science) for their own sake, separating science knowledge from science process skills, covering many science topics, and implementing inquiry as a separate set of processes.

- Place *more emphasis* on understanding scientific concepts and developing abilities to inquiry; learning science in the context of inquiry, technology, personal and social perspectives, and the history and nature of science; integrating all aspects of science content; studying a few fundamental science concepts; and implementing inquiry as instructional strategies, abilities, and ideas to be learned.

These strategies help to provide a sense of direction in meeting our national aims. The chapters that follow present additional dimensions of the standards, offer specific examples for using standards effectively, and offer support from the research base for helping learners to become scientifically literate.

chapter summary

The nature of science must be viewed holistically, and its essential characteristics must be understood. Science is more than knowledge and scientific names and facts. Assumptions about science that focus only on treating it as a body of knowledge are incomplete and incorrect. Science is possible because it is inherently human. Human attitudes provide the curiosity to begin its study, the perseverance to continue, and the necessary qualities for making informed judgments. Science process skills make it possible for children to accumulate the factual information they need to construct concepts, form scientific principles, and comprehend theories. Children are able to construct their own understanding when encouraged to inquire by exploring, questioning, and seeking.

Science has the most impact on children when they value it and are exposed to its nature in all of its forms. Science programs, science teaching practices, and assessment techniques must provide experiences that will help children to value and use science by making important discoveries for themselves. These experiences must engage learners with meaningful content in an environment that is conducive to learning where all have access and are exposed interactively to rigorous expectations. How children construct ideas and learn is a topic explored in Chapter 2.

reflect and respond

1. Think back to your primary and middle school years. What do you remember about your science classes? How do your memories compare with those of your classmates? In what ways do your recollections represent the nature of science?

2. To what extent did your teachers represent the nature of science? What do you remember about the emphasis given to attitudes, thinking skills, and science content? Why do you think your teachers emphasized (or did not emphasize) each of these characteristics?

3. Think about developmental differences observed between first-, third-, and sixth-grade students. In each grade, how much emphasis do you think should be given to emotional and intellectual attitude development? Give reasons for your answer.

4. Review the differences between basic and integrated science process skills. What is the connection between these skills and the types of science information children are expected to learn?

5. The attitudes that we carry with us are linked to experiences we have accumulated over time. Both help us to form images that we treat as our personal sense of reality. Sometimes these images represent stereotypes. For example, when you hear the word *scientist*, what image comes to mind? Draw a picture of a scientist.

6. Compare your picture of a scientist with other class members' pictures. Classify them according to such features as age, gender, amount and types of hair, eyeglasses, lab coat, laboratory apparatus, appearance (weird, out of control, and so on), and other factors. Tally the features and compute percentages to develop a class profile of a scientist. Treat this as a pretest and do the exercise again at the end of the course to look for any possible differences in stereotypes.

PEARSON
myeducationlab
Where the Classroom Comes to Life

Explore—Video Homework Exercise. Go to MyEducationLab at www.myeducationlab .com and select the topic "The Nature of Science," then watch the video "The Nature of Science," devoting particular attention to the children's expressions and postures. Complete the activity questions below.

The nature of science is a dynamic enterprise that affects all citizens and consists of the interrelationship of key components placed within a worldview context. In Chapter 1, read "What Research Says" and Tables 1.2 and 1.3.

NSES
CS-G

1. What types of attitudes seemed to be visible? What did the children do or how did the children behave that suggests these attitudes?

2. What processes were visible, and what activities verified that these skills were used?

3. What action in the video suggests that science knowledge is formed? How might what is learned be related to attitudes and processes?

Enrich—Weblink Exercise

Professional Practice. Go to MyEducationLab Resources section and select "Weblinks," then click on the links for "Kids Draw a Scientist" and "Perceptions of Scientists" to examine the children's drawings and impressions of scientists, then respond to the first three questions below. Also click on "Preschool Scientists" to review and respond to the fourth question.

NSES
TS-C, E

1. What do you notice about the "before and after" impressions? What do you notice about samples of children's perceptions from around the world?

2. Try your own research project: Use a sample of children in a school setting, and ask each child to draw a picture of a scientist. Identify distinguishing characteristics, and discuss how the pictures are or are not similar to the children. How do their pictures compare with those drawn by your college classmates? Identify reasons for similarities and differences. What are some things that you could do to help children avoid forming stereotypes of scientists?

3. Interview a sample of children with questions such as: What is science?, Is science important? If so, why? What are some interesting things you have learned from science? What types of people (including children) make good scientists? Are you a scientist? If so, why? If not, why not? Can you be a scientist? Why or why not?

4. How could you incorporate drawing to obtain insight about prekindergarten children's attitudes toward science, their basic process skills, and their preconceptions and understandings of science?

Expand—Weblink Exercise

Science Literacy. Go to MyEducationLab Resources Section and select "Weblinks," then click on the link for "Short Course on the Nature of Science" to examine the lesson plans that accompany thirteen key questions that are addressed in a free course on the nature of science on the site. It is easier to distinguish science from nonscience when one is literate about the workings of science. What appear to be essential characteristics to include in your lessons that will enable children to become scientifically literate?

NSES
PD-A

2 How Do Children Learn Science?

focus questions

- How can the research on brain development and function help teachers to improve instruction?

- How do children's prior ideas influence their ability to learn? What can be done to avoid or limit misconceptions?

- As a theory of learning, how does constructivism unite brain research, Piagetian development theory, and social learning theory?

- What teacher roles support children's attempts to make meaning, and how can those roles be used to form a model for teaching science?

$\mathbf{A}$fter teaching for some years, Jessica from the scenario in Chapter 1 has developed routines to manage her classroom duties. Her teaching methods are consistent. In math, she presents the topic, demonstrates models, explains functions and steps by giving examples, and involves some children in board work. Drill and practice come next and are followed by assigned seatwork, which is reviewed the following day.

For science, Jessica explains the point, provides a demonstration, and gives step-by-step instructions for completing the corresponding activity. She always uses visual models to help students understand complicated concepts. Each learner follows her recipe, and her methods are similar for all subjects.

Jessica is regarded as an outstanding teacher and has received several commendations. But although her students perform well on the school's standardized tests, they do not fare well on the obligatory statewide performance assessments. Jessica is frustrated. Her fifth graders do well only on memorization. They return to their own ideas when confronted with problems or questions that are not an exact replica of what they have studied in class. What can Jessica do to develop deeper, lasting understanding?

Jessica pondered this question during her vacation as she supervised the play of her two children. Her older child, Kate, was having difficulty using a pump to inflate her bicycle tires. As Kate struggled with the pump's plunger, she exclaimed, "Ouch! Why is this so hot?" She had touched the plunger that she had been rapidly moving up and down to inflate the tire. Jessica's nine-year-old son, Jonathan, was close by, riding his skateboard, and offered an explanation: "It's hot because of friction."

"What's that?" inquired his sister.

Jonathan attempted to explain: "See the wheels on my skateboard? Listen as I turn them quickly. Hear this one squeak? Now let me put a little oil on it like Uncle Gary showed me." Jonathan retrieved the oil can from the garage workbench and put a few drops of oil on the wheel's bearings. "What do you hear now?" he asked.

"I hear the wheel turning, but I don't hear the squeak," Kate replied.

NSES
PD-B

"Exactly. The wheel squeaked because of too much friction. I put on oil to take away some of it. I think there is still some friction here. That is why we hear this rolling sound of the little balls in the wheel," hypothesized Jonathan. "Let's try something. Feel the back wheel on your bike to see how cool it feels. Then hold up your bike so the back wheel is off the floor so I can turn the pedal really fast. Then hang on but drop it so the wheel hits the floor." This was done with a skidding sound and jerking motion that left a black mark on the concrete floor. "Now quick, feel the tire. How does it feel now?"

"I think it's hotter, but I'm not sure," ventured Kate.

"Yes, that's because the tire rubbed against the floor and the friction heated it. Now try this. Press your hands together so the palms are flat. Press a little, and then rub them back and forth. How do they feel now?"

"A little bit warm," replied Kate.

"Yes. Now press harder and move them faster. How do they feel now?" asked Jonathan.

"Hot!" Kate exclaimed.

Jessica was intrigued by this conversation and startled that her young son seemed to understand the idea of friction, although he did not define it exactly. "Jon, how do you know about friction? Did Ms. Glock teach you about it in school?"

"Well, I think she tried," offered Jonathan. "We studied machines in third grade, and I remember reading about friction in the book. Ms. Glock talked about it, but I can't remember much."

"Then how did you learn so much about friction?" persisted Jessica.

"Uncle Gary taught me."

Jessica encouraged Jonathan to explain and eventually uncovered his story. Jonathan had helped his uncle build a storage shed for lawn tools. His uncle had put a board in place with long screws as a temporary support, then rapidly removed the screws with his cordless drill when the support was no longer needed. Jonathan's job was to pick up the screws and put them away. His uncle had warned that the screws would be hot and that Jonathan should let them cool for a few moments. Jonathan did not understand. The screws had been cool to the touch when he had handed them to his uncle, *before* they were driven into the board. Instead of explaining, Jonathan's uncle drove some cool screws into a board and then removed them quickly. They both carefully touched the screws and noticed that they were quite warm. Uncle Gary then explained that the surface of the screw threads rubbed quickly against the wood and that the rubbing heated the screw. He showed Jonathan how to understand what happened by rubbing his hands together, as Jonathan had done with his sister.

Uncle Gary used the word *friction* to represent the idea they were investigating. He also demonstrated the same idea with a sabre saw. Jonathan carefully touched the blade of the unplugged saw and felt that it was cool to the touch. Then Uncle Gary cut a board, unplugged the saw, and touched a piece of tissue paper to the blade. The saw blade scorched the paper. Uncle Gary asked Jonathan to explain what happened by way of friction. He also asked Jonathan to get his Cub Scout book, and they looked at ways to make campfires with primitive methods that used a bow and friction. They continued their discussion of friction by trying to stand on marbles in a box and noticed that it was difficult to do since friction between their shoes and the floor was reduced, and they speculated what it would be like to try to run on slick, wet concrete with smooth-soled shoes. They discussed why oil and coolants are important to an automobile by reducing friction and removing excess heat from the motor that is caused by friction and why cars skid off rain-slicked highway curves or on snow and ice. Jonathan and his uncle worked together to identify times when friction is helpful, such as a fast-moving biker trying to cycle around a sharp curve, or a basketball player driving to the basket. The firsthand experiences and discussions had helped Jonathan understand the basic idea of friction and expanded his understanding by applying the idea in new situations, such as with his sister and the bicycle pump.

The story was serendipitous for Jessica and signaled a connection to her teaching. She decided to change her way of learning and developed a vision for presenting lessons during the upcoming school year. She consulted her college texts and journals to review the principles of child and brain development. She changed from teacher-explainer/student-receiver to teacher-guide/student-constructor. Jessica was determined to see her students through new eyes, and she considered various perspectives on how children learn and possibilities to help them form mental connections. She resolved to try different teaching approaches that would guide her students' learning—helping them learn how to learn rather than telling them what they needed to know.

NSES
TS-C

How did you learn science? Was it similar to Jessica's typical way of teaching it? Was your experience based on the teacher's instructions and explanations, vocabulary development, and memorization? Or was your experience more like an adventure, in which the exact steps to follow were as unknown as the consequences of your decisions? Did your teachers emphasize the facts, symbols, labels, and formulas of science? Or were the general ideas—concepts—developed in a way that helped you to discover the connections among the many ideas and fields of science?

How do you view science, and how do children learn to share related consequences? If you view science as a discrete body of information to be learned, you will probably bring that assumption to your teaching, which will be much like Jessica's routine. If, after reading Chapter 1, you view the nature of science as a dynamic opportunity to help children develop essential attitudes, skills, and knowledge that can benefit each of them, you will likely bring that assumption to your teaching, which may resemble Jessica's new vision. Your view of how children learn has been shaped by your teachers, and in turn your beliefs will affect the children you teach. With a little imagination, you can see the consequences or benefits of this cycle.

Jessica's routine methods did not produce the results she wanted. She decided to experiment and try other methods. In doing so, Jessica developed professionally as she changed her beliefs about learning. This chapter is about how children learn and will focus on four areas:

1. The brain's unique structure and the function it plays in learning

2. The role that children's prior ideas and misconceptions play in their learning

3. The dominant contemporary perspective on science learning and how it helps children to become self-motivated and sustain independent learning

4. The essential techniques important for constructivist teaching

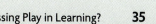

What Role Does Brain Development and Processing Play in Learning?

Simplified Brain Anatomy

NSES
PD-C

The adult brain is about the size of an oblong grapefruit, weighs about 3 pounds, consists of about 78 percent water (10 percent fat and 8 percent protein), and is covered with a one-quarter-inch-thick, wrinkled covering, resembling an orange peel, called the cerebral cortex. If unfolded, the cerebral cortex would be about the size of a newspaper page. The cortex is divided into lobes. Each lobe has a specific task with some functional overlap between lobes (see Figure 2.1). The occipital lobes process visual stimuli, the temporal lobes process auditory stimuli, the parietal lobes interpret and integrate sensory stimuli, the frontal lobes process high-level thinking such as problem solving and future planning, and deep somewhere within the cortex's lobes exists the capability to reflect and have awareness about what one thinks and does (Wolfe & Brandt, 1998). The human brain also contains the largest area of cortex (of all animals) that has no specifically assigned function, giving humans extraordinary flexibility for processing information and plasticity while learning. To assist in rapid and thorough processing, the brain's nerve cells are connected by about 1 million miles of nerve fibers (Jensen, 1998).

Simplified Brain Development and Function

NSES
PD-C

Although the brain is about 2 percent of body weight, it consumes 20 percent of one's energy (enough to light a 25-watt lightbulb). Brain energy comes from nutrients in the blood, and people need eight to twelve glasses of water each day to ensure optimal electrolytic balance of brain chemicals. Dehydration is a common problem in schools and can impair learning (Hannaford, 1995). A brain uses 20 percent of the body's oxygen. Air quality and lack of exercise can affect the oxygen richness of the blood, which can impair learning. Many people worry that schoolchildren do not exercise enough to ensure oxygen-rich blood (Jensen, 1998).

About 10 percent of a brain's cells are neurons, and these are used for thinking and learning (see Figure 2.2). *Neuron* means nerve cell and is a common name used to refer to a brain's cells. Before birth, a human fetus develops about 250,000 neurons per

FIGURE 2.1 ● **Lobes of the Brain** The cerebral cortex, a wrinkled ¼-inch-thick structure, covers the brain. Its regions are divided into lobes, each with specific functions.

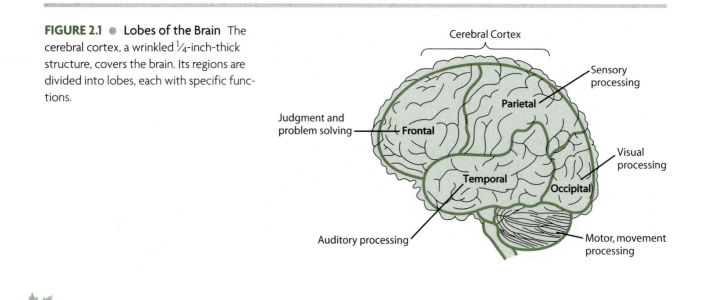

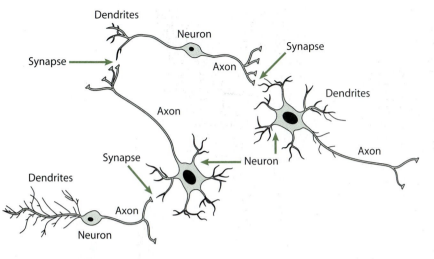

FIGURE 2.2 ● Neurons Make Connections; Connections Define Learning Neurons connect to other neurons via multiple pathways. Axons trail outward from neurons and connect with dendrites from other neurons. The connecting point is called a synapse—a space gap—across which electrochemical signals travel. Learning is believed to exist at these connections. A single neuron can connect with 5,000 to 10,000 other neurons, packing about one quadrillion connections into our brain (Wolfe & Brandt, 1998).

minute—a virtual blizzard—and at birth, a child has about 100 billion neurons (Sprenger, 1999). This number of neurons seems to be maintained throughout a lifetime, and there is some evidence that parts of our brain are capable of growing new neurons to replace those lost (Kinoshita, 1999)—a challenge to the myth that we are born with all of the neurons that we will ever have. However, the connections linking the neurons to each other change dramatically over a lifetime.

Young children's brains are like sponges, thriving on enriched stimulation. Human newborns begin to form synapses at rates far in excess of adults, so by about age four, synaptic densities have peaked and are about 50 percent greater than those of adults. Around puberty, a process that prunes away excess synapses and continues through adulthood begins, in which losses of cell neurons and synapses can occur every day through attrition, decay, and disuse (Bruer, 1998). As well, sufficient challenges and mental stimulation can increase and improve connections.

Signal Processing

Neurons have a compact cell body. They process information by converting chemicals into electrical signals and by conveying signals back and forth between other neurons; normal neurons constantly receive and send signals. Dendrites and axons are attached to the body of the neuron cell. Dendrites are like branches and extend outward from the neuron. Enriched learning environments stimulate the growth and number of dendrites, helping to afford each neuron multiple pathways for processing signals. Similar to alternative traffic routes used as detours around clogged highways or closed bridges, multiple pathways provide bypasses for each neuron; this helps learning. Axons grow out from each neuron and connect with the dendrites of other cells. Each axon helps to transport the brain's chemicals and conducts the electrical signals received by the neuron (see Figure 2.3). Each neuron receives signals from thousands of other brain cells, depending on the number of branches grown.

NSES
PD-C

The electrical signals occur because ions exchange charges possessed by nutrients in the food we eat, thus making a proper diet and hydration important for learning. Sodium, potassium, and calcium have positive charges, and chloride has a

FIGURE 2.3 ● The Synaptic Gap

An electrical charge is received by a neuron and travels to the tip of the axon, where electrical energy is converted to chemical energy by chemicals called neurotransmitters, which send a signal across the synaptic gap to the receptors on the dendrite of another neuron. The chemical signal is converted to electricity and travels through the axon of different neurons to the receptors of other neurons' dendrites. A network is established with multiple pathways for signals that travel at speeds of about 200 miles per hour.

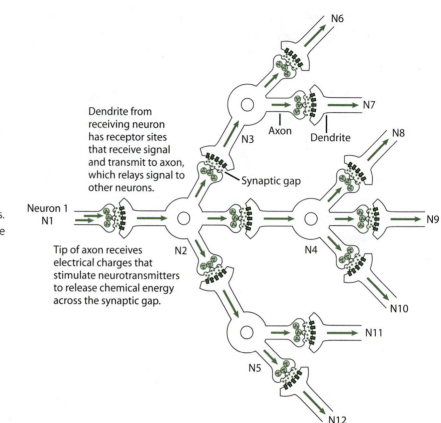

Dendrite from receiving neuron has receptor sites that receive signal and transmit to axon, which relays signal to other neurons.

Synaptic gap

Neuron 1
N1

Tip of axon receives electrical charges that stimulate neurotransmitters to release chemical energy across the synaptic gap.

negative charge. These charges are exchanged when some ions are permitted to pass through channels in the cell membranes of neurons while others are prevented from passing. Channels are openings in the cell membranes and function as types of switches, opening in response to particular chemical stimuli and closing to others.

The neurons would be nothing without nurture and sustenance, and the synapses would lose their abilities to transmit electrical signals efficiently without insulation. As you examine Figure 2.3, imagine glial cells surrounding and attaching themselves to the neurons to provide sustenance, clean up waste, and accelerate communications. The glial cells outnumber the neurons, and more glial cells are needed when neurons maintain high levels of activity. Glial cells can reproduce, and our brain can grow as many as are needed (Sprenger, 1999).

Myelin is a fattylike substance that coats the axons. This coating insulates the connection with dendrites, reduces weakening or loss of electrical signals, and helps to speed the transmission of messages exchanged with other neurons. Neurophysiologists theorize that the more often an axon fires, the more layers of myelin are added; so like a pathway through park grass, the more it is walked upon, the smoother it becomes and the easier and faster it is to travel (Hannaford, 1995). Another researcher theorizes that myelination of neurons in different regions of the brain coincides with developmental and reasoning processes from birth through adolescence very much as Piaget theorized (Healy, 1994).

Theories aside, with support from glial cells and myelin, our brain's neurons, axons, and dendrites form a system of circuits for transmitting electricity. Those electrical signals speed along at about 200 miles per hour. Each brain cell behaves like a small battery, generating electrical impulses from the potassium and sodium concentrated in cell membranes located at the synaptic gap—the small space located between the end of the axon and the tip of a dendrite. Some of these electrical signals may be new stimuli, requiring more neurons to be involved in the processing beyond the well-rehearsed pathways that are already conditioned to respond to stimuli. New stimuli encourage the growth of new synapses, which are regarded as evidence that the brain grows new connections as a consequence of learning. When the transmitted signals are related to what we already know or can do, they move along previously established neural pathways. Accumulations of pathways with recognizable patterns enhance memory retrieval and application of "remembered" (stored) material to new experiences (Krueger & Sutton, 2001). This allows the processing to be more efficient and uses fewer of the brain's neurons, but it also reinforces and makes connections stronger (Jensen, 1998). In brief, learning occurs when synaptic efficiency is enhanced.

Making Connections Makes Learning

Jensen (1998) distinguishes between learning, what we have described so far, and behavior, which is more likely governed by emotional states and memories. The brain is a soup of floating chemicals, mostly peptides, and Pert (1997) estimates that at least 98 percent of the brain and body's internal communications occur through peptides and control behavior such as attention span, levels of stress, and drowsiness.

NSES
PD-B

Experienced educators today often remark that children seem less well prepared for learning in school. There is some evidence to suggest that this is true. A developing fetus is extremely sensitive to stress from chemical and emotional effects and from poor nutrition. The effects can be huge if these stresses occur and interact during embryonic development, a time when brain cells develop rapidly.

Researchers report that emotional intelligence begins very early, and the early school grades may be a last opportunity to nurture emotional literacy (Goleman, 1995). Troubled early relationships can cause the brain to consume nutrients that are essential to cognitive functions and divert them to dealing with stress or violence. The brain can become reorganized, and the child may become more impulsive or aggressive in school or social relationships (Kotulak, 1996).

Unstimulating playgrounds, car seats that limit visual stimulation, sedentary activity while in day care, and lengthy exposure to television can impede the development of early motor skills by restricting vestibular stimulation, which can impact the brain's readiness for reading, writing, and attention (Hannaford, 1995). Restricted stimulation has been linked to learning problems such as dyslexia (Cleeland, 1984). Early stimulation in enriched environments can help the brain develop visualization (Kotulak, 1996), thinking skills (Greenfield, 1995), auditory skills (Begley, 1996), and language (Kotulak, 1993). Inadequate sleep, poor nutrition, and dehydration also affect the developing (and the developed) brain's ability to function properly in school (Jensen, 1998).

What does brain research suggest we can do to improve learning? The first thing is to focus on helping learners to grow more synaptic connections between brain cells and to strengthen, rather than lose, existing connections. Connection-making is central to learning, and enabling brain cell connections helps learners problem solve, a key to modern scientific literacy. Connections are made among and between ideas and experiences. Children will learn science more effectively if

Experiences using tools help to develop and strengthen neural pathways.

we consider their prior ideas and nurture their connection-making through constructivist principles of learning.

Reducing Stress Nurtures Learning

Enriched learning environments motivate and nurture neural connections. Brain chemistry receives a positive effect when neurotransmitters do not overly excite or impede emotions and physical activity. These suggestions help to reduce stress on teachers and learners (Sprenger, 1999):

- Play calming music, such as a classical type.
- Affirm for learners that it is fine to make errors and to learn from them.
- Promote team work and productive social learning.
- Celebrate success.
- Use stretching to incorporate movement into learning and role playing to add fun.
- Provide options and multiple outlets for expression of emotions.
- Set an example by taking care of yourself and modeling the benefits for your learners.

Where Do Children's Ideas Come From and How Do They Influence Learning?

NSES
PD-B

Rosalind Driver (Driver, Guensne, & Tiberghien, 1985) and her fellow researchers have studied this question extensively. Consider the following classroom example involving two 11-year-old students.

Tim and Ricky are studying the way in which a spring extends as they add ball bearings to a plastic drinking cup that is attached to and hangs from the spring, which is suspended from a clamp on a stand. Ricky carefully adds the bearings one at a time and measures the change in the length of the spring after each addition. Tim watches and inquires, "Wait a moment. What happens if we lift up the spring?" Ricky clamps the spring higher on the stand, measures its stretched length, and continues after he is satisfied that the length of the spring is the same as before the change in position. An observer asks Tim the reasons behind his suggestion. Tim picks up two bearings, pretends that they are pebbles, and explains his idea about weight changing as objects are lifted higher:

> This is farther up and gravity is pulling it down harder the farther away. The higher it gets the more effect gravity will have on it because if you just stood over there and someone dropped a pebble on him, it would just sting him, it wouldn't hurt him. But if I dropped it from an aeroplane it would be accelerating faster and faster and when it hit someone on the head it would kill him. (Driver, Guensne, & Tiberghien, 1985, pp. 1–2)

Tim's idea is not scientifically correct. The object's weight decreases as height increases. However, the idea is not irrational if you consider Tim's reasoning: He seems to be referring to what scientists call gravitational potential energy. The ideas children bring with them often influence what and how they learn.

Children form their own science ideas through direct experience, with social interaction.

Preconceptions

The ideas from prior experiences that children bring with them have been called a variety of names: *alternative frameworks, children's science, naive theories,* and *preconceptions.* We prefer to call them *preconceptions* because children's ideas are often incomplete preliminary understandings of fundamental science concepts that explain their everyday world. These preconceptions are influenced by hands-on, minds-on experiences, such as direct physical experiences, emotional experiences through social processes, and thoughtful efforts to make sense of the various things that exist in a child's world. Preconceptions that are brought to a new learning opportunity are important, even for adults, because the process of learning is the human activity of making connections in the brain.

NSES
PD-C

Adults and children can have a type of bias that is influenced by expectations that fit patterns already formed in the brain from previous experiences. Young children may have limited or incomplete experiences. Bias inherent in preconceptions can influence concept formation. A well-known paleoanthropologist, Donald Johanson, recognized the importance of this when he wrote: "There is no such thing as total lack of bias. . . . The fossil hunter in the field has it. If he is interested in hippo teeth, that is what he is going to find, and that will bias his collection because he will walk right by other fossils without noticing them" (Kinnear, 1994, p. 3). Another scientist, David Pilbeam, illustrates this point by explaining how his original interpretation of a particular fossil was affected by his prior expectations: "I knew . . . [the fossil], being a hominid, would have a short face and rounded jaw—so that's what I saw" (Kinnear, 1994, p. 3). Additional discoveries and further investigation revealed that the fossil did not possess the features that Pilbeam described and that it was not a hominid.

Misconceptions

Misconceptions are alternative understandings about phenomena that learners have formed. They are scientifically incorrect interpretations that learners believe or responses to problems that learners provide. "Misconceptions do not simply signify a lack of knowledge, factual errors, or incorrect definitions. Instead, misconceptions represent explanations of phenomena constructed by a student in response to the student's prior knowledge and experience" (Munson, 1994, pp. 30–31). For example, through reading and participation in class activities, including gamelike simulations, a learner may form the misconception that the top of a food chain has the most energy because it accumulates up the food chain (Adeniyi, 1985), whereas a correct scientific conception maintains the opposite: Available energy decreases as one progresses up a food chain (Munson, 1994). Students commonly believe that the summer season occurs because the earth is closer to the sun and that moon phases happen because the earth casts shadows on the moon.

NSES
PD-C

Despite sincere efforts, even some of the best students give correct answers using words they have adapted into their developing language repertoire or have memorized but do not fully understand. If we question them more closely, we can often discover misconceptions that are based on lack of understanding about the underlying concepts. Misunderstandings are quite common when one considers that children learn spontaneous concepts from their everyday experiences. While these experiences are rooted in the concrete, the expressions of understandings arise from abstractions in language. Spoken language precedes conceptualization in the everyday life of a child. As well, according to Vygotsky, thinking in science is special because new concepts that are learned in science arise from work done within a formal conceptual structure. However, a child's better-known (and trusted) informal everyday structure of play and social interactions does not reveal much that shows true understandings of science concepts, which are often invisible, abstract, or otherwise inaccessible to teachers

(Carlsen, 2007). This tension between the concrete and the abstract can be a fertile breeding ground in which misconceptions can form and grow.

Misconceptions represent a liability that affects students and their teachers. The Committee on Undergraduate Science Education (1997) described several categories of misconceptions that shed light on the basic reasons behind misconceptions and the lingering liability associated with them.

Conceptual misunderstandings may occur when learners are taught in a way that does not allow them to examine the differences between language, their own beliefs, and "real science." For example, adults may tell growing children that the "sun rises and sets," which gives children a mental image that it is the sun that moves around the earth. In school, they are taught that the earth moves by rotation and revolution, and now children face the difficult task of removing one mental image and replacing it with another. This is not easy to do, and it is not a trivial task to rearrange mental schema.

Vernacular misconceptions can arise from imprecise language that we use during explanations. For example, perhaps a teacher remarks that glaciers "retreat." As a child, could you imagine a glacier stopping, turning around, and going back in the opposite direction from which it had come? Simply substituting the word *melt* could avoid or correct this misunderstanding and help children to understand that glaciers can melt faster than they advance (this is what is meant by "retreat").

Factual misconceptions often occur at an early age based on myths and false statements that are accepted as facts, such as "lightning never strikes twice, in the same place." Lightning can strike the same place twice, and nothing prevents this from occurring; lightning does not have a mind of its own to decide where to strike.

William Philips, an earth science teacher, discovered some interesting but depressing facts about what his students knew about science—or rather, what they really did not understand. What was most troublesome was that his students thought they were correct.

Misconceptions are rarely expressed aloud or in writing and, therefore, often go undetected. Twenty years ago, shortly after I began teaching science, I encountered an outrageous misconception (or so it seemed at the time). While I was using a globe to explain seasonal changes, one very attentive eighth grader raised her hand and asked, "Where are we?" Thinking she wanted to know the location of our school, I pointed to Delaware and resumed my lecture. She immediately stopped me with another question. "No. I don't mean that. I mean, do we live inside the Earth or outside it?" The question caused several students to laugh, but most appeared to be waiting for an answer. It was all I could do to hide my astonishment. (Philips, 1991, p. 21)

Philips cites a survey in which second-grade teachers estimated that 95 percent of their students knew that the earth is a sphere. Later, the teachers conducted interviews with the children and discovered that the students actually believed that the earth is flat. Misconceptions are common, and once formed, they are held a long while. Misconceptions are linked to intuitive ideas, beliefs, or preconceptions. It is not unusual for students to go through school providing correct answers when the teachers ask for them but believing otherwise, much like the second graders mentioned above. When students give science facts correctly to questions and on tests, it does not mean that they have replaced the misconceptions they formed much earlier.

Examples of misconceptions that Philips uncovered are given in Table 2.1. Misconceptions seem to occur as students construct knowledge; they may be linked to incomplete or insufficient experiences, faulty explanations, and misperceived meanings.

Guided experiences help to reduce misconceptions.

TABLE 2.1 ● Common Earth Science Misconceptions

More than ten years' worth of research on misconceptions yielded the following list for children. Adults often harbor the same misconceptions.

The earth is sitting on something.
The earth is larger than the sun.
The earth is round like a pancake.
We live on the flat middle of a sphere.
There is a definite up and down in space.
Astrology is able to predict the future.
Gravity increases with height.
Gravity cannot exist without air.
Any crystal that scratches glass is a diamond.
Coral reefs exist throughout the Gulf of Mexico and the North Atlantic.
Dinosaurs and cavemen lived at the same time.
Rain comes from holes in clouds.
Rain comes from clouds' sweating.
Rain falls from funnels in the clouds.
Rain occurs when clouds are shaken.
God and angels cause thunder and lightning.
Clouds move because we move.
Clouds come from somewhere above the sky.

Empty clouds are refilled by the sea.
Clouds are formed by vapors from kettles.
The sun boils the sea to create water vapor.
Clouds are made of cotton, wool, or smoke.
Clouds are bags of water.
Stars and constellations appear in the same place in the sky every night.
The seasons are caused by the earth's distance from the sun.
The moon can be seen only at night.
The earth is the largest object in the solar system.
Gas makes things lighter.
Batteries have electricity inside them.
Things "use up" energy.
Wood floats and metal sinks.
Liquids rise in a straw because of "suction."
Boiling is the maximum temperature that a substance can reach.
Air and oxygen are the same thing.

Source: Excerpted from the list provided by William C. Philips, "Earth Science Misconceptions," *Science Teacher* (February 1991): 21–23. Bill Weiler (1998). University of Illinois [Online]. http://k12s.phast.umass.edu/~nasa/misconceptions.html

Joseph Novak (1991), a professor of science and education, reminds us that students must construct new meaning from the foundation of the knowledge they already possess. This means that teachers cannot afford to overlook student misconceptions because of the negative learning cycle caused by misunderstanding the simplest point. Novak also states that students can create new meaning only by constructing new propositions, linked concepts that are usually formed through discovery learning. This requires expansions of their neural networks.

What Do We Know About Children's Ideas?

Children bring many ideas to class. Their ideas represent the interpretations they have formed about the dilemmas and phenomena they have encountered. Many of these experiences occur out of school and are not connected to formal teaching, including play, conversations, and events observed through the media. Recent research on children's ideas reveals three important factors: (1) Children's ideas are personal constructions, (2) the ideas may seem incomplete or contradictory, and (3) the ideas are often very stable and highly resistant to change (Driver et al., 1985; Driver, 1996).

NSES
PD-B

Children's Ideas Are Personal. Have you ever been with a group of friends and witnessed a remarkable event, such as a concert, championship play-off, or auto accident? Or have you participated in a heated debate about a topic that was important to you? How did your perceptions of the facts or the event compare with those of your friends? Was there complete agreement on each detail? "No" is not an unusual answer. Consider children in a class, each participating in the same science activity. It is likely that the children will report diverse perceptions of what happened during the activity. Each child has seen and experienced the activity, but each has internalized the experiences in his or her own way. Our perceptions and descriptions depend as much on our original ideas as they do on the nature of the new experience or lesson. Readers do not all receive exactly the same message, even from written words.

Learners construct their own meanings. *Constructed meanings* are based on new experiences that are accumulated and compared with and processed from old ideas. Constructed meanings arise from the expanded and cross-referenced neural networks formed in the brain. The preexisting ideas are the basis for observing, classifying, and interpreting new experiences. In this way, each learner, even a very young one, continually forms and reforms hypotheses and theories about natural phenomena. We call on the mind's existing ideas to help us understand new experiences (Harlen, 1992, p. 11). What is remarkable is that although ideas are constructed independently, the general interpretations and conclusions are often shared by many (Driver, 1983).

A Child's Ideas May Seem Contradictory. Natural science is blessed with many intriguing discrepancies. Touch the flat bottom of an uncoated paper cup with a candle flame, and predictably, the paper burns after a brief time. But add water to a cup, and the

Brain-Based Learning

Marilee Sprenger suggests that you may have heard "stories about 'right-brained' people and 'left-brained' people. These are simply that—stories. People are not 'right brained' or 'left brained' unless, of course, they have had a hemisphere removed. This type of surgery is done, but only under the rarest of circumstances. We use our whole brains to function" (1999, p. 41). We benefit intellectually, emotionally, and socially when our brains receive abundant stimulation. However, just what the stimuli ought to be is complicated and cannot be prescribed for consistent classroom results. Although we are still learning about how our brains function, we are fortunate to have summaries from brain-based research that may help us to improve learning:

- We should stimulate all of the senses but not necessarily all at once.
- Science curricula should repeat concepts in a new manner or context; avoid mere duplication.
- Previous experiences and meaning affect how the brain processes new experiences and organizes new knowledge.
- Our emotions and our learning share an important relationship.
- Emotion enhances memory—a reason to include personal examples and social materials into the science curriculum.

- Learning is more than exercising the brain like a muscle. It is a true physiological experience that involves a sophisticated set of systems.
- New material will fade from short-term memory unless learners can connect it to already familiar material.
- Our brain processes and organizes many stimuli and ideas at the same time, even though we might focus on only one thing at a time.
- The significance of subject matter content depends on how our experiences are arranged and fit into patterns.
- We should present a series of novel challenges that are appropriate for development.
- Our brains process peripheral stimuli consciously and unconsciously.
- Parts and wholes are processed simultaneously by our brains, not separately or in isolation in a particular hemisphere.
- We possess spatial memories that help us to retrieve experiences rapidly and easily; for example, we might have a detailed memory of an important event even though we made no special attempt to memorize details.
- We need more practice to recall facts and to establish a level of skill when these facts are not embedded in our spatial memories.

NSES

PD-B

cup will not burn even when heated by a stronger source for a much longer time. This result challenges the mature mind to identify a coherent reason that explains the behavior of the candle and cup under all circumstances. The younger mind may see no problem and simply use another, even contradictory, explanation, unconcerned that the explanation is inconsistent with what was previously said. As Driver (1983) reminds us:

> The same child may have different conceptions of a particular type of phenomenon, sometimes using different arguments leading to opposite predictions in situations which are equivalent from a scientist's point of view, and even switching from one sort of explanation to another for the same phenomenon. (p. 3)

A child does not have the same need for coherence as an adult or a scientist has, nor does a child have a mental model to use to unify a range of different perceptions that relate to the same event. Furthermore, a child usually does not see the need for a consistent view. The constructed ideas work quite well for the child in his or her classroom practice, even though the ideas may be based on prior false conclusions.

Children's Ideas Often Resist Change. It is not simple for teachers to change children's incomplete or flawed ideas about scientific events and phenomena. Additional activities,

- Our brains respond positively to problems and challenges but are less effective under duress.
- We should allow social interaction for a significant percentage of activities.

Much of a learner's constructed meaning is accomplished through shared uses of words and language. Ernst von Glasersfeld, philosopher and regarded leader of the constructivist movement in science education, suggests that the making of meaning is not a process of giving, taking, or sharing as a commodity, such as a pencil, marker, or scissors. Meaning is achieved eventually and gradually and has a relative fit within the learner's social context; meaning is affected by a learner's culture. The meanings that children give to labels or words that are new to them are idiosyncratic and do not conform well to what a teacher may intend. To become more successful, teachers operate on these principles:

- Whatever a student provides as an answer to a question or problem is based on what made sense to the student at that time. The response must be taken seriously, regardless of how odd or "wrong" it might seem to the teacher. Otherwise the student will be discouraged and inhibited. Also, understand that the answer may be a good one depending on how the student interpreted the question.
- A teacher who wishes to modify a student's concepts and conceptual structures must try to build a mental

model of the student's individual thinking. Never assume that a student's way of thinking is simple or transparent.

- Asking students how they arrived at their given answer is a good way of discovering something about their thinking, and it opens the way to explaining why a particular answer may not be useful under different circumstances.
- If you want to motivate students to delve further into questions that they say are of no particular interest to them, create situations in which the students have an opportunity to experience the pleasure inherent in solving a problem. Simply being told "good" or "correct" does not help a learner's conceptual development.
- Successful thinking is more than "correct" answers; it should be rewarded even if it is based on unacceptable premises.
- A teacher must have an almost infinitely flexible mind to understand and appreciate students' thinking because students sometimes start from premises that seem inconceivable to teachers.
- Constructivist teachers can never justify what they teach by claiming it is true. In science, they cannot say more than that it is the best way of conceiving the situation because it is the most effective way at the moment of dealing with it.

Sources: Renate Nummela Caine and Geoffrey Caine, *Teaching and the Human Brain* (Alexandria, VA: Association for Supervision and Curriculum Development, 1991); M. Diamond, and J. Hopson, *Magic Trees of the Mind: How to Nurture Your Child's Intelligence, Creativity, and Healthy Emotions from Birth through Adolescence* (New York: Dutton 1998), pp. 107–108; Ernst von Glasersfeld, "Questions and Answers about Radical Constructivism," in Kenneth Tobin (Ed.), *The Practice of Constructivism in Science Education* (Washington, DC: AAAS Press, 1993), pp. 32–33; Alice Krueger and John Sutton (Eds.), *EDThoughts: What We Know about Science Teaching and Learning* (Aurora, CO: Mid-continent Research for Education and Learning, 2001), p. 91; Ernt von Glasersfeld, "Introduction: Aspects of Constructivism," in C. T. Fosnot, *Constructivism: Theory, Perspective and Practice* (New York: Teachers College Press, 2005), pp. 3–7.
Marilee Sprenger, *Learning and Memory: The Brain in Action* (Alexandria, VA: Association for Supervision and Curriculum Development, 1999).

comparative discussions, and even direct teacher explanations may not cause children to modify their ideas. Changing ideas is a slow process, and the necessary changes may never be complete. Children may only feel that they are to provide a certain correct answer to a teacher's questions but choose to turn off the academically correct answer in favor of the previous independent ideas once the test is over. Counterevidence presented to the child seems to make no difference. Interpretations often are based on prior ideas. Personal, if contradictory, ideas have tremendous stability and endurance (Driver, 1983, p. 4; 1996).

What Is the Dominant Perspective About How Children Learn Science?

Constructivism is the general name given to the dominant perspective on learning in science education. A constructivist perspective on teaching and learning is unlike traditional views. A teacher who embraces constructivism supports a different view of science, regards the roles of teacher and learner very differently, and selects and organizes teaching materials and the social learning environment with particular care. A constructivist perspective emphasizes the role of the learner, regarding the role as active—physically, mentally, and socially—rather than passive. The constructivist teacher seeks ways to challenge and stimulate mental connection-making in order to enhance the active participation of learners in lessons and encourage learners to construct their own understanding of their reality, which arises from their experiences. Jessica's efforts toward change illustrate a constructivist attempt.

NSES
PD-B

Jessica: A Constructivist Attempt

On the basis of her experience with her son, Jessica was determined to avoid her usual demonstration and recipe instructions. Now she distributed the materials for the science lesson *first:* clay, scissors, cardboard, rulers, string, and so on. She asked small groups of children to work together in teams to design and construct a landscape—any type of landscape *they* chose. Jessica wanted to avoid mimicry and to encourage the students not to get fixed on the definitions of a landscape, since that was not the point of the lesson. Therefore she did not define "landscape," nor did she show particular examples. When students questioned her about the task, she encouraged them to use their intuitive understanding about landscapes—their preconceptions—to think about their experiences and use what they already knew.

The groups did not begin smoothly, perhaps because the children were not accustomed to vague instructions. However, the puzzled expressions and occasional off-task behavior associated with the newfound freedom quickly subsided as Jessica maintained consistent contact with each group and challenged their thinking by asking guiding questions: "How else could you do that?" "What other features could you add?" "Where have you seen landscapes like this?" Jessica also lifted up the unique examples from single groups for all of the other groups to examine. These examples stimulated many to say, "Oh, now I see!"

After a bit more exploration, Jessica challenged each group to draw two-dimensional maps of their three-dimensional landscapes. This proved difficult until the concepts of contour and interval were constructed. Jessica guided her class in defining what these words meant and figuring out how the ideas were important to the lesson. Soon each group was applying basic math and measurement skills to construct a contour map of their own landscapes to scale. Later, the children took actual contour maps and recreated different landscapes they had never visited, again to scale.

Jessica did continue to use typical testing methods and noticed a deeper understanding of the children's learning. When she asked questions or when the children wrote answers to her tests, the responses were more detailed and appeared to be more thoughtful, and the children seemed able to use their ideas in new situations. The children seemed happier and excited about science, and this satisfied Jessica—for now.

Constructivism

Let us return to Jessica, who appears to be guided by the notion of constructivism, an emerging consensus among psychologists, science educators, philosophers of science, scientists, and others who are interested in improving children's learning. This view of learning maintains that learners (young and old and professionals such as scientists) must construct and reconstruct their own meaning for ideas about how the world works (Good, Wandersee, & St. Julien, 1993). In a very simplified way, an ancient Chinese proverb encapsulates the intent of constructivism: "I hear and I forget; I see and I remember; I *do* and I *understand*." A lot of wisdom is packed into these three phrases. One type of sensory experience alone is insufficient when we strive for understanding. Experience requires substantial stimulation of all senses and each child's mental processes if meaningful learning is to occur. Learning is influenced by a child's culture within a context of social experiences.

Childhood educators Connie Williams and Constance Kamii (1986) recommend that we strive to accomplish three things when we encourage children toward understanding:

1. Use or create learning circumstances that are indeed meaningful to the learners.
2. Encourage children to make real decisions.
3. Provide children opportunities to refine their thinking and deepen their understanding by exchanging views with their peers.

Williams and Kamii (1986) remind us that what is important is "the mental action that is encouraged when children act on objects themselves" (p. 26). Mental action is the planned or guided metacognitive activity of cognitive constructivism, a mental state influenced by physical and social interaction with the learner's world. Hence, learning is not limited to cognitive activity; emotion also influences learning.

Constructivism Defined. Constructivism is a theory of learning that assumes that real knowledge cannot exist outside the minds of thinking persons. This learning theory capitalizes on the brain's desire for stimulation and natural curiosity as it constantly seeks to make connections between the new and the known (Wolfe & Brandt, 1998). Joseph Novak (Novak & Gowin 1986) defines constructivism as the notion that humans construct or build meaning into their ideas and experiences as a result of an effort to understand or to make sense of them. Novak explains that this construction

Cognitive constructions occur as each learner attempts to make meaning.

> involves at times recognition of new regularities in events or objects, inventing new concepts or extending old concepts, recognition of new relationships (propositions) between concepts, and . . . major restructuring of conceptual frameworks to see new higher order relationships. (p. 356)

Novak describes a cognitive process that revolves around constructs, which, according to Snow, Corno, and Jackson (1996), are scientific concepts that arise from hypothetized relationships among attributes of objects and events, that is, an individual's thoughts used to represent emergent understandings. Those thoughts are communicated through spoken language through social interactions with teachers and peers. Hence, the learner's cultural context for emotional and social experiences plays an important part in the making of meaning, that is, the sense making attempted by each individual.

Constructivism emphasizes the importance of each pupil's active construction of knowledge through the interplay of prior learning and newer learning. "Learning is a process of active construction by the learner, and an enriched environment gives the students the opportunity to relate what they are learning to what they already know" (Wolfe & Brandt, 1998, p. 11). Connections are sought between the prior and the newer learning; the connections are constructed by the learners for themselves. Researchers and theorists maintain that the key element of constructivist theory is that people learn by actively constructing their own knowledge, comparing new information with their previous understanding and using all of this to work through discrepancies to come to a new understanding (Loucks-Horsley, 1990; Harlen, 1992; Peterson & Knapp, 1993; Yager, 1991). Of course, these actions are not isolated experiences occurring in a learner's mind; social interplay is also important.

Consider the possible vast difference between a scientist's ideas and those of a child. A scientist's perspective might be "A plant is a producer." In contrast, a child's perspective might be as follows:

> A plant is something that grows in a garden. Carrots and cabbage from the garden are not plants; they are vegetables. Trees are not plants; they are plants when they are little, but when they grow up they are not plants. Seeds are not plants. Dandelions are not plants; they are weeds. Plants . . . have multiple sources of food. Photosynthesis is not important to plants. (Osborne & Freyberg, 1990, p. 49)

Some concepts are correct but not inclusive. Other concepts are incorrect and merit thoughtful attention and eventual correction, stimulated by a teacher's guided interaction.

Constructivism is a synthesis of several dominant perspectives on learning. It is not entirely new. Contemporary researchers from Great Britain, Australia, New Zealand, and the United States have updated theories and methods to capture the synergy of legendary psychologists, philosophers, and researchers.

The constructivist perspective is grounded in the research and theories of Jean Piaget and Lev Vygotsky, the Gestalt psychologists; Jerome Bruner; and the philosophy of John Dewey, and is a natural extension of applied brain research. As you may imagine, the very nature and meaning of constructivism are open to interpretation; there is no one constructivist theory of learning. Some perspectives embrace the social nature of learning (Vygotsky); radical constructivists do not believe that the world is knowable (Ernst von Glasersfeld); and more conservative views advocate using constructivist principles to help learners construct accurate and useful conceptions and webs of conceptual understanding. The continuum in Figure 2.4 illustrates degrees of difference in viewpoints among constructivists and constructivist views in respect to traditional views on teaching and learning (Shapiro, 1994). Radical constructivists (not political) place greater emphasis on the individual's active, social, participation in knowledge construction and are located at the farthest left point on the continuum. Conservative constructivists use activity-based and problem-based learning experiences and teacher intervention to promote conceptual constructions, and they attempt to correct student misconceptions by helping learners construct understanding based on concepts embraced by the scientific community. Traditionalists, at the extreme right of the continuum, assume more passive learning roles for students.

Learners are
most active

Learners are
least active

Personal meaning   Scientific meaning   Memorization

*Radical
constructivists*

*Conservative
constructivists*

*Traditional
teaching/learning*

FIGURE 2.4 ● Teaching/Learning Continuum of Mental Operations

Jean Piaget's research and his cognitive development theory are regarded as the foundation of conservative constructivists' views. His contributions to constructivism arose from his theory about mental equilibration and its interplay with assimilation and accommodation.

Equilibration. According to Piaget's theory, learning is an active mental process in which each learner must construct knowledge by interacting with the environment and by resolving the cognitive conflicts that arise between what is expected and what is observed (Driver, 1983, p. 52). Each new interaction or conflict creates a dilemma in each learner's mind about how to maintain mental equilibrium.

Equilibration is a process by which each learner compensates mentally for each dilemma. Each new attempt at restoring equilibrium helps to create a higher level of functional equilibration; higher mental structures are formed. (See Figure 2.5.)

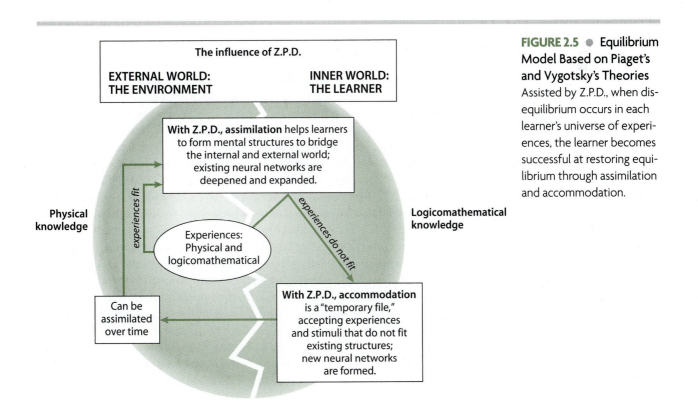

The influence of Z.P.D.

**EXTERNAL WORLD:
THE ENVIRONMENT**

**INNER WORLD:
THE LEARNER**

With Z.P.D., assimilation helps learners to form mental structures to bridge the internal and external world; existing neural networks are deepened and expanded.

**Physical
knowledge**

**Logicomathematical
knowledge**

experiences fit

experiences do not fit

Experiences:
Physical and
logicomathematical

Can be
assimilated
over time

With Z.P.D., accommodation is a "temporary file," accepting experiences and stimuli that do not fit existing structures; new neural networks are formed.

FIGURE 2.5 ● Equilibrium Model Based on Piaget's and Vygotsky's Theories Assisted by Z.P.D., when disequilibrium occurs in each learner's universe of experiences, the learner becomes successful at restoring equilibrium through assimilation and accommodation.

However, equilibrium is not a static point at which the mind rests as if on a balance beam. Instead, equilibration is like a cyclist's maintaining dynamic balance with each new challenge on the touring course. "The brain is continually seeking to impose order on incoming stimuli and to generate models that lead to adaptive behavior and useful predictions" (Yager, 1991, p. 54).

Assimilation. Assimilation is one way in which the mind may adapt to the learning challenge and restore equilibrium. If the stimulus is not too different from previous experiences and mental actions, it may be combined with or added to existing mental structures, like filing a new letter into a preexisting folder containing the same or similar information.

Accommodation. On those occasions when no preexisting mental structures (or file folders) are available to assimilate, the mind must adapt by changing or adding to its mental structures. This process of adaptation is called accommodation. The learner's thinking is adapted to accommodate the dilemma.

In practice, assimilation and accommodation are related and do not occur in isolation; each process complements the other and benefits from cooperative social interaction, as is proposed by Lev Vygotsky's views on social learning theory, particularly his notion of the Zone of Proximal Development, or Z.P.D. (Doolittle, 1997). Vygotsky's notion of Z.P.D. refers to the "distance between the abilities displayed independently and with social support" (Morris, 2007, p. 1) and proposes that children can solve challenging problems only when they are interacting with other people who are more advanced and in cooperation with peers. The challenge is to avoid both underestimating what a learner can do and having the task exceed a learner's ability by so much that it becomes incomprehensible; set the bar just beyond the learner's reach to provide sufficient challenge and motivation. As a part of the "external world" (Figure 2.5), a teacher uses Z.P.D. as a tool for helping a learner to build temporary files, as in accommodation, and gradually develop to the point of assimilating new stimuli into reliable cognitive structures, as in Figure 2.6.

Jessica: The Novelty Wore Off

NSES
PD-A

Jessica used learning groups to undertake the class's new approach to science learning. The students were very excited and cooperative—for about a week. Soon, what had been discussion, sharing and playing roles, and collective searches for meaning degenerated into arguments and stalemates over who would get materials and clean up. Normally, class time devoted to positive human relations, genuine regard, and time management would not concern Jessica. As the weeks passed, what bothered Jessica most was the growing number of students who seemed to have persistent ideas and misconceptions unchanged by the effort of problem- and project-based group work. Several individual students complained that they preferred to work by themselves rather than as a part of a group.

Concurrent reading that Jessica was doing as she experimented with her new class arrangements led her into a deeper investigation of cooperative group learning processes, constructivism, and learning models. Students wanted a flexible grouping arrangement and job assignments; they also wanted opportunities to leave a group structure. Poring over how to structure and manage all of the requests for changes, Jessica became mildly embarrassed by the sudden realization that the true spirit of constructivism would be for her to let the *students* decide how to solve their problem. The class decided to vary the number of people in groups; some contained only two, while others consisted of three to five students. Most realized that working with others was a better way to form understandings because ideas and explanations always

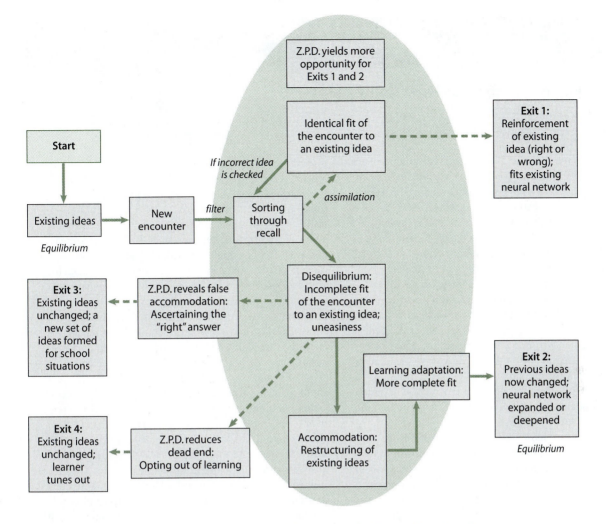

FIGURE 2.6 ● Science Education Learning Model: Z.P.D. Guides Toward Exits 1 and 2

Source: Adapted from K. Appleton, "Using Theory to Guide Practice: Teaching Science from a Constructivist Perspective," *School Science and Mathematics, 93* (5) (1993): 270.

had to be tested; cases had to be presented and pass the scrutiny of other group members.

When ideas did not fit with existing conceptions, there seemed to be four options.

1. The uneasiness many individuals in a group experienced became a source of motivation as students attempted to create minitheories to help them include the new experiences into their conceptual structures.

2. When some fit was constructed, students achieved a level of learning that was meaningful to them by regaining their equilibrium and changing previous ideas by adjusting their schema through a process of accommodation; this was regarded as the preferred learning outcome (see Figure 2.6, Exit 2). Jessica realized that a single successful experience was not enough to cause major changes in students' thinking. Recalling her son Jonathan's learning about friction, Jessica determined that multiple experiences in a variety of situations were helpful, and she used this notion to plan many opportunities for her students to expand their understanding of science concepts. She discovered that her role was important. At times, she became the

How Can You Teach Skills Now, Content Later?

by Charlotte Schartz

Grade 6, Kingman Middle School, Kingman, Kansas

NSES

TS-B, D

The year is 1977, and it is time for sixth-grade science class. There will be a unit on, let's say, the cell. We'll do lots of worksheets, with a large amount of reading. I'll lecture, assigning much vocabulary to memorize, and maybe I'll do a demonstration or two. The students are listening, I think. Individual seatwork is the norm. Talking to your neighbor is out. I am on stage telling them what to learn, what to memorize. The emphasis is on content.

That was then, this is now, and I'm learning. My evolving theory on how an adolescent learns is based on a conglomeration of articles that I have read, behaviors that I have observed, and experiences that I have had. I believe that students learn in inconsistent surges. Their rate of content absorption is in proportion to their social, emotional, and hormonal situation at any given moment.

I am becoming more and more convinced that middle school students learned something before they got to me, and they'll learn more at a later stage in their lives, but right now, they have more important things on their minds, like what to wear, who's going with whom, why Susan didn't smile today, or why she smiled at someone else. They are distracted by the unpredictable changes associated with unstable families, economic conditions, and so on. The plant or animal cell just can't compete. And after visiting with the teachers at the senior high, I learned that when they introduce that same cell, they start from the beginning, assuming that most 15- to 16-year-olds will not remember too much from middle school anyway.

I used to spend so much time on content. That's what the experts said was right at the time, I guess. . . . That was then, this is now, and I'm learning.

My teaching style has changed. I'm trying to match it to something unknown, unpredictable, inconsistent: a middle school student. If they aren't physically, emotionally, or socially able to learn and apply a bunch of big words mingled with abstract ideas and global concepts, then I must focus on something more concrete in a socially appropriate way, such as the skills that a scientist will need. In my classroom, we make observations, measure, keep records, analyze our data, make comparisons, predict based on patterns, and draw conclusions. During a project such as the design of a controlled experiment with bean seeds, my youngsters are expected to use all of the above as they construct meaning from their experiences. They work with their cooperative learning team to make their own observations, taking their own measurements, keeping their own records. They feel more of an ownership and involvement than if I had just told them about when someone else grew beans. (It's also safer to express an opinion, make a suggestion, or verbalize a revelation while working in a small group rather than in front of the whole class.) Now, are they ready to go out into the world as master bean growers? No, even though some relatively thorough content did get slipped in. But they will have practiced some useful scientific skills, constructed some important science concepts, and developed a greater ability to think, along with some critical social skills. They have a greater chance of remembering something they did rather than something they heard about. And who knows if there will even BE bean farms in fifty years?!? Look what happened to the four food groups! I do feel certain, however, that the skills of doing science and importance of constructed meaning will endure. People will still have to observe, predict, compare, keep records, and so on; people will have to think and solve problems.

source of information and explanation, although she usually functioned as a guide and questioner.

3. Despite Jessica's best efforts, some learners preferred to wait for the answer to be given—by a book, a search on the Internet, other students, or Jessica. These few students seemed to prefer to learn the answer by rote (see Figure 2.6, Exit 3). As unsatisfying as this was to Jessica, she realized that it was a beginning for these youngsters, so she resolved to help them by challenging the students to use the answer in other contexts, much as Jonathan's uncle had encouraged him to do when constructing an understanding of friction.

4. Jessica was most disappointed by the two or three children who opted out of the learning experience (see Figure 2.6, Exit 4). These learners included not only the isolated, surly types who did not consider the science topic interesting or the effort worthwhile; but also the happy social types who were present in group activities, yet—perhaps because of poor prior experiences in science or repeated failures—chose to avoid further failure by opting out of the learning situation (Appleton, 1993, p. 270). This disconcerting student behavior motivated Jessica to seek teaching guidelines and intervention strategies that would serve all learners.

What Techniques and Roles Support Constructivist Learning?

A Constructivist Learning and Teaching Model

Constructivism strives toward a deeper understanding and is served by the desire for children to experience the nature of science, as described in Chapter 1. Frontal teaching—telling and showing students all kinds of things—is minimized. According to Eleanor Duckworth (1989), all people ever have is their own understanding, and you cannot make them believe anything unless they construct it for themselves. Students can be encouraged to learn by reinventing the wheel for themselves—not a particularly time-efficient approach, but it *is* effective; retention is greater, and understanding is deeper. The learner does the discovering by forming mental connections; the teacher mediates the learning environment.

NSES

TS-E

There can be a downside, though, because not all conceptual constructions are correct, and simply choosing to believe does not make the facts correct, nor does pulling "evidence" to fit preconceptions. Donovan and Bransford (2005) suggest that it is absolutely important to engage children's preconceptions, which are resilient and ripe for improvement. We can form a plan that reminds us to draw out the ideas and experiences that children bring with them but that would not typically be made active; we can use strategic instructional guidance to expose children to surprises and discrepancies that challenge their mental impressions about how things function; and we can use narrative stories or draw examples from literature to set the stage for the nature of science and discovery.

All instruction needs a point. What point do you want learners to take with them, and how could you help learners to link new ideas to old and weave a fabric of learning that meaningfully connects to life and living? Select core concepts and organize lessons around those and plan for expanding on those core concepts—the glue that holds the learning together. Thinking about what is known or not arises from metacognitive actions. Challenge learners to think about what they know or do not know. Use a social process to test learning by asking them to communicate emergent understandings and to sort through the loose ends. How could you remember to do these things? Try an approach like the one shown in Figure 2.7 on page 56.

A learning cycle uses constructivist techniques and helps learners achieve deeper understanding through metacognitive strategies (Krueger & Sutton, 2001). Provide an opportunity for children to explore and be directly involved in manipulating objects; ask questions and encourage children to ask useful and productive questions themselves. Help children to construct best explanations from their direct experiences by finding out their ideas and encouraging them to reflect on similarities and differences, to construct connections among and between their ideas. Encourage children to expand on their ideas by using them in other settings, such as the natural world and

Learning Cycle Featured Lesson

Physical Science: Bubbles

Grades • 4–8

CONCEPTS TO BE CONSTRUCTED:

▶ Variables are those things that can affect the outcome of an experiment.

▶ To the extent possible all variables that can affect the outcome of an experiment must be identified and controlled so that the research question is answered without unintended interference.

SCIENCE ATTITUDES TO NURTURE:

▶ Curiosity

▶ Open-mindedness

▶ Cooperating with others

▶ Avoidance of broad generalizations

▶ Willingness to withhold judgment until all evidence of information is examined

Engaging Question

How can we determine which type of detergent produces the largest bubbles?

Materials Needed:

Advance Preparation: To make a soap solution for blowing bubbles, you will need 25 ml of detergent, 500 ml of water, and 7 drops of glycerin. A cleaned used gallon milk jug works well to mix the solution. It is recommended to make up the solution and let it sit 10 hours uncapped. This will allow any alcohols in the soap to evaporate. Evaporation of the alcohol and the addition of the glycerin help the blown bubbles last longer. Make up three containers of soap solution, each made from three different brands of dishwashing liquid detergent. Be sure to mark containers so that only the preparer knows which container holds which brand.

For Exploration Phase • conducted in 3–4 students per group, each group will need:

- For each team prepare three cups, labeled *unknown A, B, and C.* Half-fill each cup with the three different soap solutions.
- 3 straws for each student
- Vinegar to clean surface between unknown trials
- Paper towels for cleanup
- 1 data sheet per student to record measurements
- 1 meter stick or ruler per student

Safety: Wear goggles to avoid getting soap splashed in eyes. Be sure to clean up any soap solution that drips on the floor as quickly as possible to avoid slipping.

Exploration

PROCESS SKILLS USED:

▶ Observing

▶ Predicting

▶ Inferring

▶ Measuring

▶ Communicating

▶ Designing an experiment

Offer a scenario that asks the class to determine which type of detergent produces the largest bubbles for a planned contest. Will it be the more expensive brand? Or will an inexpensive brand do just as well? Pose the engaging question "How can we determine which type of detergent produces the largest bubbles?"

Ask the student groups to design their own experiment following general instructions. Introduce students to the materials and the requirements identified on an activity sheet that is prepared to record the measures of the diameters of at least four trials of the three different brands of detergent. The data sheet should instruct the students to measure the diameters of the soap rings left on the table surface after the bubbles are blown as large as possible and pop. Avoid telling the students the identities of the detergents until after the experiment. Take care not to structure the investigation, but encourage students to decide for themselves how to prepare the table surface, use the straws, determine duties of group members, etc. Construct a class data table using each group's record of the average diameters for each bubble solution.

Bubble solution

Explanation

Which brand *is* the best?

Compile the class's data into a table and investigate, taking care to examine the vertical columns for the range of measures and the horizontal rows for agreement or disagreement about the rank of bubble solutions by size. Identify the detergents used and the cost. Discuss questions such as "Is there a difference in the size of bubbles? Does cost affect the difference in size? What factors may have influenced the results of the experiments? Do you believe that you performed a reliable test to determine the best brand of soap solution? Why?" Use the students' answers to lead to the lesson's concept: *Variable are things that can affect the outcome of an experiment.* Deepen the students' understanding about the importance of variables and the meaning of the concept of *variables* through the Expansion phase.

Expansion

PROCESS SKILLS USED:
► Designing an experiment
► Identifying variables
► Controlling variables
► Investigating

Science in Personal and Social Perspectives

• What are some examples of variables that may cause us to get sick or become injured if left uncontrolled?

• Who needs to know about variables and use them in their daily lives? What are some examples of careers that use variables?

Science and Technology

• What are some examples of natural variables and examples that are mostly attributed to humans?

• What are some examples of technology that identify or control variables?

Science as Inquiry

1. Discuss with classmates the different variables that may have affected the outcome of our investigation. Agree how to limit the influence of at least three variables, redesign the experiment, repeat, and report results. How does the size of the bubbles now compare with those of classmates?

2. Select one of the following research questions:

a) What detergent produces the most cost-affordable bubbles?
b) What formula additives produce the longest-lasting bubble?
c) Write a description about how to design an experiment to answer the research question. Take care to identify all variables and provide a description about how to control them in order to provide the most accurate answer to the research question.

3. For the upcoming school science fair, compose a research question that will compare experimentally two or more things. Identify all variables that may affect the outcome of the experiment and describe a research design that could produce an accurate answer to the question.

History and Nature of Science

Name three scientists who have made important discoveries. At least one scientist must be a female or from a minority population. Research their discoveries. What are some examples of variables they encountered? Report on how they identified and controlled variables.

Hands-on Assessment

The students will plan a scientific investigation, conduct it, report the results, and describe in the report what steps ensured accurate and repeatable results. They should plan their scientific investigation by identifying the variables that they will control and those that they will manipulate.

Reflective Assessment

Ask the students to write a statement about the importance of controlling variables in designing an experiment.

Pictorial Assessment

Ask the students to exchange the scientific reports they created with another student team. The students will be expected to review the report for proper identification of the variables and to draw out the steps outlined in the other team's report.

FIGURE 2.7 ●

A Constructivist Learning and Teaching Model

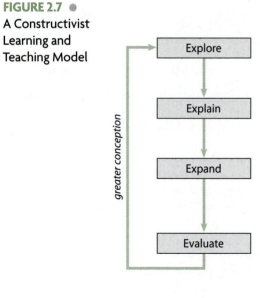

TEACHER'S ACTIVITY

Engage curiosity and provide opportunities for students to explore through all appropriate senses and to be fully involved through engaged attention. Encourage group cooperation during investigations; encourage questions.

Interact with children to discover their ideas. Question to cause them to reflect. Use the Z.P.D. to help learners use ideas formed from exploration to "construct" concepts and meaning sensible to them.

Help children to develop their ideas further through additional physical and mental activity. Help them to refine their ideas and expand their repertoire of science process skills. Encourage communication through group cooperation and broaden experience of nature and technology.

Evaluate understanding by examining changes in children's ideas and by their mastery of science process skills. Use hands-on assessment, pictorial problem-solving, and reflective questioning. Encourage children's interest in the ideas and reasoning of others. Frequent evaluation expands opportunities for using the Z.P.D. and improves each of the prior steps.

technology, and to develop process skills to enhance their thinking. Try to evaluate children's thinking by assessing any change in their ideas and process skills. Also encourage children to evaluate ideas by helping them to become interested in the explanations of others.

Constructivist Teaching Roles

Constructivism has become a popular catchword in education and often is presented as a teaching method. Teachers may mistakenly believe they are already using constructivism. However, the theory of learning must select or connect an array of teaching tools into a model of teaching if learners are to receive appropriate benefits. While hands-on science, mathematics manipulatives, and process writing share some common intentions with constructivism, applying constructivist research is much more difficult. The constructivist teacher must fill many roles but largely functions as a facilitator of knowledge construction. Young children can be encouraged to construct their own understanding if you perform these roles (Chaillé & Britain, 1991, p. 54):

NSES
TS-B

- *Presenter*—not a lecturer but one who demonstrates, models, and presents activities to groups of children and options to individuals so that direct pupil experiences are encouraged in an ongoing fashion.
- *Observer*—one who works in formal and informal ways to identify children's ideas, to interact appropriately, and to provide learning options.
- *Question asker and problem poser*—one who stimulates idea formation, idea testing, and concept construction by asking questions and posing problems that arise from observation.
- *Environment organizer*—one who organizes carefully and clearly what children are to do while allowing sufficient freedom for true exploration; one who organizes from the child's perspective.
- *Public relations coordinator*—one who encourages cooperation, development of human relations, and patience with diversity within the class and who defends this practice and educates others outside the class about the benefits for children of this approach.
- *Documenter of learning*—one who satisfies the accountability expectations and gauges the impact of these practices on each learner in terms of knowledge construction and science skill development.
- *Theory builder*—one who helps children to form connections between and among their ideas and to construct meaningful patterns that represent their constructed knowledge.

Intermediate and middle school children can benefit from these same roles, particularly if cognition is elevated to a stimulating and challenging level that is developmentally appropriate.

How Jessica Constructs Knowledge

Throughout this chapter, we have seen how Jessica wrestled with her own learning as she attempted to reconceptualize learning and teaching. When this happens to a professional or even a student, there are often several recurring actions that are important to recognize. First, Jessica was dissatisfied with her teaching and what children were learning.

NSES
TS-C

This dissatisfaction perturbed her and motivated her to seek change. Shaw and Etchberger (1993) claim that change cannot occur without some *perturbation*. Jessica's perturbation stimulated considerable thought about how children learn and how she could teach more effectively. Students too must become perturbed in order to stimulate learning.

Perturbation often encourages *commitment*—a personal decision to make a change. Commitment and progress toward change often cause additional perturbations. If you commit to a course of constructivism in your science classroom, you are likely to encounter many such perturbations that disrupt your "mental state of equilibrium" (Shaw & Etchberger, 1993, p. 264). When this happens, say Shaw and Jakubowski (1991), there are three likely pathways for you to deal with this disequilibrium: (1) block the perturbation and reduce the opportunity for meaningful change, (2) rationalize excuses for not dealing with the perturbation, or (3) form an active plan for making a change. To which pathway are you likely to commit?

A *vision* can help to keep one's commitments and steer the course toward meaningful change. This vision should be a clear, personal view of what the teaching and learning in your classroom should look like. You should be able to describe clearly to family members, supervisors, and visitors what you are trying to accomplish and the reasons for your choices. Figure 2.8 summarizes the differences between traditional and constructivist classrooms.

Reflection helps to evaluate and improve one's vision, strengthen commitment, and construct options to overcome perturbations. Thinking reflectively means to give serious and frequent consideration to the factors associated with one's vision.

NSES
TS-D

TRADITIONAL CLASSROOMS	CONSTRUCTIVIST CLASSROOMS
Curriculum	
• Presented part to whole; emphasis on basic skills	• Presented whole to part; emphasis on big concepts and thinking skills
• Fixed curriculum	• Responsive to student questions and interest
• Relies heavily on textbooks and workbooks	• Relies heavily on primary sources of data and manipulative materials
Role of students	
• "Blank slates" onto which information is etched by the teacher	• Thinkers with emerging theories about the world
• Work alone	• Work in groups
Role of teacher	
• Generally behaves in a didactic manner; disseminates information to students	• Generally behaves in an interactive manner; mediates the environment for students
• Seeks the correct anwer to validate student learning	• Seeks the students' point of view in order to understand students' present conceptions for use in subsequent lessons
Assessment	
• Viewed as separate from teaching: occurs almost entirely through testing	• Interwoven with teaching; occurs through teacher observations of students at work and through student exhibitions and portfolios

FIGURE 2.8 ● Traditional Versus Constructivist Classrooms

Source: D. C. Cantrell and P. A. Barron (Eds.). *Integrating Environmental Education and Science* (Newark, OH: Environmental Education Council of Ohio, 1994): 148.

The following questions illustrate a reflective process and can help to bring congruence to your desires, beliefs, and teaching practices: "What do students know about this topic? How are students thinking about what I am presenting to them? How do they come to think this way? How can they learn to value new ways of thinking about things? How can I help them to grasp scientific ideas? How do learners feel uncomfortable with science?" (Shapiro, 1994, p. xv).

For successful constructivist teaching and learning to occur, the teacher must become perturbed, commit to change, envision the type of change preferred, plan for change, garner the support for pursuing the vision, and reflect consistently about the progress and perturbations encountered along the path toward change. Change is a slow and deliberate process. For students, constructivist learning requires patience, persistence, and respect for another's thinking (Shaw & Etchberger, 1993).

chapter summary

This chapter is different from what you might find in textbooks on teaching science. We assume that you have completed a course in psychology or educational psychology, maybe even a course in child development. Therefore, rather than revisiting some theories you may have studied, we have recounted the emergent findings from brain research and the fundamental ideas behind the dominant belief about learning science from the perspective of a practicing teacher. How can we apply this dominant perspective on learning and teach science better?

No perspective on learning is complete without considering the potential of neural networks that arise through experiences and represent the ideas children bring to the classroom. These ideas represent preconceptions—conceptual understandings in the early stages of development—and misconceptions—conceptual understandings that do not agree with the concepts of the scientific community. These ideas are personal, may be contradictory when examined under a variety of circumstances, and are stubbornly rooted in children's minds. That children's ideas may be resistant to change poses a big challenge for teachers.

Children's learning benefits from enriching experiences that help to fulfill needs and must be considered and assimilated into a perspective on learning. As children develop over time, their needs change, and their exact cognitive capabilities are dynamic rather than static.

Experience is the one factor that unites the dominant perspectives on how children learn science. But not all experiences are equivalent, and experience alone is insufficient for helping children to achieve to their potential. As Vygotsky urged, children can achieve at higher levels of performance if they are given a boost from purposeful interaction with people who are more advanced than the learner. This process supports a view of constructed understanding.

Constructivists advocate several approaches for stimulating mental action and learning in conjunction with experience. These approaches stimulate inquiry, which is the foundation of science.

Constructivism is the contemporary concept we use to think about a child's learning. This perspective focuses on the child and what the child does during learning. It holds that knowledge cannot exist outside the mind of a learner, it cannot be directly transferred, and it must be each learner's construction of reality as meaning is made from relevant experiences—past and present.

The teaching recommendations offered should help you construct appropriate roles for yourself. If you follow these recommendations, you will find yourself covering less and guiding more, and your students will learn more in the deepest sense of the word. The chapter ends with discussion of the relationship of dissatisfaction, commitment, vision, and reflection as a process for becoming the type of science teacher you wish to be. We challenge you to envision the type of learning you wish for children and to construct a classroom that supports this vision.

reflect and respond

1. In what ways do children benefit from learning through experience? What types of materials or problems are developmentally appropriate for children in the primary grades? For the intermediate grades? For middle school youths? What similarities and differences do you detect when you compare the materials and problems for each group?

2. As may be revealed by their prior ideas, how might children's science misconceptions affect how you teach? What can you do to learn about these prior ideas and to identify misconceptions? How do you think you can help children to correct misconceptions? Do you think it is possible for learners to avoid misconceptions? Why or how?

Explore—Video Homework Exercise. Go to MyEducationLab at www.myeducationlab.com and select the topic "Teaching Strategies," then watch the video "Constructivist Classrooms," devoting particular attention to the relationships between the teacher and children. Also refer back to the "What Research Says" box and Figure 2.8 in this chapter, and then respond to questions below.

NSES
TS-E

1. How do the video images compare to the descriptions of the traditional and constructivist classrooms described in Figure 2.8?

2. How would you describe the behavior and relationship between the teacher and the students?

3. What relationships do you notice among the students? Do these relationships seem productive? Why or why not?

4. What else might you expect to see in a classroom that would fit your image of a constructivist inquiry classroom?

Enrich—Professional Practice

NSES
TS-D

1. Using Figures 2.6 and 2.7, what is it about a constructivist learning model that different from teaching and learning methods that you typically see in school classrooms? If you were using this model, what would you choose to emphasize to ensure that learners were able to "make meaning," and what would you do to ensure that their understandings were correct?

2. What are other ways in which you could teach science lessons to emphasize constructivism for learners while addressing the nature of science (Chapter 1)?

3. Select a few key science concepts from your state's standards or from the *National Science Education Standards* (see Appendix). Interview a sample of children from different age or ability groups, and determine their ideas about the concepts. What are their misconceptions? How do you think you could help to correct those misconceptions? What do you think you could do to help future learners avoid those misconceptions?

Expand—Weblink Exercise

Science Literacy. Go to MyEducationLab Resources section and select "Weblinks," then click on the following links "Brain Basics," "Neuroscience for Kids," "Misconceptions," and "Podcasts" to learn more about the topics of neuroscience and science misconceptions discussed in this chapter.

"Brain Basics"
http://www.brainconnection.com/library/?main=bbhome/main
The Brain Basics section of this free web resource provides a primer about the functions of our brains and central nervous systems through featured articles.

NSES
CS-F
PD-B

"Neuroscience for Kids"
http://faculty.washington.edu/chudler/experi.html
Neuroscience for Kids is a website with information on a level for younger learners. Learners can explore how our brains and nervous systems function, debunk myths about our brains, and experiment with models and games that simulate the science of neuroscience.

"Misconceptions"
http://www.msu.edu/user/boswort9/attempt1/cep817web/amasci/scimis.htm
Common misconceptions found in K–6 science textbooks are revealed and discussed in ways that allow readers opportunities to challenge their own science misconceptions.

"Podcasts"
http://science.ocde.us/Podcasts.html
Free podcasts discuss more than twenty common science misconceptions and help the teacher to recognize misconceptions among learners and understand what to do to reduce misunderstandings. Examples of misconceptions include that earth's highly elliptical orbit causes the seasons; primary colors are red, yellow, and blue; atoms get larger when you heat them; and fish breathe the "O" from "H_2O."

3

How Can You Improve Science Learning for Diverse Learners?

- What is the diverse range of children's cultural differences that can impede their learning of science, and what are several strategies for helping children to achieve success?

- What exceptional or special needs do learners have, and what classroom practices help them to learn?

- How can families become involved and extend learning in science?

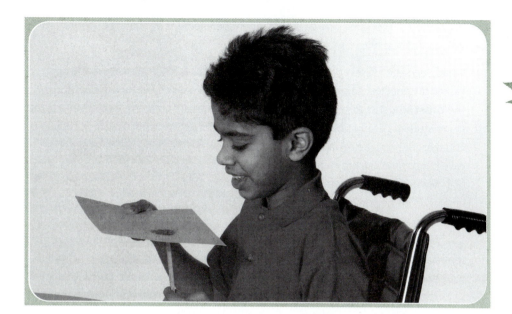

NSES
PD-B

Julie B., a recent graduate from a liberal arts, teacher preparation program, exuded confidence and passion for her first teaching position. Before the school year began, she decorated her classroom with colorful and interesting displays. Her first primary class was a dream come true after four and a half years of preservice teacher preparation and a semester of substitute teaching.

The children's names and a review of records suggested that she would have an enriched class. Julie's meeting with children and their families on the first day proved her hypothesis: Several ethnic groups and races were representative of the school's diverse community. Some children spoke English as a second language, and a number of children came with Individualized Education Programs (IEPs) to help them overcome learning disabilities. The school was committed to inclusion. A few children's records suggested the potential for giftedness.

The excitement of the new school year and the novelty of having a new teacher subsided after the first week. Toward the end of the first month, Julie noted tensions among the children that she suspected were related to differences in culture, language, gender, and social class and the children's self-perceived shortcomings in academic ability.

The autumn outdoor science projects did not progress as smoothly as Julie had planned. Some children remarked that science was too difficult for them, and some of the boys stated with derision that girls couldn't do science. The children who had learning disabilities especially concerned Julie. She had been taught and passionately believed that all children could learn. She shared her concern with a veteran teacher: "How can I teach all children when the class is so diverse?" Many children exhibited low self-perception, language was a barrier for some, and those who were gifted were impatient and constantly asked questions that seemed to take Julie's plans off track. She had also concluded that three students probably ought to be placed in a special class. Julie asked the advice of Mrs. Rice, an experienced colleague and a resource teacher. Mrs. Rice offered several practical suggestions. She gave further encouragement by sharing a story from her first years of teaching:

It had been at least seven years since my school had a science fair. Late in the fall I asked my principal if I could organize and sponsor a science fair for my class and the other students in grades four through six. My main concern was to get as many students as possible to follow a project through to completion so they could experience the reward of displaying their work. The principal immediately gave her permission and support.

My sixteen boys and one girl, aged eleven to thirteen, had reading abilities ranging from beginning first grade to high third grade. Their math skills were somewhat higher, and handwriting and spelling varied but were generally low.

According to intelligence test scores, these students had at least average potential, but they had not achieved at the same rate as most of their peers. They were placed in my class in order to receive special and individualized instruction.

The behavior and attitudes of children with learning disabilities have been described as impulsive, distractible, frustrated, stubborn, disruptive, defiant, obstinate, and extremely disorganized. One word I never used to characterize my students, though, was "unmotivated." Of course their motivation varied according to the activity at hand, but when their interest was roused, they really got into gear. Fortunately, my explanation of a science fair induced every member of the class to enter the project.

During the three months the school was involved in the science fair, I noticed some important changes in my own students and in other students and the faculty.

Learning-disabled children have difficulty getting along with one another in group situations. They are easily frustrated and tend to argue and become angry. Much to my surprise, however, this did not occur when my students worked on their science fair projects. I must stress the significance of this change in behavior. Naturally, it improved the quality of their work for the science fair, but it also demonstrated to me—and to them—that they could control themselves and cooperate to solve difficult problems.

While my students' perceptions of what they could do were changing, the attitudes of other students toward my class were also shifting. At the beginning, most of the other students in the school had little information about learning-disabled children. They only knew that my students were somehow different, and they usually called ours the "dummy class." I, of course, was the "dummies' teacher." But during preparations for the science fair, the perceptions of some of these other students began to change. They found it difficult to understand how a "dummy teacher" could run a science fair and why she'd want to. The fact that I seemed to be doing a good job created a halo effect that was important: As my image began to improve among students throughout the school, so did the image of my students. For the first time, members of my class began to develop friendships with other students.

Many teachers were as uninformed as their students about the limitations and the capabilities of learning-disabled children. These colleagues often viewed students in my class simply as behavior problems. This misapprehension was not necessarily the fault of the teachers, since many of them finished college before courses in special education and learning disabilities had become part of the curriculum.

I initiated our science fair with one goal—to have my students complete and display science projects. However, as preparations for the fair progressed, it became clear that my students were learning more than I had originally imagined possible. I was curious about their perceptions of what they were accomplishing, so I asked them.

My students did not doubt that they'd learned some valuable lessons by participating in the science fair and neither did I. In fact, it was clear that several important academic and personal goals could be accomplished by involving learning-disabled children in a science fair.

The school science fair was an extremely satisfying experience. Of the nine winners chosen by outside judges, four were from my learning-disabled class. And while getting prizes was exciting, equally important for my students were the intangible rewards of embarking on a joint enterprise with others, and discovering within themselves capabilities of which they had not been aware. (Rice, 1983, pp. 15–16)

Have you ever heard someone reason: "If you can't walk, talk, or hear, or if you look or sound different, you must be intellectually and socially inferior"? Most physical differences have no connection to one's intellect or mental capability. The biases of our hypothetical conversationalist are based on two important factors: stereotypes and a lack of information. Stereotypical thinking caused the learners without disabilities in Ms. Rice's school to refer to her students as "dummies." An uninformed teacher can stifle the intellect by holding low expectations for children with learning disabilities. Without realizing just how unfairly their expectations may affect children, teachers may actually reinforce the wider perception that learners who have disabilities or are different in some other way are dummies, and this type of teacher behavior may tend to reinforce the prejudices held by others. Julie's desire to reach for help was wise. The challenges for teachers in knowing the right things to do increase as classrooms become more diverse.

Children with learning disabilities are only one example of students who have special needs. Each child is a special case and deserves special attention and encouragement. You will be in a better position to teach, to strike down unfair stereotypes, and to serve the needs of *all* learners if you become informed about the special needs many school children have. This will be a great service for all of your students and will especially benefit those who need special assistance.

This chapter is about teaching science to serve *all* children's needs. Technically, of course, all students are culturally different; each family is unique and has its own identity. The multicultural focus of this chapter explores the special needs of culturally diverse populations (groups of students with home environments very different from society's mainstream in terms of economics, ethnicity, religion, race, and/or language) and learners who have distinct disabilities (children with differences in vision, hearing, speech, emotions, giftedness, and so on). In both instances, the science teaching techniques we recommend to help the few students in your class who may have special needs will better serve the needs of all learners.

The chapter begins with an investigation of several general factors that impede science learning and provides teaching recommendations that are beneficial for all children. The chapter is built around the question: "How can you teach science for all children?" After reading the first part of this chapter, you will be able to:

1. describe the special needs of children who are members of minority groups, culturally different, and/or multilingual;
2. practice techniques that help to meet their special needs;
3. promote gender equality in your classroom;
4. identify the different learning styles;
5. discuss management and teaching practices that encourage all learners.

The second part of this chapter should help you to:

1. identify characteristics of the exceptional students who will enrich your classes;
2. practice classroom techniques that help to meet these special needs.

The third part of this chapter explores ways to include parents in science teaching.

Science for All

NSES
TS-E

Science fulfills an important role in the education of all learners by helping children to develop abilities to think, reason, imagine, and form realistic explanations for the mysteries of their natural world. The nature of science has always encouraged all learners to advance beyond physical and sensory limitations, making science particularly appropriate for learners who have special talents, gifts, and needs (Scruggs & Mastropieri, 2007). However, special learners can become caught in the tension between two views on learning: constructed versus instructed.

Most professional organizations embrace constructed learning. Constructivist theories and child-centered perspectives on learning advocate the importance of hands-on experiences, learning through inquiry, and making conceptual meaning. Learning processes are used as tools for achieving depth rather than breadth as conceptualization and comprehension are promoted over memorization or recollection of facts. School leaders may urge instructed learning, which is aligned with a textbook that emphasizes facts and vocabulary to be learned through teacher-directed methods in response to meeting standards and achieving scores on high-stakes tests mandated by states or the federal government in which the target becomes breadth of exposure. Scruggs and Mastropieri (2007) reveal constructed versus instructed learning as a false dichotomy. Each teacher approach has limitations (see Table 3.1), and both efforts particularly help learners who have special needs.

Not all children come to school able to function effectively within a school's dominant culture. Some children lack the skills necessary to cope with the routines or rigors of schooling. These children often develop negative attitudes toward science (Weinburgh, 1995) and feel hostile toward school and toward any authority figure, especially a teacher.

Being different carries liabilities. The price of being different may be exclusion from social groups at school and prejudiced treatment from people who appear not to be different. Cultural differences can contribute to schoolchildren's difficulties and problems. The principles of cultural diversity and equity can help us to meet the needs of all children (Krueger & Sutton, 2001).

Celebrating Diversity

All children are unique and culturally distinct. Children who are culturally different from most may include those of nonmajority races or children who have special needs. Cultural differences may also include those of race, religion, economic level, ethnic background, the primary language used by the child, and in some instances

TABLE 3.1 ● Constructed Versus Instructed Science: Implications for Learners

NSES

TS-B

Constructed Learning	
Benefits	**Liabilities**
Learners enjoy and value hands-on investigations.	Some learners do not function well within unstructured learning activities.
Achievement overall increased through hands-on science.	Independent, active reasoning strategies are difficult for some children to use without direct guidance or teacher intervention.
Hands-on learning approaches accommodate inclusion efforts of teachers or intervention specialists.	Strategies for mastering vocabulary and retaining facts will need to be added and made explicit.
Coaching strategies benefit learners and assist development of higher-order thinking.	Pacing is slower and may not be rapid enough to cover broad content for tests.

Instructed Learning	
Benefits	**Liabilities**
Direct instruction covers more material.	Learners who have disabilities or language limitations have difficulty learning independently from a text.
Learners benefit from mnemonic and vocabulary acquisition strategies.	Many learners do not benefit from a focus on breadth over depth.
All learners benefit from text enhancements and processing strategies.	Learning outcomes are limited when structured learning conditions exclude independent thinking.
Classwide peer tutoring and differentiated curriculum benefit learners in inclusion classes.	Teacher-directed instruction without hands-on opportunities negates the recommendations of professional organizations.

Source: Adapted from T. E. Scruggs and M. A. Mastropieri, (2007). "Science Learning in Special Education: The Case for Constructed Versus Instructed Learning," *Exceptionality,* Vol. 15, No. 2, p. 70.

gender. Hence, teachers must value the contributions and uniqueness of children from all backgrounds and be aware that a country's welfare is ultimately dependent upon the productivity of all its people. All children can learn and be successful in science, and our nation must cultivate and harvest the minds of all children and provide the resources to do so (Kahn, 2003). In this spirit, the National Science Teachers Association (2000) urges that:

- schools provide science education programs that nurture all children academically and physically and develop a positive self-concept;
- children from all cultures have equal access to quality science education experiences that enhance success and provide the knowledge and opportunities for them to become successful participants in a democratic society;
- curricular content incorporate the contributions of many cultures to our knowledge of science;
- science teachers be knowledgeable about and use culturally related ways of learning and instructional practices;
- science teachers accept the responsibility to involve culturally diverse children in science, technology, and engineering career opportunities; and
- instructional strategies selected for use with all children recognize and respect the cultural differences students bring.

All children benefit from learning science.

Although the challenge can be great, preparation in science can lead to higher-paying careers, more critical thinkers, and a greater number of future technical workers who can fill vital vacancies and support our nation's economy (Linn, 1994).

Who Makes Up Culturally Diverse Populations? Often, an African American child who is poor is envisioned as a typical example of a child who is culturally different. This is an inaccurate stereotype of African Americans. Although the example does apply, culturally different children are as likely to come from the hills and mountains of Appalachia, Spanish-speaking communities of Florida or the Southwest, French settlements of the northernmost regions of Maine, Asian communities of the West Coast, or recent immigrants from Latin America who have settled in the Midwest. Let us not overlook the Native Americans who once were the majority in this land. They, too, are now culturally different from a changed mainstream society. In fact, each of us can become culturally different when we enter a community or region where our identity is not among the majority of the residents.

How Can You Use Cultural Differences to Promote Greater Science Understanding? Science classes can reflect greater cultural diversity if instruction reflects contributions made by people from all over the world. Often our print materials and media leave the impression that science is a recent white European construct. In fact, this impression is very wrong.

Over 5,000 years ago in Egypt and Mesopotamia, copper was being extracted from its ores, glass was made, and fabrics were dyed with natural colors . . . . Iron swords are known to have been produced over 3,000 years ago. . . . Distillation was used in Mesopotamia as far back as 1200 B.C. for the production of perfumes. . . . Many of the techniques and much of the terminology of modern chemistry derives from ancient times; for example, *alkali* from the Arabic *al qality*—the roasted ashes; *soda* from Arabic *studa*—a splitting headache. (Williams, 1984, pp. 133–146)

You can promote diversity education in your science class by doing the following:

- *Developing science themes related to conservation and pollution, disease, food and health, and population growth and teach with consideration for humankind as a whole.* Develop an understanding among your students about the interdependence of people and unequal distribution of natural resources.

- *Selecting classroom teaching examples that address the contributions and participation of people from a range of backgrounds, cultures, and genders.*

- *Considering carefully any issues of race, gender, and human origins by exploring the myths that surround them* (Antonouris, 1989, p. 98).

- *Challenging inaccurate statements students make about ethnic minority communities and people.* Statements may refer to different physical features, countries of origin, religion, language, and customs (Antonouris, 1989). For example, you may have heard myths about the strengths and weaknesses of blacks, Asians, women, and so on. As educated adults, we understand that these alleged qualities cannot be applied to a group and that beliefs like these arise from ignorance. We know that human beings are much more alike than they are different. Use science teaching as an opportunity to refute these myths if children repeat them.

How Can You Meet the Needs of Children from Diverse Backgrounds? All children seem to share some characteristics. Here are some tips for meeting the needs of culturally different children:

- *Share different activities.* What most of us take for granted may be completely lacking from the childhoods of children who are culturally different, minority, low-income, or disabled. For example, herds of domestic animals, menageries of pets, and/or wild animals that roam at will may be as foreign to a city dweller as piles of wind-tossed convenience packaging, crowds of densely packed people, and smog are to a farmer or rancher. Classroom activities, videos, and field trips with planned comparative discussions help to build awareness about and tolerance for differences by adding new experiences. Yet real experiences are a better choice. Activity-based science learning has long been proven to help the students who are culturally different to reach higher levels of science achievement, develop better process skills, and develop more logical thought processes (Bredderman, 1982).

- *Use science demonstrations rather than words.* Few children who are multilingual or multicultural will be patient enough to listen to long instructions or descriptions. Get to the point. Provide simple, direct demonstrations and concrete experiences. Indeed, all children benefit from clarity and directness.

- *Introduce science vocabulary.* The rough, blunt street talk or backwoods language of some children can cause quite a shock if you do not share the culture. In the same way, the child with limited English proficiency who speaks haltingly may have difficulty following a normal conversation. Children need a vocabulary that is suited to the mainstream if they are to become competitive in the workplace. Science offers abundant opportunities for developing vocabulary and effective communication skills.

- *Use simple, clear instructions.* Children can become frustrated and misunderstand the purpose of an activity if there are too many choices or if your instructions are too flexible. Some children may live in cultures in which they are not encouraged to make many of their own decisions. Be definite and clear with your instructions.

- *Develop genuine relationships.* Be empathetic rather than sympathetic. Looking down on the students' different social or economic standing is demeaning despite your best intentions.

- *Show children how to control their own results.* Poverty tends to produce feelings of hopelessness and desperation. Children who are culturally different, in the minority, low-income, or disabled may feel that they have little or no control over their lives and may look for immediate gratification. Fate control is defined as the belief that you cannot control what happens to you. Many children from culturally different backgrounds believe that what happens to them happens by chance or that their future lies in the hands of others who are more powerful and beyond influence. Science experiments help children to learn that variables can be manipulated to produce different outcomes. Educators have realized for decades that children can apply this understanding about variables to themselves and eventually use their understanding to help shift the locus of fate control to a point at which they perceive the power to control their own lives (Rowe, 1974).

How Can You Help Non-English-Speaking Students?

Having a shortcoming in using the language spoken by a majority may not indicate a lack of intelligence. It is possible that the non-English-speaking student possesses what Howard Gardner calls "linguistic intelligences," the capacity to use native language to express thinking and to understand other people (Checkley, 1997). Therefore,

NSES
TS-B

children can be helped if your efforts are focused upon helping them to use the second language proficiently. The following tips can assist non-English speakers in your classes.

Help Students to Help Themselves. Students will learn to help themselves from these approaches:

- *Distribute a vocabulary list and/or copy of the curriculum guide at the beginning of each unit.* This material helps students to know exactly what will be expected of them and will give them additional time to master the difficult terms.

- *Ask students who are readers of their native language to carry pocket dictionaries (English-to-native language and vice versa).* At times, simple words create communication barriers. Pocket dictionaries can solve the problem and help to create the self-sufficient habit of looking up unfamiliar words. English-speaking students can be encouraged to do the same as a way of learning words in another language.

- *Invite the students who are uncomfortable with English to ask questions.* This personal invitation, in a nonthreatening environment, will help students to overcome fear of using the new language. The joy of being successful at expressing opinions or asking questions becomes a positive reinforcer.

- *Be patient.* Wait-time (see Chapter 6) is particularly important for multilingual speakers, to allow them to form their questions or answers.

- *Encourage the children to write their own translations of words in their notes.* As you examine lab notebooks and see translations, you will be aware that the student has looked up the words and probably understands them better.

- *Encourage students to read science articles and books in their own languages.* Additional supplemental readings such as those available from *Scholastic* provide brief, popular articles and photographs that encourage additional practice with the language.

I Hear and I Forget. For those times when you feel that you must lecture, try the following techniques to help students remember (Kahn, 2003).

- *Speak slowly and enunciate clearly.* All students benefit from this because the technical words of science at times seem like a foreign language.

- *On the chalkboard, whiteboard, or digital display, provide an outline or definitions, descriptions, or figures to add meaning to your spoken words.*

- *Add emphasis to the main ideas.* Underline concepts or highlight the important meanings. Non-English speakers will remember to look them up later, while other students will treat the emphasis as a study cue. Concept mapping also helps (see Chapter 4).

I See and I Remember. A picture really is worth a thousand words. It provides another mode for learning, and it is helpful for memory retention. Try these suggestions:

- *Use visual aids as often as possible.* The problem in science education is deciding what to teach and what materials to use, not the availability of interesting, useful materials. Check the school district's resource center or curriculum library or the education resource co-op that serves your school. There is a wealth of films, videos, DVDs, bulletin board ideas, computer programs, models, posters, and charts. Old, discarded science textbooks or magazines can be salvaged for useful visual aids.

- *Nurture animals and plants.* They add excitement and can also make superior visual aids.

- *Use artwork.* Add your own artwork, and invite talented student artists to contribute to your notes, digital images, transparencies, learning activity illustrations, and lab activities. Stick figures with details are fine too.

I Do and I Understand. All three learning approaches—hearing, seeing, and doing—are important, especially when all five senses are stimulated. Combined approaches provide better opportunities for understanding than a single approach. The power of activity learning stimulates improved communication as well as greater levels of science achievement, process skill development, scientific attitudes, and logical thinking than does traditional teaching, where teacher talk and student reading dominate (Shymansky, Kyle & Allport, 1982).

Demonstrate—Group Investigate—Individual Investigate Teaching Language Model. By demonstrating a concept, you create interest as well as stimulate curiosity. A demonstration gives students an opportunity to listen and observe before having to produce any language. Student group investigation can help learners comprehend and practice communication skills with peers. Language skills develop naturally as students observe and communicate with others. Independent individual student investigation helps students to explore questions that are related to the concept that is already familiar to them. Table 3.2 provides some examples of this teaching and learning model.

- *Have students do hands-on, lab-type learning activities often.* The minds-on experiences that accompany hands-on learning can contribute to language and reading development. Some non-English-speaking students may not understand a lecture,

NSES
TS-A, B

TABLE 3.2 ● Language Development Model

Teacher Demonstration	Group Investigation	Individual Investigation
Concept: **Electrical energy causes motion.**		
Use an inflated balloon to pick up small pieces of paper.	Use an inflated balloon to cause another balloon to move.	Use an inflated balloon to test what objects it will pick up.
Concept: **Rapid motion causes the temperature of objects to rise.**		
Rub a wooden block over sandpaper to show how the temperature of the block goes up.	Bend a paper clip rapidly back and forth, and use cheeks to test for temperature change.	Find other objects (e.g., saw, chisel, file) outside the classroom that change temperature after rapid motion, and test them for temperature change.
Concept: **Animals move in different ways; some animals move by stretching.**		
Use earthworms to show how they move by stretching because they have no legs.	Observe earthworm activity when these are placed in a carton of soil.	Find examples of other animals without legs outside the classroom or in pictures. Name and classify them according to how they move.
Concept: **Rapidly moving air causes some objects to rise.**		
Hold a long piece of paper to the bottom lip and blow hard across the top of the paper to show how it moves up.	Blow hard across the top of a balloon, and then try to explain why it rises and what makes airplanes rise into the air.	Use a fan to see what objects you can lift up into the air.

Source: A. K. Fathman, M. E. Quinn, and C. Kessler, *Teaching Science to English Learners,* Grades 4–8 (Washington, DC: National Clearinghouse for Bilingual Education, 1992), p. 13 (ERIC Document Reproduction Service No. ED 349 844).

discussion, or teacher demonstration, but once they have done it themselves, the experience is easier for them to link with language. Focus on one or two language functions that are particularly appropriate for the planned activities. "Language functions are specific uses of language for accomplishing certain functions. . . . For example, *directing* (giving and following directions) may be emphasized in an activity in which the teacher first gives directions on how to build a rocket" (Fathman, Quinn, & Kessler, 1992, p. 16) and then has students work in groups to direct each other in building their own paper rockets. Table 3.3 shows several language functions that are commonly used in science classrooms.

- *Coordinate your teaching with the English as a Second Language (ESL) teacher.* Blend the grammar and vocabulary used in both classes so that the students have a double exposure to the science vocabulary.

- *Link science concepts with the students' background experiences.* Learn what you can about the children's countries of origin, and refer to geographical locations, climate conditions, fauna and flora, and so on to link new science concepts with what the students already know. For example, always mention the Rocky Mountains or the Mississippi River. The rest of the class will benefit from the geography enrichment.

- *Use appropriate guest speakers and field trips.* These additions will help multilingual students become more accepted and feel at home in their new environment and with science. Include all children in the full range of activities. Invite speakers from the students' countries of origin to help classmates become familiar with people from other cultures.

Try to Reduce Test Anxiety. Children from other countries often attach more importance to testing and achievement than native-born American children might. The mere mention of a test can evoke much anxiety because of its importance in determining children's academic futures, and a test in English can pump anxiety to counterproductive levels. The following suggestions offer some ideas for reducing test anxiety:

- *Try puzzles.* Crossword puzzles assist spelling and provide additional cues for correct answers. Students seem to do better when they know how many letters to expect in an answer. A list of words helps, too, for crosswords and fill-in-the-blank questions.

- *Encourage children to draw.* Invite children to draw answers rather than write. This is a good way to communicate ideas as the child gets around the temporary language barriers.

TABLE 3.3 ● Language Functions

NSES
TS-B

Language functions are specific uses of language for accomplishing certain purposes. Teachers can help students develop an understanding of these functions by building them into their lessons. Verbal ("What to Discuss") and written ("What to Record") exercises can be included in teacher demonstrations and student group and individual investigations.

Directing	Refusing	Describing	Disagreeing
Praising	Requesting	Accepting	Expressing opinions
Advising	Cautioning	Questioning	Defining
Agreeing	Suggesting	Encouraging	

Source: A. K. Fathman, M. E. Quinn, and C. Kessler, *Teaching Science to English Learners,* Grades 4–8 (Washington, DC: National Clearinghouse for Bilingual Education, 1992), p. 13 (ERIC Document Reproduction Service No. ED 349 844).

- *Encourage students to check their work.* At the end of each test, consider allotting 3 to 5 minutes for students to check answers. Permit them to use books, notes, and class handouts.
- *Try bonus points for extra credit.* Offer bonus points for student creations. Science-oriented jokes, riddles, poems, and songs that use the concepts and vocabulary being studied can be a great way to encourage review and creativity. Permitted as homework, creations for extra points can be a good way to promote language study between the child and parents.

Is Gender Equality a Special Need?

Though gains have been made, females still report unequal access and encouragement to pursue careers in science. This it is not a women's problem; it appears to be a cultural problem linked to how females are socialized in the mainstream of society; often, males and females, by age 11, have developed strong sex-stereotyped attitudes concerning socially appropriate behavior and gender roles in society (Chivers, 1986). Although improvements have been made, many people still attribute cultural differences to gender. Cultural gender differences play an important role in career selection.

NSES
TS-E

How Does Culture Affect Females in Science?
There may be cultural disincentives for women to pursue careers in science, technology, and mathematics. Proportionally fewer women and minorities have been encouraged to develop a sufficient background for scientific careers, and they are underrepresented in these careers, although more women are employed in science careers today than during the prior decade.

The current concern for gender inequity has arisen from several factors, some of which still persist despite the enlightened efforts of many to improve conditions and to encourage more females to pursue science. Consider the following:

- Parents, teachers, school counselors, and peers discourage females from pursuing scientific careers (Elfner, 1988).
- Most early childhood elementary teachers are women who lack a strong background in science; their lack of confidence can reinforce children's beliefs that women are not supposed to like science (Chivers, 1986; Shepardson & Pizzini, 1992).
- A shortage of appropriate female science and engineering role models reinforces the belief that science is a male domain (Jones & Wheatley, 1988; Hammrich, 1997).
- Though studies do report inconsistencies, young males tend to report more positive attitudes toward science than young females do; females report less confidence and more fear of success in careers like engineering; females report that physics courses are too difficult (Jones & Wheatley, 1988; Kahle & Rennie, 1993; Hammrich, 1997).
- Some studies suggest that females may not be socialized at home or at school to develop and demonstrate scientific skills and may not be encouraged to develop practical ability, independence, and self-confidence. Several studies reveal that skills and characteristics associated with scientists consist of high intellectual ability, persistence at work, extreme independence, and apartness from others. Females may be hesitant to pursue science because they do not wish to fit these common perceptions of scientists (Jones &

Females now receive equal encouragement and access to science.

How Can You Teach Science for All Children?

by Joan M. Yospin

Grade 5, Franklin Elementary School, Newton, Massachusetts

NSES
PD-B

Science, more than any other subject, allows children to connect to their own lives, something that is essential to involvement, interest, and motivation. Beginning the school year with a study of some aspect of our planet—climate regions, topographical features, oceans, rivers, ponds, or forests—lets children connect their own lives to the greater environment. Some have visited mountains, some have been to the city park, but all are aware of local plant and animal life and can understand where they might expect to find similar life forms. Children are fascinated to learn of their close connection to our planet; that their bodies contain proportionally as much water as the earth is often a new idea and helps them see that they are special beings, uniquely suited to living in their environment. That life forms are suited to the place where they live is meaningful to all children, regardless of gender, race, or language spoken at home. Most are eager to participate in reflective discussions about their place in the world.

Any of the big "why" questions produce similar interest and involvement: Why is the sky blue? Why are leaves green? Why are the days longer in the summer? Some students may have no idea of the reasons, some may provide partial information, some may have long, involved misconceptions that they share with the class. Discussing and getting some to think about the questions is a goal for my science classroom. Students who do not speak English or who are very quiet may be left out of discussions unless they are provided with interpreters or pocket dictionaries (and help to use those dictionaries), so it is important to have frequent discussions and keep them short.

Exposure to the language and to the vocabulary of science is helpful to non-English speakers; many of my ESL students copy words from the board and discuss the vocabulary at home with their parents. All students keep an "interactive notebook," or science journal, where they record ideas and vocabulary that are discussed in class. The left side of the page is for the student's own use of symbols, drawings, or words that will help them to remember the vocabulary or idea that is written on the right side of the page. Students should come away from a 10-minute discussion with a written record and with the idea that exchange of ideas and brainstorming are valued as part of scientific inquiry. Not all students will have a chance to participate during each short session, so the teacher must not allow one student or group of students to monopolize the time. Students must understand that everyone's ideas and opinions are welcome and needed by the group but that proceeding to the day's hands-on activity limits the time for discussion.

Science is "asking and doing," and focusing on an area of earth science—pond life, for example, or earthworms—allows students to learn more about a particular environment, while developing science process skills. The manner in which a topic is presented and students are asked to approach its study can ensure that all students are interested and involved. Science lessons must focus on developing the investigative skills that will be used at any level of scientific inquiry, and that will be valuable tools throughout life. Observing, recording, formulating questions, making predictions, drawing inferences, and classifying are process skills that must be practiced and developed regardless of the topic; the topic is the frame inside of which the skills are practiced.

A trip to a pond lets children observe that environment; making a sketch and detailed drawings of plants, insects, or

Wheatley, 1988; Shepardson & Pizzini, 1992; Hammrich, 1997). Even the toys that are typically given to boys require more assembly and manipulation than the toys that are given to girls.

- When women have problems, some suggest that they tend to blame themselves for the problems or the inability to solve them, whereas when men have difficulties, they tend to place the blame outside themselves (Jones & Wheatley, 1988).

- Teachers reflect the values and expectations that are thrust upon them by the dominant society and can unintentionally perpetuate gender stereotypes in science. In addition, gender bias can be observed in the practices of teachers and the assignments of science teachers. Female science teachers usually are assigned to introductory science classes and biology, whereas males more often are high school department chairmen and are assigned to teach such advanced science classes as chemistry and physics (Jones & Wheatley, 1988; Kahle & Rennie, 1993).

the surface of the pond are ways to gather and record data. If there is no pond or puddle to observe, the teacher can provide pond water and examples of plant life for a "classroom pond" in an aquarium. Field guides can be used to identify plants, either at the pond or back in the classroom. Students who are gifted at drawing and those who have made detailed observations use those strengths to advantage. Students who do not speak English can excel at detailed drawings and share their work with others who have the skills to use a field guide. In this way, students learn to draw on individual strengths and work cooperatively with others.

Working together is not only acceptable in science learning, it is essential. When microscopes or other science materials must be shared, students need to take turns, express their findings verbally, and help one another. Assigning roles in a group helps students understand the tasks that must be done and gives them an opportunity to gain skill in different roles. The recorder does the drawings or makes the tally marks for the group; the equipment manager gathers the materials for the group; the messenger asks questions or shares information with other groups. Next time, each student will be assigned a different job. Students who have strong skills in one or another area have a chance to model those skills for others and practice in areas where their skills are weaker. Working cooperatively is a life skill, valued in the workplace as well as in the family and classroom. Physically handicapped, severely learning disabled, and non-English-speaking students may not be able to perform their jobs without assistance, but assistance is at their side, provided by other members of the group as needed.

Working in pairs is another technique to ensure that all students develop needed skills, and varying the partnerships keeps students interested. Girls are often more interested in keeping peace with a partner or getting to know someone new than in finishing an assigned task. Boys may not have strong relational skills and may be more task oriented. Same-sex partnerships can give girls the opportunity to get into a task, where a male partner might upstage them. Girls who are used to taking a backseat may be thrilled to have the job "all to themselves," or they may need encouragement to get started. Boys paired with boys have to listen to each other and work together to accomplish a task. It is important to create mixed gender partnerships, too, because that is what one finds in the "real world"—men and women working together as equals.

One of my most successful partner activities has been a Mystery Skulls observation lesson, done during our study of the human body, with our first-grade buddies. Together, as cross-age pairs, the students handle and make observations about several animal skulls, draw a skull, and discuss what kind of animal they think it is. Fifth graders are full of pride as they ask their young buddies questions about placement of the eye sockets or call attention to the animal's teeth. They are making inferences about what the animal eats, whether it is a predator, and practicing questioning skills. Being a teacher is satisfying for us; it is an equally satisfying feeling for a ten-year-old.

Hands-on activities, partner work, animated discussions, group presentations—these are the methods science teachers use to ensure success for all their students. Not every student will be fully engaged by every lesson, but a variety of working arrangements and levels of activity and opportunities to go beyond assigned work, such as researching an area of interest or point of contention in the library or on the Internet, will help learners achieve the habits of mind and process skills necessary for success in science study.

How May Teachers Contribute to Gender Problems in Science? Although the role of teachers perpetuating sex-role stereotypes has not been fully explored, the literature indicates that teachers are not consciously and intentionally gender stereotyping students. Many teachers do try to treat males and females fairly and equally—it is the "equally" portion that is the problem. Few things in life are as unequal as providing the same for females as for males. Koch (2007) suggests that the rigor of science is not the deterrent to female participation but that the teaching method neglects making science relevant to students' lives. This claim is supported by research showing that many school-aged girls and boys are disenfranchised by science when it makes few connections to their lived experiences (Meyer, 1998).

Often, teachers say that they want all children to develop to their full potential. However, family members, school counselors, other teachers, social workers, books, and television have taught teachers (even you!) that certain behaviors are appropriate for females and others are appropriate for males (Sadker, Sadker, & Thomas, 1981; Shepardson & Pizzini, 1992; Hammrich, 1997; Pollina, 1995; Shakeshaft, 1995). Bias by gender will begin to change only when you are able to recognize the subtle messages that steer males and females toward particular behaviors and career choices. Please be aware that overcompensation for females can provide unintended disadvantages for males (Sadker & Silber, 2007).

Considerable evidence indicates that teachers' expectations affect students' performances and that elementary teachers may perceive males to have higher scientific ability than females. This perception usually sends a negative message to females, influences the self-perceptions of females, and determines the tasks and responsibilities that teachers assign to students during scientific activities (Shepardson & Pizzini, 1992). More likely, females are given passive roles to perform during group activities (Baker, 1988; Kahle, 1990; Shakeshaft, 1995), which reinforce teachers' perceptions that females are less interested and less capable in science (Shepardson & Pizzini, 1992). Cooper's model (1979) is based on this evidence and explains how differences in achievement may stem from differences in teacher expectations (see Figure 3.1). The model, which consists of the following steps, can be useful for overcoming gender stereotypes and encouraging high performance for *all* learners.

Step 1. Form different expectations for students.

Regardless of gender, hold high but realistic expectations for all students.

Step 2. Believe that all children can learn science.

Do not assign class roles or jobs on the basis of beliefs that females are better note takers and writers and males are better handlers of equipment.

Step 3. Encourage all learners to take the lead in activities, to make lab decisions, to take measurements, and to handle equipment.

Do the same for females and males but without leading them to believe that one gender is more capable than the other.

Step 4. Strive for equal amounts and types of nurturant contact with females and males.

Several studies in preschool and elementary classrooms indicate that males often receive more attention from teachers and more feedback about their performance

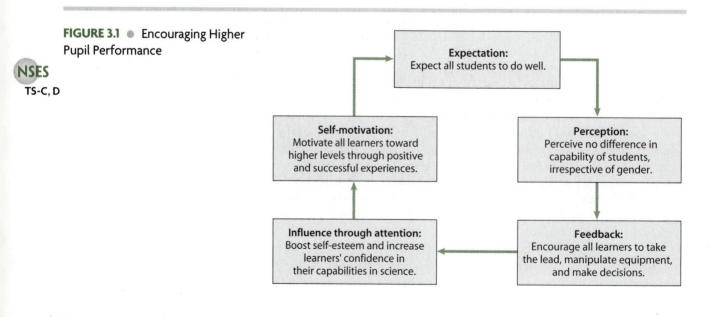

FIGURE 3.1 ● Encouraging Higher Pupil Performance

(Jones & Wheatley, 1988; Shepardson & Pizzini, 1992). Added attention can bolster students' beliefs about the importance of their effort and encourage them to work harder.

Step 5. Provide opportunities for success.

As children master classroom tasks, they become more motivated to strive for even higher quality. Females will undertake and excel at physical science study instead of achieving dramatically less than males do by the seventh grade.

What Can You Do to Overcome Gender Inequality in Science? The earlier a teacher can address gender bias, the better the chances of having an impact. From early childhood, males are often treated as if they are expected to be more independent, creative, and manipulative. These early experiences may affect their development of spatial and verbal abilities (Levine & Ornstein, 1983). Males often have more opportunities to experience science-oriented activities than females, although females have the interest to become more involved in science if given the opportunity (Kahle & Lakes, 1983; Kahle & Rennie, 1993; Shakeshaft, 1995). To help promote gender equality in your science class, include the following:

- *Strengthen your science preparation.* Strive to strengthen your experience with science. Project the importance of science for all students. Your attitude toward the subject will have a powerful effect on all the children.

- *Strive to become aware of your own subtle biases and different expectations for students.* Examine how you assign classroom tasks and the daily life examples you use of science at work for evidence of subtle gender bias.

- *Experiment with single-gender class groups.* Until you can create and maintain a nonsexist learning environment, females may receive less-biased treatment if they are not paired with males for small-group activities. Females in mixed groups have been found to spend more time than males watching and listening, whereas in same-sex groups, females spend the same amount of time as males in same-sex groups on hands-on science processes and experimental tasks (Rennie & Parker, 1986; Shepardson & Pizzini, 1992; Rop, 1998).

- *Have high expectations for both genders.* Examine your reinforcement for equality, fairness in discipline, and encouragement of nonverbal behavior toward females, especially during science class. Ensure that both males and females participate fully in all science activities.

- *Be aware of the difficulties some children may experience when using equipment that is unfamiliar to them.* Logical-mathematical, spatial, and bodily kinesthetic intelligences (Gardner, 1983) are essential in science; however, they are not confined to one gender. Rather, differences in social expectations often lead families to give different types of toys to boys and girls and encourage different types of social interactions through games and sports. Young males are often encouraged to manipulate objects that are very similar to the tools and equipment of science. Young females may not have been encouraged by their families to use a variety of tools and could have some initial difficulty with science equipment. A little extra time and encouragement early on will help females to build their confidence so that they can cope easily (Pollina, 1995) and develop important skills.

- *Hands-on learning is a great equalizer.* Science process–oriented learning tasks help both genders to acquire manipulative experiences, making access to science learning more equitable (Humrich, 1988; Shepardson & Pizzini, 1992).

- *Treat science as gender-free.* Do not always refer to scientists as males; lift up female scientists as role models.

- *Invite female science role models.* Males will be well served too, because they will see new opportunities for females.

- *Help all learners to develop personal characteristics that are associated with success in science.* Encourage them to break away from any submissive behavior patterns and encourage them to become more independent and self-reliant. Also encourage learners to explore new topics and materials and to test out their new ideas and interests (Kahle & Rennie, 1993; Shepardson & Pizzini, 1992).

- *Screen teaching materials.* Examine all print materials and media for gender bias. Posters, textbooks, videos, and other media should have equal representations of males and females.

Similarities in Learning

NSES
TS-D

Children from other cultures or who are not speakers of English benefit from specific management and teaching techniques. Indeed, most children can benefit from the suggestions that are recommended for special groups of learners. Children benefit when they are taught with the learning styles they prefer (Krueger & Sutton, 2001).

Multiple Intelligences and Learning Preferences. The theory of multiple intelligences (MI) is a popular psychological and educational concept that embodies an effort to understand how cultures and disciplines shape human potential by studying how individual learners respond to different types of content and solve problems or construct something that is valued (Checkley, 1997). Eight intelligences are recognized: linguistic, logical-mathematical, spatial, bodily kinesthetic, musical, interpersonal, intrapersonal, and naturalist. Each intelligence has a particular representation in the brain, and each individual may be particularly good or impaired in one or more of these intelligences (Gardner in Checkley, 1997). MI is focused on content or products of learning (Silver et al., 1997), whereas learning styles focus on the processes of learning—how learners think and feel as they solve problems, interact, and create products that represent learning (Silver et al., 1997).

The concept of learning styles arises from the general acceptance that we all learn in preferred ways (processes), that those ways can be identified, and that teachers can teach in ways that capitalize on student preferences. If they begin from a position of strength (preferred learning style), learners can be exposed to other ways of learning and expand their repertoires as they overcome weaknesses.

Teaching to accommodate different learner preferences helps teachers to reach each individual. Students who need special assistance receive instruction through their preferred learning style during the intervention process. Children learn about how they learn and are encouraged to use their strengths. All benefit from the variety of approaches. Teachers also plan instruction carefully to make certain that all children have an opportunity to learn through their own preferred styles.

Types of Preferences. Learner preferences are often classified by function. As learners, we have different modes of perception, we prefer various environments, we are motivated by different things, we express

Children perceive in different ways and prefer various learning environments.

ourselves uniquely, we think differently, and we prefer various levels of mobility as we learn. True individualization is a challenge. At least nine learning styles can be identified by function (Dunn & Dunn, 1975) and are considered widely representative of children's preferences for processing information:

1. *Visual*—prefer to perceive by reading and seeing words, numbers, charts, models, and objects.

2. *Auditory*—prefer to perceive meaning by hearing and listening.

3. *Bodily kinesthetic*—prefer tactile, hands-on involvement.

4. *Individual learners*—prefer to work alone. These students may be more confident in their own opinions than in the ideas of others.

5. *Group learners*—prefer to learn with at least one other child.

6. *Oral expressive*—can easily speak or explain their ideas and opinions. They may know more than they can reveal on a written test.

7. *Written expressive*—write fluent essays or good answers on tests. Their thoughts are organized better on paper than they are presented orally.

8. *Sequential*—have the ability to arrange thoughts and ideas in a linear, organized fashion.

9. *Global*—have the ability to be spontaneous, flexible thinkers. These learners may be quiet and intuitive and order their thoughts randomly, preferring to do things their own way.

Learners do not all fit exclusively into one style, and an outstanding performance using one or more of these styles may indicate a strong, specialized intelligence. Many children share strong preferences among several styles. All students can be served better when learning opportunities are provided in multisensory, multiexpressive, and multienvironmental modes. The following suggestions can help a wide variety of learners, particularly those who have special needs:

- *Establish classroom and study routines.* Many children are unable to organize unaided, and traditional school learning cannot occur until organization is established. You can provide a helpful model for children if you are well organized and consistent in your classroom. Children will then know what to do and how to do it.

- *Limit choices.* Democratic learning and cooperative learning encourage choices, but this approach may not help children who get confused easily. Asking, "Would you like to . . ." implies choice. As an example, if your intention is to have a child put science equipment back on the storage shelf or follow a specific instruction, it is better for the child if your instructions are explicit and/or provide limited choices.

- *Make certain the children are attending to what is going on.* Asking students to repeat instructions or information, requesting a response to a specific question, requiring that a child complete a specific motor task, and maintaining eye contact are some ways to determine the extent to which a child may be attending. Focus on each child often.

- *Give clues to help remembering.* Use mnemonic devices, rhymes, auditory associations, linking associations, and visual clues to help the child remember. Help the children construct personal memory devices.

- *Sequence instruction carefully.* Concept mapping (Chapter 4) and task analysis can help you to find the most logical sequence of any task. The four Ws help to begin a task analysis: *what* to teach, *where* to begin, *when* the objective has been met, and *what* to teach next.

- *Separate teaching and testing.* Use activities assignments as a type of reinforcement, not as a test. Provide instructional assistance to encourage learning and to help lower the failure rate. An example at the top of an activity guide or a list of guiding questions can transform the assignment from a test into a learning task. Also provide models, cues, verbal and written prompts, and correct answers as feedback.
- *Be specific with criticism and praise.* Tell the child exactly why a response is correct or wrong. When part of an answer is correct, tell the child; also identify what is not correct.
- *Provide time clues.* Some children may have difficulty remembering time sequences, estimating time intervals, and determining the amount of time needed to complete tasks. By routinely displaying schedules in prominent places and referring to time in the classroom, you can help students learn to structure their school work.
- *Confer with special education teachers, intervention specialists, second-language teachers, and gifted and talented coordinators.* Continuity of content and consistency of management and routines help many children. Coordinate your classroom activities with those of other classes the child attends.
- *Show empathy, encouragement, sensitivity, and understanding for each child's attempts to learn, to remember, and to conform to your routines.* Point out the child's abilities and respect the child as a human being.
- *Provide kinesthetic experiences, practical hands-on learning activities with concrete, relevant materials.* Children who are experience-deficient will benefit, as will children who prefer this type of learning. Hands-on experiences stimulate minds-on learning.
- *Identify desired behaviors, set clear expectations, and reduce distractions.*
- *Simplify.* Break each task down into its simplest steps; assist the students with step-by-step instructions.
- *Give frequent feedback.* Small improvements deserve praise, and precise direction helps children continue to improve.
- *Use the preferred learning mode.* If the child has a dominant mode of learning (visual, tactile, auditory), use it. Regard the preference as a strength and try to build success on it. Then use this preference to help build self-esteem on successes before tackling learning weaknesses.

Science for Exceptional Children

Public Law 94-142 of 1975 (Education for All Handicapped Children Act) was part of a federal law (Individuals with Disabilities Education Act, IDEA, renewed in 2004 as IDEIA: Individuals with Disabilities Education Improvement Act) that helped to ensure a place for students with disabilities in American public schools. IDEIA aligns with No Child Left Behind to ensure that all children with disabilities have access to a free, appropriate public education in the least restrictive environment. The law includes specific categories of thirteen disabilities, including deafness, hearing disability, mental retardation, orthopedic impairment, other health impairment, serious emotional disturbance, specific learning disability, speech impairment, and visual impairment.

NSES
PD-B
TS-D

The least restrictive environment is encouraged so that students with disabilities are educated in regular classrooms where appropriate. Placement decisions are based on extensive assessment, parental consent, and decision making among school personnel that must follow due process of law.

The presence of students with disabilities in regular classrooms does not mean that the curriculum must be the same for all children. Federal law states that the schooling of children with disabilities must be differentiated according to their special needs and provided with necessary support. This may require a degree of individualized education not usually found in typical classrooms. The Individualized Education Program (IEP) prescribes goals for the school year based on present performance levels, specific educational services the school must provide, the extent to which the student participates in the regular classroom, and schedules and procedures for evaluation, which can include as many as 47.4 percent of school-aged youths (Kirch et al., 2007). Indeed, many educators believe that the intent of the IEP benefits all children, yet only about 32 percent of educators feel prepared to address the needs of students with disabilities (Kirch et al., 2007). Table 3.4 provides a brief description of adaptations that help students who have special needs.

Teaching Children Who Have Learning Disabilities

A child with a learning disability has the intellectual potential to succeed in school. But for some reason, the child's academic achievements are significantly below the expected level of performance in a specific subject, such as reading or mathematics. Krueger and Sutton (2001) suggest that restricted access to science causes this difference. Understanding learner needs and modifying lessons can help children to succeed.

NSES
TS-D

A child can be identified as having a learning disability if a school evaluation team finds a severe discrepancy between the child's achievement and intellectual ability in one or more of these areas: oral expression, listening comprehension, written expression, basic reading skill, reading comprehension, and mathematics calculation (Hallahan & Kauffman, 2000). The child may perform at or above the expected level in some school subjects but poorly in others. When this happens, it is especially frustrating for the child and makes identification of the disability difficult. The child may develop failure-avoidance techniques that surface as behavior problems to draw attention away from areas of academic failure.

Over 11.5 percent of U.S. students have a disability and are served by an IEP (U.S. Department of Education, 2002), and at least 5 percent of school-age children have learning disabilities (Hallahan & Kauffman, 2000). The number of schoolchildren who have a learning disability has increased over time, in part because of greater sensitivity in assessment and diagnosis, teacher alertness for possible learning disabilities, and increases in poverty. For example, the number of children who live in poverty has increased from 15 to 19 percent since the 1970s (U.S. Office of Education, 1977; Hallahan & Kauffman, 2000). Nationwide, nearly 30 percent of the students who receive special education services attend regular classrooms (Hallahan & Kauffman, 2000).

Learning disabilities are not diseases. There is no single learning disability. Disabilities include dysgraphia, disorders in written language; dyscalculia, disorders in arithmetic; dyslexia, disorders in receptive and expressive language and reading; and difficulties in perception of spatial relations and organization. Some famous people who have had learning disabilities include Thomas Edison, Albert Einstein, Winston Churchill, Cher, and Tom Cruise.

Structure is the most important concept in teaching children with learning disabilities. These children have perceptual and cognitive difficulties that may make it impossible for them to mask out

Exceptional children learn science with the proper type of support and encouragement.

TABLE 3.4 ● Teaching Children Who Have Special Needs

Special Need	Environmental Adaptation	Materials Adaptation	Teaching Adaptation	Assessment Adaptation
Attention-deficit hyperactivity disorder (ADHD)	Seat student at front of room with back to rest of class to limit distractions. Place good peer models close by.	Use recording sheets. Maintain structure and focus. Organize materials to encourage self-monitoring progress.	Remove excess materials, use audible cues (such as beeps or timers) and eye contact with succinct verbal instructions.	Provide daily assignments. Test knowledge, not attention span. Reward for on-task behavior. Maintain written communication with parents.
Cultural	Carefully select visuals and nonprint materials for cultural inclusion. Represent plural culture. Maintain clear classroom organization. Establish empathic relationships.	Use culturally representative materials. Avoid cultural stereotypes. Use broad themes to include all cultures.	Set explicit expectations, and give explicit instructions. Use divergent questions to encourage pluralism and inclusion. Challenge inaccurate statements. Include careful consideration of issues. Use experience-rich methods.	Provide and accept diverse contexts for assessment activities.
Non-English-speaking	Be patient. Use visual aids to help communicate. Provide direct experience. Encourage high levels of activity.	Maintain a conceptual focus. Enrich vocabulary development.	Be verbally clear. Maintain written clarity; use outlines. Emphasize concepts. Link concepts to experiences. Use guest speakers and field trips. Reduce test anxiety.	Encourage the use of pocket translators and dictionaries. Use pictorial assessment devices, puzzles, and performance tasks.
Gender	Nurture independence and self-confidence. Use hands-on learning activities. Use female role models in the sciences.	Identify and eliminate gender bias in materials. Use a wide variety of manipulatives.	Experiment with heterogeneous and single-sex grouping. Use cooperative learning techniques. Maintain high but realistic expectations for all. Provide frequent progress feedback.	None
Learning style preferences	Include all styles.	Select a balance of visual, auditory, kinesthetic, oral, and written materials.	Provide activities to match preference for individual, group, sequential, visual, verbal, auditory, and global learners.	Assess concepts through verbal, written, kinesthetic, individual, and group opportunities.

NSES

PD-B, C

TS-D

TABLE 3.4 ● Continued

Special Need	Environmental Adaptation	Materials Adaptation	Teaching Adaptation	Assessment Adaptation
Learning disability	Show empathy. Seat student away from distractions during introduction and when giving instructions. Focus attention by putting student with well-behaved student for activity.	Use concrete manipulatives. Screen out irrelevant materials and distractions.	Show clear expectations. Simplify; give cues and specific praise. Use dominant learning mode and multisensory activities. Use concept analysis.	Provide specific criticism and praise. Try oral tests. Modify reading and writing exercises if needed.
Cognitive visability	Limit visual and verbal distractions.	Select appropriate reading level. Use concrete, relevant manipulatives.	Use concept analysis. Simplify. Praise. Use repetition. Maintain eye contact. Engage in physical activity. Give feedback, use cues, cooperative learning. Use examples and nonexamples. Use brief periods of direct instruction.	Verbal tests. Provide assistance with written tests. Provide small-step progress checks.
Visual	Provide clear, predictable traffic pathways. Maintain organized, predictable locations for materials and storage. Provide good lighting. Seat student near activity. Sighted student tutor can assist.	Use voice tapes and audiotapes. Print materials should be large, clear, and uncluttered with numerous colors and geometric designs. Adapt materials to special equipment students may have to use.	Emphasize uses of other senses. Taped instructions or science information can be provided. Pair with sighted students.	More verbal assessment. Assist with written assessment. Assist with physical manipulation of objects during performance assessment.
Hearing	Seat so vision is not obstructed. Seat away from distracting background noises.	Modify for making observations through other senses. Use captioned films and videos. Use printed text to accompany audiotapes. Model or illustrate spoken instructions.	Face the child when speaking. Speak distinctly; do not shout. Use written outlines.	Avoid spoken forms of assessment.
Orthopedic	Identify and remove physical barriers. Provide adequate space for movement. Seat near exits for safety. Check tables and desks for proper height.	Identify devices that assist handling of objects, such as spring-loaded tongs, accountant's pencil grips, test tube racks.	Encourage physical manipulation of objects. Pair with nonimpaired student peer. Provide student training time with equipment prior to use.	Provide assistance with writing and manipulation of materials.

(continued)

TABLE 3.4 ● Continued

Special Need	Environmental Adaptation	Materials Adaptation	Teaching Adaptation	Assessment Adaptation
Behavior	Seat away from distractions. Provide well-lighted quiet space for study.	Train in use prior to providing special equipment.	Use brief activities. Give praise and cues. Reinforce desired behaviors. Obtain attention and establish eye contact prior to discussion or giving instructions.	None
Gifted	None	Advanced reading materials. Greater application of technology.	Emphasize problem solving. Accelerate pace. Arrange mentorships. Emphasize processes, mathematics, and uses of technology.	Increase expectations for analysis, application, and hypotheses. Use open-ended assessment devices.

unnecessary stimuli such as sights and sounds in the background of the classroom. Ways to promote structure include class and study routines, limited choices, focused attention, memory clues, sequenced instruction, clear distinctions between instruction and testing, specific criticism and praise, time clues, conferences with special education teachers, and empathy and encouragement (Coble, Levey, & Matthies, 1985).

Learning disabilities can be difficult to diagnose, and teachers can be left alone to respond to a child's off-task or aggressive behavior resulting from learning frustrations. A school's community may have resources that can help to mitigate some of these frustrations and help children to seek topics of interest and demonstrate their special talents. For example, the World Forestry Foundation, based in Portland, Oregon (*www.worldforestry.org*), sponsors the Forestry Discovery Center in real and virtual settings. The center focuses on forestry concepts of the Pacific Northwest that are widely generalized to most temperate forests. Tours and education programs are available for teachers and children that focus on urban and forest trees and tropical rain forests. All learning opportunities and educational kits are correlated to national and state science standards.

On the East Coast in Port Clyde, Maine, the Herring Gut Learning Center (HGLC) (*www.herringgut.org*) strives to educate local youths about aquaculture and mariculture in a North Atlantic community. HGLC offers summer and school-year programming, correlated to state science standards and unique to its locale, to "fill in the blanks" of school science programs. Led by marine science specialists, preschool through high school youths are treated to interesting field-based programs, such as marshes and mudflats, rocky-shore geology, tidal pools, and island life. Older youths use the alternative science education programs to overcome learning differences and behavioral difficulties, while progressing with mathematics and reading. Life skills are developed, school attendance is improved, and dropout rates are reduced, as a potential new generation of fishermen and lobstermen and women discover marine science careers.

The Great Smoky Mountains Institute at Tremont (*http://www.gsmit.org/*) is nestled in the national park within the Appalachian Mountains south of Knoxville, Tennessee. Although its mission is broader than serving school youths, Tremont provides residential programs in science and nature studies for students and teachers, annually, serving over 4,000 youths from thirteen states. The Great Smoky Mountains National Park is used as a classroom for studies of aquatics, geology, fauna, and flora in order to connect people and nature, foster stewardship, and celebrate diversity. Custom hands-on interdisciplinary programs are designed to provide opportunities for all children to learn in a natural setting through day excursions, extended hikes, and stream studies. The programs are uniquely delivered through cooperative efforts of the Tremont staff and the children's teachers to ensure that learners' needs are met and lasting connections are made with the school curriculum.

Each program, in a different setting, illustrates a real-world example of unique community-based resources available to teachers and schools for helping youths with the learning difficulties that are experienced in typical school settings. Whether you are based in a densely populated urban center or the rural heartland, consider contacting the local chamber of commerce or educational resource center to discover the unique opportunities that are available to help the children of your community.

Teaching Children Who Have Cognitive Disabilities

Some children in your classes will have cognitive disabilities; these children may also be referred to as learners with *mental retardation.* There are different categories of cognitive disabilities, and each has a range of different functions. The American Association of Mental Deficiency describes children who have cognitive disability as having subaverage intelligence and being deficient in behavior and responsibility for their age-related cultural group. These limitations affect academic and motor skills. Children with cognitive disabilities are capable of learning some academics, acquiring social skills, and developing occupational skills.

NSES
TS-D

Children with a mild cognitive disability requiring intermittent support may be included in a general education science classroom. *Educable mentally retarded* (EMR), a term that has been used to describe this level of intelligence, applies to about 11 percent of special needs children in U.S. public schools (Cheney & Roy, 1999).

By acquiring as much information as you can about a child, you will be able to emphasize strengths while teaching to overcome weaknesses. School-support services and special-education personnel can make situation-specific suggestions to assist any particular child. The recommendations in Table 3.4 on pages 82–84 can help enhance a child's academic skills.

Teaching Children Who Have Physical Disabilities

Physical disabilities include visual, hearing, and orthopedic impairments. Conservative estimates suggest that less than 0.5 percent of schoolchildren may have a physical disability; about half of those have multiple disabilities, one-fourth have a chronic health problem, and one-fourth have an orthopedic impairment without other serious complications (Hallahan & Kauffman, 2000).

NSES
TS-D

What Barriers Do Children with Physical Disabilities Face? Children with physical disabilities carry burdens that often limit their access to science education. Most of these burdens arise from the barriers the children encounter, such as:

- family members and school advisers who perceive children with physical disabilities through stereotypes and low expectations,
- classroom structures that limit accessibility and exposure to tactile, manipulative experiences, which are critical to basic science learning,
- science programs that have not been modified or adapted to meet the needs of children with physical impairments,

- teachers who may harbor fearful or negative attitudes or who may treat the children in an overly protective or cautious manner.

Why Is Science Important for Children Who Are Physically Disabled? Science instruction should begin at an early age and continue throughout schooling for children who are physically disabled. As early as 1983, the National Science Board Commission on Precollege Education in Mathematics, Science, and Technology offered three reasons for early and sustained education in science:

1. Science emphasizes hands-on experience and exploration of the environment. It can help to fill some experiential gaps that may have evolved because of extensive hospital stays and/or overprotectiveness of schools or parents. Science can help to develop the individual's independence and overall positive self-image.

2. Recent scientific and technological advances have provided tools such as computers, talking calculators, control systems, versabraille hook-ups to computers, and special telephone systems. These advances can help to mitigate the limitations imposed by a physical disability and can enable the individuals to become independent, contributing members of society. Science instruction that emphasizes making observations, collecting and organizing information, and making conclusions can help develop the individual's mental and manipulative readiness for using new technology.

3. Job opportunities will require knowledge and understanding of technological devices. Computers will continue to be an important part of many jobs. Advances in technology have helped children with physical disabilities learn and have provided new employment opportunities. Children with physical disabilities will need the background, training, and self-confidence to seek these opportunities.

Visual Impairments. Children who are *educationally blind* and *partially sighted* are increasingly benefiting from regular education experiences. They must learn from voice, audiotapes, braille, and other devices designed for the visually impaired. Children who are partially sighted may require printed materials larger than standard school print size. Magnifying devices can be used to enlarge standard print.

Children with severe vision problems are identified at an early age. However, less severe problems often go undetected for years. Regular classroom teachers may be the first to notice sight problems. Some behaviors that may indicate vision loss include squinting at the chalkboard, holding a book closer or farther away than most other children, blinking or otherwise distorting the eyes, holding the head at an odd angle, and unusual sensitivity to light. Refer all children who demonstrate any of these behaviors to the school official who can arrange a vision screening. Parents and children appreciate early notification.

Teaching Children with Visual Limits. An audio-tactile teaching approach may help children who have visual limits. Lessons can be audiotaped for later playback, written assignments and tests can be tape-recorded, and a personal recorder with headphones can be used by children who are educationally blind without disturbing the rest of the class. (Be certain to provide verbal or tape-recorded feedback about answers too.) Magnified print materials and visual aids with high contrast can help children who are partially sighted.

Science process skills (Chapter 1) can provide helpful tactile experiences for the student with a visual impairment. Tactile experiences are more helpful than passive participation. Ideas include:

- modeling various birds and habitats with clay,
- illustrating the carbon cycle of a forest with papier-maché,

- constructing leaf print books from old newspapers,
- designing constellations by constructing paper stars,
- illustrating the food chain by using natural objects,
- designing cloud formations from cotton balls,
- building bridges and other structures using drinking straws,
- building a replica of a coral reef,
- illustrating an electromagnetic wave by using iron filings and magnets, and
- constructing replicas of prehistoric tools.

Instruction that stimulates the greatest range of senses (multimodal instruction) is vital for children with physical impairments. Commercial materials exist and may be modified to assist the student who is visually impaired. Programs such as the Elementary Science Study and Science: A Process Approach II have been used with over 3 million students. Teacher supplements are available with suggestions for modifications for students with disabilities. Adapting Science Materials for the Blind (ASMB) was developed from two Science Curriculum Improvement Study units for use with visually impaired children in mainstreamed classrooms. Science Activities for the Visually Impaired (SAVI, http://www.lawrencehallofscience.org/cml/saviselph/) have been designed especially for elementary and middle-level children.

Pair children who have visual disabilities with sighted children. Several researchers have found that this approach enables the child with a visual impairment to achieve on par with nondisabled peers. The sighted member of a team can translate the class experiences to the child with a visual disability, who can obtain an understanding through other senses. Together, both can report the results of an experiment or activity.

Hearing Disabilities. *Deaf* and *hard of hearing* are two types of hearing impairments. Regular classroom teachers occasionally work with children who have profound hearing losses but more often have students with some lesser degree of hearing loss. Common types of hearing impairments concern volume and pitch. Another type is intelligibility—the volume of a sound may be adequate, but the sound is garbled. Hearing aids, lipreading, expressions, and gestures help the child with a hearing disability succeed in the regular classroom.

Deafness is often identified early in childhood, but mild hearing losses frequently go undetected. The following behaviors may signal a hearing impairment that should be referred to school personnel for screening: odd positioning of the head while listening, inattention during discussions, often asking the speaker to repeat, and asking classmates for instructions.

Teaching Children Who Have Hearing Limits. Language development is one of the major problems for children who are hearing impaired. Direct experience with objects is essential if children are to develop language sufficiently, and objects from a child's environment enhance learning of scientific concepts. When we provide rich experiences, children who have hearing impairments can improve

> language performance, observing and listening skills, vocabulary, the learning of science concepts and development of cognitive skills through direct experiential experiences in science. In order for this learning to occur, students must have the opportunity of "doing science" by hands-on, inquiry, real-life experiences through direct physical manipulation of objects that focus attention on patterns of interaction in physical and biological systems. The pairing or coupling of disabled and nondisabled children also seems to be an effective means for students to learn science. (Brown, 1979, p. 89)

Observations that students must make can be adapted. For example, auditory observations may be changed to visual observations, as in the case of the sounds made by different sizes of tuning forks. Have the child transfer the sound wave to water or sand and compare what happens as an alternative to hearing. Other techniques that teachers can use are similar to those used for multilingual children, including seating the child near the front of the room so that vision is not obstructed, looking directly at the child and obtaining his or her attention before speaking, shaving beards or mustaches so that lips are visible for the student's lipreading, speaking loudly and distinctly without shouting, pairing students, and using a written outline for activities that require several steps.

Orthopedic Disabilities. Orthopedic impairments are disabilities that are caused by diseases and deformities of the muscles, joints, and skeletal system. Examples include cerebral palsy, spina bifida, amputations, birth defects, arthritis, and muscular dystrophy. Temporary injuries are not covered by federal law because they can be corrected. A child with an orthopedic impairment may require an appliance such as a wheelchair, a walker, crutches, or skeletal braces.

Teaching Children Who Have Orthopedic Disabilities. An orthopedically disabled child generally requires adjustments that are physical rather than educational. Be aware of and attempt to remove physical and psychological barriers in your classroom. Examine the curriculum materials and activities, and modify them to include the child with a disability without sacrificing their purpose or science content. Do not underestimate the child's capabilities. Become familiar with the function and maintenance of any appliance the child uses.

Teaching Learners Who Are Gifted and Talented

Children who are gifted or talented may make up 3–5 percent of the U.S. school population (Hallahan & Kauffman, 2000) and are not included in the federal law. However, federal legislation does encourage states to develop programs and support research for students who are gifted and talented (Hallahan & Kauffman, 2000). Gifted or talented children do have special needs that are not usually served well by the instruction that is given to most children. Most teachers have gifted and talented children in their classrooms, and authorities have questioned the wisdom of pulling gifted children out of the regular classroom for special instruction.

Some of the problems that these children experience parallel disabling conditions described earlier. The definition and processes that are used to identify children who have special gifts involve similar difficulties that exist for children who have mental retardation or learning disorders. Whereas most people may feel a moral obligation to help those who have a disadvantage, the child with a special gift may be presumed to find a way to excel on her or his own (Hallahan & Kauffman, 2000).

However, like children who have disadvantages or who are different in other ways, children who are gifted and talented benefit from a balanced view of humanity and become prepared to work and live in the greater society. Children who are gifted should be considered as individuals who have unique needs and abilities, and their education should attend to those specific needs and abilities.

Who Are Gifted and Talented Learners? Children who are gifted and/or talented show promise of making superior progress in school. These children may demonstrate advanced progress in academic achievement in a school subject or exceptional ability and creativity in the arts. Their special intelligence and talents are observed and may be verified by achievement and IQ tests or superior performance in a subject or artistic area. In addition, gifted children may demonstrate other traits, such as sensitivity to the needs of other children, a need for independence, a predisposition for expression, a capacity for social leadership, broad interests in different school areas, apparent natural talents in the arts, and such noticeable behaviors as intensity, persistence, self-assured introversion, or detachment from what they believe are mundane topics.

Children who are gifted and talented have a wide range of characteristics. This range makes it difficult to generalize about all gifted children. Gifted and talented children can represent a tremendous challenge to the science teacher.

Academically gifted children may appear to become easily bored with instruction offered to the rest of the class. If you have not majored in science, you may have some anxiety about having a scientifically gifted child in your class. Fear not. Feeling unprepared in science should not stop you from teaching gifted children. Perhaps your anxiety will be eased if you can keep the issue in perspective. Remember that you are an adult who teaches children, and the experiences of adulthood provide advantages when working with the student who is gifted. Despite all the knowledge a young gifted learner may have, he or she is still an elementary or middle school student, and the student's social, emotional, physical, psychological, and cognitive development is not complete. As an adult, you still have much to offer. All learners enjoy seeing their teacher get excited about their students' work. Having a gifted child in your science class is reason to rejoice and will give you a wonderful opportunity to become a real facilitator and guide rather than a messenger.

Teaching Learners Who Are Gifted and Talented. Children who are gifted in science often are capable of accelerated and more detailed learning. You can enrich their experiences by encouraging them to pursue the subject to a greater depth. You may also accelerate their instruction by drawing on topics from advanced grades or by arranging for the child to work with a mentor (perhaps an older student, another teacher, or a science career professional) on special science topics. It is not uncommon for gifted students to perform two or three years above grade level in the subject or area where they show talent (Hallahan & Kauffman, 2000; Piburn & Enyeart, 1985). Therefore, more flexibility in written assignments and higher expectations for verbal communication are necessary. Try having gifted learners engage in more speculation about scientific events, hypothesize, and develop arguments and counterarguments that pertain to scientific/social issues. Have gifted learners demonstrate the application of science as well as the relationships between science and material learned in other subjects. The following teaching strategies are often appropriate for gifted learners.

- *Develop open-ended learning activities.* Children who have learning and intellectual disabilities benefit from narrowly focused, sequential activities. Children who are gifted should be challenged to develop their intellectual reasoning through open-ended activities that have many possible outcomes. These activities avoid step-by-step recipe procedures and do not have predetermined results. Several of the cooperative inquiry teaching methods and the tools of questioning in Chapter 5 are useful in working with gifted learners.

- *Use gifted students as classroom leaders.* These children may become reliable informal teachers of their peers who can greatly enhance the classroom

When encouraged and supported, exceptional children can overcome exceptional challenges.

NSES

PD-B, C

Teaching Students Who Have Exceptionalities

Who has the wisdom and ability to predict which of our students will succeed and which will not? People who have disabilities are often erroneously thought to be mentally deficient, but the prevailing social attitude has slowly changed. Thanks to federal laws, inclusion, and local school efforts to service better the special needs of children are greater than at any time in the history of schooling. All children are given more encouragement and are provided with more opportunities to achieve their full potential.

After decades of turning away students with disabilities, universities learned to accept them for scientific career training and removed physical and psychological barriers. A three-year survey by the American Association for the Advancement of Science reported a resource group of more than 700 scientists with disabilities. People with disabilities *can* do science. But our schools still must do more. Robert Menchel, a senior physicist for the Xerox Corporation who has been deaf since the age of 7, has visited many schools. He says:

The lack of development of a basic science curriculum from kindergarten to the twelfth grade is a national disgrace and one that puts the deaf child at a disadvantage in comparison to the nonhandicapped child. Furthermore, these students are still being pushed into stereotyped job roles and dead-end jobs. For the female students it is even worse.

Robert Hoffman, a researcher who has cerebral palsy, speaks about the effects of isolation due to a disability:

When one is born with a disability severe enough so society shoves him into a special program (which nonhandicapped people develop), one becomes separated from "normal" persons. All through his school years, he learns from other disabled students, and the teachers design studies to fit the limitations of his physical disability.

John Gavin, a research scientist with a physical impairment, cautions those who have no apparent disability:

atmosphere. Children who are gifted can also be used as resource people, researchers, science assistants, and community ambassadors for exciting school programs.

- *Use technology, science processes, and mathematics.* Scientific observation can be enhanced through mathematics. Encourage gifted children to use higher forms of mathematics and statistics as often as possible. Engage them in more precise measures and more extensive uses of science process skills. Technology will challenge gifted students to expand research capabilities as well as quantify and communicate their scientific findings.

- *Reinforce and reward superior efforts.* Some school programs for gifted and talented children use pull-out approaches: learners are placed in special programs or given accelerated instruction. Inclusion can also benefit children who are gifted. Adaptations of science content and changes in instruction with more options for the gifted learners can provide suitable instruction in the regular classroom. Science content adaptations could include emphasizing higher levels of thinking, abstraction, and independent thinking. The challenge is fundamentally the same as with any other child: Help the child learn how to learn. Reinforcement and rewards for effort and work well done are usually all that is necessary to help gifted children keep their high level of motivation for learning. Some suggestions for reinforcing and rewarding superior effort include public recognition for effort, extra credit or waiver of standard assignments, positive teacher comments, extra leadership opportunities and/or classroom responsibilities, and encouraging students to do real research projects.

One of the least desirable traits of the human condition is our propensity to avoid those among us who are afflicted with overt physical disabilities. While this may be an inherent psychological carryover from those days of survival of the fittest, it is more likely we do not wish to have a reminder that we are potentially and continually eligible to join them.

Teachers become the key. A caring teacher with a positive can-do attitude is consistently ranked highly by children with disabilities. Teachers who care seem to expect that their students can learn at a high level. These teachers try to see that all children fulfill the high expectations held for them.

Language development is one of the major problems of children with hearing impairments. Researchers report that direct experience with objects is essential and that utilization of objects from a child's environment enhances his or her learning of concepts.

The most significant changes needed for teaching children who have visual impairments are related to the adaptation of educational materials and equipment to take advantage of each child's residual vision.

Children who are orthopedically disabled are a heterogeneous group, and it is difficult to prescribe general methods and adaptations that will serve each child well. However, pairing a child who has an orthopedic impairment with a child who has no disabilities helps both. The child who is impaired still needs direct physical experience with the science phenomena to the greatest extent possible. For example,

> a magnet can be taped to the arm or leg. Another student can bring objects in contact with the magnets. The child should be able to feel and see which objects interact with the magnet and which do not. In this way, the child [with a disability] is involved in the decision making and discovery that is the major emphasis of [the] lesson.

Dean Brown's groundbreaking research showed that children with physical disabilities learned to understand science concepts and that they developed higher levels of reasoning skills if given the opportunity. Children with disabilities need direct, experiential, sensory experiences in science. Many researchers have repeatedly expressed the need for doing science through hands-on, inquiry-based, real-life experiences.

Source: Adapted from the literature review by Dean R. Brown, "Helping Handicapped Youngsters Learn by 'Doing,'" in Mary Budd Rowe (Ed.), *What Research Says to the Science Teacher* (Washington, DC: National Science Teachers Association, 1979), Vol. 2, pp. 80–100; and D. P. Hallahan and J. M. Kauffman, *Exceptional Learners* (Boston: Allyn & Bacon, 2000).

- *Provide extracurricular or cocurricular learning opportunities.* Your classroom will have limited teaching resources, and your time will also have limits. Out-of-class or out-of-school learning options may also help the gifted student continue to learn science. Use community library resources or make arrangements for the child to do special work at a community college or nearby university. Develop and utilize community resource personnel: Construct a network of science-related resource people and arrange mentor-intern relationships. Start a science club for students with special interests. Begin an after-school science lab, and encourage the learners to design and pursue experiments. Student teachers or field experience interns from a nearby university may be able to assist with the science lab instruction and programming.

How Can Families Help Meet Children's Special Needs?

More families are realizing the importance of science, and involving parents and caregivers helps to increase children's success by

- encouraging greater achievement in school;
- increasing family participation in school activities;
- supporting positive changes in school climate;

NSES
TS-C, E

Learning Cycle Featured Lesson

Physical Science: Magnets

Grades • K–2

Engaging Question

What is a magnet and what does it do?

Materials Needed

For Exploration Phase • for teacher introduction you will need:

- 2 bar magnets, 1 suspended from a table top by an 18-inch length of string

For Exploration Phase • conducted in pairs, each pair will need:

- 2 bar magnets

For Expansion Phase • conducted whole class, you will need:

- Magnets in a variety of shapes, such as horseshoe, disk, button, and rod
- Masking tape
- An assortment of materials from the classroom, including steel and iron objects; nonmetal objects; and metallic objects such as coins, aluminum cans, tinfoil, and brass

Safety: Refrain from using iron filings. If iron filings are used, require that students wear goggles to avoid filings getting lodged in their eyes. Adaptation for a student with visual impairment: Glue or tape a small object, such as a button, on one end of the bar magnets. The tactile relief will assist in identifying the "same" ends of the magnet.

Exploration

Teacher Introduction

Suspend two bar magnets from a thread from a small table and demonstrate how one magnet can make another spin or swing or change position.

Ask: "Why do magnets seem to push or pull at each other? Do you suppose they always do this?"

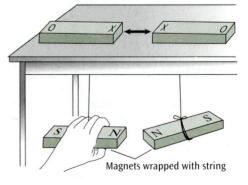

Magnets wrapped with string

Student Activity

Provide the student pairs with two bar magnets that have had the N and S stamps on the end of the magnets covered with masking tape. Encourage the children to investigate the behavior of two bar magnets by pushing and pulling them toward each other on a flat, nonmetal table. Ask the children to use a crayon or marker to place an X on the end of one of the magnets and an O on the other end. Now ask them to place the labeled bar magnet on the table top. Ask them to move the unlabeled bar magnet toward the X end of the bar magnet sitting on the table. Tell them that if the magnet they are moving gets pushed away they should label the end that got pushed away X; if their magnet was pulled toward the X end of the magnet sitting on the table, they should label that end O. Ask them to continue manipulating the two bar magnets.

They will eventually notice that the X's and the O's repel each other and the X + O ends will attract each other.

Avoid dropping the bar magnets; they will tend to lose their strength. However, the magnetic forces can be strengthened if you have a magnetizer available from a science supplier.

Explanation

Compose and use questions that cause the children to describe their experiences, such as:

1. Which ends of the magnets seemed to pull together? [The X to the O ends.]

2. Which ends seemed to push away? [Both of the X's and both of the O's.]

3. What kind of pattern did you notice? [Those with the same label will push away from one another; those with different labels will move toward one another.]

Ask the students to remove the masking tape from the ends of the magnets and point out the N and S stamped on the bars. Ask the students to fill in the sentences that represent the concept:

Magnets _____ (push) away from each other when the ends are the same.
Magnets _____ (pull) together when the ends are not the same.

Develop vocabulary, if appropriate, for students by using "attract" and "repel" or "pull" and "push."

Expansion

PROCESS SKILLS USED
▶ Classifying
▶ Communicating
▶ Inferring

Continue to use the language "pull" or "attract" and "push" or "repel" as children investigate the behavior of different types of magnets. Ask them:

• Can you find a way to use the disk magnets and make them roll away from or toward another disk magnet?

Encourage the children to use a variety of magnets to examine the behavior of common metallic and non-metallic objects from the classroom.

Challenge the children to group the objects and explain their reasons and to communicate their findings by making a chart to illustrate the types of objects that a magnet attracts.

Discuss with the children where magnets exist in their homes and what these magnets do.

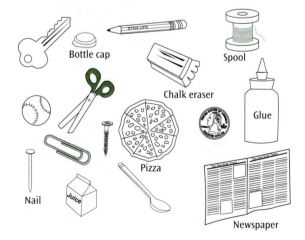

Bottle cap
Spool
Chalk eraser
Glue
Pizza
Nail
Juice
Newspaper

Hands-on Assessment

The students, when given a magnet, will be able to identify like and unlike poles. The students will then be asked to predict and test objects that may be attracted to a magnet.

Reflective Assessment

The students will be required to use the concepts of push and pull or attract and repel appropriately to describe the behavior of magnets.

Pictorial Assessment

When given a set of pictures of various objects, the students should be able to classify them as "attracting" or "repelling" a magnet. The students will also be able to view the following drawing and respond to these questions about the picture:

This picture shows a hand pushing Magnet 1 toward Magnet 2.

- The magnets are on a flat table. What do you think will happen to Magnet 2?
- Why do you think this will happen?

- improving student attendance;
- decreasing the school dropout rates;
- decreasing substance abuse, violence, and antisocial behavior; and
- increasing the collective efforts among school personnel, parents, and families toward greater productive partnerships. (Krueger & Sutton, 2001, p. 92)

Science skills develop over time, and development builds on older skills. "If you don't use it, you'll lose it" applies here. The science foundation that is laid during childhood will increase each individual's potential for later success. Also, science depends on mathematics. Students should be encouraged to study mathematics every school year.

All students learn science through hands-on, minds-on experiences. Children should be encouraged to handle physical objects, make measurements and direct comparisons, and ask frequent questions about what they observe and experience.

How Can Families Help Their Children Study and Prepare for Science?

NSES
TS-E

Parents, caregivers, and other family members are invaluable when it comes to educating children. They are closest to the special needs their children may have. Families can help their children to succeed in science by following these suggestions:

- *Stimulate interest in and foster feelings for science.* Families can help their children to realize that science can be fun and help them to experience success, with its feelings of excitement, discovery, and mastery.
- *Include science in the child's everyday experiences.* Children can be asked to count and form sets of utensils at dinnertime and can help to measure ingredients. Include children also in repairing broken appliances or building a model airplane.

94   chapter 3   How Can You Improve Science Learning for Diverse Learners?

- *Establish a regular study time and provide a designated space for study away from distractions.* Work with the teachers to develop effective ways to communicate with children who have vision and hearing disabilities. Equipment modifications can be developed for children who have physical disabilities, and these can be shared with the school.

- *Check with children every day to make sure homework and special projects are completed.* Families should ask to see completed homework and any tests or projects that have been graded or returned.

- *Offer to read assignment questions.* Even if a family member does not know the answers, the result will be a stronger bond. The child will benefit from an interested adult role model, forming the impression that school, homework, and effort are important.

Science is found in all aspects of life and is important to children's successful futures.

- *Ask whether children have any difficulties with science or mathematics.* Families should talk often about any difficulties and then follow up if there appear to be continuing problems.

- *Use a homework hotline if the school has one.* This may be school-based or supported by individual teachers during designated hours.

What Are Some Ways in Which Families Can Help Their Children?

NSES
TS-E

Some teachers, even entire schools, arrange home-based science activities to supplement school instruction. Family members become enthusiastic and develop a stronger bond with the school. They often say, "Let's have parent involvement programs more often." "It helps me keep in touch with my child." "The activities didn't take too much time, so it was simple to include them into our busy evening schedule." "I think it's great to get the parents involved. Each activity we did benefited our older child and our younger child who is not even in school!" (Williams-Norton, Reisdorf, & Spees, 1990, pp. 13–15). Meaningful activities can be found for young children in magazines such as *Click* and *Dragonfly*.

The rich variety of science teaching resources makes it easy to suggest home study extensions. Giving options help families to overcome limits of time and materials. When making suggestions for families, keep these criteria activities in mind (Williams-Norton et al., 1990, p. 14):

- *The activities should be at grade level and developmentally appropriate for the child.* Select options with the special needs of the children in mind.

- *Activities should require materials that are available at home.* No family will welcome traveling to gather together materials, and many cannot afford the expense.

- *The activities should supplement what is taught in school, not duplicate it.* Do not expect family teaching to be a substitute for your own responsibility.

- *Provide complete and accurate instructions including instructions for safety.* Try the activities yourself before sending them home. Can a child do the activity with minimal adult guidance?

- *Select activities that emphasize simple and accurate concepts.* Cross-check the concepts of the activity with those of your textbook or science program. Are they consistent? If they are different, modify them or select another activity. Choose activities that emphasize a main science idea, and encourage the family to continue emphasizing this main idea.

- *The activities should be fun.* Families will enjoy a special time together when the activity is fun. Encourage families to share the joys and mysteries of science. Positive attitudes toward science from families will benefit school science.

- *Develop the concepts of sink or float and density* by floating common objects such as straws and plastic buttons in plain water and in salt water. Because the density of salt water is greater, objects that sink in plain water often float in salt water. Try adding different amounts of salt to water to explore the effects of salt concentration on density and floating.

- *Explore primary and secondary colors.* Following the directions on food coloring packages, prepare different colors, and arrange them in glass jars. Dye macaroni or paper to represent the colors of a rainbow. Combine the three primary colors to produce every color.

- *Demonstrate magnetism* by having children compare the effects of magnets on different objects in the kitchen. Let the children predict which objects will and will not be attracted to the magnets.

- *Use building blocks to develop the concepts of set and order.* Lay a foundation of three blocks; then place two blocks on the next layer and one block on the top layer. Ask the children to count the blocks and to estimate how many blocks would be necessary to build towers six and ten blocks high.

chapter summary

A single science teaching method by itself is insufficient. Each hands-on science lesson must be accompanied by adaptations to suit the needs of each special student.

There is no single method or science program that can be used to teach all children. One single factor does benefit *all* children: hands-on science—where all children have abundant opportunities to benefit from multisensory stimulation in cooperative settings. This approach has the potential to become the great equalizer, specifically when coupled with teacher instruction for the minds-on connection. Children who are culturally different may acquire missed experiences through hands-on

science. Non-English-speaking children can use science to learn and develop language skills. Young females can overcome skill deficits, gender stereotypes, and career limitations through hands-on, minds-on science. Exceptional children are given new opportunities because of hands-on science and its ability to include all children in minds-on experiences. Gifted and talented children also benefit as they are introduced to new experiences and are motivated to process these experiences at an advanced intellectual level.

Families play a vital role with students who have special needs. Teachers should inform parents about the importance of science and offer activities to strengthen the school–home learning connection.

reflect and respond

1. Cultural differences can have a positive impact on the social climate of a classroom. What are some ways in which you can encourage the expression of differences and make a positive impact on all children?

2. Take the picture of a scientist that you drew in Chapter 1, and draw another one now. How do the pictures compare? What features are similar? How many of these same features do you observe: male, middle-aged, bald,

96   chapter 3   How Can You Improve Science Learning for Diverse Learners?

glasses, facial hair, lab coat with pocket protector, test tubes? How do these features reflect bias, attitudes, stereotypes, and values? Where did the impressions portrayed in the pictures come from? What types of multicultural education concepts are reflected in the picture? How can social context and media influence impressions? How are the impressions you have of science and scientists likely to influence young children?

3. Blindfold yourself, or attend a class while wearing earplugs. How is your ability to function impaired? What long-term cumulative effects could result from your temporary disability if it were to become permanent? How could these effects influence your ability to function in a regular classroom?

4. Brainstorm ideas that are suitable for teaching science to gifted students. What differences are found on your list according to grade level? How would you work with a youngster who is gifted and who also has a cultural or language difference and/or a disability?

5. Brainstorm ideas related to classroom organization. How can a typical self-contained room be converted to better suit the special needs students? Look especially for barriers that might limit the inclusion of children who have physical disabilities. What complications might a teacher encounter? What are some ways to overcome these complications?

6. Complete the survey on pages 92–98 "How Equitable Is Your Science Program and Your Teaching?" What do you conclude about your willingness or ability to provide equitable science teaching and learning?

Directions: Answer each question with a yes or no. If a question does not specifically or completely pertain to you, try to offer a yes or no response based on what you know and think you would do. If possible, respond to each item as a member of a multicultural, gender, and exceptional representative team including parents, learners, administrators, and other teachers. If uncertain, try to collect the necessary information in order to substantiate your answers.

NSES

TS-F

The General Science Education Program Survey

Does the school's science instruction and curriculum:

_____ 1. Use hands-on activities on a regular basis?
_____ 2. Include grouping and cooperative learning activities routinely?
_____ 3. Emphasize content and the processes of problem solving equally?
_____ 4. Encourage learners to talk about their science learning?
_____ 5. Relate written class materials to science in the everyday lives of a culturally diverse society?
_____ 6. Include information on a regular basis about careers using science?
_____ 7. Include role models who represent both genders and persons of different racial, cultural, linguistic, and exceptional (disabled and gifted) groups for students to interact with on a regular basis?
_____ 8. Provide access for all students to technology and ensure equal experiences with it?
_____ 9. Integrate science content and processes with other core subjects, such as language arts, social studies, and mathematics?
_____ 10. Strive to develop and encourage positive attitudes toward science for all teachers, administrators, parents, and students?
_____ 11. Develop partnerships with science and industry that include participants who represent both genders and people of different racial, cultural, linguistic, and exceptional (disabled and gifted) groups?
_____ 12. Assess what students know and can do in science with performance-based criteria that emphasize the open-ended nature of science and the importance of using language for description and questioning?
_____ 13. Ensure that all counselors, teaching staff, and parents are aware of strategies that encourage equitable participation of female, minority, and exceptional students in science?
_____ 14. Monitor all teaching materials for equal representation of both genders and people of different racial, cultural, linguistic, and exceptional groups in the science community?

Source: Adapted from the work of Martha A. Adler: How Equitable Is Your Science Education Program? The Checklist. (*Dwight D. Eisenhower Mathematics and Science Education, 4, 1,* 1994): 6–8.

Science in Pre-K Through Upper Elementary

_____ 15. Provide professional development for all teachers to update and improve their science teaching skills?

_____ 16. Support and train teachers who are uncomfortable teaching science?

_____ 17. Emphasize accountability for teaching science on a regular basis in all classrooms?

_____ 18. Encourage and facilitate out-of-school learning experiences at all levels and for all skills groups?

_____ 19. Monitor extracurricular activities for equitable representation of students of both genders and of different racial, cultural, linguistic, and exceptional groups?

_____ 20. Establish guidelines for science fair projects that deemphasize the "wow" effect of experiments and encourage children to formulate their own questions and explore science in their own natural environments?

_____ 21. Publicly acknowledge strong commitment to science as an integral part of the school curriculum rather than as enrichment or an option?

_____ 22. Provide assistance for teachers in obtaining the necessary materials and equipment for teaching science with an experiential emphasis?

_____ 23. Form partnerships with parents to define their roles in supporting science education for their children?

_____ 24. Deemphasize the textbook approach to science in favor of an experience-based approach?

_____ 25. Include outreach efforts to parents who are representative of the entire student population on decisions regarding science activities and explorations with children?

Scoring

If you have scored as an individual, then credit one point for each question you answered yes.

- **20–25 points:** Congratulations! Share what you do with other schools and take a look at what is happening at the secondary level in your district.

- **10–19 points:** Good start, keep working at it! You have the elements of a good beginning. Check to see if your negative responses form any pattern. What is working for the school at this grade level? What is missing? Share the checklist with others and discuss a plan of action for improving.

- **0–9 points:** It's never too late. Examine your positive responses and try to build on your successes. What has made it possible for these to be incorporated in science education in your school? Then, examine the questions where you provided a negative response. Try to identify barriers and speculate about potential solutions to help your school to elevate its science program to a more equitable level for all students.

PEARSON
myeducationlab
Where the Classroom Comes to Life

Explore—Video Homework Exercise. Go to MyEducationLab at www.myeducationlab .com and select the topic "Diverse Learners," then watch the videos "Lesson on Birds" and "Science for All," noting the characteristics of the learner and strategies used by the teacher. Respond to the questions below.

NSES

PD-B

1. How does equitable access to high-quality science experiences help to develop future citizen-participants in a democratic society?

2. How might cultural influences deter children from developing the skills they will need for a future in science?

3. What experiences have you had in a culturally diverse setting? How did your experiences contribute to a better understanding of the diverse needs of learners?

Enrich—Professional Practice

1. Interview a teacher whose students are culturally different from himself or herself. Inquire about how the science program or instruction has been modified to recognize and use cultural differences in a positive way. What effects have the teacher's efforts had on all of the children?

2. Examine several science textbooks from different publishers. Report observations about possible gender bias, omitted discussion of cultural differences, and potential for adaptation for non-English-speaking, disabled, and/or gifted children. What suggestions are provided in the teacher's guide?

3. Choose any lesson from a science text or hands-on program. Demonstrate how you would adapt it to provide special instruction for one or more children who have the types of special needs described in this chapter.

NSES
TS-D

Expand—Weblink Exercise

Science Literacy. Go to MyEducationLab Resources section and select "Weblinks," then click on the link for "Disabilities, Teaching Strategies and Resources" for information about a wide range of disabilities, teaching strategies, and resources. Study the characteristics, behaviors, and indicators for the disabilities. What are the learner benefits if the teaching strategies are used?

NSES
TS-D

How Do You Plan for the Inquiry-Based Classroom?

- How do standards support inquiry and help teachers to plan lessons?

- How does concept mapping relate to standards, and how may it be used as a tool for planning, teaching, and assessment?

- What is a learning cycle lesson, and how does it benefit learners and teachers?

It was spring, and Jennifer was near the end of her first year of teaching fourth grade, a position that she had won over forty-two other applicants. Jennifer did not believe that she was better prepared for the position than the other applicants, especially since some had several years of teaching experience. Midway through her first semester, Jennifer learned that she had impressed Mr. Emerson, the principal, and the teaching staff with her views on teaching and that the science demonstration lesson that she taught was perceived by the staff as being on the cutting edge of meeting her state's standards which were stimulated by the National Science Education Standards. Mr. Emerson and her fourth-grade teaching team of three other teachers had high expectations for Jennifer. The fact that she was a first-year teacher did not tempt them to make excuses for her; the school's staff had its focus on providing what was best for the students in order to meet state achievement test standards.

Jennifer did not disappoint anyone. She proved her value among her teammates, and her self-effacing ways made her a joy to collaborate with. Jennifer read widely, eagerly collected teaching ideas, and was genuinely grateful for suggestions. She was flattered when other teachers indicated interest in her science lessons and how those lessons could interface with some of the topics taught by her teammates who specialized in one subject, which was taught to all fourth-grade students who rotated through the mod. Jennifer thought that her teammates were only being kind, but they recognized considerable skill and potential for teacher leadership and recommended that Mr. Emerson appoint her to the Professional Development Council (PDC).

Jennifer accepted the appointment to the school PDC, although she thought the appointment should be given to someone with more experience. Science was the topic for next year's PDC agenda. The school had recently revised its curriculum to fulfill the state and National Science Education Standards. Curriculum decisions for the school district were made by the school board using site-based management. The state recommended a general curriculum model and materials that schools might use but let the schools determine how best to devise and implement the curriculum. The standards made it difficult to select a single

NSES
PD-B
TS-B

textbook and still be able to prepare students well for the statewide mandatory achievement test that was given to all grades each year. The test was designed to measure progress toward fulfilling the standards. The PDC was concerned with the teachers' needs that were identified on a survey the committee had taken. The survey spoke of high frustration levels and a desire for extensive professional development teaching toward the standards.

Coincidentally, the school's student achievement test scores were received the same day as Jennifer's first meeting with the council. Teacher comparisons were discouraged but were unavoidable. Jennifer's students were the only ones who had scored above the norm. Was this a fluke, or did this first-year teacher do something different to encourage higher student performance?

Jennifer felt somewhat defensive at first but soon realized that her colleagues' questions were professional and were asked in the spirit of schoolwide collaboration. Did she feel overwhelmed by the standards? What science concepts did she teach, and how did she decide when and how to teach them? Was there an order that worked best? How did she bring some balance from the science disciplines into her lessons? What did she do with the four new dimensions of science: science as inquiry, science and technology, science in personal and social perspectives, and history and nature of science? How could she possibly fit them into science lessons?

Jennifer described the frustrated feelings that she too had experienced at first. The standards advocated covering fewer concepts but expected teachers and students to go to greater depth in science than had ever been attempted. Jennifer explained that desperation motivated her to think back to her experiences during teacher preparation. She had found a way to connect certain experiences and use them as tools for dealing with the expectations set by the standards.

Jennifer described a tool called *concept mapping* that helped her to sort and organize the science content concepts into story lines regarding specific themes. One teacher thought that the concept mapping technique seemed like brainstorming and webbing, as used in language arts, but Jennifer demonstrated that mapping was much more than that and explained how the techniques helped her to find a focus for individual lessons. Jennifer designed each of her lessons for a single concept but planned comprehensively to help students construct their understanding of the concept and to connect it with other concepts from other lessons. Over time, students seemed to think differently and to be able to make many connections to what they learned and become more confident in responding to new problems and challenging questions. Students even learned to make their own concept maps to illustrate their understanding. Jennifer used these maps to conduct formative evaluations of her teaching and her students' learning.

Jennifer also described a *learning cycle model* that she used to foster a culture of inquiry and to plan the sequence of student activities to ensure that the concept was built from direct student activity and then expanded to connect with the new content outcomes indicated by the science standards for her specific grade level.

Jennifer shared some of her lesson plans with the other PDC members. They easily understood what it meant to *engage* the learner, but some asked her to explain what she meant by *explore, explain, expand,* and *evaluate.* They were curious why Jennifer had students do activities first without explaining the point of the lesson and why she did not always test students at the end of her lessons, although the "evaluate" part of her planning model seemed to indicate that she would assess student learning at the end of each lesson.

Her lesson plans contained several activities that were related to each other, in a sequence over several days, sometimes requiring that almost a whole day be devoted to science. Of course, these special occasions were supported by Jennifer's teammates, and at times, they helped her teach science to all of the 100 fourth graders whom they shared. The PDC concluded that the ideas that Jennifer learned and used might help other teachers, and they decided to plan next year's professional development agenda around concept mapping, learning cycle planning, inquiry, teaching techniques, and authentic embedded assessment. Jennifer was consulted often about how to do this and to suggest where the PDC might find assistance.

You might think that this scenario is too far-fetched? Rest assured, it is not. We find that many new teacher graduates experience situations very much like this one. They have skills that are different—in some ways more sophisticated—than those of more experienced teaching professionals and that make them in demand when schools and teachers find themselves facing the challenges afforded by change and meeting the pressures of public accountability.

Rising expectations for students and teachers require new ways of thinking and teaching, guided by state and national standards, which can be addressed through purposeful planning. One new challenge is to convert typical planning processes into an approach that helps learners to "make meaning" from the inquiring experiences that they acquire. How can you plan interesting, high impact lessons, and what is a potent tool that you can use to help make decisions about what and how to teach? In this chapter, we

1. examine National Science Education Standards for content to identify the concepts to be taught,

2. explore the use of concept mapping as a planning and assessment tool, and

3. investigate a constructivist inquiry-based learning cycle for planning lessons that specifically addresses the NSE standards for content in a direct and effective manner.

Using the National Science Education Standards for Content and Promoting Science Inquiry

"What should learners understand and be able to do?" is a fundamental question that educational commissioners (who establish standards) and all teachers ponder. This is an outcomes-based question whose answer is the heart of lesson planning and improving achievement through educational reform (Lee & Paik, 2000). The question is consistent with the inquiry intentions of the National Science Education Standards and the science standards of most states. If our desire is to embrace and use those standards, then we subscribe to a goal of helping children to become scientifically literate. This means that the lessons that we select or plan will involve learners in numerous processes of inquiry and the development of essential thinking and problem-solving skills. The experiences that we plan and provide for children will help develop and nurture scientific attitudes, which will motivate intellectual inquiry and result in an understanding of scientific concepts. Processes, attitudes, and concepts (commonly called the knowledge of science) are emphasized in our lessons.

NSES
TS-A

The National Science Education Standards outline important concepts for grade level clusters and are a place to begin to make decisions about what you may wish learners to understand and be able to do. Table 4.1 provides an excerpt taken from the National Science Education Standards for content for K–4 Physical Science. The rest of the related standards are provided in the Appendix.

TABLE 4.1 ● K–4 Physical Science Standards: Standard B

NSES
CS-B

All students should develop an understanding of:

- Properties of objects and materials*
- Position and motion of objects*
- Light, heat electricity, and magnetism*

Properties of objects and materials concepts:

- Objects have many observable properties, including size, weight, shape, color, temperature, and the ability to react with other substances. These properties can be measured using tools such as rulers, balances, and thermometers.
- Objects are made of one or more materials, such as paper, wood, and metal. Objects can be described by the properties of the materials from which they are made, and these properties can be used to separate or sort a group of objects or materials.
- Materials have different states—solid, liquid, and gas. Some common materials such as water can be changed from one state to another by heating or cooling.

*See Appendix.

Source: NRC. Science content standards. *National Science Education Standards* (Washington, D.C.: National Academy Press, 1996): 123.

Examine your state documents or the National Science Education Standards. You will notice that these documents do not precisely describe everything that you may be expected to teach or how you should teach, nor may those standards be used as a checklist; mastery of what the standards describe requires multiple exposures. Try sketching the relationships among the concepts, as in Figure 4.1, as a tool to understand expectations

NSES
CS-B

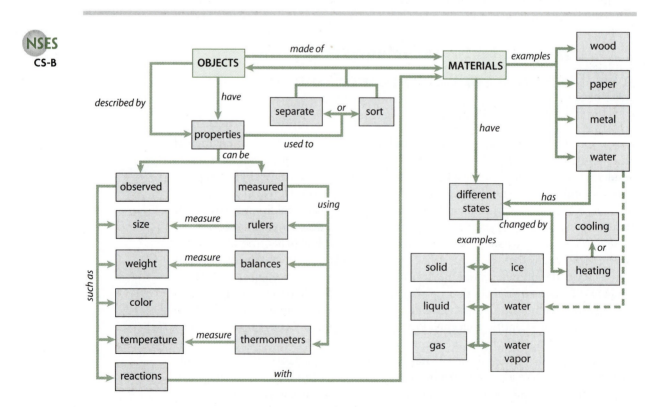

FIGURE 4.1 ● K–4 Properties of Objects and Materials

and for translating standards and outcomes-based documents into a general plan of topics, concepts, and sequences. This tool is called a *concept map*.

Concept Mapping

NSES
TS-F

State documents may refer to "benchmarks" to be addressed or "indicators" to be achieved. Collectively, these labels may be thought of as *outcomes*—the intended learning that results from teaching. "Outcomes are high quality, culminating demonstrations of significant learning in context" (Spady, 1994, p. 18). William Spady reminds us that *demonstration* is the operative word. Outcomes identify in general terms the end product that we expect students to develop or achieve. The National Science Education Standards and other reform movements (such as Project 2061's Benchmarks) identify the essential contexts and the types of high-quality end products that we should expect from scientifically literate students. Sometimes these end products—outcomes—are described for a particular grade level, but most often they are listed for a cluster of school grades. The grade-level placement, order, fit, and process of the steps that are required for successful demonstration of these end products might not be defined. This planning chore is the duty of the curriculum developers or, more likely, each teacher. Several of the questions that were asked of Jennifer in our chapter scenario reflect the anxiety and uncertainty that this chore can cause for teachers.

As was shown in the scenario, concept maps are essential tools for planning and teaching, and they can help students to improve concept constructions, while helping to avoid misconceptions (Haney, 1998). Concept mapping is becoming widely used as constructivist-inquiry learning models are pervasive in science education, particularly as a tool for diagnostic, formative, and summative assessment of students' conceptual understandings (Bell, 2007).

Concept mapping helps students to gain high-quality and meaningful learning outcomes in science. Maps provide concrete visual aids to help organize information before it is learned. With a teacher's leadership, young children contribute ideas that reveal the preconceptions of a class or group as they learn. These ideas can take the form of a bulletin board or key words placed on a felt board or magnet board with relationships discussed and sentences formed to display fuller, richer representations of the lesson's target concept. Students learn to make their own maps while they learn, and examine the changes in their thinking as they construct their understanding. Maps can also be made as a type of assessment at the conclusion of lessons.

Science textbooks are beginning to use concept maps to introduce chapter materials, and concept maps are among their end-of-chapter activities. Teachers who have used them have found that concept maps provide a logical basis for deciding what main ideas to include in (or delete from) their lesson plans and science teaching. Concept maps can be developed for an entire course, one or more units, or even a single lesson. We have developed concept maps for each chapter of this book. These maps introduce you to the dominant ideas and illustrate the relationships among the chapter's concepts. These maps are available in the instructor's manual and are provided at the MyLabSchool site. Please ask your instructor for copies.

A concept map is a tool that illustrates the conceptual connections understood by the map's creator. Each person may construct a different map, depending on how he or she understands the subject of the map. Never try to memorize a concept map. Instead, study it for the conceptual story that it tells, paying attention to the main ideas and the relationships among them.

Necessary Definitions

Some definitions must be provided before we can proceed. The fundamental purpose of education is to help students find new meaning in what they learn and to make meaning

NSES
PD-A

from what they do. We refer to this as *meaningful learning*. Meaningful learning implies that as a result of instruction, individuals are able to relate new material to previously acquired learning. This means that learners see new knowledge in the light of what they already know and understand; hence they find new meaning. Knowledge continually grows but in a fashion that encourages connections with what learners already know. If these connections are missing, learners may regard the ideas they are taught as useless abstractions that only need to be memorized for a test. David Ausubel (1968) contrasts meaningful learning with rote learning, which is the result of many disjointed lessons.

Concept maps use three types of knowledge: facts, concepts, and generalizations.

Facts. A *fact* is a singular occurrence that happens in the past or present and that has no predictive value for the future. Thus, the information that you are now reading in this book at a specific time of day is a fact, just as a statement about what you ate for lunch or dinner yesterday is a fact. These facts may be completely isolated events that give no indications about your study or eating habits. On the other hand, if you regularly read your science methods book at the same time or if you consistently eat salad for lunch and chicken or fish for dinner, then these seemingly isolated facts have much in common with your similar actions at other times.

Concepts. Common attributes among facts can be described, and facts that form related clusters of ideas can be named. The name that is given represents a *concept*. Interestingly, your behavior today or yesterday can be described by a single word or brief phrase. Words such as *magnet*, *pole*, *attract*, and *repel* are examples of names of concepts that are based on an accumulation of facts. The definitions of these concepts may include descriptions, such as "You read your textbook before and after the science methods class" or "You try to eat foods that are low in calories, fat, and cholesterol." A concept covers a broader set of events than a singular occurrence that might happen at random. Therefore, concepts by their nature are abstract. Other examples of concept names are *computer*, *animal*, *mineral*, *vegetable*, *food chain*, *solution*, *conservation*, and *buoyancy*. All examples require that we know the definition of the name to understand the meaning of the concept. In fact, most words in the dictionary represent concepts. All learners, especially young children, need to experience many examples of singular occurrences or facts before they can develop the abstract understanding necessary for conceptualization. But once they learn the concept, they do not need to learn isolated facts that are subsumed in it. They can reconstruct these facts when they need them.

Generalizations. *Generalizations* are broad patterns between two or more concepts that have predictive value. Generalizations are rules or principles that contain more than one concept and that have predictive value. Thus, a statement such as "Like poles in magnets repel each other and opposite poles attract" is a generalization, and it can predict what would happen if two magnets were brought next to each other. Learners must know the concepts of *magnets*, *poles*, *attraction*, and *repel* before they can fully understand the meaning of the generalization.

What Are Concept Maps?

Concepts are abstract ideas. Concept maps are concrete graphic illustrations that indicate how a single concept is related to other concepts in the same category (see Figure 4.2). As you begin to learn about concept maps, you may prefer to think of them as sophisticated planning webs that reveal what concepts children must learn and how the concepts must be related. Curricula are designed primarily to teach concepts that students do not already know. Therefore, teaching and learning will be greatly enhanced if we know which concepts should be included and which need to be excluded from instructional programs.

Concept maps show relationships among different smaller and larger concepts. By looking at a concept map and considering the level of the children's abilities and other

NSES

PD-A

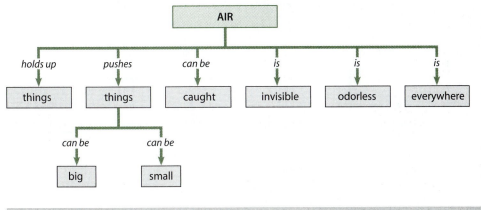

FIGURE 4.2 ● Concept Map for Air

Source: This figure represents concepts found in the first-grade text (published by Addison-Wesley) described by John R. Staver and Mary Bay in "Analysis of the Conceptual Structure and Reasoning Demands of Elementary Science Texts at the Primary (K–3) Level," *Journal of Research in Science Teaching* 26, no. 4 (1989): 334. Reprinted by permission of John Wiley & Sons, Inc. Copyright © 1989 by John Wiley & Sons, Inc.

instructional factors, you can make a decision about the scope of the concepts you need to cover in an instructional program. Recent research suggests that Piaget underestimated the capabilities of young children to deal in abstract ideas, which we commonly call *concepts*. Novak's (1990) twelve-year longitudinal study verified that primary grade learners could acquire understandings of any basic science concept, including challenging concepts such as *energy* and *energy transformations*, if the instruction was carefully designed. As well, primary grade children are very "capable of developing thoughtful concept maps which they can explain intelligently to others. The challenge we face as [teachers] is primarily how to organize better instructional material and how to help students learn this material" (Novak, 1990, p. 941).

A concept map's visual illustration of main ideas is the primary advantage that it provides over other ways of planning instruction. A concept map shows hierarchical relationships: how various subordinate concepts are related to the superordinate concepts. A relationship can descend several levels deep in the hierarchy of concepts. The relationship between superordinate and subordinate concepts is shown in Figure 4.3.

A concept map is different in several ways from the outline or table of contents generally found at the beginning of a book. First, outlines do not show any definite relationships between concepts; they simply list the material in an organized way. Concept maps, on the other hand, show a definite relationship between big ideas and small ideas, thus clarifying the difference between details or specifics and the big idea or superordinate concept. This can be helpful when a teacher must decide how much emphasis to give to specific facts as compared to concepts in a lesson.

The second difference is that concept maps provide visual imagery that can help students to recall information and see relationships between concepts. Outlines do not provide such imagery. Outlines do serve a useful function: They indicate a sequence of different steps. Concept maps, on the other hand, show hierarchies of ideas that suggest psychologically valid sequences. These hierarchies may not match the linear sequence or outline that a teacher has decided to use for a presentation.

Third, concept maps can show interrelationships between ideas, or *cross-links*. These help to "tie it all together," as students often remark.

Why Develop Concept Maps?

Concept maps help teachers to understand the various concepts that are embedded in the larger topic they are to teach. This understanding improves teacher planning and instruction (Starr & Krajcik, 1990). Since the science knowledge domain is vast and most of us have acquired it in pieces at different stages, we are not likely to see the important connections between the separate ideas we teach. As a professional development exercise, mapping provides an opportunity to express our understanding about various concepts and to show gaps or incomplete understandings. Mapping helps teachers

NSES
TS-A

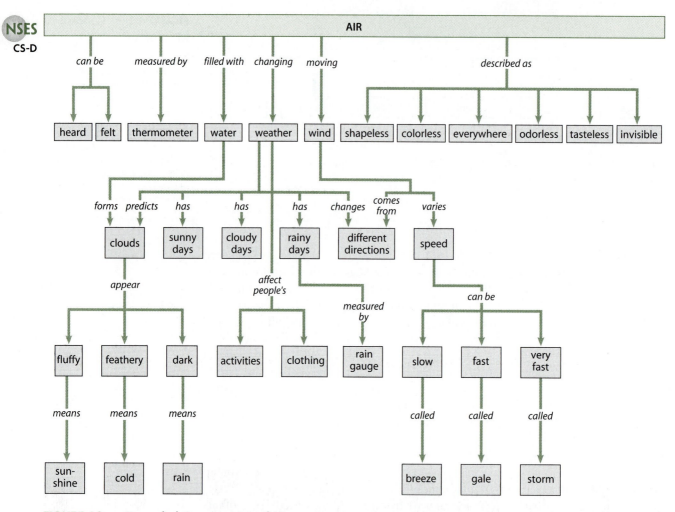

FIGURE 4.3 ● Expanded Concept Map of Air

Source: The figure shows the relationship of several levels of subordinate concepts as provided by John R. Staver and Mary Bay, in "Analysis of the Conceptual Structure and Reasoning Demands of Elementary Science Texts at the Primary (K–3) Level," *Journal of Research in Science Teaching* 26, no. 4 (1989): 339. The researchers examined the contents of the Merrill first-grade science text. Reprinted by permission of John Wiley & Sons, Inc. Copyright © 1989 by John Wiley & Sons, Inc.

to envision an array of lessons through larger topics or units (superordinate concept) that become hierarchically arranged. This arrangement shows facts at the bottom and subordinate concepts arranged in relationships with each other in the body of the map (see, for example, the details of Figures 4.2 and 4.3). Our experience with thousands of teachers and students has convinced us that they gain new insight from developing concept maps when they structure what they know around a superordinate concept. This observation is also supported by Novak and Gowin (1986): "Students and teachers often remark that they recognize new relationships among concepts that they did not before" (p. 17). As well, concept maps help learners to encode information into meaningful networks that enhance long-term memory (Eggen & Kauchak, 1992) and help to reduce students' anxiety while improving achievement and enhancing self-worth (Jegede et al., 1990).

Concept mapping is one of the most crucial steps to take while deciding what to include in a curriculum, unit, or lesson plan. Clear mapping can help to avoid student-formed misconceptions (Czerniak & Haney, 1998). Without concept maps, teachers choose to teach what they can remember or what they prefer. The topics that they select in this manner may be appropriate at times, especially for teachers who have had previous successful experiences with the material, but this process revels a major psychological flaw in the process of curriculum development and lesson planning. The concepts or topics that are chosen may be so disconnected from each other that learners are baffled and see no connections. Learners may also fail to receive new meaning because they cannot link the new material with what they have previously learned. As a result, learners may resort to memorizing isolated facts, treating the experiences and ideas with less thought than we prefer. This mental inaction would defeat the modern science goal of developing new habits of the mind.

Although some material must be memorized, sustained memorization has questionable value in science. Taking the time to identify concepts yields clear science topics and helps to determine which topics are worth learning. Mapping concepts suggests specific objectives that teachers must establish for pupils. Concept maps can help you to see the logic of the relationships among specific concepts. Once you see this logic, you can decide how much depth or breadth to include in lessons so that students will see the same conceptual relationships. These decisions consist of choosing the proper activities and learning aids as well as selecting the appropriate type of pupil evaluation.

You can also use concept maps to organize the flow of the classroom lessons. We have used concept maps as advance organizers to focus students' attention and guide them along to seeing a bigger picture and for use as a mental scaffolding for organizing their thoughts and discoveries. You can use concept maps as road maps to indicate the direction in which instruction is to proceed in your classroom—up, down, and across the map. Students can be shown concept maps several times during instruction so that they can see what has been covered and how it fits with the rest. Creative primary teachers have used concept maps as a reading and metacognitive tool by posting sight words that represent the science idea of the day on a large bulletin board, then discussing cumulative meanings with children and inviting them to suggest organizational relationships between and among the words. Over time, the class of young learners cooperatively constructed a class concept map that illustrated their emergent and changing conceptions.

Another way in which you can use concept maps is for student evaluations. For example, display large pieces of newsprint in a conspicuous place and use them daily to show the science ideas students have learned and how these ideas interrelate. This daily effort is an example of formative evaluation. You could ask primary grades children to "fill in the blanks" of a constructed map using a familiar word bank or ask intermediate and middle school children to develop their own maps at the end of instruction to reflect what they understand, a process called *summative evaluation.*

Steps for Developing a Concept Map

A concept map can be developed for the entire course for a year or semester, for a single unit, or even for a single lesson. Figure 4.4 shows the relationship of concepts in a concept map. Ultimately, a concept map "tells" a story by revealing the relationships among key ideas. The following steps work for creating concept maps:

1. List on paper all of the concepts (names of topics) that pertain to a general area you will teach. Only the names are needed at this stage. No descriptions are necessary. For example, let's say that you have examined your

The structure of a map tells a conceptual story.

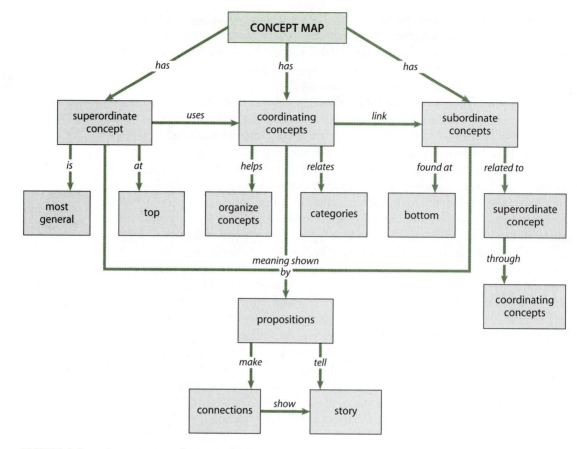

FIGURE 4.4 ● Concept Map for Concept Maps

next science chapter or module and have listed the following topics: air, weather, clouds, storms, and effects of weather.

2. Note any specific facts (examples) that are either essential for students to learn or that you find especially interesting. The facts and examples you list might include that air moves, measurements are used to track air movement, moving air causes weather, weather can be helpful or harmful, and weather helps us decide what clothes to wear.

3. From the list of concepts, choose what you find to be an overarching concept (superordinate), and place it at the top of your paper or computer screen. (You may want to use a large sheet of newsprint or other suitable drawing paper.) Suppose you decide that the overarching concept is *weather*. It seems that all other ideas relate to it. Satisfied, you now line up the other concepts by going to Step 4.

4. Arrange the first level of subordinate concepts underneath the superordinate concept. Generally, this stage requires the use of propositions or linking words such as *provides, types, contains,* and *can be* to develop the appropriate connections between subordinate concepts. Refer to the second line of boxes in Figure 4.4. (The first level of subordinate concepts is known by another term, *coordinate concepts,* because they link or coordinate the superordinate concept and the subordinate concepts found lower in the hierarchy. Each coordinate concept is related to the same superordinate concept, but it is distinctly different from other concepts arranged at that level of the hierarchy.)

5. After the first level of coordinate concepts has been identified, start arranging other subordinate concepts that are directly related to the level above. Similarly, you can develop further hierarchies by going down several levels. You will find that specific facts will be examples of certain individual subordinate concepts that will most likely be at the bottom of the hierarchy. See, for example, in Figure 4.3 that *clouds* is a subordinate concept connected to coordinate concepts of *water* and *weather,* and the concepts *fluffy, feathery,* and *dark* are connected to *clouds* to show other subordinate concepts in the hierarchy; each concept relates back to the superordinate concept, *air.*

6. Draw lines and arrows to show relationships among the subordinate, coordinate, and superordinate concepts. The entire hierarchy should resemble a pyramid. Write linking words (propositions) on the lines to show relationships among concepts. These relationships help to make the map's story clear and serve as expressions of scientific principles. Refer to Figure 4.4, and notice the connecting lines with propositions, for example, *has, uses,* and *through.*

7. After the entire map has been developed, mark or circle certain subordinate concepts that are particularly appealing for your students or are at the appropriate difficulty level. These would generally constitute your course or unit for the given time period.

There are three more important points. First, try to minimize jumping around the entire map; that is, try not to select topics without a strong rationale. The strongest reason for a choice of topic is to build on the knowledge the children have already acquired. During the appropriate phases of your instruction (called *concept construction* and *expansion,* which are explained later in this chapter), you need to help children link the new concept with previous learning.

Second, balance the number of specific details you teach in terms of how well they contribute to overall concept development. Remember, the factual information sits at the bottom of the map, and your purpose is to have children understand what rests at higher levels of the map. Teaching factual information alone does not help children to develop concepts at a higher level unless you make specific attempts to move up the hierarchical ladder.

Third, use Figure 4.5 to self-evaluate your concept map. The criteria of the rubric will help you to move from a novice level of mapmaking toward a level of mastery and integration of conceptual understanding of science into your graphic portrayal of abstract ideas.

Planning Constructive Inquiry Science Lessons

Reform efforts, such as the National Science Education Standards, direct our attention toward teaching to the goal of scientific literacy. Documents for reform do vary in their conceptions of science achievement and expressions of expectations for teachers and learners (Lee & Paik, 2000). Collectively, these documents do identify what can be considered to be standards of aspiration and outcomes to be accomplished. Standards identify numerous outcomes that we attempt to help students achieve. Embedded in the outcomes are dozens of essential science concepts, skills, values, and cross-disciplinary science knowledge that students are expected to demonstrate. Constructivist learning theory and inquiry research caution us against attempting the futile effort of frontal teaching. How can we address the new expectations held aloft for science teachers and students?

NSES
TS-F

NSES

AS-A, D, E

4 Integrating	
• Map has frequent branching. • Cross links are frequent and logical. • Linking words are present and appropriate. • Concepts are logically presented and show various levels.	• All concepts are included on the map and others are added to support related concepts. • Examples are abundant and relevant.

3 Mastering	
• Map has frequent branching. • Cross links are present and logical. • Linking words are usually present but not always appropriate.	• Most concepts are logically presented and show various levels. • Most concepts are included on the map. • Examples are present and relevant.

2 Developing	
• Map has some branching. • Cross links are few and not necessarily logical. • Linking words are used sparingly and are not always appropriate.	• Concepts are not logically presented and/or lack various levels. • Several concepts are not included on the map. • Examples are sparse.

1 Novice	
• Map is rather linear. • Cross links are not evident and/or are not logical. • Linking words are not evident and/or are inappropriate.	• Concepts are not logically presented and/or lack various levels. • Large gaps exist in concept representation. • Examples are not evident or are irrelevant.

FIGURE 4.5 ● Holistic Scoring Rubric for Concept Maps

Source: J. Haney, (1998). "Concept mapping in the science classroom: Linking theory to practice," *The Agora*, Vol. VIII, September, p. 6.

Using Standards for Selecting Performance Outcomes and Developing Curriculum

NSES

PD-B

Concept maps (see Figure 4.6) illustrate clusters of concepts that share relationships with other science concepts. These relationships make it possible to identify or construct a unifying theme that can help us to construct units of science experiences for learners. The standards' outcomes help to provide parameters that are useful for selecting learning outcomes and developing a curriculum that encourages full, active participation and student conceptual constructions. See the Appendix for a list of science content outcomes for grades K–4 and 5–8. The standards, outcomes, and concept maps are tools for making prudent selections to avoid the "fill-up-the-empty-time" approach. Used appropriately, mapping and planning can help to make wise choices so lessons have clear expectations, abundant opportunities for students to construct understanding through inquiry, and expanded contact with science in many contexts. Some general planning principles can help us help students to develop their thinking skills and learn meaningful science:

1. *Provide a variety of activities for learning.* Activities that provide children opportunities to experience and manipulate real objects are essential. Emphasize direct physical and mental involvement for children in primary and intermediate grades. Help learners to develop language skills by giving opportunities to explain what they experience and to communicate this to others in written and spoken language. All learning activities should be expanded to address as many of the goal clusters as possible.

2. *Introduce concepts and specialized vocabulary after children have gained firsthand experiences with the object or concept.* As a general rule, teachers should talk less and involve students more. One way of doing this is to tell less and ask more. Questions are devices for encouraging children to use their minds. Chapter 6 is devoted to the uses of questions.

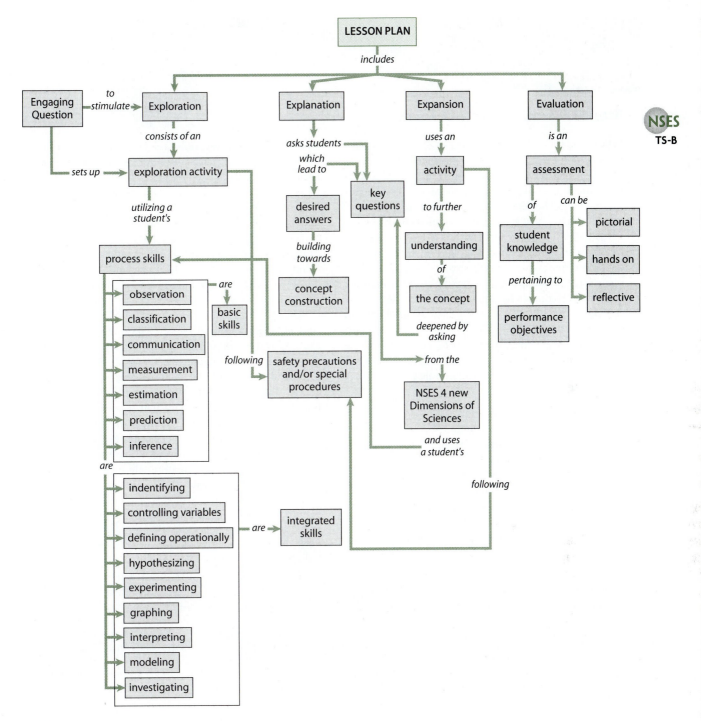

FIGURE 4.6 ● Concept Map of Inquiry Lesson Plan

3. *Interact with children, and have them interact with each other.* Questions stimulate interaction, interaction encourages thinking, and communication develops language. Ask children to describe what they have done or observed. Encourage children to ask each other questions about their experiences and to ask *why* questions.

4. *Focus learning experiences so that children are encouraged to discover and construct concepts.* Focusing on concepts, the main ideas behind learning, helps children learn connections more easily and removes the learning barrier of disconnected facts.

NSES

PD-A, B

Standards-Based Science Lesson Planning

Why spend time planning detailed science lessons when there could be simpler and less time-consuming ways to plan? The big picture for thoughtful science lesson planning comes from the Glenn Commission Report, *Before It's Too Late*. The report challenges us to keep in mind four reasons to focus carefully on planning effective, standards-based lessons so that learners can become proficient in science: (1) A rapidly changing workplace within a global economy demands a strong understanding of science, (2) everyday decision making requires scientific and technical competency among all citizens, (3) national security is dependent upon science and technology, and (4) science shapes and defines human history and culture. Collectively, these reasons comprise a compelling goal of pursuing scientific literacy for *all* students, which requires that primary and middle school science lessons:

- help learners understand the important and fundamental ideas of science,
- stimulate active learning through inquiry-based, question-driven lessons,
- motivate learner-constructed connections across the scientific disciplines,
- orient all learners about potential future careers, and
- use learning strategies and mental tools that help students with personal decisions related to issues in science.

These requirements may be met in using a planning and teaching model undergirded by processes for knowledge construction while regarding the importance of the interplay between language and action as children learn in social settings. As Glasson and Lalik point out, "To construct knowledge, students must identify and test their existing understandings, interpret meaning of their ongoing experiences, and adjust their knowledge frameworks accordingly. . . . Teachers must find ways to understand students' viewpoints, propose alternative frameworks, stimulate perplexity among students, and develop classroom tasks that promote effort at knowledge construction."

Successful science lessons are planned to provide all students with opportunities to learn, meaning that student-centered, real-world contexts and uses of inquiry processes afford each learner an opportunity to use preferred styles of learning for building confidence and self-esteem about successful performance, and sufficient challenge for developing additional skills that reside outside their comfort zones. Lessons must be well balanced in opportunities to learn. Individual tasks should be complemented with group investigations and cooperation; an array of skills must be developed to stimulate mental, physical, social, and emotional dexterity. While planning for learning, teachers strengthen students' achievements if they plan to teach around the cycle: balancing the challenges and instructional methods so that all children are met partly in their preferred style, but also gain confidence in learning with less preferred modes. Planning for a learning cycle can help to ensure that teachers sufficiently challenge, motivate, and support all of their learners, and avoid the limitations of unidimensional teaching.

Source: National Commission on Mathematics and Science Teaching for the 21st Century, *Before It's Too Late: A Report to the Nation from the National Commission on Mathematics and Science Teaching for the 21st Century.* Washington, DC: U.S. Department of Education. A. Krueger and J. Sutton (Eds.). *EDThoughts: What We Know About Science Teaching and Learning* (Aurora, CO: Mid-continent research for education and learning, 2001). G.E. Glasson and R. V. Lalik (1993). "Reinterpreting the Learning Cycle from a Social Constructivist Perspective: A Qualitative Study of Teachers' Beliefs and Practices." *Journal of Research in Science Teaching, 30*(2), pp. 187–207.

Planning the Lesson: A Learning Cycle Model

NSES

TS-B, D

Effective science lessons have a central focus and clear expectations for student performance. The *lesson concept*—the main science idea—is the central focus, and is the heart of a learning cycle inquiry lesson plan: Select or develop it first. Your planning in other education courses may have taught you how to write objectives. Lesson objectives help define the expected types and levels of performance (or what and how the students are to demonstrate that they understand the concept) and can apply their understanding to useful matters. Objectives are important for helping to evaluate what learners know and can do. To have lasting value, conceptual understanding must be applied to the student's world. This application expands the depth of learning and helps to fulfill the new dimensions of science

114 chapter 4 How Do You Plan for the Inquiry-Based Classroom?

outcomes: experiencing science as inquiry, understanding the interrelationships of science and technology, using personal and social perspectives to understand science, and comprehending the nature of science throughout its history. These expected outcomes are shown in Chapter 1.

The planning model presented here revolves around a central concept, helps learners to construct meaning, encourages students to expand understanding of that fundamental meaning, and evaluates student performance in authentic ways. Called a *learning cycle* (see Figure 4.7), this series of planning and teaching steps helps teachers to encourage learners to construct meaning from direct experiences, then expand that understanding through direct treatment of the new dimensions of science. The lesson planning model in this chapter closely follows the original format of the Science Curriculum Improvement Study, which major research studies credit with the greatest student achievement gains and significant improvements in student science attitudes and inquiry skills when compared to similar experimental science programs and traditional science curricula (Bredderman, 1982; Shymansky et al., 1982).

Effective science lessons stimulate learners' minds, shape attitudes, and provide learning opportunities for physical manipulation of learning materials.

Our planning model embraces the array of national science standards for content, teaching and learning, and assessment and has been modified to stimulate a full range of student inquiry, reflect cognitive and social constructivist learning expectations, support inquiry, and emphasize appropriate student evaluation. This approach is a simple model that is thorough and has considerable potential to effect improvements in students' learning. The planning model also becomes the teaching method. A detailed description of the teaching method is described in Chapter 5. The elements of planning are given here.

The fundamental phases of the science planning and learning cycle provide most of the structure for planning an effective science lesson. Once you identify the concept that is to be learned, you can structure the learning activity to take advantage of the learning cycle. Then

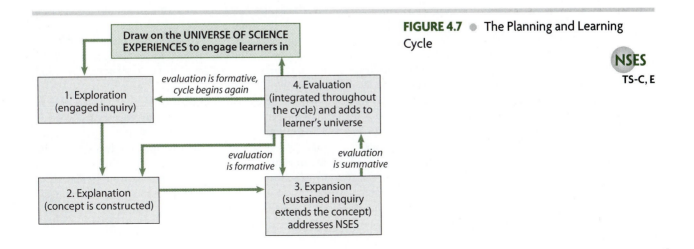

FIGURE 4.7 ● The Planning and Learning Cycle

NSES
TS-C, E

you can add descriptions of the proper ways to evaluate what the children learn. Consider these questions to see the big picture as you begin your lesson planning:

- How can I identify and get to "the point"?
- How can I engage my learners in a productive inquiry?
- How can I faithfully model what science is and help the children experience holistic science?
- How can I address specific standards?
- How can I promote science safely?
- How can I teach effectively and in a manner that fits children's learning?
- How can I evaluate authentically what children know and can do?
- How can I pull the answers to all of these questions into a single plan that also becomes my method for teaching?

The planning steps are recommended: engaging question, exploration, explanation, expansion, and evaluation. The following questions should help you plan for each step of the learning cycle as you write the lesson plan. The parenthetical remarks suggest the aspects of science and teaching strategies that may be used. A sample science learning cycle lesson plan is shown in the Feature Lesson on page 118.

teachers on Science Teaching

Providing Creative Learning Opportunities for Science

Jessica Martin and
Amy Mullins
Grade 2
Granville Elementary School
Granville, Ohio

As teachers, we are bound by national and state standards, but we strive to be creative and engaging. We want children to become intellectually active learners; this means finding ways to use their natural curiosity to explore and achieve academically. It is also important to us, as new second grade teachers, to create opportunities for teacher collaboration as we plan lessons to help children fulfill the indicators for our grade level, as set by our state in its compliance with national standards.

For example, when developing a solar system unit for our classrooms, we began our planning with the Ohio Academic Content Standards as the basis for identifying key concepts to be learned and skills to be developed. From these standards, we selected the grade-level indicator for the concept of "the universe." We then constructed different exploration activities that embraced the various learning styles our students preferred. Before teaching the unit, we identified what students already knew so that we could build new explanations that connected to their background knowledge. We also planned ways to expand their understandings using various enrichment materials such as books, posters, diagrams, and models on the subject.

As we began instruction, our learners were encouraged to freely explore the wide variety of materials before we began our research and study of the the concept. This encouraged our learners to construct a basic foundation for understanding because they were able to develop an initial familiarity with the topics; this most likely led to the formation of preconceptions. In most cases, we began engaging our learners by asking fundamental questions, such as "What *do you know* about _____? What *do you think* you know about _____? What *do you want to know* about _____?" These questions were accompanied by a type of graphic organizer, which was displayed in our classroom and used as a visual reference for the students throughout the course of study. For example, a KWL chart was used as an introduction to the moon phases. Students referred to the KWL chart as their learning progressed and added to it as more information and experiences were obtained.

With the information that we gained, we were able to plan interactive lessons to reach our goals as teachers that also continued to engage the students' attention and excitement about the topic. For example, while studying the moon phases, children were assigned a continuous project in which they were encouraged to become "scientists at home" while observing the moon nightly and describing its appearance through their writing with illustrations on a

Step 1: Developing an engaging question

Much of scientists' business deals with questions that arise from a problem, curiosity, societal need, dilemma, or discrepant event (Chapter 5). Encourage children to become scientists. Grab children's attention, and focus their thinking toward the nature of science (Chapter 1), and in doing so, set their motivation toward wanting to investigate, reason, and discover. A good question will tease learners into an inquiry, which is taken up by other parts of the lesson. Consider the following:

- What local event, phenomenon, change, or interesting topic will help me to form an engaging question?

- How can I use children's literature or other subjects to identify a seed for investigation?

- What is it about the investigation and interactive learning activities that will plant a seed for thinking if I express it in the form of a question?

- How can I express our target or purpose in a way that is captured by the form of a large, interesting question?

- How can my question encourage learners to share preliminary ideas and set them about a path for exploration?

chart. Our intention was to encourage our students to learn by physically observing, charting, analyzing, and describing the data they collected on a daily basis. With this, the learners were able to prove that they had constructed their knowledge that the moon changes over time, which is a grade-level indicator established by our state. Students used several learning modalities during this project, which helped us to differentiate the lessons for each individual learner and enabled us to modify activities and assessments for children with special needs. For example, on each day of the chart, the moon was predrawn, and a student needed only to shade in the part he or she saw during observation and then verbally describe what happened to the shape of the moon over time.

We created additional learning opportunities by encouraging learners to develop social and academic skills. Children embraced their jobs as scientists by forming research teams (a small carefully selected group) to investigate the different planets. The research teams chose a planet as their main focus and were asked to conduct structured research using various resources (texts, posters, and the Internet). The students were given a set of basic questions as a guideline to help them complete the research. As a result, our learners were able to acquire specific vocabulary, which helped to strengthen their language and writing skills. They became "experts" on their topic as a consequence of their teamwork and investigative efforts. Our learners were then asked to share their newly acquired expertise by creating a pamphlet or brochure stating important facts about their planet that included student-created illustrations

and diagrams. They presented their projects orally to the class and then designed an interactive bulletin board for the hallway. The interactive bulletin board displayed the projects, and teachers and students could physically take the project off the bulletin board to read it, then put it back before moving on to the next one. This project gave children a creative way to illustrate what they had learned and helped to reveal to us possible misconceptions and provide us with opportunities to intervene and reverse those mislearnings. This project provided other grade-level teachers and students with opportunities to view the learning and projects that occurred during the unit and stimulated considerable professional discussion about how we could meet the state standards and our individual goals for learners.

Through collaboration, we met state standards, allowed students to explore learning by encouraging their natural curiosity, and differentiated instruction that provided students with opportunities to show their learning through alternative assessments. Our projects also helped us to connect our teaching with other school curricula, such as language arts. For example, students gained an important element in the prewriting process by becoming familiar with using graphic organizers to organize and clarify their thinking. We encouraged children to explore ideas before the actual "point" was taught, which helped our students to create new and engaging learning opportunities for themselves. As teachers, we can always strive to create meaningful learning opportunities for students, but we must also remember the importance and future benefits of student-led learning.

Learning Cycle Featured Lesson

Physical Science: Air

Grades ● K–1

NATIONAL SCIENCE EDUCATION CONTENT STANDARDS– PHYSICAL SCIENCE—GRADES K-4

▶ Properties of Objects and Materials. Objects have many observable properties, including size, weight, shape, color, temperature, and the ability to react with other substances.

CONCEPTS TO BE CONSTRUCTED

▶ Air takes up space

SCIENCE ATTITUDES TO NURTURE

▶ Curiosity
▶ Open-mindedness
▶ Perseverance
▶ Positive approach to failure
▶ Cooperating with others

Engaging Question

How do we know that air is real?

Materials Needed

For Exploration Phase ● for teacher introduction you will need:

- 1 balloon
- 1 kitchen-size garbage bag
- 1 child's party horn

For Exploration Phase ● conducted whole class, each student will need:

- 1 Styrofoam cup
- 1 straw
- 1 container of soap solution

For Explanation and Expansion Phase ● conducted whole class, you will need:

- 1 large plastic tub or an aquarium
- 1 plastic cup
- 1 bendable drinking straw per child

🛈 **Safety:** Wear goggles to keep soap bubbles from popping in eyes. Avoid sucking soap solution into mouth.

Exploration

PROCESS SKILLS USED

▶ Observing
▶ Identifying
▶ Comparing

Teacher Introduction

- Set the stage for exploration by demonstrating how to blow a balloon and to make "music" with the escaping air. Engage the children by asking: "What do you think is inside the balloon? What do you think makes this music?"

- Answers may differ, but most will refer to breath or air in the balloon. Pose the question: "Do you think air is real? Why?"

- Use the student's variety of answers to convey the need to investigate in order to find out whether air is real. Avoid discussing the concept at this point.

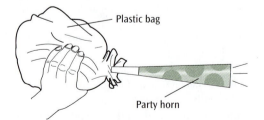

Plastic bag

Party horn

- Investigate by filling a plastic bag, about the size of the kitchen garbage can bags, with air. Close the open end of the bag over the small "blow into" end of a child's party horn. Hold the bag closed against the horn and gently squeeze the bag to blow the horn (like a bagpipe). Pose open-ended questions to the children about what they think makes the horn sound, what filled the bag, where the air came from, etc.

Student Activity

Provide each student with a Styrofoam cup. Ask the students to punch a hole the size of the diameter of a straw 1 inch from the bottom of the cup. Invert the cup, and dip it into a soap solution. Insert the straw into the hole. Encourage the

students to blow through the straw. Larger bubbles will result when the cup is inverted.

Caution the students to avoid sucking up the soap solution, and demonstrate how to change their breathing to make the bubbles larger and smaller.

Question: "What do you think is inside your bubble? How do you think the air got inside the bubble? How do you think you could remove the air from your bubble?"

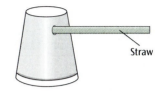
Straw

Explanation

Demonstrate how to fill a plastic cup with water and invert it in a water tank or a clean aquarium. (You can use a large plastic tub or classroom's water table, if available.) Ask the students prediction questions, such as "What do you think may happen to the water in the cup if you blow air into it?"

Demonstrate how to use a bent straw to blow air into the filled cup while the cup is in the water and inverted.

Ask the students to explain what they observe. Invite some of the students to try the same demonstration, or allow all to try. Discuss what happened in each of the investigations and how air behaved the same as in this demonstration. Use a sentence starter and invite the students to offer ideas to complete it: "Air takes up _____."

The desired answer is *space,* and the sentence represents the *concept* that is common to each investigation in this lesson. Ask the students: "How do we know air is real?"

Relate the question to the concept statement and use the concept statement throughout the rest of the lesson.

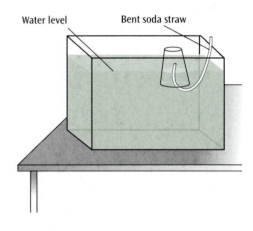
Water level   Bent soda straw

Expansion

- Permit all the students to practice the demonstration as described in the Explanation phase. Encourage all students to describe the property: Air takes up space.

- Set up an additional investigation that will be used for the Evaluation phase. Partially fill several clear plastic shoeboxes or small clean plastic aquaria. Have several small potted plants on hand with dry soil. Immerse one plant into the water, and observe the air bubbles as they emerge from the dry soil. (You can substitute a small cup of dry sand for the same effect.)

- Discuss: "What do you think causes the bubbles? Where do you think the bubbles come from?"

- Answers should reveal that the students understand the lesson's concept, are able to use it in their spoken communication, and can use it in a new setting. Continue to question and encourage the students to communicate their findings as they investigate by placing the following dry objects into the water:

Small piece of wood

Small rocks

Pine cones

Popsicle sticks

Sponge pieces

Pieces of brick or fish tank gravel

Leaves

Sidewalk chalk

Classroom chalk

Aluminum foil (flat, folded, and crumpled)

Crayons

Paper

Clay

Cloth

Paper

- Use cooperative groups to predict and investigate what happens when the objects are immersed in water. Use a pictograph to classify objects as having air or no air. Pose the question again: "How do we know air is real?"

Evaluation

Hands-on Assessment

The students should be able to observe changes to the balloons and water in the cups, predict what they think will happen when changes are proposed, and communicate their observations. They should also be able to classify objects as having air or no air.

Reflective Assessment

The students should be able to give a response to the question "How do we know if air is real?" and a reason for their answer.

Pictorial Assessment

The students should be able to describe and illustrate examples of objects or conditions in which "air takes up space."

Step 2. Planning for student exploration

Children must have opportunities to explore, use language, and form preconceptions if they are to form clear concepts. The learners must become engaged in the context of the inquiry and be stimulated by the teacher and objects to undertake free and guided inquiry. Use these guiding questions:

- How can I help my learners to experience the nature of science?
- What do I want the children to learn? (concept, attitudes, processes)
- What main concept will be explored? (science products)
- What must I do to engage the learners' thinking and involve them in inquiry processes?
- What activities must the children do to find and to construct the needed data? (processes, information, answers to questions)
- How will I stimulate the learners to remain engaged in the processes of inquiry?
- What kinds of records should the children keep? (process skills)
- What kinds of instructions and encouragement will the children need? (attitudes)

Begin the lesson by directing the children's activities and suggesting what kinds of records they should keep. *Do not tell or explain the concept—it will be constructed later*. State the instructions succinctly. Plan this step carefully so that it is student centered and student activity based.

Step 3. Planning for explanation

The main purpose of this phase is to restore mental equilibrium (Jean Piaget, Chapter 2) through productive interaction (Vygotsky, Chapter 2). Equilibrium is reached when learners' thinking is guided, meaning is made from personal and social experiences, and a new concept is formed and/or linked to previously understood related concepts. Interactive and reciprocal uses of language are helpful for forming learners' explanations through classroom dialogue (Glasson & Lalik, 1993). Here students must focus on their primary findings from exploration, and the teacher must help them by introducing proper language or concept labels. The original learning cycle called this step *concept invention*. The teacher's task is to guide students through a discussion so that students can discover the concept by inventing it for themselves. The teacher's technique is to question skillfully so that students use the experiences of their explorations to construct scientific meaning. The teacher acts as a facilitator and introduces any special vocabulary that must accompany the concept. Plan this step carefully so that it does not become completely teacher centered or dominated by lecture. Use these questions as you plan for this part of your lesson:

- What kinds of information or findings are students expected to provide? (products, process skills)

- How will the students' activities in using their observations and records from the exploration phase be reviewed and summarized? (teacher questioning, pupil discussion, graphing, board work)

- How can I guide the students' findings and refrain from telling them what they should have found, even if students' findings are incorrect or incomplete? (teacher questioning, guided construction, attitudes)

- What are the proper concept labels or terms that must be attached to the concept? (products)

- How can I use a sentence starter to involve the students in using language to explain what the concept means?

- What reasons can I give the students if they ask me why the concept is important? (teacher exposition, lesson expansion)

The last question automatically leads to the next phase: expansion.

Step 4. Planning for expansion

The purpose of this phase is to sustain the inquiry by helping students organize their thinking and by applying what they have just learned to other ideas or experiences that relate to the lesson's concept and to help the students to expand their ideas. It is very important to use the language of the concept during the expansion-of-the-idea phase. Plan this phase for continued student involvement, such as in a cooperative group, and to limit misconceptions by refining the concept. Consider using these questions:

- What previous experiences have the children had that are related to the concept? How we can connect the concept to these experiences? (new activities, questioning)

- What are some examples of how the concept and the activities encourage the students' science inquiry skills? (learning activities, questioning)

- What activities and key questions can be used to illustrate the interrelationship of science and technology and the contributions of each to society and the quality (or problems) of life? (discussion, readings, uses of multimedia, class projects)

- In what ways has science benefited the students personally? (class projects, reflective questioning)

- How has science affected the children and influenced our society, policies, and laws? (linkages with social studies, current events, children's literature)

- What have been the dominant ideas of science throughout recorded history, and how have those ideas and the nature of science changed over time? (linkages with social studies, documentaries, class projects, discussion, biographies)

- What new experiences do the children need in order to expand on the concept? (processes, attitudes, activities)
- How is the next concept related to the present one? How can I encourage exploration of the next concept? (products, processes)

Step 5. Planning for evaluation

The purpose of this phase is to go beyond standard forms of testing. Learning must occur in small increments before larger leaps of insight are possible. Your evaluation of students can be planned in terms of meeting the explicitness of your state's grade-level indicators, standards-based outcomes, and pupil performances and can illustrate what learners know and can do, relevant to your lesson's concept. Several types of records are necessary to form a holistic evaluation of the students' learning and to encourage conceptual understanding as well as process skill development. Evaluation can occur at any point in the lesson. Consistent evaluation can help to reveal misconceptions before they become deeply rooted. Chapter 7 delves more deeply into ways to assess learning. For purposes of completing your plan, ask yourself the following questions:

- What key questions should I ask to encourage purposeful exploration that promotes inquiry? (processes, attitudes)
- What questions can I ask to help students think about their data in an effort to construct realistic concepts? (processes)
- What questions will expand conception and achieve selected science standards and outcomes? (processes, products)
- What behavior (mental, physical, attitudinal, social) should I expect from the students? (attitudes, processes)
- What hands-on assessments can the students do to demonstrate the basic skills of observation, classification, communication, measurement, prediction, and inference? (processes)
- What assessments can students do to demonstrate the integrated skills of identifying and controlling variables, defining operationally, forming hypotheses, experimenting, interpreting data, and forming models?
- What pictorial assessments can students do to demonstrate how well they can think through problems that require both knowledge and the integration of ideas? (products)
- What reflective question assessments will indicate how well the students recall and use what has been learned? (products)

chapter summary

The National Science Education Standards ushered an era of exciting learning opportunities for students and instructional challenges for teachers. Constructivist teaching and inquiry-based learning require careful planning that places conceptual focus, acts of created understanding, essential experiences, language development, and authentic assessment in a carefully balanced dynamic system. In this chapter, we used a learning cycle to illustrate a planning model that will help you meet the new challenges.

Concept mapping is a tool that helps teachers to identify essential concepts and the relationships among concepts. The tool is helpful for making fundamental planning decisions in order to fulfill the outcomes of the content standards. Concept mapping is also a useful evaluation tool.

The learning cycle provides a dynamic planning system that balances student-centered exploration with teacher-guided conceptual construction. Expansion nurtures understanding as the new dimensions of science learning are fulfilled. Evaluation is continual and is fit to the task.

reflect and respond

1. Contemporary movements in education usually embrace the preference for students to demonstrate learning outcomes focused upon concepts and skills. Performance or behavioral objectives may be used for this purpose. What advantages or disadvantages do you see with this type of objective?

2. In what ways will the concepts from the Appendix and the outcomes from Table 4.2 help you to decide what children should know and be able to do?

3. How could Vygotsky's concept of zones of proximal development (Chapter 2) promote for you and your learners the interplay of language and action, and how could you include this in your lesson plan?

PEARSON
myeducationlab
Where the Classroom Comes to Life

Explore—Video Homework Exercise. Go to MyEducationLab at www.myeducationlab.com and select the topic "Lesson and Unit Planning," then watch the video "Concept Mapping 2" describing the many uses of concept maps. Consider how the message in the video correlates to that of this chapter, and respond to the questions below.

1. What are the various ways in which concept maps can be used? How do you think the process and form of a map could be modified for young learners?

2. What benefits could concept maps provide for users?

3. Think back to Chapter 2. How do the processes of making and using concept maps seem to be compatible with how children learn?

4. Think back to Chapter 3. What types of benefits do you think concept maps could provide for learners who have special needs?

5. If you first map the concepts and relationships among science topics and then plan a series of lessons, how might you think differently or teach differently while leading lessons for learners?

NSES
PD-A, B
TS-B

Enrich—Video Homework Exercise. Go to MyEducationLab Resources section and download the Learning Cycle Lesson Plan template. Then select the topic "Inquiry," and watch the video "The Learning Cycle," and respond to the second question below.

1. Examine a science text, science module, or teacher's manual for any grade level you choose. Construct a concept map for the material. What is your opinion about how the printed materials' organization corresponds to the insight expressed by the MLS teacher? How well does the printed material make connections between associated concepts?

2. Prepare a learning cycle lesson. How many lesson activities do you have, and where do they fit into a cycle? What dimensions of the National Science Education Standards do you include? How do you evaluate students' learning?

NSES
PD-B

Expand—Weblink Exercise

Science Literacy. Go to MyEducationLab Resources section and select "Weblinks," then click on the links for "Constructivism and the 5Es" and "Brain-Based Research" to expand your understanding of science and the importance of planning and teaching in ways that support how children learn.

NSES
CS-A, F

5

What Inquiry Methods Help Learners to Construct Understanding?

focus questions

- What factors encourage the development of scientific literacy?

- What are the important attributes of inquiry, and how does learning science through inquiry benefit learners?

- What are the chapter's featured teaching methods, and how do their pedagogies contrast respective to inquiry?

- What roles do learner cooperation and socialization play within each of the featured teaching methods, and what are several recommendations for managing learning?

NSES
TS-B

Mrs. Myers has loved science since she was very young, and her love is communicated to her students through her positive attitude and enthusiasm. She tries to connect each lesson with her students' experiences by involving each child in a personal way. Her third-grade classroom is an active place. Sometimes visitors mistake her lessons for play. When queried, she always refers to play as a way to make an important point. In fact, her young scientists can be overheard asking each other about "the point" because they are accustomed to looking for a focus in each lesson. A "minds-on" focus guides each hands-on lesson. Mrs. Myers's classroom consists of individual desks clustered into research groups of four. Her classroom walls are alive with brilliant colors, usually the children's artwork and projects but also commercial posters carefully selected to illustrate a variety of careers and diverse role models for the young scientists as well as to illustrate various forms and uses of technology. Plants and small mammals are positioned in the research corner near the aquarium and the desert climate terrarium.

Mrs. Myers begins the day's science lesson by asking the children to count off from 1 to 4 and reminds each child to remember his or her number. Having a small frame, Mrs. Myers often safely joins the children in the physical activities. She says, "OK, scientists. Today we are going to begin an investigation of a very important idea. Would you all please gather in a circle around me?"

In no particular order, Mrs. Myers gently directs the twenty-four children into a tight circle, each standing shoulder-to-shoulder. Humor and gentle prodding accomplish the task and provide a nice link to the geometry lesson they learned in math class last week.

"Where are the number 'ones' standing?" asks Mrs. Myers. "All of the 'ones' will represent 'food' during our activity. What does the number 'one' mean for us?"

"Food!" answer the scientists with enthusiasm.

"All of you will represent a special role. Who are the 'twos'?"

Exuberant "mes" identify most of the "twos," and a few gentle jostles of classmates remind the other "twos" to identify themselves.

"The 'twos' will be 'water,'" informs Mrs. Myers. "The 'threes' will be 'shelter.' The 'fours' will be 'space.'"

A brief practice session ensures that everyone understands her or his role. Some tightening of the circle and turning in a common direction place all children appropriately, with hands grasping the shoulders of the scientist in front.

"Now for the physical challenge. When I count to 3, our mission is to hold our positions, bend our legs, and gently sit on the knees of the scientist behind us." Mrs. Myers takes some time to offer assurance and make the process clear. The 1-2-3 count is given, and success happens fleetingly until pandemonium breaks out when the seated circle breaks apart and children do a controlled fall with enthusiastic exaggeration.

"Everybody up! Let's talk about this. Why do you suppose we had trouble keeping our circle together?"

"I couldn't find Sasha's knees!" quips Sachiko.

"Brent fell down and so did I," offers Jon.

"So what happened to the rest of us when Brent fell?" asks Mrs. Myers.

"We all fell!" responds a chorus of voices.

"That's right. We depend on one another. We have a system of parts, and when one part falls, the others also soon fall. Let's try this again and see whether we can set a record. What do you suppose we could do to make it easier for us to keep our circle together when we sit?"

A number of suggestions are offered, and after incorporating them into the arrangement, Mrs. Myers gives the physical challenge again. The children count to 30 before Mrs. Myers gives the signal to stand. Not one child drops out of the circle. Mrs. Myers continues her lesson:

"All animals need a habitat in order to survive, and all habitats contain the food, water, shelter, and space unique for the animal. In today's activity, we each play an important role—food, water, shelter, space—and when we keep our circle together, we provide a 'pretend' habitat for an animal." Mrs. Myers continues the discussion by asking the children to identify the parts of a habitat needed for a common animal such as a robin, fish, cow, dog, or squirrel.

"What's a habitat?" she asks, testing the young scientists. The children put into their own words their operational definitions and descriptions of food, water, shelter, and space as examples for some other animals familiar to them.

"Let's do our activity again, and this time let's pretend we have a drought," offers Mrs. Myers. The children are told that each of the "waters" will leave the circle, one at a time, while all are seated, and try to keep the circle together as long as possible. Some of the children predict that all of the "waters" can leave and they can still keep the circle together, while the skeptics don't think any "waters" can leave without the circle falling.

"What do you think we might have to do to keep our circle together?" asks Mrs. Myers. After some discussion, the children offer that they might be able to "adapt" by scooching together to take up the empty space and avoid falling.

The lap sit is repeated. After the first "water" slips out, the strain of the void can be felt around the entire circle, but all adapt and manage to keep the circle together. Mrs. Myers asks the children to think about the effort before the next "water" is invited to leave. Barely successful after the next departure, the circle collapses when the third "water" slips aside.

Mrs. Myers led a discussion that was rich with understanding about the importance of a habitat in which all components are available in sufficient supply and suitable arrangement. Children were asked to think about how common wild animals and outdoor domestic animals could be affected by a drought or a loss of other essential components of their habitats. Other variations were attempted to simulate stresses placed on human habitats, including famine, overcrowding, and shelter lost to natural disasters. Notions of interdependence and the need to adapt or relocate emerged from the ideas. In the days that followed, books were read, videos were viewed, Internet searches were conducted, and information was organized to help the children observe the habitats of local animals and plan suitable habitats for crickets, ants, and earthworms to be placed in classroom terraria.

NSES
AS-E

Mrs. Myers is unique and understands that each individual student must integrate a complex mental structure of many types of information in order to construct his or her own understandings of science. She believes that her intentions are important to help her learners develop a strong foundation for higher learning as one effort to prepare youth for higher levels of achievement. The Trends in International Mathematics and Science Study (TIMSS) and the National Assessment of Educational Progress (NAEP) have been the objects of many popular press articles describing the science achievement of school youth. General reports of elementary children reveal relatively good performance at achieving basic proficiencies in science. However, a decline is apparent as students move into high school and are expected to meet higher goals. The U.S. science curriculum is described as covering too many topics at each grade without sufficient depth; repetition seems to prevail as children advance through school. The science curriculum is believed to be insufficient, and teaching methods are criticized for their failure to prepare learners to meet more rigorous proficiencies.

Why do children underachieve in school? Rosalind Driver (1997) reveals a mistaken conventional view that has long been held by policymakers and by many school leaders and teachers when they consider what it takes to "make" children learn the things they should know. Views about learning are deep-seated. Conventional wisdom holds this view: As long as experts tell a clear story or convey accurate loads of information and as long as children pay attention, the children's understanding will automatically accumulate and replicate an understanding similar to that of the expert. However, contemporary views taken from the research of cognitive science, psychology, and science education reveal the falsehood; children do not simply offload understanding from experts. Children may appear to be attentive to the expert or to be reading for understanding, but what children learn is construed in many ways that are different from what the expert source intends.

Mrs. Myers uses active, interpretive, and interactive processes to help her learners strive toward becoming scientifically literate. She realizes that helping students to develop ideas from experiences is a complex series of processes that require sufficient time to think and reason and encouragement for students to express their understandings. Therefore, Mrs. Myers encourages each child to explore the ideas of science, looking for relationships among ideas and the reasons for these relationships. Children are encouraged to use their formative ideas to explain natural phenomena and to solve problems. Each lesson is multifaceted and requires each child to make observations, ponder and pose questions, examine books and other sources of information to discern what is already known about a topic, plan investigations, gather data and analyze and interpret data, and suggest explanations and answers for problems and experimental outcomes. Mrs. Myers encourages her learners to be active inquirers in their pursuit of scientific literacy.

"How can you support your learners in becoming scientifically literate as they inquire and construct scientific meaning?" We use this question as the focal point for organizing this chapter: Our response to this question helps you to:

1. examine the meaning of scientific literacy,
2. explore several teaching methods that use inquiry to promote student conceptual construction and self-discovery,
3. investigate techniques that promote student cooperation, and
4. identify conditions that enhance students' learning of science.

What Is Scientific Literacy?

NSES
AS-B

A literate person has a fundamental command of the essentials: what one needs to know and be able to do to function as a contributing member of a society. Not long ago, the standard refrain in education was that a literate person commanded the basics of reading, writing, and arithmetic. But this view is too narrow to provide an education that helps our youngsters to survive in a complex world with its wonders of technology and sophisticated social, economic, and political problems.

On an international rating scale of scientific literacy, the United States ranks at number 14 with a score of 499, just below a weighted average of 500. South Korea (552), Japan (550), Finland (538), the United Kingdom (532), and Canada (529) rank as the top five countries. Within the United States, California, New York, Texas, and Illinois rank as the top four states, with their value of scientific and technical services ranging from nearly $7 trillion to $2.4 trillion and contributing significantly to the economy. Employees in scientific and technical careers from those states earn salaries totaling downward from $4.6 to $1.8 trillion. Clearly science and its affiliated fields are important to the present and future (NationMaster, 2007). Tomorrow's leaders and policymakers must know more, have a different worldview, and possess an impressive array of skills. What does a scientifically literate person know, and what is that person able to do in a modern society?

Defining Scientific Literacy

Many definitions of scientific literacy have been written. We refer to the definition advocated by the National Science Education Standards set by the National Research Council (NRC):

> Scientific literacy means that a person can ask and find or determine answers to questions derived from curiosity about everyday experiences. It means the ability to describe, explain, and predict natural phenomena. It means the ability to read with understanding articles about science in the popular press and engage in social conversation about the validity of the conclusions. Scientific literacy implies that a person can identify scientific issues underlying national and local decisions and express positions that are scientifically and technologically informed. A literate citizen should be able to evaluate the quality of scientific information on the basis of its sources and the methods used to generate it. Scientific literacy also implies the capacity to pose and evaluate arguments based on evidence and to apply conclusions from such arguments appropriately. (NRC, 1996, p. 22)

Promoting Scientific Literacy

NSES
PD-C

The NRC also reminds us that scientific literacy is not an all-or-nothing happening; a person may be scientifically literate in some fields or topics of study but not in others. Furthermore, scientific literacy is developed over a lifetime. Schooling is important, but literacy continues to develop during the adult years. The development of scientific literacy is influenced, as the details of its description suggest, by the attitudes and values of the individual, as well as the habits of mind and conceptual understandings that the individual uses and knows. Very broadly, then, a scientifically literate person has a capacity to use essential scientific attitudes, processes, and reasoning skills, and science types of information to reach reasoned conclusions and use the ideas of science in meaningful ways. This is representative of an ancient proverb's wisdom: "Teach a person how to fish, feed the person for a lifetime." Various reform efforts in science education pursue lifelong learning through efforts that strive to develop attitudes, skills, and knowledge. In other words, educators are encouraged to believe that if they teach a person how to learn, the person will learn for a lifetime.

Science helps to improve our lives.

Scientific Attitudes.

Positive scientific attitudes—persistence, curiosity, humility, a healthy dose of skepticism—motivate learners to approach a task or problem with enough interest to find solutions for themselves. There is a relationship between attitudes, interest, achievement, and perception of one's successes, summed up by the saying "Success breeds success." Anyone who has ever persisted with a problem long enough to solve it knows the sweet feeling of achievement and the "can-do" perception that accompanies success. The relationship among these factors appears to be cumulative and conveys the notion that children's achievement increases as they develop more positive attitudes and more interest in science (as well as other subjects). As achievement increases, motivation and desire stimulate the development of new learning skills, and that leads to greater understanding of the information, which is accumulating at a dizzying pace. Therefore, the processes of science are the skills by which the learner acquires observations and constructs meaning. Processes can provide the type and quality of the science experience that is desired for children in which thinking is expanded and improved.

Scientific Skills.

Process skills, as literacy-building tools, have tremendous carryover value in and out of school (see Chapters 1 and 7). They are also vital to adult living. They are the mechanisms by which problems are identified, explored, and solved. Whether the adult mission is to improve or improvise on a recipe; determine the cause of a blown fuse (or tripped circuit breaker); troubleshoot the cause of a car's failure to start; plan the best route to run a new line for an extension telephone; identify evidence and separate it from opinion while listening to a political candidate; or determine how to thread a sewing machine, the processes of science contribute to solving the problem.

Children are naturally interested in science and associated science topics. Surveys done in elementary schools show that children choose science a majority of the time when given lists of school topics from which they can choose. Parents report, too, that their children list science as one of their favored school subjects (Mechling & Oliver, 1983a).

FIGURE 5.1 ● Traditional Disciplines and New Content Dimensions An appropriate science lesson may be focused on a single concept within a specific science discipline and can expose learners to relationships with all of the new dimensions of science.

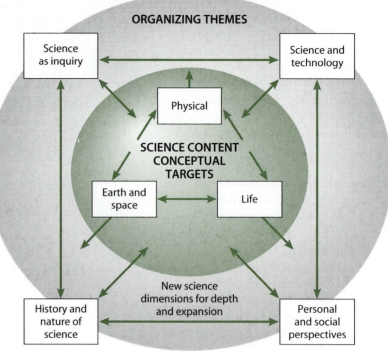

Scientific Knowledge. Like you, children cannot escape the importance of science; it affects every aspect of their lives. However, the intent of scientific information is that it be a means, not an end. Science content can help children to become responsible consumers and personally learn how to benefit more from learning science. If science content is applied to real circumstances, scientific information and areas of study provide meaningful contexts for developing literacy skills. Recommendations from science organizations, such as the National Science Teachers Association, urge that children have daily opportunities to relate science to their own lives and that science study not be limited to science time. Other organizations, such as the American Association for the Advancement of Science and the National Research Council, urge that science lessons be focused on meaningful standards that address the historical, social, technological, and interdisciplinary nature of science (see Figure 5.1). The information, attitudes, and skills of science can be used to enrich other school experiences, and times of reading, art, music, social studies, writing, mathematics, discussion, physical education, and so on can be used to deepen an understanding of science. Science is central to the education of literate citizens.

Science as Inquiry for Literacy

NSES

PD-C

Inquiry means the use of the processes of science, scientific knowledge, and attitudes to reason and to think critically. Inquiry assists in constructing an understanding of scientific concepts, learning how to learn, becoming an independent and lifelong learner, and further developing the habits of mind associated with science. Learning outcomes for inquiry require students to be able to understand inquiry and do a variety of types of science activities in order to learn the uses and skills of inquiry and develop a greater capacity to inquire.

Inquiry is the process that students should use to learn science. They should be able to ask questions, use their questions to plan and conduct a scientific investigation, use appropriate science tools and scientific techniques, evaluate evidence and use it logically to construct several alternative explanations, and communicate (argue) their conclusions scientifically (NRC, 1996). Learners who are scientifically literate:

- have the age-appropriate knowledge and understanding of scientific concepts and processes required for participation in a digital society;
- can ask, find, or determine answers to questions that arise from curiosity rooted in their everyday experiences;
- develop and maintain the ability to describe, explain, and predict natural phenomena;
- are able to read with understanding and to discuss articles about science in the popular press with awareness about the validity of the conclusions;
- have age-appropriate awareness and can identify scientific issues underlying national and local decisions and can express age-appropriate positions that are scientifically and technologically informed;
- are able to evaluate at an age-appropriate level the quality of scientific information on the basis of its source and the methods used to generate it; and
- have the capacity to pose and evaluate arguments based on evidence and to apply conclusions from such arguments appropriately (adapted from enGauge, 2007).

NSES
TS-E

The Importance of Scientific Inquiry

The National Science Education Standards (NSES) (National Research Council, 1996, p. 32) list, among specific teaching standards, several points that encourage teachers to:

- focus and support inquiries while interacting with students;
- orchestrate discourse among students about scientific ideas;
- challenge students to accept and share responsibility for their own learning;
- recognize and respond to student diversity and encourage all students to participate fully in science learning; and
- encourage and model the skills of scientific inquiry, as well as the curiosity, openness to new ideas and data, and skepticism that characterize science.

Inquiry as Cornerstone. Inquiry is the cornerstone of these standards for teaching, and according to the NSES (NRC, 1996, p. 4), good teachers at all age and grade levels are expected to be able to plan inquiry-based science lessons and science programs, take proper actions to guide and facilitate learning, assess teaching and learning, and develop and maintain classroom environments and learning communities that enable children to learn science. Even so, teachers hold diverse views about what inquiry is (Bybee et al., 1997), and many teachers report familiarity with inquiry, yet their actual teaching practices suggest that they do not understand deeply the purposes and processes of inquiry (Lederman & Neiss, 1997; Mullis et al., 1997).

Science goals focus on the interrelationships of learners, their inquiry processes, society, technology, and the history of science.

For children, inquiry refers to the activities—the processes—that children experience in which they develop testable ideas and construct understandings of real-world scientific ideas. Inquiry activities usually involve:

- pondering and posing questions;
- using tools to make and classify observations;
- examining sources of information;
- investigating, analyzing, forming answers, and explanations; and
- communicating outcomes and conclusions.

Inquiry Is More Than Hands-On. Hands-on activities alone do not guarantee inquiry. Inquiry is dependent on a set of interrelated processes guided by questions. Inquiry is a process of interrelationships between the object of the inquiry and the people who do the inquiring. Inquiry refers to the process of the cognitive effort used to explore questions, ideas, and phenomena. The result of the effort is a discovery that is new to the child in school science but already known by scientists and teachers. Children are able to inquire when they are given hands-on learning opportunities, appropriate materials to manipulate, puzzling circumstances or problems for motivation, enough structure to help them focus or maintain a productive direction, and enough freedom to compare ideas and make personal learning discoveries.

Inquiry methods can take several forms, yet all strive to promote a healthy dynamic between hands-on, minds-on learning processes. This dynamic has been found to improve children's spatial ability and help to reduce early differences between genders respective to imagining and manipulating objects with moving parts (Solomon, 1997). In this section of the chapter, we invite you to explore a learning cycle method, scientific experimental method, Suchman's inquiry method, playful discovery, and problem-based learning. All of these methods make use of inquiry techniques to stimulate conceptualization and discovery of meaning. As simple as each method appears, you will benefit from cumulative experiences, reflection and self-evaluation, and revision in using these methods.

Methods That Use Inquiry to Promote Student Concept Formation and Discovery

How can you accomplish all that is expected in this age of multiple literacies, curriculum and teaching standards, academic content outcomes, increased public expectations, and expanded calls for accountability? A clearly focused lesson plan, authentic forms of assessment, and sensible teaching tools all help to provide the answer. Chapters 4 and 7 focus on planning and assessment. We devote most of this chapter to illustrating methods that use inquiry to help children discover and understand. Figure 5.1 on page 130 presented the different forms of science content and the multiple interactions to be taught across the primary, intermediate, and middle grades. National and state science standards embrace the view that science ought to be learned and understood authentically through inquiry methods.

A Science Learning Cycle

NSES
TS-B, E

A learning cycle is a method for planning lessons, teaching, learning, and developing curricula. This multipurpose method was originally designed as a teaching method for the Science Curriculum Improvement Study and has produced the largest achievement gains among the experimental elementary science programs of the 1960s. These increases are largely a result of the learning cycle as an inquiry teaching and learning method, because the cycle is a way of thinking and acting that is consistent with how pupils naturally inquire and make discoveries.

The science learning cycle originally consisted of three phases: exploration, concept invention, and discovery. Several modifications have been made to the original learning cycle over the past four decades, and the literature reports several popular iterations. Perhaps a 5-E model is most recognized. We recommend emphasis on at least 4-Es, with specific focus on accommodating all of the new science goals that emphasize mastery of specific concepts, developing reasoning and problem-solving skills, and addressing new dimensions of science and accountability (see Figure 5.2). A complete learning cycle consists of engagement, exploration, explanation, expansion, and evaluation. Each phase, when followed in sequence, has sound theoretical support from the cognitive development theory of Jean Piaget (Renner & Marek, 1988; Marek & Cavallo, 1997) and applies constructivist learning procedures (see Chapter 2). A focused version has produced significant gains in pupil achievement, skills, and scientific attitudes during the authors' successful Lead Teacher Project (1990–1993) for K–6 science funded by the National Science Foundation and in pupil achievement and attitudes toward elementary science (Ebrahim, 2004). Table 5.1 on page 134 presents an overview of the cycle's phases, which are described in more detail below.

Phase One: Engagement. An effective lesson stimulates interest, motivates curiosity, and sustains learner inquiry. Many times, teachers will begin a lesson with this phase and then use principles of engagement strategically within other phases to guide learner investigations and thinking (see Figures 5.2 and 5.3). Strategic questions can serve to stimulate interaction between teacher and learners and drive an inquiry. Questioning and supportive interaction can also encourage learners to reveal preconceptions and misconceptions, which can be addressed, modified, and possibly corrected as the lesson progresses. Discrepant events (see later in this chapter) and children's literature can be used to pull in and focus children's attention.

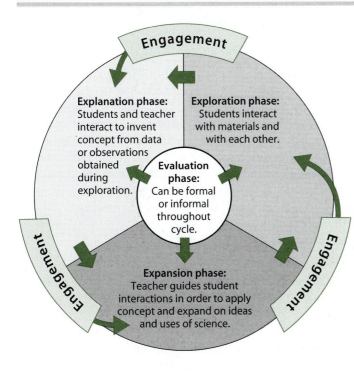

FIGURE 5.2 ● The 5-E Science Learning Cycle

Source: Adapted from a figure by Charles Barman, "The Learning Cycle: Making It Work," *Science Scope* (February 1989): 28–31.

TABLE 5.1 ● A Learning Cycle Summary

Phase	Focus	What Students Do	What Teachers Do	Outcome
Engagement	Thoughtful attention Curiosity Motivation	Respond to questions and problems	Pose questions Stimulate interaction	Preconceptions proved and misconceptions revealed
Exploration	Inquiry Engaged learning	Hands-on investigations Use process skills and tools Cooperative investigation	Establish the inquiry Interact with student groups Guide exploration Informal assessment	Process skill development Preconceptions formed and explored
Explanation	Engaged reasoning with convergent thinking for conceptualization Processing the Exploration	Respond to teacher's guidance Examine collected information Respond to questioning Form the concept	Direct investigation of the information Use questioning Coach with explicitness Identify the concept Form operational definition for concept	Concept identified and described
Expansion	Interaction to expand understanding of concept Address new dimensions of the National Science Education Standards	Teacher-directed activity Student-directed projects Use concept and skills in new situation Think, reason, apply	Direct additional activity Guide student projects Continue the inquiry Questioning Practical applications Informal assessment	Deeper conceptual understanding Substantive accomplishment of standards
Evaluation	Discern what students know and can do	Respond to teacher Demonstrate understanding Demonstrate skills Express attitudes	Interact with students and groups Focus on what students know and can do Plan next step	Demonstration of conceptual understanding, proficiency in using skills, degree of attitudes

NSES

TS-E

Phase Two: Exploration. The exploration phase is student centered, stimulates learner mental disequilibrium, and fosters mental assimilation. The teacher is responsible for engaging and sustaining the learners' curiosity by using inquiry questions, offering sufficient instructions and using materials that help learners to interact in ways that are related to the concept and form intuitive understandings. The teacher's directions must not tell students what they should learn and must not explain the concept; this occurs later. The teacher's role is to:

- pose the lesson's central question,
- engage the learners in the inquiry,
- answer students' questions,
- ask questions to guide student observations and to cause students to engage in science processes or thinking skills (see Figure 5.3), and
- give hints and cues to keep the exploration going.

Students are responsible for exploring the materials and for gathering and recording their own information. Teachers rely on questioning skills such as those

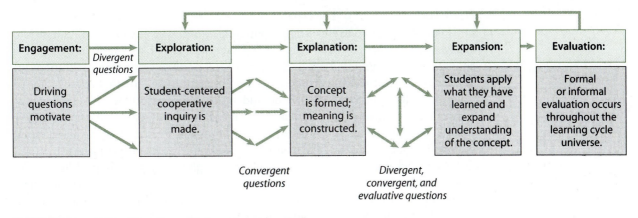

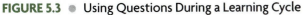

FIGURE 5.3 ● Using Questions During a Learning Cycle

shown in Figure 5.3 to guide the exploring and assisting learners in making observations and collecting data that will be used in the next explanation phase to construct the concept.

Phase Three: Explanation. The explanation phase may be less student centered and provides for learner mental accommodation. The teacher refrains from lecturing or too much telling but uses this phase to help learners form the conceptual explanation for the lesson's inquiry question through intellectual engagement. The main purpose of this phase is for teachers to guide student thinking so that the concept of the lesson is constructed cooperatively, not merely given by the teacher. To accomplish this, the teacher selects and sets the desired class environment. The teacher asks students to give the information they have collected and helps students to process and mentally organize the information by using interactive examination of the data and skillful uses of questioning.

Once the information is organized, the teacher introduces the specific language needed for the concept, as Mrs. Myers did in the chapter's opening scenario *after* her students observed and explored what happened to them during the lap sit when different variables were introduced. Teachers help students to identify the lesson's concept and to construct and attach meaning to the concept. Often, learners benefit from Vygotsky's concept of zones of proximal development (Chapter 2), and this action can be simplified by using a sentence starter including the concept label and asking the learners to call upon the experiences and intuitive understanding to help form an operational definition for the class.

This phase helps to lead to mental accommodation, as described by Piaget. Here, students must focus on their primary findings from their firsthand explorations. The teacher must introduce language or concept labels to assist in mental accommodation. These questions may help you to think about your mission and help you to guide students' thinking so that they construct their own explanations of the concept:

- What kinds of information or findings should the students talk about?
- How can I help students to summarize their findings?
- How can I guide the students and refrain from telling them what they should have found, even if their understanding is incomplete? How can I help them to use their information to construct the concept correctly?
- What labels or descriptions should the students attach to the concept?
- What reasons can I give the students if they ask me why the concept is important? This question automatically leads to the next phase: expansion.

Phase Four: Expansion. The expansion phase should be student centered as much as possible and organized to encourage group cooperation. The purpose of this phase is to engage learners mentally to organize the experiences they have acquired by forming connections with similar previous experiences and by discovering new applications for what they have learned. Constructed concepts must be linked to other related ideas or experiences. The purpose is to take the students' thinking beyond where it is currently, and planning for this part of your teaching can be helped through concept mapping (see Chapter 4). You must require students to use the language or labels of the new concept so that the students add depth to their understanding. This is a proper place to help students apply what they learned by expanding examples or by providing additional exploratory experiences for stimulating students' science inquiry skills, encouraging them to investigate science-technology-society interrelationships, and understanding the history and nature of science. (See goals in Chapter 1 and the science content interactions illustrated in Figure 5.1.) The expansion phase may provide new opportunities for engagement and can automatically lead to the exploration phase of the next lesson; hence, a continuing cycle for teaching and learning is established. The Feature Learning Cycle lesson shows how to do this.

Teachers help students to organize their thinking by relating what they have learned to other ideas or experiences that relate to the constructed concept. It is very important to use the language of the concept during this phase to add depth to the concept's meaning and to expand the range of the children's vocabulary. Consider these questions:

1. What previous experiences have the students had that relate to the concept? How can I connect the concept to those experiences?

2. What are some examples of how the concept encourages the students to see science's benefits to themselves? To help them understand the relationships among science, technology, and society? To help them develop science inquiry skills? To help them be informed about the history and nature of science?

3. What questions can I ask to encourage students to discover the concept's importance? To apply the concept? To appreciate the problems it solves? To understand the problems it causes? To identify the careers influenced by it? To understand how the concept has been viewed or used throughout history?

4. What new experiences are needed to apply or expand the concept?

5. What is the next concept related to the present one? How can I encourage exploration of the next concept?

Phase Five: Evaluation. The purpose of this phase is to overcome the limits of standard types of testing; Chapter 7 presents several tools to use. Evaluation should occur throughout the entire cycle and not be reserved for the end of the lesson. Learning often occurs in small increments before larger mental leaps of insight are possible, and frequent assessment nurtures learning. Therefore, evaluation should be continual, not a typical end-of-chapter or end-of-unit approach. Several types of measures are necessary to form a holistic evaluation of the students' learning and to encourage mental construction of concepts and process skills. Evaluation can be included in each phase of the learning cycle. Ask yourself these questions:

1. What appropriate learning outcomes should I expect?

2. What types of hands-on evaluation techniques can the students use to demonstrate the basic skills of observation, classification, communication, measurement, prediction, and inference?

3. What techniques are appropriate for students to demonstrate the integrated science process skills of identifying and controlling variables, defining operationally, forming hypotheses, experimenting, interpreting data, and forming models?

4. How can I use pictures to help students demonstrate how well they can think through problems that require understanding fundamental concepts and the integration of ideas?

5. What types of questions can I ask students to help them reflect and to indicate how well they recall and understand what has been learned?

Scientific Method: How Can You Use Principles of Scientific Investigation While Teaching?

Scientific method is defined as the systematic pursuit of knowledge involving the recognition and formulation of a problem, the collection of data through observation and experimentation (the experiential element), the formulation of a hypothesis, and the testing and confirmation (or rejection) of that hypothesis (Fields, 1989, p. 15).

NSES
TS-B

What went through your mind as you read the definition? If the scientific method was taught in your high school, it was probably taught in a science class apart from actually doing science. Some scientists and educators object to the notion of a scientific method and, justifiably, cite that all scientists do not think or investigate in such a linear way. Often, a method is memorized as a series of steps like these:

1. Define the problem.
2. Find out what is already known about the problem.
3. Form a hypothesis or educated guess.
4. Conduct an experiment to test the hypothesis.
5. Use the results to reach a conclusion.

Unfortunately, many textbooks and teachers have treated these steps as a recipe for doing and learning science. The new vision presented by the National Science Education Standards (NSES) encourages inquiry beyond the "science as a process" approach. The principles of scientific experimentation encourage learners to combine science skills (such as observing, classifying, predicting, and experimenting) and scientific knowledge by reasoning and thinking to develop their understanding of science. According to the NSES, students who inquire through scientific experimentation:

- construct understanding of science concepts,
- "know how we know" in science,
- develop an understanding of the nature of science,
- develop many skills necessary to become independent inquirers about their natural world, and
- develop mental habits of using their skills and abilities (NRC, 1996).

The principles of scientific inquiry and experimentation offer ways to form cooperative problem-solving groups, particularly when the principles are used flexibly to

Learning Cycle Featured Lesson

Physical Science: Make a Sinker Float: Clay Boats

Grades ● 4–6

► Motion and Forces. If more than one force acts on an object, then the forces can reinforce or cancel one another, depending on their direction and magnitude. Unbalanced forces will cause changes in the speed and/or direction of an object's motion.

CONCEPTS TO BE CONSTRUCTED

► If the upward force of the liquid is greater than the downward force of an object, the object will float because it is buoyed (lifted up or supported) by the water. This concept is called buoyancy, and it explains why some heavy objects, such as steel ships, will float in water.

SCIENCE ATTITUDES TO NURTURE

► Open-mindedness
► Cooperating with others
► Avoiding broad generalizations
► Willingness to withhold judgment

Engaging Question

Why can heavy objects float?

Materials Needed

For exploration phase ● conducted in teams of three or four, each team will need:

- 1 small tub or bucket filled with water
- Small objects that will sink or float in the water,
- 1 lump of modeling clay (Plasticine)

For explanation and expansion phase ● conducted whole class, you will need:

- 1 large plastic beaker or container with a lip, that will drain into a smaller beaker
- 1 lump of modeling clay (Plasticine)
- 1 spring scale

Safety: Have students notify you in case of spills. Use a room with a nonskid floor surface if possible.

Exploration

PROCESS SKILLS USED

► Observing
► Estimating
► Predicting

Student Activity

- Have the students examine the variety of objects given to them and predict whether each object will sink or float in the

water. Have the students write their predictions on organized data sheets that you provide. Use as one of the objects a lump of clay about the size of a tennis ball. Provide time for the students to test their predictions, and then gather the students together to explore what their predictions reveal.

Explanation

If objects of different sizes and weights are used in the exploration phase, students will discover that heaviness is not the factor that determines whether an object sinks or floats. For example, a large piece of 2 × 4-inch wood will be heavier than a glass marble or a metal washer, but it will float, while the marble and washer will sink.

Explain that Archimedes, a Greek philosopher, is credited with discovering that an object immersed in a liquid (water) will appear to lose some of its weight.

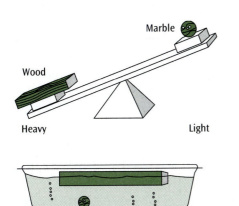

Ask students to speculate why this seems to be. A suitable explanation may be: If the upward force of the liquid is greater than the downward force of the object, it will float because the object is buoyed (lifted up or supported) by the water. This factor is called *buoyancy* and is the conceptual focus of the lesson.

Steel has been given a special shape (the ship) that gives it a greater volume, which helps to spread the ship's weight across a larger amount (volume) of the water, making it possible for the buoyant upward forces of the water to be greater than the downward force of the ship's weight.

How might buoyancy be affected by the amount of cargo a ship carries?

Why is it important to keep a ship from taking on water? What were you able to do with the clay to help it to float? What did you do to the clay's mass respective to the volume of the container's water?

Expansion

PROCESS SKILLS USED:
▶ Inferring
▶ Measuring
▶ Hypothesizing
▶ Investigating

• Weigh the lump of dry clay and the smaller container to be used to catch the water spill, and record the measures. Take the lump of clay, and use the device as illustrated. Carefully lower the clay into the container of water, and measure its weight while it is submerged. Catch the water that spills out of the container, and weigh the container again. Subtract the dry container weight to determine the weight of the water displaced by the sinking clay.

The weight of the submerged clay should be less than the dry weight because of the upward (buoyant) force of the water. Challenge the students to find a way to change the shape of the clay so that it will float in the water. Challenge them to see who can make a clay boat that will carry the largest amount of cargo before it sinks.

Have students draw pictures of their boats' shapes and/or measure the size of the boats' bottoms.

Capable students could calculate the surface area of the boats' bottoms and graph the amount of cargo carried (before sinking) as a function of area.

Ask students to observe carefully what happens to make their clay boats sink and to describe later what they observe.

Science in Personal and Social Perspectives

Ask the students why the Coast Guard requires flotation devices on boats and why these devices make it possible for a person to float who otherwise might sink. Why does the Coast Guard set passenger limits on pleasure craft?

Science and Technology

Ask the students to search for other inventions that apply the buoyancy principle. Ask how these uses have had an impact on people. Examples might include floats connected to switches or valves that control pumps or appliances, seat cushions on airliners that are removable and can be used as flotation devices, and channel buoys for navigation or to mark danger zones.

Science as Inquiry

• Ask the students to identify other examples of buoyancy in liquids and to describe differences. As examples, ask the students to redo their sink-or-float tests in denatured or isopropyl alcohol, a mixture of alcohol and water, or water with different amounts of salt added. (This can lead to another concept and another lesson on specific gravity.)

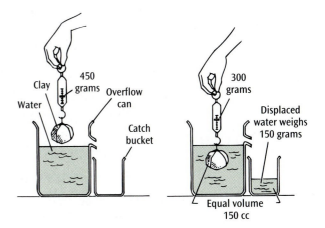

- Ask the students to explain why a submarine can sink and float and how it is possible for a submarine or a SCUBA diver to remain at a particular depth.

- Construct a Cartesian diver using a 2-liter soft drink container filled with water. Place a glass medicine dropper in the container, and put the cap on tightly. Squeeze the sides of the container, release, and watch what happens to the dropper. Why does the dropper sink and rise? What is necessary to keep the submarine dropper at a constant depth in the container?

- Ask the students to explain why it is easier to swim and float in salt water than in fresh water.

History and Nature of Science

- As an expansion assignment, have the students search for pictures and examples of careers that require some knowledge of the buoyancy concept. Examples may include ship builders, navy and marine personnel, fishermen, marine salvage crews, plumbers, and SCUBA divers. How have the inventions used by these changed over time?

- Read Pamela Allen's *Mr. Archimedes' Bath* (1991) to the class, and discuss what the author needed to know about science to write this children's book.

Evaluation

Hands-on Assessment

The students should be able to use the ball of clay and/or the Cartesian diver to demonstrate and explain the concept of buoyancy.

The students will also be able to demonstrate the proper use of the balance when weighting the clay, measure and calculate the area of clay boats, and graph the maximum cargo carried as a function of the surface area of the boat.

Reflective Assessment

The students should be able to explain in their own words why and how a clay boat or a steel ship will float. They will also research the buoyancy inventions used by a single career over a period of time (perhaps over fifty years) and explain how different understanding of buoyancy and technical advancement influenced persons in these careers.

Pictorial Assessment

The students should draw a picture of what happens when their clay ball is placed in water as a ball and when its shape is changed.

help learners design a procedure they wish to follow. Most children need structure and considerable guidance until they develop the mental habits of thinking like a scientist. Begin simply, perhaps by saying that science deals with answering questions or solving mysteries, or as Fields (1989), says, "Science invents stories and then sees if they are true" (p. 15). Use thoughtful questions to guide classroom discussions and pursue answers to those questions and soon you will find students asking their own questions, inventing their own stories, and pursuing those stories to see whether they are true. These questions usually serve to define the problem and point out what needs to be known and imply how the inquiry ought to occur.

The Principles of Scientific Inquiry as a Teaching Method

NSES
TS-B

The teaching strategy can have five steps that parallel those listed above. Steven Fields's fine article in *Science and Children* (Fields, 1989) provides many practical examples of how the steps you have memorized can be turned into a motivating, interactive, and effective teaching method. We paraphrase his ideas as follows:

STEP 1. Have students conclude that experimenting will provide the best answer to the science question.

If a child shows interest in a topic by asking a question or if children become curious about a topic after you ask a question, look for a way to discover the answer by acting on it. For example, how can you discover the answer to a question such as "If rudders (and flaps) steer an airplane in flight, which rudders steer it in which direction?" (See Figure 5.4.) Problem questions such as this can make good challenges for cooperative group investigations in which each learner has a specific duty to fulfill.

STEP 2. Focus the science question to seek a specific answer.

Try a brainstorming session. Accept all ideas related to the question, then limit the question to the kernel of the problem it poses. Identify a hypothesis from the ideas offered. Help the student groups to find out all they can about the problem; then encourage them to make and test predictions. Continuing with Steve Fields's airplane example, some predictions could include the following:

- Wing rudders control up-and-down movement.
- Tail rudders control movement to the left and right.
- When rudders are set in any given way, the plane will fly up and down or side to side.

STEP 3. Guess the answer to the science question, and use references to try to find out if the answer is already known.

Individual students and groups can brainstorm and decide the best way to find out the answer. Guiding questions can steer their thinking. Examples include the following:

- "Can you find the answer in a book? If 'yes,' what kind of book?"
- "Who do you know who might already know the answer?" (Other children, teachers, outside resources, experts, and so on.)
- How could you find helpful information on the Internet?

If these questions do not help, try "How can you (we) design a test to find out the answer?" For older children, this a good place to discuss variables that can affect the outcome and reliability of an experiment.

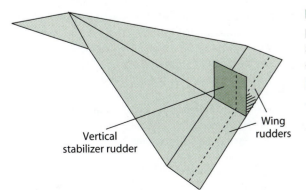

Vertical stabilizer rudder

Wing rudders

FIGURE 5.4 ● **Paper Airplane Illustration** On this paper airplane, the wing rudders and vertical stabilizer rudder are located as shown. Of course, creating various models of airplanes is a scientific endeavor in its own right. Let students experiment with making planes and rudders themselves.

Source: Steve Fields, "The Scientific *Teaching* Method," *Science and Children* (April 1989): 15. Reprinted with permission from NSTA Publications, copyright 1989 *Science and Children,* 1742 Connecticut Ave., N.W. Washington, DC 20009.

STEP 4. Follow the procedures suggested by the guiding questions in Step 3 to find the answer to the science question raised in Step 2.

Help children during this stage by limiting their temptation to overgeneralize. For example, if the wing rudders are set up and the plane flies up, guide the students to the conclusion that these settings *probably* affect all planes the same way. One could not know for certain that larger planes are affected the same way unless they also are tested.

STEP 5. After experimenting, interpreting, and concluding, have the students use what they have learned.

Focus on everyday experiences, and have the children apply the main ideas they have learned—the concepts—to things they can understand. The rudder example applies to paper airplanes as well as kites, model rockets and planes, spoilers on racing cars, and rudder steering on conventional boats and swamp or airboats.

Like most other inquiry approaches, this method requires more time and planning to cover concepts. Equipment is needed, although often simple and inexpensive materials

NSES
PD-B

what
Research Says

The Science Learning Cycle

According to Glasson and Lalik, learning cycles have proven to be *the* utility tool—a framework for planning and teaching and for using student ideas as a foundation for learning. Treagust's synthesis of research on learning cycles confirms that they are effective instructional strategies that provide many advantages respective to achievement, attitudes, learning processes, and learner motivation when compared to traditional instruction. Learning cycles have also provided some additional advantages. Musheno and Lawson have found positive effects and improved comprehension when learning cycles are used with texts. Marek and Methven have found improved teaching and pupil performance.

Jean Piaget's research on cognitive development helped to establish the first two phases of the learning cycle: exploration and explanation (concept invention). Mental activities in these phases promote what Piaget called *assimilation* and *accommodation*. Imagine the mind as a file cabinet; faced with information, the mind seeks a place to put it. Placing new information in an existing file with similar information would be an example of assimilation, as the mind adds to what already exists. However, when it does not find a file with information similar to that to be stored away, the mind must create a new file.

However, a learner does not always function independently or in isolation from a social system. A learning cycle promotes timely and strategic interaction among peers and with teachers and materials. As a model for learning, the cycle is served well by Vygotsky's theory, which emphasizes

the importance of social interaction in the broad range of thought processes and in lending assistance to individual learners for increased comprehension. Glasson and Lalik have found that these interactions have produced improvements in language acquisition and usage.

Robert Karplus, director of the Science Curriculum Improvement Study (SCIS), is credited with adding a third phase to the learning cycle. He named this phase *discovery* and then later changed the name to *concept implementation*. Some science educators prefer to call this the *application phase*. John Renner and Edmund Marek have made improvements and call the third phase *expansion of the idea*. There is considerable research to support uses of the learning cycle for improving children's science achievement and process skill development.

Renner and Marek note that the SCIS program relies on the learning cycle to organize its materials and to guide its teaching methods. Consequently, they have used the SCIS materials to conduct their own research.

Renner and Marek have used Piagetian mental conservation tasks to design experimental studies that indicate what effect the learning cycle may have on the intellectual development of young children. They found that when the learning cycle was used, children in an experimental group significantly outperformed other children who learned within a traditional textbook control group. Number, weight, liquid amount, solid amount, length, and area were the measures of conservation. The researchers believe that "the data support the conclusion that the rate of attainment of conservation will do. Certain concepts lend themselves to experimentation more easily than others. The emphasis on concepts, however, is precisely what makes student comprehension greater and retention last longer. The cooperative group problem investigation approach helps to leverage the students' ideas by stimulating new approaches to the problem.

Suchman's Inquiry: How Can You Get Students to Think and Question?

Science magic? Dressed in cape and top hat, Mr. Martinez was ready to deliver his promised special treat to the fourth-grade class. With the theatrical flair of an amateur magician, he proposed to take his very sharp magic wand (the straight steel shank cut out of a coat hanger and filed to a pin-sharp point on one end) and pass it through a balloon without bursting it. Mr. Martinez played the crowd. He blew up a balloon, tied it off, and enlisted the aid of the audience by having them chant, "I believe! I believe!" and then, on his signal, say the magic words. As the supersharp pin was about to touch the stretched side of the balloon, several children furrowed their brows and covered their ears. And with good reason: Pop!

NSES
TS-B

reasoning is significantly enhanced by the experiences made possible by [the first graders who learned through a learning cycle]." They also claim that the learning cycle enhances the intellectual development of young learners.

The learning cycle has also been used to test the ability of children to use science processes. In a study that investigated fifth graders who were controlled (via a matched-pairs design) for intellectual development, chronological age, gender, and socioeconomic level, Renner and Marek found that all differences in the performance of science process skills favored the group that used the learning cycle. The researchers concluded that the learning cycle helped children learn to use the processes of science much better than did a traditional program using a conventional science textbook.

In still another study, Renner and Marek investigated the influence of the learning cycle in a science program on student achievement in mathematics, reading, and social studies. They discovered that children learned *just as much and just as well* from the learning cycle as those who learned from a traditional program on understanding mathematics concepts, learning mathematics skills, learning social studies content, and understanding word meaning. However, they conclude that the *learning cycle was superior* for helping children apply mathematics; master social studies skills that involve interpreting graphs, tables, and posters and assimilation of data for problem solving; and determine paragraph meaning. In yet another study, Renner and Marek discovered that the learning cycle used in the SCIS first-grade program helped children outperform other children in a reading program on reading readiness skills.

The researchers maintain that the learning cycle is a natural way to learn and that it fulfills the major purpose of education: helping children learn how to think. Furthermore, Renner and Marek state that their research provides a rebuttal to teachers and administrators who say, "We just don't have time or cannot afford to invest in the resources to teach science." They conclude: "The truth of the matter is that any school that teaches science using the learning cycle model is teaching much more than good science; it is also teaching reading, mathematics, and social science. In fact, schools cannot afford *not* to teach science using [the learning cycle model]."

Sources: Adapted and quoted from J. W. Renner and E. Marek, *The Learning Cycle and Elementary Science Teaching* (Portsmouth, NH: Heinemann, 1988), pp. 185–199. See also E. A. Marek and A. M. L. Cavallo, *The Learning Cycle: Elementary Science and Beyond* (Portsmouth, NH: Heinemann, 1997). G. E. Glasson and R. V. Lalik (1993). "Reinterpreting the Learning Cycle from a Social Constructivist Perspective: A Qualitative Study of Teachers' Beliefs and Practices." *Journal of Research in Science Teaching, 30*(2) pp. 187–207. E. A. Marek and S. B. Methven (1991). "Effects of the Learning Cycle Upon Student and Classroom Teacher Performance." *Journal of Research in Science Teaching, 28*(1) pp. 41–53. B. V. Musheno and A. E. Lawson (1998). "Effects of Learning Cycle and Traditional Text on Comprehension of Science Concepts by Students at Differing Reasoning Levels." *Journal of Research in Science Teaching, 36*(1) pp. 23–37. D. F. Treagust (2007). "General Instructional Methods and Strategies." In S. K. Abell and N. G. Lederman (Eds.), *Handbook of Research on Science Education.* Mahwah, NJ: Lawrence Erlbaum Associates.

The giggles were meant to tell Mr. Martinez "I told you so," but he persisted with remarks about not all of them believing or not selecting the right magic words. "Let's try again," he said as he began working the crowd again. Martinez blew up another balloon, tied it, and then remembered that he should add a drop of elixir from an oil can to his magic wand. They all went through the routine again, and this time, to the amazement of the children, the wand pierced one end of the balloon and slowly came out the other—a perfect axis through the top of the balloon and at the bottom near the knot (Figure 5.5). The children clapped and immediately wanted to know how he did it.

Mr. Martinez explained that he was not aware of any magic that really worked and that his buildup was only an act. He emphasized that there are usually scientific explanations for the discrepancies we observe. But he assured the children that the balloon trick was no illusion. To convince them, he passed the balloon around for the children to inspect and then said, "You usually expect me to ask *you* questions, but today is a special opportunity for *you* to ask the questions. Let's pretend you are super sleuths who are going to find out the explanation for this balloon trick. You can ask me all the questions you want, but there are some special rules you must follow. First, you can only ask me questions I can answer with a 'Yes' or 'No.' Second, begin by asking questions to establish the facts of what you have just seen. Don't take anything for granted: Verify that it was done as you *think* you saw it. Finally, after you think you have all the facts you need, tell me the reason you think this trick was possible. Let's begin. Lucinda?"

"Did you do anything special to the second balloon, like make it stronger?"

"No."

Then other children asked: "Were they the same kind of balloons?"

"Yes."

"Were they the same size? I mean when you blew them up?"

"Yes—I tried to have them the same."

"Did you let a little air out of each one?"

"Yes."

"Does the oil make it work?"

"That sounds like an explanation type of question to me. Let's hold that one a while until after we uncover some more facts," said Mr. Martinez. Then the lesson continued until eventually the children discovered the *real* answer, and it wasn't because of the oil. The answer was related to the position, thickness, and strength of the balloon's fabric.

FIGURE 5.5 ● Balloon Discrepant Event

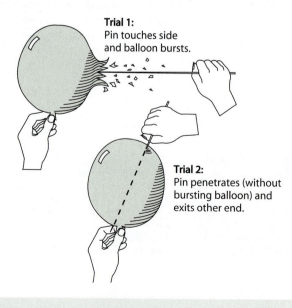

Trial 1:
Pin touches side and balloon bursts.

Trial 2:
Pin penetrates (without bursting balloon) and exits other end.

Discrepant Events. This inquiry technique, developed by J. Richard Suchman (1962), relies on the use of discrepant events. *Discrepancies* are differences from what we normally expect, such as the sharp pin penetrating the balloon without bursting it. Most often, the human mind is intolerant of discrepancies and needs to maintain consistency. This belief refers to an inconsistency between two cognitions—cognitive dissonance—between what one observes and what one believes. The balloon is a good example: Everyone knows sharp objects cause balloons to pop, but this one didn't!

The Method. Your students' need for cerebral consistency can motivate even those who are less alert and attentive. Why not use it to your advantage and teach science concepts with it? Suchman's method uses inquiry to help children construct theories (best explanations) for the discrepancies they observe. The approach is student centered and requires children to ask the questions—possibly a difficult task because it requires considerable thought to ask useful questions and to build the answers into some order that will explain the discrepancy. Take a cooperative approach, and divide the class into detective teams to organize questions, conduct research, and form scientific explanations. Use convergent questions, to be answered with either a *yes* or a *no*. (See Figure 5.6 on page 146 for a visual map of how the inquiry is structured.) These are the phases of Suchman's method:

1. Present the discrepant event.
2. Students ask yes/no questions to verify the events and collect information.
3. Students discuss ideas and do library research or further investigations to gather additional information to help them form explanations or theories.
4. The teacher reconvenes the class and leads a discussion to help students give and test their explanations or theories.

Suchman's approach is successful with intermediate and middle school children, but younger children need more teacher guidance. With K–2 children, we have successfully used versions of the game Twenty Questions to accomplish the same outcome. Familiar objects placed in mystery boxes work well with younger children, as youngsters delight in questioning teachers, gathering clues, and solving the "mystery."

Demonstrations for Inquiry

A little panache can enliven the class, as in the demonstration for Suchman's inquiry. However, we do not suggest that you must be an entertainer. Demonstrations can be effective teaching tools for stimulating inquiry and can be appropriate if used to:

NSES
TS-B, D

- avoid putting students in danger by using a demonstration as a safer alternative;
- help students learn skills, such as the proper ways to use equipment or handle and care for plants and animals;
- focus on engaging learners in inquiry or for concept development;
- overcome equipment shortages when there is not enough equipment for all children to benefit firsthand from the exercise;
- arouse student interest, raise important inquiry questions, or pose learning problems that require critical and creative thinking;
- help solve academic problems;
- apply what has been studied to new situations by expanding understanding through new experiences; and
- encourage slow learners and challenge rapid learners.

FIGURE 5.6 ● Discrepant Event Map

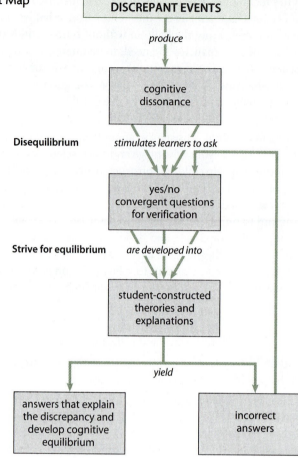

Your demonstrations can be safe and effective teaching tools if you follow these recommendations:

1. *Have a specific purpose for the demonstration.* The purpose must *be clear* to all learners. Focus on the point to be learned, and make it evident in the demonstration. Also discuss how it relates to past or future lessons. If it is intended only to entertain and not teach a concept, the demonstration has little value.

2. *Plan carefully.* Collect all the necessary materials and practice the demonstration in advance. Follow the instructions and inspect them for inaccuracies. Modify the demonstration, if necessary, for safety.

3. *Involve the students when possible.* Let the students participate in the demonstrations or permit them to conduct the demonstration. Interactive teaching techniques such as questions and guess-making stimulate thinking, enthusiasm, and participation in the inquiry.

4. *Stimulate thinking and discussion.* "What do you think will happen if . . . ?" questions help to stimulate original thinking and bring forth children's ideas for productive discussion. This technique also keeps you from giving away too much information before the demonstration and running the risk of destroying interest.

5. *Repeat the demonstration.* A rapid flash or a loud bang is sure to get attention and will demand a repeat performance. During the repeat, students will pay closer attention, and their powers of observation will be keener. Also, they will be

given chances to acquire ideas or form mental connections that seem simple for adults but are difficult for children because of their limited experiences.

6. *Use simple materials.* Unfamiliar equipment may distract the students' attention. Familiar objects and equipment will help them to focus on the cause of the action or the purpose of the demonstration rather than on the gadgets being used. Students may also choose to try the demonstrations for themselves. Importation of high school equipment for elementary classroom use should be selective, and the equipment should always be screened for safety (see Chapter 10).

7. *Keep the demonstration easily visible.* A cluttered demonstration table will distract children from seeing what you intend. Similarly, objects that are too small to be seen by those who are sitting beyond the first row will frustrate viewers and cause them to lose interest. Use a tall table or counter, gather the students around when feasible (and when safe), or consider using such projection devices as the overhead projector or computer.

8. *Connect with the students' environment.* Interact to connect the point of the demonstration with the children's personal interests, community, or social issues to expand the benefits of the demonstration and the scientific concepts or principles.

9. *Rely on quality, not quantity.* Avoid a large number of demonstrations. A single well-designed, timely demonstration can communicate powerful ideas more effectively than an overwhelming number of entertaining shows. Focus on a central concept.

How Can Children Learn Science Through Play?

Young children are natural scientists, and their time spent at play with common objects helps to reveal their intuitive grasp of simple scientific processes. Sand, water, and block play areas are in demand, suggesting that children usually do not need external motivation to probe into nature. However, teachers and adult helpers can encourage exploratory play and help to nurture a solid foundation of scientific inquiry by providing children with time, place, and simple equipment for investigating the natural world. Ross (1997, p. 35) offers teachers and adult helpers play-based tips that consist of:

NSES
TS-D

- supporting open-ended inquiry;
- supplying instruments of play;
- supervising to ensure safety;
- seizing the moment to capitalize on natural interest;
- offering inviting places for discovery to occur;
- providing access to relevant information through tapes, video, picture books, and computer programs;
- sharing respect for life (even the small, innocent insect!);
- seeking to develop a community for involvement; and
- celebrating wonder.

The method of playful discovery illustrates how these principles can be put into a simple teaching model. Playful discovery is based on the innate curiosity of very young children, in which play is the method for learning science. The method uses some of the elements of inquiry, but it is much more open-ended. Children are natural investigators. Combine a child's interest with some adult encouragement and opportunities to play around with interesting materials, and playful discovery enables very young children to form initial fundamental science concepts they can build on for the rest of their lives (McIntyre, 1984; Lind, 1999). The method also encourages cooperation among very young learners.

Playful discovery is based on the theories of John Dewey and Jean Piaget, who stated that young children learn best through active involvement with interesting and meaningful materials. Dewey and Piaget, however, reminded us that we as teachers must go beyond simply passing out interesting materials and letting children play with them. Both believed that teachers should direct the hands-on learning through encouragement and guiding questions. Dewey was most concerned about the quality of this hands-on experience, about which he wrote, "Everything depends upon the quality of the experience which is had. The quality of the experience has two aspects. There is an immediate aspect of agreeableness or disagreeableness, and there is an influence upon later experiences" (Dewey, 1937, p. 27).

Versions of playful discovery strive to provide young children with a variety of rich and immediately agreeable experiences. The method is used in childcare centers and preschools with three- to five-year-old children and in progressive kindergarten classrooms. Playful discovery is stimulated initially by teacher-planned experiments that are based on phenomena, substances, and/or materials that are interesting and familiar to the children. For science, the learning activities can promote positive attitudes, lay the foundation for learning simple science concepts, and stimulate development of such process skills as observation, comparison, classification, prediction, and interpretation. The following scenario (Rogers, Martin, & Kousaleos, 1988, p. 21) helps to illustrate the method. Figure 5.7 briefly describes its six stages.

Christopher: A Blossoming Scientist.

Mrs. Kousaleos invited her group of four- and five-year-olds to gather by her and experiment with ice cubes in hot and cold water. Five small children were arched over the two containers of water observing and comparing the effects. Christopher suddenly announced with obvious excitement, "Look! The ones in hot water are really getting small." At Mrs. K's suggestion to check the water with their fingers, the children were surprised to discover how very cold the formerly hot water had become.

A week later, after repeating the ice activity, Mrs. K suggested another experiment to find out how to melt an ice cube quickly. Eager children generated ideas, then tested them by several methods. Putting ice cubes into mouths and breaking ice cubes into smaller pieces were by far the most popular methods. Midway through the experiment, however, Christopher, eyes wide open and a "Eureka" tone in his voice, proclaimed, "Let's try hot water!"

After duplicating the ice experiments with slight variations (such as exploring effects of amounts of water, numbers of ice cubes, and sizes of containers), the children began to ask permission to conduct their own experiments, Christopher in particular. These requests usually meant making ice in some uniquely shaped container, mixing various ingredients together, or adding a variety of materials to water.

During one of Christopher's self-initiated experiments, he noted that pouring salt into a container of water made the water "lift out." Since Christopher seemed intrigued with this phenomenon, Mrs. K planned some activities on displacement.

Later, when Christopher took a vacation, his parents sent a postcard to Mrs. K that said, "Christopher is spending much time on the beach experimenting with water, observing changes as he adds shells and sand." Christopher had become fascinated by how the water "came out" when he and his dad jumped into their vacation swimming pool.

When Christopher returned, his class did a displacement experiment, using different sizes of containers and different amounts of water with marbles to assess and extend some of his vacation learning. After exploring the effect of adding marbles to water in narrow and wide containers, Christopher observed, "When the water's up high, the marbles lift the water out." He later concluded in response to a question about the difference between the narrow and wide containers, "In a fat one, the water spreads out. In a thin one, it goes up to the top."

FIGURE 5.7 ● Six Stages
of Playful Discovery

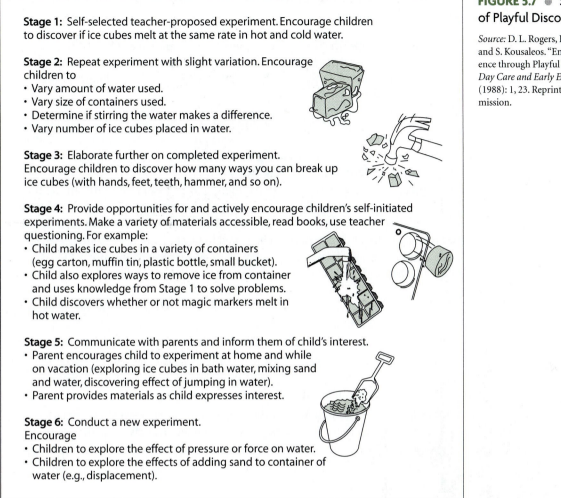

Stage 1: Self-selected teacher-proposed experiment. Encourage children to discover if ice cubes melt at the same rate in hot and cold water.

Stage 2: Repeat experiment with slight variation. Encourage children to
• Vary amount of water used.
• Vary size of containers used.
• Determine if stirring the water makes a difference.
• Vary number of ice cubes placed in water.

Stage 3: Elaborate further on completed experiment. Encourage children to discover how many ways you can break up ice cubes (with hands, feet, teeth, hammer, and so on).

Stage 4: Provide opportunities for and actively encourage children's self-initiated experiments. Make a variety of materials accessible, read books, use teacher questioning. For example:
• Child makes ice cubes in a variety of containers (egg carton, muffin tin, plastic bottle, small bucket).
• Child also explores ways to remove ice from container and uses knowledge from Stage 1 to solve problems.
• Child discovers whether or not magic markers melt in hot water.

Stage 5: Communicate with parents and inform them of child's interest.
• Parent encourages child to experiment at home and while on vacation (exploring ice cubes in bath water, mixing sand and water, discovering effect of jumping in water).
• Parent provides materials as child expresses interest.

Stage 6: Conduct a new experiment. Encourage
• Children to explore the effect of pressure or force on water.
• Children to explore the effects of adding sand to container of water (e.g., displacement).

Source: D. L. Rogers, R. E. Martin, Jr., and S. Kousaleos. "Encouraging Science through Playful Discovery," *Day Care and Early Education* 16 (1988): 1, 23. Reprinted with permission.

The Playful Science Classroom. Christopher's response is an example of what can happen when sensitive teacher guidance and well-planned experiences are combined to set the stage for the high-quality "later experiences" John Dewey wrote about. Numerous and different ongoing experiments will be evident in the playful discovery classroom. Many experiences will be based on common activities that use ordinary materials such as sand, water, and blocks.

Playful discovery gives young children opportunities to explore freely and to begin to understand the nature of materials before more structured lessons try to teach them concepts. Figure 5.7 outlines the six stages Mrs. K followed. First, she stimulated interest by proposing class experiments; later she stimulated sustained learning and experiential elaboration by permitting children to self-select experiments. Children will function at different stages at different times. For example:

> Some children may not go beyond Stage 1 because of lack of interest or understanding, and the teacher must proceed to Stage 6 for them. Others may spend a great deal of time on Stages 1 and 2, but not be able to make the leap to Stages 3 and 4. In this case it may help to skip these stages and go to Stage 5, so as to promote elaboration and self-initiation [by] suggesting that parents provide experiences in "science experiments" at home. (Rogers et al., 1988, p. 23)

Is this approach worth the effort? How long do the experiences endure? Perhaps you will find the answer here:

> Even months after the [first ice] experiment, a mother of one of the children [said] that when she was trying to figure out how to get ice cubes in a small-necked thermos, her four-year-old daughter suggested she could melt them a little in hot water first so they would fit. (Rogers et al., 1988, p. 23)

Playful discovery works best when the experiments chosen deal with phenomena and substances that the children encounter every day. The everyday environment adds a practical aspect to science by showing its usefulness, and it helps the children to construct a better understanding of their own world.

Objects from the everyday environment can be assembled into simple tools or explorer kits. These kits should be built on topics that interest the children and serve the science content recommendations offered by the National Science Education Standards (see the Appendix). Kit materials can be stored in plastic tubs; color-coordinated stickers help children learn to clean up after themselves. Management and storage ideas may be found in Chapter 10. Ross (1997) offers kit ideas such as the following:

- Exploring light with prisms, crystals, sheets of Mylar or chrome tubes, lenses, kaleidoscopes, and spectroscopes;
- Creating a disassembly line while wearing goggles and using screwdrivers and pliers to remove loosened screws from broken appliances (electric plugs removed) such as old clocks, radios, computers and modems, VCRs, CD/DVD players, cassette players, toasters, and irons;
- Digging soil in designated outdoor or indoor areas with various sizes of food containers, cookie cutters, molds, magnets, strainers, trowels, small shovels, or spoons;
- Investigating (with a respect for life) roly-poly insects—commonly called pill bugs—typically found under rotting logs or leaf litter, by using magnifying lenses, soil tubs, watercolor brushes, toothpicks, or pipe cleaners;
- Seizing the moment by exploring playground puddles and windy days with pinwheels, kites, and vessels made from paper, straws, aluminum foil, or common craft supplies.

Problem-Based Learning

The new age of science teaching recognizes that basic skills are important, yet reformers argue that future citizens must also have a command of key scientific ideas, be able to solve problems, and think critically (NRC, 1996). An emphasis on inquiry-based learning methods and student construction of understanding takes time, vision and cooperation, and often interdisciplinary treatment of school subjects. The National Science Education Standards suggest that desirable long-term inquiry activities include formation of arguments, explanation, and communication of ideas to others while using a wide range of procedural, manipulative and cognitive skills (Marx et al., 1997). Problem-based learning approaches are useful for:

- enhancing students' abilities to attend to and store information in closer proximity to what they already know with potential for avoiding misconceptions;
- situating newly constructed understanding within a realistic experiential context;
- promoting productive social interaction and learning through collaboration;
- stimulating the uses of cognitive tools, such as podcasts, CD learning programs, websites, personal computer simulations, concept maps, and problem-posing/decision-making structures (Marx et al., 1997).

Marx, Blumenfeld, Krajcik, and Soloway (1997, pp. 344–346) recommend to teachers five important features of their project-based science model that is exemplary of many problem-based learning approaches in science.

1. Help students form a *driving question* in order that projects have a focus. Driving questions should be worthwhile (connected to a curriculum framework); pose real-world problems that students find meaningful and feel ownership over; problems that are feasible and within the learners' realms of experience, knowledge, and skills.

2. Engage students in *investigation*—the real work of science—that consists of planning and designing investigations and conducting real-world research to collect and analyze information so that the students may form inferences and conclusions about the driving question.

3. Guide students toward the collection and creation of *artifacts,* which are tangible, real results of an investigation. Artifacts can consist of air- and water-quality samples, documents from corporations and science agencies, multimedia materials obtained from Internet searches, and so on.

4. Help students to *collaborate.* When students labor together to plan and complete tasks, they benefit from the collective intelligence of all members of the group and learn to value the ideas of others.

5. Expose learners to *technological tools.* Investigations become more authentic when students use tools to measure, gather, and process information by themselves. The entire classroom environment becomes more authentic and inquiry becomes more serious through real-time data collection. Students learn to make models and extend their inquiry and collaboration to other groups outside the home base of their classroom.

Figures 5.8 and 5.9 illustrate some of the tools that are used to nurture students' cognitive skills and to encourage the formation and analysis of driving questions. A teacher using these tools can consult the National Science Education Standards for

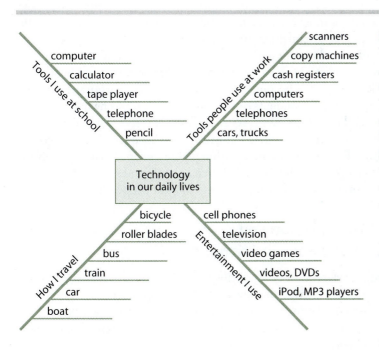

FIGURE 5.8 ● Spider Map for Investigating Technology's Influence on Our Daily Lives.
A spider map can be used to help students list and organize the various ideas they have about a topic. You could draw the basic sketch of the spider and add the legs (we have used just four, but more could be added). You might also suggest the labels for the legs and then ask the children to offer examples, which you list. From the ideas and examples, driving questions may emerge, which can be organized into a framework for investigating a problem as shown in Figure 5.9.

Source: The idea of the spider map is used in *Breakthroughs: Strategies for Thinking* series. Columbus, OH: Zaner-Bloser, 1992.

Question Box	Important Information Box	Decisions of Solutions Box
What is technology? How does technology affect me? What kinds of problems or solutions does technology create? How can I use technology?	Technology helps people to make new tools. People have used technology for a long time. Technology can help to keep me healthy. Technology can be misused and cause harmful things to happen to people and animals. All kinds of people use technology. You do not have to be a scientist to use and understand technology. Technology can make work easier. Sometimes technology can help people to do more work in less time.	The students' decisions or problem solutions should reflect their understanding about science and technology and a balance among positive and negative effects.

FIGURE 5.9 ● Problem-Based Learning Decision-Making Framework

content and curriculum framework ideas. The standards help to guide learners in the direction of worthwhile questions and applications to their daily lives. The figures illustrate the investigation of technology, a new science content area included in the standards.

Techniques for Promoting Student Cooperation

NSES

TS-E

Science inquiry encourages learners to construct their understanding from direct physical experiences and guided thinking. The methods have risks and potential difficulties. If all teachers were responsible for only one student at a time, these constructivist, inquiry approaches to science education would be rather simple to manage. Problems arise when two or more learners independently attempt to inquire. That students or a group may pursue several different questions and work on various projects at the same time presents management and organization difficulties for most teachers. Sufficient resources may also be in short supply. Postponing or even canceling lessons are options if the initial difficulties become too much to risk. With encouragement and time to develop the needed skills, students can become confident posing questions and need less help researching their answers. With practice, you too will become more skilled at managing the busy class activities and will know what questions and needs to anticipate. You will also learn many fascinating things about science that you probably never had a chance to investigate. One procedure that can help you manage the inquiry from children's questions is associated with learning teams or cooperative groups.

What Roles Do Socialization and Cooperative Learning Have in Science?

Science teachers frequently group students during science activities to manage crowded classes and stretch precious materials that always seem to be in short supply. Cooperative learning, even if used mostly for science management, is more than asking students to group their desks together, however. F. James Rutherford and Andrew Ahlgren, writing in *Science for All Americans,* tell us

The collaborative nature of scientific and technological work should be strongly reinforced by frequent group activity in the classroom. Scientists and engineers work mostly in groups and less often as isolated investigators. Similarly, students should gain experience in sharing responsibility for learning with each other. In the process of coming to common understandings, students in a group must frequently inform each other about procedures and meaning, argue over findings, and assess how the task is progressing. In the context of team responsibility, feedback and communication become more realistic and of a character very different from the usual individualistic textbook-homework-recitation approach. (Rutherford & Ahlgren, 1990, p. 189)

Questions from children help motivate further inquiry, encourage discovery, and offer a basis for cooperation.

Scientists and engineers work in an environment that is more cooperative than competitive. Roger Johnson and David Johnson (1991) and Robert Slavin (1995), well-known promoters of cooperative learning methods, maintain that the research base for cooperative learning (in its many forms) indicates that students would learn more science, like it more, and feel more positive about their performance if more of their science experiences were obtained through cooperative learning. In their extensive review of the research on instructional strategies for teaching science, Tobin, Tippins, and Gallard (1994) remind us that cooperative learning should not be viewed as a panacea. Rather, it is valuable because of the potential for students to clarify, defend, elaborate, evaluate, and argue their constructed thoughts with one another. Table 5.2 on page 154 compares the advantages of cooperative learning teaching and management techniques over those of customary small groups. This comparison illustrates that clear learning outcomes and systematic management procedures are keys to success.

Cooperative Inquiry Groups

Three to five is a functional number of students for inquiry groups or cooperative learning groups. When each group member has a special job, the group inquiry process can be both effective and functional. The research on this management approach shows that "students who work in groups learn concepts just as well as those who work individually, with the added bonus that students who work together can develop both interpersonal skills and a sense of group responsibility" (Jones, 1985, p. 21).

Form groups, assign roles, and give each child a job description. The *principal investigator* (PI) is in charge of managing the group. Duties are to check the assignment and ask the teacher any clarifying questions, then lead the group by conducting the activity for the rest of the group or by assigning duties to the other group members. The PI is also in charge of safety.

The *materials manager* is in charge of picking up and passing out all equipment and materials that are necessary. Inside the classroom, the materials manager is usually the only student who has a reason to be moving around.

The *recorder* is in charge of collecting the necessary information and recording it in the proper form: graph, table, tape recorder, and so on. The recorder works with the principal investigator and the materials manager to verify the accuracy of the data.

The *reporter* is in charge of reporting the results, orally or in writing, back to the teacher or the entire class.

The *maintenance director* is in charge of cleanup and has the power to involve others in this group responsibility. Equipment must be returned and consumables must be cleaned up.

What Is a Question Box?

NSES
PD-A

by Mary Ann Sloan

Grade 1, Paumanok Elementary School, Dix Hills, New York

My first-grade classroom can best be described as a whole science classroom, where cooperative learning takes place throughout the day. I have found that cooperative learning is a powerful tool. In my classroom, science provides the platform for an interdisciplinary approach. The children raise questions; make predictions; devise plans; obtain, organize, and analyze data; and make many decisions while they gain experiences in using science inquiry skills. All of this is the result of the introduction of a very simple device—a question box!

The question box has helped me to begin the process of transforming the class into groups of cooperative learners. This strategy takes full advantage of the children's natural curiosity and allows them to become active participants in the learning process.

To make the question box, cover a cardboard box about the size of a mailbox with dazzling foil paper. Then cut out five-inch question marks from bright construction paper. Be sure to have one for each child and one for you too. To introduce the question box to your class and to provide a model for the first questions, select an exciting book to read to the whole class. One of the books that I have used with great success is *Papa, Please Get the Moon for Me,* by Eric Carle. After reading the story, I ask the children what questions they would ask Monica, the main character, if she could come to our classroom and visit them. I record the questions they ask. Now I take out the question box. I explain that the question box is the place where they can put any questions they would like to have answered, that they can write their questions on their own or have someone help them, and that I will set aside time each day to work with the question box. I invite each child whose questions I recorded to put his or her question into the box. While we decorate our paper question marks, I move from table to table, modeling the kind of on-task behavior I expect. As I decorate my question mark, I think aloud of questions I might put into the question box and ask them about the questions they may be considering.

After a few days of working with the box—reading the questions aloud and adding more questions—I randomly

The roles of recorder and reporter can be combined, as can the roles of materials manager and maintenance director for groups as small as three. Badges, sashes, headbands, photo IDs, or other role-identifying management devices can be used to limit confusion. Rotate the roles and form different groups often to promote fairness and

NSES
TS-E

TABLE 5.2 ● Benefits of Cooperative Science Groups

Cooperative Groups	Small Groups
Positive interdependence; students sink or swim together; face-to-face verbal communication.	No interdependence; students work on their own, often or occasionally checking their answers with other students.
Individual accountability; each pupil must master the material.	Hitchhiking; some students let others do most or all of the work, then copy.
Teachers teach social skills needed for successful group work.	Social skills are not systematically taught.
Teacher monitors students' behavior	Teacher does not directly observe student behavior; often works with a few students or works on other tasks.
Feedback and discussion of students' behavior are integral parts of ending the activity before moving on.	No discussion of how well students worked together, other than general comments such as "Nice job," or "Next time, try to work more quietly."

Source: P. E. Blosser, "Using Cooperative Learning in Science Education." Columbus, OH: ERIC Clearinghouse for Science, Mathematics, and Environmental Education, 1993, ERIC Reproduction Document No. ED 351 207, p. 4.

select a question to be answered. Our first question was "Are elephants afraid of mice?" The children made a list of what they already knew about elephants. When we reread the list, they decided that they needed to know more. They wanted to know: "How big are elephants and their trunks?" "Why does an elephant have a trunk?" "Had anyone ever seen a mouse attack an elephant?" We made predictions and developed a plan of action. The children began to meet in their cooperative learning groups. Each group worked on answering one of the questions. Now science became what we do to find answers, and the children loved it!

One product that developed from their explorations was a full-size painting of an African elephant and an Indian elephant, with attention to the length and width of the trunks, which demanded measuring with many different devices. Three charts showing objects bigger, smaller, and the same size as an elephant were completed, requiring lots of comparisons. Two world maps showing where elephants and mice are found were drawn by using the overhead projector. A diorama, using clay and construction paper, was created to depict an elephant habitat. Drawings of the kinds of foods elephants eat were labeled. Clocks were made to show when elephants sleep, eat, and travel. One group found that elephants don't breathe through their trunks and that it takes lots of food to keep an elephant healthy. This news

helped the group that was working to determine how elephants actually use their trunks. They made paper bag elephant costumes and put on a play. The last group wrote letters to the Big Apple Circus, the Bronx Zoo, the Washington Zoo, and the San Diego Zoo. None of the zoo personnel had ever seen a mouse attack an elephant. In fact, they wrote to say that in their experiences, mice seemed to be afraid of elephants. We made elephant T-shirts that the letter-writing group designed. This group was also responsible for keeping a record of money collected. They enlisted a mom to help them buy the shirts. She also helped with the stenciling.

This was just the beginning of the question center. Throughout the year, many questions are answered, and the children have many opportunities to classify, create models, generalize, form hypotheses, identify variables, infer, interpret data, make decisions, manipulate materials, measure, observe, predict, record data, replicate, and use number and language skills. You will know when your class is a community of cooperative learners. I promise this center will never be empty. The children will not want to leave for recess or lunch, and three o'clock will come too soon. They will miss school on weekends and won't be able to wait until Monday mornings, when they can put more questions into or take another question out of the question box.

group responsibility. This group technique can be used with any inquiry method in which groups are used. Robert Jones provides further tips in Table 5.3 on page 156.

Successful, problem-free science lessons can occur if each member of the group understands the importance of his or her role. In a cooperative learning environment, the groups purposely comprise boys and girls of different ability levels. Each student realizes that on any given day, he or she could serve in any capacity as a member of the cooperative group. Therefore, each member is responsible for learning the material. The grade earned by participating in the lesson is a reflection of the group effort, not an individual's. The group is interdependent; its members will sink or swim together. The students within a group need to communicate to one

Children learn responsibility by sharing tasks in cooperative groups.

another problems, observations, and successes before they go to the teacher with them. Courtesy, respect, and encouragement are interpersonal skills needed by each member of the cooperative group.

One useful cooperative method is known as a *jigsaw approach* (Watson, 1992). Use it, for example, when you are teaching third-grade students about the state tree, flower, and bird. Within each cooperative group, a different member will be assigned one of the following tasks:

1. Determine the criteria for becoming the official state tree.
2. Determine the criteria for becoming the official state flower.
3. Determine the criteria for becoming the official state bird.
4. Find out who suggested the state tree, bird, or flower and where these are found in the state.
5. Learn what the state tree, bird, and flower are in one bordering state.

Students in the cooperative groups should decide which student will take on each of the five tasks. Once these students are determined, then all of the students in the class assigned to task 1 should get together to find answers to that task, those assigned to task 2 should do the same, and so on. After a sufficient amount of time has passed (for this topic with third graders, two or three 35- to 40-minute class periods should be enough time) the students should have found answers for their task. They must now return to their original cooperative groups to share their information. The success of the cooperative group will depend on how well the expert gets his or her information across to the members of the group. After two class periods of sharing information from the five tasks, it is time for the quiz. This can be done by having student experts for task 1 move to different cooperative groups. Those experts will then quiz each member of a different cooperative group individually on task 1 information. After the task 1 experts quiz the students and record their results, the task 2 experts will do the same, and so on. The success of each student will be reflected by how well his or her cooperative group expert prepared the group for the quiz.

NSES

TS-E

TABLE 5.3 ● Tips for Cooperative Group Inquiry Activities

- Let each group choose a name for itself. It is a good social activity, and the names will help you identify the different groups.
- Change group members from time to time. Try out introvert-extrovert or boy-girl teams; experiment with cultural and racial mixes; form academically heterogeneous groups.
- Talk only to the principal investigators about the activity. This will set up a chain of command and prevent a repetition of questions. The students should discuss questions and problems among themselves so that it will be necessary for you only to clarify points with the principal investigator.
- Employ both indoor and outdoor activities. Badges work well indoors; armbands and headbands are more visible on school grounds. Handheld walkie-talkies (inexpensive children's type) are also useful and (if they are available) should be used by the principal investigators.
- Use groups of three when working outdoors or on a field trip. This size group is better for safety.
- To ensure clear communication, post class rules, group names, job descriptions, and any other important information on a bulletin board in the classroom.
- Develop a system for rotating roles.
- Use job descriptions for classroom management and discipline. Most of the time you will simply need to ask which person has which role to resolve problems.
- Develop a worksheet, data recording sheet, or some other instrument for each activity.
- Make yourself a badge and join in the fun.

Source: R. M. Jones, "Teaming Up," *Science and Children* (May 1985): 23.

Recommendations for Enhancing Students' Learning of Science

All of the inquiry methods that we have presented are student centered to various degrees. They engage children in active thinking and learning and differ only in approach, but despite these procedural differences, each method guides children through inquiry toward making discoveries. The methods are successful when teachers help students to construct understanding. What elements unite these different procedures, which lead to a common outcome (Rakow, 1986)?

NSES

TS-D, F

1. Successful constructivist teachers *model scientific attitudes.* The scientific attitudes we most wish to develop in children must be evident in the people who teach them. Successful inquiry teachers must be curious, open-minded, tolerant of different viewpoints, skeptical at times, willing to admit when they do not know answers to all questions, and able to view those occasions as opportunities to expand their learning.

2. Successful constructivist teachers are *creative.* Effective teachers find ways to make deficient materials effective. They are masters at adapting others' ideas, and they become comfortable taking risks with the unknown. They encourage creativity in students by being creative themselves.

3. Successful constructivist teachers are *flexible.* Inquiry takes time. Students need time to explore, think, and ask questions. Successful constructivist teachers are patient and use time flexibly to afford children the time they need for effective inquiry learning.

4. Successful constructivist teachers use effective *questioning strategies.* Types of questions used, wait-time, and proper uses of praise, reinforcement, and encouragement are the fodder of inquiry learning.

5. Successful constructivist teachers *focus* their efforts on preparing students to *think* in order to construct meaning. The constructivist teacher wants students to develop an ability to solve problems. Successful problem solving depends on numerous thinking skills that arise from the processes of science that guide all phases of the inquiry. The end result of the inquiry process is the construction of scientific concepts. The end justifies the means, but exclusive focus on the end product does not provide the means for future problem solving.

Take the first step by beginning small. Trying to adapt all lessons into a constructivist approach is an overwhelming task and can be frustrating. If yours is a conventional textbook science program, focus on only one or two chapters at first by mapping the concepts (see Chapter 4). Then develop the material into good inquiry activities or find other supplementing resources. Add more each year, and soon you will have developed an effective collection of material. Combine your efforts with those of other teachers (particularly those who teach the same grade level), pool your materials, improve them, and help your program become more effective. Read journals, such as *Science and Children* for elementary teachers and *Science Scope* for middle school and junior high teachers. These journals, available from the National Science Teachers Association, contain activities reported by experienced teachers and describe new materials available through government-sponsored programs and commercial publishers.

chapter summary

The physical, life, and earth/space science content is an important context for developing scientific literacy. The standards require four new dimensions of science learning to ensure that real progress is made toward helping students experience the nature of science and achieve literacy. These new dimensions challenge us to help students understand science through processes of inquiry, understand the interrelationships between science and technology, benefit from science personally and understand the social perspective of science, and understand and appreciate the history and nature of science. Parts of the many outcomes for these new dimensions predictably overlap and complement learning. The challenge will be to find a way to link all of these dimensions of science learning and literacy to the content context.

Inquiry-based science teaching methods are interactive: Students and teachers investigate together and share many responsibilities that are carried only by the teacher in conventional classrooms. Construction of understanding is encouraged by a family of science teaching methods that promote student inquiry in a hands-on, minds-on way. Inquiry is a process, a way of pursuing learning. The outcomes of its methods are students' discoveries. Discoveries are mental constructions. All constructivist methods are based on a belief about the power of experience and socialization. The methods rely on effective questioning to promote concept development.

Several inquiry-based science teaching methods are described in this chapter. The science learning cycle is appropriate for concept development in all grades and is particularly well suited for implementing the new goals in science education described in Chapter 1. A feature lesson is included in this chapter.

Principles of scientific inquiry help us to develop an approach for turning what once were memory exercises into a powerful teaching and learning method. This approach is most suitable for the intermediate through middle school grades and lends itself to cooperative inquiry groups.

Suchman's inquiry method makes use of puzzling phenomena—discrepant events—that permit teachers to build on intrinsic motivation and turn children into questioners and pursuers of explanations. Playful discovery is a little-known inquiry method that was developed for very young children. Preschool and kindergarten children benefit from its playful atmosphere, accumulating agreeable and valuable experiences that help them build concept structures for later study. Problem-based learning revolves around children forming and pursuing solutions to meaningful problems. Classroom management can become challenging; therefore, we offer practical recommendations for using cooperative learning groups.

Effective teachers who use inquiry methods demonstrate several common attributes: They model science attitudes, are creative in their approaches to science material and flexible in classroom management, and tend to focus on developing children's abilities to think rather than on mere acquisition of subject matter. Research verifies the superior effects of student-centered constructivist approaches over traditional text-based teaching methods for science achievement and the attitudes and skills of scientific inquiry.

reflect and respond

1. What arguments support using inquiry science teaching methods? What barriers seem to limit the acceptance and use of inquiry in elementary classrooms? Will you use some of the methods described in this chapter? Why or why not?

2. What are the similarities and differences in the approaches described in this chapter? Under what circumstances would you favor any one approach over the others?

3. Why is it that as children get older and presumably more capable of thinking independently, they appear to rely more on an authority figure for information than on their own experiences for discovering it?

4. Inquiry methods tend to promote greater independence among learners. What are several things you can do to help students become more independent learners?

5. Inquiry teaching strives to accommodate individual student differences. Individual differences do, however, tend to complicate teaching. What are some things you could do to manage the diversity of individuality without losing your cooperative focus?

6. How do inquiry methods help children who are slow or fast learners?

Explore—Video Homework Exercise. Go to MyEducationLab at www.myeducationlab
.com and select the topic "Inquiry," then watch the videos "The Learning Cycle"; "Explanation"; "Expansion"; and "Evaluation." After viewing this series of videos that examine the
various phases of the learning cycle model, respond to these questions.

1. What roles did the teacher play during the various phases of the cycle?

2. How is the Exploration phase different from the Expansion phase?

3. How did each teacher use the students' experiences from the Exploration phase while
   striving for concept construction during the Explanation phase?

4. How do you think the teachers checked for student misconceptions during the learning
   cycle?

NSES

TS-B

Enrich—Video Homework Exercise. Go to MyEducationLab and select the topic "Inquiry," then watch the video "The Learning Cycle." Respond to the questions below.

1. Try teaching a science lesson using the method featured in the video. Determine the extent to which learners obtained and retained the points of the lesson. What does your
   analysis reveal? Which of the methods described in this chapter could you use, and how
   might you alter them to fit your learners' needs?

NSES

PD-B

Expand—Weblink Exercise

Science Literacy. Go to MyEducationLab Resources section and select "Weblinks," then
click on the link for "Rapid Changes in Biotechnology" for a complete explanation of why
you should be concerned about scientific inquiry within the context of the rapid changes in
biotechnology and the impact on citizens and public leaders; click on the link "Inquiry and
the Nature of Science" for a full description about inquiry and the nature of science to better
understand the processes that lead to discovery; and click on the link "Lesson with Primary
Aged Learners" for a lesson in developing inquiry skills among K–2 learners.

1. Why should you be concerned about scientific literacy?

2. Try this lesson with children in kindergarten through second grade and discuss with
   your methods class.

NSES

PD-A

CS-A

CS-F

How Can You Use Questions to Foster Scientific Inquiry?

focus questions

- How do questions support inquiry in science?

- How may different types of questions be used, and how do different questions benefit learners?

- How may teachers improve their questioning skills?

- How may children's questions be improved and used to reveal the nature of science?

Mrs. Barcikowski extended warm greetings to each child running into the lab. A table in the middle of the room was piled with rocks of many different types, colors, shapes, and sizes. Each child was encouraged to pick up several samples and look at them carefully. The children rubbed the samples, held them up to the light, and used magnifying glasses to make closer inspections. The room was buzzing with activity, including the predictable horseplay of a few students, and the buzz was punctuated with the exclamations of scientific discoveries. All the while, Mrs. B expressed her interest by asking many different questions that helped the children to sharpen their observations.

NSES
PD-B

Then she had the children gather around her. When all were seated, Mrs. B began making conversation with such casual questions as "How many of you have a hobby? How 'bout your parents or brothers or sisters? What are some of your hobbies?"

After a few minutes of listening and encouraging, Mrs. B said, "It seems that many of you collect different things for a hobby. Right?" Smiles and nodding heads gave her an entrance. "I do too. In fact one of my favorite things to do on vacation is to look for unusual rocks to add to the collection I've been sharing with you today. Would you like to see one of my favorites?" Holding up a smoothly polished, quarter-sized sample for all to see, and passing around others for them to hold, Mrs. B said, "We've been studying the concept of *properties* for many of our lessons. Let's use properties to help us study rocks. What kinds of properties do you observe in this rock?" The children's observations were accepted with encouragement and occasional praise. Another key question Mrs. B asked was, "What other rocks from our pile seem like this one?"

After noticing variety in the color, size, and shape of the other samples, a child pointed out that some of them were more different than alike.

"True," Mrs. B confirmed. "I guess we need to focus a bit. What property appears to be the same in each of the samples?"

"Crystals?" offered a child.

"That's right! This type of rock is known especially for its crystals. What kind of rock do you think this is?" Mrs. B reminded the children to refer back to their observations while they tossed ideas around among themselves. She watched them closely and then invited Elizabeth, who seemed unsure, to venture a guess.

"Well, it looks kinda milky so I guess it's called . . . a 'milk rock?'" asked Elizabeth as she groped for an answer. The other children laughed, but Mrs. B reminded them to be polite; then she smiled as she saw how a connection could be made.

"I know you go to the grocery with your parents. What sizes of containers does milk come in?"

Elizabeth thought to herself: gallon? Half gallon? Somehow those didn't seem right. Then an idea came to her. "A quart rock?" Elizabeth hesitantly asked.

"Good try. Almost, Elizabeth, just one more letter," encouraged Mrs. B as she wrote the word *quart* on the lap chalkboard and held it up for all to see. "Let's add a *zzz* sound to this and see what we have. *Q-u-a-r-t-z*. What does that spell, Elizabeth?"

"Quartz!" exclaimed Elizabeth, with emphasis on the *z*.

"Now everyone," encouraged Mrs. B.

For the next several seconds, the class spelled and pronounced the new word like cheerleaders. Then Mrs. B referred them back to the samples and continued her questions, always waiting patiently, and encouraging and building on the children's ideas. She paused periodically to add a point or two of her own. By the lesson's end the children had learned that quartz is a common mineral found in rocks and comes in many different colors. When polished smooth, quartz may be used in jewelry as a semiprecious stone, and quartz crystals are used to manufacture prisms, lenses, watches, computer chips, and other electronic gadgets. They even learned that the scientific name is silicon dioxide, SiO_2.

In teaching science through inquiry processes, scientific literacy is not regarded as a collection of facts and recipelike steps to follow; science is a way of thinking, reasoning and making meaning from essential experiences (Van Tassell, 2001), so the essence of inquiry lies "in the interaction between the student and the materials, as well as in the teacher-student and student-student interactions that occur dozens of times each and every class period" (NRC, 2000, p. 90). Within an inquiry-based framework, questions are tools for planning, teaching, thinking, and learning. What do you know about classroom uses of questions and your own questioning skills? It is typical for teachers to use questions intuitively or even out of habit. Some may even achieve satisfactory results. Yet considerable research suggests that many teachers do not realize that modest improvements in their questions can result in substantial gains for their students. In science, the students' questions play an important role in the nature of their inquiry and in their learning; they need to be encouraged. The National Science Education Standards' Teaching Standard B (NRC, 1996, p. 32) prompts teachers to guide and facilitate learning by:

- focusing and supporting inquiries while interacting with students;
- orchestrating discourse among students about scientific ideas;
- challenging students to accept and share responsibility for their own learning;

- recognizing and responding to student diversity and encouraging all students to participate fully in science learning; and

- encouraging and modeling skills of scientific inquiry, as well as the curiousness, openness to new ideas and data, and skepticism that characterize science.

Effective teachers use productive questions to help students advance in their thinking. Effective teachers use questions to focus on what is important, orchestrate productive discussions, sharpen process skills, build positive scientific attitudes, and increase understanding (Krueger & Sutton, 2001). Effective questioning enables a teacher to construct a mental framework for helping students to construct their own understandings. How can you develop and use productive questions to promote science inquiry?

The mission of this chapter is to:

1. raise questions about questions and report the effects that questions have on students' achievement, attitudes, and thinking skills;

2. explore the different types and uses of questions;

3. investigate how questions can be used to foster inquiry;

4. offer some suggestions you can use to monitor and improve your own questions; and

5. provide a rationale and suggestions for using students' questions as an important part of your teaching for inquiry and discovery.

Questions on Questions

NSES
PD-C

What is a question? We use questions often, but do you know much about their proper uses and effects? Following are seven important questions about questions. Try answering them from what you already know. Then read on to check your answers. How well informed are you about this most potent teaching tool?

1. What kinds of questions do teachers ask, and what kinds of answers do they require?

2. Why do teachers use questions?

3. How do questions affect students?

4. How are teacher questions and student answers related?

5. How do teachers use questions to involve *all* students?

6. What is wait-time, and why is it important?

7. What types of questions are used most in elementary science books and tests?

What Kinds of Questions Do Teachers Ask and What Kinds of Answers Do They Require?

According to studies of typical science classrooms, most questions demand little of students, and the preponderance of questions are low level. Examples of low-level questions include: yes/no, guess, remember facts, leading and rhetorical, and questions answered by the teacher (Krueger & Sutton, 2001). Research verifies that elementary teachers use questions more than any other teaching tool. For example, one study reports that third-grade teachers asked reading groups a question every 43 seconds (Gambrell, 1983); while another study found that teachers ask as many as 300 to 400 questions each day, the average being 348 (Levin & Long, 1981). Most researchers agree that the number of teacher questions depends on the nature of the activity. Even so, teachers ask between 30 and 120 questions per hour (Graesser & Person, 1994). Most of these questions are asked in a rapid-fire question-answer pattern. The pattern and extent of question use have changed little in nearly seventy-five years, with teachers asking about 93 percent of all questions and children receiving little time to respond or opportunity to ask their own questions. This type of limited questioning is ineffective and does not support inquiry.

Knowledge and comprehension of content make up at least 70 percent of the questions, and questions that require application, analysis, synthesis, or evaluation thinking are used much less often (Martin, Wood, & Stevens, 1988). In the context of the National Science Education Standards, teachers who ask for facts appear to be poor role models for productive questions that stimulate inquiry (Graesser & Person, 1994). It has been shown, over time, that teachers who ask for answers to facts actually encourage fewer students to ask fewer questions (Marbach-Ad & Sokolove, 2000). However, as students mature, they do ask more questions, but this occurs outside of the classroom (Dillon, 1988). The culture of inquiry that teachers hope to establish is often limited by these uses. Progress toward inquiry can be made by thinking about how we wish to use questions and the impact that our questioning can have on learners.

Why Do Teachers Use Questions?

According to Mary Budd Rowe (1973), a science educator, teachers use questions for three main purposes:

1. to evaluate or to find out what the pupils already know,
2. to control the functions of the classroom: inquisition used as a classroom management strategy or to reduce off-task behavior, and
3. to instruct children by suggesting resources and procedures, focusing observation, pointing out differences and discrepancies.

Questions have other uses as the stock-in-trade of teachers, and the potential far exceeds Rowe's three fundamental uses (see Table 6.1).

How Do Questions Affect Students?

Teachers' questions influence students in three areas: attitudes, thinking, and achievement.

Attitudes influence how students participate, think, and achieve. Students with positive attitudes tend to look more favorably on a subject, teacher, or method of teaching.

TABLE 6.1 ● How Can Teachers Use Questions?

• To arouse students' interest and motivate participation	• To provide listening cues for students with difficulties and to focus inattentive students' attention
• To determine students' prior knowledge before a lesson begins	• To diagnose students' strengths and weaknesses
• To determine students' thoughts and other information essential to a problem before it is explored	• To help students develop concepts or see relationships between objects or phenomena
• To guide students' thinking toward higher levels	• To review or summarize lessons
• To discipline disruptive students by asking them to explain their behavior	• To informally check students' comprehension
	• To evaluate planned learning outcomes, such as performance objectives

What other uses can you add to this list?

Students with negative attitudes often link them to a subject, school experience, or teacher and tend to resist and perform poorly. From his research, William Wilen (1986) concludes that teachers' uses of questions play an important part in shaping children's attitudes, thinking, and achievement. "Students must develop positive attitudes toward higher-level questioning if instructional approaches such as inquiry are to be effective," Wilen (1986, p. 21) writes.

Forty years ago, Hilda Taba (Taba, Levine, & Elsey, 1964) discovered that teachers' questions influenced students' levels of thinking. Teachers expected students to think at a certain level (according to Bloom's taxonomy of the cognitive domain), composed and used questions for the expected level, and then awaited responses from students that matched their expectations. Teachers can and do control the thought levels of students (Arnold, Atwood, & Rogers, 1973). In fact, Gallagher and Aschner (1963) reported that a mere 5 percent increase in divergent questioning can encourage up to a 40 percent increase in divergent responses from students. Divergent thinking is important for problem-solving tasks and for learning that requires creativity. Also, high-level questions help students to evaluate information better and improve their understanding of lower-level facts (Hunkins, 1970).

Appropriate questions can improve children's attitudes, thinking, and achievement.

How pupils think must match the requirements of teachers' methods if students are to become confident learners. The questions learners ask are indicators of the thinking they are doing and of the impact of teachers' questions.

Questions can make the difference between learning from *meaningful* manipulation of materials and from *meaningless* messing around. This belief is based on a process-product model of classroom learning, in which specific teaching behaviors provide useful pupil learning experiences. The product of this process is pupil achievement. This model suggests that "increases in the quantity and quality of pupil behaviors should result in concomitant increases in pupil achievement" (Tobin & Capie, 1982, p. 3). The assumed increases are attributed to the quality of verbal interaction. For example, teachers and students are reported to talk about 71 percent of the time in activity-based classrooms, compared to 80 percent of the time in nonactivity-based classrooms. In average activity-based elementary science classrooms, 29 percent of the questions are at a high level, while only 13 percent of teachers' questions are high level in average nonactivity-based classrooms (Bredderman, 1982).

Do the changes in verbal interaction make a difference? Apparently, yes. The studies here are limited, but the results show that a teacher's questions can produce pupil achievement that is superior to levels attributed to written questions found in textbooks and on worksheets (Rothkopf, 1972; Hargie, 1978). Some earlier studies appear to conflict with this conclusion (Rosenshine, 1976, 1979). However, more recent studies suggest that key ingredients of effective verbal interaction may have been missing in the earlier research. For example, Kenneth Tobin (1984) describes increased achievement for middle-school students in science when teachers redirected questions, used probing strategies, and used wait-time to increase students' discourse and reaction. Higher-level questions seem to stimulate greater science achievement when combined with a longer wait-time (Riley, 1986).

How Do Questions Create Independent Thinkers?

by Ursula M. Sexton

Grades 1–5, Green Valley Elementary School, Danville, California

NSES

TS-E

I have moved away from pouring information, most of which students forget, to facilitating discussions, providing opportunities for explorations and ways to assess our progress and goals. I guess you could say I've gone from being an informational witness to becoming a thinking coach.

I am now defining my teacher role as one who provides the means for my students to make connections with big ideas; guides them through process oriented activities; demonstrates circumstances that would otherwise be dangerous, foreign, or inaccessible to them; and who is the listener and facilitator. This role works best when students are given situations, open-ended explorations, dynamic roles, and the tools or options to build, to research, to communicate, and to share their thinking. I tell my students our most frequently used questions should be: "Why do you think so?" "How can you support it?" "What do you mean by that?" "How does it work and why?" and "What do you think would happen if . . .?"

Some ideas foster a climate not only for higher-thinking questions and answers but for inclusion of all students:

• Set the stage like a mystery scene, in which students are given the clues, and they need to prove that these clues are valid to solve the mystery, or they need to use them to

find further clues (process skills). They share with the class their approaches and solutions, back them up, and record them on graphs, videotape, illustrations, journals, or portfolios.

• Provide scenarios to visualize, make mental images, or think of characteristics by which they can describe an object, animal, plant, place, person, or situation. We make and brainstorm umbrellas of big ideas for categorization, such as color, weight, time, location, traits, extinct or not, parts, functions, habitats, means of survival, and so on, and hang them around the room for reference.

• Give plenty of opportunities and different materials and means to classify and label their sorting. This one is especially dear to me, because it was my wake-up call to learn to encourage and understand the children's thinking. One day, my little first-grade scientists were reviewing the process of classification by sorting ourselves into three groups. I would point to a child and direct him or her to an assigned area in the classroom, within clear sight of the rest of the class. To play, they could not call out the answer to the rule or pattern being sorted, but had to point to the team they thought they belonged to, once they studied it and recognized the rule. If they were correct, they would stand with the team. If not, they would remain seated for a

How Are Teacher Questions and Student Answers Related?

Raising the level of questions is all well and good, but it makes a difference only if students actually think and respond on the level elicited by the questions. Is this what happens?

Greater use of higher-level questions may be a significant difference between hands-on science learning and traditional teaching, according to Ted Bredderman (1984). He reports a direct relationship between the level of questioning and the level of response in elementary science lessons. Bredderman observed specially trained teachers raising the level of questioning in reading lessons. His research suggests that questioning levels "can be raised through activity-based science training, which could have the effect of raising the cognitive level of classroom discourse and could result in increased achievement" (Bredderman, 1984, pp. 289–303). Other researchers found that higher-level questions had a positive influence on the language development of young children and on skills such as analytical thinking (Koran & Koran, 1973; Kroot, 1976). What is the general conclusion? There is a positive relationship between higher-level questions later turn. At the end, everyone was standing in one of the teams. As I inquired what their team characteristic or pattern was, most children called out what I, as the chooser, had made for the rule. "We all have turtlenecks," called one. "We all have collars," said the others. Finally, in the third team, the speaker said, "We all have jackets." At that moment, one of the girls in the middle team said, "I thought I was here because we all have red and none of the other teams do." Indeed, she was right! So I decided to capitalize on the thought and asked the rest of the class, "Can you think of any other ways by which we all might be sorted while in the teams we are in now?" Oh! it was just wonderful to hear their reasoning! They were very proud of themselves. These are the circumstances that teachers need to act upon repeatedly throughout the day and not in isolated instances. Becoming aware of them takes a little self-training and practice.

- "What ifs . . . ?" are just wonderful, open-ended questions that can be connected to real-life circumstances.
- Have a discovery corner with manipulatives and questions promoting scientific processes.
- Have the children design new questions to go along with the discovery corner boards for another class to try out.

One of the most important elements of science instruction is the teacher's attitude toward science. Your own attitude toward learning will be the underlying gift you pass on to your kids. If and when you need to be the guide, do it with enthusiasm. Facilitate in a motivating, nonthreatening, and enthusiastic manner. If you were asked to write a newspaper advertisement for a science classroom guide and facilitator, what would you write? Check how this description matches the way you teach in the classroom. Take notes on your style if you need to focus more in this direction. You will probably be pleasantly surprised to see how much you really do to foster the children's previous knowledge and their questions. When you introduce new concepts, ask yourself, "New to whom? To a few? How new? New to me? What questions might they have that will definitely show growth when we are done learning about them? What am I learning from this process?" Listen to their discussions and their questions; take notes. Make comments, bring to light awesome and small achievements, discoveries, questions that foster further questioning. With ownership of their thinking processes, they'll become independent thinkers. As far as assessment, remember that tests are merely a reflection and a tool to tell how well you've conveyed a message and how well they have received it. This is why assessments should be ongoing—by observation, cooperation, participation, and communication.

I have learned so much from my students' attitudes about learning, their questions, their inquisitiveness or lack of it, and their experiences. The gifts they bring on their own are assets to all. It is because of them that I enjoy teaching. They challenge me on a daily basis. I grow with them on a daily basis.

and higher-level student answers (Barnes, 1978). We recommend using more advanced questions to obtain more thoughtful answers from children.

How Do Teachers Use Questions to Involve *All* Students?

Exemplary teachers treat different pupils equitably and are capable of adapting instruction according to student needs, including the levels of questions they use. How equitable is the questioning treatment that is found in typical elementary classrooms?

Studies done in urban classrooms show that teachers call on students whom they perceive as high achievers more frequently than on students they perceive as low achievers. Also, teachers are less likely to react to the responses received from low achievers. Usually, when high achievers hesitate to answer, they are given more time to think. Low achievers often receive less time to think and respond, perhaps out of regard for the students' feelings. High achievers also receive more opportunities to exchange ideas with teachers at higher thought levels (Krueger & Sutton, 2001). Similar data show questioning differences between Caucasian and African American students, with

African American males most deprived of opportunity (Los Angeles Unified School District, 1977).

Unfortunately, girls may feel shortchanged because they often perceive that they are given fewer opportunities than boys to answer questions. As well, some classrooms reveal that boys may be treated preferentially by their teachers and are involved more often in higher-level questions than girls. The result can be that boys feel a more positive experience and form a more positive attitude (Altermatt et al., 1998).

However, perceptions and reality of the research on gender and questioning appear to be misaligned. Altermatt, Jovanovic, and Perry (1998, p. 516) provide a historical summary of widely perceived interaction differences between children and their teachers. For example, as in prior studies reported, it is widely believed that:

- boys report more positive interactions with their teachers than girls do;
- boys report more opportunities to answer questions than girls do;
- boys perceive more individual treatment, encouragement, and feedback from their teachers;
- boys are involved in more higher-level questioning than girls are;
- many teachers spend more quality academic time with boys than with girls;
- perceived differences in pupil-teacher interactions, as related to gender, contribute to differences in achievement and attitudes; and
- teacher bias exists when teachers call more on boys than on girls at rates that are disproportionate to the numbers in classrooms.

Interestingly, more recent research suggests that the differences are not so systematic as to fall along lines of gender; rather, the "students themselves may play in influencing the numbers and types of questions to which they are asked to respond" (Altermatt et al., 1998, p. 524). When adjusted for volunteers in proportion to the number of males and females in the same classes:

- boys and girls are asked similar questions;
- teachers do not consistently demonstrate overall bias toward boys;
- teachers are influenced by the proportion of students who volunteered to answer questions;
- teachers do call more often on boys when the volunteer pool is dominated by boys; and
- teacher perceptions and gender preference do not seem to influence the opportunities for classroom interaction, but inequities do remain and tend to exclude some learners, particularly those who are not assertive or who do not volunteer.

What Is Wait-Time and Why Is It Important?

Pause for a few seconds, and think about what happens when you are the student and a teacher asks you a question. Unless you have memorized the answer, you must decode the meaning of the question (no small task if it is unclear or if multiple questions are used); think, "What do I know?" about the question's possible answer; ask, "How can I say the answer without sounding foolish?"; actually form the answer; and then give the response to the teacher. All of these steps take time, as Figure 6.1 suggests.

Wait-time is defined in different ways, but two types of wait-time are usually recognized. *Wait-time 1* refers to the length of time a teacher waits for a student to respond. *Wait-time 2* is the length of time a teacher waits after a student has responded before the teacher reacts to what was said. Several teachers have improved student thinking by

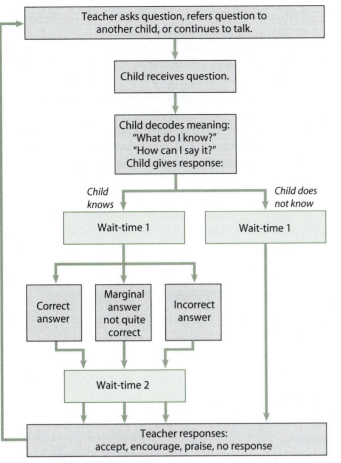

FIGURE 6.1 ● Questioning Map: Students Need Time to Think What happens after a learner asks a question?

Teacher asks question, refers question to another child, or continues to talk.

Child receives question.

Child decodes meaning:
"What do I know?"
"How can I say it?"
Child gives response:

Child knows

Child does not know

Wait-time 1

Wait-time 1

Correct answer

Marginal answer not quite correct

Incorrect answer

Wait-time 2

Teacher responses:
accept, encourage, praise, no response

"practicing quietness through longer wait-times, attentive silence, and reticence" (van Zee et al., 2001).

How long do teachers typically wait? Rowe (1974) first researched this topic and reported that an average for wait-time 1 was 1 second. Wait-time 2 was equally short, with teachers often only parroting the students' answers or providing very low-value feedback such as, "Okay," "Uh-huh," or "Good." Many teachers wait about 1 second for students to respond, without any adjustment for the difficulty of the question and then almost immediately react to what the students have said without giving the response much thought. "Evidently students are expected to respond as quickly to comprehension questions as they are to knowledge-level questions," and teachers believe they can accurately predict what students will say (Riley, 1986). Under what conditions do you think wait-times of 1 second or less *are* appropriate?

There is a growing list of advantages we can expect from increasing the length of wait-times. Kenneth Tobin (1984) reports increases in the length of student responses, increases in student achievement, and changes in teacher discourse. Teachers tend to "probe and obtain further student input rather than mimicking pupil responses" (p. 779). Yet there is a possible threshold effect; a certain optimal length of wait-time exists depending on the type of question, advises Riley (1986). Tobin and Capie (1982) recommend an overall wait-time of

By allowing appropriate wait-time, teachers can encourage students to think carefully before answering. How might volunteerism affect who is selected to respond?

about 3 seconds with an approximate mix of 50 percent lower-level questions and 50 percent higher-level questions to produce optimal pupil responses. They advise us to establish the facts first to give the students something worthwhile to think about before we build on the base of knowledge by using higher-level questions. Tobin (1984) even suggests that an effective strategy is to ask the question, wait, call on a student to answer, wait, then redirect the question or react accordingly (see Figure 6.2).

Some teachers encourage cooperative types of learning by using the think-pair-share approach. A teacher asks the question and waits; students think about possible answers for 10 to 20 seconds; students then pair up and compare answers. A student pair is then asked to share its answer with the class.

Students might find the waiting time awkward at first and misinterpret your intentions. We have had considerable success with learners by telling them about wait-time and why we are going to use it, then cueing them to think before responding. Try waiting at least 3 seconds before you respond, and you may discover the benefits reported by Rowe (1970):

- Student responses can become 400 to 800 percent longer.
- The number of appropriate but unsolicited student responses increases.
- Failure of students to respond decreases.
- Pupils' confidence levels increase.
- Students ask more questions.
- Low achievers may contribute up to 37 percent more.
- Speculative and predictive thinking can increase as much as 700 percent.
- Students respond and react more to each other.
- Discipline problems decrease.

FIGURE 6.2 ● A Questioning Strategy for the Whole Class There are times when questions should be used with the whole class. This questioning strategy can maximize student involvement.

Source: This strategy is based on the research of Kenneth Tobin (1984) as reported in "Effects of Extended Wait-Time on Discourse Characteristics and Achievement in Middle School Grades," *Journal of Research in Science Teaching,* vol. 21, no. 8, pp. 779–791.

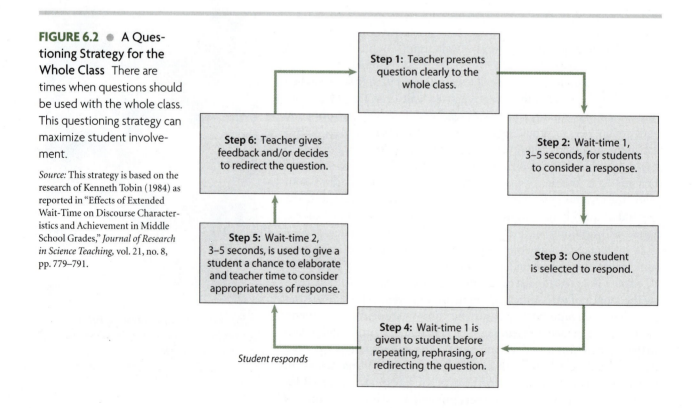

Step 1: Teacher presents question clearly to the whole class.

Step 2: Wait-time 1, 3–5 seconds, for students to consider a response.

Step 3: One student is selected to respond.

Step 4: Wait-time 1 is given to student before repeating, rephrasing, or redirecting the question.

Step 5: Wait-time 2, 3–5 seconds, is used to give a student a chance to elaborate and teacher time to consider appropriateness of response.

Step 6: Teacher gives feedback and/or decides to redirect the question.

Student responds

What Types of Questions Are Used Most in Elementary Science Books and Tests?

Textbooks have a profound impact on curriculum, teachers, and instruction because student texts and teacher guides often determine the level of questions. The accuracy and import of texts on learners remain a concern (Shepardson & Pizzini, 1991; Budiansky, 2001; Raloff, 2001). Questions, as we have learned, influence the extent of thinking and learning that takes place. Low-level questions have been consistently used in textbooks for several school subjects, but high-level questions have seldom been found. For example, of the more than 61,000 questions in history textbooks, teacher guides, and student workbooks, more than 95 percent were devoted to recalling facts (Bennett, 1986). Another researcher found that only 9 out of 144 lesson plans in the teacher guides from the basal readers of four major publishers contained questions distributed over Bloom's various cognitive levels (Habecker, 1976). Overall, elementary science textbooks are no better, but recent improvements are encouraging as publishers enact the science standards. Excellent resource experiment books are also available; they pose questions based on the science processes (see Figure 6.3).

These findings also raise concern for tests and the printed materials they represent. What types of test items are provided? Tests supplied by text publishers appear to be devoted to low levels of thought as well. Gregory Risner (1987) studied the cognitive levels of questions demonstrated by test items that accompanied fifth-grade science textbooks. When they were rated on Bloom's taxonomy, Risner found about 95 percent of the test questions were devoted to knowledge or comprehension, about 5 percent used for application, and 0.2 percent used for evaluation;

The questions below are representative of those found in books for children. Use these science processes to label the questions: observing, communicating, hypothesizing/experimenting, measuring, comparing/contrasting, and generalizing/predicting.

Process	Question
_____	1. Which plants seem to be sturdier: ones left in the sun or ones left in the shade?
_____	2. Most rain in clouds comes from the ocean; why doesn't it rain over the ocean and nowhere else?
_____	3. Which plant do you think will grow better?
_____	4. Do the creatures react to such things as light or shadows or an object in their path?
_____	5. What was the temperature?
_____	6. Which length works best?
_____	7. What can you move with the air you blow through a straw?
_____	8. Which seeds stick to your clothes as you walk through a weedy field?
_____	9. What happens to the number of breathing movements as the temperature drops?
_____	10. How long does the solution bubble?

Answers: 1. Observing; 2. Hypothesizing/experimenting; 3. Generalizing/predicting; 4. Observing; 5. Communicating; 6. Measuring; 7. Hypothesizing/experimenting; 8. Comparing/contrasting; 9. Generalizing/predicting; 10. Measuring.

FIGURE 6.3 ● Science Process Questions

*For a complete discussion, see Sandra Styer, "Books That Ask the Right Questions," *Science and Children* (March 1984): 40–42, or W. Harlen, *Teaching and Learning Primary Science* (London: Paul Chapman Publishing, 1993), pp. 83–86.
See sources for Figure 6.3 on page 190.

Using Questions in Science Classrooms

NSES
TS-E

One function of teaching science is to help learners develop higher levels of thinking. To do this you must facilitate better communication with and among your students. One way to encourage communication is by asking questions. Teacher questions can serve a variety of purposes, such as:

- managing the classroom ("How many of you have finished the activity?"),
- reinforcing a fact or concept ("What name is given to the process plants use to make food?"),
- stimulating thinking ("What do you think would happen if . . . ?"),
- arousing interest ("Have you ever seen such a sight?"),
- helping students develop a particular mindset ("A steel bar does not float on water; I wonder why a steel ship floats?").

Science teachers are concerned about helping students to become critical thinkers, problem solvers, and scientifically literate citizens. If we want students to function as independent thinkers, we need to provide opportunities in science classes that allow for greater student involvement and initiative and less teacher domination of the learning process. This means a shift in teacher role from that of information giver to that of a facilitator and guide of the inquiry and learning process.

Few children are able to construct their own understanding from an activity without teacher guidance. Productive questions help teachers to build a bridge between learning activities and student thinking. According to Mary Lee Martens, productive questions help learners to:

- focus their attention on significant details (What have you noticed about . . . ? How does it feel/smell/sound?);
- become more precise while making observations (How many . . . ? How often . . . ? Where exactly . . . ?);
- analyze and classify (How do they go together? How do these compare?);
- explore the properties of unfamiliar materials, living or nonliving, and of small events taking place or to make predictions about phenomena (What about . . . ? What happens if . . . ?);
- plan and implement solutions to problems (What is a way to . . . ? How could you figure out how to . . . ?);
- think about experiences and construct ideas that make sense to them (Why do you think . . . ? What is your reason for . . . ?).

Central to this shift in teacher role are the types of questions that teachers ask. Questions that require students to

analysis and synthesis questions were neglected completely. All types of questions are important, but consistent overuse of any one type can limit learning. You must be able to identify questions necessary for stimulating desired levels of thought and then build those questions into your teaching.

What Are the Different Types of Questions?

NSES
PD-B
TS-B

"Many innovative scientists would never have made their most important discoveries had they been unable to think divergently in their pursuit of the new. Through thinking nontraditionally and divergently, scientists like Copernicus, Galileo, Pasteur, and Salk discovered solutions, formulated theories, and made discoveries that revolutionized the modern world. The need for divergent thinking did not die with their achievements." (Pucket-Cliatt & Shaw, 1985, pp. 14–16)

These scientists learned to think divergently—broadly, creatively, and deeply about many possibilities. They learned how to ask the right questions at the right time. "Wrong questions tend to begin with such innocent interrogatives as why, how, or observe characteristics, recall data or facts have a different impact on pupils than questions that encourage pupils to process and interpret data in a variety of ways.

The differential effects of various types of teacher questions seem obvious, but what goes on in classrooms? In one review of observational studies of teacher questioning, spanning 1963–1983, it was reported that the central focus of all teacher questioning activity appeared to be the textbook. Teachers appeared to consider their job to be [seeing] that students have studied the text. Similar findings have been reported from observational studies of teachers' questioning styles in science classrooms. Science teachers appear to function primarily at the recall level in the questions they ask, whether the science lessons are being taught to elementary students or secondary school pupils.

Why doesn't questioning behavior match educational objectives? One hypothesis is that teachers are not aware of the customary questioning patterns. One way to test this hypothesis is to use a question analysis system.

You can do several things if you want to improve your questioning behavior by using a wider variety of questions. First,

> locate a question category system [you] can use comfortably and then apply it, during lesson planning and in postlesson analysis. Because of the variety of things that go on

during a lesson, a post-lesson analysis is best accomplished by tape-recording the lesson or at least those parts of the lesson containing the most teacher questions.

Are the kinds of questions you ask different? What kinds of teacher-student interaction patterns seem to exist? Are some patterns of interaction more effective than others? Compare your written and oral questions. Do they accomplish what you intend? If you use a variety of oral questions to promote different levels of thinking, quiz and test questions should do the same. Students quickly figure out what you value and then strive for it.

George Maxim offers practical suggestions for helping young children to improve their thinking through productive questioning:

- Use age-appropriate questions to stimulate children to think about concrete objects in order to form simple abstractions.
- Use questions to help children interpret the sensory information they received by manipulating objects and encourage them to exchange points of view with adults and peers.
- Encourage children who are entering the period of concrete operations (7–11 years) to uncover reflective abstractions by challenging them to answer "Why?" questions.

Sources: P. Blosser, "Using Questions in Science Classrooms," in R. Doran (Ed.), *Research Matters . . . to the Science Teacher,* vol. 2 (1985) (ERIC document no. 273490); M. L. Martens (1999, May). "Productive Questions: Tools for Supporting Constructivist Learning." *Science and Children, 53,* pp 24–27; G. Maxim (1997). "When to Answer the Question Why?" *Science and Children, 35*(3), pp. 41–45.

what" (Elstgeest, 1985, p. 37). Elstgeest provides an excellent example in this brief story:

> I once witnessed a marvelous science lesson virtually go to ruins. It was a class of young secondary-school girls who, for the first time, were free to handle batteries, bulbs, and wires. They were busy incessantly, and there were cries of surprise and delight. Arguments were settled by "You see?" and problems were solved with "Let's try!" Hardly a thinkable combination of batteries, bulbs, and wires was left untried. Then in the midst of the hubbub, the teacher clapped her hands and, chalk poised at the blackboard, announced: "Now, girls, let us summarize what we have learned today. Emmy, what is a battery?" "Joyce, what is a positive terminal?" "Lucy, what is the correct way to close a circuit?" And the "correct" diagram was deftly sketched and labeled, the "correct" symbols were added, and the "correct" definitions were scribbled down. And Emmy, Joyce, and Lucy and the others deflated audibly into silence and submission, obediently copying the diagram and the summary. What they had done seemed of no importance. The questions were in no way related to their work. The rich experience with the batteries and other equipment, which would have given

Questions can encourage children to develop science process skills.

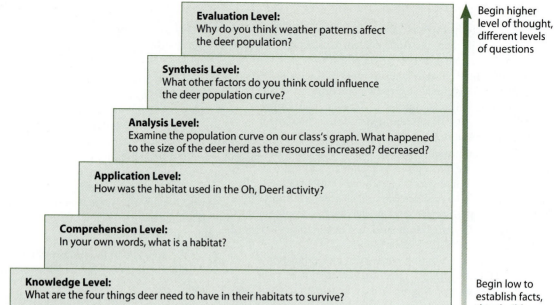

FIGURE 6.4 ● Bloom's Taxonomy of Cognitive Domain

Source: B. S. Bloom, *Taxonomy of Educational Objectives, the Classification of Educational Goals, Handbook I: Cognitive Domain* (New York: Longman, 1956).

them plenty to talk and think about and to question, was in no way used to bring order and system into the information they actually did gather. (pp. 36–37)

Elstgeest defines *good questions* as those that take a first step toward an answer, like a problem that actually has a solution. The good question stimulates, invites the child to take a closer look, or leads to where the answer can be found. The good question refers to the child's experience, real objects, or events under study. The good question invites children to show rather than say an answer. Good questions may be modeled after the science process skills in which learners are asked to take a closer look and describe what they find. Try matching the questions and skills in Figure 6.3.

There are several additional ways to classify questions. When presenting information from the research on questions, we have often referred to Bloom's taxonomy of the cognitive domain. It is possible to write questions for each level of the taxonomy. Figure 6.4, which gives examples of each level of taxonomy, is elaborated below:

- *Knowledge-level* questions request the memorized facts.
- *Comprehension-level* questions stimulate responses of memorized information in the students' own words.
- *Application-level* questions cause students to use information while thinking about how to put what they have learned to use in a new context.
- *Analysis-level* questions require that students break down what they know into smaller parts to look for differences, patterns, and so on.
- *Synthesis-level* questions stimulate children to consider variety, new ideas, or original possibilities.
- *Evaluation-level* questions require children to make choices and provide reasons.

The taxonomy suggests that learners cannot make a learned judgment until they know the facts, understand the facts, can apply the facts, can dissect the facts, and can reorganize the facts so that new perspectives are revealed (Bloom, 1956; Morgan & Saxton, 1991).

Educators often disagree about the level at which a question is written. This can make Bloom's taxonomy difficult to use, but it is worth learning. Spreading your questions across the taxonomy's range can make you a more effective teacher.

Gallagher and Aschner (1963) offer a simple and useful method for classifying questions. This method has four types of questions that address all of Bloom's levels and incorporate the science processes. The simplicity of this method makes it useful for all subject areas. Table 6.2 provides a level-of-thinking context; Figure 6.5 on page 176 provides examples of the following kinds of questions:

- *Cognitive memory questions* require students to recall facts, formulas, procedures, and other essential information. This is similar to Bloom's knowledge and comprehension levels and helps students to establish the facts before moving toward higher levels. Memory questions also assist observations and communication. *Examples:* "Do you see the bubbles rising from the liquid?" "What is the common name for acetic acid?"
- *Convergent thinking questions* cause students to apply and analyze information. To do this successfully, children must have a command of cognitive memory types of information. Convergent questions assist in problem solving and are useful for the basic science processes: measuring, communicating, comparing, and contrasting. *Example:* "What kind of chart, graph, or drawing would be the best way to show our class's results?"
- *Divergent thinking questions* stimulate children to think independently. Students are given little teacher structure or prior information; they are encouraged to do possibility thinking by combining original and known ideas into new ideas or explanations. Questions of this type require synthesis thinking and promote creative problem solving and the integrated science processes (hypothesizing and experimenting). *Example:* "Why do you think these seedlings are taller than those?"
- *Evaluative thinking questions* cause students to choose, judge, value, criticize, defend, or justify. Often the simple question "Why?" or "How?" propels thinking to this level after students are asked simple choice or yes-no types of questions. Processes stimulated by evaluation questions include making predictions, reaching conclusions, and forming generalizations. *Example:* "What things make a difference to how fast the seeds begin to grow?"

Science for many children, unfortunately, may be an exercise in closed thinking in which memory and convergent questions are emphasized. Children are prodded to seek

TABLE 6.2 ● Levels of Thinking Questions Require

Question Type	Level	Type of Thinking Expected
Closed questions	Low	Cognitive memory operations; convergent operations
Open questions	High	Divergent thinking operations; evaluative thinking operations

Source: A comparison of Gallagher and Aschner's questions as adapted from P. Blosser, *How to Ask the Right Questions* (Washington, DC: National Science Teachers Association, 1991), p. 4.

QUESTION CATEGORY			SAMPLE QUESTION PHASES
Evaluative Thinking	**Bloom's Evaluation Level:** • Make choices • Form values • Overlap critiques, judgments, defenses	**How and Why Reasonings:** • Choose, appraise, select, evaluate, judge, assess, defend, justify • Form conclusions and generalizations	• *What do you favor...?* • *What is your feeling about...?* • *What is your reason for...?*
Divergent Thinking	**Bloom's Synthesis Level:** • Develop own ideas and information • Integrate own ideas • Plan, construct, or reconstruct	**Open-Ended Questions for Problem Posing and Action:** • Infer, predict, design, invent • Hypothesize and experiment • Communicate ideas	• *What do you think...?* • *What could you do...?* • *What could you design...?* • *What do you think will happen if...?*
Convergent Thinking	**Bloom's Application and Analysis Level:** • Uses of logic • Deductive and inductive reasoning • Construct or reconstruct	**Closed Questions to:** • Focus attention, guide, encourage measurement and counting, make comparisions, take action • Use logic, state relationships • Apply solutions • Solve problems • Hypothesize and experiment • Communicate ideas	• *If "A", then what will happen to "B"...?* • *Which are facts, opinions, and inferences...?* • *What is the author's purpose...?* • *What is the relationship of "x" to "y"...?*
Cognitive Memory	**Bloom's Knowledge and Comprehension Level:** • Rote memorization • Selective recall of facts, formulas, instructions, rules, or procedures • Recognition	**Managerial and Rhetorical Questions:** • Simple attention focusing, yes-no responses **Information:** • Repeat, name, describe, identify, observe, simple explanation, compare	• *What is the definition of...?* • *What are the three steps in...?* • *Who discovered...?* • *In your own words, what is the meaning of...?*
Intended mental activity →		←	Key function or science process

FIGURE 6.5 ● Composing the Correct Level of Questioning: Higher Levels of Thought

the so-called right answer or to verify the correct results. Teachers should use both open and closed types of questions. *Open questions* are those that encourage divergent and evaluative thinking processes. Because they are traditional and expedient, *closed questions* have been used most often by teachers. Yet there is a danger associated with overuse of closed questions. "Convergent questions sacrifice the potential for many students to be rewarded for good answers, since their focus is a search for one right or best answer" (Schlichter, 1983, p. 10). Because science is a creative process, much more divergent thinking must be encouraged. Try your hand at classifying convergent and divergent questions in Figure 6.6, and experiment with both while you teach. Be advised that there are risks for teachers who use divergent or open-ended questions.

"The risks for the teachers who ask divergent questions should not be underestimated: an open-ended question can alter the day's schedule, spark discussion on topics the teacher may not be prepared for, and shift the teacher's role from guardian of known

Convergent questions mean to elicit the single best answer, while divergent questions encourage a wide range of answers without concern for a single correct answer. Use the letters C and D to classify the following questions:

_____ 1. What kinds of food make your mouth water?

_____ 2. What name do we call the spit in your mouth?

_____ 3. What is another name for your esophagus?

_____ 4. How do volcanoes form?

_____ 5. What do you think could be done to make it safer to live near an active volcano?

_____ 6. How many weights do you think you can add to your structure before it falls down?

_____ 7. Are you kept warm by radiation, conduction, convection, or all three?

_____ 8. Why does sound travel faster through solids and liquids than it does through air?

_____ 9. What kinds of uses does a balloon have?

_____ 10. How does electricity work?

Answers: 1. Divergent, because *how many different kinds of food make your mouth water?* 2. Convergent, saliva; 3. Convergent, gullet; 4. Convergent, distinct earth processes; 5. Divergent, numerous creative ideas are encouraged; 6. Divergent, because this question asks for a prediction that depends on several factors that stimulate many different answers; 7. Convergent, because you are asked to select an answer from those given; 8. Convergent, because a specific concept is used to answer the question; 9. Divergent, because who knows the answer to this one? Only your imagination limits the possibilities; 10. Convergent, because descriptions about electron energy transfer rely on a specific concept.

FIGURE 6.6 ● Identifying Convergent and Divergent Questions

answers to stimulator of productive (and often surprising) thinking. But they are risks well worth taking." (Schlichter, 1983, p. 10)

There are risks associated with using *any* type of question. What can you do to limit the risks? How can you learn to use questions more effectively?

What Are the Keys to Effective Questioning?

Plan specific questions. Take the time to write specific questions before you teach. List six to eight key questions that cover the levels of thinking you wish to promote, and then use the questions as a guide for what you teach. The questions should help to establish the knowledge base of information and then help to build toward higher levels. Avoid yes-no questions unless that is your specific purpose; instead, focus the questions on the lesson topic by building toward the objectives. Open-ended questions can stimulate exploration, and convergent questions can focus concept invention. Both, along with evaluation questions, can contribute to expansion of the lesson's main idea. Pay attention to the types of questions used in children's books; then select books and materials with many different types, and supplement them with your own questions for special purposes.

Ask your questions as simply, concisely, and directly as possible. Make your purpose clear, and use single questions. Build upon previous questions once they have been answered, and avoid multiple, piggy-backed questions. These confuse students and indicate that the question is not well defined in the teacher's mind.

Ask your question before selecting who should answer. This helps to keep all learners listening and thinking. Pause briefly after asking the question so that everyone can think about it. Then select an individual to respond. Give both high and low achievers a chance to answer, and try to provide equal and genuine feedback. Involve as many different types

NSES

PD-B

TS-B

Earth/Space Science:
Investigating Soil

Grades • 5–8

NATIONAL SCIENCE EDUCATION CONTENT STANDARDS–PHYSICAL SCIENCE—GRADES 5-8

▶ Earth/Space Sciences. Soil consists of weathered rocks, decomposed organic material from dead plants, animals, and bacteria. Soils are often found in layers, with each having a different chemical composition and texture.

Engaging Question

What is soil and how is it formed?

Materials Needed:

For exploration phase • conducted in teams of three or four, each team will need:

- Soil samples from local area
- Newspaper
- 1 sheet of white construction paper
- 1 magnifying glass/hand lens per student
- 1 pair of goggles per student
- 1 hammer
- Pieces of local rock

For expansion phase • conducted in teams of three or four, each team will need:

- 2 transparent plastic containers with lids
- Local soil samples with considerable amount of organic matter present

CONCEPTS TO BE CONSTRUCTED:

▶ Soil is made from finely ground rock and organic material.

SCIENCE ATTITUDES TO NURTURE:

▶ Open-mindedness
▶ Cooperating with others
▶ Investigating and analyzing science questions.

ⓘ *Safety:* Students must wear goggles while smashing rocks with hammers. Wrap the rocks in newspaper, and then strike them with a hammer. This will prevent rock pieces from flying and causing injury.

If you choose to take the students outside to collect soil samples, be sure that proper safety procedures are followed. Pair the students, and make sure they know the boundaries for soil sample collection.

Exploration

PROCESS SKILLS USED:

▶ Observing
▶ Classifying
▶ Recording data

Student Activity:

- Engage the class by posing the engaging question and involving the students in predicting answers. Explore by providing the class with soil samples collected from the local area, or, if possible, take the students around the school grounds to collect soil samples.

- Ask the students to cover their desktops with old newspapers and then place the white construction paper on top. Ask the student teams to use the magnifying glasses to make detailed observations of the individual particles found in the soil sample. Encourage the students to draw or write a description of their observations. Pose divergent questions to stimulate observations using basic process skills.

- After the students have made as many observations as possible, ask them to try to separate their soil samples into different parts. *Divergent question to ask: "How many different ways do you think you can use to separate the soil samples?"*

- Give each group a hammer and several pieces of local sedimentary rocks such as sandstone or limestone. Remind students to put on and keep on goggles at all times during this section of the activity. On top of the newspaper, ask the students to wrap the rock sample in more newspaper and then pound the rocks with hammers. Ask: *"How do the rock samples compare to the sediments you separated from the local soil?" (Open-ended evaluative question to stimulate independent thought)*

Explanation

Ask the students to share the results of their observations. As they share, use the following line of questioning to help the students invent the concept:

1. What kinds of things did you observe? (Convergent question—implies specific answers based on their observations)

2. How did the components of the soil compare in size? Shape? (Encourages detailed observations to respond to the convergent close-ended question)

3. How many different ways did you separate your soil samples? Suggestions may include size or color, rocklike, or plantlike. (Open-ended evaluative question)

4. What did your rock look like before you crushed it with the hammer? Afterward? (Convergent question—implies specific answers based on their observations)

5. How do the crushed rock and your soil sample compare? (Evaluative question asking for analysis and synthesis of results)

Continue using questions, moving from divergent types from the exploration phase to more convergent and evaluative questions to help the students create a working definition for soil: "Soil is made from finely ground rocks and organic material."

Expansion

PROCESS SKILLS USED:
- ▶ Observing
- ▶ Inferring
- ▶ Manipulating materials
- ▶ Classifying
- ▶ Estimating
- ▶ Predicting

Provide each cooperative group with two transparent plastic jars with lids. Ask the students to label one jar "*local soil*" and the second jar "*homemade soil.*" Ask the students to fill the first jar halfway with one of the local soil samples. Ask the students to place in the second jar some of the crushed rock they just smashed, some sand, and some grass clippings or leaves or some organic soil so that half the jar is filled. Into both jars pour enough water to cover all of the solid materials. Place the lids on the jars, and shake them vigorously. Solicit predictions about what will happen in each jar after it sits for one hour, for three hours, and overnight. Ask the students to record their predictions, and then place the jars where they will not be disturbed for the times indicated.

Use the following questions to help the students conclude that the rocks and plants found in the local area will determine the kind of soil that is formed. Weathered sandstone will create a sandy soil, more finely ground particles will create a silty soil, and very fine particles will create a clay soil.

Note that the questions start as close-ended, convergent questions. This is to help the students to focus on the expansion activity. Next they move into more open-ended divergent and evaluative questions—all designed to help the students create an understanding of the relationship between local rock and type of soil formed in the area:

- What did the two samples look like after one hour? After three hours? The next day?

- If you did not look at jar labels and just at samples, how could you tell the difference between the soil in the two jars? How are they similar? How are they different?

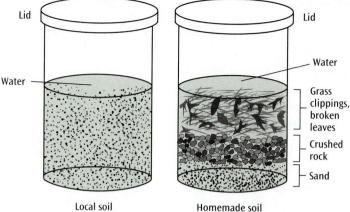

Local soil | Homemade soil

- Look at the settled materials. How much of the sample do you estimate is sand? Silt? Clay?

- On the basis of your estimates how would you classify the soil?

- What do you think will happen to the grass or leaves if you let the jar sit for one week, one month, or three months? Solicit predictions, and then set the jar in a safe place so that students can observe it over a three-month period.

- What do you conclude about the local rock found in the area and the soil type after looking at your results and the results of the whole class?

Science in Personal and Social Perspectives

- What kind of soil is found around your home? What types of plants would grow well in the soil? What types would not grow well? How might soil types affect agricultural decisions?

- Should people be concerned about farmers using excessive amounts of fertilizers in soils? Why or why not? What can be done to prevent excessive use of fertilizers?

- Do you think it is better to have a sandy soil or a silty soil in your garden? Why? Do you put fertilizers on your soil? If so, why?

Science and Technology

- As you have discovered, soils are not all alike. Do you think it was important to keep this fact in mind as tractor tires were developed? If so, why?

- What do you think *no-till* means, and why would farmers be urged to use this method of farming?

Science as Inquiry

- What are at least three components of soil?

- What influence does local bedrock have on the type of soil found in an area?

- How might the rate of weathering and erosion in an area affect the formation of soil?

- Where do you think the minerals that are found in soils come from?

History and Nature of Science

- What are the responsibilities of a soil agronomist?

- How important is it for a land developer to understand soil formation?

- What is organic farming? How do these methods of farming differ from other methods?

Evaluation

Hands-on Assessment

The students will be able to take a soil sample and demonstrate the steps necessary to estimate the amounts of sand, silt, and clay in the sample.

Reflective Assessment

The students will be able to explain in their own words how the type of soil that is found in a local area is dependent on the local bedrock and ground cover. They will also be able to write a persuasive argument on why grass is necessary to cover soil or on how soil is different from dirt.

Pictorial Assessment

The students will be able to draw and label the results of what happens to a sample of soil rich in organic matter when it is placed in a jar, filled with water, and shaken, then left to sit for three hours.

of students as possible, volunteers and nonvolunteers. The entire class shouting out answers could create discipline problems. Limit rapid-fire, drill-and-practice questions to times when specific facts need to be gathered or reviewed. Avoid parroting the students' answers, but do try to use the students' ideas as much as possible.

Practice using wait-time. Wait-time 1 is often 1 second or less. Practice waiting at least 3 seconds for students to respond to most questions, especially if students are exploring or trying to expand on the lesson's main idea. Wait-time gives the children opportunities to think, create, and demonstrate more fully what they understand. Higher-level questions may require a wait-time longer than 3 seconds.

Wait-time 2 may need to be longer than wait-time 1. Rowe (1974) believes that this wait-time is more important, especially when the occasion calls for critical or creative thinking. Quality and quantity of student responses increase, low achievers respond more, and the teacher has more time to think carefully about the questioning sequence.

Listen carefully to your students' responses. Encourage students nonverbally and verbally without overdoing the praise. Make any praise or encouraging remarks genuine. Check to make certain the children's responses match the level intended by your questions, and prompt them if the level is not appropriate. Do not always stop with the right answer. Probing benefits students who are partially correct and helps them to construct a more acceptable answer. As a general rule, do not move on to another student before giving the first student a chance to form a better answer. This is a great opportunity to gather clues about students' misconceptions, incomplete information, or limited experiences. A brief questioning sequence may be all that is needed to overcome important learning problems.

Try using questions to produce conceptual conflict. Piaget's research (Wadsworth, 1996) suggests that learners should be in a state of mental disequilibrium to help them adapt or add new mental constructions to their thinking:

- *What do you think will happen if* we add more weight to the boat?
- *If* we add a drop of soap, *then* what could happen to the surface tension?
- *How would you* design a test to determine the effects of fertilizer on plant growth?
- *What evidence do you have to support* your identification of the limiting factors?
- *What other ways are possible to* explain the effects of sunlight on plant growth?
- *How can you explain* to the others what you did and what you discovered?
- *What do you think causes* newsprint to look larger when viewed through a water droplet?

Talk less and ask more, but make your questions count. Ask, don't tell. Use questions to guide and invite your students to tell you. Work with students by exchanging ideas instead of conducting an inquisition. Try to make discussions more conversational by asking students to share thoughts and react to each other.

Try to use questions that yield more complete and more complex responses. Given consistently adequate wait-time, students should give longer and more thoughtful answers. The effectiveness of any specific question you use is never any greater than the answer you are willing to accept. Establish a base of information first; then build on it by asking questions that require more complex answers. Ask students who give short, incomplete answers to contribute more.

Ask different types of questions to encourage all children. Some learners seem unprepared for or incapable of answering high-level questions. If this is the case, try beginning your questions at a low level before attempting a higher level; build upward. Recalling information with frequent low-level questions for review, recitation, and drill helps children to experience success, develop confidence, and establish a reliable

Listen carefully; ask concise, direct questions; practice wait time; and match the level of the questions to the level of the child.

foundation on which to build higher thinking. But do not let your questioning stagnate. Begin with closed questions to establish a firm footing, and then move on to more open-ended questions. Use divergent and evaluative questions less often initially, and increase their use over time if your students have difficulty responding as you desire.

Learners who have already had more successful and satisfying school experiences are eager and appear more capable of responding to higher levels of questions sooner. Reflective discussions that mix convergent, divergent, and evaluative questions can form a strategy for critical and original thinking. Yet despite the type of student, several studies show that lower-level questions promote greater achievement gains for all primary children when learning basic skills.

Several learning theorists and researchers remind us about differences in how primary and upper elementary children think. Each group processes information differently because of differences in mental development. Yet appropriate experiences can help mental development reach its full potential in each group. Questions related to the processes of science provide the momentum for this development.

For younger children in the primary grades (ages 5 to 10), use questions that stimulate.

- Observation of basic properties. *Example:* "What do you see happening to the Silly Putty?"
- Classification based on similarities and differences. *Example:* "Which of these animals is an insect?"
- Communication to show thoughts and increase the value of the experience as well as to develop cooperation and interpersonal relations. *Example:* "What are you observing?" "How do you feel about what you see?"
- Measurement, using numbers and time. *Example:* "What is the final temperature?" "How much time did it take to reach that temperature?"
- Prediction to form guesses based on what is known. *Example:* "What do you think will happen to the brightness of the bulb if we use a longer wire?"

For older children in the upper elementary and middle grades (ages beyond 11), use questions that fall into these categories.

- Identification of variables. *Example:* "What variables did we keep the same?"
- Control of variables. *Example:* "What variables seemed to affect the size of your soap bubbles?"
- Formation of operational definitions based on verified information. *Example:* "From what we did in this experiment, how should we define 'force'?"
- Formation and testing of hypotheses to reach conclusions. *Example:* "Why did the electrical resistance increase in this experiment?"
- Interpretation of data from experiments. *Example:* "What do the green and pink color changes of the purple cabbage juice indicate?"
- Formation of models to explain occurrences or represent theories. *Example:* "What kind of relationship between the species is suggested by their population graphs over the same length of time?"

Determine whether the children are providing answers equal to the level of your questions. To do this you will need to monitor your questions and your students' responses.

Realize when not *to ask a question.* According to Morgan and Saxton (1991), times when it may not be appropriate to ask questions include:

- when students have insufficient knowledge and experiences from which to draw an answer (this is a good time to encourage children to ask *their* questions);
- when children are making progress on their own and your question would be an intrusion that impedes productive work;
- when students seem to be despondent or having personal problems. Instead of asking a question to which a student may feel obliged to respond, try making an observation such as "Tina, you seem quiet today" and then become an active listener if Tina chooses to do the talking.

How Can You Improve Your Questioning?

You can improve your questioning with training and practice. One way to improve is to videotape or tape-record a lesson in which you use questions, play back the recording, identify the questions, and analyze them. Observation instruments or checklists such as those in Table 6.3 on page 184 can be used. A more informative approach is to structure your observation and analysis around these questions.

NSES

PD-C

TS-B

- What kinds of questions were the most stimulating for learners to engage in the inquiry?
- What questions best nurtured development of process skills?
- How did you use questions to help learners construct conceptual understanding?
- What types of questions sustained or expanded the inquiry?
- How often did you use cognitive memory questions?
- How does this number compare to your use of convergent, divergent, and evaluative questions?
- How are your questions phrased? Do you avoid yes-no questions as much as possible?
- How do you know your questions are at the appropriate level for your students?
- What evidence do you have that you adjust questions to the language and ability levels of the students?

TABLE 6.3 ● How Effective Is Your Questioning?

Record a lesson, and use this checklist to help you examine your questioning skills.
When you teach and question, do you:

_____ 1. plan and record questions when preparing your lessons?

_____ 2. compose and choose different questions for a variety of purposes, such as exploring, observing, clarifying, redirecting, summarizing, explaining, expanding?

_____ 3. begin your lessons with questions to stimulate inquiry?

_____ 4. avoid using yes-no questions unless that is your specific intention?

_____ 5. focus your questions on searching for student understanding by removing emphasis from correct or incorrect answers?

_____ 6. use wait-time 1 effectively?

_____ 7. encourage students to ask their own questions?

_____ 8. help students improve their own questions?

_____ 9. use wait-time 2 to help you listen carefully to students' questions and answers?

_____ 10. expand on students' ideas?

_____ 11. avoid asking multiple or piggybacked questions?

_____ 12. avoid answering your own questions?

_____ 13. ask students to clarify, summarize, compose the conceptual explanation?

_____ 14. avoid repeating your questions and rephrase questions that are misunderstood or unclear?

_____ 15. talk less and ask more?

_____ 16. model self-questioning by thinking outloud about a problem?

_____ 17. use good grammar on a level understood by the students?

_____ 18. avoid using questions to punish or embarrass?

_____ 19. stop productive discussions after receiving the correct answer?

_____ 20. avoid repeating student answers and sounding like a parrot?

- Are your questions distributed among all learners regardless of ability, gender, socioeconomic status, and where they are seated?

- How often do you call on nonvolunteers? How do you decide which nonvolunteer to call upon?

- How often do you use probing to encourage students to complete responses, clarify, expand, or support a decision?

- How long do you wait? How do you use wait-time? What benefits do you receive from using wait-time? How does your use of wait-time 1 compare with your use of wait-time 2?

- How well do the written questions on your plan match the verbal questions you use in class? Do your test questions represent the same levels as questions used in class?

- How often do children ask questions? What types of questions do they ask? Under what circumstances do they ask questions?

Why Use Students' Questions?

"The children's questions worry me. I can deal with the child who just wants attention, but because I've had no science background I take other questions at face value and get bothered when I don't know the answer. I don't mind saying I don't know, though I don't want to do it too often. I've tried the let's-find-out-together approach, but it's not easy and can be very frustrating." (Jelly, 1985, p. 54)

Why Bother with Students' Questions?

"Can one black hole swallow another?"
"Why do fireflies light up?"
"How does a steel ship float when it weighs so much?"
"Why are soda cans shaped like a cylinder and not a rectangle?" (Pearlman & Pericak-Spector, 1992, pp. 36–37)

Children's questions give precious insight into their world and illustrate topics of interest. Their questions can surprise teachers who might underestimate the ability of particular children and can suggest that certain learners have more ability than is evident from their reading and written work. The questions that students ask also offer a guide to what they know and do not know, and when they want to know it. These questions give clues about what science content is understood and the level of concept development—if we are willing to listen closely. Questions could also indicate an anxious child, or simply reveal a habit formed by one who has been reinforced to ask questions (Biddulph, Symington, & Osborn, 1986).

Questions help students focus and gain knowledge that interests them. Incessant "why?" questions can be a method of gaining attention, but unlike the two-year-old, the school-age child who asks, "Why?" reveals an area in which understanding is lacking and is desired. Questions help young children to resolve unexpected outcomes or work through problem situations; they can also be a way of confirming a belief. Children's questions also help them to learn more quickly. "When they are following their own noses, learning what they are curious about, children go faster, cover more territory than we would ever think of trying to mark out for them, or make them cover" (Holt, 1971, p. 152).

Children's questions can become the center of inquiry. Children's questions reveal their ideas about a science topic, and they can be used to generate interest (Chin, 2007). Basing inquiry on children's questions:

- helps them to gain understanding,
- provides them a powerful incentive to improve their own information-processing skills,
- helps them learn to interact with ideas and construct meanings for themselves from an interesting situation or topic, and
- gives them occasional opportunities to learn from their own mistakes.

Encouraging students to ask questions develops a useful habit: reflection. Habits take time to form, and asking questions is a habit that can enrich a school's curriculum. Time spent in contemplation helps form this habit. Asking oneself questions and hazarding guesses about their answers stimulate creative thinking, provide a means for solving critical problems, and can help a child learn "to find interest and enjoyment in situations that others would see as dull or boring" (Biddulph et al., 1986, p. 78).

How Can You Stimulate Students' Questions?

Four factors stimulate children to ask questions. If you want children to ask more questions, you should provide adequate stimulation, model appropriate question asking, develop a classroom atmosphere that values questions, and include question asking in your evaluations of children.

Stimulation. Direct contact with materials is a first step. What kinds of materials stimulate curiosity in children and provide them opportunities to explore? The best indicator is the materials that children bring in spontaneously. The sharing has a built-in curiosity

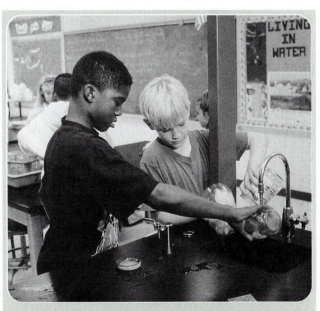

Children's questions can be used to develop interesting problems for science inquiry and to encourage the useful habit of reflection.

factor and requires little effort to conduct discussion; simply invite them to share and ask questions. The mind will be on what the hands are doing.

Modeling. Teacher question asking is modeling. Learners must be shown how to ask good, productive questions. Showing genuine enthusiasm and consideration for what interests others can show children how to do the same. Consider some of the following ways to bring this modeling into the routine of your classroom (Jelly, 1985).

Share collections and develop classroom displays, much as Mrs. B did in the opening scenario. Link these activities to regular classwork and organize them around key chapter questions. Use one of the question classification systems described earlier in this chapter to help you ask questions at many different levels. Invite children to share their own collections and create class displays while building questions into the discussion the children share with classmates.

Establish a problem corner in your classroom or use a "Question of the Week" approach to stimulate children's thought and questions. These approaches can be part of regular class activity or used for enrichment. Catherine Valentino's (1985) Question of the Week materials could be a good place to start until you acquire enough ideas of your own. Consider one of her examples, "I Lava Volcano," a photo of an erupting volcano, which asks these questions: "Do volcanic eruptions serve any useful purpose?" "Over millions of years, what changes would occur on the earth if all volcanic activity suddenly stopped?" Valentino's full-color weekly posters and questions stimulate curiosity and inquiry.

Prepare lists of questions to investigate with popular children's books. Encourage students to add their own questions to the list.

Use questions to organize teacher-made activity cards that learners may use independently. Encourage children to think of their work as an investigative mission and to see themselves as clue seekers.

Try a KWHL chart. Marletta Iwasyk (1997) describes the importance of modeling curiosity and productive questioning at the beginning of discussions by focusing basic questions on the topic of study and recording the children's answers to four basic questions (Figure 6.7).

For primary-grade learners Neil Dixon (1996) offers the "Planning House" as a metaphor for stimulating children to inquire and to record questions systematically. The roof of the house represents the outcome of the inquiry, which results from the planned steps taken, whereas the lower levels of the house show how children began the inquiry and then worked their way up toward the outcome question (Figure 6.8).

John Langrehr (1993) recommends two additional tools that teachers can use to model effective questioning and help learners improve their thinking and question-asking skills. Figure 6.9 provides sixteen question starters that should help any student to design focused, thoughtful questions. Consider the topic of insects. Using the question starters shown in the matrix, students should be able to expand their inquiry by

FIGURE 6.7 ● A KWHL Chart

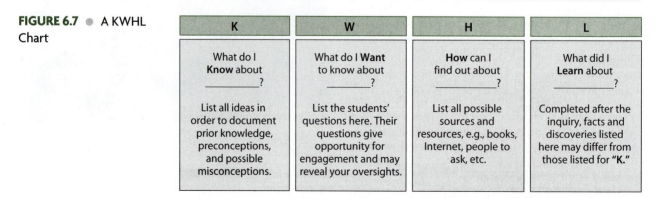

K	W	H	L
What do I **Know** about _____?	What do I **Want** to know about _____?	**How** can I find out about _____?	What did I **Learn** about _____?
List all ideas in order to document prior knowledge, preconceptions, and possible misconceptions.	List the students' questions here. Their questions give opportunity for engagement and may reveal your oversights.	List all possible sources and resources, e.g., books, Internet, people to ask, etc.	Completed after the inquiry, facts and discoveries listed here may differ from those listed for "K."

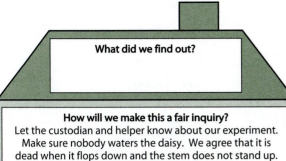

FIGURE 6.8 ● The Planning House

What did we find out?

How will we make this a fair inquiry?
Let the custodian and helper know about our experiment.
Make sure nobody waters the daisy. We agree that it is
dead when it flops down and the stem does not stand up.

What will we need?
A fully grown daisy in a pot.
A sunny window.

How will we find out?
We will keep the daisy inside in the classroom
window, and we will not water it. We will look at it each
day and draw pictures of how it looks.

What do we want to investigate?
How long can a daisy live without water?

asking questions such as: *What is* an insect? *How is* an insect different from a spider? *What can* insects do that humans cannot? *Where would* you expect to find insects? *Why might* insects be better able to survive a forest fire than mammals? and so on.

Langrehr also recommends that we show students how to use a *connection map* (Figure 6.10) to improve their questioning and construction of mental connections among and between the various ideas that may be illustrated by the map. Less able thinkers tend to think more generally, while more capable thinkers tend to think more abstractly. As a tool, the connection map encourages each student to record several key words in boxes that surround a central idea. Encourage students to write connecting words between the boxes that form simple sentences that make sense. This student-designed map can help you peer inside the thinking of the student. Simple questions such as "Why?" or "How?" can encourage students to construct more thought-provoking questions that stimulate productive experimentation.

	Object/Event	Situation	Reason	Means
Present	What is …?	Where is …?	Why is …?	How is …?
Possibility	What can …?	Where can …?	Why can …?	How can …?
Probability	What would …?	Where would …?	Why would …?	How would …?
Imagination	What might …?	Where might …?	Why might …?	How might …?

FIGURE 6.9 ● Question-Formation Matrix

Source: S. Langrehr, "Getting Thinking into Science Questions," *Australian Science Teachers Journal* 39 (4), (1993): 36.

FIGURE 6.10 ● Question Connection Map

Source: Adapted from J. Langrehr, "Getting Thinking into Science Questions," *Australian Science Teachers Journal* 39 (4), (1993): 36.

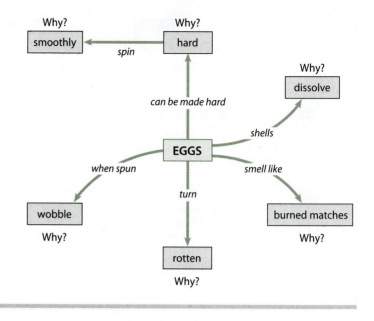

Classroom Atmosphere. Suchman (1971) believes that students inquire only when they feel free to share their ideas without fear of being censored, criticized, or ridiculed. Successful teachers listen to children and do not belittle their curious questions. Establish an atmosphere that fosters curiosity by praising those who invent good questions; reinforce their reflective habits. You can provide opportunities for questions by:

- using class time regularly for sharing ideas and asking questions as learners talk about something that interests them,
- having children supply questions of the week and rewarding them for improvements in their question asking,
- helping children to write lists (or record lists for nonreaders) of questions they have about something they have studied. These questions can be excellent means for review, for showing further interest, and for providing an informal evaluation of how clearly you have taught a topic.

Question Asking and Evaluation. Have students form questions as another way of evaluating their learning. This factor can stimulate habits of question asking and is different from if you, as teacher, ask questions children must answer. Include a picture or description of a situation in a test occasionally, and call for children to write productive questions about it. Another approach is to have students list questions they believe are important for a more complete understanding of the material they have just studied. Lists of their questions can be evaluated for the number and quality of the questions; quality should refer to the relevance of the question to the topic as well as the thought required to answer it.

How Can You Use Students' Questions Productively?

When children ask, focus your listening on the ideas represented by their questions. You will need to help them clarify their questions until they learn to ask better ones by themselves. Jelly (1985) offers a strategy you can use to turn children's questions into productive learning opportunities. Figure 6.11 is based on Jelly's recommendations.

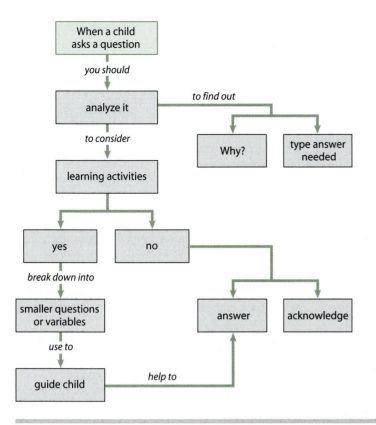

FIGURE 6.11 ● How Should You Respond to Children's Questions?

chapter summary

If there is a universal teaching tool, the question is it. Questions provide unique opportunities for teachers and students to become involved in productive dialogue; questions invite both teachers and learners to think and respond in many different ways.

We know that the potential of questioning is underused and that many teachers' questions are closed and stimulate low-level thinking. Questions may be misused if the wrong types of questions are used before children are capable or ready to respond at the level desired. Know when not to question. Productive questions stimulate productive thinking and curiosity. Effective questions contribute to students' improved attitudes, expanded capability for thinking, and increased achievement.

As teachers, we need to afford all learners equal opportunities to learn through our questioning techniques. Old habits may have to be changed. We must strive to give children adequate time to think by expanding wait-time; screening textbooks, tests, and other print materials for evidence of good questions; and helping them through the habit of inquiring and reflecting to ask their own questions.

Questions are not all equal; they come in many different types, such as Bloom's taxonomy, open and closed, science processes, memory, and evaluation. Questions should be selected or composed for specific purposes.

You can question well by using the keys for good questioning described in this chapter. Periodically analyze how you use questions and form a plan for self-improvement. Check your skills against your plan and revise as necessary.

Students' questions provide benefits for teachers, children, and the science program. Teachers can encourage learners' questions if they use materials and activities that stimulate questions, model good questioning skills, provide a supportive classroom atmosphere, and include children's question asking in evaluation techniques.

reflect and respond

1. On the basis of your experiences in classrooms, what differences have you noticed about how your teachers used questions? How do your elementary, secondary, and college teachers compare on using questions?

2. What types of questions do your teachers usually ask? How well do the questions match with the teachers' intentions? Justify your answer.

3. How do the teachers you have observed use questions to begin a lesson? To focus children's observations? To lead children toward conclusions? To bring closure to a lesson?

4. What priority do you believe teachers should give to children's questions? What strategy should they use?

5. How important is it for teachers to monitor their own uses of questions? What are some effective things you could do?

6. Observe a science lesson. Record the number and types of questions asked by the teacher, and try to measure the average wait-time. How do your observations correspond to the average uses of questions and wait-time described in this chapter?

7. If you were writing a letter to the teacher in question 6, what suggestions would you offer to help improve the teacher's questions?

Sources for Questions for Figure 6.3:
1. Seymour, S. (1978). *Exploring fields and lots: Easy science projects.* Champaign, IL: Garrard Publishing. 2. Bendick, J. (1971). *How to make a cloud.* New York: Parents' Magazine Press. 3. Seymour, S. (1970). *Science in a vacant lot.* New York: Viking Press. 4. Zubrowski, B. (1979). *Bubbles: A children's museum activity book.* Boston: Little, Brown. 5. Seymour, S. (1978). *Exploring fields and lots: Easy science projects.* Champaign, IL: Gerrard Publishing. 6. Renner, A. G. (1979). *Experimental fun with the yo-yo and other scientific projects.* New York: Dodd, Mead. 7. Milgrem, H. (1976). *Adventures with a straw: First experiments.* New York: E. P. Dutton. 8. Selsam, M. E. (1957). *Play with seeds.* New York: William Morrow. 9. Seymour, S. (1969). *Discovering what frogs do.* New York: McGraw-Hill. 10. Zubrowski, B. (1981). *Messing around with baking chemistry: A Children's Museum activity book.* Boston: Little, Brown.

PEARSON
myeducationlab
Where the Classroom Comes to Life

Explore—Video Homework Exercise. Go to MyEducationLab at www.myeducationlab.com and select the topic "Questioning Strategies," then watch the video "Questioning"; select the topic "Laboratory and Demonstrations," then watch the video "Cooperative Learning"; select the topic "Inquiry," then watch the video "Inquiry Learning"; select the topic "Questioning Strategies," then watch the video "Animal Classification." Skillful questioning guides learners toward making meaning from essential experiences and requires thoughtful design, use, and timing. After viewing this series of videos, respond to the questions below.

NSES

PD-A

TS-B

1. What are the different ways in which teachers can use questions? (Table 6.1 should be helpful.)

2. What examples of these uses did you notice in the video?

3. Consider what you understand about wait-time. What types of wait-time did the teacher use? How long did she wait? Did her wait-time seem appropriate? Why or why not?

4. Consider what you understand about inquiry. In what ways did the teacher help children to inquire? If you were teaching the lesson, what are some things you would do differently to promote inquiry?

Enrich—Weblink Exercise. Go to MyEducationLab Resources section and select "Weblinks," then click on the link for "SCENE: The Inquiry Process" to investigate the role of questioning in the inquiry process. Respond to the questions below.

1. In what ways do questions fit into and sustain the inquiry processes? What is it you notice about the purposes of questions (when used for inquiry) that stimulate and sustain a system of inquiry?

NSES
PD-C

2. KWL is a common graphic process for helping learners to interact with text to be read. The KWL process can be modified and used successfully to improve questioning and inquiry in science, such as KWHL. However, some learners are reticent to offer questions or find it difficult to pose productive questions. What is an alternative described at the MLS link, and why is this alternative recommended?

3. Try each method with children during your field experience or internship: *KWL* and *I notice, I wonder.* Report your results. Is one better than the other for obtaining productive questions? If so, why?

4. Investigate the Question Tree. How does it compare with the Chapter 6 techniques for using and improving children's science questions?

Expand—Weblink Exercise

Science Literacy. Go to MyEducationLab Resources section and select "Weblinks," then click on the link for "Using a Question to Start Inquiry" to learn more about how to create specific questions and how to use questions with learners to develop an experimental design.

NSES
CS-A
CS-G

How Do You Develop and Use Authentic Assessment?

NSES
TS-C

Late one February afternoon, as Jim Kestel, a first-year teacher, was completing the lamination of his fifth-grade students' science projects, he was dismayed by the comments he heard in the teachers' workroom. Two fourth-grade teachers were talking about the upcoming state achievement tests. "Well, I think I'm about ready to stop teaching for a while and get these students prepared for the upcoming state tests," stated Kim Carlson, one teacher. "Yeah, I know what you mean," said Al Rodriguez, the other teacher. "I've already stopped work on all of my students' science projects just so I can grill them on everything we've learned so far and give them practice taking multiple-choice tests. Most of the other teachers have already started prepping their students for them."

Jim sought the perspective of Joe Pokorny, another fifth-grade teacher, "Is it true that teachers stop *good teaching* just to get their students ready to take the state achievement tests? I always thought as long as I consistently challenged my students and gave assessments that required them to use higher-order thinking skills, like analysis, synthesis, and application, regardless of whether I *covered all* of the content, my students would be prepared to take these state exams! Am I wrong?" Joe just looked at Jim in amazement and said, "Oh, you poor, naïve, new teacher!" and walked away, shaking his head and laughing.

Worried that he was doing his students a disservice, Jim went home that evening and called his friend Kathy del Vecchio, who had been teaching science in a neighboring school district for over ten years. "So, do you think I'm wrong for not stopping teaching like the others to spend time grilling my students on all of the science I've taught them so far this year?" Jim asked Kathy, who was also a fifth-grade teacher. "Well, Jim, that really depends on what you've been doing as far as assessing your students this year. What does a typical test for your science class look like?"

"Well, I've actually used a number of strategies. In the beginning, when I wanted to find out how much they knew about a new topic, I tried pretests, but those soon became overused, since the students started feeling as if they had to get a perfect score. Then I stopped and taught them how to make a concept map when we completed our unit on rocks and minerals. So then, when we began a unit on electricity, I tried the idea of a concept map as a pre- and post-assessment. It was really neat to see how the maps changed from the beginning to the end of the unit."

"Okay. Those were pretty good strategies to find out what they knew to start with. How else did you know whether your students were learning the science content?" Kathy asked Jim.

"Well, as you know, I really believe in giving all students as many opportunities as possible to show me what they know and what they can do in science. So for each lesson I created, I followed a learning cycle format, making sure I had assessment built into every phase of the lesson. I identified the process skills the students used during the exploration and expansion phases of the lesson and placed those into a spreadsheet. Throughout the lesson, I just kept my computer open to that spreadsheet with the skills listed across the top and the students' names in the first column. When I saw that a student had mastered that skill, I just entered that into the spreadsheet. If I noticed someone was having troubles, I jotted a note to myself in the spreadsheet about that student, then tried to work one on one to help master those skills. Basically, I was assessing the students throughout every phase of my lesson."

"Wow, that sure seems like a lot of work," Kathy noted.

"Not really," said Jim. "Once I set up the initial spreadsheet, it was easy to just copy and paste for each new unit the skills I wanted to address. The hard part was disciplining myself to log in what I observed each day. Sometimes I'd walk around with Post-it notes and jot down things I observed on each student, then log in those notes later in the day."

"Okay, so that took care of the science process skills. What about content knowledge? How have you been assessing that?" asked Kathy.

"Well, for each unit, I really try to make sure I address just about every possible learning style by having a performance assessment—some sort of hands-on activity in which the students have to apply the science content to a new situation. I also include a picture that they have to interpret, or a picture for them to draw and explain the science concept. Then there's always a reflective question, something that causes them to think about the content in a way not used in class. Hmm . . . maybe I should try to include some multiple-choice questions in there so my students can handle those on the upcoming state proficiency tests."

"Whoa, Jim, don't be so quick to change what I'd call good assessment strategies. It sure sounds as if your students are really learning some science. Even if you don't *cover* every possible topic they might see on that state exam, it sounds as if your students have been challenged to think about what they're learning and how it's applied in other contexts. If you have a chance, go to the state department of education's website or the National Assessment of Educational Progress website. You'll be able to download some of the past years' tests. I think you'll be pleased to find that even though those tests are written in a multiple-choice and extended-response format, the kinds of things they want the students to do are no different from what you've been challenging your students with this year. If you are tempted to add some multiple-choice questions as an assessment, then please make sure they're not just written at the pure memory level. If you keep in mind what you told me earlier—that you're pushing for higher-order thinking skills—then be sure to write test questions that require those skills in order to provide a

194 chapter 7 How Do You Develop and Use Authentic Assessment?

correct response. I think you're on the right track, Jim, for a first-year teacher. The best advice I can give you is to ignore what you hear in the teacher's workroom. Continue to do what you *know* is good science teaching, and you and your students will be successful."

Assessing students' performance is essential if we really want to know our students have learned and can apply their understanding of the content in a new context. How *can* you assess student learning? Do you want to *test* your students, in the strictest definition of the term—to measure their worth? Or do you want to do, as the term *assessment* connotes—sit with the learner to determine what they know and what they can do with a particular concept? I doubt that the other teachers in the scenario who stopped regular instruction to give students multiple-choice tests that would provide practice in test taking would say they were measuring how *worthy* their students were. Like many teachers caught up in the *fears* that standardized testing brings to the schools, they think they are being *good* teachers by preparing their students to be successful on the exams.

Mr. Kestel's examples of assessment reflect the view that assessment is a means of gathering information about students—what they know and can do. Jim's assessment is authentic. He looks for habits of mind, rather than habits of recall. He uses assessment to monitor how well his students are doing and how he is doing as a teacher. His assessment supports exemplary science teaching. It is consistent with inquiry and constructivist teaching practices. Jim's assessment strategies require students to be active in their learning and in their assessment; and that teachers and parents play a more active role in collecting meaningful data about student performance. The assessing strategies that Jim described more accurately reflect and measure what we value in education.

How can you determine what the learners know and can do? In this chapter, we help you to:

1. explore the purposes and limits of evaluating learning;
2. investigate the need for alignment of lesson and assessment; and
3. compare the benefits of different assessment tools.

Evaluating Student Learning

Children learn more completely when they are focused on learning outcomes and objectives teachers want them to achieve because planning, teaching, and evaluation go hand in hand. This philosophy of assessment is consistent with the National Science Education Standards for assessment, as identified in Chapter 5 of the document (NRC, 1996). The five assessment standards state the following:

Standard A: Assessments must be consistent with the decisions they are designed to inform.

Standard B: Achievement and opportunity to learn science must be assessed.

Standard C: The technical quality of the data collected is well matched to the decisions and actions taken on the basis of their interpretation.

Standard D: Assessment practices must be fair.

Standard E: The inferences made from assessments about student achievement and opportunity to learn must be sound.

Purposes and Limits of Assessment

NSES

AS-A

Since the NSE standards were written in 1996, the quality of the standardized assessments that are used to determine student achievement in science has vastly improved. In looking at and analyzing the sample science test items that are shared on the department of education websites for many states in the United States (Sexton, 2006), it is evident that the test developers no longer rely solely on multiple-choice or true-false test items designed to address the lowest rung of the Bloom's taxonomic scale of questioning: pure content knowledge. Items are written to capture the higher-order thinking skills of analysis and synthesis—the practical applications of scientific content knowledge.

An analysis of items presented to fourth- and eighth-grade students in the 2005 National Assessment of Educational Progress (NAEP) Science exam reveals that multiple-choice test items are not the only type of questions that the test takers must answer. The students receive varying levels of multiple-choice questions from easy to medium to hard. They are expected to provide short constructed responses for some items and extended constructed responses for others. They are assessed in their abilities to know and apply scientific investigations, practical reasoning, and conceptual understanding (NAEP, 2007).

A good example of an easy multiple-choice item from the fourth-grade 2005 NAEP assessment as found on the National Center for Educational Statistics website (http://www.nces.ed.gov/nationsreportcard), the homepage for the NAEP, is as follows:

Which of the following is NOT a form of precipitation?

A) Hail

B) Wind

C) Rain

D) Snow

The following question, while still multiple-choice, is identified as a hard item for a fourth grader to respond to:

The surface of the Moon is covered with craters. Most of these craters were formed by:

A) Eruptions of active volcanoes

B) The impacts of many meteoroids

C) Shifting rock on the Moon's surface ("moonquakes")

D) Tidal forces caused by the Earth and Sun

Some critics would argue that items like these prove that national assessments do not provide an accurate picture of what children know and are capable of doing. The developers of NAEP have responded to those critics through short and extended constructed response items. An example of a *short* constructed response from the 2005 fourth-grade NAEP is as follows:

Sally is swimming in an outdoor pool. She hears thunder. What is the safest thing for Sally to do?

A) Stay in the water

B) Stand under a tree

C) Go into a building

D) Dry off and stand by the water

From what you have learned in science, explain why your choice is the safest.

An example of an *extended* response item on this assessment is:

List four ways that the Earth is different from the Moon.

Extended response items are scored as complete, essential, partial, and unsatisfactory/incorrect. Test items such as these require more time during testing and longer time for scoring; thus, they increase costs in the delivery and analysis of the tests.

Many states argue that they cannot afford to assess all of their students using the types of test items and analysis of the items that the NAEP employs. This is the most limiting factor of statewide assessments. Teachers then often become critical of the testing results when test items rely on habits of recall over habits of mind. Others argue that this type of summative assessment has little reflection on classroom instruction and student learning (Lee and Abell, 2007). It has been said that there is no substitute for a well-made teacher test to truly show what a student knows. Others will reply, "That's great and wonderful, but how do you know that you're truly testing what the state and/or national standards say the children should know?" The next section examines how assessment can be aligned with standards-based lessons.

Alignment of the Assessment and the Lesson

Exemplary science teaching requires students to be actively engaged in their learning. If they are immersed in a learning environment that gives them ample opportunities to demonstrate their understanding of the science content, their grasp of the science skills, and the formations of essential attitudes for science, then it is inconsistent to fall back on paper-and-pencil, pure knowledge types of tests that require recall of facts, or rote memorization, to determine understanding of what was taught. Authentic assessment strategies are designed to reveal what students can *do* instead of emphasizing their weaknesses. Students benefit when there is flexibility and variety in their learning activities. They also benefit when they are given multiple opportunities to demonstrate what they have learned by participating in those activities. The lesson "Simple Circuits," found in the feature lesson, gives students numerous opportunities to learn the concept of a *circuit* and to practice applying their understanding in various ways. How the student's knowledge is assessed is reflected in the learning outcomes stated in the evaluation phase of the lesson plan. These outcome statements reflect the kinds of activities the teacher directs the students to do throughout the lesson.

For a novice teacher, the question becomes "How can I write these outcome statements to be true to the meaning of authentic assessment and at the same time ensure that my students are proficient in the standards identified in the lesson?" One strategy to follow that helps to give "precision and clarity to teaching" is called a *table of specifications* (Guskey, 2005, p. 34). It can be used as a planning tool to describe the "knowledge and abilities that students must master to meet a particular standard" (Guskey, 2005, p. 34). Table 7.1 provides an excellent format to follow in completing a Table of Specifications. When appropriately applied, the outcome statements that are written in the Evaluation Phase of the learning cycle lesson plan will reflect each of the categories found in the table. Table 7.2 is an example of a Table of Specifications for the Simple Circuits Learning Cycle Lesson provided in this chapter. We have expanded on the "Knowledge of Facts" category, adding the term "concepts" to capture our belief that a conceptual approach to lesson development is more consistent with constructivist teaching principles. This completed table became the guide for writing the outcome statements in the Evaluation Phase of the lesson.

Evidence of understanding the concept of a *circuit* is not left for the end of the lesson, where a multiple-choice test would require the students to define the word *circuit* and the various types of circuits. While quizzes and/or prompts—such as homework

NSES
AS B-C
TS-C

Learning Cycle Featured Lesson

Physical Science: Simple Circuits

Grades • 4–6

Engaging Question

What does it take to make a lightbulb light?

Materials Needed:

For exploration phase • conducted whole class, each student will need

- 1 dry cell (D battery)
- 1 10- to 12- inch length of wire with ends stripped of insulation
- 1 flashlight bulb

For expansion phase • conducted in teams of three or four, each team will need

- 1 dry cells (D battery)/student
- 2 10- to 12- inch lengths of wire with the ends stripped of insulation per student
- 1 bulb holder and flashlight bulb per student
- 1 wire stripper
- 1 Phillips head screwdriver and a knife switch
- Scissors
- Aluminum foil
- 1 paper clip per student
- 2 paper fasteners per student
- Masking tape
- Small pieces of cardboard
- 1 cardboard tube (toilet paper tube) per student

⚠️ *Safety:* Students should be instructed not to use more that five dry cells in the same circuit to limit shock potential and to preserve light bulbs.

Exploration

Student Activity

Teacher's instructions to students: You have been given a
wire, a battery, and a bulb. Use
them in any combination to

light the bulb. Once you are successful, find three other ways to light the bulb. You can use only the three pieces of equipment you have been given. Carefully draw a picture of each method you used to try to light the bulb. Label your drawings *Will Light* and *Will Not Light*. Be certain to show exactly where your wire is touching and how your bulb is positioned with the battery.

Explanation

Have students draw their pictures on the chalkboard. Use your finger to trace the path that electricity from the battery flows through when the bulb lights and when it does not light. Tell the students that this path is called a *circuit*.

Using the students' own ideas and words, construct an explanation that a circuit is a pathway that electricity follows from the power source to the bulb and back to the power source. Show the students that contact with the bulb must be made in two specific places.

For the bulb to light, the path must be complete from the battery through the bulb and back to the battery. A key question to ask is "*In how many places must metal touch the bulb for it to light?*" The answer is "*Two; the side and bottom conductors of the bulb must be included in the circuit.*"

Expansion

Challenge the students to light more than one bulb; combine batteries for more power; and add equipment such as a bulb holder, a switch, and more wires. Ask what happens to the other bulbs when one is unscrewed.

Challenge the students to make a circuit so that all bulbs go out when one is unscrewed—a series circuit. Then challenge them to make a circuit so that the other bulbs remain lighted when one bulb is unscrewed—a parallel circuit or several separate series circuits. Look carefully to determine whether they truly created a parallel circuit. Construct a paper clip switch and demonstrate its function.

Science in Personal and Social Perspectives

• Name some devices you use that require an electrical circuit. What type of circuit is needed?

• What would your life be like without electricity controlled by circuits?

• How is electricity "made"? What resources are necessary? How has demand for electricity changed with population growth?

Science and Technology

A set of car headlights is one example of a specific circuit that is used for safety purposes. When one light burns out or is broken, the other remains lighted.

• What are other examples in which the type of circuit used is important for safety or convenience?

• A flashlight uses a simple series circuit and is an example of technology. How has the simple flashlight improved or affected your life? Your community? The world?

• Use the idea of a circuit to make a flashlight out of these materials: cardboard tube, wire, two D-cell batteries, flashlight bulb, paper clip, two brass paper fasteners, plastic milk cap, tape.

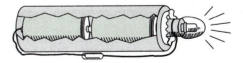

Science as Inquiry

Plan, conduct, and explain investigations that illustrate short circuits, open and closed circuits, and series and parallel circuits. Identify new concepts in new lessons, such as resistance, cell versus battery, and electromagnetism. Use the concepts of open and closed circuit to solve circuit puzzles.

History and Nature of Science

• Thomas Edison experimented hundreds of times before he successfully found a material that was suitable as a filament that could be used to complete the circuit in a lightbulb. How would our world be different today if Edison had never succeeded?

- Who needs to know about circuits? Name careers, and have students identify the careers that they previously did not know about that rely on some knowledge of electrical circuits. Some possibilities include electrician, appliance repair person, architect, city planner, electric power producer, computer engineer, car/truck repair person.

- How has the knowledge base changed over time for people in their careers?

Evaluation

Hands-on Assessment

Upon completing the activities, the students will be able to:

- Construct a working switch from cardboard, two paper fasteners, a paper clip, and two wires.

- Construct, demonstrate, and describe the operation of a series circuit and a parallel circuit. Each circuit must include at least two bulbs and be controlled by the paper clip switch.

- Construct a flashlight that functions properly. Students must show the teacher that the switch turns the light on and off.

- Cooperate with group partners, volunteer to assist peers who may need help in constructing the circuit, and demonstrate a positive approach when having difficulty with manipulative tasks.

Reflective Assessment

Upon completing the activities the students will be able to:

- Correctly identify all of the circuits as complete or incomplete by marking them *will light* or *will not light.*

- Describe three ways to use circuits and identify at least two different inventions that control the flow of electricity through those circuits.

- Use inquiry skills to solve correctly four circuit puzzles.

- Describe at least three safety precautions to avoid accidents with electricity.

Pictorial Assessment

Upon completing the activities the students will be able to:

- Accurately draw a diagram and correctly label the parts of the circuit they use to make their flashlights.

assignments and questions on key terms—can be given, they are *not* the only means of assessing the student's understanding of the concept of a *circuit.* The lesson plan demonstrates that the students are given multiple opportunities to demonstrate their understanding of the concept and that they are able to apply that understanding in a new context. This means of assessment is consistent with exemplary science teaching that reflects constructivist teaching practices.

Selecting the Tool for the Task

Evaluation, testing, assessment, performance assessment, and *authentic assessment* are terms that educators frequently use interchangeably, but they are not the same. The evaluation phase of the learning cycle lesson reminds us to select the most appropriate and timely tool for determining what students understand and can do so

TABLE 7.1 ● Table of Specifications

	Knowledge of			Translation	Application	Analysis and Synthesis
Terms	Facts	Rules and Principles	Processes and Procedures			
New vocabulary: Words Names Phrases Symbols	Specific information: Persons Events Data Operations	Relations Guidelines Organizational cues	Patterns Sequences Order of events or operations Steps	Identify Describe Recognize Distinguish Compute	Use Illustrate Solve Demonstrate	Compare Contrast Explain Infer Combine Construct Integrate

Source: Thomas R. Guskey, "Mapping the Road to Proficiency," *Educational Leadership* 63(3): 32–38 (November, 2005).

that modifications can be made to instruction, or appropriate intervention can be given to correct possible misconceptions among students. The evaluation of student understanding and performance should be ongoing and cumulative (formative), rather than only a summative function that occurs only at the end of units or chapters. Periodic, focused assessments become the tools of evaluation. Some educators refer to this practice of continual assessment as embedded assessment. "Embedded assessment 'blurs the lines' between teaching and assessment. Many assessment activities become effective teaching activities and many effective teaching activities also are very useful

TABLE 7.2 ● Table of Specifications for Simple Circuits Learning Cycle Lesson Plan

	Knowledge of			Translation	Application	Analysis and Synthesis
Terms	Facts and Concepts	Rules and Principles	Processes and Procedures			
Circuit Switch Bulb Conductor Insulator Open and closed circuits Series and parallel circuits Electricity	Electrical circuits require a complete loop through which the electrical current can pass. A circuit is a pathway that electricity follows from the power source through the bulb and back to the power source.	Metal must touch metal on the bulb in two places for the bulb to light; the side and bottom conductors of the bulb must be included in the circuit.	Use inquiry skills to solve circuit puzzles. Apply basic safety principles in conducting experiments using electricity. Identify safety precautions to avoid accidents with electricity. Cooperate and collaborate with peers in all activities.	Correctly identify complete and incomplete circuits. Describe ways to use circuits, and identify inventions that control the flow of electricity through the circuits.	Draw a diagram and label the parts of a circuit used to construct a simple flashlight.	Construct a working switch. Construct, demonstrate, and describe the operation of a series vs. parallel circuit. Construct a working flashlight, applying understanding of switch and circuit.

teachers on Science Teaching

Embedded Assessment

by Mary Walsh Trant

Grade 2, Mark Twain School, Chicago, Illinois

As a teacher of a very diverse group of second graders with varying degrees of English proficiency, I am always looking for new ways to assess their knowledge of science and be sure they can relate what was taught to their everyday experiences. I try to have them see science in their life experiences. I constantly try to reinforce the fact that we are always acting as scientists. For instance, during reading, when I introduce a story, I ask the students what they think the story may be about simply by looking at the title, pictures, and using prior knowledge. The students are encouraged to make predictions. Also, the students are asked to use context clues to help them with new vocabulary words. They make observations, use clues, and infer. The students are asked to explain how this reading lesson was like being a scientist as a way of evaluating their knowledge of the scientific method. After a unit on food chains, I will ask the students to choose one piece of food they had at lunch and create a food chain back to the sun, using a picture graph. After being displayed, the graphs are put in the students' portfolios. I also encourage students to bring in books for me to read to the class, or they may choose to read to the class. They must be able to tell how the story relates to science. For example, one student brought in the story "If You Give A Mouse a Cookie" and told us that it showed the mouse's habitat.

"The Snowy Day" can relate to evaporation, condensation, heat, etc. You can also pick a book and see if the students can identify the way the story relates to science.

I encourage students to look outside the classroom and bring in things that relate to what they learned in science. They must be able to explain how these things relate to a particular science concept. It is amazing some of the things students bring in, but more amazing is how well they relate to what they learned in science. This transfer of knowledge seems to have deeper and more lasting effects than simply memorizing concepts and spitting back facts on a test. I try to tape the children's presentations whenever possible. They love to watch themselves and really enjoy bringing the tapes home to share with their families.

Each student has a science portfolio. At the beginning of each new unit, the children write or create an audiotape of what they would like to know about the topic and what they already know about the topic. At the end of the unit, they do a similar activity stating what they learned and what they still want to learn. I design a very simple rubric at the beginning of each unit. We discuss the rubric so the students know what I expect them to learn. As the children bring in books and complete activities, I use the checklist-type rubric as a form of assessment.

---

sources of assessment data" (Treagust et al., 2003, p. 37). How this is put into practice is discussed in Teachers on Science Teaching.

Treagust and colleagues suggest embedded assessment follows a cycle within a lesson that answers the following questions:

NSES

AS-A

TC-A

- How can I obtain information on students' ideas and reasoning on the topic of instruction?
- What does this information tell me about students' understanding and how they make sense of this topic?
- What action should I take to help students advance their understanding? (2003, p. 37)

The Learning Cycle Feature lesson on page 198 requires timely and continual teacher assessment of student understanding and skills. Table 7.3 lists several appropriate assessment types that support the expectations for students during each phase of the learning cycle. Most of the effects offered by these assessment types cluster into three types of teacher-designed assessment devices: pictorial assessment, reflective questioning, and hands-on assessment. These approaches were invented by the Full Option Science System (FOSS) of the Lawrence Hall of Science in Berkeley, California, as special techniques

TABLE 7.3 ● Types of Appropriate Evaluations for the Learning Cycles

Phase	Purpose of Evaluation	Type of Evaluation
Explore	Determine possible misconceptions.	Questioning and student answers, pictorial assessment
	Document students' uses of process skills.	Process skills checklists
	Encourage exploration.	Record observations, make predictions, ask observation questions
	Improve social skills and interactions.	Teacher observations, checklists
Explain	Clarify concept constructions.	Group discussions, data processing, picture drawing, constructing models, reflective questioning
	Document conceptual change.	Concept mapping, interviews, pictorial assessment
Expand	Document ability to use integrated process skills.	Reflective questioning, hands-on assessment
	Determine students' abilities to transfer learning to new situations.	Inventions, writing activities, presentations
	Stimulate new interests, make connections to previous learning.	Projects and activities that address standards outcomes, portfolios

to support constructivist teaching and learning through authentic assessment. We used the original version of FOSS as a model for designing authentic assessments for the lesson that is featured in this chapter.

Pictorial Assessment

Pictorial assessment requires students to complete reasoning tasks that differ from traditional fill-in, multiple-choice, and one-answer tasks. The nature of the analysis depends on the types of pictures (or illustrations) used and the context associated with the pictures. Pictorial assessment encourages students to demonstrate their capability to use science process skills appropriately. Some tasks that students may be asked to do could include estimating, predicting, comparing, classifying, identifying properties, determining sequences of events, and designing an experiment.

Pictorial assessment uses pictures to represent familiar objects and events. The assessment device couples well with learning activities and can be completed concurrently. Students are required to apply what they have learned and to communicate what they understand. Often, more than one correct answer or solution is possible on an assessment task. Some tasks encourage students to estimate their answers, then do a hands-on task that permits them to check their estimations. Other assessments may ask students to complete a pretest and then use a similar activity as a pictorial assessment posttest, such as those shown in Figures 7.1 and 7.2. Figure 7.3 is another type of pictorial assessment; both complement the learning cycle plan in the feature lesson.

Reflective Questioning

This type of assessment consists of written tasks that expect students to respond to a wide range of intellectual tasks. Use of basic and integrated science process skills may be necessary. For example, students may have to recall essential information, analyze

FIGURE 7.1 ● Pictorial Assessment
of Simple Circuits

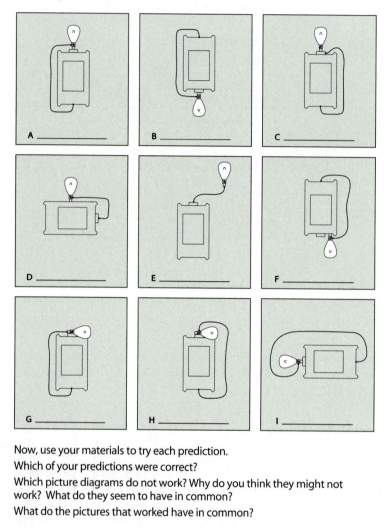

Pretest

Will the bulb light or not? Below each picture, make your prediction
by writing either "Yes" or "No."

A _____   B _____   C _____

D _____   E _____   F _____

G _____   H _____   I _____

Now, use your materials to try each prediction.

Which of your predictions were correct?

Which picture diagrams do not work? Why do you think they might not
work? What do they seem to have in common?

What do the pictures that worked have in common?

information that is provided, apply what they have learned to new but related circumstances, and integrate information to construct answers to unusual situations. Students
will find it necessary to read instructions carefully and then follow the directions. Students may list responses, construct illustrations, select the best response from choices
given, defend their choices, or write extensive responses that can be evaluated for language arts concepts and skills as well as science.

Reflective questioning assessments require students to reflect on the lesson's content
and to use their knowledge in a way that is different from the way it was experienced in
the lesson. This type of assessment encourages students to use a variety of approaches to
solve a problem. Problems often require more than one step in arriving at a solution,
and teachers must be prepared to accept all reasonable and correct answers. We have
been delighted to observe students discover creative or unique answers and solutions
that we did not have in mind when devising the reflective questioning assessment.

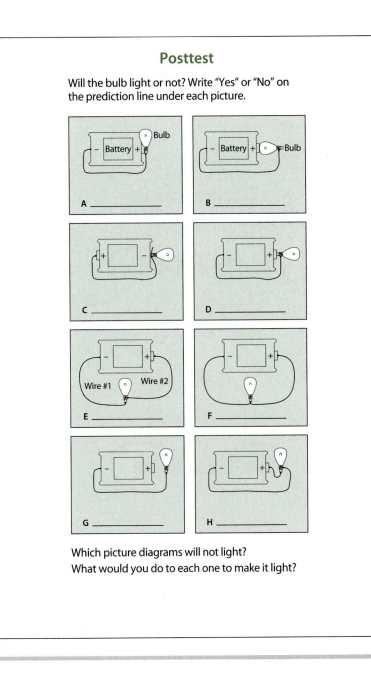

FIGURE 7.2 ● Pictorial Assessment of Simple Circuits

Posttest

Will the bulb light or not? Write "Yes" or "No" on the prediction line under each picture.

Which picture diagrams will not light?

What would you do to each one to make it light?

Figures 7.4 (page 207) and 7.5 (page 210) illustrate this type of assessment tool; both complement the learning cycle plan in the lesson.

Hands-On Assessment

Hands-on assessment requires what the term implies: Students must manipulate materials from the lesson to complete tasks that enable them to demonstrate what they understand. Hands-on assessment permits a teacher to observe how well a student can perform. (*Performance assessment* is another name for this tool.) Students must use their knowledge and skills in a practical way to solve a problem. Students often must use integrated process skills to identify variables, design investigations, gather information, and demonstrate outcomes of their investigations.

Please examine the pictures carefully. These objects were used in class and contain some parts that relate to concepts that we studied in earlier classes: *insulation* and *conduction*. Other parts and functions represent concepts that we are now studying.

Use the word bank to identify the parts shown by the arrows. Words may be used more than once, or not at all. Write your answers on the blank line by each arrow.

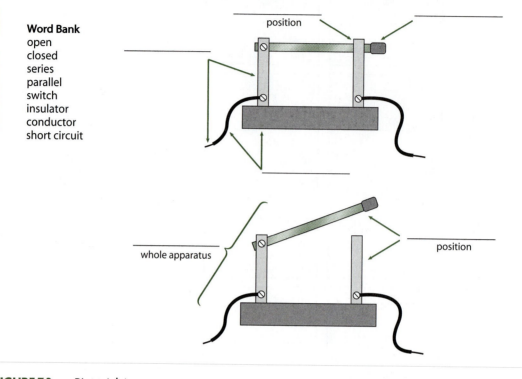

Word Bank
open
closed
series
parallel
switch
insulator
conductor
short circuit

position

whole apparatus

position

FIGURE 7.3 ● Pictorial Assessment

Hands-on assessment gives a teacher opportunities to determine how well students use science tools and science thinking. This type of performance assessment directly pursues the science as inquiry and the nature of science dimensions of the National Science Education Standards. Students are encouraged to create their own problems and use their own data in identifying solutions. They are required to think about and analyze science in a practical context: physical science, life science, and earth/space science content standards. Hands-on assessment is easily expanded through the complementary technique of reflective questioning. Figures 7.6 and 7.7 (page 211), and 7.8 (page 212) illustrate the tools of hands-on assessment and complement the learning cycle plan in the Feature lesson.

Teacher Records and Observations

NSES

AS-E

While good assessment will include hands-on, pictorial, and reflective components, teachers must understand that there is more to good formative assessment than just these graded components. Good assessment will place the emphasis on the learning, not the teaching. Continuous collection of data on what the learner is getting out of the teaching will help teachers to adjust instruction to meet the needs of the learner. Research by Black and Wiliam found that "students taught by teachers who used assessment for learning achieved in six or seven months what would otherwise have taken a

Pictures A, B, C, and D show batteries, bulbs, wires, and sockets. These pictures represent some of the circuits that we constructed in class. Examine each carefully and answer the questions below the pictures.

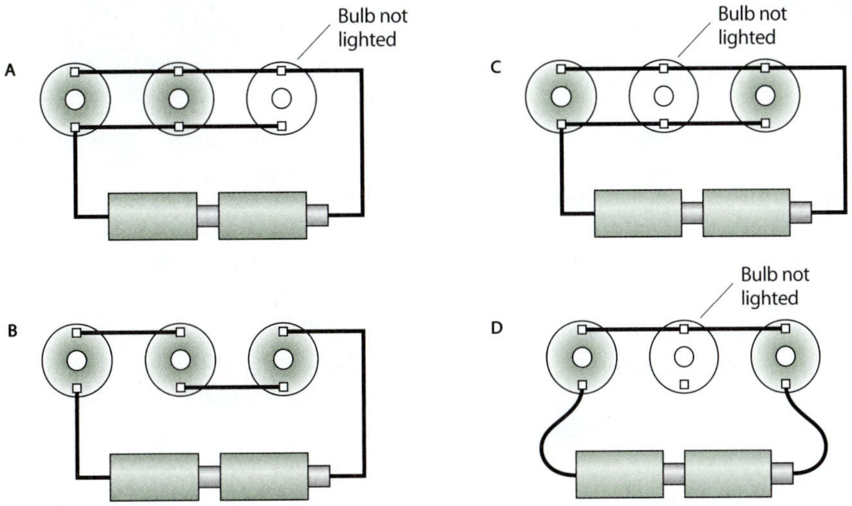

What type of circuit is shown for each picture (series or parallel)?

A _____   C _____

B _____   D _____

Why do you think the bulbs do not light in A, C, and D? There might be many reasons, so please organize your work and explain completely.

What would you do to make the unlit bulbs light in circuits A and C? Please describe all possibilities you can think of.

Go back to circuit D and trace a pathway to show how you would rewire it to make the bulb light. You may remove some wires or add extra wires if you need them.

FIGURE 7.4 ● Reflective Questioning Assessment of Simple Circuits

year" (Leahy et. al. 2005). To this end, it makes sense that tangible records are kept and used to reveal what students know and can and cannot do. Useful records can include the successes and difficulties a child has with homework assignments and notations about the quality of a completed science project, written report, class notes, activity data sheets, and so on. Your teacher records are important because they can reveal the interplay among memorizing, understanding, and using scientific concepts. Emphasis on practical application encourages hands-on, minds-on interaction and helps to address the various dimensions of the science program. Figure 7.9 (page 212) shows a record-keeping system a teacher might use to complement the sample lesson plan on basic electricity. This type of record keeping is useful because it helps to focus a teacher's observations of a child on the concepts and processes to be learned. Figure 7.10 (page 213)

what Research Says

Assessment: What to Emphasize?

Recent research and publication of the National Science Education Standards (NRC, 1996) illustrate the need for envisioning systemic changes in the activities and methods used to assess science learning. For example, the assessment standards of the National Science Education Standards (NRC, 1996, p. 100) urge teachers to place:

Less Emphasis on	More Emphasis on
• Assessing what is easily measured	• Assessing what is most highly valued
• Assessing discrete knowledge	• Assessing rich, well-structured knowledge
• Assessing scientific knowledge	• Assessing scientific understanding and reasoning
• Assessing to learn what students do not know	• Assessing to learn what students do understand
• Assessing only achievement	• Assessing achievement and opportunity to learn
• End-of-term assessments by teachers	• Students engaged in ongoing assessment of their work and that of others
• Development of external assessments by measurement experts alone	• Teachers involved in the development of external assessments

In the spirit of changing emphasis, fourth-grade teachers in a Concord, New Hampshire school district took on the task of annually assessing their students' ability to "think and behave like scientists." After an extensive review of the literature, the teacher teams took on the task of developing performance-based assessments for science. Data were collected and analyzed on the success of their instrument. The concerns their peers shared about this type of assessment were as follows:

- Let teachers correct their own tests. (Others suggested a paid committee of teachers to score student responses from across the district.)
- More anchor papers (examples of responses at each of the four levels) are needed to help with scoring.
- There is too much emphasis on grammar and spelling.
- A student-friendly rubric is needed.
- Spread the tasks out over the year in order to determine growth.
- It takes a lot of time to do one task.
- It is difficult to conduct the driving test in the confines of the classroom.

Indeed, performance-based assessment administered as a standardized assessment tool is not without its problems. Providing the tests is only half the battle. Working on the mindsets to accept this form of testing will take a lot longer. As the authors of this study conclude, "Most paper-and-pencil assessments provide adequate insight into students' ability and can help effectively guide instruction.

shows a generic form that is suitable for an entire class. It may be used as a checklist to keep track of who has and has not demonstrated mastery of the concepts or preferred science skills. This format can be used to record students' progress on the pictorial, reflective questioning, and hands-on assessment techniques.

Recording students' progress is not enough. Recent research shows the importance of teacher feedback to student motivation (Chappuis, 2005; Leahy et al., 2005; Lee & Abell, 2007; Valdez, 2007). Teachers must first learn to listen to their students to understand what students are thinking and not just to hear whether the students are giving the correct answer. If we are to change students' misconceptions, we have to learn to listen to the responses students give and the reasoning behind their responses. Practice in listening to students will give us insights into the types of questioning strategies we should plan for before we teach the lesson: asking probing questions for clarification, using wait-time to allow the learners to expand on their ideas, and allowing for student-driven questions to help in extending knowledge.

While mastering the skill of *listening* to your students during both teacher-student interaction and student-student interactions, you must also address the *written* feedback

A well-designed, performance-based assessment propels a science program beyond this level of adequacy and guarantees that teachers are making curricular decisions based upon a more complete picture. After all, if science literacy is going to be measured in terms of what students know and are able to do, then the tests we give them better allow students to *do* something."

The federal *No Child Left Behind* legislation of 2002 expects school districts to have strategies in place so that *all* children will succeed. The National Science Education Standards' shifting emphasis for assessment suggest that the learner plays a more active role in assessment. Providing authentic assessment for *all* students does not mean excluding those with learning disabilities. In his research on inclusive classrooms, Konstantinos Alexakos, a high school physics teacher in New York City, offers several suggestions on how *all* students can participate in authentic assessment, from prerecording the test questions for auditory learners to having a student aide read the questions. Alexakos suggests that "Assistive technology, such as computers equipped with touch-sensitive screens or speech synthesizers and voice recognition software, should be employed when appropriate. Such technology can decrease the feelings of separation and isolation of learners with disabilities, reducing their frustration, and increasing their self-esteem."

Alexakos's research suggests that the evaluation of what students should know and be able to do, in an inclusive classroom, does not have to rest solely on individual performance. In fact, the rubrics he created to assess the students' ability in a lab situation stressed the value he placed on teaming. A sample lab evaluation sheet developed by Alexakos follows:

Sample lab work evaluation sheet

A. Written team report (28 points)
____ of 4 points   Need for such experiment
____ of 4 points   Safety precautions
____ of 5 points   Collection of data
____ of 5 points   Calculations
____ of 5 points   Analysis
____ of 5 points   Neatness

B. Team work (24 points)
____ of 8 points   Safety
____ of 8 points   Collaboration
____ of 8 points   Individual participation

C. Verbal assessment (24 points)
____ of 12 points   Team comprehension
____ of 12 points   Individual comprehension

D. Individual written report (24 points)
____ of 12 points   Essay evaluating the particular experiment and outcome
____ of 12 points   Suggestions and criticisms concerning the experiment

Total: ____ of 100 points

Comments:

Note: Specifics of rubrics should be discussed before being made final so students can express their concerns and suggest changes.

Source: Adapted from Konstantinos Alexakos, "Inclusive Classrooms." *Science and Children* (March, 2001): 40–43.

Source: Adapted from Chris Demers, "Beyond Paper and Pencil Assessments," *Science and Children* (October 2000): 24–29, 60.

you provide on students' work. If you are assessing the students' ability to write up a lab report in which the learner is expected to use the data that were collected to draw conclusions about a science concept and to explain through the analysis of those data their understanding of the concept, then be sure to provide feedback that does more than evaluate the quality of the work. Placing a grade of a C+ on the paper without any explanation as to why it merited a C+ does little to change student practice. An explanation such as "You did not use the data you collected to support the conclusions you drew. How do your data support or negate the hypothesis you started with?" will give the student greater insight into the grade you put on the page. According to Bloom (1984), effective feedback will identify the successful aspects of the document and offer details on any recommended changes.

Rubrics

Providing descriptive feedback that offers details for recommended changes to a project, a homework assignment, or a lab report can be time consuming. Science teachers from the middle grades up often see over 120 students a day. Combine that with several

Imagine that a storm has passed, it is nighttime, and you are walking down the street with a flashlight. The street lights are not working and many houses are dark, but you do notice light coming from some houses. You see a loose electrical wire with one end on the ground and the other end attached to a utility pole. What are three safe things you might do?

1. _____
2. _____
3. _____

What are three electrical devices that you use regularly? List them below and identify the types of circuits that they have (series, parallel, or both). Also for each, list inventions that control the flow of electricity to or within the device. You must identify at least two different inventions overall.

Electrical devices	Type of circuit used	Invention that controls
_____	_____	_____
_____	_____	_____
_____	_____	_____

Imagine that our community has a power failure for one week. Life must go on, including school! What things would change in your daily routine in which you usually use electricity, but now cannot? Describe your day without electricity, beginning with your morning wake-up and preparation for school, time spent getting to and from school, and your evening until you go to sleep.

_____

_____

_____

_____

assignments per week, and you will soon learn why one of our graduate students concluded, in her research project on the value of journaling in science teaching and daily descriptive feedback by the teacher with those journals: "Through my research I learned that students who were provided daily descriptive feedback in their journals achieved higher test scores than students who did not receive the descriptive feedback. While I know that is good for science learning I found the task exhausting. I'm not sure I'd do this all the time in my classroom!" (Hurd, 2003).

One strategy that can be as effective to descriptive feedback is the use of rubrics. *Rubrics* are devices, such as checklists, scales, or descriptions, that identify the criteria used to evaluate a student's work. Paul Smith (1995), a middle school science teacher, recommends using rubrics that have been created by the students for students, with teacher guidance. Since students are part of the design process, they clearly understand the expectations and use this understanding to improve their work. The creation of the rubrics also affords additional teaching opportunities.

For written work, Smith (1995) asks students to consider two questions: "What information should go into the written response?" and "How should the information be presented?" He uses a peer and parental review system that encourages students to prepare and improve written drafts. Parents and caregivers appreciate the rubrics because the rubrics help them to improve guidance they offer while helping with homework.

Find out what is in the six mystery boxes A, B, C, D, E, and F. They have five different things inside, shown below. Two of the boxes will have the same thing. All of the others will have something different inside.

Two batteries:

A wire:

A bulb:

A battery and a bulb:

Nothing at all :

You can use your bulbs, batteries, and wires any way you like. Connect them in a circuit to help you figure out what is inside.

When you find out what is in a box, fill in the spaces on the following pages.

Box A: Has _____ inside.

Draw a picture of the circuit that told you what was inside Box A.

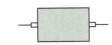

How could you tell from your circuit what was inside Box A?

Do the same for Boxes B, C, D, E, and F.

FIGURE 7.6 ● Hands-On Assessment: Electricity Mystery Boxes

Source: R. J. Shavelson and G. P. Baxter, "What We've Learned about Assessing Hands-on Science," *Educational Leadership* (May 1992): 20–25. Reprinted by permission of the Association for Supervision and Curriculum Development. Copyright © 1992 by ASCD. All rights reserved.

FIGURE 7.7 ● Hands-On Assessment: Electric Circuit Boards

Below are the pictures of four circuit boards you will find in your science center. Design a simple circuit tester from a battery, bulb, socket, and wires. Test the four boards to determine which points (A, B, C, and so on) are wired into the same circuit. Draw lines on the circuit picture showing where you believe the wires make a connection between the points. Show your teacher your work, and then open the circuit folder and check the results. Were you correct?

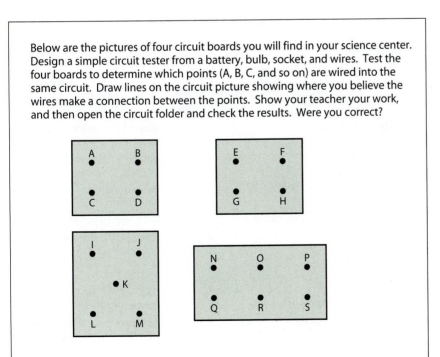

FIGURE 7.8 ● Hands-On Assessment: Help Me Out!

Yikes! I'm lost in a cave and I'm using a small candle that is about to burn out. What I really need is a flashlight—one that can withstand the drafty and damp cave—to help me find my way out. All I have is:

2 size "D" dry cells
1 small 3-volt bulb
1 thin piece of insulated wire, 30 centimeters long (about 12 inches)
1 metal paper clip
2 metal paper fasteners
1 cardboard tube, 15 centimeters long (about 6 inches)
1 roll of masking tape
1 plastic bottle cap
1 small knife

1. Use the materials to sketch a picture of how these things could be assembled to make a temporary flashlight. Make certain you draw your circuit carefully. (Draw your picture here.)

2. Now help me by testing your plan. Did the light work? Keep trying! Now show me my new light and explain to me how it works.

FIGURE 7.9 ● Student Progress Report

Student's Name: Raul
Lesson or Unit: Basic Electricity

Concept Number	Description of Activity or Skill	Teacher Rating Low 12345 High	Teacher Comments
1	Open circuit using one bulb, wire, and dry cell	5	Was the first in the group to do it
2	Closed circuit using same materials	3	Had difficulty, needed my help
3	Closed circuit with bulb socket	4	Easily done after I helped with clips
4	Series circuit, 2 or more bulbs	5	Done independently
5	Parallel circuit	2	Having difficulty, made 2 series circuits
6	Short circuit	4	
7	Use a knife switch	5	Easily done
8	Make a paper clip switch	5	Concept easily shown
9	Construct a flashlight	4	No circuit trouble, difficulty with bulb connections only

FIGURE 7.10 ● Class Record-Keeping System

Unit: Basic Electricity

Children's Names	Objective, Concept, Skill, or Activity Number											Comments
	1	2	3	4	5	6	7	8	9	10	11	
Emerson												
Frankie												
Jaclyn												
Jana												
Jay												
Julie												
Joy												
Marilyn												

Note: This format is easily managed by a spreadsheet program if a value number is assigned to each object. Some teachers prefer a coding system that shows progress, such as + for entirely correct, *n* for partially correct, *u* for mostly incorrect, and – for entirely incorrect.

This is a scoring rubric for a learning-cycle lesson on simple circuits. A score of three indicates what the class believes all students should be able to do. A score of four indicates that the students exceeded expectations.

Content scale

0	1	2	3	4
• No work completed	• Few concepts • Models not used in explanation • Some awareness of safety • Some awareness of technology uses	• Some concepts explained • Three common safety examples • Three common technology examples	• Uses circuit model to explain differences • Identifies differences in series, parallel, open, closed circuits • Uses concepts from previous lessons, e.g., conductor, insulator, etc.	• Uses additional concepts to explain differences, e.g., switch, resistance, energy flow • Unusual safety and/or technology examples

Style scale

0	1	2	3	4
• No work completed	• Poor organization • Many misspellings • Punctuation missing or inappropriate	• Clear organization • Very few misspellings	• Appropriate punctuation	• Extremely clear, concise writing

First reviewer's name: _____

Score for content: _____   Score for style: _____

Comments:

Second reviewer's name: _____

Score for content: _____   Score for style: _____

Comments:

FIGURE 7.11 ● Reflective Questioning Assessment Rubric

Criteria	Exceeds expectations (5 points)	Meets expectations (3 points)	Fails to meet expectations (1 point)
Communication	• Raises relevant questions and shares ideas with peers • Offers clear and concise oral and written presentation of personal ideas and understanding, indicating that time has been devoted to thinking about the topic	• Occasionally participates in group discussions, but rarely initiates or accepts a leadership role in guiding the group • Does not elaborate on his or her understanding • Often does not complete expression of his or her thoughts or ideas	• Provides no oral or written evidence of understanding activity or discussion topics • Never or rarely raises relevant questions • Never or rarely provides oral or written communication
Sharing sources and resources	• Brings sources of information to the class to share with teachers or peers • Brings resources such as activities, materials, or literature that can be used to extend the learning activities of the class	• Makes reference to outside sources of information and resources but does not take the initiative to bring them to class to share with others • Is unable to provide evidence that he or she has looked for outside sources and resources	• Never or rarely brings in outside resources that could enhance the learning experiences of others
Openness to learn	• Accepts class assignments and requirements with a positive attitude • Actively seeks (by asking questions or speculating) connections between course requirements and goals	• Reluctantly accepts class assignments	• Rejects or dismisses class assignments as meaningless or boring • Cannot make connections between class requirements and goals of the instructor
Respect	• Listens to others; encourages others to contribute ideas; accepts alternative perspectives; is tolerant of the shortcomings of others; and helps others to succeed in class	• Is tolerant of others but often dominates the group activity or discussion • Listens to the ideas of others but generally maintains personal views and ideas	• Dismisses the thoughts and ideas of others; possibly uses rude or abusive language to ridicule • Offers ideas that are limited to his or her personal opinions

FIGURE 7.12 ● An Assessment Rubric for Class Participation

Source: John A. Craven III and Tracy Hogan, "Assessing Student Participation in the Classroom," *Science Scope* (September, 2001): 36–40.

Smith claims that students are able to make better sense of what they learn and that student satisfaction is very high with this participatory approach.

Rubrics can help a teacher to encourage students to give better responses to reflective questioning assessments. The rubric shown in Figure 7.11 (page 213) has been generalized for use with reflective questioning assessments. It illustrates Smith's recommendations. Figure 7.12 provides a general rubric that can be used for a variety of science tasks.

A variety of websites are designed to help teachers build rubrics that objectively evaluate student work; some websites even help in identifying "student-friendly" descriptors. Three such sites that can help you build rubrics for all sorts of topics are the Landmark Project's Rubric Builder (http://landmark-project.com), Eduscapes (http://eduscapes.com/tap/topic53.htm), and Rubristar (http://www.rubristar.com). Whether you choose to use a website that helps in building the rubric or use your own descriptors, there are two important things to keep in mind. First, create descriptors that

Criteria	Exceeds expectations (5 points)	Meets expectations (3 points)	Fails to meet expectations (1 point)
Accepts and provides constructive criticism	• Positively accepts constructive criticism and incorporates it into his or her approach to learning • Offers constructive criticism and critiques, including viable suggestions for improvement, to his or her teacher and peers	• Accepts constructive criticism but does not incorporate it for improving targeted behaviors	• Often or always rejects constructive criticism • Offers no viable alternatives to others' suggestions
Material preparedness	• Makes class materials readily available and accessible without causing interruption of activities or discussions	• Regularly forgets some materials or does not prepare fully; or prepares for class but is unable to retrieve his or her materials without disruption	• Consistently is unprepared for class
Academic preparedness	• Refers to relevant literature or readings to support ideas and arguments during discussions • Demonstrates awareness of course and teacher expectations	• Refers to concepts or topics related to the activity or discussion topic but provides incomplete written or oral responses • Expresses opinions that may have merit but is unable to support them with evidence from classroom work	• Is unable to respond correctly to questions regarding required readings • Offers responses that are consistently wrong or meaningless • Expresses surprise or confusion when probed for his or her understanding
Class Presence	• Frequently volunteers to participate in classroom activities • Demonstrates his or her focus on classroom activities by appropriate eye contact and alert posture	• Occasionally participates in group discussions • Provides ideas or comments that are largely restricted to reiterations of others' ideas or comments	• Sits passively in class • Does not participate in group discussions • Does not pay attention to classroom activities

Score: ___/40

FIGURE 7.12 ● Continued

are clearly written, using language that the students can understand and that explicitly states what you expect students to know and/or be able to do. Also, use care in your selection of criteria and descriptors so that there is room to reward points for work that is above and beyond what is required. A good rule of thumb is to ask yourself "Could a student with mediocre work still score high using this rubric?" When in doubt, add a category called "the wow factor." This gives you an opportunity to award points based on student work that has gone well beyond just meeting the basic criteria.

Systematic Observation

The types of records that are shown in Figures 7.13 and 7.14 (page 216) require systematic teacher observation. Systematic observation is another source of information that is helpful to meaningful evaluation. Teachers always make observations, but systematic observation goes beyond being aware that Rosa is interested in birds, Joel asks questions all the time, and Ali creates messes. Systematic observation is illustrated in this example:

NSES
AS-E

FIGURE 7.13 ● Recording
Science Process Skills

Note: The process skills can be
changed and the form expanded to
address better the science skills your
lessons emphasize.

Directions: Circle the number that best represents the skill level you have observed. Number 1 means *having difficulty*, 2 means *fair*, 3 means *good*, 4 means *outstanding*.

Name	Observation	Classification	Communication	Measurement	Prediction
Sam	1 2 3 4	1 2 3 4	1 2 3 4	1 2 3 4	1 2 3 4
Wanda	1 2 3 4	1 2 3 4	1 2 3 4	1 2 3 4	1 2 3 4
Herman	1 2 3 4	1 2 3 4	1 2 3 4	1 2 3 4	1 2 3 4
Kara	1 2 3 4	1 2 3 4	1 2 3 4	1 2 3 4	1 2 3 4

A teacher divides the class into working groups to figure out a way to test the strength of different brands of paper towels. As the children work on the problem, the teacher walks about the room, listens carefully to the questions the children ask each other, and observes how they approach the task. The teacher notes who does nothing, who appears to have difficulty, who has trouble measuring, who asks the most interesting questions, and who offers the most interesting ideas.

Systematic observation is guided by a structure; the teacher's observations are focused on specific tasks. These tasks include trying to determine how well the children demonstrate their understanding of the science ideas, how well the children use the science process skills, and what types of scientific attitudes the children demonstrate. Figure 7.13 illustrates an observation form for science skills and Table 7.4 defines the attributes of the skills.

Science learning improves when student attitudes are positive (Yager & Penick, 1987). There are dramatic differences between traditional science classrooms and exemplary ones in which teaching and assessment involve all aspects of science. Positive attitudes about science greatly influence students' achievement levels and process skills, as is shown by research on exemplary science classrooms (Yager & Penick, 1987). These results are now prompting teachers to question the traditional view that attitudes are inconsequential. Figure 7.14 shows one way in which you can evaluate and record the levels of your students' science attitudes.

Social skills are important to science learning. Karen Ostlund (1992) tells us that we are not born with a set of instinctive behaviors that help us to interact well in social settings. Social skills are learned. If we expect students to work together in cooperative science activity groups or on science projects in smaller teams, then we must assess the

FIGURE 7.14 ● Evaluating and Recording Science Attitudes

Check those attitudes or record the number of times each student demonstrates the desired scientific attitudes during the observation period.

Name	Is curious	Cooperates	Persists	Is open-minded	Safely uses materials
Celeste	✓✓✓	✓✓	✓	✓	✓
Jen	✓	✓✓✓✓	✓	✓✓✓✓	✓✓✓
Tikara	✓✓✓✓	✓✓✓	✓✓✓✓✓	✓✓	✓✓✓
Jon	✓	✓✓✓	✓✓	✓✓	✓✓
Sara	✓✓	✓✓	✓✓✓	✓✓✓✓	✓✓✓✓

Basic Processes

Observation: involves active engagement with the manipulation of objects and the use of the senses, directly or indirectly, with simple or complex instruments. This process:

- describes objects' attributes,
- describes changes in terms of actions,
- describes changes with accuracy in terms of patterns and relationships.

Classification: systematically imposing order to data based on observational relationships. This process:

- creates groups by using a single attribute to express linear relationships,
- creates groups and subgroups using one attribute to express symmetrical relationships,
- creates groups using several attributes together to express symmetrical relationships among different groups.

Communication: exchanging information through a variety of media. This process involves:

- expressing opinions,
- explaining using sense data (touch, taste, hearing, sight, and smell),
- explaining causal relationships.

Measurement: describing an event by using instruments to quantify observations. This process:

- uses nonstandard instruments, such as paper clips, hands, and feet,
- uses standard instruments, such as rulers, balance scales, and graduated cylinders,
- uses standard instruments with precision, such as measuring within tenths or hundredths when using the metric system.

Prediction: stating future cause-and-effect relationships through manipulation of objects. Accuracy of prediction is based on information gathered through observations. This process includes:

- guesses from minimal supportive evidence,
- guesses based on limited observable facts,
- guesses based on an accurate understanding of cause-and-effect relationships.

Questioning: raising uncertainty. This process:

- focuses on the attributes of objects,
- focuses on relationships and patterns within an experiment,
- focuses on events and patterns abstracted from an experiment.

Using numbers: expressing ideas, observations, and relationships in figures rather than words. This process:

- uses numbers to express ideas without relating them,
- uses numbers to express relationships,
- uses numbers to express relationships in precise terms.

(continued)

TABLE 7.4 ● Continued

Integrated Processes

Interpreting data: finding patterns or meaning not immediately apparent among sets of data that lead to the construction of inferences, predictions, and hypotheses. This process:

- identifies a single pattern among objects within an experiment,
- uses accuracy to identify a single pattern among objects within an experiment,
- uses accuracy to identify multiple patterns among objects.

Controlling variables: identifying and selecting factors from variables that are to be held constant and those that are to be manipulated in order to carry out a proposed investigation. This process involves managing:

- one manipulative variable without holding others constant,
- several manipulative variables and holding at least one variable constant,
- several manipulative and constant variables at the same time.

Designing experiments: planning data-gathering operations to determine results. This process involves:

- collecting data through trial-and-error processes;
- testing questions and hypothesizing with an attempt to identify and control variables;
- using organized, sequential plans to test hypotheses and interpret results in measurable terms.

Inferring: providing explanations, reasons, or causes for events based on limited facts. Inferences are of questionable validity because they rely heavily on personal judgment. This process:

- explains by making guesses,
- explains using observable data,
- explains using quantifiable observable data.

Defining operationally: describing what works. This process:

- explains how to measure variables in an experiment,
- states relationships between observed actions to explain phenomena,
- explains relationships by generalizing to other events not observed.

Hypothesizing: tentatively accepting an explanation as a basis for further investigation. Constructing generalizations that include all objects or events of the same class. The hypothesis must be tested if credibility is to be established. This process involves making:

- statements based on opinions,
- statement based on simple sensory observations without explanations,
- statements used to create concepts through explanations.

Formulating models: describing or constructing physical, verbal, or mathematical explanations of systems and phenomena that cannot be observed directly. Models may be used in predicting outcomes and planned investigations. This process:

- creates one-dimensional explanations,
- creates multidimensional models,
- creates scalar multidimensional explanations.

Source: G. W. Foster & W. A. Heiting, "Embedded Assessment," *Science and Children* 32, 2 (1994): 30–33. Reprinted with permission from NSTA Publications, copyright 1994 from *Science and Children,* National Science Teachers Association, 1840 Wilson Boulevard, Arlington, VA 22201-3000.

TABLE 7.5 ● Science Social Skills

Science social skills can be observed and recorded by a teacher, or used as a part of a student self-evaluation. As an example, for student self-evaluation you could ask students to rate how often or how well they do the following.

Cluster skills: *How often do you*

- move into groups quietly?
- stay with your group?
- use a quiet voice to speak within your group?
- call the people in your group by their names?
- look at the person in your group who is talking?
- keep your hands and feet to yourself?
- share materials with your group mates?
- wait and take your turn?
- share your ideas?

Camaraderie skills: *How often do you*

- avoid saying "put-downs"?
- encourage others in your group to participate?
- give each person in your group a compliment?
- show your support to others with words or actions?
- describe how you feel when it is appropriate?
- try humor or enthusiasm to help energize your group?
- criticize the idea, not the person?
- allow each person in the group to talk before you talk again?

Task skills: *How often do you*

- ask questions of your group members about the task?
- ask for help from group members?
- ask group members to explain what you do not understand?
- offer to explain things to another group member?
- check for understanding with group members?
- state the purpose of the task and make certain others understand it?
- watch time and let others know when time is short?
- offer ideas about how best to do the task?
- value other group members' contributions?
- summarize the material to help others in your group?
- develop ways to help the group remember important details?
- encourage other group members to share their thinking?
- ask others to plan out loud how they would solve a problem?
- compare viewpoints when there is a disagreement and try to reach agreement?
- combine parts of different persons' ideas into a single point of view?
- ask others to explain their reasons?
- help other group members reach a conclusion?
- check your group's work against the instructions?

Source: Adapted from K. L. Ostlund, "Sizing Up Social Skills," *Science Scope* (March 1992): 31–33.

extent to which the learners develop those skills. Table 7.5 (page 219) lists important social skills that students can learn if we encourage them. Systematic record-keeping formats (similar to those shown in Figures 7.13 and 7.14, page 216) can help us to monitor the status of students' social skills.

According to Ostlund (1992), science social skills fall into three groups:

1. *Cluster skills:* behaviors that involve a student's ability to move into a science learning group quickly and quietly and get the task started.

2. *Camaraderie skills:* behaviors that help all learners feel better about themselves and about each other as they work together. These skills build a sense of cohesiveness and encourage stable operation of the science group.

3. *Task skills:* behaviors pertaining to management chores, ranging from those necessary for mastering a task to those that use critical thinking to construct a deeper level of understanding.

Student Self-Assessments

Student self-assessments are an important part of the authenticity in constructivist science teaching. Self-assessments can range from the informal collections of reflective tape-recorded (for nonreaders) or written journal notes to more formal efforts, such as self-evaluation ratings. A student portfolio is also a common technique that is used to organize and present the self-assessment.

A *portfolio* is a selection of student work that is collected over a period of time (Hein & Price, 1994). A portfolio's purpose is often to tell a story about the student's science activities. The contents of a portfolio may be focused on illustrating a student's abilities to solve problems, show thinking and understanding, illustrate content and capability of written communication, and reveal science connections that a student is able to make across many lessons and the views that students have of themselves in science (Glencoe Science Profession Series, 1994).

Oftentimes, the teacher may get caught up in the *collecting evidence* aspect of the portfolio and miss its use as a tool for learning in itself. With technology now being more readily accessible in the classroom, the focus of portfolio development can easily shift from a collection of student artifacts to an electronic, continuous source of assessment, which represents growth over time. The "electronic portfolios (e-portfolios)— digital collections of student work—are flexible, motivating, and extremely useful teacher tools that can address a range of needs from student assessment and professional development to creating connections between teachers, students, and parents" (Garthwait & Verrill, 2003, p. 22).

Key to making portfolios a tool for learning in themselves is aligning the selection of materials placed within the portfolio with the standards. Identifying standard for the students and then asking them to select work that they think best demonstrates their understanding of that standard is a great way to find out how that student is interpreting the standard. For a student to select artifacts that are appropriate for a given standard, the teacher must be sure that portfolio-worthy assignments, aligned to specific standards, are assigned to the students. The quality of the artifacts that the student chooses can only be as good as the quality of the assignments designed by the teacher to address given standards (Niguidula, 2005). Asking the students to write and include goal statements for themselves and then to identify how their portfolio meets their personal goal adds to the learning value behind the use of portfolio as assessment.

A student *journal* is a type of self-assessment. A journal can assist the reflective process when students are encouraged to record what they have done and what they

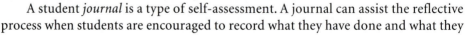

NSES
TS-C

have learned. A journal may provide a written summary that is helpful for planning and constructing a portfolio. The following examples are appropriate for a portfolio:

- written report of a project or investigation,
- responses to open-ended questions,
- examples of problems that have been formed or solved,
- journal excerpts,
- science art,
- individual student's contribution to a group report or project,
- photographs or drawings of science models,
- teacher check sheets and recorded observations of student performance,
- analyses of a video of the student's group behaviors and conversations while planning and performing an experiment,
- uses of science tools, equipment, and suitable technologies to solve problems or to complete an activity,
- examples of how science is important to the student,

FIGURE 7.15 ● Portfolio Evaluation Form

Source: Glencoe Science Professional Series, *Alternative Assessment in the Science Classroom* (1994). (ERIC Document Reproduction Service No. ED 370 778), p. 37.

Portfolio Topic _____

Student: _____

Teacher: _____ Date: _____

1. Concepts, procedures, process skills explored: _____

   _____

2. Areas of growth in understanding: _____

   _____

3. Unfinished work or work needing revision: _____

   _____

4. Assessment of the following areas:

   (a) Problem-solving work: _____

   _____

   (b) Reasoning and critical thinking: _____

   _____

   (c) Use of language: _____

   _____

   (d) Other: _____

   _____

Student Self-Evaluation Checklist

Name: _____ Date: _____

Did the circuit problems
Finished some   Finished them all

Worked with the materials
Messy   Always careful

Recorded and described in my journal
Wrote a little   Wrote a lot

Practiced important safety rules
Some of the time   All of the time

Discussed ideas and results with the class
Some of the time   All of the time

Worked well with classmates
Some of the time   All of the time

Used time well
Wasted time   Worked hard

Learned from the lesson
Learned a little   Learned a lot

Things I liked or did well: _____

_____

Things I did not like: _____

_____

FIGURE 7.16 ● Student Self-Evaluation Checklist

Source: Adapted from G. E. Hein and S. Price, *Active Assessment for Active Science: A Guide for Elementary School Teachers* (Portsmouth, NH: Heinemann, 1994).

- descriptions of safe science practices learned and applied in another setting, such as at home,
- linkages of science history and how views have changed as a result of study,
- examples of how science is used in the community and careers that use the science topics that have been studied.

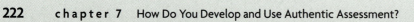

Self-Evaluation Rating Scale

Name: _____ Date: _____

Directions: Rate yourself. On a scale of one (low) to ten (high), how well did you do each of the following activities?

Making a switch
Didn't understand what to do   Made a great one

| 1 | 2 | 3 | 4 | 5 | 6 | 7 | 8 | 9 | 10 |

Making circuits
Had trouble   Easy to do

| 1 | 2 | 3 | 4 | 5 | 6 | 7 | 8 | 9 | 10 |

Solving circuit puzzles
Had trouble   Easy to solve

| 1 | 2 | 3 | 4 | 5 | 6 | 7 | 8 | 9 | 10 |

Electricity mystery boxes
Did some   Did all

| 1 | 2 | 3 | 4 | 5 | 6 | 7 | 8 | 9 | 10 |

Making the flashlight
Could have tried harder   Did my best

| 1 | 2 | 3 | 4 | 5 | 6 | 7 | 8 | 9 | 10 |

Overall feeling about the electricity lessons
Liked them a little   Liked them a lot

| 1 | 2 | 3 | 4 | 5 | 6 | 7 | 8 | 9 | 10 |

Things I liked or did well: _____

_____

Things I did not like: _____

_____

FIGURE 7.17 ● Student Self-Evaluation Rating Scale

Source: Adapted from G. E. Hein and S. Price, *Active Assessment for Active Science: A Guide for Elementary School Teachers* (Portsmouth, NH: Heinemann, 1994).

Portions of a portfolio may be evaluated by the teacher individually or collectively within the portfolio package. Items in the portfolio should invite student self-evaluation. Figure 7.15 provides a format that invites students and teachers to have input into the evaluation in an open-ended way. Figures 7.16 and 7.17 illustrate specific student self-evaluation approaches that may be used to inform teachers and caregivers about how students perceive their own learning.

chapter summary

When assessment is left only for the end of a lesson or unit of study, when it requires the students to rely on habits of recall rather than habits of mind, and when it engages students only in lower-order thinking skills, which require rote memorization, then it is of no value in the teaching/learning process. It should answer the question of what we want teachers to teach and how, and what we want students to learn and how. Effective assessment becomes a lever for change. It is consistent with the National Science Education Stan-

dards and provides a means of collecting data on students about their understanding of the National Science Education Standards.

Tools for authentic assessment include pictorial analysis, hands-on performance tasks, reflective questioning, and systematic observation. Many illustrations show various types of teacher records and student products, including portfolios that verify the types and levels of understanding. These techniques are pragmatically illustrated by supporting a central lesson throughout the chapter.

reflect and respond

1. Contemporary movements in education usually embrace the preference for students to demonstrate learning outcomes. Performance or behavioral objectives may be used for this purpose. What advantages or disadvantages do you see with this type of objective?

2. How is the idea of *embedded assessment* consistent with the National Science Education Standards for assessment?

3. What is the advantage of having students create a rubric to assess their work over a teacher-developed rubric? What would be the disadvantages?

4. Devise a rubric for scoring a pictorial assessment. To what extent did you struggle with this task? Given your

response to the previous question, does it make sense to use only one kind of assessment, such as pictorial assessment, to determine what your students know and are able to do?

5. Create a reflective assessment question, and share it with your classmates. Ask them to answer your question without any further prompts from you. Did they respond in the manner you intended when you wrote the question? If not, what do you think you will need to change in the question to get the response you intended?

Explore—Video Homework Exercise. Go to MyEducationLab at www.myeducationlab .com and select the topic "Assessment," then watch the video "Informal Assessment" for a brief glimpse of informal assessment. The literal definition of the term *assessment* is "to sit with." What better way is there of finding out what science your students learned than to sit down and ask them to tell you what they know and understand? After viewing this video, respond to the questions below.

NSES
AS-A
AS-C

1. What kinds of questions did the teacher use to promote more student responses?

2. How did the teacher respond to the students once they answered her questions?

3. Do you think the responses the teacher gave to the students were appropriate? Why or why not?

224 chapter 7 How Do You Develop and Use Authentic Assessment?

4. How might the questioning skills of the teacher, including student feedback, contribute to the overall classroom atmosphere and how the students feel about assessment?

5. What would you do with this class to move from the informal assessment to a more formal assessment? Provide an example of how you could involve the students in creating and scoring a more formalized assessment. Take a lesson that you have created, and develop a formal assessment for that lesson.

Enrich—Video Homework Exercise. Go to MyEducationLab and select the topic "Assessment," then watch the video "Standardized Tests" for a thorough description of such high-stakes assessments. Respond to the questions accompanying the video in MyEducationLab, and complete the activity below.

NSES
TS-C
AS-D

Often, teachers will state that a standardized test does not accurately reflect the content they taught their students during the past school year. Interview classroom teachers who must give their students standardized tests. Are their understandings of these tests similar to that shared in the video? If not, how do their views differ? Do they have misconceptions about standardized assessment? What would you share to change their views?

Expand—Video Homework Exercise. Go to MyEducationLab and select the topic "Assessment," then watch the videos "Forms of Assessment" and "Observing Children in Authentic Contexts." Respond to the questions within each video. Then select "Weblinks," and click on the link for "Source for Authentic Assessment," which provides links to numerous resources to help create authentic assessments.

NSES
AS-B
AS-C
AS-E

In the video *Forms of Assessment,* what kind of systematic data did the eighth-grade teacher collect as evidence that the students know the science content? How are the data that he collects on student performance similar to the systematic data that the early childhood educator collected in the video *Observing Children in Authentic Contexts?* How is it different? How can each teacher claim that he or she is collecting evidence of student learning?

How Do You Integrate Technology That Enriches Science Learning?

- Why is technology used in the science classroom?

- What technology tools can be used to help all students learn science?

- How can technology remove classroom walls to expand learning?

- How can technology be applied in the context of science teaching?

Scenario 1: Elementary Students with Access to a Wide Variety of Educational Technologies

A small group of Ms. Ramirez's fifth-grade students were sprawled on the floor, poring over several pages of data on stream quality that they had just pulled from a centralized Internet database. Another group was in the corner near the sink, doing a separation test on a soil sample that they had taken from the bottom of their local stream. A third group was at the computer, entering new data and creating colored bar graphs from the data. A fourth group was transferring digital images of the stream in question from the digital camera to the computer. After forty minutes had passed, Ms. Ramirez pulled the group together.

"Okay, students, I'd like to spend a few moments having each team give me a status report. Kevin, how far along is your team on their stream study project?"

"We just need to check one more source on the Internet to verify these figures, and we'll be ready to put our electronic presentation together. We'd like to go to Mr. Hill's room after school some day this week so he can help us edit our video and digitize it for our presentation. Could you find out which night he can work with us?"

"I'm happy to hear how much progress your team has made during the past two weeks. I'll check with Mr. Hill to determine when he's available to work with you. Are there any other groups that need to work with Mr. Hill?"

"Oh, Ms. Ramirez," said Carla, "our team also needs to edit its video. We still need to scan in some still images we took with Sam's camera and add those to our presentation. Our group worked on graphing the data we collected and made graphs that compared our data to data we pulled from that national database you identified for us on the Internet. We're starting to see some interesting comparisons."

"That's great, Carla. What about your group, Ronaldo? How much work does your team have left to complete?"

"We'll probably need a few more days before all of our work is ready to share with everyone. Our team just scheduled a videoconference with an aquatic biologist from the

NSES
TS-D

ISTE-NETS
1, 2, 4

university. We're going to use the desktop conferencing equipment in the library tomorrow afternoon and link to the scientist right at his desk. Mrs. Sadlowski from the library set that up for us and taught us how to make the video phone call at 2 P.M. tomorrow. We're still figuring out how to videotape that session. Charles and Keisha talked to Mr. Hill about it at lunch today. He said he'd have to think about it, but that he'd try to find a way to capture some of the conference on video for us. We'd like to use that in our presentation."

"So, let me see—Kevin, Carla, Ronaldo. Sally, you've been awfully quiet. What's your group been up to?"

"Well, Ms. Ramirez, our group's been as busy as the others. We're just struggling with one problem. We have some data that seems like it's wrong. We're not sure if it was the pH meter that didn't work right, if the meter wasn't hooked to the computer and calibrated right to give us an accurate reading, or if those of us that read the meter messed up. Do you think if we went out today and got another pH reading that we could just plug that number into our data, or would we have to collect all the other data we're using to make our conclusions as well?"

"You've raised an interesting problem, Sally. I'd like to pose that to the entire class. What do you think about this team's problem? To help them come up with a solution, I'd like all of you to think about that article we found on the Internet last week. Remember the one about the scientists at three different labs, who assumed that they were doing exactly the same thing with rats in their study and still got different results. What kind of conclusions would they draw from their data if one of the scientists decided to just change one number because it didn't look right? Especially if they didn't inform the others."

NSES
TS-D
TS-F

A lively discussion ensued in this technology-rich, fifth-grade classroom. The debate ranged from e-mailing several scientists to get their ideas, to doing an Internet search on the use of accurate data, to having the students demonstrate to the class exactly how they used the pH meter complete with the computer hook-up, just in case they had done it right and their original data were correct.

ISTE-NETS
1, 2, 4

Scenario 2: Elementary Students with Access to a Few Educational Technologies

"Ms. King, are we meeting with your class this afternoon?" shouted three kindergarten students across Marshfield Elementary School's playground to the sixth-grade teacher.

"Of course! If you're ready to share your experiences, my students are ready to listen," replied Ms. King.

As Rachel King walked back into her sixth-grade classroom, a smile came over her face. All of the planning she did this past summer with the kindergarten teacher, Tom Denton, was paying off. Even after fifteen years of teaching in elementary schools, she was still excited when she discovered new ways to get students interested in science. This year, she collaborated with Tom to help the children in the primary grades move beyond thinking science was just "playing with stuff" to giving them opportunities to explain their understanding of the "science" behind the "play." For her sixth-grade students, it was an opportunity to review the science they learned over their years of elementary school before taking the statewide proficiency test at the end of sixth grade.

Rachel and Tom developed *kinderpals,* pairings of her sixth-grade students with kindergarten students in an effort to have a real audience for the sixth-grade students to share their understanding of the science they learned throughout their years at Marshfield Elementary. The project also gave the kindergarten students an opportunity to share their understanding of what they were learning through their science activities even before they had developed the ability to write down their understandings. The sixth-grade students would "capture" the thoughts of the kindergarten students through what looked like play and conversation to the kindergarten students. Before their weekly visits to Mr. Denton's class, Ms. King's class would do the activity that Mr. Denton was going to do with his class. Ms. King would explore with her students the science behind the activity and assign them some additional reading on the given concept or concepts as a refresher for them on previously learned material.

The plan called for starting with the kindergarten and sixth-grade students this year and expanding it up and down the grade levels over subsequent years. As constructivist educators, both Tom and Rachel believed in the value of building on their students' experiences, yet they struggled with getting those experiences into proper conceptual formation. Using even the lowest of education technologies that were available to them in their school—cassette recorders, some old donated computers, and two newer computers with Internet access in the library—proved to be a real asset to their data collection needs.

Rachel's thoughts were interrupted by her own students' animated conversations as she entered her classroom. Ron was engaged in a heated debate with Sarah and Carmen. "But Jimmy really did get the idea of surface tension after we talked about all the things he did with bubbles," stated Ron.

"I thought you were just supposed to tape the two of you having a conversation about what he did with the bubbles," Sarah said.

"I did do that, but while I was typing up some of his ideas so I could practice my keyboarding skills, something I heard Jimmy say on the tape had me puzzled. The next time we went to Mr. Denton's room, I asked Mr. Denton if Jimmy and I could play over at the water table. I started asking Jimmy some questions about the bubbles he made last week, and then I asked him if we could try to make bubbles with just plain water. After stirring up water in a cup, we started playing around to see how many things we could put in a cup of water without it overflowing. I remembered the activity we did in our own class with paper clips in a cup to explore surface tension, so I started telling Jimmy about it. All I know is that when I then took a bowl and shook pepper on the top of the water, Jimmy told me it must be surface tension that kept the pepper on top. You should have heard him scream when I put a drop of soap into the bowl and all the pepper fell to the bottom!"

Ms. King could not help jumping in with the comment "What do you plan on doing the next time you go down to Mr. Denton's class with your *kinderpal* Jimmy? Have you thought about going to the library with him and jointly generating a picture of Jimmy's experiences using the KidPix Software?"

"I didn't think of that—but what a great way to help Jimmy remember what surface tension is!"

At that suggestion, other students jumped into the conversation, some wanting to use the Internet connection in the library with their kindergarten charges to find out more information on various topics they were exploring in their class and others wanting to jointly create e-mail letters to community partners with their *kinderpals* that question the partners on how they use, in their jobs, some of the science that the kindergarten students were learning. The bell interrupted the enthusiastic sixth graders as they headed over to Mr. Denton's kindergarten class to complete their plans.

The students in Ms. Ramirez's class from the first scenario are not as unusual as some may think. Technology initiatives throughout the United States have spent millions of dollars to bring educational technology into the K–12 schools, right down to the classroom level. The students at Marshfield Elementary in the second scenario are not as fortunate. As evidenced by the *kinderpal* plan of Ms. King and Mr. Denton, even low-end technology can also offer useful tools for data collection and analysis. Whether you are an advocate of the technology being accessible in the classroom or moving the students down the hall to the lab, there is no doubt that the tools available for the twenty-first century classroom will dramatically change the way classrooms function. The artifacts of student work that we collect no longer rely on paper, pencil, and chalk. The artifacts that are created in today's classroom provide the students with multiple opportunities to construct knowledge and to demonstrate what they know.

In this chapter we:

- provide a rationale for using educational technology,
- describe a variety of digital technologies useful for supporting inquiry science, and
- provide standards and tools for making informed selections of technology and of software- and web-based instructional materials.

Those who are resistant to applying educational technology at the elementary level should reflect on the nature of technology itself and how those applications have benefited society. As an example, for one of this book's authors, growing up in the city produced an idealized view of farm life. The author envied "country kids," thinking it would be like *Rebecca of Sunny Brook Farm* every day, getting up when the rooster crowed to feed the chickens, checking under their nests for eggs, and bringing them back in a tidy basket, smiling and humming a happy tune. Many years later, good friendships were formed with those "country kids." They laughed at the author's romantic view of farm life. The horror stories they shared about the backbreaking labor were nothing to be dreamed of longingly. On the bright side, they talked of how advances in technology actually saved them hours of hard labor. Now chickens are raised in tight quarters in which all food and water are carefully measured. Eggs automatically drop down onto conveyor belts that move them along for easy collection. Egg production is not the only technological advancement on the farm. Baling hay, planting and picking crops, and grain storage have changed dramatically with advances in technology.

While we tend to think of technology for schools in terms of computers, just about any artifact of our modern world is really technology. The preceding examples demonstrate the real-world applications of technology. The opening scenarios share some uses of educational technology in the elementary school. This chapter is

Older learners can become technology mentors for younger children.

designed to help you think about how to use education technology in the classroom and apply it in a real-world context, much as the students in Ms. Ramirez's, Mr. Denton's, and Ms. King's classes did. It answers the questions of *why* one would use educational technology and *how* one could apply it in the context of science teaching. This chapter does this by examining the National Educational Technology Standards, the varying skill levels for the teacher and student in using educational technology, and by providing examples of how to apply the National Educational Technology Standards to science lessons designed to meet the National Science Education Standards.

Why Use Technology in the Science Classroom?

Chances are that in a school that is rich in educational technology, a teacher like Ms. Ramirez is given more opportunities to enhance her technology skills and is able to incorporate the available technology into her student's classroom experiences. However, as Ms. King and Mr. Denton demonstrated, even in a setting in which access to educational technology is difficult, the decision to apply educational technology in the learning environment is often driven by the task at hand, not the available technology.

Educational technology can be seamlessly incorporated into a classroom whether you are a teacher who is more comfortable using classroom content strictly prescribed by the school curriculum or you are in a school environment in which creating content based on statewide learning outcomes is encouraged. Even though you may be an expert at using one computer application, you may be a novice at another. Teachers must overcome the notion that they must be experts in using all educational technology before their students are given a chance to use it. As Ediger's (1994) studies on *Technology in the Elementary Classroom* have revealed, applying technology in the classroom does several things to student learning: (1) It increases interest even in rote tasks; (2) it provides purpose for learning; (3) it can attach meaning to an ongoing lesson; (4) it provides opportunities to perceive knowledge as being related, not isolated bits; (5) it allows for individual student differences; and (6) it can affect students' attitudes toward learning.

Teachers in today's classrooms are experiencing students who are "digital natives." These students have grown up with technology and often are more proficient in its use than their teacher is. These students also have no understanding of why technology would *not* be used in the classroom. Parents of these digital natives believe that technology provides a way to enrich their children's social lives and academic abilities.

Parents, teachers, and students are living in an age of information overload. According to the North Central Regional Education Laboratory (NCREL), parents have high expectations that students will "learn high-level skills such as how to access, evaluate, analyze, and synthesize vast quantities of information" (NCREL, 2005, paragraph 1) needed for future employment. In contrast, "teachers are evaluated by their ability to have students pass tests that often give no value to these abilities" (NCREL, 2005, paragraph 1).

Expectations about students' abilities to solve complex problems are often incompatible with the teaching and learning of isolated skills and information that must be taught by teachers for testing purposes. Finally, teachers are expected to meet the needs of all students and help them reach their full potential when high-stakes assessment tests are the primary measure of student and school success (NCREL, 2005).

Technology can assist with some of these expectations and make teachers—and their students—more successful. As the world becomes more complex, teachers must "continue to shift from teaching and learning isolated skills and information within each content area, to teaching skills that enable students to solve complex problems across many areas" (NCREL, 2005, paragraph 1). "Students in today's Web-dominated environment need to learn how to prioritize and manage a dizzying array of information coming at them through Web sites and e-mails, how to think critically about what they find, and how to use multiple media to communicate well, among other skills" (Vadero, 2007, p. 32). "Educators must prepare for a technology-rich future and keep up with change by adopting effective strategies that infuse lessons with appropriate technologies." (NCREL, 2005, paragraph 1).

National Educational Technology Standards

The artifacts of student learning—anything created by our students as evidence of their understanding of a given concept—can be created in a variety of formats as teachers provide opportunities for students to use educational technologies in the creation of such artifacts. As shared in the opening scenario, using instructional software on computers is not the only use of educational technology. The International Society for Technology in Education (ISTE) has established National Educational Technology Standards (NETS) for Students: The Next Generation for grades K–12. These six standards, which are listed in Table 8.1, define what students need to know and be able to do with technology to "learn effectively and live productively in a rapidly changing digital world" (Knezek, 2007, p. 4).

Applying these skills within the context of a science lesson can strengthen the understanding of the science concepts if we recognize and value the experiences students bring with them and then use the technology to clarify any misconceptions and stimulate proper concept formation (Nickerson, 1995). Conceptual understanding will come when the student's interaction between the educational technology and the science content is purposeful. Choosing software or websites that promote active mental processing and student discoveries is vital and must ensure for students a state of mindfulness while they interact with the technology and must motivate and engage the students to enable them to form appropriate conceptualizations. Computer software, be it instructional software such as the multitude of titles created to address a specific science topic or application software designed to create a document or draw a picture, is no substitute for active teaching and learning. It can, however, become an essential part of that teaching and learning, a means for creating student artifacts of the concepts studied.

Computers help young children to expand uses of their senses.

Technology Tools for Science

Utilizing a computer in a science classroom seems like a contradiction of constructivist science teaching. As modeled in the opening scenarios, when appropriately used as a learning tool, computers can help

TABLE 8.1 ● National Educational Technology Standards for Students: The Next Generation K–12

1. Creativity and Innovation

Students demonstrate creative thinking, construct knowledge, and develop innovative products and processes using technology. Students:

a. apply existing knowledge to generate new ideas, products, or processes.
b. create original works as a means of personal or group expression.
c. use models and simulations to explore complex systems and issues.
d. identify trends and forecast possibilities.

2. Communication and Collaboration

Students use digital media and environments to communicate and work collaboratively, including at a distance, to support individual learning and contribute to the learning of others. Students:

a. interact, collaborate, and publish with peers, experts or others employing a variety of digital environments and media.
b. communicate information and ideas effectively to multiple audiences using a variety of media and formats.
c. develop cultural understanding and global awareness by engaging with learners of other cultures.
d. contribute to project teams to produce original works or solve problems.

3. Research and Information Fluency

Students apply digital tools to gather, evaluate, and use information. Students:

a. plan strategies to guide inquiry.
b. locate, organize, analyze, evaluate, synthesize, and ethically use information from a variety of sources and media.
c. evaluate and select information sources and digital tools based on the appropriateness to specific tasks.
d. process data and report results.

4. Critical Thinking, Problem Solving, and Decision Making

Students use critical thinking skills to plan and conduct research, manage projects, solve problems, and make informed decisions using appropriate digital tools and resources. Students:

a. identify and define authentic problems and significant questions for investigation.
b. plan and manage activities to develop a solution or complete a project.
c. collect and analyze data to identify solutions and/or make informed decisions.
d. use multiple processes and diverse perspectives to explore alternative solutions.

5. Digital Citizenship

Students understand human, cultural, and societal issues related to technology and practice legal and ethical behavior. Students:

a. advocate and practice safe, legal, and responsible use of information and technology.
b. exhibit a positive attitude toward using technology that supports collaboration, learning, and productivity.
c. demonstrate personal responsibility for lifelong learning.
d. exhibit leadership for digital citizenship.

6. Technology Operations and Concepts

Students demonstrate a sound understanding of technology concepts, systems and operations. Students:

a. understand and use technology systems.
b. select and use applications effectively and productively.
c. troubleshoot systems and applications.
d. transfer current knowledge to learning of new technologies.

Source: International Society for Technology in Education (ISTE), NETS*S 2007, http://cnets.iste.org/students/NETS_S_standards-1-6.pdf

learners to construct an understanding of complex concepts. At the most basic level, software applications can be used to observe scientific phenomena directly. The software can provide a concrete example of an object, provide facts, or recall basic information. Users of educational technology can easily use drill-and-practice software. As Berger and colleagues' (1994) study notes, mindfulness is rarely associated with this type of computer-assisted instruction.

A teacher can use software applications that supply scientific information found on CD-ROM encyclopedias and atlases or software applications to evaluate student performance, keep records, or guide students to resources.

As students are given more opportunities to apply the technology in their regular classroom activities, they become more proficient through practice in various computer tools and advance to another technology level. Many of the productivity tools that assist in the creation of multimedia productions require students to have more than a simple working knowledge of the software application.

Webquests provide great problem-solving opportunities for students and allow teachers to create engaging, interactive web-based materials. Students can engage in a cooperative learning quest to solve a real-world science problem. Bernie Dodge, the creator of the webquest, has created a page for teachers to use in building webquests for their classrooms. The page, the WebQuest Portal (http://webquest.sdsu.edu/), can provide training and searchable webquests that can be matched to the science curriculum. Kathy Schrock's *WebQuest in Our Future: The Teachers' Role in Cyberspace*, (http://kathyschrock.net/slideshows/webquests/frame0001.htm) provides an overview, PowerPoint-based instructions, and a template for building a webquest to use in your classroom (Schrock, 2007). Webquests provide a way for teachers to incorporate cooperative learning, critical thinking, authentic assessment, and technology integration into inquiry-based science lessons.

Other cooperative learning tools for the science classroom include wikis and blogs. Each allows students to work with a team to publish on the Internet. Blog sites such as Blogger (https://www.blogger.com/start) or Class Blogmeister (http://classblogmeister.com/) provide educators with protected web space for students to work safely on the Internet and still have an opportunity to publish thoughts about science, share science information, and publish scientific work with photos. Wikis allow students, teachers, and experts to edit, comment, and publish on the web in a collaborative web-based effort. Wikis create an environment in which multiple student authors work on team projects and post their information for others to see and critique. Wikispaces (http://www.wikispaces.com) is a teacher-created and free wiki space for educators. It also contains a tutorial to help you or your students develop your first wiki for science.

It is important to remember that as teachers and students work on the web, issues of ownership of content and information taken from websites must be considered. Plagiarism and copyright issues are often overlooked in the classroom. Teachers and students must be careful to correctly cite all work from the Internet. A number of sites offering teachers and students information on plagiarism and copyright are available on the Internet. Parents should also be part of this discussion, as younger students "cut and paste" often to locate content for research papers.

As a final note, any teacher who is integrating technology into the classroom should establish acceptable use policies for computer and Internet use. Social spaces such as Facebook and MySpace offer opportunities for students to network with other students around the world. While most schools block such sites from school use, creative students often e-mail and connect on these sites from their home computers. It is important for every teacher to understand the possible ramifications of social networks and their impact on the classroom. Students may become victims of cyber-bullying and peer pressure through contact with others on social networks. Two websites that can help teachers to become aware of the issues of social networks are OnGuard Online (http://onguardonline.gov/socialnetworking.html) and Get-NetWise (http://www.getnetwise.org/). Each contains extensive information that can help teachers, students, and parents to be aware of safety issues surrounding Internet use. Teachers can play a major role in educating parents on the safe use of the Internet, thus providing an opportunity for parents to understand home computer use by their son or daughter.

The limits of handheld technologies are just beginning to be tested in the classroom.

Although computer simulations are no replacement for actual experimentation, simulations do "provide a valuable conceptual tool which should be augmented with actual experiments in the classroom," according to McKinney (1997). Software simulations typically require more than beginner-level skills.

Simulation software applications may provide a pictorial, verbal, numerical, or graphical representation of reality. Simulations that integrate all four forms of representation appear to offer the best opportunity to stimulate conceptual change. *Rainforest Researchers* (Tom Snyder Production, 2005a) and *The Great Ocean Rescue* (Tom Snyder Production, 2005b) are popular programs that effectively integrate all four representations. These interactive programs, designed primarily for middle school students, make use of video, print, and computer software to engage students in an interdisciplinary unit.

Computer-based laboratories, which effectively integrate numerical and graphical data as quickly as a probe attached to the computer can record them, often require technology skills beyond the novice level. Small devices such as the HOBO® data logger can be used to monitor both indoor and outdoor conditions such as temperature, relative humidity, rainfall, and sunlight and can connect to third-party sensor devices. The HOBO® has the ability to connect to a computer or be used as a stand-alone digital device. Sensors and timing devices attached to a computer, students can do such things as monitor heart rate; detect strength and direction of external forces; determine the strength of magnetic fields; record temperature; record pH of liquids; measure amplitudes of audio sources; sense and record humidity changes; imitate the spectral response of the human eye; sense and record changes in pressure; and use an ultrasonic motion detector to measure distance, velocity, and acceleration (Arbor Scientific Company, 1996).

Students who are proficient in all six categories of the National Educational Technology Standards are at a level of technological literacy at which they can use software applications that simulate experiments in which variables may be manipulated and extended beyond ordinary phenomena. Microworlds (http://www.microworlds.com) are computer-based laboratory experiences that simulate real-world phenomena. Students can explore undefined phenomena when given proper guidance and intervention by the teacher. Students can be given "what if" predictive situations to evaluate and reflect on scientific theories, pose problems that can be solved only through computer-enhanced simulations, and construct the meaning of concepts based on computer-simulated evidence. An inquiring science educator can bring the use of computers to their highest level of application by using microworld environments to give students opportunities to explore and discover scientific theories by using problem-solving strategies to ask, "What is the real problem?" "How do we know it's a problem?" "How can we go about solving the problem?" Microworlds truly embody the spirit of constructivism in its application.

There are many methods that science teachers can use to integrate the ISTE National Educational Technology Standards into their lessons. Some examples are as follows:

- Use a digital camera to take pictures each week of a plant's growth and place the measurements of the plant's growth on a bulletin board.

- Classification activities help students to increase their vocabulary, observation skills, and critical thinking.
  1. Create a chart (spreadsheet) that shows the characteristics of pets that students in the class have at home.
  2. Use websites to locate different animals found around the world and identify these characteristics compared to the students' pets.
  3. Create a chart (spreadsheet) that shows the number and characteristics of trees on the playground.
- Keep a scientist's journal about local habitats.
  1. Use drawings created in KidPix and other drawing software.
  2. Download images from the web or scan copyright-free pictures.
  3. Write observations in a journal concerning a particular habitat and the interaction of organisms in that habitat.
  4. Record activities of organisms in the habitat with a video recorder or digital video camera and share with the class and parents.
  5. Compare and contrast the observations seen in the video at different times of day.
- Use concept mapping software such as Inspiration® to assess students' understanding of concepts presented in a unit of study.
- Use PowerPoint to create presentations containing pictures, demonstrations, and explanations of students' investigations.

Young scientists enjoy investigating the world around them. Digital cameras and digital video cameras can help improve observation skills and help students become more aware of the world in which they live.

Removing Classroom Walls to Expand Learning

NSES
PD-B, D

The Internet allows teachers and students to move beyond the classroom walls into a wide variety of environments, including virtual tours, databases containing real-time data, web content pages, wikis, blogs, and social environments for learning. Each of these unique environments provides opportunities for students to connect with other students, become publishers on the web, and connect to experts in the field.

Teachers now have greater access to additional information, knowledge, and content experts by eliminating barriers of time and place. Internet connectivity encourages teachers' professional development, collegial consensus building, and development of shared ideas related to professional teaching. Teachers find that skills in using the Internet can provide them with opportunities to link with other practicing teachers through sites such as the Global Learning Portal (http://www.glp.net) or Globe Project (http://www.globe.gov/globe_flash.html).

Science standards for every state, the National Science Education Standards (http://www.nap.edu/readingroom/books/nses/html/overview.html), and science associations found on the web can provide support for the first-time science teacher for job interviews. Teacher grant award competitions and competitions for students may be found as well (O'Brien & Lewis, 1999).

Various national databases exist to support science teaching. Some national services include the National Science Teachers Association (NSTA), the National Consortium for Environmental Education and Training (NCEET), the National Aeronautics and Space Administration (NASA), the National Oceanic and Atmospheric Administration (NOAA), and the National Park Service. These sources provide websites filled with lessons, resources, and knowledge of various science topics. Science NetLinks (http://www.sciencenetlinks.com/) contains lessons, a list of resources that have been carefully evaluated, interactive tools, and K–12 science literacy goals as outlined by AAAS's Project 2061.

teachers on Science Teaching

Bringing Students Eureka! Moments

by Louise Sayuk
Grade 4, The Kinkaid School, Houston, Texas

"Robotics was lots of fun! Every day I looked forward to it."

"I really loved learning computer graphing. It was cool how those numbers could turn into a chart."

"What did I like about robotics? Everything . . . cool models, the challenge, racing, and the computer programming was really nifty!"

"Computer graphing was super. I not only learned how to make graphs, but now I am so much better at reading them."

"It was such fun changing the graphics of graphs!"

"Google Images is the best. I can now find pictures of EVERYTHING!"

"I enjoyed programming the robots. After this unit, I tried other programming on my own. It was almost like magic how you could move things from the computer to the Lego brick. Where else could someone my age make something come to life?"

"Eureka! moments" are what science is all about, and the quotes above from some of my students show how technology has brought more and more of these moments to our elementary school classroom. Two years ago when our school's technology committee decided to provide computer carts with twenty laptops for classroom use, our world of technology opened considerably. Now all students had their own computer and could connect to the Internet from their desk. There was ample opportunity for everyone to do research, graphing, or robotics. Not being a computer whiz myself, I have to admit I was hesitant. However, after our first exploratory work, the students and I have all been thrilled with the possibilities. Computer graphing, robotics, and Internet research are all standard parts of our curriculum. In addition we use flex cams to show work on our classroom TV and have digital cameras available for recording data.

What value did adding technology contribute to our classroom experience? Students have learned the value of persistence in a project. "Try, try, again" is often the motto when working through how the computer program they have written translates into the movement of the robot. The excitement evidenced by all when it finally responds as planned permeates the classroom. Students from other groups come running to celebrate with the designer, often questioning the strategies used by the inventing group for success.

Girls have learned that they can be just as successful as boys in designing prototypes and programming. Girls working in groups have often become the leaders in writing programs and working on designs. It is evident that they feel very proud of their achievements. What a great boost for self-esteem!

Robotics and graphing seem to offer students success no matter what their learning styles. Some children excel at the programming, some at the designing, and some at embellishing the graphics. All of the projects seem to offer everyone some area where they can make a valuable contribution.

Technology has enhanced the creativity of the students. Once students begin to work on these projects, there is no limit to where their imaginations can take them. The different ways to use robotic sensors and solar panels especially seem to get the creative juices flowing. Availability of the Internet has provided a plethora of information that formerly would have been difficult to keep available in the classroom. In addition, sites such as Google Images allow the teacher to show pictures on virtually any science topic. Our computer is linked to our classroom TV screen, giving us the equivalent of a file of millions of classroom posters.

Technology empowers both the teacher and the students to be their best. What a great opportunity for students to coach teachers while teachers are coaching students. Working on these projects not only increases the communication and critical thinking skills of students in the group, but also puts them at ease with technology. When new projects come along in middle school, they will be ready to dive right in!

Several states have developed websites that provide outstanding resources that have been peer reviewed and evaluated by experts in science and education. Development of web-based sites makes resources readily accessible to the teacher. One such website is the Ohio Resource Center (www.ohiorc.org). The Ohio Resource Center (ORC) for Mathematics, Science, and Reading is a "virtual" best practices center. Materials at the ORC site provide web-based content, instruction, and professional resources for science, mathematics, and reading which exemplify teaching to high standards. The ORC provides a rubric to use when evaluating best practices and contains numerous links to web-based lesson plans on the Internet.

With more than one billion websites available for use, the web is becoming a primary source of information for teachers and students. Teachers must take care to review each website for appropriate content before bringing it into the classroom. Many websites seem harmless at first but upon careful scrutiny are found to contain information that is incorrect or—worse—harmful. Teachers and students must learn to critically evaluate each website that they use during information gathering. This digital literacy skill is considered by ISTE NETS to be one of the most important skills for today's society. Web pages should be evaluated for their authenticity, applicability, authorship, bias, and usability (Schrock, 2007). A great location on the web to use for evaluating websites and to gain more information on the process for evaluating websites is Kathy Schrock's Guide for Educators, available at http://school.discovery.com/schrockguide/eval.html. This site contains a complete guide to evaluating websites for each grade level: elementary, middle, and high school. The pages of the evaluation are downloadable in PDF format for easy use by teachers and students.

Teachers should critically review any electronically accessed lesson, no matter which website is accessed for science resources. Just because a source is "published" on the Internet does not necessarily mean it is worthwhile. Table 8.2 suggests evaluation criteria for judging the worthiness of electronically accessed lessons. Please use this table to help you sort and separate the safest and most promising lessons.

TABLE 8.2 ● Is This a Worthy Task?

Is the task based on sound and significant content?
- Identify the concepts and/or skills.
- Is the content accurate?

Is the task based on knowledge of students' understandings, interests, experiences, and the range of ways that diverse students learn?
- Identify why the task might appeal to your students.

Are all safety measures properly addressed and followed in any lessons that are provided? If not, can appropriate safety measures be easily applied to the given task? If you answer no to this second question, do *not* use this lesson.

In your opinion to what extent would the task:

	a lot				not at all
• engage students' intellect?	4	3	2	1	0
• actively involve students?	4	3	2	1	0
• develop students' understandings and skills?	4	3	2	1	0
• stimulate students to make connections to other disciplines?	4	3	2	1	0
• stimulate students to make connections to the real world?	4	3	2	1	0
• call for problem formation, problem solving, and reasoning?	4	3	2	1	0
• promote communication/interaction among students?	4	3	2	1	0

For students, Internet environments provide real-world applications of science concepts. Collecting data that will be shared in a nationwide database, such as the *Everglades Information Network and Digital Library* or the *Journey North: A Global Study of Wildlife Migration,* encourages students to be more careful in applying proper scientific procedures when they collect their data on a local level to be shared nationally.

Learn NPs, an interactive project funded primarily by the National Park Service, is designed to promote greater understanding and appreciation of the natural and cultural heritage of the United States and to develop sustainable partnerships among parks, schools, and communities. Through *Learn NPs,* data are collected to monitor air, water, and land resources on parklands. This interactive project can simulate landform changes and cycles in populations within the parks (National Park Service, 2007).

Technology helps learners to explore and understand social, ethical, and human issues.

The National Geographic Society offers *National Geographic Explorer,* a combination of weblinks designed to meet curricular needs, telecommunications' access to classrooms around the world, teacher guides and lesson plans, homework support, and access to activities and experiments (National Geographic Society, 2007). There are various problem-based links to join.

Although national projects can be accessed and joined, having access to a wide area network within the classroom can encourage students and teachers to start their own science research projects and to invite schools throughout the nation to join the research effort. Collaborative projects can be designed to explore bodies of water, landfills, groundwater movement, seasonal changes per latitude, or any local problem or issue that may have global impact. The impact of projects like these is best stated by one teacher who responded to the question "What are your most compelling reasons for integrating educational technology into the curriculum?" as posed by Randy Knuth on the Internet in September 1995:

> I think we should go beyond integration into the classroom and create a new context for learning that maximizes the learning potential of technology and telecommunications. From my perspective . . . the reason is relevancy. We can extend learning beyond the walls of the classroom . . . to do real stuff with real people for compelling reasons . . . with real results that have real significance. Students are not dumb . . . they know when it matters and when it is simply an exercise. . . . Connect them to their communities through technology! And give them economic viability! (Knuth, 1995)

Using educational technology as a communication tool goes beyond transporting graphics and text. Depending on the connectivity, students can participate in networks that transport voice, video, and data. Schools throughout the nation are linking together to share in scientific explorations with full motion video and voice interface. From the primary level through college, students are linking with content providers to enrich and enhance the lessons that are studied within the classroom. Zoos, museums, and cultural institutions are revamping the way in which they present their content to take advantage of the visual medium offered through interactive video networks. Linkages like these promote greater student interaction and discussion of concepts. Providing students with as many opportunities as possible to articulate their understanding of concepts will promote greater conceptual construction and retention. Advancing technologies offer students opportunities on an ever-increasing basis.

Emerging Technologies in the Science Classroom

NSES

PD-A

TS-D

Emerging technologies are technologies that are at the leading edge; in other words, these are technologies that are just beginning to be found in K–12 classrooms and are being explored as new tools to help students gain a better understanding of science and to improve student achievement. With the recent improvements in wireless technologies, more portable personal computers, and the Internet, schools are examining the use of personal digital assistants in their classrooms. Personal digital assistants are often referred to as PDAs or handheld computers. Many of you will recognize these devices under the brand names of Palm®, PocketPC®, and iPaq®.

These small personal computers may be held in the palm of a student's hand, are lightweight and portable, and have enough memory to carry out many of the same function that are available on a typical desktop computer. The portability of the handheld computer allows the student to carry a computer to a wide variety of sites for fieldwork and data collection. Word processing, spreadsheet, and database software found on most handhelds is similar to the software on a desktop. The student can enter field notes into the word processor file or collect data into a database file and then transfer the files to his or her classroom desktop at a later time.

With the advent of the handheld computer, there has been a resurgence in the use of probeware in elementary classrooms. Sensor probes such as the Vernier LabQuest® allow for the real-time capture and display of data to create new possibilities for learners to explore and understand the world in which they live. The ability of the handheld device to take the data collected from the probe and display them in a symbolic manner can greatly increase comprehension of difficult to learn concepts (Tinker, 2003).

Creating theories and testing them in the real world are important activities of science. The use of handheld devices and probeware can help young students to develop measurement skills and to translate the physical environment in a visual environment that tests conceptual understanding. These small, battery-operated devices give students the freedom to explore their homes, playgrounds, museums, and field environments without being tied to the electrical outlet on the wall (Bannasch & Tinker, 2002).

Teachers find that these small handhelds can be used as an assessment tool in the classroom and as a management tool for keeping track of student assignments, lesson plans, and organizational needs in the classroom. While some teachers feel that it is difficult to integrate handheld devices and probeware into the classroom, many companies that sell handhelds and probeware are developing lesson plans to help teachers overcome their anxiety about this emerging technology. Teachers using handheld devices and probeware are able to integrate technology into a science curriculum that focuses on inquiry, problem solving, and conceptual understanding.

Assistive Technologies in the Science Classroom

Assistive technology refers to "any item, piece of equipment, or product that is used to increase, maintain, or improve functional capabilities of individuals with disabilities" (Technology-Related Assistance for Individuals with Disabilities Act of 1998; Assistive Technology Act, 1998). The Assistive Technology Act was amended in 1998 to provide for wider implementation in classrooms across the nation. Classroom are being transformed within education from lecture-based and teacher-centered learning to a more student-centered, constructivist model for education. The focus is to understand how different people perceive, transform, and convey concepts by placing the student at the center of learning. Technology can offer tools to apply the principles of cognitive theory to teaching and learning (Landmark College, 2006).

Assistive technology connects a student's cognitive abilities to an educational opportunity. Technology helps students with disabilities to accomplish tasks such as these:

- *Master grade-level content:* Technology presents the material in different forms (visually, auditorily, etc.).
- *Improve writing and organizational skills:* Technology can enable students with learning disabilities or autism to do such things as develop a concept map for a research paper and write using grade-level vocabulary words that they would not use without a computer because of poor spelling skills.
- *"Read" grade-level text:* The computer either reads the text digitally or presents it at a lower grade level for students with reading disabilities or visual impairments.
- *Take notes:* Many students with disabilities have difficulty taking notes in longhand because of poor spelling, writing, and/or eye-hand coordination skills.
- *Master educational concepts that would have been beyond their reach:* Students can experience abstract concepts such as the metamorphosis of a flower through three-dimensional simulations (Jendron, 2007, paragraph 1).

Assistive technologies come in a wide range of equipment that can improve access to technology in the science classroom. Special devices such as modified keyboards, head pointers, and keyguards can be connected to computers to improve a student's control over the device. Devices to improve vision, hearing, and computer-aided instruction can also be found in science classrooms to connect the student to learning. Several great websites offer teachers and parents information about the types of equipment that can be used in a classroom and how the equipment can be located or purchased. The National Center for Improved Practice (http://www2.edc.org/NCIP/) has an extensive list of technologies and resources for students with special needs. "Web Toolboxes for Educators," (http://www.ed.sc.edu/caw/toolboxvendors.html) by Dr. Cheryl Wissick at the University of South Carolina College of Education, offers help with the integration of technology in education with links for software related to web access, talking word processors, and text-to-speech tools (Jendron, 2007, paragraph 1). Assistive technologies cannot guarantee academic success but provide students with alternative ways of learning through the use of advanced technologies.

How Can Technology Be Applied in the Context of Science Teaching?

The National Science Education Content Standards provide a list of concept statements for the three science divisions, Physical, Life, and Earth and Space Sciences. One would never think of having students simply memorize the concept statements. In fact, the Science Standards provide many suggestions for effective science teaching, all strongly encouraging active student exploration to construct an understanding of the science concepts. The lessons that are provided in the back of this textbook serve as examples of how the standards can be explored through student-centered inquiry activities within a learning cycle format.

NSES

TS-A, D

Learning Cycle Featured Lesson

NATIONAL SCIENCE EDUCATION CONTENT STANDARDS—GRADES 5–8

Life Science

▶ Populations and Ecosystems Concepts. For ecosystems, the major source for energy is sunlight. Energy entering ecosystems as sunlight is converted by producers into chemical energy through photosynthesis. Energy then passes from organisms in food webs.

NET Student Standards

▶ Technology operations and concepts—using tech tools to collect data.

▶ Digital citizenship—social, ethical and human issues and discussion of advantages of using tech tools to collect data.

▶ Communication and collaboration tools— using technology to communicate results of study.

CONCEPTS TO BE CONSTRUCTED

▶ Light is a necessary factor for life by way of photosynthesis.

▶ The intensity of light varies throughout canopy levels within a forest.

SCIENCE ATTITUDES TO NURTURE

▶ Open-mindedness

▶ Cooperating with others

▶ Tolerance for the opinions of others

PROCESS SKILLS USED

▶ Hypothesizing

▶ Observing

▶ Collecting and recording data

▶ Manipulating materials

▶ Interpreting data

▶ Designing an experiment

▶ Drawing conclusions

Life Science: Impact of Light in the Forest

Grades • 5–8

Engaging Question

Does the light intensity affect the type of vegetation that is found in an area?

Materials Needed

For exploration phase • conducted in teams of three or four, each team will need

- 1 Palm® with Vernier Light Sensor and an ImagiWorks Interface and one-prong interface sensor adaptor **OR**
- 1 HOBO® device with built in light intensity sensor.
- Computer with software for the data collection device used, Microsoft Word, Excel, and a web browser.

For expansion phase • conducted in teams of three or four, each team will need

- Same materials as listed for exploration phase.

Safety: Handle all equipment with care. Broken equipment should be reported to the teacher immediately. Do not take the equipment near water. Use caution when working in poorly lighted area. Always walk, do not run, in the classroom or out in the field of study area.

Exploration

Student Activity

- Group students, providing each team with a Vernier probe and Palm® or a HOBO®.

- Ask the students to measure the amount of light in different areas of the room with the lights off and only one window with open curtains.

- Students measure light, collect data, and analyze data from three specific areas and three areas which the students choose.

- Results should be graphed in a model to be put on the chalkboard for whole class review.

Mini Explanation—check for understanding on using probes to collect light intensity data

As the students maneuver through the introduction activity, they will find that areas away from the window have less light. Wave properties of light will be seen when light is detected even behind obstacles.

- Where is the intensity of the light greatest and where is it least?

- Why is the light greatest or least there?

- How does light get around obstacles?

- How does light move? (straight lines? curves?)

- Does light bend? Explain.

Begin the next activity once the students demonstrate they can use the light probes with the Palm® or use the HOBO® correctly to collect light intensity data.

- Divide the students into research groups, and provide each team with three growing bean plants, already potted. Ask the teams to think about the results of light intensity data they collected earlier.

- On the basis of the analysis of those data, ask them to select three study areas in the room to place their growing plants where:

    1) they found the light intensity to be the greatest,

    2) they found the light intensity to be the least, and

3) they found the light intensity to be between the greatest and the least.

- Before they place the plants in their three study areas, have the students create a data sheet to record the condition of their plants before being placed in the test areas.

- Allow the teams to pick which variables they will record as to the *condition* of their plants. Remind them about manipulating only the variable of light through placement in three different study areas. Since they are manipulating the amount of light, all other variables should remain constant; for example, the amount of water provided to each plan, how often each plant will be watered, amount of nutrients given to each plant (if any), conditions of plant that will be recorded (e.g., height, number of leaves, sturdiness of stem).

- Ask the teams to record light intensity on their plants and the condition of their plants on a daily basis.

- After two weeks, ask the teams to create a graph that compares the conditions of their three plants over time.

- Ask the teams to draw conclusions on the relationship between light intensity and the condition of their plants.

- Share the results with the entire class.

Explanation

Ask the student teams to share the results of their data analysis. Ask the students to reflect on their exploration activity to answer the following:

- Was there a difference between the plants that grew where the light intensity was the greatest and the plants that grew where the light intensity was the least?

- What did you observe about the growth of the plants in the "in-between" area?

- On the basis of the data you collected, what could you conclude about the relationship between light intensity and plant growth? (Students should conclude that too

much or too little light intensity would stunt plant growth.)

Once the students can articulate that plant growth depends upon light intensity, explain to them that light is necessary for plant growth in that it stimulates food production and that this process is called photosynthesis. At this point, the teacher can develop a presentation on photosynthesis, explaining how light energy is converted to food energy for the plant. Background knowledge on photosynthesis will help the students to respond to the inquiry question posed in the beginning of the lesson and explored in the expansion phase of the lesson.

PROCESS SKILLS USED
▶ Observing
▶ Hypothesizing
▶ Experimenting
▶ Recording and analyzing data
▶ Cognitive thinking
▶ Drawing conclusions

Light Intensity and Photosynthesis

Assign the student teams to a field study area within the forested school land lab, in the open prairie area, and in an area right next to the school void of vegetation.

• On day one, as a team, the students will go to all three of their assigned study areas and record the type and amount of vegetation found within each area. Teams should develop a data table to collect and record this data.

• A schedule will be set up so that at specific times during the school day, different students in the group will be responsible for going to those three study areas and collecting data on light intensity, using the light probes. They will record the light intensity data on their record sheets (Note: This can be created on the Palm® through Excel or even by using the ImagiProbe® software on the Palm®.)

• Teams should record their data at the same times throughout the day for five consecutive days. The inquiry question behind this study is "Does light intensity affect the type of vegetation that is found in an area?"

Once the students have collected and analyzed the data, the teacher will use that information to get into a discussion on photosynthesis, asking how students think varying levels of light affect the rate of photosynthesis and how light intensity affects the types of plants that are found within the study areas.

Science in Personal and Social Perspectives

• How will your understanding of light intensity affect where you place the plants you have growing in your homes?

• When you see a houseplant with yellowed leaves, what do you think the plant is telling you?

Science and Technology

• What is the benefit of using the probes with the Palm Pilots in the field or the lab?

• Can you come up with any uses for the light intensity probe other than collecting information on plant growth?

Science as Inquiry

• Why do we need plants?

• Can we live without plants?

History and Nature of Science

• Why is it important in conducting an experiment that you manipulate only one variable and control all of the others?

Hands-on Assessment

The students will be able to design an experiment that shows the relationship between light intensity and plant growth.

Reflective Assessment

The students will be able to explain the importance of light in the process or photosynthesis. They will also be able to explain why plants that are found on a deciduous forest floor grow earlier in the spring compared to the trees of the forest.

Pictorial Assessment

When given a picture of a rain forest, the students will be able to explain why plants that are found on the forest floor compete for sunlight compared to members of the canopy.

Just as the National Science Education Standards make recommendations for how a science concept may be best learned, so does the International Society for Technology in Education strongly suggest that the teaching of the National Educational Technology Standards not take place void of context. Chapter 8 of the companion website contains a section called *Technology Ideas for Meeting the NETS: The Next Generation.* This website provides examples of how the National Educational Technology Standards for students can easily be incorporated into each science lesson without an added burden to the teacher and allows the student to develop technology skills while learning a particular science concept.

The lessons that are found in Section II of this textbook can be accomplished without the use of educational technology. However, as you read through the tables and recall Ediger's six findings on what educational technology can do to enhance learning, you will discover that if you apply a few of these suggestions to the lessons, educational technology can truly enrich the learning experience.

chapter summary

Some time in the future, you and your students might pick up a newspaper and read a headline such as "Genetic Engineering Unravels the Aging Process" or "Antartic Ice Increases Rate of Melting." The stories following these headlines will be important to both you and your students. They will deal with important quality-of-life issues that you, as citizens, may need to form an opinion about or make a decision about concerning your future. Being able to understand the consequences of your choices is important to you and to your students.

As a teacher, you will need to ask yourself whether you have done your best to provide your students with the skills they will need to make these future decisions. Emphasis on student inquiry through questioning, research, issue resolution, and higher-order thinking skills must be constantly practiced as well as consistent use of educational technology to create the artifacts that demonstrate the students' ability to perform such skills.

Scientific and technological knowledge is changing so rapidly that it is becoming more difficult to prepare students for this complicated task. Textbooks cannot keep pace with the new discoveries in science; however, as a classroom teacher, you can supplement your textbook and your program with experiences and opportunities from the Internet.

Stimulate learning by serving as the bridge between the resources that are relevant and available to you and the students in your classroom. Appropriate applications of educational technology can extend the learning environment beyond the confines of the classroom. Only your imagination and energy limit your uses of educational technology, which can provide inquiry-based learning opportunities that stimulate your students and provide an atmosphere for scientific discovery.

reflect and respond

1. Review the National Educational Technology Standards provided in Table 8.1. Visit the International Society for Technology in Education website at cnets.iste.org to review the specific performance indicators for each standard at a given grade range. Do you think these are realistic expectations for all students? Why or why not?

2. Defend the notion that the National Educational Technology Standards provided in Table 8.1 are not linear.

Do you believe it is possible for your students to be more proficient in some technologies than you are? Would that intimidate you? Explain your feelings. Identify one educational technology tool you'd like to become more proficient in and establish a plan for reaching proficiency.

3. Discuss what criteria you may use to choose instructional science software. What criteria will you use to make your decision?

4. Locate two web sources that you could use with students in your grade level. Using the ABC's of Website Evaluation found at http://school.discovery.com/schrockguide/pdf/weval_02.pdf, evaluate the websites you have chosen. Did you make a good selection of websites? If not, which area of the evaluation was the most difficult to meet?

Explore—Video Homework Exercise. Reread "Teachers on Science Teaching" box in this chapter. Then go to MyEducationLab at www.myeducationlab.com and select the topic "Technology," then watch the video entitled "Lesson on Birds"; and the video entitled "Technology" with particular attention devoted to the types of technologies presented and how the technologies are used. Respond to the questions below.

NSES
TS-A
TS-D

1. What types of technologies are shown in the video? Can you identify a way in which each technology that is shown can be used to support concept development in science?

2. We often think of technology as only a computer. What other types of technologies can be used to engage learners in science?

3. In the video, the teacher spoke of going to centers. How can a center be used to promote the integration of technology into a science lesson?

4. Create a personal statement about the use of technology in your science classroom.

Enrich—Weblink Exercise. Go to MyEducationLab Resources section and select "Weblinks," then click on the links for "Introduction to Assistive Technology" and "National Educational Technology Standards (NETS)."

NSES
TS-D

1. Using the Internet and being safe on the Internet can be daunting for teachers. Locate two websites that can be used to support teachers in determining ways in which safe access to technology can be achieved in the classroom. What issues of copyright must be adhered to in using material from the Internet?

ISTE-NETS
5-A, B, C, D

2. Assistive technologies can help to eliminate barriers to learning and provide support in helping the teacher in the classroom meet the needs of all students. Identify three ways in which you could use technology to help students with disabilities in today's science classroom.

3. Identify a science concept for a particular grade level from the National Science Education Standards provided in the Appendix or from the link found in My Lab School.

Create a learning cycle lesson plan for a given concept. Include activities that require the students to practice each of the six National Educational Technology Standard for Students (NETS).

Expand—Weblink Exercise

Science Literacy. Go to MyEducationLab Resources section and select "Weblinks," then click on the link for "Building Websites for Scientific Literacy" to read several revealing definitions and discussion of how definitions of scientific literacy can be used to evaluate websites.

How Do You Plan for and Integrate Science with Other Disciplines?

focus questions

- What is integration?

- How do I go about integrating science with other content areas?

- What is an *across the standards* approach to integration? How do I do this?

- What is a *driving question* approach to integration? How do I do this?

- What are the school system challenges to integrating the curriculum?

- How can I overcome those challenges?

Shaundra Lewis is a newly hired first-grade teacher at Wilton Elementary. The day she signed her contract, the principal handed her four thick books of standards for each of the major content areas: science, mathematics, language arts, and social studies. She went home rather bewildered, trying to figure out how she would survive her first year of teaching and meet every standard identified for first grade. Excited about her new position, Shaundra planned to spend the summer determining how she would address each of the standards throughout the school year.

Shaundra started by creating a calendar and marked when she would address each of the indicators for the different disciplines' standards. She soon became overwhelmed with the list of things to cover and called her principal in despair.

"I just can't figure out how I'm going to meet all of these standards within one school year, especially if all of my first graders do not come prepared to begin where the kindergarten standards left off. How do the other teachers do it all?"

"Whoa, Shaundra! I never meant to overwhelm you with the standard guides. I meant for you to review them so that when you meet with the other first-grade teachers this summer, you'll be up to speed understanding the standards. The other teachers spent the spring quarter looking at the newly adopted state standards for each of the disciplines. Their plan for the summer was to review the standards for overlapping concepts and to determine which units and lessons they could develop integrating the standards across the disciplines."

"How am I going to do that?" Shaundra asked.

"A strategy that we found worked well with fifth-grade teachers was to create a chart of the standards for each discipline and then look for similarities, even when different terms describe the big ideas. For instance, the science standards address science as inquiry. When you read the description for what is meant by inquiry, and examine the specific indicators for your grade level on what inquiry means, you should see an overlap between those descriptions and the problem-solving standard in mathematics. Also, in the language arts standards, for instance, the students are expected to conduct research, pose questions, and gather, evaluate, and synthesize data. The fifth-grade teachers saw a link between these skills and what is described as the history and nature of science in the science standards."

"So, basically, what you're saying is that the more I can familiarize myself with the individual standards for each of the disciplines, the easier it may be for me to make the links across them," Shaundra said. "Then in our upcoming planning meetings we can begin to write lessons that incorporate standards from two or more disciplines. Wow, I'm so relieved! The idea of integration encourages me. I may just be able to address all of these standards in one year."

Having to "do it all" can be an insurmountable task even for veteran teachers. Teachers are faced with meeting national standards each day for the four major disciplines of science, mathematics, language arts, and social studies and standards for the arts, physical fitness, and technology at least weekly. How can one address the standards for each of the disciplines without treating them like a "to do" list? What does it mean to integrate the disciplines? Is it possible to integrate, and if so, how can it happen so that science is not neglected? In this chapter, we help you to:

- explore the meaning of integrated learning;
- examine two integration methods that support inquiry; and
- understand the unique challenges of integrated planning, teaching, and learning.

What Is Integration?

NSES

TS-F
PD-B

It is not uncommon for classroom teachers of the same grade level to plan units together—much like the teachers in our opening scenario. It becomes problematic, however, when teachers are all using the same terms, but understand them to have different meanings and intentions. Integration of the disciplines should not be confused with planning topic-based units. At the primary level, the problem arises when teachers decide that everyone will use dinosaurs as the topic for the upcoming unit or when they all try to use a topic such as pumpkins when the seasons change from summer to autumn. Using a topic to teach each subject is *not* the same as planning integrated lessons.

Integrated instruction also requires more than a superficial understanding of the standards for each discipline. Shaundra, the teacher in the opening scenario, was correct to begin reviewing the standards documents the principal gave her upon signing her teaching contract. A quick review, however, is not enough. One should be able to understand what is meant by the term *standards* for each discipline and what subdivisions are found under those standards. Does one discipline follow the standards with grade-range benchmarks and then more specific grade-level indicators, or do they simply provide generalizations for grade-level ranges below the standards? Having an understanding of how each discipline organizes its standards helps in looking for recurring big ideas or concepts across the disciplines.

In the literature, integrated instruction is also referred to as *cross-curricular instruction* or *thematic instruction* (Holdren, 1994; Vogt, 1995; Lake, 2001). In those interpretations, integrated or "thematic instruction seeks to put the teaching of cognitive skills such as reading, mathematics, science, and writing in the context of a real-world subject that is both specific enough to be practical, and broad enough to allow creative exploration" (McDonough, 2001). "Blended science instruction" is another way of defining the term *integrated instruction.* Through blended science instruction, lessons or units are planned in which the discrete science subjects are connected throughout the lesson (McComas & Wang, 1998).

Whatever terms one uses, *cross-curricular, thematic, or blended,* integrated instruction requires choosing a key concept for a theme that sets a clear focus for all instruction, learning, and assessment. The National Project Learning Tree Environmental Education Guides (http://www.plt.org) offer many standards-based lessons that serve as models for integration using key environmental concepts. A good example of a key concept they offer is *pollution.* "Pollution is considered any contamination of the air, water, or land that affects the environment in an unwanted way." This key concept is developed through the learning cycle lessons featured as Lessons A and B in this chapter. Both lessons do as Vogt suggested when describing the use of key concepts in thematic instruction: "This key concept guides all activities and lessons, and the reading selections emerge naturally from it. It is expected, by the end of the theme, that all students will begin to internalize, build upon, and transfer this key concept to their own lives" (Vogt, 1995).

Successfully integrated lessons require the writing of clear and succinct concept statements. A novice teacher may need to work on several lessons within the individual disciplines until he or she has gained experience with the standards for each of the disciplines to make the leap to integration. Planning and delivering lessons for only one discipline help the teacher to personally struggle with the interpretation of the standard, allow the teacher to thoughtfully apply the individual standards within a lesson, and, by reflecting on the lessons after they are taught, provides feedback on how the students struggled with the concepts and where the misconceptions may remain. Being aware of children's misconceptions in individual disciplines can help the teacher to focus the key concept statement of an integrated lesson and to avoid reinforcing student's misconceptions.

The key to successful integration is not to *force* it. If the links across the disciplines are not evident as the lesson is being developed, do not add an extra task just to address a given discipline's standard if it doesn't fit with the rest of the lesson. This strategy leaves the impression that you're treating the standards like a checklist, something to be covered to force integration. The beauty of creating an integrated lesson is that it allows for revisiting the content that may have been taught in isolation (as just one discipline) to show the links among and between the disciplines.

Approaches to Integration

Across the Standards Approach

Much like the team of fifth-grade teachers mentioned in the opening scenario, one way to purposely plan to integrate multiple disciplines within one lesson plan is to complete a Standards Similarity Analysis (Table 9.1). By first determining what was meant by standards for each discipline and next determining the indicators for those standards— what the children are expected to know and be able to do—it became evident that the standards could be classified into five categories: content, skills, technology, the nature of the discipline, and real-world connections.

Analysis of the standards revealed that each discipline has unique content knowledge. In Table 9.1, the Standards Similarity Analysis, unique content is placed in the first row. Also, found within the standards are skills that at first glance may appear to be

NSES

CS-unifying
Concepts
PR-D

TABLE 9.1 ● The Standards Similarity Analysis

Similarity	Science	Mathematics	Language Arts	Social Studies	Technology
			Disciplines		
Content	• Life • Physical • Earth/Space Science	• Algebra • Geometry • Numbers and operations	• Write, speak, and visually represent to create text • Range of materials and purposes for reading	• People, places, and environments • Power, authority and governance • Production, distribution and consumption	• Technology productivity tools
Skills	• Inquiry	• Measurement • Data Analysis and Probability • Problem Solving • Reasoning and Proof	• Research and inquiry • Reading strategies, language use, and conventions	• Individuals, groups, and institutions	• Technology research tools • Technology problem-solving and decision-making tools
Technology	• Technology			• Production, Distribution and consumption • Science, Technology, and Society	• Basic operations and concepts
The Nature of the Discipline	• History and nature	• Communication • Representation	• Purposes for spoken, written, and visual language	• Time, continuity, and change • Civic ideals and practices	• Social, ethical, and human issues • Technology communication tools
Real-World Connections	• Personal and social	• Connections	• Language diversity and competency	• Culture • Individual development and identity • Individuals, groups, and institutions • Global connections	• Technology problem-solving and decision-making tools

unique to the discipline, but upon careful examination, one may find similarities with the skills that are developed within another discipline. Overlapping skills can be addressed in an integrated lesson.

In many of the disciplines, there is a standard that addressed the link between that discipline and technology. This is not to be confused with computer-based technology; rather, *technology* is a term that is globally defined as "*any manmade invention that alters or changes our environment and/or has impacted the environment in some way.*" In mathematics and language arts, technology as defined above is not addressed, and it is left blank in Table 9.1. These disciplines

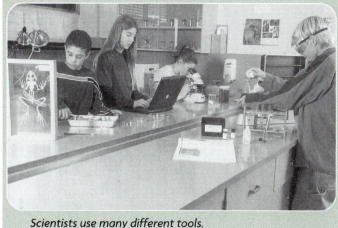

Scientists use many different tools.

do, however, as part of their underlying principles behind their standards, address the power of computer-based technology in learning. For instance, the National Council of Teachers of Mathematics (NCTM) states: "Technology enriches the range and quality of investigations by providing a means of viewing mathematical ideas from multiple perspectives" (NCTM, 1991).

A careful examination of the standards for each of the disciplines also revealed that there are concepts which reflect the history of the discipline; that is, the role the discipline has played in the development of humanity. These standards imply that there is something inherent in the nature of the discipline that should be developed through the experiences and activities we provide our students in our lessons.

The last *similarity category* is the real-world connections that are emphasized within each of the disciplines. In life, it is rare that we encounter a specific event or phenomenon whereby the standards of only one discipline can be used to explain the event. It is essential in planning an integrated lesson to understand how the disciplines are applied in the real world, and to provide a real-world context for those lessons.

For integration to occur, it is important to dig deeper within each discipline to identify specific benchmarks or indicators that reveal the expectations for each grade level when applying that standard. Using the *Across the Standards* approach to integration, one content area is chosen as the vehicle for addressing standards within each of the disciplines. A concept within that discipline is identified and then the following questions are asked:

- To what extent will the concept be developed by this lesson?
- Do I need to build in a discipline-specific activity to develop a rich understanding of the concept before I apply it across an integrated lesson?
- Will this integrated lesson develop the understanding of the concept?
- Is this lesson going to reinforce the student's understanding of a previously learned concept?
- While I'm teaching this concept within a given discipline, what similar standards will I address from the other content areas?

Feature Lesson A (page 258) models an *Across the Standards* approach for integration. A specific science concept is identified as the *key concept.* However, while the key concept *pollution* is being developed, standards from mathematics, language arts, social studies, and technology can be reinforced. The *Standards Similarity Analysis* (Table 9.1) selected standards from each of the other disciplines that were addressed within this lesson. These standards are listed in Table 9.2. Before you look at that list, read the lessons

TABLE 9.2 ● Standards Addressed in Feature Lesson A: Across the Standards Approach

Similarity	Disciplines				
	Science	Mathematics	Language Arts	Social Studies	Technology
Content	• All organisms cause changes in their environment where they live. Some of these changes are detrimental to themselves or other organisms, whereas others are beneficial. • Humans depend on both their natural and their constructed environment. Humans change environments in ways that can either be beneficial or detrimental for other organisms, including the humans themselves.	• *Algebra* Understand patterns, relations, and functions; represent and analyze patterns and functions, using words, tables, and graphs. • *Geometry* Use visualization, spatial reasoning, and geometric modeling to solve problems—recognize geometric ideas and relationships and apply them to other disciplines and to problems that arise in the classroom or in everyday life.	• *Range of Materials and Purposes for Reading* Students read a wide range of print and nonprint texts to build an understanding of texts, of themselves, and of the cultures of the United States and the world; to acquire new information; to respond to the needs and demands of society and the workplace; and for personal fulfillment. Among these texts are fiction and nonfiction, classic and contemporary works.	• *People, Places, and Environments* In the early grades, young learners draw upon immediate personal experiences as a basis for exploring geographic concepts and skills. They also express interest in things distant and unfamiliar and have concern for the use and abuse of the physical environment.	• *Technology Productivity Tools* Students use productivity tools to collaborate in constructing technology enhanced models, preparing publications, and producing other creative works.
Skills	• Scientific investigations involve asking and answering a question and comparing the answer with what scientists already know about the world. • Scientists make the results of their investigations public; they describe the investigations in ways that enable others to repeat the investigations.	• *Measurement* Apply appropriate techniques, tools, and formulas to determine measurements; develop strategies for estimating the perimeters, areas, and volumes of irregular shapes. • *Data Analysis and Probability* Formulate questions that can be addressed with data and collect, organize, and display relevant data to answer them—collect data using observations, surveys, and experiments; represent data using tables and graphs such as line	• *Research and Inquiry* Students conduct research on issues and interests by generating ideas and questions, and by posing problems. They gather, evaluate, and synthesize data from a variety of sources (e.g., print and nonprint texts, artifacts, people) to communicate their discoveries in ways that suit their purpose and audience. • *Reading strategies, Language Use, and Conventions* Students adjust their use of spoken,		• *Technology Research Tools* Students use technology to process data and report results.

plots, bar graphs, and line graphs; develop and evaluate inferences and predictions that are based on data—propose and justify conclusions and predictions that are based on data and design studies to further investigate the conclusions or predictions.
- *Problem Solving* Select and use various types of reasoning and methods of proof.

written, and visual language (e.g., conventions, style, vocabulary) to communicate effectively with a variety of audiences and for different purposes.

Technology
- Abilities of technological design

- *Science, Technology, and Society* Young children can learn how technologies form systems and how their daily lives are intertwined with a host of technologies. Young children can study how basic technologies such as ships, automobiles, and airplanes have evolved and how we have used technology, such as air conditioning, dams, and irrigation to modify our physical environment.

The Nature of the Discipline
- Although men and women using scientific inquiry have learned much about the objects, events, and phenomena in nature, much more remains to be understood. Science will never be finished.

- *Communication* Organize and consolidate their mathematical thinking through communication. Communicate their mathematical thinking coherently and clearly to peers, teachers, and others; analyze and evaluate the mathematical

- *Civic Ideals and Practices* During these years, children also experience views of citizenship in other times and places through stories and drama.

- *Technology Communication Tools* Students use a variety of media and formats to communicate information and ideas

(continued)

TABLE 9.2 ● Continued

Similarity		Disciplines			
	Science	Mathematics	Language Arts	Social Studies	Technology
The Nature of the Discipline (continued)		thinking and strategies of others. ● *Representation Standard* Create and use representations to organize, record, and communicate mathematical ideas. Use representations to model and interpret physical, social, and mathematical phenomena.			effectively to multiple audiences.
Real-World Connections	● Changes in environments can be natural or influenced by humans. Some changes are good, some are bad, and some are neither good nor bad. Pollution is a change in the environment that can influence the health, survival, or activities of organisms, including humans. ● People continue inventing new ways of doing things, solving problems, and getting work done. New ideas and inventions often affect other people; sometimes the effects are good and sometimes they are bad. It is helpful to try to determine in advance how ideas and inventions will affect other people.	● *Connections* Recognize and use connections among mathematical ideas. Understand how mathematical ideas interconnect and build on one another to produce a coherent whole. Recognize and apply mathematics in contexts outside of mathematics.			

and go to the national standards for each of the disciplines provided by the National Council for Teachers of Mathematics (NCTM), the National Council of English Teachers (NCET), the National Council for the Social Studies (NCSS), and the National Educational Technology Standards (NETS). Which standards from those disciplines do you think were used to support concept development through this integrated lesson plan? Did your selection agree with those identified in Table 9.2?

The *Across the Standards* approach used in Feature Lesson A explicitly developed the standards for science, while the standards for the other disciplines were implicit. Oftentimes, implicit planning leads to disagreements. While the authors of the integrated lesson plan believe that the standards identified in Table 9.2 were also reinforced through the lesson, another reader of the written plan may not readily see that link or may see where a different standard is developed. It is important in using this approach and sharing lessons with other teachers that you walk others through the lesson, clarifying where and how you see the links to the other disciplines within the lesson.

Driving Question Approach

Integrated instruction is an interdisciplinary approach to teaching that combines knowledge from different disciplines and encourages students to examine a topic deeply, read from a variety of sources and materials, and engage in a variety of activities. Often, the topic is presented in an extended time frame allowing students to engage in inquiry that leads the students to a deeper understanding of the topic and its connection to their world. Well-designed, integrated, interdisciplinary units set high standards and expectations for all students (NCREL, 2003).

NSES
PR-B
PR-E

> It is taken for granted, apparently, that in time students will see for themselves how things fit together. Unfortunately, the reality of the situation is that they tend to learn what we teach. If we teach connectedness and integration, they learn that. If we teach separation and discontinuity, that is what they learn. To suppose otherwise would be incongruous. (Humphreys, Post, & Ellis, 1981, p. xi)

Brain research indicates that to develop long-term memory or a true understanding of concepts, the information that is acquired must make sense and have real-life meaning to the student. Content integration provides a framework that assists students in making connections between the new information and the previously learned information. This allows for deeper understanding and concept formation. This is not a new idea. John Dewey, in 1938, warned that isolation in all forms is to be avoided and connectedness would better support the processes of learning (Mid-continent Research for Education and Learning, 2001).

Questioning is a basic process of science; it is a basic process of inquiry and a natural result of human curiosity. When we question, we progress into unknowns and uncertainties; we develop hypotheses and test ideas and find solutions. Questioning allows us to extend our knowledge and share similar goals of inquiry, observation, problem solving, experimentation, and communication across content areas.

Planning integrated learning experiences using a problem-based learning model helps students develop scientific thinking for solving problems in real life. The connection of the lessons to the students' real life creates an understanding of the commonalities between and among diverse topics, develops the students' ability to perceive new relationships, and provides a motivational tool for learning (Mid-continent Research for Education and Learning, 2001).

Teachers developing problem-based learning environments often use a *driving question* to help support integration across content areas. A driving question is a single

Learning Cycle Featured Lesson

Life Science: Pollution Search: Across the Standards Approach

Grades ● K–4

NATIONAL SCIENCE EDUCATION CONTENT STANDARDS–PHYSICAL SCIENCE—GRADES K-4

▶ Organisms and their Environments Concepts. All organisms cause changes in the environment where they live. Some of these changes are detrimental to themselves or other organisms, whereas others are beneficial.

NCTM Standards, Language Arts, Social Studies, and NET for Students also addressed. Refer to national content groups for specific standards.

CONCEPTS TO BE CONSTRUCTED

▶ Pollution is considered any contamination of the air, water, or land that affects the environment in an unwanted way.

SCIENCE ATTITUDES TO NURTURE

▶ Open-mindedness
▶ Curiosity
▶ Perseverance
▶ Cooperating with others
▶ Positive approach to failure

Engaging Question

Who is responsible for pollution?

Materials Needed

For exploration phase ● conducted whole class, you will need:

- Dr. Seuss's *The Cat in the Hat Comes Back* (New York: Random House, 1958)
- Large poster paper, whiteboard, or chalkboard
- Markers or chalk

For expansion phase ● Indoors conducted whole class, you will need:

- Large poster paper, whiteboard, or chalkboard
- Markers or chalk

Outdoors conducted in student groups of four or five per group, each group will need:

- 1 clipboard with a data record sheet
- Computer software to create a data table and to create graphs (such as Excel or graph-making software) or create charts with pencil and paper
- Journal or word-processing software (optional)

① Safety: Remind students to respect the reader and the other students while the story is being read. Be sure that there is a proper student-to-adult ratio when taking students outdoors. Remind students to always walk, not run, during outdoor field study.

Exploration

PROCESS SKILLS USED

▶ Observing
▶ Predicting
▶ Communicating
▶ Problem solving
▶ Designing an experiment

Student Activity

Ask the students to gather around you as you read *The Cat in the Hat Comes Back* by Dr. Seuss. As you read the story, use the poster paper or a whiteboard to write the story's events. Ask the children to summarize what happens at each stage of the story.

1. The cat shows up at the house.
2. The cat takes a bath and leaves a bathtub ring of pink stuff.
3. The cat uses a dress to get the pink stuff off the tub and ends up getting it all over the dress.
4. The cat gets the pink stuff on the wall and uses shoes to clean it off.
5. And so on . . .

Explanation

Use the sequence of story events to have a discussion about how a story like this might be real. Be sure to refer to the list of events as you ask the students questions such as these:

- Out in the playground when people just throw their trash around, we consider that behavior polluting our environment. What in the story might represent pollution?
  - Where did the pollution come from?
  - How did the cat deal with the pollution?
  - Did that help to solve the pollution problem?

- What did the little cats do? Did they help with the pollution problem?

- Who finally cleaned up the pollution, and how did that happen? Share with the students examples in real life of how pollution problems, such as major oil spills, get cleaned up.

Use the students' answers to make a summary statement about pollution. Ask the students to complete this sentence starter: *When we put things into the air, water, or land that affect our environment in an unwanted way, this is considered ___ (pollution) or Pollution is ___.*

Expansion

PROCESS SKILLS USED

▶ Observing
▶ Planning an investigation
▶ Recording and analyzing data
▶ Comparing and contrasting
▶ Problem solving
▶ Drawing conclusions
▶ Communicating findings

Indoors

Prepare the class to go on a local pollution sources search. Remind the students about the story and how the "pink stuff" spread, making a mess of the house. Ask them whether the pink stuff was pollution, contaminating the house. What might that look like if it contaminated the water? The air?

Ask the students, since we don't have to worry about a Cat in the Hat, what other ways might our surroundings get polluted? Collect a list of these suggestions. Draw two intersecting circles on the board. Label one circle *inside,* for those pollutants found inside buildings; label one circle *outside,* for the suggested pollutants found outdoors. Explain to the children that the area where the two circles intersect can be labeled *both* to represent the pollutants from their suggested list that are found both inside and outside. Explain to them that what they have created is called a *Venn diagram.*

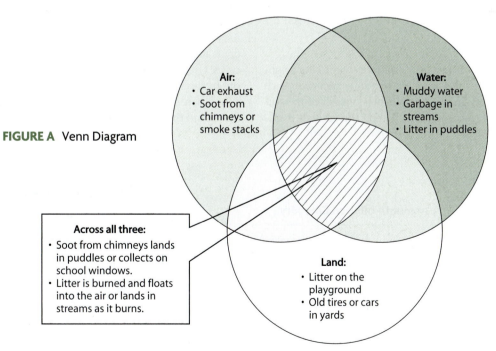

FIGURE A Venn Diagram

Air:
- Car exhaust
- Soot from chimneys or smoke stacks

Water:
- Muddy water
- Garbage in streams
- Litter in puddles

Across all three:
- Soot from chimneys lands in puddles or collects on school windows.
- Litter is burned and floats into the air or lands in streams as it burns.

Land:
- Litter on the playground
- Old tires or cars in yards

Field Data

Name of Pollution Source	Where It Was Found	Size or Amount	Type
Fast-food wrapper	In playground by swing set	1 wrapper	Land
Soot from chimney	Coming from house on Elm Street	Watched chimney for 5 minutes and soot was coming out entire time.	Air
Oil slick	Floating on the surface of a puddle on Grant Street	Since it was an irregular size, we estimated the area of the oil slick to be about 15 cm x 22 cm.	Water
Candy wrappers	In front of house on Lee Place	5 wrappers	Land

FIGURE B Field Data

Ask the students to look at the Venn diagram and see whether there is another way they could look at the pollutants so that they draw three circles that overlap. Lead the students toward these three groups: air, water, and land (see Figure A). Make three new intersecting circles, and label them with the terms. Ask the students to take the items from the previous Venn diagram and place them in the appropriate new circles. Tell them that they will use these categories to search for evidence of pollution—called pollutants—as they work in teams in the neighborhood around the school.

Outdoors

Assign student teams to a field study area within the neighborhood around the school. Have adults supervise each student team. Assign cooperative roles to each of the students (reporter, recorder, etc.). Direct the student teams to walk around the school neighborhood looking for pollution or pollutants and to record what they see on a data sheet. Figure B is an example of such a sheet.

When the students encounter litter that can be collected in their neighborhood, instruct them first to record the data and then, using rubber gloves and garbage bags, to collect the litter for disposal once they return to school.

Back in the classroom, have the students work in teams at computers to record their data into a spreadsheet. Ask them to make a new Venn diagram of the three pollution types: air, water, and land. Ask them to graph the data by those categories. If graphing software is available, have students use their data to create a bar graph of the pollution types. Use the individual team data to create a bar graph of the entire class data set.

Discuss with the class the pollution types that were found and the sources for them. Solicit potential solutions

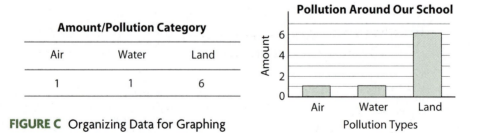

Amount/Pollution Category

Air	Water	Land
1	1	6

FIGURE C Organizing Data for Graphing

Pollution Around Our School

to eliminate the pollutant. Have each team write an informational story to be shared in a newsletter that will be distributed to the local community about the data they collected and the results of the data analysis. Be sure that each team includes data to back up their story. Ask each team to offer suggestions on what the students in the school can do to reduce pollution and what members of the local community can do as well.

Science in Personal and Social Perspectives

- What suggestions can you provide members of the local community to reduce the amount of pollution your team found around the school?
- What kinds of things can you do to eliminate a pollution source around the school or your home?

Science and Technology

- Did you identify any pollution sources that were originally made to make a person's life easier? If so, what were they? (e.g., using a Styrofoam cup instead of a glass one when traveling)

- Do you think we can live without this technology? If not, do you have any suggestions as to how it can be changed to make less pollution?

Science as Inquiry

- On what other things or events in our life can we collect data to make informed decisions?
- Does it help to follow a sequence of events to figure out how to solve problems? Why?

History and Nature of Science

- Are scientists the only people who collect data and make informed decisions based on the analysis of the data? In what other careers is the ability to collect and analyze data important?

Evaluation

Hands-on Assessment

Upon completing the activities, the students will be able to:

- Create and distribute a news story to the local community explaining the various sources of pollution that were found around the school. They should describe what all members of the community can do to reduce the amount of pollution, using graphs and charts to identify the location of the pollution sources, the types of pollution, and amounts and size of pollutants found from their local pollution search.

Reflective Assessment

Upon completing the activities, the students will be able to:

- Describe a source of pollution and provide a plan for how that source could be eliminated or at least reduced.

Pictorial Assessment

Upon completing the activities, the students will be able to:

- When given a picture of an area with obvious pollution problems, identify the possible pollution sources and speculate as to possible sources if none is found within the picture.

Integration and the Curriculum

NSES

PR-A

Integration of instruction, thematic approach, synergistic teaching, and *interdisciplinary curriculum* are all terms that relate to a growing understanding of the complexity of today's problems and the need for students to engage in an educational experience that integrates a broad knowledge base. An integrated curriculum is one that links subject areas and meaningful learning experiences to support a greater understanding of conceptual relationships.

The term *integrated curriculum* is used synonymously with *interdisciplinary curriculum. Interdisciplinary curriculum* is defined in the *Dictionary of Education* as a "curriculum organization which cuts across subject-matter lines to focus upon comprehensive life problems or broad based areas of study that brings together the various segments of the curriculum into meaningful association" (Lake, 1994). This provides the student with a classroom that is linked to language arts, social studies, mathematics, science, music and art in such a way that knowledge and skills are developed and applied to solve real life problems. This definition supports the view that an integrated curriculum is "an educational approach that prepares children for lifelong learning" (Lake, 1994).

The debate surrounding curriculum integration has continued well over fifty years. The growth of scientific knowledge, changes in teacher education requirements, and the fragmentation of teaching schedules have made many teachers feel that they will "never be able to teach it all" or that "each year more and more material is added to the curriculum." The increased pace of today's classroom coupled

with increased external pressures on schools to provide a workforce with the ability to problem solve in a global environment is one of the motivations behind the development of an integrated curriculum. "More and more schools are coming to an understanding that facts cannot be taught in isolation and are moving toward a more constructivist view of learning, which values in-depth knowledge of subjects" (Lake, 1994).

In the science classroom, an interdisciplinary curriculum may pair the cognitive processes of predicting, classifying, identifying cause and effect, sequencing, inference, and summarizing with similar processes presented in the context of language arts, social studies, and mathematics. Greene (1991) found that in the science classroom, an interdisciplinary curriculum motivated learning and improved attitudes toward science. Greene determined that the cognitive processes of science along with student-centered planning for learning created an environment in which students had higher attendance, higher levels of homework completion, and a better conceptual understanding of the connections of science to other content areas.

Science and language arts provide ample opportunities to interpret and communicate ideas through reading, writing and predicting, inferring, comparing and contrasting, and examining cause and effect relationships. "Many of the process skills needed for science inquiry are similar to reading skills, and when taught together reinforce each other" (Krueger & Sutton, 2001, p. 52). The integration of reading

question, which will lead the student to investigate the problem from a variety of viewpoints and through inquiry, build the science concept being studied.

One teacher in a fourth-grade classroom posed the following question to her students: "How do human beings and industry change an environment over time?" In past conversations with her students, the teacher realized that her students did not understand the relationship of the Ohio River to the environment, industry, history, and society of the community in which the students lived. By creating cooperative teams of students to answer the driving question, the teacher provided an opportunity for her students to understand the environmental issues surrounding a large river, and to see the impact the river had historically on the economy of the community as well as the societal impact of immigration to the region. Students were supplied with computers and scientific probeware to measure flow rates, pH, and oxygen levels and they maintained a field journal of observations concerning the riverbank area over the course of a school year. Math skills were strengthened as the teams of students charted information from field trips onto posters that described the monthly changes of the river over the school and writing as a component of inquiry-based science has been shown to increase vocabulary not only in science content but also in fluency as measured on standard language tests (Krueger & Sutton, 2001). Science journals and reports that communicate observations and data collected through inquiry serve as a natural fit for improving reading and writing competence. The integration of mathematics through the drawing of graphs and charts to represent collected data adds value to the math skills students are learning elsewhere in the curriculum. When the use of technology is integrated to access, gather, store, retrieve and organize data, the teacher is able to meet standards not only for language arts, science and mathematics but for technology as well. "Technology can help teachers reach all students with inquiry-based science content and processes that reflect the connected and digital world" in which today's students reside (Krueger & Sutton, 2001, p. 70).

Student success in reading can be a great motivator to stimulate reading, writing, and oral communication as the student pursues science inquiry in greater depth. Teachers should use a wide variety of literature, including trade books, texts, fiction, extensive illustrations, and nonfiction to cover science topics in greater detail to motivate and engage students to speak, ask questions, explore, and engage in science inquiry. Helping students to make connections across the curriculum is an important learning outcome for early childhood and middle grade students. Integration of content can enable students to develop a broader understanding of concepts and improve teaching and learning for all.

The structure of the school day is often cited as a barrier to integration. Teachers feel helpless in convincing district administrators that a common planning time is essential for curriculum planning and lesson development, or administrators and teachers do not see the value of putting energy into this kind of effort. The research on the use of integrated units bear out that there is value in pursuing a change in the organization of the school day and in changing the negative attitudes some teachers may have toward integration. Research by Schubert and Melnick showed that an integrated curriculum increased the student's positive attitudes toward school and their self-concepts. Lawton found that eighth-grade students in an interdisciplinary course outscored their peers in single-discipline subjects by fifty-eight points. Kostelnik, Soderman, and Whiren found that thematic units motivated not only students but the teachers as well. Whenever teachers are provided common time to sit and discuss the content they are teaching, they find that their understandings of the content become richer, and connections between the disciplines become more evident when discussed openly among peers.

Sources: Adapted from K. Lake. *School Improvement Series—Research You Can Use: Integrated Curriculum* (Northwest Regional Educational Laboratory, Office of Educational Research and Improvement (OERI), U.S. Department of Education. #RP91002001.May 1994). Retrieved online October 10, 2003, www.nwrel.org/scpd/sirs/8/c016.html. L. Greene, "Science-Centered Curriculum in Elementary School," *EDThoughts: What We Know about Science Teaching and Learning* (Aurora, CO: Mid-continent Research for Education and Learning, 2001). M. J. Kostelnik, A. K. Soderman, & A. P Whiren, *Developing Appropriate Curriculum: Best Practices in Early Childhood Education.* Upper Saddle River, NJ: Merrill, 2004. E. Lawton (1994). "Integrating Curriculum: A Slow but Positive Process." *Schools in the Middle* 4(2), pp. 27–30. [EJ 492 890]. M. Schubert and S. Melnick, *The Arts in Curriculum Integration.* Paper presented at the Annual Meeting of the Easter Educational Research Association (Hilton Head, SC), 1997. [ED 424 151]

year. During critical points in the school year, students made predictions about the anticipated changes in the river and what impact the changes might have on industries, recreational pursuits, and families that live downstream.

As a teacher or team of teachers develops the unit, a series of standards-based essential questions should be formed to frame the process of interdisciplinary learning. Assessment goals should align with these essential questions.

The driving question approach in the previous example addressed standards from the content areas of mathematics, science, language arts, and social studies. In the driving question approach to integration the teachers first identified the driving question. Then teachers used a standards similarity analysis (see Table 9.1) to predict from which of the

By planning integrated lessons, teachers provide real-world context for learning.

Learning Cycle Featured Lesson

NATIONAL SCIENCE EDUCATION CONTENT STANDARDS–PHYSICAL SCIENCE—GRADES K–4

▶ Organisms and their Environments Concepts. All organisms cause changes in the environment where they live. Some of these changes are detrimental to themselves or other organisms, whereas others are beneficial.

NCTM Standards, Language Arts, Social Studies, and NET for Students also addressed. Refer to national content groups for specific standards that address the above concept statements for each discipline.

CONCEPTS TO BE CONSTRUCTED

Science concept

▶ Pollution is considered any contamination of the air, water, or land that affects the environment in an unwanted way.

Mathematics concept

▶ Data can be communicated through the use of bar graphs.

Language Arts concept

▶ Fictional children's' stories can be used to communicate the negative impact human's actions have on the environment.

Social Studies concept

▶ Children can be advocates for social change by the way in which they communicate the analysis of data on a pollution search.

Technology concept

▶ The computer can be used as a tool to communicate information.

SCIENCE ATTITUDES TO NURTURE

▶ Open-mindedness
▶ Curiosity
▶ Cooperating with others

Life Science: Pollution Search: Driving Question Approach

Grades • K–4

Engaging Question

Does our school neighborhood have a pollution problem?

Materials Needed

For exploration phase • conducted whole class, you will need:

- Dr. Seuss's *The Cat in the Hat Comes Back* (New York: Random House, 1958)
- Large poster paper, whiteboard, or chalkboard
- Markers or chalk

For exploration phase • *Indoors conducted whole class, you will need*:

- Large poster paper, whiteboard or chalkboard
- Markers or chalk

Outdoors conducted in student groups of four or five per group, each group will need:

- 1 clipboard with a data record sheet
- Computer software to create a data table and to create graphs (such as Excel or graph-making software) or create charts with pencil and paper
- Journal or word-processing software (optional)

🛈 *Safety:* Remind students to respect the reader and the other students while the story is being read. Be sure there is a proper student-to-adult ratio when taking students outdoors. Remind students to always walk, not run, during outdoor field study.

Exploration

Student Activity

Ask the students to gather around you as you read *The Cat in the Hat Comes Back* by Dr. Seuss. As you read the story, use the poster paper, whiteboard, or chalkboard to write the story's events. Ask tne children to summarize what happens at each stage of the story.

1. The cat shows up at the house.
2. The cat takes a bath and leaves a bathtub ring of pink stuff.
3. The cat uses a dress to get the pink stuff off the tub and ends up getting it all over the dress.
4. The cat gets the pink stuff on the wall and uses shoes to clean it off.
5. And so on . . .

Explanation

Use the sequence of story events to have a discussion about how a story like this might be real. Be sure to refer to the list of events as you ask the students questions such as these:

- Out in the playground when people just throw their trash around, we consider that behavior polluting our environment. What in the story might represent pollution?
- Where did the pollution come from?
- How did the cat deal with the pollution?
- Did that help to solve the pollution problem?
- What did the little cats do? Did they help with the pollution problem?
- Who finally cleaned up the pollution, and how did that happen? Share with the students examples in real life of how pollution problems, such as major oil spills, get cleaned up.
- What might we do to look for sources of pollution in our school community?
- What kind of data might we collect on pollution sources, and how might we communicate the results of the data we collected?

Use the students' answers to make a summary statement about pollution. Ask the students to complete this sentence starter: *When we put things into the air, water, or land that affect our environment in an unwanted way, this is considered* ___ (pollution) or *Pollution is* ___.

Expansion

Use the following summary activity to make the integration explicit after the expansion activities as described in the *across the standards approach to integration lesson plan* found in this chapter.

Once the public display of the results of the pollution search in the school neighborhood has been completed, reconvene the class, and ask the students to reflect on all of their experiences. Suggested questions to ask student to make the connection to each of the disciplines addressed in the lesson include the following:

- What is pollution? (*Designed to address the science concept.*)
- What math skill did you need to communicate or show what you found? (*Looks for an understanding that data can be communicated using a bar graph.*)
- Who was your audience when you wrote about the results of your pollution search around the school neighborhoods? Why was it important to keep your audience in mind? (*Designed to address the identified language arts concepts.*)
- In our social studies class, we learned that throughout time people will endure great hardships to bring about a social change, such as the Pilgrims coming to America to start a new society that would allow them to practice freedoms that they did not have while living in Europe. How do you think the activities we just completed show that you can become an advocate for social change? How do you think you might start some changes to reduce pollution in the local community? (*Designed to address the identified social studies concepts.*)

The remainder of the lesson can follow the across-the-standards approach to integration lesson plan found in this chapter.

disciplines the students may have to draw to solve the problem. While writing the lessons, the teachers anticipated which of the standards from each discipline would help solve the problem. They guided the students through the inquiry so that those standards were specifically addressed. Concepts from across the disciplines were explicitly developed.

Feature Lesson B represents a model for the driving question approach to integration with slight modifications. This is accomplished by identifying specific concepts from each of the disciplines that the teacher will help the students to understand in the exploration and expansion activities. Any questions that are asked during the explanation phase should guide students to develop each of the desired concepts. To solve the problem, the students complete their public communication on pollution within the community by considering the driving question. This action also makes specific the knowledge needed for each discipline.

Challenges to Integration

NSES
SS
A-G

As schools move to a more constructivist view of learning, greater value is placed on indepth knowledge and less on the teaching of isolated facts. Twenty-first century students will require flexibility in their ability to apply knowledge and manage the complex systems of global interdependence (Damian, 2002). Children do not encounter problems in the real world that can be solved with isolated bits of information. Providing students with learning experiences that require the application of rich, contextualized understanding of content knowledge from across the disciplines should be planned for during classroom time.

teachers on Science Teaching

NSES
TSA-B
PD-C
PR-B

Science Comes to Life for Students and Teachers

by Debby Todd
Grade 5, Slate Hill Elementary, Worthington, Ohio

Science in the elementary school needs to leap off of the textbook pages and lab instructions to come in to the lives of the children. Our students need to know that science is a continuing story of discovery, inventions, history, art, music, movement, and new theories. Children need to be made aware that science is found in all areas of their lives by immersing them in projects that will encompass all of the academic areas.

When a child in my classroom begins to study ecosystems and positive and negative impacts on ecosystems, he or she should be filled with curiosity and wonder. Where did these ideas come from? Who were the people who came up with these ideas? Why did they think about them? How did they use them? How did they impact the world? What is their story?

In the classroom I have found four critical elements that support achievement on science standards and encourage inquiry learning of every child:

1. Make all children think critically.
2. Tell a good story through literature including fiction/nonfiction and writing.
3. Bombard their senses through the integration of all academic and related arts areas.
4. Give them ownership.

Science is definitely an area in which all students can be included. Developing lessons with critical thinking components is key to making the lesson flexible enough to be tiered when integrating math, social studies, reading, and writing. This approach meets the needs of all levels of students. All assignments require every child to meet certain minimum standards. Every assignment integrates two or more of the following areas: math, social studies, reading, and writing. All students then have an opportunity and are encouraged to extend their learning with additional challenges that are provided. These challenges are higher in thinking skills not in the length of the assignment. This

Teachers who use an integrated approach for meeting content standards describe one common barrier: *time.* Planning and teaching an integrated curriculum require more time. Teachers working together to build integrated lessons need a common planning time to explore themes, locate resources, discuss student needs, and coordinate daily schedules. Locating an effective and coherent theme/key concept on which all agree can be challenging. When teachers work together to identify content knowledge, skills, standards, and themes with appropriate connections to the content areas, the time issue is reduced by the gains found through the division of labor with teamwork. Remember Shaundra in our opening scenario. When working in isolation, she found the task of addressing all of the standards overwhelming. Grade-level teams, working together, can more easily identify the areas of integration that may not be so obvious when working in isolation. The efforts of good planning, flexible schedules, and an empowered team of teachers can produce outstanding lessons that engage learners in inquiry.

When teachers work together in grade-level teams, they can identify areas of integration that may not be so obvious when working alone.

As was demonstrated in Feature Lessons A and B, teachers can "do it all" without making the task overwhelming or insurmountable. Essential to integration is making the decision on whether it will be implicit, as the across-the-standards approach to integration suggests, or explicit, as explained by the driving question approach.

component of choice and ownership gives the children pride and a sense of accomplishment when lessons are completed. The students become very motivated to succeed and try another level.

Reading exposes students to science concepts and the people behind those ideas through a story. Here they have an opportunity to experience the hopes, dreams, joys, and disappointments of life. They see conflicting points of view and choices being made, and they think critically. They learn about the impact that science has had on human beings and the integrity of people to use or not use a newly developed idea. They make the idea their own and decide what position to take—pro or con.

Bombarding the children's senses through related arts programs allows me to bring many abstract concepts into the child's real world and creates an opportunity for brain development by making use of the children's multiple intelligences. All the teachers of the school work with the related arts teachers to support and extend many of the lessons throughout the year. Following is one example of how my colleagues and I accomplish this goal.

When the students begin their study of ecosystems and populations, the art teacher presents lessons on animal structure, sculpture, and design; the music department teaches how animal movement and behavior can be represented through music and also shows music of different geographical areas; and the physical education teacher uses physical activities and games that imitate animal movement. The kids use these experiences in class to enhance their study of animal movement, adaptations, and survival in different ecosystems. The children have many personal experiences from these areas to use for discussion and activities in the classroom.

In art class, they create an animal sculpture that is displayed in the school and in the classroom. They incorporate music in an assigned hyper-studio research project on ecosystems and adaptations for enhancement. My students have ownership and control of their learning. I have found that these activities increase their motivation to achieve specific goals for the classroom and increase inquiry attitude and enthusiasm in the classroom.

chapter summary

Being responsible for teaching all of the disciplines can look like an insurmountable task. This chapter encouraged you to look at it as an asset. Having to teach all of the disciplines provides you the luxury of addressing standards from a variety of disciplines within a single lesson plan. The integration of the standards across the disciplines can be done implicitly through an *Across the Standards Approach* or explicitly using a *Driving Question Approach*. The differences between the two approaches as defined and modeled in this chapter make our task of having to teach the standards of each discipline within a school year less daunting and quite doable. And most important, for the learners, it does not leave the connections among and between the disciplines to happenstance. Purposeful, well-planned, contextualized learning allows the learners to confront problems as they see them in the real world.

reflect and respond

1. How is an integrated lesson different from a topic-based unit?

2. Why do you think it is important to understand how each discipline organizes its standards?

3. Do the different disciplines such as mathematics, language arts, or social studies define the term *standards* differently? Why or how?

4. Examine your state standards for the content areas of science, mathematics, language arts, and social studies. Create a Standards Similarities Analysis. Compare yours to Table 9.1. Did you identify similar categories? Where do your state standards differ from the national standards?

5. Examine your state standards for the content areas of science, mathematics, language arts, and social studies. What are the standards within each content area for which technology could be used to help meet the content standard?

Where the Classroom Comes to Life

Explore—Video Homework Exercise. Go to MyEducationLab at www.myeducationlab .com and select the topic "Cross-Curricular Connections," then watch the videos "Integration" and "Planning for Instruction;" and finally select the topic "Questioning Strategies," then watch the video "A Scientific Investigation in Preschool: From Tadpole to Frog." Respond to the questions below.

NSES

TS-F
PD-B
PR-B

1. Science lessons often take a back seat to the teaching of mathematics and reading, which are heavily emphasized in many schools; instead, time could be spent in planning and teaching cross-disciplinary units. What are some of the suggested approaches to curriculum integration?

2. What approach do you think the two social studies teachers are using in the "Planning for Instruction" video?

3. Listen to ideas the two teachers are sharing. How can this lesson be used as an integrated unit? What science standards do you think could be addressed in this unit?

4. How would you formally integrate those science standards into this social studies unit?

5. In "A Scientific Investigation in Preschool: From Tadpole to Frog," what content areas are addressed in the lesson you are observing? What techniques is the teacher using to make the concepts from the different subject areas concrete? What other content knowledge can be addressed through this lesson? What content areas do you think you could integrate if you were the teacher? How would you formalize the integrated content?

Enrich—Video Homework Exercise

Professional Practice. Go to MyEducationLab and select the topic "Cross-Curricular Connection," then watch the video "Emergent Curriculum Built on Children's Interests," which provides a thorough description of how one teacher developed an integrated unit in her preschool class. Respond to the questions below.

1. How can you employ the brainstorming strategy that the classroom teacher used in this video to plan an integrated lesson? Do you think you could involve your students in planning an integrated unit?

2. What strategies did the teacher in the video share to successfully integrate student ideas with the standards that she must address in her curriculum?

3. Select a "big idea" that will work well for integration. Develop a brainstorming web on that idea. What will be the next steps that you should follow to turn this into a standards-based integrated unit? Can you use a driving question approach? What might that driving question be? How might you use student suggestions to plan the unit?

Expand—Weblink Exercise

Science Literacy. Go to MyEducationLab Resources section and select "Weblinks," then click on the links "Integrating Music into Any Subject," "Integrating Physical Education," and "Integrating Multicultural Issues" to find out more about the value of integrating subjects or to find strategies and sample lessons specifically designed to integrate the often forgotten subjects such as music, physical education, or multicultural education.

Then click on the link "Integrating Snakes and Sentences in the Primary Grades" to read an article that provides ideas on integrating language arts and science. Finally, click on the link "Integration of the World Wide Web" to get to a site devoted to web-integrated lesson plans.

10

How Can You Design and Manage a Safe Inquiry-Based Science Classroom?

focus questions

- What safety hazards must you foresee and avoid?

- What are the essentials you must know and practice for a safe inquiry science program?

- How can you safely and efficiently store science equipment and materials?

- How can you help children to develop an attitude of safety?

NSES
PD-B

In 1992, the District of Columbia was offering a summer school program designed to provide hands-on education to gifted and talented eight- and nine-year-old students. Dedrick Howell was a nine-year-old student enrolled in the program. Louis Jagoe, a Ph.D. candidate at the American University, was teaching a class on making sparklers.

> The children scooped the chemicals, including potassium perchlorate, out of jars, ground up the mixture in mortars. While they were combining the chemicals, Jagoe ignited three different chemical mixtures at the front of the room with a butane lighter. . . . The children continued to grind the material, while a counselor distributed pieces of metal hangers to be dipped into the mixture at a later time. Dedrick Howell was specifically told not to dip the hanger material until instructed to do so. Moments later the chemicals exploded in front of Dedrick. The chemicals burned at 5000 degrees Fahrenheit and Dedrick was burned over 25 percent of his body including his hands, arms, chest and face. (District of Columbia v. Howell, 1992)

The jury found the District of Columbia negligent under several alternative theories.

Do you think the court was right? Why or why not? How could the accident have been avoided? What guidelines should teachers follow when having an outside guest presenter in their room for science?

► As you read the following scenario, can you identify the safety issues associated with the activity?

Twanna returned from the supply table of the second-grade classroom with her hands full of materials.

"Did you get the paper, iron filings, hand lens, and magnets?" asked José.

"Yes I did," responded Twanna. "Let's get going."

"First, we need to be sure that we have plenty of room to perform this activity," said José, who was the manager and recorder for the science activity. "Are you sure that you have all the materials now, Twanna?"

Twanna, the materials manager for the activity, ran off to get a box. In a few minutes she returned from the supply table with a shoebox with one end cut out of it.

"Now," stated José, "lay the shoebox flat on the table and place the white paper over it. While I am doing that, Twanna, you need to pour some iron filings onto the second sheet of paper and examine them with your hand lens."

José went about his work while Twanna poured the filings from the glass jar onto the paper. "Wow!" she squealed. "Look at these things! They look like baby fish hooks and spears. Why are they so jagged?"

"Maybe they were simply made using a file on an old piece of pipe," said José. "My father makes them all the time when he puts new pipes in people's houses."

"Okay," said Twanna. "Are you ready for the filings now?"

"Si," replied José. "Put them on the paper covering the shoebox now."

Twanna poured half her filings onto the paper and leaned forward to watch José, who picked up the large bar magnet and reached under the paper with it. "Watch to see what happens to the iron filings as I move the magnet around under the paper," he stated.

Both students were peering at the shoebox from opposite sides, their eyes on the same level as the filings. Just as José touched the lower right edge of the paper with the magnet, Twanna sneezed. Several of the iron filings sprayed into José's face, with a few of them entering his right eye. "Oowww!" shrieked José as he twirled from his chair, eyes buried in his hands. "Help me, please!!!"

How could this accident have been prevented? Were there any oversights that you noticed?

The Roosevelt sixth-grade class finally arrived at its destination, the old Wilson farm. As the bus rolled to a stop, Mr. J addressed the class: "Please remember our purpose here today. We are visitors to these animals' homes, so do not disturb them or the plants. In science we observe, measure, and record; we don't destroy or disrupt. Let's review our lesson plans for today's environmental science."

Following a five-minute clarification of the outcomes and precautions for the activity, Mr. J answered student questions. "Now for our safety guidelines," he stated. "Are there any questions concerning the safety items on your activity page, such as equipment operation, accident procedures, and the buddy system? Remember to stay with your buddy and never allow yourself to be separated from myself, Mr. P, Mrs. M, or Ms. O by more than 50 meters in this pasture area. If you need help in an emergency, please use your whistles. We adults were here earlier this morning checking out the area and found no hazards to worry about during this mapping exercise. But please be careful, just in case."

Mark and Alicia filed off the bus, confident of their purpose.

"Let's see," said Alicia. "We need to proceed 50 meters to the northeast to pick up our first marker, then 60 meters to the east for our second one. Do you have the map, compass, and whistle ready, Mark?"

"Yes, I do," replied Mark. "Put on your helmet."

As the students proceeded about 20 meters into the trees, they noticed that the terrain became more rugged and difficult to negotiate.

"See these little lines, Alicia?" remarked Mark, looking at the map. "They are the little hills we are walking over now. Another 30 meters and we should spot the first marker."

Just as they came over the next small hill, they both spotted a green plastic lid, partially hidden in the leaves.

"What is that?" asked Mark.

"I don't know. Let's check it out," replied Alicia.

As they cautiously lifted the lid, it broke into several pieces. Before them was a deep hole about 1 meter in diameter. It did not appear to have a bottom, although you could see water down about 2 meters.

"Let's explore it," suggested Alicia.

"No way! Let's get help!" replied Mark.

"Don't be silly," said Alicia. "We can check it out, finish our assignment, and return before anyone knows. It could be our secret."

"What if the water is over your head?" persisted Mark. "How long do you think you could stay afloat? We'd better get some help to make sure nothing will fall into it."

"I guess you're probably right," agreed Alicia. "We'd better use the whistle!"

What was the difference between the safety emphasis in this scenario and those in the first two? Can you credit the judgment simply to the older ages of the students?

The scenarios provide teachers with "food for thought" when considering active student involvement in science. Teachers must be reasonable and prudent in their decisions when attempting to protect young students from potential injury. The initial scenario reminds teachers that there are certain standards that should be met when considering the involvement of outside presenters in their classrooms. Conservative attitudes and careful inquiry into the guest's background are essential.

The second and third scenarios point out the need for teacher anticipation of what could go wrong and preparation for the foreseeable safety situations. In addition, it is immediately apparent that teachers must provide for appropriate protective safety equipment and a setting that can accommodate the excitement created by inquisitive students stimulated by active science learning.

Inquiry is the basis to most science that students love to pursue. Inquiry involves students physically and mentally. In many cases, all senses are engaged in the processing of information and the interaction of mind and body. The National Science Education Standards (National Research Council, 1996) define inquiry as the process that students should use to learn science. These include asking questions, planning investigations, utilizing physical tools and techniques, assessing their evidence, and applying these to develop explanations and communicate them in a verifiable format.

As stated earlier in this text, inquiry is the cornerstone of the National Science Education Standards, exhibited through acceptable student techniques and procedures that help guide and make possible scientific methodology from both the teacher's perspective and that of their students. However, anytime students are actively involved in their own learning through inquiry, there will be safety implications that MUST be anticipated and addressed by the teacher and applied by students. Students can become so excited about the processes of science that they forget to think about the safety implications of some decisions.

Safety in elementary science teaching, and student learning, is not a new concept. In 1983 Downs and Gerlovich focused on this issue in the preface to *Science Safety for Elementary Teachers:*

> At the elementary level children learn best by active participation. Knowledge is gained by using fundamental learning processes essential to comprehension. Research by Jean Piaget indicates that an experimentally based (hands-on) science program is preferred, together with an inquiry approach that capitalizes on the student's natural curiosities.

Some level of risk is inherent in many science activities. The problem is to determine an acceptable level of risk for all planned activities contained in the science curriculum. Safety principles enable us to choose between experiences that are unproductive or even foolish and those that enrich our lives and make them worthwhile.

This chapter uses these organizing questions: *What are the foreseeable hazards associated with valued educational activities? What materials are necessary for educational activities? What safety practices need to be implemented in an inquiry-based science classroom?* This chapter helps you construct answers to these questions by:

1. encouraging you to develop a philosophy of safe science teaching;
2. helping you understand your legal responsibilities;
3. helping you understand when and how to use safety equipment;
4. encouraging you to perform safety assessments of your classroom, lab, field site, or working space;
5. examining the tasks necessary for safe and efficient storage of equipment and materials;
6. suggesting methods for distributing, maintaining, and inventorying science materials.

In *Exploring Safely: A Guide for Elementary Teachers* (Kwan, Texley, 2002) the authors recommend setting high expectations for all science teaching/learning endeavors. It sets the tone for this chapter.

> As any veteran teacher knows, high achievement is the satisfying reward for setting high expectation for our students. This is as true for the use of safe procedures as for any other expectation. The more you make students responsible for using and enforcing safe laboratory and fieldwork procedures, the more easily safe practice becomes habit. Once you have established a classroom climate that is based on the expectation that students be as vigilant as you are in spotting safety hazards and eliminating them, you might find that fewer rules work better than rules for every step and procedure. The ultimate safety rule should be: Don't do anything that you know or think might be unsafe to yourself or others.

Recommendations for Safe Science Experiences

The National Science Education Standards (NSES) (National Research Council, 1996) state that students at K–4, 5–8, and 9–12 levels should know and be able to "utilize safety procedures during scientific investigations." Teaching Standard D of the NSES states:

> Teachers of science design and manage learning environments that provide students with the time, space, and resources needed for learning science. In doing this, teachers ensure a safe working environment.

These standards provide a blueprint for improving the teaching and learning for *all* students based on an inquiry-based, student-centered curriculum. They also demand a greater understanding of applicable laws, codes, and professional standards for ensuring safety for students. To probe these standards in greater detail, you may wish to review the complete document on line at www.nap.edu/readingroom/books/nses.

In recent years there has been a great deal of inquiry surrounding the conditions of safety in science settings throughout the United States. In the fall of 1999 and spring of 2000, a yearlong science safety project was completed in Wisconsin (Gerlovich, Whitsett, Lee, Parsa 2001). As part of that effort, teachers were required to complete a pre-training survey of their facilities, equipment, and understanding of their legal and professional obligations towards safety. The results were disturbing and confirmed earlier studies by Gerlovich (1997) indicating that few teachers were aware of their legal and professional obligations for safety within their science settings. The study also supported safety conclusions that emerged from a 1998 Iowa study (Gerlovich, Parsa, & Wilson, 1998) which indicated that poor facilities and equipment combined with inadequate understanding of legal and professional obligations resulted in increased numbers of accidents and lawsuits.

With increasing emphasis on hands-on, minds-on inquiry instruction at all levels in the National Science Education Standards (NSES) and most state frameworks of courses of study, it becomes more incumbent upon elementary teachers who teach science to be as knowledgeable as possible about laboratory safety issues and their own responsibilities. As teacher role model, you are expected to display good safety habits at all times and to set appropriate safety expectations for your students. Unfortunately, when you increase the amount of inquiry instruction in your classroom, you also increase the likelihood of accident. The document *Science and Safety: It's Elementary!* (CSSS, 1999) is intended to educate and reassure you, the user, that liability concerns can be minimized when you are knowledgeable of your duties and take appropriate precautions and preventative actions to avoid or minimize foreseeable hazards and accidents.

With an inquiry-based science program, you are likely to encourage students to experiment, observe, and explore on their own, in addition to following your step-by-step instructions. However exploratory, the work must be done in a safe manner. There can be no experimentation with safety rules. When it comes to safety instructions and safe procedures, you need to be explicit and exacting. While safe practices support inquiry-based science, it is totally inappropriate to let students learn by trial and error when it comes to matters of safety. If you catch your students quoting you—you've succeeded.

The National Science Teachers Association Pathways to the Science Education Standards reinforces the critical nature of inquiry in the learning process of elementary age students.

NSES
TS-A

The most important tool that children at the primary level use is observation. Curiosity makes students eager to explore by working with objects and asking questions. They learn about objects by grouping and ordering them. Such exploration provides early experiences in organizing data and understanding processes. (Lowery, 1997)

For additional information concerning the Pathways document, check out this website: http://www.nsta.org.

Students who participate in meaningful laboratory and field experiences assimilate the inquisitive spirit of science. Not only are hands-on laboratory and field activities vital for students to learn science, there is a critical minimum amount of time required for these active learning experiences. The National Science Teachers Association (NSTA) recommends minimum amounts of instructional time be devoted to doing science where students are observing, manipulating, measuring, organizing information, reasoning analytically, communicating findings, and conceptualizing scientific phenomena (NSTA Position Statement on Laboratory Science, 1993). Elementary students should spend a minimum of 80 percent of their science learning time doing hands-on activities. Reading about science, computer programs, and teacher demonstrations is valuable, but should not be substituted for hands-on experiences. Middle-school students should spend a minimum of 60 percent of their science instruction time on laboratory-related experience including pre-lab instruction, hands-on activities, and a post-lab period involving analysis and communication. High-school science students should spend 40 percent of their time on laboratory-related experiences including pre- and post-lab instruction. Table 10.1 provides the NSTA recommended minimum percentage of time that should be allotted for students' hands-on activities.

Common Factors That Influence Science Classroom Accidents

West et al. (2001) suggest that there are several patterns in research data that identify factors linked to an increase in the seriousness, the number, and the most prevalent accidents. Safety research findings can be grouped into four areas: 1) overcrowding; 2) state characteristics; 3) district/school characteristics; and 4) teacher characteristics. We will address only two of these: overcrowding and teacher characteristics.

Overcrowding and Class Size

NSES

TS-D

"Collaborative inquiry requires adequate and safe space" (NRC, 1996, p. 218). Overcrowding is a complex issue, as well as a serious issue, because adequate and safe space concerns two issues: 1) the class size, and 2) the amount of physical space per student.

TABLE 10.1 ● Minimum Instructional Time for Laboratory or Field Activities Recommended by NSTA

Level	% of Instructional Time
Elementary	80
Middle school	60
High school	40

Source: National Science Teachers Association, *Position Statement on Laboratory Science* (Arlington, VA: National Science Teachers Association, 1993).

TABLE 10.2 ● Professional Organizations' Recommendations for Class Size

Organization	Class Size	
	Elementary	Middle School
National Science Teachers Assoc. (NSTA) www.nsta.org/	24	24
National Science Educational Leadership Assoc. (NSELA) http://www.nsela.org/ positionstatements/crowding.html	24	24
Council of State Science Supervisors (CSSS) http://www.csss-science.org/ recommendations.shtml	24	24

Brennan (1970) found that class enrollment and laboratory space have a significant relationship to laboratory accidents; the higher the classroom enrollment and the smaller the laboratory space, the higher the frequency of accidents. Eliminating overcrowding is the one change that will most affect safety in science classrooms.

There is ample evidence that more accidents occur as the class size or the number of students per teacher in any one class increases (Macomber, 1961; Brennan, 1970; Young, 1972). Teachers consistently rate overcrowding as their number one safety concern (Horton, 1988; Rakow, 1989; West et al., 2001).

The National Science Teachers Association and the Council for State Science Supervisors recommend class size be limited to 24 students. Several research studies at the secondary level emphasize this recommendation. According to West et al. (2002), as secondary class size increased, so did the number of mishaps. The percentage of incidents and accidents increased from 27 percent to 36 percent when class size increased from 22 or fewer to 24 or fewer students. The number of incidents increased to an even more dramatic 58 percent when class size increased to more than 24 students.

Based on the safety research and the experience of science teachers over the years, most American and international professional organizations and states recommend a maximum science class size limit of 24 (see Table 10.2).

The National Science Teachers Association has also provided recommendations for the gross minimum room sizes. These would be the room dimension from wall to wall, not subtracting for any fastened furniture or other obstructions (Biehle et al. 1999, 22) (see Table 10.3).

The issue of building adequate science facilities is so great that the National Science Foundation (NSF) funded a project that established a website (www.labplan.org) that provides a process that can be used to plan and design science facilities.

TABLE 10.3 ● NSTA's Recommendations for Minimum Room Size for a Class of 24

Classroom Type	Room Size	
	Elementary	Middle School
Multiple use Classroom	1,080 ft^2	1,440 ft^2
Pure Science Room	960 ft^2	1,080 ft^2

Source: J. Biehle, L. Motz, and S. West. *NSTA Guide to School Science Facilities.* (Arlington, VA: National Science Teachers Association, 1999).

Teacher Characteristics

NSES
CS-A

The National Science Education Standards recommend that safety become an essential factor for all science teachers, especially in this age of scientific inquiry. The characteristics of these individuals are clearly delineated in their safety premise and are best expressed in this statement:

> Safety is a fundamental concern in all experimental science. Teachers of science must know and apply the necessary safety regulations in the storage, use, and care of the materials used by students. They adhere to safety rules and guidelines that are established by national organizations such as the American Chemical Society and the Occupational Safety and Health Administration, as well as by local and state regulatory agencies. They work with the school and district to ensure implementation and use of safety guidelines for which they (school and district) are responsible, such as the presence of safety equipment and an appropriate class size. Teachers also teach students how to engage safely in investigations inside and outside the classroom. (NRC 1996, p. 44)

It may be overstating the obvious, but individuals who are well prepared in their content fields and who have more experience tend to have fewer accidents. West, et al. found that

> Individual teacher characteristics, such as inadequate content preparation, less teaching experience, poor classroom management, allowing student access to chemicals and lack of safety training, all link to unsafe science teaching and learning experiences. Usually accidents can be attributed to one or more of the following: inadequate safety knowledge, poor safety attitudes, and insufficient safety skills.

How Do You Plan for Safety?

NSES
PD-A

Children are natural scientists because they are curious about everything in their physical world. Given the opportunity, they will investigate events and objects of all types and see beauty and intrigue in events that adults accept as mundane. Sometimes it is difficult for children to separate danger from fascination. The teacher's responsibility is to balance these two factors, with information from publishers, science experts, peers, and considerations from their own teaching environment (student abilities and maturities, equipment available) in order to ensure that science learning is effective yet safe.

Natural events provide effective learning opportunities for elementary students. Ice storms, tornadoes, thunderstorms, floods, the first snowfall, a gentle rain, and the changes of the seasons are all natural phenomena which elementary students are curious about. When these events happen around them, students become even more curious about the causes and are receptive to learning about what causes the events.

In order to keep students safe while attempting to construct an understanding of science concepts through hands-on science activities, teachers must have a simple yet effective safety philosophy that guides students. It is important to identify appropriate grade-level concepts and worthwhile explorations in order to enact an effective safety philosophy. Once these are clearly identified, the teacher must ask, "What are the foreseeable hazards associated with valued educational activities?" Ask yourself, "Would a respected peer use the same materials or activity I have selected?" "What adjustments might another teacher make to fit the needs of students according to their emotional, social, and academic abilities?" "What group size or class setting would a reasonable teacher use to make the activity effective and safe?"

Activities should be selected based on the developmental level of the students involved. You must think about any foreseeable hazards your students may encounter as they participate in your activities. Be sensitive to such issues as chemical problems, areas in which you may have insufficient knowledge, fire hazards, potential eye injuries from sharp objects or flying projectiles, and overcrowding. If the foreseeable hazards exceed the educational value of the knowledge or experience students could gain from direct participation, you have some choices to make:

1. Provide additional safety parameters, such as safety goggles, fire blankets, eyewashes, and additional supervision.

2. Limit the activity to a teacher demonstration, in which you are the only one who manipulates the equipment, and students become active observers. (In many instances this is the most logical and educationally responsible choice.)

3. Eliminate the activity entirely from the curriculum. Unless you have recently performed a detailed assessment of the entire science curriculum across grades, you might be surprised at how many duplicate activities of little value exist in science classes that are taught primarily because of tradition. (Gerlovich et al., 2003)

The National Science Teachers Association recommends the following in *Exploring Safely* (Kwan & Texley, 2002):

Lesson plans often have great continuity but fall short in the real world. Every day there is someone absent in almost every classroom. That means that your safety precautions must consider the consequences of both teacher and student absences.

Remember that you are responsible for the program offered by your substitute. Because the substitute is unlikely to have your knowledge of the subject matter or the same level of classroom control, it is usually not a good idea to have them conduct complex activities or those with potential hazards. Many teachers have a special substitute folder for one-day unexpected absences containing safe activities that would fit almost any part of the year.

When students are absent, they often miss safety directions, so it is important to have a written version and to begin every class with a short review. Be sure that all your safety lessons and directions are included in your lesson plan book.

Students who are absent often need access to the supplies the next day. To save your sanity, you may want to organize these supplies in labeled boxes containing all the supplies for a particular unit. Place a laminated card with the relevant safety rules in the box with the supplies.

In an inquiry-based science program, teachers encourage students to observe, experiment, and explore on their own as much as possible. It is vital, however, that this be guided freedom performed with a safety first attitude. Safety should be explicit and targeted at the scientific investigation being performed. The following lesson plan examplifies how safety can be planned for and reiterated throughout a lesson.

What Are Your Legal Responsibilities?

Although this section focuses on tort law as it relates to science teaching, the principles and philosophy apply to all school subjects. There are several legal concepts you must be familiar with in order to understand your legal responsibilities.

NSES
TS-A, C, D, F

Earth/Space Science: Cooling Crystals

Grades • 5–8

▶ Structure of the Earth's system. Changes in the solid earth can be described as the rock cycle. Old rocks are buried, then compacted, heated, and often recrystallized into new rock.

Engaging Question

Why do some rocks, made of the same materials, have different names?

CONCEPTS TO BE CONSTRUCTED

▶ The rate at which a crystal cools affects the size of the crystal.

▶ Rocks like granite, rhyolite, and obsidian are essentially made of the same material yet they look different because of the rate at which the crystals cooled to form each varied.

SCIENCE ATTITUDES TO NURTURE

▶ Curiosity·
▶ Perseverance
▶ Open-mindedness
▶ Cooperating with others

Materials Needed

For exploration phase • conducted in teams of three or four, each team will need:

- 2 500-ml beakers
- 3 glass caster cups
- 3 small test tubes (10-ml)
- Test tube holder
- Paradichlorbenzine (PDB) flakes
- 1 150-ml beaker
- Heat proof glove
- Hot plate
- Water
- Crushed ice

For expansion phase • conducted in teams of three or four, each team will need:

- Samples of igneous rocks, such as rhyolite, granite, and obsidian
- 1 hand lens/student
- Grease pencil
- Crushed ice
- Tongs
- Paper towels

🛈 *Safety:* Review with the students proper use of heating equipment—such as hot plates used in this activity. Remind them the hot plates purposely have short cords so that they are plugged in close to the wall. No extension cords should be used. Keep the table that the hot plate is on close to the wall to minimize the risk of someone tripping over the cord.

- Extreme care should be used near the hot plate and in handling the hot water and the PDB.
- Goggles should be worn at all times, NO excuses.
- Be sure the room is well ventilated when melting the PDB.

PROCESS SKILLS USED
▶ Observing
▶ Predicting
▶ Manipulating materials
▶ Recording data
▶ Drawing conclusions

Student Activity

As safety is very important with this activity, it is important to conduct this as a *Guided Discovery Activity*. Lead the student teams in a step-by-step process:

1. Ask the students to fill one of the 500-ml beakers with 300-ml of water. Place a caster cup in the beaker. Boil the water on the hot plate. Again, remind the students to place the hot plate flat on the table as close to the wall as possible to avoid anyone tripping over the cord. Fill the other 500-ml beaker with crushed ice. Place the second caster cup in the beaker. Leave the third caster cup at room temperature.

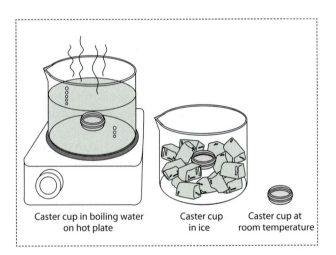

Caster cup in boiling water on hot plate   Caster cup in ice   Caster cup at room temperature

2. Ask the students to observe some PDB flakes. Be sure to remind students that goggles are to be worn at *all* times and that these observations are made in a well-ventilated area of the room. If no fume hood is present, be sure windows are opened. Ask the students to record their observations.

3. Once the water in the beaker begins to boil, ask one student from the group to put on the heat-proof glove and carefully remove the 500-ml beaker from the hot plate. Set it on a heat-proof surface, away from risk of getting knocked over while the students perform Step 4.

4. Again, in a well-ventilated area, ask the students to fill each of the three small test tubes with PDB flakes, and to half-fill the 150-ml beaker with water. Place the three test tubes in the beaker containing the water. Place the beaker on the hot plate. Heat the beaker gently until the PDB melts. Be sure a team member is carefully watching for the PDB to melt and that goggles are still on *ALL* students.

5. Instruct students to go back to the 500-ml beaker and using the tongs carefully remove the caster cup from the boiling water. Dry the cup and label it A. Once the PDB flakes have melted in each of the test tubes, instruct one student from each team to use the test tube holder to carefully remove one test tube from the beaker and pour the liquefied PDB into the caster cup. Ask the students to time how long it takes for the PDB to completely become a solid, to record the time, and to record their observations for the PDB as it was placed in the caster cup and what happened to it over time.

6. Ask the students to now remove the second caster cup from the beaker with ice. Dry the cup quickly and completely. Label it B. Ask another student from each team to use the test tube holder to carefully remove another test tube from the beaker and pour the liquefied PDB into the caster cup labeled B. Ask the students to time how long it takes for the PDB to completely become a solid, to record the time, and to record their observations for the PDB as it was placed in the caster cup and what happened to it over time.

7. Ask the students to take the third caster cup which was sitting at room temperature and label it C. Then ask another student from each team to use the test tube holder to carefully remove another test tube from the beaker and pour the liquefied PDB into the caster cup labeled C. Again, ask the students to time how long it takes for the PDB to completely become a solid, to record the time, and to record their observations for the PDB as it was placed in the caster cup and what happened to it over time.

Encourage the teams to use the hand lens to draw pictures of the now cooled PDB in each of the caster cups—A, B, and C.

Explanation

Ask the students teams to help create a set of class data on cooling rates for the liquefied PDB in cups A–C. Collect student drawings of the cooled PDB from the cups to share with the entire class. Use the following questions to help make the concept behind the guided activity concrete:

- Which caster cup took the longest for the PDB to solidify? Which took the least amount of time?

- Was there a difference in the PDB when it solidified in the hot cup A compared to the cold cup B?

- Look at the various drawings of the solidified PDB in casters A–C. How are they different? What caused this difference? What conclusions can you draw?

- How does the rate of cooling affect the size of the crystals?

The students should conclude that the rate at which a crystal cools affects the size of the crystal formed.

Expansion

PROCESS SKILLS USED:
▶ Observing
▶ Recording data
▶ Generalizing
▶ Formulating models

This expansion activity can be completed as an open discovery once the students are reminded of the safety issues and proper teacher supervision makes sure that the students follow them. The student teams can be free to explore at their own pace. Remind students to wear goggles during the expansion phase in case rock samples are dropped, to avoid getting rock chips into eyes.

Ask the students to observe the crystals in the samples of granite, rhyolite, and obsidian with a magnifying glass. Have them draw the crystals in each sample on paper. Can they even see separate crystals in the obsidian? Ask them to compare the crystals in the caster cups with the samples of granite, rhyolite, and obsidian, and to respond to this question in their journals: Which PDB crystals are most similar to the crystals in the rock samples? [Cup A, granite; cup B, obsidian; cup C, rhyolite).

Granite, rhyolite, and obsidian are igneous rocks essentially made of the same material. Ask the students to use what they learned in the exploration phase to provide an explanation as to why they look different. Ask the students to record team responses to the following questions in their journal so that responses can be shared once all the student teams have completed their observations: Where would igneous rocks have a chance to cool slowly? Where would igneous rocks cool rapidly? If you saw a rock that contained large interlocking crystals, what would you say about the way it was formed? Some suggested answers are: The more slowly a crystal cools, the larger the crystals are. Granite cooled slowly and crystals were able to form. Rhyolite cooled more rapidly than granite, but more slowly than obsidian; thus crystals are evident, just not as large as those found in granite. Obsidian cooled quickly, thus it is difficult to see the crystals. Igneous rocks cool slowly deep in the Earth. They cool rapidly on the surface. Large interlocking crystals form slowly inside the earth.

As a class, ask the students to respond to the engaging question: Why so some rocks made of the same materials have different names?

Science in Personal and Social Perspectives

- What kinds of crystals do you eat regularly? [salt and sugar]

- How does the size of the crystal determine its quality? Do you think your knowledge of how crystals form will assist you in determining the quality of precious rocks and gems?

Science and Technology

- The strength and quality of rocks are important in construction. What is the best type of rock for long-lasting buildings?

- How has the scarcity of quality gems on the market affected your life, your community, the world?

Science as Inquiry

- What kinds of rocks are found in the area where you live? Can you classify them according to their crystal structure?

- Are crystals found in sedimentary rocks? Why or why not?

History and Nature of Science

- What kinds of careers would use information on crystal formation? Some possibilities include geologist, geophysicist, volcanologist, jeweler, sculptor, and geographer.

- Choose one of the career suggestions from the above question and research the skills necessary to enter that career. Provide an oral report to the class.

Evaluation

Hands-on Assessment

The students will be able to examine samples of igneous rocks and explain why they have different sized crystals.

Reflective Assessment

The students will be able to explain how the prices of precious jewels are affected by the process of crystal formation.

Pictorial Assessment

The students will be able to use drawings of crystals of different shapes and sizes and identify where the crystal cooled (on the earth's surface, or inside the earth) by the shape of the crystals. They will be able to identify which drawings are of crystals that cooled quickly or slowly.

Safety Precautions

The following are examples of safety precautions associated with this experiment. What other precautions did you identify?

Safety Precautions

- Review with the students proper use of heating equipment—such as the hot plates used in this activity. Remind them the hot plates purposely have short cords so that they are plugged in close to the wall, NO extension cords should be used. Keep the table/desk that the hot plate is on close to the wall to minimize the risk of someone tripping over the cord.

- Extreme care should be used near the hot plate and in handling the hot water and the PDB.

- Goggles should be worn at all times, NO excuses.

- Be sure the room is well ventilated when melting the PDB.

Tort

A *tort* is a wrong, or injury, that someone has committed against someone else. The injured party generally wants restitution for the injury or damages. The resolution of such conflicts between litigants (*plaintiffs* being those who bring the claim and *defendants* being those against whom the claim has been filed) generally occurs in a court, involving lawyers, a judge, possibly jurors, and witnesses, and is referred to as a *lawsuit*.

Remember, as a teacher you are acting in place of the parents (in loco parentis). The courts point out that you assume these responsibilities because you are a professional educator. *Exploring Safely* (Kwan & Texley, 2002) spells out these responsibilities.

| Prepare: | Keep up to date with continuing education and activities within professional organizations and school policies and procedures. |
| Plan: | Use best strategies to ensure your students learn effectively and safely and you think ahead to determine how best to work with their strengths and limitations. |

Protect: Assess hazards and review procedures for accident prevention and teach and review safety procedures with every student when a hazard is anticipated.

Protect: Check your facilities for the presence and accessibility of correctly operating safety equipment and protective devices, demonstrate their proper use, and maintain these records.

Reasonable and Prudent Judgment

The U.S. legal system does not require educators to be superhuman in the performance of their duties. It is expected only that they be *reasonable and prudent* in their judgment when performing their duties with students. Educators need only do what reasonable persons with comparable training and experience would do in similar situations. They must ask themselves whether their peers would endorse these activities being performed with students. Proceed with confidence if questions are answered affirmatively. If not, add more safety features, limit the activity to a teacher demonstration, or eliminate it entirely. As science teachers, we must attempt to anticipate reasonable hazards, eliminate them, or be confidently prepared to address them.

Foreseeability

If you discover something amiss in your teaching environment, you should request corrections, preferably in writing, as soon as possible (see Figure 10.1). Essential items, such as fire extinguishers, fire blankets, eyewashes, or safety goggles, need to be obtained or repaired immediately; less important items, like nonskid floor wax, can be discussed with administrators for future correction. All known hazards and appropriate emergency measures should be explained to students as well.

The foreseeable hazards of all activities, as well as appropriate emergency reactions, should be completely explained to students *prior* to an activity. Field trip sites should be

FIGURE 10.1 ● Request for Correction of Safety Concern

Source: Gerlovich et al., *The Total Science Safety System CD (New Hampshire Edition).* (Waukee, IA: JaKel, Inc., 2006). Excerpted, with permission.

Date filed with administrator: _____

Secretary's initials: _____

Request for Correction of Safety Concern

Date: _____   Room: _____

The following is a safety concern in the science area:

_____   _____
       (Teacher name)   (Signature)

CC: Teacher, Dept. Chair

reviewed very carefully by the teacher before students arrive. Ask the owner or proprietor of the field site about any known hazards or potential hazards to students. Any sensitivities to foods the class might be working with should be ascertained before the activity begins. Any phobias should be identified before students are placed in potentially frightening situations. The teacher *must* know about any medical problems that students may have—for example, medication schedules, allergies, fears, and anxieties. Before ever involving students in activities, ask yourself, **"What could go wrong with this activity, and am I prepared to address the problem?"** If you can answer the questions affirmatively, proceed with confidence.

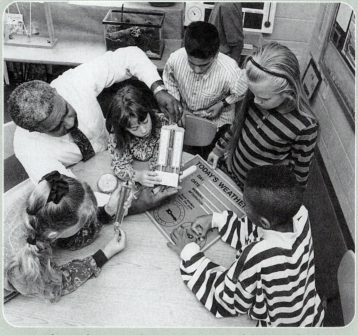

Prudent judgment and proper supervision fulfill most legal responsibilities.

Negligence

Before you can be held accountable for personal injury accidents, it must be proven that you were negligent. *Negligence* has been defined as "conduct that falls below a standard established by law or profession to protect others from harm" (Iowa Annotated Code, 2000). It is sometimes described as failure to exercise due care. What are your professional standards? Refer to Table 10.2 (Professional Organizations Recommendations for Class Size) for additional information.

Due Care

Due care may be defined as your duty to protect your students (Iowa Code Annotated, 2000). For younger or disabled students, the degree of care provided must be increased. It is recommended that every student with a disability (temporary or permanent) should be viewed by the teacher as occupying two student seats (JaKel, Inc. 2006). You must remember that you are the authority in the classroom. You, or an equally qualified adult substitute, must be with students at all times, especially when the potential for injury exists. During science activities, when materials and chemicals are being manipulated, your presence is essential. If you need to leave the room during such activities, you must make certain that an equally qualified person assumes this responsibility. Due care is often summarized in three teacher duties: instruction, supervision, and maintenance (Iowa Code Annotated, 2000).

Instruction. You must ensure that the instruction is appropriate for the physical and mental development levels of your students. Since textbooks form the basis of many science programs, you would be wise to ensure that safety is an integral and conspicuous component. Strive to select textbooks that parallel your safe science teaching philosophy.

All activities which involve students should be weighed for their educational value versus the hazards involved in having students perform them. If the foreseeable dangers outweigh the educational value of the activity, limit the demonstration to the teacher, add more safety features, or eliminate the science activity (Gerlovich et al.,

FIGURE 10.2 ● General Safety Rules for Students

Source: T. Kwan and J. Texley. *Exploring Safely: A Guide for Elementary Teachers* (National Science Teachers Association, 2002).

NSES

TS-B

Always review the general safety rules with the students before beginning an activity.

1. Never do any experiment without the approval and direct supervision of your teacher.
2. Always wear your safety goggles when your teacher tells you to do so. Never remove your goggles during an activity.
3. Know the location of all safety equipment in or near your classroom. Never play with the safety equipment.
4. Tell your teacher immediately if an accident occurs.
5. Tell your teacher immediately if a spill occurs.
6. Tell your teacher immediately about any broken, chipped, or scratched glassware so that it may be properly cleaned up and disposed of.
7. Tie back long hair and secure loose clothing when working around flames.
8. If instructed to do so, wear your laboratory apron or smock to protect your clothing.
9. Never assume that anything that has been heated is cool. Hot glassware looks just like cool glassware.
10. Never taste anything during a laboratory activity. If an investigation involves tasting, it will be done in the cafeteria.
11. Clean up your work area upon completion of your activity.
12. Wash your hands with soap and water upon completion of an activity.

2003). As a service to teachers, newsletters are supplied by safety-conscious scientific supply companies. Many equipment supplier newsletters include safety columns and hints as well as more effective safety equipment ideas for young students.

Rules should be clearly written and explained to students. Copies of the most important rules should be written in large print using age appropriate language and posted conspicuously throughout the room. To help assure the safety of students, the National Science Teachers Association (Kwan & Texley, 2002) recommends that teachers post, in conspicuous places visible to students, General Safety Rules for Students, outlined in Figure 10.2.

Public Law 94-142, also known as the Individuals with Disabilities Education Act (IDEA), is a federal law approved in 1975 and reauthorized in 1990. It mandates that students receive a free public education that is appropriate to their level of disability. In addition, these students must be educated with peer students who do not have disabilities. The Americans with Disabilities Act (ADA) also prohibits discrimination against persons with disabilities. Teachers must be extra cautious to assure that neither equipment nor facilities discriminate against these students while at the same time keep them safe. One way that this can be accomplished is through targeted science lesson plans and safety contracts. It is best to check with your state department of education for specific guidelines.

NSTA recommends that teachers in the upper grades (4–6) develop a safety

Determine the educational value of an activity before doing it.

STUDENT SAFETY CONTRACT		

My teacher told me, (student)_____, about these safety items in my science class.

Safety Things	Do You Understand These? Yes/No
Safety Rules	
	Do you know how to find and use these?
Safety Equipment	
Fire extinguisher	
Fire blanket	
Goggles	
Eyewash	
Heat sources	
Candle	
Alcohol lamp	
Microwave oven	
Other	
Electrical equipment	
Telephone or intercom	
What to do:	
During a fire	
During a chemical splash to the body	
When disposing of chemicals	
During an accident	
When performing experiments	
During an eye emergency	
Following a chemical spill	
During an electrical emergency	

Teacher:_____ Parent/Guardian_____
          Signature/Date   Signature/Date

Student is wearing vision correcting contact lenses   (Yes____ No____)

FIGURE 10.3 ● Student Safety Contract: Sample 1 for Upper Elementary Classrooms

Source: J. Gerlovich & D. McElroy, *The Total Science Safety System: Elementary Edition,* computer software (Waukee, IA: JaKel, Inc., 2007). Excerpted, with permission. JaKel, Inc. (2007). Total Science Safety System, National Edition CD-ROM.

contract (Figure 10.3 and 10.4) with their students and have parents read it aloud and review it with their children at home early in the year, and then sign and return the document to the teacher. A student between the ages of 7–14 may be held accountable to such contracts providing the contract was clear and there is some indication the student understood it. Children younger than age 7 cannot be held accountable to these contracts. It might be helpful to everyone to go over the

NSES
TS-E

FIGURE 10.4 ● Student Safety Contract: Sample 2

Source: T. Kwan and J. Texley. *Exploring Safely: A Guide for Elementary Teachers* (National Science Teachers Association, 2002).

I am learning to be a good scientist. I know that I must be organized, neat, and well behaved to learn science best. I promise to:

- Prepare for activities: I will listen to directions and make sure I understand them before I start.
- Care for equipment: I will handle objects carefully and put them away when I am done.
- Follow directions: I will do each step in order, and I will not try unknown things.
- Observe carefully: I will be as quiet and calm as possible so that I can learn more.
- Keep careful records: I will write down my observations.
- Clean up afterwards: I will wash my hands and my workspace.
- Follow all safety rules.

I will share good science safety with students and family so that I can be a good investigator:

(Signed) _____ / (Signed) _____
                          Student   Parent

importance and implications of this document with parents at a scheduled parent-teacher conference. It's a good idea to update and repeat the contract process each quarter to semester.

Discipline during science activities should be fair, consistent, and firmly enforced. Safety is so important that no one should be exempt. The only exceptions should be based on a student's obvious physical or mental limitations. Students will support teachers in their activities a great deal more if they feel that everyone is treated fairly. You may also wish to involve students in the safe science and discipline rules for the class.

You are a role model. You set the safety expectations for your class by example. Students cannot be expected to take safety seriously if you do not observe all guidelines. Be especially careful to wear safety equipment items (goggles) and observe all safety rules. Explain all safety considerations and have all safety equipment items available before beginning any activity. Safety should be something that students expect you to enforce.

If you are considering having an outside presenter in your room, you may want to check on the individual's background and follow the guidelines provided by the National Science Teachers Association in their Outside Presenter's Form (Figure 10.5, page 289).

Consider simulating age appropriate foreseeable emergencies—for example, a student who receives a chemical splash on his or her clothing, face, or eyes; a classroom or clothing fire caused by science items; finding another adult to give emergency assistance; evacuating the room—and proper safety responses as part of your daily teaching. Following instructions, you might evaluate students on their proper and expeditious performances. Accent the positive; emphasize what you want students to *do*. Be careful to protect students from any hazards during the simulations.

Should an accident or incident occur, collect as much information as possible from witnesses (student and staff). An accident or incident report (see Figure 10.6, page 291) can help focus the report should legal repercussions arise from the incident. These accounts are powerful, firsthand evidence of what actions were taken and the teacher's commitment to safety. Some states set limits on the length of time, after an incident occurs, wherein legal action can be taken. When the statute of limitations for legal actions passes

Science safety is an integral part of science education and serves as a preparation for life. Accordingly, the _____ School District encourages teachers to assure meaningful and safe science experiences both inside and outside the classroom. The intent of the safety guidelines that follow is to promote safe science practices at all school-sponsored activities.

NSES
PD-B
TS-F

The Following Situations May Not Be Part of Any School Science-Related Activity Under Any Circumstances:

1. Parts of the body are not to be placed in danger, such as placing dry ice in the mouth or dipping hands or fingers into liquid nitrogen or molten lead, or exposing the hands and face to micro-organisms. Demonstrations such as the following shall not be conducted: walking on broken glass or hot coals or fire with bare feet, passing an electric current through the body, and lying on a bed of nails and having a concrete block broken over the chest.
2. Live vertebrate animals may not be used in demonstrations or for experimental purposes. Such animals may be used only for observational purposes provided the animals have been lawfully acquired, are housed in proper containers, and are handled in a humane way. Any certification papers or vaccination documents shall be made available upon request.
3. Animals are to be used for educational purposes and not for the exploitation of the animal for advertisement, commercial purposes, or sensationalism. This includes use of animals in an exhibit hall.
4. Live ammunition, firearms, or acutely dangerous explosives, such as Benzoyl peroxide, Diethyl ether, Perchloric acid, Picric acid and Sodium azide, may not be used. Commercially available fireworks and blasting caps shall never be used.
5. Plants with poisonous oils (e.g., poison ivy), saps (e.g., oleander), or other plants known to be generally toxic to humans are not to be used.
6. Experiments or demonstrations with human blood/body fluids may not be conducted.
7. Radioactive powders, liquids, or solutions are not to be used except in a laboratory facility designated for the type of radioactive material. Arrange for proper shielding and protection for demonstrations which involve radiation. Only low-level radioactive sources shall be employed.

Guidelines for Preparing Your Presentation:

1. Practice all demonstrations or workshop procedures BEFORE presenting them to an audience or having participants try them.
2. Research and understand the properties, chemical reactions, and dangers involved in all demonstrations. Plan to use correct handling and disposal procedures for all chemicals and biohazards used. Arrange to have a fire extinguisher available whenever the slightest possibility of fire exists. Be aware of emergency and fire escape routes for your site.
3. Prepare a handout that gives participants detailed instructions about the procedures, safety precautions, hazards, and disposal methods for each demonstration and workshop. Have Material Safety Data Sheets (MSDS) for chemicals and biohazards available upon request.
4. Prepare photographs, slides, videotapes, and so on, that show safe science practices. When preparing these materials, safety goggles and equipment shall not be removed for aesthetic considerations.
5. In planning demonstrations and/or workshops, keep quantities of hazardous materials to a minimum. Use only those quantities that can be adequately handled by the available ventilation system. Do not carry out demonstrations that will result in the release of harmful quantities of noxious gases into the local air supply in the demonstration or other rooms. The following gases shall not be produced without using a fume hood: nitrogen dioxide, sulfur dioxide, and hydrogen sulfide. Volatile toxic substances such as benzene, carbon tetrachloride, and formaldehyde shall not be used unless a fume hood is available.

FIGURE 10.5 ● NSTA Guidelines for Outside Presenter's Form

Source: National Science Teachers Association Board of Directors. *Outside Presenter's Form* (August 1994; revised July 2000).

for the incident, dispose of the materials. These reports can also be very effective learning tools when used with other classes.

Supervision. The duty of supervision, as part of due care, can be a significant challenge. Teachers should always be in the classroom when scientific equipment or chemicals are accessible to students. The only exceptions to this rule are times of extreme emergencies or

6. Make sure your glassware and equipment are not broken or damaged. The use of chipped or cracked glassware shall be avoided. If glassware is to be heated, Pyrex™ or its equivalent shall be used.
7. Thoroughly check motor-driven discs that revolve at moderate or high speeds. Make sure the disc is sturdy, that it contains no parts that may come free, and that the safety nut is securely fastened.
8. Arrange to use a safety shield and/or eye protection for audience members and interpreters for any demonstration(s) in which projectiles are launched or when there is the slightest possibility of an unsafe explosion. Do not allow direct viewing of the sun, infrared, or ultraviolet sources.
9. Make sure any lasers to be used in demonstrations are helium-neon lasers with a maximum output power rating not exceeding 1.0 milliwatt. At all times, avoid direct propagation of a laser beam from a laser into the eye of an observer or from a reflected surface into the eye.
10. Secure pressurized gas cylinders by strapping or chaining them in place or by using proper supports, i.e., lecture bottles.
11. Obtain in advance, the necessary state and/or local permits needed for the firing of model rockets. Activities involving the firing of rockets must be well planned and follow Federal Aviation Agency (FAA) regulations, state and local rules and regulations, and the National Association of Rocketry's (NAR) Solid Propellant Model Rocket Safety Code.
12. Arrange for appropriate waste containers and for the disposal of materials hazardous to the environment.
13. Plan to dress safely for your presentation or workshop.

During the Presentation:
1. Comply with all local fire and safety rules and regulations. Follow the NSTA Minimum Safety Guidelines.
2. Wear appropriate eye protection, an apron, ear protection, and similar protective gear for all chemical demonstrations or when appropriate for other demonstrations. Provide eye protection, aprons, and safety equipment for participants who will be handling chemicals, hazardous substances, or working with flames.
3. Do not select volunteers from the audience. Assistants used in demonstrations shall be recruited and given the proper instructions beforehand.
4. Warn participants or audience to cover their ears whenever a loud explosion is anticipated.
5. Use a safety shield for all demonstrations that involve the launching of projectiles, or whenever there is the slightest possibility that a container, its fragments, or its contents could be propelled with sufficient force to cause injury. Shield moving belts attached to motors. Use caution when motor-driven discs revolve at moderate or high speeds. Shield or move participants to a safe distance from the plane of the rotating disc.
6. Follow proper procedures for working with pressurized gases and when heating all forms of matter.
7. Use appropriate gloves and shields when working with hazardous chemicals and biohazards, cryogenic materials, hot materials, radioactive substances, vacuums, electromagnetic radiation, and when presenting animals for observation.
8. Do not taste or encourage participants to taste any nonfood substances. A food substance subjected to possible contamination or unsafe conditions shall never be tasted.
9. Alert the audience clearly at the beginning of the program to the presence or production of allergenic materials, such as strobe lights, microwaves, lycopodium powder, or live animals.
10. Maintain a clear exit during the demonstration or workshop.
11. Emphasize and demonstrate appropriate safety precautions throughout the presentation or workshop.
12. Distribute a handout that will give participants detailed instructions about the procedure, safety precautions, hazards, and disposal for each demonstration and workshop.

FIGURE 10.5 ● Continued

when the supervision has been delegated to another equally qualified person. Overcrowding, classroom size, and field trips are matters that require specific supervisory attention.

There is increasing evidence that *overcrowding* is the root cause of accidents in science settings. Supervision should increase when the danger level of the activity increases, the number of students with disabilities in the class increases, and the learning environment differs from the conventional classroom setting. Teachers must be aware of overcrowding and initiate corrections as soon as possible.

FIGURE 10.6 ● Teacher Accident/ Incident Report

Source: JaKel, Inc. (2007), *The Total Science Safety System* National Edition CD-ROM.

1. Staff member completing the report: _____

2. Date of accident/incident: _____

3. Time of the accident/incident: _____

4. Location of the accident/incident:

5. Staff/student(s) involved in the accident/incident:

   (a) Staff (report attached)   (b) Student (report attached)

   _____   _____

   _____   _____

   _____   _____

   _____   _____

6. Teacher description of the accident/incident:

7. Immediate action taken to deal with the emergency:

8. Corrective action taken to avoid a repeat of the accident/incident in the future:

_____   _____
       (Date report completed)   (Signature of person completing report)

The classroom teaching environment has a significant influence on the safety that can be provided to students. In its 1989 safety guide, the Texas Education Agency recommended two types of floor plans for teaching elementary school science that may provide a model for the nation. Emphasis was placed on:

- Safety equipment
- A maximum of twenty-four students during science activities
- Extensive open space leading to a least two exits
- Adequate room for students to move about without bumping into each other or equipment
- Students need to be easily supervised by the teacher from any point in the room
- No blind spots in the classroom

Adult volunteers enhance due care through supervision on field trips.

Field Trips

Item	Date Satisfied
The teacher has visited the field trip site prior to involving students there.	_____
The activity is a well-planned part of the science course.	_____
The activity is appropriate for the mental and physical age of the students.	_____
Transportation is via school or school-sanctioned vehicles only.	_____
Teachers, assistants, and drivers have complete lists of participating students.	_____
Teachers have cell phones, CB-radios, etc, for emergency communications.	_____
Clear, appropriate rules of behavior are established and understood by students.	_____
All field trip dangers are pointed out to students in advance and again when students arrive at the site.	_____
Students are dressed according to the demands of the environment and weather. (Parents are notified of such clothing and supplies to be taken on the trip in advance.)	_____
In tick and mite areas, students' arms, legs, and necks are covered.	_____
Following field trips, in areas where ticks are common, students are checked for ticks when they return to school.	_____
Any field trips to water environments require at least one person in each group to be familiar with lifesaving, CPR, and artificial respiration techniques.	_____
Approved life jackets are available for all students who venture out into the water.	_____
Approved adult/student ratio never exceeds 1:10.	_____
Supervision is increased according to the novelty and danger inherent in the field trip environment.	_____
All safety equipment is in proper state of repair.	_____
Equipment is designed for the mental and physical ages of the students using it.	_____
Students know how to use the equipment properly.	_____
Glass collecting equipment is avoided if possible.	_____
The buddy system, pairing students in teams, is used to help ensure safety and mutual responsibility.	_____
The teacher is congnizant of any "known" student medical needs (allergies, medication schedules, phobias, etc.).	_____
Signed parent or guardian permission forms have been received and processed.	_____
Alternative activities are planned for those not attending the field trip.	_____
For extended field trips, appropriate student medical and liability insurance cards have been obtained.	_____
For extended field trips, teacher/supervisors have obtained telephone numbers for contacting parents or designees at any time. A copy of the student's insurance coverage card is also provided to the teacher/supervisor.	_____
Appropriate first-aid kits are appropriately stocked and available.	_____
All safety procedures are demonstrated and understood by students.	_____
The teacher has talked with the landowner or other knowledgeable persons concerning hazards prior to involving students at the site.	_____
The teacher has checked that the weather is safe for student participation.	_____

A

FIGURE 10.7 ● Field Trip Checklist for Teachers

Source: J. Gerlovich et al., *The Total Science Safety System CD, New Hampshire Edition* (Waukee, IA: JaKel, Inc., 2006). Excerpted with permission.

For field trips, obtain parent or guardian release forms or waivers for all students and apprise the administration of the event (Figures 10.7 A, B, and C). The activity should be an integral part of the course. Teachers should use only school-sanctioned and insured vehicles. On field trips, increase supervision to one teacher or other quali-fied adult to ten students. It is imperative that teachers and other assisting adults pre-view the field site for hazards *before* students are involved. Students should be apprised

Field Trip Permission Request Form

Date: _____ School: _____

Your child's class is planning a school field trip on (date) _____ to _____ as part of their science class studies. The class will be traveling via school vehicles and departing from the school at _____ and returning to the same location at _____. They will be under the direct supervision of their regular teacher as well as additional "qualified" chaperones.

If you prefer not to have your student participate, please contact me so that alternative activities can be arranged. No student will be allowed on the trip without this signed form returned to me by (date) _____.

If you have questions related to the trip, or specific information concerning your child that would be helpful for the teacher to know (medications, allergies, medical ailments, handicaps, etc.), please contact:

_____ at _____
                (Teacher)   (Telephone number)

Principal _____

Supervising Teacher _____

B

Field Trip Permission Form

I give permission for my child _____ to participate in the science field trip on (date) _____ to _____, understanding that all foreseeable precautions have been taken to ensure his/her safety.

I have provided my child with the $ _____ recommended to cover meals and other field trip related expenses.

I may be contacted at any time during my child's field trip at the following telephone numbers: _____ (Home) _____ (Work).

Date _____

Parent or Guardian _____

C

FIGURE 10.7 ● Continued

of any known hazards and appropriate responses in an emergency, such as described in the opening third scenario. Be careful to consider poisonous plants and plants with thorns or other irritating parts, and check for poisonous or biting animals. On the school grounds, look for broken glass, holes, drug paraphernalia, and other unexpected items. Remember to be aware of insects that carry diseases, such as Lyme disease, encephalitis, and yellow fever. Check with local medical authorities for updates. If an insect repellent is to be used, check that it contains DEET and that no students are allergic to it.

What must a teacher do to ensure safe field trips?

Implement the buddy system on field trips, pairing students and holding them responsible for each other (Rakow, 1989). Buddies can apprise adults of any problem. Very young students (grades K–3) should not be separated from adult supervision at any time. The teacher should arrange for upper elementary students to meet at prearranged times and these times should be adhered to explicitly. Increase adult supervision for young learners.

Maintenance. Maintaining an educational environment is the third teacher duty. It is imperative that you attempt to foresee hazards and expedite their correction. You are not expected to be superhuman in your identification or make the repairs yourself. However, a logical, regular review of the teaching environment is a reasonable expectation. The information available in the safety equipment and safety assessment sections of this chapter can help you with maintenance. For additional information concerning legal concept and case studies, visit the American Association of Law Librarians website at www.aallnet.org.

Federal and State Legislation

Eye Protective Equipment. A vital state law or statute about which you should instruct students relates to eye protective equipment (safety goggles) (Iowa Annotated Code, 2000). You must insist that appropriate eyewear approved by the American National Standards Institute (ANSI, 2000) is provided to all students whenever the potential for eye injury exists. These federal equipment criteria were established to ensure minimum quality standards. You must insist that such eyewear meets ANSI standards and that you and your students wear them.

Compliance with these federal equipment standards is ensured when you see "Z87" printed on the goggle. The teacher is responsible for insisting that the purchasing agent order only goggles that conform to these standards. Goggles that do not meet ANSI Z87 standards, that do not fit the students, or that have scratched faceplates, missing vent plugs, or damaged rubber moldings or headbands should not be used.

In addition to the eye protective equipment (goggle) legislation for your respective state, you need to investigate and, likely, comply with appropriate federal and/or state Occupational Safety and Health Administration (OSHA) standards that directly impact all school science instruction, such as Bloodborne Pathogens, Right-to-Know legislation, and the Lab Standard–Chemical Hygiene Plan. Each of these is described briefly below; however, for additional information concerning your state, check the OSHA website at www.osha.gov or contact your state department of education for questions.

Bloodborne Pathogens. On December 6, 1991, OSHA issued its final Bloodborne Pathogens Standard. It mandates engineering controls, work practices, and personal protective equipment that, in conjunction with employee training, are designed to reduce job-related risk for all employees exposed to blood. Employers must establish a written exposure control plan that identifies workers with occupational exposure to blood and other potentially infectious material and specify means to protect and educate these employees. Other requirements include hepatitis B vaccinations and applicable medical followup and counseling following personal exposure. The standard became effective May 30, 1992. Under 29 Code of Federal Regulations (CFR), Part 1910.1030, Subpart Z, the Department of Labor, OSHA released the *Bloodborne Pathogens Standard Summary Applicable to Schools* (1992).

> The intent of this standard summary is to offer schools an overview of the OSHA standard to eliminate or minimize occupational exposure to Hepatitis B virus (HBV), which causes hepatitis B, a serious liver disease; Human Immunodeficiency Virus (HIV), which causes Acquired Immune Deficiency Syndrome (AIDS) and other bloodborne pathogens. Based on a review of the information in the rulemaking record, OSHA has made a determination that employees face a significant health risk as the result of occupational exposure to blood and other potentially infectious materials because they may contain pathogens. OSHA further concludes that this exposure can be minimized or eliminated using a combination of engineering and work practice controls, personal protective clothing and equipment, training, medical surveillance, Hepatitis B vaccination, signs and labels and other provisions. This summary includes scope and application, definitions, exposure control, methods of compliance, Hepatitis B vaccination and post-exposure evaluation and follow-up, communication of hazards to employees, recordkeeping, and effective dates.

Right-to-Know. The OSHA Hazard Communication Standard or Right-to-Know (RTK) legislation, pertaining to hazardous chemicals in the workplace, was originally drafted as Final Rule in 1983 and became effective November 25, 1985.

All RTK legislation is designed to help employees recognize and eliminate the dangers associated with hazardous materials in their workplace. The legislation requires that a *written program* be developed for all public and private educational institutions and that all affected employees know its contents. The details of such legislation will vary from state to state. Check with your state department of education, federal or state OSHA office, or Department of Labor (chemical emergency procedures and right-to-know questions at 1-800-424-9346). The program need not be detailed; however, it must include the following items:

1. Written hazard assessment procedures
2. Material safety data sheets (MSDSs) for all hazardous chemicals
3. Labels and warnings
4. Employee training

Laboratory Standard–Chemical Hygiene Plan. As of January 31, 1991, laboratories engaged in activities that encompass the definition "laboratory use" must have in place a written Chemical Hygiene Plan (CHP) outlining how the facility will comply. This is according to *OSHA Occupational Exposures to Hazardous Chemicals in Laboratories Chemical Hygiene Plan,* (29 CFR, 1910.1450). This OSHA standard applies to all employers engaged in the laboratory use of chemicals. "Laboratory use" means:

> chemicals are manipulated on a laboratory scale where the chemicals are handled in containers designed to be safely and easily manipulated by one person; multiple chemical procedures are used; procedures are not of a production process; protective laboratory equipment and practices are in common use to minimize employee exposure.

The plan requires that employers, *including schools,* develop a comprehensive plan for identifying and dealing with chemical hazards. The plan must include all employees who could be exposed to these chemicals and it must be updated annually.

Material Safety Data Sheets. Elementary teachers should use only "over-the-counter" chemicals. Avoid use of any donations, hand-me-down, or concentrated chemicals. The federal government requires that manufacturers of chemicals create Material Safety Data Sheets (MSDS) for all of their products. MSDSs typically provide the following types of information:

- General Material Identification (common name, chemical name, supplier information)
- Ingredients
- Physical and Chemical Information (boiling point, solubility, density)
- Fire and Explosion Hazard (equipment, procedures, flash points)
- Reactivity (conditions to be avoided, etc.)
- Health Hazard (primary routes of entry into the body, acute/chronic reactions)
- Disposal (environmental information, emergency management)
- Special Protection Information (protective equipment, first-aid procedures)
- Precautions (warnings, special hazards, handling)

MSDSs are available not only for exotic chemicals associated with high-school and college-level science courses but also for items common to elementary schools including glues, paints, markers, cleaning supplies, crayons, etc. These documents must be supplied to the school district upon purchase. Be certain to ask your administration for them. Teachers should be familiar with these vital documents and be careful not to use concentrated chemicals, soaps, or cleaners with students.

MSDS sheets can be found at the following websites:

http://www.ehs.cornell.edu/

http://www.msdsonline.com

http://chemfinder/camsoft.som/

http://www.chemcenter.org

http://www.sargentwelch.com/

http://www.umt.edu/research/files/environ/appendic.htm

http://www.ilpi.com/msds/index.htm

http://www.hazard.com (focus on household/general chemical names). (JaKel, Inc. 2006)

Be careful to keep all potentially hazardous chemicals under lock and key and out of the sight of students. Do not keep any chemicals that you do not know well. Watch for expiration dates and be certain to dispose of them before that date.

Teachers should consider these ideas for any chemicals they have in school:

- Date all chemicals.
- Anything over two years of age should be purged using appropriate means of disposal.
- Do not take used chemicals from others.
- Store chemicals properly.
- Store only essential chemicals—purge others using appropriate means of disposal.

- Watch for changes in the appearance of chemicals and get rid of them if they change.

- Do not use chemicals that you do not know.

Safety Equipment

NSES
TS-D

Certain safety equipment items are essential when teaching science activities. Much of this equipment may be necessary for upper elementary classrooms. Primary classrooms should reconsider the appropriateness of the activity if any of this equipment is needed. You should be confident that such items are immediately accessible when needed, that you and students can operate them, and that the items are appropriate for your students. The critical nature of this level of understanding is demonstrated by the results of a 2003–04 safety study completed by Gerlovich, McElroy, et al. of Kentucky elementary science teachers. The study found:

- 45 percent of the classes had enrollments of 26 students, or more, all in rooms of less than 1000 square ft.

- 50 percent of the teachers did not know if their electrical outlets, near water, were GFI or GFCI protected.

- 73 percent had, or were aware of, "approved" eye protective equipment for their students.

- 53 percent of respondents had never received any safety training.

- 61 percent of the teachers observed the professional standards of a teacher: student ratio of 1:10 or less during field trips.

- 62 percent of responding teachers included safety procedures in their science lesson plans.

- 42 percent did not know the three duties that teachers must satisfy to show that they are not negligent in a student injury case.

Gerlovich and several colleagues corroborated these results in several other states including: Alabama (2001), Arkansas (2007), Iowa (1998, 2002), Kentucky (2004), Nebraska (2001), North Carolina (2001), South Carolina (2003), Tennessee (2004) and Wisconsin (2001). Students should also be taught proper operation and location of all safety equipment items they might need to use, including fire extinguishers, fire blankets, eyewashes, safety goggles, and a telephone or intercom, if available. You might need duplicate safety items in more than one location in the room. Every student should have a set of goggles during science activities when eye protection is needed.

Eye Protective Equipment

Require students to wear the goggles or safety glasses whenever there is the slightest chance that someone could sustain an eye injury in your classroom. Remember that injuries can happen even when students are walking about the room while others are performing science activities. Think also about injuries that could happen with simple chemicals, such as salt or vinegar, or with flying objects like rubber bands or balloons. Attempt to foresee such problems and act accordingly.

Most state statutes require that goggles be cleaned before students wear them. Such equipment should be stored in a relatively dust-free environment, such as a box or cabinet. (Secure a copy of your state's eye protective equipment legislation from the state department of education or school administration, and check for specific details.) Remember, in many states this is the law.

Goggles

Ground fault interrupter

Electrical Equipment

Whenever possible, hot plates with on-off indicator lights should replace open flames. This simple change could eliminate many fire situations from science rooms. You should not have to use extension cords for hot plates, since the room should have sufficient electrical outlets. Extension cords on the floor create tripping hazards unless they are in cord protectors. Do not allow cords to be draped across desks or other work areas in order to prevent students from inadvertently upsetting apparatus. Electrical outlet caps should be in place when the outlets are not in use. In primary grades, outlets should be covered at all times so students cannot stick metal items in the plug holes, which could cause electrocution or burns.

Elementary classrooms make regular use of electrical power. The science curriculum can increase that need significantly. Teachers should be careful that all outlets are safe for students by ensuring that outlets have ground fault interrupters (GFI) on them. The purpose of a GFI is to shut off electrical power to an outlet in the event that electricity seeks ground through a student, etc. The accompanying graphic provides a visual image of a GFI. Note the three-prongs for grounding and the reset switches in the event the breaker trips. Some circuits are protected by Ground Fault Circuit Interrupts (GFCI) that protect a circuit of several outlets. These would not likely have reset switches on each outlet, but rather only intermittently on select outlets. They would, however, provide the same protection. Check with your building engineer or administration to find out for certain.

Heating Equipment

Alcohol lamp

Open flames are periodically necessary; be certain that emergency fire equipment is functioning properly and is immediately available. If alcohol lamps, sterno cans, or candles are used, place them in pie pans filled with damp sand. Should a spill occur, the pie pan will prevent flaming liquids from spreading to clothing, tables, and other items. Alcohol looks like water; be sure to keep it off items where it might be treated like water. If you put alcohol in lamps, add a small amount of table salt so that the flame burns a bright orange color. Large quantities (1/2 liter or more) of alcohol or other flammable liquids should never be brought into the classroom or lab, and students should never have access to quantities of these liquids. Teachers should be solely responsible for refueling burners.

Flammable Liquid Storage

If you are storing flammable liquids, such as alcohol, do so only in small quantities in the manufacturer's original container or in an approved *safety can*. A safety can is made of heavy-gauge steel or polyethylene. It has a spring-loaded lid to prevent spilling and to vent during vapor expansion caused by a heat source. It also has a flame arrester or heat sump in the throat of the spout to help prevent explosions.

Loose Clothing and Long Hair

Safety can

Loose clothing (especially sweaters) and long hair should be restricted when students are working with open flames. This seems obvious, yet clothing and hair commonly cause accidents. Be careful to pull long hair back so that it does not hang down over the flame, and restrict loose clothing by pushing up sleeves and securing them with pins or elastic (nonrestricting rubber bands) to keep clothing from falling into open flames.

Aprons and Gloves

Many activities require the use of materials that can stain or damage clothing. The use of lab aprons can provide lab participants a layer of protection for clothing and body. Some materials can act as a skin irritant or stain. Protective gloves should be used whenever students will be handling such materials. The teacher should use great discretion in choosing activities that require such materials.

Fire Blankets

Fire blankets should be of the proper type and size and in the proper location. They should not be so large that students cannot use them in an emergency. Check to be certain that they are placed in conspicuous locations and easily retrievable by all students and staff, including those with disabilities. Unless otherwise recommended by the fire marshal, these blankets should be made of wool. Fire blanket display and storage containers should be carefully checked for proper function. Be sure to eliminate containers with rusted hinges and latches, blankets still stored in plastic wrappers, and blankets made with asbestos fiber. Six-foot vertical standing fire blanket tubes should be avoided since they can result in facial burns. Do not attempt to extinguish torso fires by wrapping a standing student in the fire blanket. Because of the chimney effect, heat is pushed across the student's face, causing facial burns. The stop-drop-and-roll procedure endorsed by fire departments appears to be the most effective at extinguishing body fires and presents the fewest drawbacks.

Fire blanket

Fire Extinguishers

ABC triclass fire extinguishers are usually preferred by fire departments because they can extinguish most foreseeable fires, such as fires from paper products, electrical items, and grease that are likely to happen in elementary science.

It is a good idea to have fire department personnel come into your classroom to demonstrate age-appropriate fire procedures and equipment to students. You should be confident and comfortable in using fire equipment items. You should also establish the habit of checking the pressure valve on fire extinguishers in or near your room to ensure that they are still adequately pressurized. It is also wise for students to learn to hold or lift extinguishers, unfold and use a fire blanket, and rehearse foreseeable emergencies involving fire. Refer to the video on *MyEducationLab* for additional details in the proper use of a fire extinguisher.

First Aid Kit

For most elementary programs, a common *First Aid Kit* should be compiled that addresses all common, foreseeable emergencies. It can then be moved from room to room, within the building, and be used wherever hands-on, inquiry-based science activities are being undertaken by the students. It is

Fire extinguisher

Eyewash Station

imperative that teachers consult with their school nurse or medical authority for specific items that can and cannot be used with students.

Eyewash and Shower

It is recommended that 15 minutes (2.5 gallons per minute) of aerated, tempered (60–90 degrees Fahrenheit) running water be deliverable from an eyewash to flush the eyes of a person who has suffered a chemical splash. At the elementary- and middle-school level, eye irritants may include salt, vinegar, sand, alcohol, and other chemicals. You should explore the installation of the fountain fixture type eyewash station. It is not expensive ($60–70) and is easily installed by screwing it into an existing gooseneck faucet. The fixture allows the plumbing to be used as both an eyewash and a faucet simply by pushing a diverter valve. Should traffic patterns or room designs change, fountain fixtures can be moved to other faucets easily. On a temporary basis, you can stretch a piece of surgical tubing over a gooseneck faucet in order to deliver aerated, cool running water to the eyes of a chemical splash victim. In the event of chemical spills on other and/or larger parts of the body, drench showers are recommended. Again, it is critical that such equipment be easily accessible to all staff and students. Be certain that the hot water faucet handle has been removed from any sink's eyewash to prevent accidental burns that could be caused by hot water.

Bottled water stations are not recommended because they can become contaminated, and they cannot deliver 15 minutes of aerated running water. They should be used only when there is no alternative, such as in field settings, and where you maintain strict control of them.

Critical safety equipment, such as fire blankets, fire extinguishers, eyewashes, and drench showers, should be located within 30 steps or 15 seconds of any location in the science room. These vital equipment items should be checked for proper operation every three to six months.

Performing Safety Assessments

NSES

TS-C, D, F

Teachers must foresee safety hazards by regularly performing safety inspections (audits) of their room, equipment, and safety techniques. They should learn to document identified problems and inform the administration of necessary changes. This process has been significantly improved through the utilization of the computer. Gerlovich and others have been working for twenty years to automate this process as much as possible. These science education researchers have created an interactive, cross-platform CD-ROM that provides elementary and secondary science teachers with a complete resource addressing safety issues, forms and checklists for performing audits, and chemical databases for addressing chemical problems. In addition videos and safety graphics are provided to address certain safety techniques, and hundreds of web links take teachers to other resources. Figure 10.8 provides an example of one of the checklists. For additional information concerning The Total Science Safety System CD, contact JaKel, Inc. at www.netins.net/showcase.jakel.

General Safety Procedures Checklist.

Item	Date Satisfied	Item	Date Satisfied
Students are encouraged to report any safety concerns to the teacher immediately.	_____	Student groupings should be limited to a size that can work effectively without causing confusion or accidents. Groups of two are recommended for the primary grades, and groups of three to five for the upper elementary grades	_____
Teachers should be a positive role model for students by always practicing appropriate safe behaviors and using necessary personal protective equipment (safety goggles, aprons, gloves, etc.)	_____	Students are instructed to keep their hands away from face (eyes, nose, mouth) whenever doing science activities	_____
Students are instructed in the proper usage and hazards associated with all science equipment before use	_____	Long hair and loose clothing (especially sweaters) should be restricted when using open flames or chemicals	_____
Teachers should monitor students for any food or contact allergies associated with science activities	_____	Foreseeable emergencies are rehearsed with students	_____
Students are instructed to always keep their work area clean and clear of unnecessary material (bags, books, lunches)	_____	Students never have access to chemical storage areas	_____
		Students never dispense hazardous chemicals	_____
Students understand all hazards associated with the activities conducted	_____	Eating and drinking are prohibited whenever any scientific investigations are being conducted, unless otherwise directed by the teacher	_____
At the primary grades, students use only non-pointed, safety scissors. When students are carrying scissors, tips should be pointed toward the floor	_____	Whenever substances have been heated, the hot container is placed on a ceramic plate	_____
Students are never allowed to conduct any unauthorized experiment or to work alone or unsupervised	_____	Liquids spilled on hardwood or tile floors are wiped up immediately to prevent slipping and falls	_____

FIGURE 10.8 ● Science Safety Checklist

Source: Gerlovich, J., D. McElroy, et. al., JaKel, Inc. (2007). National Edition – Total Science Safety System: Elementary Edition, CD-ROM. (Waukee, IA). Excerpted with Permission.

What Materials Are Necessary for the Activities?

While preparing for a science lab activity, determine appropriate materials you will need and any associated foreseeable hazards. Identify readily available items, and locate where any additional items can be obtained. A good suggestion is to divide the remaining items into categories: items to be purchased through a scientific supplier, items that can be purchased locally through a discount or hardware store, and items that can be made for little or no cost from recycled materials.

NSES
CS-G

FIGURE 10.9 ● Science Activity Planner Form

Concept to be taught: _____

_____

Material needs: _____

_____

Safety concerns: _____

_____

Items available through school inventory: _____

_____

Items available at no cost/recycle: _____

_____

Scientific supplier (indicate vendor name, catalogue number, description, number needed, cost per unit, total cost):

Local store (indicate store name and exact cost):

A Science Activity Planner form (Figure 10.9) will facilitate your ordering needs. Fill out this sheet at least six weeks before you teach the lesson to allow time for vendor shipping and/or the steps your order must go through for approval of purchase and appropriation of funds in your school district. Figure 10.10 provides an example of how this form can be used.

Items Purchased Through a Scientific Supplier

Microscopes, slides, cover slips, thermometers, magnets, and electrical bulbs are the typical kinds of materials supplied by many reputable science equipment vendors. Science teachers in your school may already have suppliers they regularly deal with. Talk with fellow teachers about companies they have used in the past. If you are uncertain, request supply catalogs from companies.

Do not be quick to order from the vendor. Be a wise shopper, and compare prices and quality. Ask questions of others who may have previously ordered materials from a particular vendor. "How good is their service?" "Are they willing to meet needs quickly or slow in processing orders?" "What type of return policy do they have?" "Are they willing to take a purchase order or do they need to be paid up front?" A complete listing of science vendors, updated yearly, is available from the National Science Teachers Association.

Does your current textbook publisher supply prepackaged kits to accompany their activities? If so, will it be necessary to replenish materials in these kits? Is there a specific supplier you should order these kits from? If your answer to these questions is yes, then determine which items need to be replaced and if it is possible to replace only the used items or necessary to order a new kit. You may often come across prepackaged general science kits, such as one that supplies all materials you will need to do a unit on electricity. Under both circumstances, you must determine your needs. Will you use all of the materials provided in the kit? Will it be less expensive to order the items individually?

Carefully examine the supply catalogs. You may spot items that could enhance a lesson—an item you did not even think of in your original list of materials. Perhaps

FIGURE 10.10 ● Science Activity
Planner Example

Concept to be taught: The circular path electrons follow is called a *circuit*.

Material needs: *For each student:* Battery, flashlight bulb, insulated copper wire, switch, bulb socket, cardboard tube (toilet paper tube), paper clip, two brass fasteners, plastic cap from a gallon milk container or a 35mm film can.

Safety Concerns: Can you identify the safety concerns associated with this activity?

Items available through:

School inventory	Bulbs, switches, wire
No cost/recycle	Cardboard tubes, milk caps, film canister caps
Scientific supplier	Delta Supply, Nashua, New Hampshire 57–020–9769, Bucket of batteries, 30, $29.95, $29.95 57–020–5644, Bulb sockets, 30, $4.85/pkg. of 6, $24.25
Local store	John's Dollar Store on Main Street 1 box of paper clips, 79¢ 2 boxes of brass fasteners, $1.45

you found the item in two different catalogs, each at a different price. As you gain experience in ordering, you will find that companies differ in prices on equivalent items. If you are placing a big order with one company, it is usually more economical to purchase the higher-priced item from it along with the rest of your order. The money you may save on the price of the item with a different vendor could be spent on shipping charges. The task of ordering supplies with school money can vary from district to district. Teachers should explore proper procedures to assure that all appropriate steps are followed to help assure expeditious receipt of materials. This is especially critical when ordering live materials.

Items Purchased Locally

Consumable items—paper cups, bags, straws—are some of the common items purchased from local vendors. If you teach in a community that is very supportive of its local schools, you may be able to get donations of consumable items from local restaurants, grocery stores, or discount stores. Even the local lumber yard may be willing to supply a class with yard- or metersticks or scrap lumber.

Discount stores that specialize in overruns are an excellent source for science supplies. As you walk up and down the aisles, scan the shelves thinking about science concepts you could teach with various items. You may be surprised at what you come up with. Simple toys like yo-yos, ball and jacks, paddle balls, and rubber balls can be used to teach a variety of scientific concepts. Paper clips, masking tape, batteries, or wire can start you on the way to a terrific electricity unit (see Chapter 5).

Local stores may already have agreements with your school district, such as charge accounts or cash credit accounts. Check with the school district treasurer. You may be able to charge the items at those stores. Other stores may take purchase orders. Occasionally you may have to provide your own money. If this is the case, find out the procedure for reimbursement in your school. Does the principal have a fund from which you can immediately be reimbursed upon turning in your receipt? Is a receipt necessary? Do you need a petty cash voucher from the school before you make a purchase? What kind of information does the vendor need to supply on that voucher? Do you need to supply the vendor with a tax-exempt number from the school so that you are not charged sales tax? Ask all of these questions *before* you go out and spend your own

Local restaurants, grocery stores, or discount stores are usually willing to donate items such as paper cups, containers, or straws to meet your science activity needs.

money. You do not want to find out after the fact that since you did not complete the proper paper trail, you will not be reimbursed.

Items Made from Recycled Materials

You've been caught again rummaging through the bin at the local recycling center. Embarrassed? There is no need to be when it's done in the name of science! What was it this time? Looking for cans to paint black for a unit on heat? Was it a plastic soda bottle to make another Cartesian diver? Do you need various size jars for a sound unit? Whatever the science topic, usually one or two items can be found in a recycling bin. Of course, you can avoid those embarrassing moments by encouraging your students to bring in materials they ordinarily throw away. Setting up a recycling area in your classroom will provide a quick source for those necessary items and teach students the importance of recycling.

Cans are not the only useful recyclable item. Styrofoam plates from prepackaged meats are useful in many activities. They make great placemats for messy activities that involve liquids. Styrofoam egg cartons can be turned into charcoal crystal gardens in no time, or they can be used to stack small items like rock collections. Toilet paper and paper towel tubes can be used in making flashlights, and aluminum pie plates are useful for heating water. Plastic containers with lids, such as the ones that food comes in at the grocery store, can be used for storage. Your imagination is your only limit when it comes to deciding what to do with recycled materials.

Live Items

The National Science Teachers Association (Kwan & Texley, 2003) recommends that teachers consider these factors when planning for plants and animals in the elementary classroom (Table 10.4):

Plants. Plants should be kept in areas where they can thrive, be readily viewed, and be protected. Be careful to study only plants about which you are knowledgeable. Do not use plants that present hazards from oils (poison ivy, poison oak, poison sumac, poin-

TABLE 10.4 ● Selecting Organisms for Your Classroom

Type of Organism	Level of Care	Potential Problems
Plants	Low: Need light and water, can be left during vacations	• Molds bother some sensitive students • Some plants are toxic
Aquarium fish, protests (amoebae, paramecia, euglena)	Low: Can be left during vacations	• Slight risk from bacteria in tank • Temperature controls may be required during vacations
Crustacea and snails	Moderate: Simple foods, intolerant of heat	• Moderate risk of bacterial contamination
Insects, butterflies	Moderate: Cultures can become moldy	• Stings • Exotic species endanger the environment
Reptiles (snakes, lizards, turtles)	High: Require live food, intolerant of cold	• Bites • Salmonella infections • Moldy food • Sensitive to temperature change
Rodents and rabbits	High: Can't be left unattended during vacations	• Allergenic dander • Odor from droppings and bedding • Bites and scratches • Human disease carriers

Source: T. Kwan and J. Texley, *Exploring Safely: A Guide for Elementary Teachers* (National Science Teachers Association, 2002).

settia, and other local plants) or hazards from saps (oleander, stinging nettle, and other local plants). In addition, no plants that are poisonous if eaten should be accessible to students, including those shown in Table 10.5.

For additional information, check the College of Veterinary Medicine & Biomedical Sciences, Dept. of Clinical Sciences, Colorado State University—*Guide to Poisonous Plants,* website: www.vth.colostate.edu/poisonous_plants/. Another excellent database resource for plants and animals of the world can be found on the following United States Geological Survey (USGS) website: www.npwrc.usgs.gov/resource/. The online guide provides information on more than 100 poisonous plants. Information for each plant includes: common and botanic name; color photograph; description; habitat; animals (including people) affected; toxic principle; gastrointestinal, nervous, integumentary, and other system symptoms; and treatment. The National Gardening Association site, www.kidsgardening.com/hydroponicsguide/toc.asp, provides an excellent overview of hydroponics (growing plants without soil) gardening for kids. Lesson plans are included.

Animals. Whenever animals are used in science activities with students, it is imperative that care be exercised to protect both the animals and the students. It is obvious that animals stimulate learning in many life science and biology classes. They can, however, present some unique hazards to students. Teachers should anticipate such hazards as much as possible so that neither students nor animals are injured. Be careful, for instance, not to allow animals to be handled when they are eating.

TABLE 10.5 ● Plants That Are Harmful if Eaten

Some fungi (many mushrooms)	Daffodil (bulb)	Iris	Nightshade	Sumac
Aconite	Dieffenbachia	Jack-in-the-Pulpit	Oleander	Sweet Pea
Azalea	Elderberry	Japanese Yew	Philodendron	Tansy
Buckeye	English Ivy	Jimson Weed	Poinsettia	Tomato
Belladonna	False Hellebore	Jonquil (bulb)	Poison Oak	Virginia Creeper
Bloodroot	Four-O'Clock	Lantana	Pokeweed	Wild Tobacco
Buttercup	Foxglove	Lily-of-the-Valley	Potato (sprouts)	Wild Tomato
Caladium	Herbane	Mayapple	Privet	Wisteria
Castor Bean	Holly	Milkweed	Rhododendron	Yellow Jasmine
China Berry	Hyacinth	Mistletoe	Rhubarb	
Croton	Hydrangea	Morning Glory	Scotch Broom	
	Indian Tobacco	Moutain Laurel	Skunk Cabbage	

Source: Gerlovich et al, *The Total Science Safety System CD, Kentucky Edition* (Waukee, IA: JaKel, Inc., 2003). Excerpted, with permission.

Do not allow dead animals in the room, as the exact cause of death may not be determinable. Many warm-blooded animals carry and transmit diseases to humans through ticks, mites, and fleas. Heavy gloves should be used for the handling of animals that might bite. Be certain that adequately sized and clean cages are provided to all animals. Cages should be kept locked and in safe, comfortable settings. Since most supply houses are required to quarantine animals and check them for disease before sale, it would be wise to obtain study animals only from these dealers. If any are purchased locally, check for general health of all animals before purchase.

Students should wash their hands immediately and thoroughly when finished working with animals; this will help prevent students from inadvertently transmitting germs. If an animal dies unexpectedly, have it examined by a local veterinarian. This is cheap insurance in helping prevent disease complications.

Guidelines on the use of live animals in the classroom are available from the National Association of Biology Teachers (NABT). They are well developed and provide the teacher with more depth of understanding in deciding what animals to bring into the classroom and under what conditions. The guidelines can be found on the NABT website at www.nabt.org. For additional information concerning the responsible use of animals in the classroom, you may want to check the *National Science Teachers Association Handbook* (NSTA, 1996) or NSTA's website at www.nsta.org/about/positions/animals.aspx.

Storage

Central or Classroom Storage Access

NSES
TS-D

The biggest task is over—or so you think. The materials have been ordered and are beginning to arrive. So where do they go? Does your school have a central storage area for science materials? Are the materials you ordered solely for your classroom use, or will you be sharing them with other teachers? Who will be allowed access to the materials? Do you have space in your classroom to store materials? Before you begin stocking your classroom shelves, find the answers to these questions.

Central Storage Area. Some schools designate one room or area in the school to keep all science materials. If this is the case at your school, find out who is responsible for maintaining that area. Careful inventory should be maintained of the items stored there.

FIGURE 10.11 ● Science Equipment Checkout Form

Science Equipment Checkout Form

Name: _____

Grade and/or subject area: _____

Room number: _____

Date of checkout: Expected date of return:

_____   _____

Items borrowed:

_____

_____

_____

Signature: _____

It is best if one person is responsible for keeping the inventory current. Teachers who borrow materials should be held responsible for their return. One person should have the authority to request the return of borrowed materials after a reasonable time period. Sign-out sheets (Figure 10.11) should be completed by any staff member who uses materials from the central storage.

The teachers should determine who will have access to the central storage area:

- Will only science teachers be allowed to use it?
- Will other teachers have access?
- Will students be allowed to borrow items from central storage?
- Who will be responsible for disseminating the materials? Will it be done on an honor system?

These questions may appear trivial, but once you count on items for a particular activity only to find that someone has borrowed them without signing them out, you will not be too happy. Often it becomes a wild-goose chase to find out who used the materials last. If the search comes up short, you may end up omitting a valuable lesson for lack of supplies. Some ground rules can avoid any unnecessary searches or hard feelings.

Classroom Storage. If you store materials in your classroom, plan where the materials will be located. The first consideration is who will have access to those materials. Will the students be allowed access to everything, or will safety reasons prohibit total access? Where can you store materials that you consider dangerous to students? Ideally, any hazardous materials should be stored in locked cabinets.

Think about the storage of live specimens. If plants are brought into the classroom, is an area available near windows to facilitate plant growth? Is shelf space available near a window, or will you have to appropriate a table or bookshelf to set up near a window? Can artificial lights be used on the plant? If window space is minimal, where will this designated artificial light be? Should the students have access to these plants? Do they present any potential harm to the students if ingested?

If you know that students will need access to certain materials, arrange materials so that they are on shelves or in cabinets within easy reach. If there are certain mate-

Proper materials storage makes preparation and replacement easier.

rials, such as chemicals or cleaners, that need to be out of the students' reach, a locked cabinet or cupboard is a necessity. Plan to make shelves or cabinets if they do not exist in your classroom. Rather than looking at your classroom negatively and simply deciding that there is no place to put anything, think creatively. Would an unused corner make an ideal storage area? Can you get a local business to donate some unused bookshelves or storage cabinets? Can the school's maintenance personnel make some shorter shelf units for student access? Try to have these problems solved before the materials arrive.

Not all items will be stored. For instance, if you have a learning center that constantly requires the use of a balance, leave the balance out and do not store it. Other activity areas may be set up where materials are always left out. The students should know that they are free to move items from one center to another.

Freedom to move materials creates a learning environment that is adaptable to the students' needs. To avoid creating an inventory nightmare, establish some simple task assignments. Most children like to be useful and help the teacher. In the primary grades, the teacher can create a poster for each center with a picture of the necessary items. Older students can have a written supply list for each center. Students can be assigned to the different centers on a rotating basis and be responsible for making sure that at the end of the school day the items for their assigned center are in place. When consumable items are needed, the students should write them on a master list for the teacher, indicating which items are needed at each learning center. The teacher can then use this list to obtain the materials, then give the items to the student responsible for that center to put in their proper place. Gentle reminders to students about returning items to the place where they found them will facilitate the task of taking inventory.

Storing and Dispensing Materials

No matter where materials are stored, you will need to decide how to store them. Will they be arranged according to units, such as electricity, weather, and simple machines, or will the items be stored separately? Once you make this decision, choose from among numerous ways to arrange the items, from shelves to shoeboxes to plastic storage bins. Table 10.6 identifies the advantages and disadvantages of several storage possibilities.

Whether items are kept in a central storage area or in the classroom, you still need to think about how the students will collect them for a particular activity. When items are stored in a central location, you may want to collect the materials at least a day ahead of time to make sure everything needed for a given activity is still available. Decide how many of what item you will need. Once the items are in the classroom, appoint students to arrange the materials for the various working groups.

In a safe and efficient activity-based science classroom, the teacher does not have to do all of the advance work for a particular science activity. The teacher can appoint responsible students to collect the science materials. A simple way to disseminate the materials is to have a materials list posted for the activity, assign particular students

TABLE 10.6 ● Materials Storage

Materials Stored	Advantages	Disadvantages
As units	All material together Can present lesson at any time without rummaging through shelves for necessary materials	Question of who is responsible for replacing consumable items Scarce resources cause unit to be picked apart and used for other activities
Individually	Ideal storage in schools where resources are scarce Works well when materials are centrally stored, easier to collect	Time needed to pull several items together for each teaching unit Additional storage space necessary to store individual items in classroom
On shelves	Items can be shelved alphabetically for quick and easy retrieval Efficient method for storing glassware and large items	Difficult to determine where one letter ends and the next begins Difficult to store items in multiple quantities With multiple users, need to rearrange shelves frequently
In plastic bags	Sealable bags are ideal for small items Can be labeled with permanent markers Available in a variety of sizes to accommodate various sized materials	If seal not made, items fall out and get lost With extended use, labeling wears off Tear with frequent use
In shoeboxes or cardboard boxes	Inexpensive way to store multiple items like thermometers, magnets, and marbles Easily labeled and can be covered with an adhesive plastic for prolonged use An ideal size for storing on shelves	Since opaque, necessary to open to determine contents Even covered, eventually wear out
In plastic storage bins	Available in a variety of shapes and sizes Clear so items stored are visible Can be labeled with permanent markers Many guaranteed to last at least five years	Better-made containers are costly Lids crack on less expensive containers if heavy things are stacked on top
Using color coding	Ideal for identifying hazardous materials by using colored safety stickers Identifying quickly consumed items with one color facilitates reordering needs	Advantages lost if all teachers do not understand or remember color codes If color code key not posted, difficult to locate material

NSES
TS-D, F

to gather materials, and provide those students with buckets or plastic bins to put the collected materials in for that activity. Each materials manager for the day should be responsible for collecting the correct number of items for his or her group to do the activity and be responsible for counting the materials at the end of the lesson, collecting them in the bucket, and returning them to their proper place. If the materials go back to a central storage area, the teacher should make sure they are returned to their proper place as soon as possible. Other teachers may be counting on the use of those materials.

Keep safety concerns in mind when returning used materials. Students should not be responsible for the relocation or disposal or these materials. Many common household items used at the elementary level in science activities could fall into these categories—such items as bleach or ammonia, carpet shampoos, window cleaner, paints, and glues. Does your school have an appropriate system to handle disposal of these wastes? Which materials can be recycled? What procedures should be followed to dispose of used materials? Remember that hazardous waste improperly handled can pollute drinking supplies, poison humans, and contaminate soil and air. The teacher should be responsible for disposing of used hazardous materials. If you are uncertain about disposing of a particular item, check with the local fire marshal or local office of the Environmental Protection Agency. These agencies will be able to instruct you on proper disposal. Many local fire departments are equipped to handle low-level toxic waste. All high schools should have a plan in place for handling waste from chemistry classes. Check to see if your district has one. If it does not, work with local agencies to develop a safe and reliable disposal system.

Room Arrangement

Carefully planned lessons and ample supplies are not enough to carry off a successful inquiry-based science activity. The physical arrangement of the classroom is also an important consideration. Barriers such as classroom size, traffic patterns, blind spots, poles, and walls will require a teacher to be creative about utilizing the available space. Before you begin moving furniture around, draw a scale floor plan of your classroom. Ask yourself the following questions when deciding how to arrange the classroom:

NSES
TS-D

- What is the best way to utilize the space I have available?
- What kinds of activities will my students be involved in?
- What kinds of materials will be used?
- What type of furniture do I have in my classroom?
- Will I need any additional furniture, or should I eliminate some of the furniture that is already in there?
- What kind of flooring does the classroom have? Is it appropriate for the activities my students will be engaged in?
- Where are the entrances and exits in the classroom?
- Do I have clear access to the exits? (NSTA recommends at least two, five foot wide outward opening doors.)
- Where are the electrical outlets?
- What kind of traffic patterns do I wish to develop?
- What are the potential hazards with the arrangement I have in mind?

These questions are designed to help you arrange your classroom to maximize your students' science experiences while allowing you to maintain flexibility to accommodate the teaching of other subject areas.

Large-Group Science Activities

Flat surfaces offer the best means of engaging in science activities when working with an entire class. If you are in a classroom with tilted desk tops, you will need to be creative; child-sized tables are one alternative. Another is to designate space on the floor for children to participate in science activities.

Divide the class into small working groups of three or four students each. Current recommendations are that elementary school classrooms should provide at least 45-square feet of space for each student and have no more than twenty-four students for labs and activities. Although elementary science classes are not laboratory based, if all students are to have sufficient feedback and guidance in science projects, twenty-four students is a manageable number. While the physical constraints of your classroom may not allow you this much area or your class size puts you beyond the twenty-four-student limit, whenever possible optimum space should be allocated and ideal class size should be maintained.

Whether the students are working at small tables, several flat-topped desks pushed together to make a larger working area, or on the floor, consider the type of flooring in the classroom. A nonslip tile floor is best but not a necessity. Carefully taping down an inexpensive vinyl floor remnant in the designated science area will save a carpet from messy spills and facilitate clean-up.

Create an area where you can collect materials for science activities before the class uses them. This place should also function as an area where science demonstrations occur. Preferably, this area should be close to the science storage area.

chapter summary

By asking, "What are the foreseeable hazards associated with valued educational activities?" What safety practices need to be implemented in an inquiry-based science classroom?" and "What materials are necessary for the activities?" teachers can be successful in creating an efficient, safe environment for activity-based science. Once the concepts to be taught are clearly identified and grade-level-appropriate activities are chosen, decisions about materials needed to teach these concepts, storage of the materials, and safe practices while handling them must be decided upon. Generally storage decisions depend on school building space restrictions and the safety philosophy embraced by the teaching faculty.

Teachers must attempt to foresee problems posed by activities and address them; teach appropriately for the emotional, physical, and intellectual levels of their students; and provide adequate supervision applicable for the environment and the degree of hazards anticipated, in addition to ensuring that the environment and equipment items are properly maintained. Teachers who are sure that they have addressed all of these concerns can proceed with confidence. If they cannot, adjustments should be made—adding more safety features, limiting the activity to a teacher demonstration only, or eliminating the activity.

The physical arrangement of the classroom directly affects the success of the activity-oriented science lesson. When physical barriers impede the completion of an activity, the students can become frustrated. If materials are not readily available to bring a child from a state of disequilibrium to equilibrium, a teachable moment may be lost. A flexible learning environment, carefully planned and designed to promote student exploration, will greatly facilitate science learning.

> There needs to be a renaissance, a reawakening, around school laboratory safety. The problem is ignorance of what the regulations are and the age-old problem of money ... but safety has to be job one, and in too many cases it is not. (Colgan, 2002)

reflect and respond

1. You are planning a field trip with your first-grade class to the local prairie ecosystem (or other special local ecosystem) to study plants. All parent and guardian release forms have been returned with the exception of one. Would you allow the student to attend the activity anyway? Give three reasons for your answer.

2. A student in your third-grade class asks you if he can bring his pet northern banded water snake to class to show during your reptile unit. What would be your response? What information would you want to support your decision? Where would you secure such information?

3. You are preparing to do a simple chemistry experiment with your sixth-grade class. A student says that she has new safety glasses provided by her optometrist and would rather wear them than your safety goggles. What would be your response? Why?

4. Visit an elementary school that has a central storage area for science materials. Does this area appear well maintained? Is someone responsible for checking materials in and out? Who keeps the inventory of supplies? How well managed do you think the storage area is? What recommendations would you make?

5. During a unit on insect behavior, several children bring to school both live and dead insects. What should be done with the dead insects? The live ones? Should the students be encouraged to bring insects into the classroom? Why or why not? What do you believe your responsibility is to the insects and to the students' attitudes toward insects?

6. In 1992, the jury found the District of Columbia's summer school program negligent under several alternative theories. Do you think the court was right? Why or why not? How could the accident have been avoided? What guidelines should teachers follow when having an outside guest presenter in their room for science?

Explore—Video Homework Exercise. Go to MyEducationLab at www.myeducationlab .com and select the topic "Safety and Classroom Management," then watch the videos "Safety Goggles," "Heating Use of Alcohol Burner," "Use of a Wool Fire Blanket," "Use of an Eyewash," "Use of a Fire Extinguisher," "Electrical Safety Outlets and Covers," "Use of a Hot Plate," and "Field Trips and First Aid Kits." After viewing the series of brief video demonstrations to help you become comfortable and confident in knowing what to do and how to use common safety items for science, respond to the questions below.

1. How do you handle a fire blanket, and what can you use to improvise in the absence of an approved fire blanket?

2. Why should one put a few grains of table salt into an alcohol burner, and how can you safely use an open flame?

3. Why are safety goggles important? What features should you look for when purchasing goggles? How can you safely clean goggles?

4. What are the limits to eyewash bottles? How does an eyewash station function, and why is it superior to an eyewash bottle?

5. What should you know about safely operating hot plates? Is it safe to use an extension cord? Why or why not?

6. What items should you consider essential for a first aid kit? Why?

7. How do you operate a fire extinguisher? What are the different types? Where are your school's fire extinguishers located?

Enrich—Weblink Exercise

Professional Practice. Go to MyEducationLab Resources section and select "Weblinks," then click on the link "H. Animal Hazards" to learn more about safety concerns related to keeping live animals in the classroom.

NSES
PD-A, C
CS-C

1. What are the common types of hazards you could expect from caring for animals in the classroom?

2. What types of animals should never be housed in your classroom?

3. Describe the appropriate safety practices for common mammals and fish.

Expand—Weblink Exercise

Science Literacy. Go to MyEducationLab Resources section and select "Weblinks," then click on the links "Peer-reviewed Safety Resources"; "Guide for Using Animals in the Classroom"; and "Resources for Science Fairs, Animals in Education and Research" to consult professional sources to prepare you for making decisions about classroom safety and the humane treatment of living organisms.

NSES
CS-A, E

What Materials and Resources Promote Inquiry-Based Science?

focus questions

- What was learned from past programs, and how do those findings shape modern science experiences for children?

- What issues should be considered in selecting and using tests and trade books?

- What is a "best practice," and how can you determine whether resources exemplify it?

- How can science centers and bulletin boards serve as a source of best practice?

- What kinds of human resources can be used in a science classroom, and what should be done to use them effectively?

Professor Marjorie Becker divided the science methods class into research teams. Each team's purpose was to pick a science topic and locate all the materials available on that topic in the lab, library, and college curriculum collection. The team members were to examine and compare the materials, classify them by intended purposes, and then use their findings to speculate about what makes an effective science lesson. The teams were told to generalize beyond single lessons because the class would attempt to identify the characteristics of an effective science program. Groans were prompted by the requirement to select and use research-based, practice-proven materials. Those groans subsided when Professor Becker demonstrated the speed and ease of using a free web-based resource center containing professionally reviewed lessons, videos, applets, and simulations (see www.ohiorc.org).

Professor Becker reconvened the class and asked the groups to report. She listed the features that the students found most often among the materials: objectives, suggested teaching methods, materials needed, background information, illustrations, assessment devices, and ideas for extending the activities. Many recent lessons were correlated with the National Science Education Standards and the standards of many host states. These lessons frequently contained references to themes, conceptual frameworks, skills to be developed, ideal group sizes, key vocabulary, lesson rationales, competencies, and subjects with which the lessons could be integrated. When she asked for the groups' ideas about effective programs, she received replies such as "They [programs] emphasize subject matter most and produce higher test scores," "Effective programs are those that children like," and "You can tell the program is effective if more children take science in high school and if more want to enter scientific careers." These replies fell short of Professor Becker's hopes, so she guided the class into a discussion of the assignment, pressed them to give specific examples of what they had found, and repeated the assignment's central question: What are the best practices that compose or support an effective science program?

We are likely to repeat mistakes of the past if we are ignorant of the history that brought us to the present. In fact, the National Science Education Standards' history of science content standards encourages a historical development perspective of science. Looking back, we see considerable similarity among the recommendations that arose from several science education reports during the mid-1940s, again during the late 1950s and early 1960s, and still again during the late 1980s and mid-1990s. *No Child Left Behind* and 21st century blue-ribbon panels of experts call for more intellectual rigor, increased standards, elevated expectations, improved student discipline, increased classroom time on task, improved test scores, and enhanced teacher/subject expertise. The TIMMS video analysis (National Center for Educational Statistics, 2006) of science teaching in classrooms throughout the globe verified that despite years of research-based recommendations for effective science programs, these goals have yet to be reached.

Indeed, devoting more time to intellectual subject matter in science is a common and worthwhile goal, but when it is the only expectation, it falls short of fulfilling the larger goal of more effective science programs. The key to effective science instruction is selecting and using intellectually engaging experiences with the proper mix of science content and processes.

Calls or mandates for improved pupil achievement and recommendations for producing these improvements may be naively based on uninformed right-wrong perspectives or faulty assumptions about what should be taught and learned and about how children learn and should be taught. But what role are you expected to play? You will be involved, at some point in your career, with science program development. More immediately, your concern is to select the best materials available to plan and teach effective lessons. Can you afford to ignore the lessons of the past? This chapter provides:

1. a report of lessons learned,
2. a viewpoint on selecting and using textbooks, and
3. a description of best practices and suggested resources.

Lessons Learned

Legacy of the Past

NSES
PR-A

Biology, chemistry, physics, and *earth science* are common school science curricula. Even in general science and elementary science courses, these subjects persist as topics or units of study. They arose from scientific research disciplines, which were popular during the 1800s. However, since about 1900, these disciplines have not accurately represented the important areas of science. Thousands of diverse scientific journals now report experimental findings from a countless number of new fields of science and technology. Distinctions among the different fields of science are now made more by the type of problem being researched than by the discipline being served. Today, there is simply too much—too many facts of science to be learned in a school science program.

The amount of scientific information continues to double about every five years. So what should be taught? At times, this question has been answered with an issues-and-problems approach.

A specific problem in science education has always been to resolve the issue of how the schools could best prepare "citizens to live in a culture most often described in terms of achievements in science and technology" (Hurd, 1986, p. 355). In the 1930s and 1940s, elementary schools tried to resolve this issue by teaching in a "prescribed authoritative manner almost exclusively through single-author textbooks" (Sabar, 1979, pp. 257–269). Basically, science was a reading program that covered a large body of information and used the subtle but powerful forces of conformity and consensus to control the direction of American society and to aid citizens as they tried to adjust to society's new directions. The important facts, concepts, and theories of science that were taught were based on the consensus of specialists. Specialists told previous generations of teachers what was important to know and teach.

Teacher emphasis on pupil conformity and learning science by reading is still highly visible today. Another emphasis from the past that is still widely supported is the cry to get back to basics, with emphasis on reading, writing, and arithmetic. This chant began after World War II for the same reasons that can be heard today: the perceived overall low success of high school graduates as shown by their declining achievement scores and poor job skills and the need for citizens to keep pace with scientific and technological breakthroughs of other advanced countries (Sabar, 1979, p. 258). Ironically, this last factor makes the study of science a basic need for all. Educators with a bigger view of scientific literacy think that there is much value in teaching the science disciplines with a blended curriculum. When science disciplines are blended, our understanding of the concepts are more consistent with how we apply science content knowledge in our daily lives. This means that the study of science is more than a basic need; it is a basic literacy subject that must be present in the school curriculum (Sousa, 1996; McComas & Wang, 1998), as described in Chapter 5.

Past programs prepared children to become scientists.

Efforts began earlier, but it was the launching of the Soviet satellite *Sputnik* in 1957 that caused the most serious attempts at science curriculum reform. During the twenty-five years after *Sputnik,* $2 billion dollars were spent to support mathematics and science education in elementary and secondary schools. The main goal then, as many believe it should be now, was to prepare future scientists and engineers, mostly out of a concern for national defense. As important as this goal is, we now know that defense issues rise and fall in urgency and that "this is a goal that is appropriate for only 3 percent of high school graduates, and a goal where we have traditionally spent 95 percent of our time, efforts, resources and attention" (Yager, 1984, p. 196).

Alphabet-Soup Programs

The decade after *Sputnik* is known for alphabet-soup elementary science programs. Three programs that were developed during this period are worth mentioning now because of their goals, their effects on children's learning, and the eventual improved quality of modern textbooks and other curriculum materials. Several assumptions on which the programs were based have been supported over time by a growing body of research, while other assumptions have fallen from favor. These programs are known as SAPA, SCIS, and ESS.

Science—A Process Approach (SAPA), Science Curriculum Improvement Study (SCIS), and the Elementary Science Study (ESS) were regarded as innovative programs in their day. Designed and field-tested during the 1960s and then revised during the 1970s, these experimental programs had several features in common:

- They were developed by teams of scientists, psychologists, educators, and professional curriculum specialists rather than written by single authors or single expert specialists.

- Federal funds were widely available for development, research, field testing, dissemination, and teacher inservice training.

- Each project was developed from particular assumptions about learning drawn from prominent theories and used to form a specific framework for each project. Behavioral and cognitive-development psychology had major influences.

- Each project was developed from what were assumed to be the ways in which children learned best. Specific teaching approaches were emphasized and were used to help children learn the ways and knowledge of science and to develop the attitudes of scientists.

- Active pupil learning was assumed to be very important. Each project provided hands-on learning experiences for all children because it was assumed that manipulatives help children to learn best.

- The projects did not provide a standard textbook for each child. In fact, a workbook for recording observations was as close as some children came to anything that resembled a textbook.

- There was no attempt to teach all that should be known about science. Specific science processes or content areas were selected for each project, thus narrowing the field of topics to a specialized few.

- Attention was given to the basic ideas of science—the concepts and theories—with the intention of increasing the number of citizens who would seek careers in science and engineering.

- The programs were conveniently packaged. Equipment was included with curriculum materials. This made the programs easier to use and reduced teacher preparation time by eliminating the need to gather diverse equipment.

- Mathematical skills were emphasized. The programs were more quantitative than qualitative. Emphasis was placed on student observation, careful measurement, and the use of appropriate calculations to form ideas or reach conclusions.

- Science was taught as a subject by itself and was not associated with social studies, health, or reading. At times, science was treated as a pure subject that was believed to have inherent value for all children.

- The teacher's role changed. Teachers used less direct methods of teaching such as inquiry and functioned as questioners and guides for students. They avoided lecturing or more didactic forms of direct instruction. The teacher was *not* to be an expert who told children what they should memorize.

Significant Gains

Table 11.1 shows the results of extensive meta-analyses. When compared to comparable learners in traditional textbook-based science programs, students in the three experimental science K–6 programs demonstrated significant gains in achievement,

TABLE 11.1 ● Performance Improvement for Students in Classrooms Using ESS, SCIS, or SAPA as Compared to Students in Traditional Classrooms

Performance Area	Percentage Points Gained		
	ESS	SCIS	SAPA
Achievement	4	34	7
Attitudes	20	3	15
Process skills	18	21	36
Related skills	*	8	4
Creativity	26	34	7
Piagetian tasks	2	5	12

*No studies reported

Source: James A. Shymansky, William C. Kyle, Jr., and Jennifer M. Alport, "How Effective Were the Hands-On Science Programs of Yesterday?" *Science and Children* (November–December 1982): 15.

process skills, and scientific attitudes. An important lesson was learned: Effective science programs favor a holistic view of science and include features that aim to improve children's science attitudes, science skills, and science content knowledge.

What the three most used programs have in common is an inquiry-based, hands-on curriculum and teaching approach. Despite what is widely believed and practiced, inquiry learning approaches are superior to the traditional direct, textbook-based approach. James Shymansky and his colleagues (1982) tell us that synthesis of the abundant research shows conclusively that children in a hands-on science program achieve more, like science more, and improve their problem-solving skills more than do children who learn from traditional textbook-based programs. The hands-on approaches help the children's minds to grow and construct meaning. These conclusions endured resynthesis even though the original statistics have been revised to yield results of greater precision (Shymansky, et al., 1990).

Ted Bredderman (1983) adds support to this view. Bredderman's research arose from *Project Synthesis,* a massive research effort funded by the National Science Foundation to determine the results of past experimental programs so that present and future science education goals could be revised. Bredderman's research collected the results from sixty studies that involved 13,000 students in 1,000 elementary classrooms over fifteen years. He analyzed the results of these studies carefully through meta-analysis procedures to sort out conflicting findings reported in the literature. His conclusion clearly shows what works:

> With the use of activity-based science programs, teachers can expect substantially improved performance in science process and creativity; modestly increased performance on tests of perception, logic, language development, science content, and math; modestly improved attitudes toward science and science class; and pronounced benefits for disadvantaged students. (Bredderman, 1982, pp. 39–41)

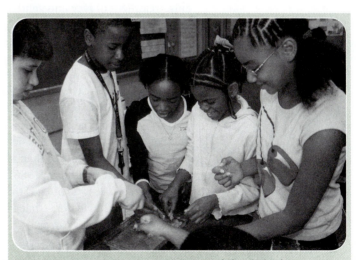

Interaction is an important inquiry tool that helps learners to construct meaning from materials and experiences.

Inquiry learning makes the difference. Exploring, investigating, and discovering are essential to meaningful learning and effective science teaching. When children solve problems and make discoveries, they are learning how to learn and constructing meaning for themselves. Jerome Bruner (1961) points out the benefits for children as they make discoveries through active learning:

- As children's intellectual potency is increased, their powers of thinking improve.
- Children's rewards for learning shift from those that come from the teacher or someone else to those that are found inside themselves from the satisfaction they feel.
- Children learn the procedures and important steps for making discoveries and find ways to transfer these to other learning opportunities.
- What children learn takes on more meaning, and they remember it longer.

Selecting and Using Textbooks

NSES

PR-B

PR-D

If you had taken a look in a large number of elementary classrooms where science is taught more than two decades after Shymansky and Bredderman's research, what do you think you would have seen? Would you have witnessed a massive change toward the kinds of inquiry-based active and interactive learning? No. Instead, it is likely that you would have observed what Donald Wright reported: "Fifty to 80 percent of all science classes use a single text or multiple texts as *the* basis for instruction. For students, knowing is more a function of reading, digesting, and regurgitating information from the textbook or lab manual than it is of analyzing, synthesizing, and evaluating" (1980, p. 144). In the 21st century school, science is still largely dependent upon a single text even though texts continue to be criticized for their shortcomings (Kirk et al. 2001; Stern & Roseman, 2001; Holliday, 2002).

Shortcomings and Differences in Textbooks

Although authors and publishers have made dramatic improvements over recent years, science textbooks vary considerably on factors, such as readability, reading and study aids, treatment of race and gender, and emphasis given to vocabulary versus concepts. Readability studies show greater levels of difference mostly for the upper elementary and middle grades. Students' science achievements decline when they use textbooks that are written above their reading ability levels. Reading and study aids, such as chapter headings, help pupils comprehend and recall, particularly when children are taught to use these features. Gender bias has been reduced, with more balance now seen toward female representation. However, people who have disabilities and nonwhites often do not receive substantial recognition in textbooks. Science vocabulary continues to be emphasized much more than science concepts, even though researchers report that emphasis on concepts rather than vocabulary results in *increased* science achievement (Meyer, Greer, & Crummey, 1986). In contrast to this finding, Paul D. Hurd (1982) has found that science texts often introduce "as many as 2,500 technical terms and unfamiliar words" (p. 12). He notes that a beginning foreign language course attempts to cover only half as many new words.

Who decides what material science textbooks will include and how they will be organized? Recommendations from credible sources such as the National Research Council, the National Science Teachers Association, or the American Association for the Advancement of Science do not always drive the development or revision of printed materials like school textbooks. Authors, teachers, editors, marketing staffs in publishing houses, boards of education, and textbook censors have less influence than you may imagine. Texas, California, Florida, and North Carolina all have statewide textbook adoptions. The combined student population of these states accounts for 25 percent of the United States' school-age population; the powerful textbook selection committees of these states tremendously influence the content that most publishers choose to put into their books (Kirk et al., 2001). Hence, a few states tend to determine the content and features offered to the rest of the nation. Approaches and material that appear radical or unconventional stand little chance despite their academic merits, origin, or proven effects.

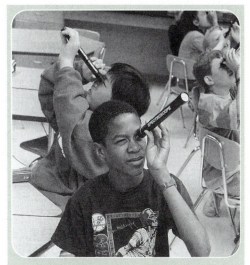

Student activities can enhance the use of a textbook.

If it seems unlikely that textbooks will be dramatically improved and some errors will be inevitable, what options do you have? You *do* have a choice of programs. The choices you make will influence the direction you use to guide your students and the extent of the positive impact on their interactive learning experience. You can:

- enhance the textbook in use,
- change the sequence of topics to reflect better the concepts to be learned, or
- select the textbook that most closely represents the needs of your students and fulfills the recommendations for effective science teaching and learning.

Enhancing the Textbook

Each teacher can enhance the textbook to include more effective learning activities and interesting information rather than waiting for authors and publishers to do it. You can add enhancements that are timely and that match learner interests and abilities. These are some other ways in which you can use textbooks to foster constructivism:

1. Combine the best elements from published programs. Use old editions or the most interesting materials from unadopted examination copies of textbooks. Cut out pictures, information, and activities to make minibooks or a resource file by topic.

2. Select relevant supplements from laboratory programs and web-based materials. Experimental programs may have been used by your school in the past and then discarded. Remnants might be found stored away. Conduct an inventory of equipment and teaching materials from the past, and select useful materials relevant to the concepts you are teaching.

3. Identify local resources. School and community professionals, local businesses, parks and recreation facilities, libraries, and museums all provide rich resources for classroom speakers and field trips. These enhancement resources also help to demonstrate the relationship of science and everyday life as well as update or fill in gaps not covered by dated textbooks.

4. Check with your state's department of education. Some states compare commercial materials and keep on file survey-style coverage of important science findings and laboratory programs that make fine enhancements for standard textbook programs.

5. Screen supplementary materials for the appropriate reading level and context accuracy. Deemphasize use of a textbook that is written on too high a reading level by substituting suitable materials. Use accelerated material if the writing is too simple.

6. Select evaluation devices that reflect the preferred outcomes. If your desire is development of a particular process skill, select performance-based evaluation tasks

that require the children to demonstrate the skill. Carefully screen all textbook questions and written exercises, and select those that match the intended level of thinking and skills. Adapt project ideas, and improve the types of questions that are used in the textbook or teacher's guide.

7. Work to organize building- or district-level committees in which teachers form supplement teams. More hands make lighter work, and more heads generate a greater number of effective ideas. Teams of teachers can share the research and swap ideas.

8. Attend professional conferences. States have affiliates of the National Science Teachers Association, and large cities have their own science education organizations. Attend their annual conferences, and listen to other teachers to get ideas for your own classroom. Adapt these ideas to your science program. Remember that your ideas are just as important as those of others. Why not make your own presentation at a conference or provide a workshop for other teachers?

9. Relearn the concepts and processes of science. Take workshops or courses to learn about the most recent ideas in science and its teaching. This continues your education and professional development; both can help you to enhance the science textbook. Request a staff development program for yourself and for helping the other school staff members relearn and elevate their own levels of scientific literacy. Other teachers will be more likely to enhance the textbook if they feel more confident and informed.

teachers on Science Teaching

How Toys Can Enhance Your Teaching

by Michael E. Cawthru
Grade 5, Kyffin Elementary School, Golden, Colorado

NSES
PD-B

There are literally dozens of books out on the market to help teachers bring science demonstrations into the classroom. I know, I'm on the mailing list for all of them. But it is worth it to have an assortment of ideas at your fingertips. Don't let anyone tell you that you must teach the textbook and never vary from it. Textbooks are nice, but you have to be yourself. Go for it!

When you start to do classroom demos, make certain you have practiced and are prepared. Nothing can kill the demo faster than the teacher's leaning over the file cabinet or searching through the closet muttering, "Just a second, kids, I'll have what I need. Just sit still." Yeah, right. Before you can turn around, Johnny is all over the room and into everything you had out for the demo. Likewise, nothing can get and hold their attention like all the equipment laid out on the table.

Speaking of equipment, it would be great to have thousands of dollars' worth of glassware, burners, chemicals, and such. But you can also use mason jars and propane torches and check out the chemicals that are sold over the grocery store counter. Ping-Pong balls—I keep at least a dozen on hand for all sorts of demonstrations:

atomic structure (color them and give kids colored marshmallows for their set so they can eat them at the end), planets, physics—well, you get the idea. A globe and a ball, the diameter of which is the same as the distance from San Francisco to Cleveland on your globe, will be the perfect model for the earth and the moon. Also include a string that has been wrapped around the globe ten times; that's the distance from the earth to the moon. And never underestimate the toy department. Oh boy, my wife won't let me go in unescorted. Slinkies, cars, marbles, magnets, and models—models of space shuttles, human bodies, eyes, just about anything.

Yes, I must admit, my room looks like a toy store. But the bottom line is this: Are the kids learning? You bet your atom they are. Because I also don't just sit. When kids with Ping-Pong balls are walking around the room imitating electrons moving about the nucleus, and another kid is trying to hit a ball with a marshmallow, they understand the reason electrons pass through matter without hitting anything, that atoms are mostly empty space. Yeah, they learn. And that is the whole point, the "ah-hah" moment we all live for, when Suzy says, "I get it, Mr. C!"

Changing the Sequence

The textbook's chapter order and the organization of the information within chapters may not be what is best for your students. Perhaps some simple resequencing will bring improvement in science achievement, attitudes, and interest and help you to help learners make clearer and stronger conceptual connections.

Cognitive scientists emphasize the importance of anchoring ideas to the learner's mental structure. New information becomes more meaningful when it can be attached to concepts that are already in the children's minds. Science material is better understood when it interrelates "in such a way as to make sense to the learner" (Hamrick & Harty, 1987, p. 16). Resequencing material so that ideas relate in ways that make more sense to the children adds meaning. In a study of sixth graders,

> the findings revealed that students for whom content structure was clarified through resequencing general science chapters exhibited significantly higher science achievement, significantly more positive attitudes toward science, and significantly greater interest in science than students for whom general science content was not resequenced. (Hamrick & Harty, 1987, p. 15)

Concept mapping is a method of sequencing the ideas of a lesson, and a version of it can be used to sequence the text effectively. A concept map shows ideas graphically according to their relationships. (See Chapter 4 for more information.) The relationships communicate important connections that show an intended mental structure to be formed about the map's topic. Consider the following when resequencing:

1. Proceed from the smallest to the largest ideas or from the simple to the complex when resequencing a text. Researchers recommend that rearrangements first be made into an interrelated pattern based on the size of the ideas (Hamrick & Harty, 1987). A hierarchy of ideas is formed; perhaps physical science leads to life science topics, which progress to earth and space science concepts. See Table 11.2 for an example of a typical textbook sequence of topics with a revised sequence. You can determine the children's hierarchical views of the material by doing a webbing exercise in which they refer to the table of contents or chapter titles of the text and

TABLE 11.2 ● A Sample of Textbook Content Sequence and Revised Textbook Content Sequence

Textbook Sequence	Revised Content Sequence
Animals with backbones	Matter (elements and compounds)
Classifying animals without backbones	Sources of energy
Plants	Light
Life cycles	Electricity and magnetism
Matter (elements and compounds)	Communications
Electricity and magnetism	Energy outcomes and the future
Sources of energy	Energy for living things
Light	Plants
Communications	Life cycles
Climates of the world	Classifying animals without backbones
Energy for living things	Animal with backbones
Energy outcomes and the future	Climates of the world

Source: L. Hamrick and H. Harty, "Influence of Resequencing General Science Content on the Science Achievement, Attitudes Toward Science, and Interests in Science of Sixth Grade Students," *Journal of Research in Science Teaching* 24(1) (1987): 20. Reprinted by permission of John Wiley & Sons, Inc.

connect these in a web that makes sense to the children. Begin at the chalkboard with a single word such as *science*, and have the children refer to the ideas in the chapter titles and sections within chapters to add the ideas of science to the chalkboard. Engage the children in a discussion of how they see these ideas of science connected; ask for their reasons. Your prompts can help them to order material from the simple to the more complex in a way that is more understandable. At the same time, you will be reinforcing higher levels of thinking.

2. Convey the interrelated structure to the students. An overview of the restructured material can be made on a student handout, placed in a notebook, and used for clarification, reinforcement, and review throughout the year. Children can check off the major concepts as they are studied. This serves as a structure of information for learners, gives you an opportunity to teach for concepts, and provides a ready guide for reinforcement.

3. Help learners to clarify the content of the structure. They will not absorb all of the ideas of the resequencing overview at once. Take advantage of any opportunity to discuss the structure of the material you have chosen for your class. Be aware of how many levels of complexity exist once all chapter resequencing occurs and chapters are mapped. Does the textbook take into account the difficulty children may have in developing relationships among and between the concepts? Help learners to paint the big picture and to see how the smaller ideas fit into a pattern with the larger ideas.

Selecting the Best Textbook

Teachers are becoming more selective, and it may be that their efforts to identify the best textbooks are having effects on changes. Textbooks are often selected because they offer many activities, worksheets, tests, and programmed teacher's guides. They appear busy or glitzy and may require little more than reading and writing exercises. Such textbooks may fall short of meeting recommendations for effective science instruction and do not support inquiry-based, constructivist learning. What can you do to select a better textbook or to use the one you have in ways that improve the experience for students? As a starting point for screening textbooks, ask yourself:

- What does the textbook expect my students to do?
- Does the textbook include important content and related information?
- What should my students be able to do after they study the textbook that they could not do before?
- For every student activity, project, or question, ask: "What kind of thinking is required?" "How does this address the National Science Education Standards?"
- Examine the textbooks for inclusion of the NSES content standards (see Appendix) and ask: "To what extent is each new dimension emphasized?" and "How is it included in the textbook?" "How well do the textbook's concepts represent these recommendations?"
- Summarize your initial screening by asking: "Will this textbook really help my students reach the goals I have set for them—or is it going to waste their time?"

Look again at the textbooks that pass the initial screening. Now is the time to be more critical. An effective textbook should motivate students; it should involve children in the processes of science by guiding them toward making discoveries. It should include materials that can be adapted to fulfill local needs. How does the textbook help students to experience the history and nature of science within the local context? The activities should not be cookbook recipes that encourage learners to follow the steps mindlessly. Focus on the student activities, sample several from each book, and ask these questions:

- Are students required to make careful observations?
- Are students encouraged to make inferences?
- Is classification a skill that is used in the experiments?
- How often are students asked to make a prediction based on observation or data?
- How often are students encouraged to display data in a systematic way that will enhance their ability to communicate?
- What kinds of weblinks or enhancements does the publisher offer, and how do those enhancements fulfill your state or national standards?
- What resources are offered to assist learners who have special needs?

The best science textbook will challenge children to improve their thinking.

These questions will help you to select a textbook that delivers a strong blend of expository information and productive interaction through sound activity-based learning. Table 11.3 provides a brief instrument for screening textbooks and printed curriculum materials.

We cannot force students to learn. We can help them to make discoveries and form connections for themselves, and our guidance is an important factor. Go slowly, and guide with purpose. Avoid merely covering information without ensuring students' understanding. Strive for quality rather than quantity. Remember the maxim "Less is more." Listen to students more, and talk less. Try to emphasize student cooperation instead of competition. Blend learning activities to include discovery opportunities, group work, and learning that requires different types of information processing—thinking. Try to concentrate on students doing right thinking rather than getting right answers. If you must use a textbook and teacher-centered approaches, incorporate several of the suggestions offered in this chapter to make your classroom more interactive. Chances for effective teaching will be greater through your efforts, and your reward will be improved student achievement, positive attitudes toward science, and greater interest in school through more student-centered, constructivist teaching practices.

Using Trade Books

Using trade books or children's literature is another way to bring content-focused science material to class. While science textbooks focus on the factual and analytical aspects of reading, the trade book can provide an aesthetic or emotional dimension to learning (Rice, 2002). Often, this combined approach helps to address specific, real-world uses of science and is an approach that favors the inclusion of females and minorities. The trade book is not a substitute for skills-directed instruction in teaching reading skills or science concepts. However, a trade book can involve a wider audience and offer an applied setting for learning science.

Trade books may include biographies of scientists; reference books on particular types of animals, plants, or environmental issues; natural science concepts; or specifically focused single publications on physical science topics, science theories, or natural causes, such as volcanoes and tornadoes. Trade books may contain fictional characters but illustrate specific science concepts. Textbook publishers have begun identifying

NSES
TS-D
TS-F
PD-A

TABLE 11.3 ● Screening Texts and Other Printed Curriculum Materials

You can learn about the science program by examining the textbooks and other written curriculum materials available.	Yes	No	?

Science Content

1. Is there a balanced emphasis among the life sciences, earth sciences, and physical sciences? ___ ___ ___
2. Do the materials include study of problems that are important to us now and in the future? Examples: acid rain, air and water pollution, technology's impact, energy production and availability, medical research, world hunger, population, deforestation, ozone depletion. ___ ___ ___
3. Do materials require students to apply major science concepts to everyday life situations? ___ ___ ___
4. Are the materials accurate? ___ ___ ___
5. Do the materials encourage an in-depth examination of concepts and issues? ___ ___ ___
6. Other: ___ ___ ___

Science Processes

1. Do the materials include liberal amounts of hands-on investigations and activities that the children can do in order to experience the nature of science? ___ ___ ___
2. Is scientific inquiry an important part of the materials the children will read? Examples: observing, measuring, predicting, inferring, classifying, recording and analyzing data, etc. ___ ___ ___
3. Do the materials encourage children to explore, discover, and construct answers for themselves rather than tell them how things should turn out? ___ ___ ___
4. Do the materials require children to use scientific reasoning, to apply science processes to problem-solving situations, and to construct conclusions? ___ ___ ___
5. To what extent do the materials help learners to build thinking skills? ___ ___ ___
6. Other: ___ ___ ___

Other Considerations

1. Are the materials consistent with the science goals of your school? (Or, in the absence of such goals, those of the National Science Education Standards or your state framework of science goals.) ___ ___ ___
2. Are the materials well designed, clearly written, accurate, up to date, and easy to use? ___ ___ ___
3. Do the materials proceed from the simple to the complex and are they designed for the children's appropriate developmental levels? ___ ___ ___
4. Is the information written at the proper grade level? ___ ___ ___
5. Do the materials for children appear interesting and relevant to their levels? ___ ___ ___
6. Are there opportunities for children to learn about the history and nature of science and science-related careers? ___ ___ ___
7. Are valid evaluation materials used or included? Examples: performance demonstrations, pictorial assessment. ___ ___ ___
8. Is a teacher's guide included and is it helpful for using the materials? ___ ___ ___
9. Do the materials include enough application of science content and processes to make science meaningful to students? ___ ___ ___
10. Is technology included and do children have to use appropriate forms of technology to access or process the science material? ___ ___ ___
11. Are different cultures, races, genders, social groups, ages included with respect and equity? ___ ___ ___
12. Do the materials promote teaching methods that promote an effective, interactive learning environment? ___ ___ ___
13. Other: ___ ___ ___

Source: Originally adapted from Kenneth R. Mechling and Donna L. Oliver, *Characteristics of a Good Elementary Science Program* (Washington, DC: National Science Teachers Association, 1983) and updated by the authors of this text to reflect contemporary expectations and the National Science Education Standards (NRC, 1996).

trade books to be used with their textbook series (Rice, 2002). The annual March issues of *Science and Children and Science Scope,* published by the National Science Teachers Association, list the most outstanding science trade books for children. These books pass scrutiny for having substantial science content; clarity; and freedom from gender, ethnic, and socioeconomic bias. More recently (March 2007), the NSTA journals have provided detailed reviews of trade books published in Spanish.

Teachers must be aware that trade books have their limitations. Some teachers may use trade books to introduce or to complement a lesson, such as during a learning cycle's *Explanation* phase to support the vocabulary and help to develop the concept. Trade books should be scrutinized carefully, just as you would do for a textbook, because some researchers report numerous factual errors and information and illustrations that encourage the formation of misconceptions (Rice, 2002).

Trade books for children help to expand conceptualization and to support habits of scientific literacy.

Best Practices

The field of education is replete with labels containing multiple meanings, and the term *best practice* probably qualifies for multiple perceptions and meanings. As the label implies, there can be a qualitative distinction between the value of one practice versus another. In science teaching and learning, we use the term *best practice* to convey a clearly defined basis for making an evaluation about a resource's or a practice's impact on learning. A best practice consists of superior teaching materials that are used with effective teaching methods. Choosing and using a best practice should result in a significant impact on student learning.

NSES
PR-B
PR-D

Identifying Best Practices

The lessons that have been learned from the rich history and research base of science education mean that a best practice in science uses effective principles of curriculum design, psychology, cognition, assessment, and teaching. A modern best practice is a teaching resource, such as a lesson, that:

- is aligned with specific content, teaching, and assessment standards,
- has a research base,
- has accurate content and is developed in a way that promotes student understanding,
- implicitly or explicitly supports equity,
- engages the interests of most students using methods of inquiry and requires active participation for learning to occur,
- frames the content in a learning context that students find meaningful and significant,
- may be specifically targeted upon a special need,
- is adaptable to a variety of learning settings and promotes discourse leading to constructed understanding,
- uses appropriate technology in highly effective ways,

Emphasis on Excellence

NSES

PD-B

The National Science Education Standards provide criteria for excellence in developing K–8 science programs and improving science teaching, learning, and assessment. The standards for excellence are grounded in five assumptions:

1. The vision of science education described by the Standards requires changes throughout the entire system.
2. What students learn is greatly influenced by how they are taught.
3. The actions of teachers are deeply influenced by their perceptions of science as an enterprise and as a subject to be taught and learned.

4. Student understanding is actively constructed through individual and social processes.
5. Actions of teachers are deeply influenced by their understanding of and relationships with students (NRC, 1996, p. 28).

Achieving these standards for excellence requires several changes throughout the system of science education. Therefore, the excellent science program must encompass the following changes in emphases (NRC, 1996, p. 224):

Less Emphasis On

- Developing science programs at different grade levels independently of one another
- Using assessments unrelated to curriculum and teaching
- Maintaining current resource allocations for books
- Textbook- and lecture-driven curriculum

- Broad coverage of unconnected factual information

- Treating science as a subject isolated from other school subjects
- Science learning opportunities that favor one group of students
- Limiting hiring decisions to the administration

- Maintaining the isolation of teachers

- Supporting competition

- Teachers as followers

More Emphasis On

- Coordinating the development of the K–12 science program across grade levels
- Aligning curriculum, teaching, and assessment
- Allocating resources necessary for hands-on inquiry teaching aligned with the Standards
- Curriculum that supports the Standards and includes a variety of components, such as laboratories emphasizing inquiry and field trips
- Curriculum that includes natural phenomena and science-related social issues that students encounter in everyday life
- Connecting science to other school subjects, such as mathematics and social studies
- Providing challenging opportunities for all students to learn science
- Involving successful teachers of science in the hiring process
- Treating teachers as professionals whose work requires opportunities for continual learning and networking
- Promoting collegiality among teachers as a team to improve the school
- Teachers as decision makers

- includes tools for helping teachers to conduct assessments of increased student learning, and
- may innovate, motivate, and hold high expectations for learners.

A Site for Best Practices

Fortunately, the list of qualities shown above is built into an evaluation rubric for reviewing web-based science resources (www.ohiorc.org/rubric/), which is used to locate hundreds of high quality lessons. The *Ohio Resource Center for Mathematics, Science and Reading* (ORC) is a free web-based center supplying lessons for improving teaching and learning. The ORC resources are used by teachers, school leaders, policy makers and university faculty; children benefit. The ORC provides links to peer-reviewed instructional resources that have been identified by panels of experienced educators. Lessons promote best practices and are correlated to the national standards and Ohio's academic content standards. Correlations with national standards make the resources attractive to educators in any state and may be accessed from any Internet connection any place, any time. The ORC is not a clearinghouse and includes only materials that have passed the most rigorous review. The ORC may be accessed on www.ohiorc.org. The resources may be browsed by topic, grade level, or standard. The resources may also be searched by using basic or advanced techniques. An example of a best practice using a learning cycle can be seen by viewing this review record and using the direct link. The ORC record can be found easily by using the search features and searching on key words, topics, or record number.

Supported Beliefs about Effective Elementary Science Programs

A science program consists of more than a collection of individual lessons, even if they are classified as best practices. An effective science program, whether it is based on a single text or multiple resources, will be based on the supported beliefs that have arisen from reputable research and decades of classroom-based impact. According to numerous publications from the National Science Foundation and the National Science Teachers Association, the following list describes the intentions, dispositions, and characteristics of high impact programs. Fortunately, numerous resources are available.

1. The National Science Foundation's experimental elementary science programs and new approaches to teacher preparation have been successful, even though a low percentage of schools (30 percent) have used the programs and an even smaller percentage of teachers (7 percent) have received direct training.

2. Effective elementary science programs keep pace with changes in science, society, knowledge, and trends in schooling.

3. Most current elementary school science programs do not serve all children well. Effective programs have meaning for diverse audiences.

4. Effective science programs strive to promote children's personal development; to help children explore the interrelationships among science, technology, and society; to continue academic preparation through inquiry; and to build awareness of the history and nature of science.

5. Effective programs have no single author but are developed by teams with teacher involvement. Extensive classroom testing and program revision are necessary and must be done frequently.

6. Students learn successfully in different ways; multiple views on learning add diversity and help to balance the effective science program.

7. Programs that emphasize conceptual learning appear to be most effective overall and produce the greatest and most enduring gains in achievement when conception is a learner's construct.

8. Multiple teaching methods are useful, and hands-on learning opportunities are necessary for all children. Overall, inquiry methods and learning cycles are useful methods for helping children learn science concepts.

9. What is taught—the substance of science—must be useful and relevant for each child. Publications such as the National Science Education Standards help guide content selection.

10. Packaging the program is helpful and reduces teachers' preparation time. New generation science curriculum supplements have several common features that add impact to the materials. They identify relevant themes, define purposes or objectives, give background information, list materials needed, state procedures for teaching, identify essential vocabulary, offer ideas for evaluation or lesson expansion, and so on.

11. The history and nature of science make it possible to integrate topics into other subject lessons. Science's diversity enriches other parts of the school curriculum and adds to its power as a literacy subject.

12. A less direct, teacher-as-guide instructional role is effective because students are encouraged to assume greater responsibility for their own learning.

13. Conceptual learning takes time and should not be rushed; effectiveness rather than time efficiency should be the driving force of the curriculum.

14. Learners in constructivist science programs achieve more, like science more, and improve their problem-solving skills more than children who learn from traditional textbook-based programs. Innovative newer generations of science textbooks incorporate many of the features of the effective experimental programs.

15. Effective science programs promote children's intellectual development by improving their thinking through inquiry and problem-solving processes.

16. Materials and learning activities must match the child's level of development to have the greatest impact.

17. Students receive intrinsic rewards from the personal discoveries they make through firsthand learning experiences with manipulatives.

18. Science students who learn from effective programs are better able to transfer their learning to other circumstances, obtain more meaning, and remember what they learn longer.

Resources for Best Practices

NSES

SS-D

TS-D

PD-A

Lessons from the past have helped to improve the wonderful new resources that are available to teachers. This exciting era of curriculum and program development has helped to renew interest in science through uses of best practices. Science programs are attempting to keep pace with changes in the fields of science and technology and to investigate the impact of each on our society through the eyes and experiences of children.

The new generation of science programs strives to serve the needs and interests of all learners, not an intellectual elite. New programs often emphasize conceptual development through constructivist techniques, use multiple teaching methods to fill multiple student interests, and incorporate multiple views on human diversity. Many programs promote additional science outcomes, such as students who are skilled at science inquiry and problem solving; investigations of interrelationships among and between science, technology, and society; awareness of the history and tentative nature of science; and an expanded awareness of career opportunities in science.

The direct and sustained involvement of classroom teachers is one of the greatest factors shaping new science programs, particularly in working to match students' levels of development to appropriate learning experiences and to strengthen the conceptual constructions of learners by connecting learning experiences and central concepts to science themes. Common thematic similarities among the new science programs are patterns of change, structure and scale, systems, diversity, and models. There are few differences among the newer programs, the biggest gap being under the term *form and function.* That theme is identified in the National Science Education Standards, yet it is not explicitly called out as a major theme in any of the newer science programs. Careful inspection shows that many of those programs lump form and function with structures. Continual classroom testing of materials and lessons and frequent revision through formative evaluation assist these programs through rapid stages of evolution. Hence, conceptual flaws are reduced, and supported assumptions about learning are expanded.

Although there are numerous small-scale efforts to produce the next generation of science programs, space permits us to share only a sample of the larger efforts that have endured rigorous evaluation and received national (often international) attention.

Programs and Print Resources

The Lawrence Hall of Science Resources. Many publishers and vendors supply science resources; very few have developed standards-rich, engaging materials for grades pre-K–12 that have withstood the test of time. Over the years, the leader in the development of rich science resources has been The Lawrence Hall of Science (LHS) at the University of California, Berkeley (http://www.lawrencehallofscience.org/). Curricular materials that they have developed include FOSS, GEMS, MARE, PEACHES, SAVI, SEPUP, and Seeds of Learning. Following is a brief description of each. Details for each program are found on the LHS website.

FOSS (Full Option Science System) has twenty-six grade K–6 modules and nine courses for departmentalized middle schools (grades 6–8). The elementary components provide student equipment kits and print materials. The strength of this program is its thorough assessment component. Children *do* science, construct concepts, and perform direct evaluation exercises in the areas of life, physical, and earth science and scientific reasoning and technology. All materials are correlated to the NSES standards and are available through their website. The FOSS Science Stories are also available in Spanish. The middle school FOSS materials are in-depth units that require 9–12 weeks to teach.

GEMS (Great Explorations in Math and Science) is designed for students K–12. Science and mathematics are integrated in teacher activity publications and student project booklets. Several old GEMS units have undergone a transformation, with additional information on current pedagogical research and standards. Detailed content knowledge on each topic is provided to the teacher, and assessments are embedded throughout the unit. Some GEMS titles are *Crime Lab Chemistry, Color Analyzers, In All Probability, Oobleck, Algebraic Reasoning, Early Adventures in Algebra,* and *Living with a Star.* GEMS kits are available from Carolina Biological Supply Company.

MARE (Marine Activities, Resources, and Education) focuses each grade on a different aquatic habitat. Primary grades focus on near-shore habitats (pond, rocky seashore, sandy beach, and wetlands). The intermediate grades explore offshore marine habitats that are conceptually more abstract (kelp forest, open ocean, and islands), and the middle school students explore coral reefs and the polar seas. Thus, each grade level experience is built upon over the years. The program provides an interdisciplinary approach, by addressing the NSE earth, physical and life science standards, as well as inquiry, language arts, environmental issues, art, and music. Formative assessment occurs throughout the activities.

PEACHES (Primary Explorations for Children and Educators in Science) is designed for children ages 4–6 (grades pre-K–1). Numerous science and mathematics activities and projects are designed to present concepts in developmentally appropriate ways.

Literature, language acquisition, drama, art, role-play, and environmental awareness are woven into the activities.

SAVI/SELPH (Science Activities for the Visually Impaired/Science Enrichment for Learners with Physical Handicaps) were originally designed to address effective science education for students with disabilities in grades 3–8. These programs have been found to be effective for *all* learners at these grade levels. The goal of SAVI was to produce science activities for blind and visually impaired grade 3–8 students. Specialized equipment and new procedures to ensure full access to science learning for blind students were also developed. The SELPH project started out adapting and modifying SAVI materials and procedures for students with orthopedic disabilities and students with learning disabilities. Both programs are interdisciplinary and multisensory.

SEPUP (The Science Education for Public Understanding Program) provides modular based materials for children in grades 6–12. The original program, CEPUP, emphasized chemical education. Current modules address physical, earth, and life sciences and science processes. SEPUP kits are available. They address topics such as pollution, household chemicals, and chemicals in food. The Chem-2 SEPUP program is designed for grades 4–6. These modules strive to make science concepts relevant to the learner's world.

Seeds of Science/Roots of Reading™ program consists of two series: a collection of integrated science and literacy units and a parallel collection of literacy units, each paired with a set of four-color student books. Currently, there are four *Seeds of Science/Roots of Reading* units designed for second- and third-grade students. When complete, the entire series will include twelve units from grades 2–5. This is one of the newest programs developed at the Lawrence Hall of Science. It was developed in response to the large emphasis placed on reading skills in the public schools.

Environmental Education Resources.   Many environmentally based local resources are typically made available through the individual state departments of natural resources or the state agricultural extension offices and/or websites. Various groups have published books, posters, or pamphlets with environmental activities identified. Few have endured in print form over the years to the extent that Project Learning Tree, Project WILD, and Aquatic Project WILD have. These resources and Project WET are described below.

PLT (Project Learning Tree) is perhaps the oldest of the Environmental Education Resources. PLT provides a pre-K–8 guide designed to help learners better understand the forest community and its relationship to the day-to-day lives of people and animals. Each lesson is classroom-tested, linked to a specific science theme, and supported by conceptual story lines. Themes include diversity, interrelationships, systems, structure and scale, and patterns of change. The student pages for each activity and the glossary pages within the guide have Spanish translations. Modules addressing specific subjects, such as forest ecology and risk, are designed for secondary students. PLT also provides supplemental resources such as the energy and society program, which provides formal and informal educators with tools and activities to help students in grades pre-K–8 learn about their relationship with energy and investigate the environmental issues related to energy's role in society. In addition to hands-on activities, it engages kinesthetic learners in energy concepts through music and dance.

PLT has collaborated with the U.S. Department of Interior's Bureau of Land Management and the National Interagency Fire Center to provide workshops of wild land fire education. These workshops make use of pre-K–8 activities as well as the secondary PLT modules and fire education supplements such as the CD-ROM "Burning Issues" produced by the Science Education Department from Florida State University. PLT also provides partners for *GreenWorks* grants, specifically designed to encourage student involvement with local community spring initiatives that focus on wild land fire prevention, safety, and restoration. The activity guides are available only through training sessions. Information about Project Learning Tree can be obtained by contacting PLT at the American Forest Foundation, 1111 19th Street, N.W., Suite 780, Washington, D.C. 20036 (www.plt.org).

Project WILD and Aquatic, two different versions of a great idea, emphasize wildlife and aquatic life, respectively. Interdisciplinary and for grades K–12, the environmental guides address major school subjects and skills areas by involving children in direct and simulated wildlife experiences. The purpose is to increase awareness first, then to build toward making personal decisions and taking responsible human actions. The teacher-designed materials make it easy to bring outdoor wildlife concepts into the classroom. The activity guides are available only through training sessions. Information can be obtained by contacting Project WILD (www.projectwild.org).

Project WET (Water Education for Teachers) helps teachers to explore water issues with students. One hundred multidisciplinary activities support this resource, which is also supported by such supplements as special topic modules, models, children's literature books, and living history materials. The activity guides are available only through training sessions. Information can be obtained by contacting Project WET (www.projectwet.org).

Miscellaneous Resources.   There are a few other resources worth mentioning in this section. They have been selected because of their unique focus.

AIMS (Activities Integrating Mathematics and Science) publishes elementary and middle school curriculum materials that integrate mathematics and science for grades K–9. These materials provide field-tested teacher manuals. Workshops and seminars are available through the AIMS organization. For each grade and discipline (earth, life, and physical Science), AIMS provides 20–30 hands-on, inquiry-based activities. Titles include *Bats Incredible, Cycles of Knowing and Growing, Floaters and Sinkers, Primarily Physics,* and *Budding Botanists.* Some titles are available in Spanish.

Delta Education is in a unique situation in that it serves as the distributor for many of the LHS products, yet it creates and sells over forty science modules ranging from *Air* to *Observing an Aquarium* to *You and Your Body*. Their lessons are suitable for intermediate and middle school grades, provide easy-to-follow instructions that help teachers guide students through constructivist learning opportunities, and offer reasonable authentic assessments. Modules may be purchased separately or as a set. Kits of hands-on materials are available at additional cost. This vendor has an extensive catalog of science and math materials. Details can be found at http://www.deltaeducation.com.

National Geographic KIDS is one of the better web-based resources available for school-aged children. At this site, students can find videos, stories, activities, and games on a variety of science topics. Students can read and react to blog postings as explorers travel the globe and record their experiences in their blogs. The website is found at http://kids.nationalgeographic.com/.

TOPS (Task Oriented Physical Science) Learning Systems materials have been around for over twenty-five years. This organization prides itself in offering activities which explore physical science concepts with low- or no-cost materials. They have over forty modules for grades K–10. Each module comes with reproducible masters that include detailed instructions for hands-on, concept-based activities around a given theme. They offer several sample activities for free via their website at http://topsscience.org/.

Learning Cycle Featured Lesson

Physical and Earth/Space Science: Water Cycle

Grades • 5–8

▶ Transformations of Energy. The sun is a major source of energy for changes on the earth's surface.

EARTH/SPACE SCIENCE— GRADES 5-8:

▶ Populations and Ecosystem Concepts. The number of organisms an ecosystem can support depends on the resources available and abiotic factors such as light and water, range of temperatures, and soil composition.

CONCEPTS TO BE CONSTRUCTED

▶ The *water cycle* is a system in which the earth's fixed amount of water is collected, purified, and distributed from the environment to living things and back to the environment.

SCIENCE ATTITUDES TO NURTURE:

▶ Cooperating with others
▶ Obtaining reliable sources of information
▶ Avoiding broad generalizations

Engaging Question

Living things need and use a lot of water, so why isn't the earth's water supply used up?

Materials Needed

For exploration phase • conducted whole class, you will need:

- The national environmental resource *Project Learning Tree—K–8 Guidebook for the Activity Water Wonders*.
- Sentence statements about a drop of water as it moves through the water cycle. The sentences should be cut into strips, placing about three different possible pathways in an envelope. Provide one envelope to each student.
- Signs posted around the room identifying possible stopping points for a drop of water as it moves through the water cycle: a cloud, a lake, the air, the soil, etc.

For expansion phase • conducted whole class, you will need:

- A video on the water cycle, such as *The Wonders of Weather* from Discovery Films.
- From National Project Learning Tree, the video and the CD *Energy and Me with Billy B*. This demonstrates the water cycle as well as other energy transfer systems.

Safety:

- Remind the children to walk as they move around the room simulating a water drop as it moves through the water cycle.
- If the PLT activity is used from Part B in *Water Wonders*, require the students to wear goggles while making the watering can. Enforce no eating.

Exploration

PROCESS SKILLS USED

▶ Communicating
▶ Predicting
▶ Inferring
▶ Identifying variables

Student Activity

- Modify the PLT activity *Water Wonders©* to fit a learning cycle format.

- Present the word *cycle* to the class, and ask the students to help construct a list of all words they can think of containing the word *cycle*. Without drawing special attention to the words *water cycle*, develop a general description of what the word *cycle* means. Use guided imagery, and ask the students to imagine that they have a glass of water and to divide it into its smallest part: a water molecule. Prepare the students to take a pretend journey as a water molecule, following the instructions and using the water station's materials as provided in the Project Learning Tree lesson, *Water Wonders*. Information on this resource can be found at *plt.org*.

- A brief description of this part of the PLT lesson is that sentence strips are prepared that give statements that describe a possible path the water molecule took as it moved through the water cycle. One example is, "*I was swallowed by a human and moved through their body and flushed into the sewer system*" OR "*I fell to the ground as rain and landed on a leaf.*" In the classroom, the teacher should hang signs designating the various locations where the water molecule could land. The students should number their sentence strips as they remove them from the envelope. Students should write on the back of the strip the place they moved to per the sentence statement. After about four rounds, ask the students to return to their seats and to draw a picture showing their movement as a water molecule.

Explanation

Take the signs from the various stopping stations for the water molecule, and hang them in the front of the classroom in a circular shape. Point to the various stations; for instance, ask the students to describe where they were prior to the cloud and where they went after the cloud. Do this for all stations and web the diagram. Discuss the meaning of the diagram and what it represents: *a water cycle*.

Ask the students to describe what they think a water cycle is based on their exploration experiences. What does it do, and how does it function? Encourage them to apply names to the processes that occurred as the water molecule moved through the cycle. For instance, if the sentence strip said, "*I fell from the clouds and landed on the leaf,*" add the term *precipitation* to describe that process of falling from the cloud. If the sentence strip stated, "*I moved from the ground up into a cloud,*" use the term *evaporation* to describe that process.

Consult the water cycle figure in the Project Learning Tree lesson. Develop the concept that a water cycle is a system in which the earth's fixed amount of water is collected, purified, and distributed from the environment to living things and back to the environment.

Expansion

PROCESS SKILLS USED:
▶ Observing
▶ Recording data
▶ Generalizing
▶ Formulating models

Use Part B of the PLT lesson and the enrichment activity to expand the children's conception of the water cycle. Supplement the discussion with questions provided in order to address many of the National Science Education Standards' *New Dimensions*. The expansion can also be supplemented with a video such as *The Wonders of Weather*, available through the Discovery Channel. Also available from Project Learning Tree (*plt.org*) is the *Energy and Me* CD and video by Billy B., which demonstrates the water cycle, among other energy transfer systems.

Resource Used and Modified into a Learning Cycle and used with permission: Copyright 2003, American Forest Foundation. Reprinted with permission from Project Learning Tree © PreK-8 Activity Guide ©, Activity #44, *Water Wonders*. Permission to reprint should not be interpreted in any way as an endorsement of these materials by the American Forest Foundation/Project Learning Tree ©. The complete Project Learning Tree PreK-8 Activity Guide can be obtained by attending a Project Learning Tree © workshop. For more information about Project Learning Tree © please visit http://www.plt.org.

Evaluation

Hands-on Assessment

The students will be assessed as they choose their sentence strips and move through the cycle that their water molecule followed. The teacher will be looking for the students' ability to determine where a water molecule will end up on the basis of the clue in their sentence strips.

Reflective Assessment

The students will be able to explain in their own words and on the basis of their lesson experiences what a water cycle is, using key terms involved in the process.

Pictorial Assessment

The students will be able to construct a concept map of the water cycle.

The National Science Teachers Association (NSTA) provides many print and video resources. Their journals that are most enjoyed by elementary science teachers are *Science and Children* for the primary grades, *Science Scope* for the middle to junior high grades, and *The Science Teacher* for high school. NSTA members can access past articles from those journals via their website. The NSTA also sells many resources rich with science activities or the latest on research in science education. Their website is http://www.nsta.org.

Science Learning Centers

NSES
TS-D

We often think of resources as books or websites to which the classroom teacher can go to get ideas for our lessons. What about our learners? Is their access to resources limited to a weekly trip to the school library? Extend your students' learning opportunities by bringing the resources to the classroom through science learning centers.

When working with the entire class for a science lesson, a teacher who is committed to the learning cycle and constructivist approaches will find that science learning centers satisfactorily accommodate additional expansion activities for each lesson. You can design the learning center so that it focuses on a particular concept brought out in a class lesson and provides additional experiences to enable a greater understanding of the concept. All students should be encouraged to use the learning center at their convenience, to engage in activities that provide additional experiences with a particular science concept. Once all of the students have had sufficient time to participate in the expansion activity, change the activity to address a new concept.

Another approach to science learning centers is to design them so that students gain greater experience in the processes of science. When you present science lessons to a large group of students, the chances that each student has adequate time to make observations, predictions, measurements, and so on are slim if a more-skilled peer blurts out the answer first. The learning center can be designed so that each child has a chance to work in the area, gain experience in solving problems, measuring, predicting, using scientific instruments, and so on. You can change the learning center weekly, with different process skills as the focus (see Figure 11.1).

A science learning center can also be designed as a *discovery area*—a place where children create inventions from a variety of provided materials. The center can be considered a challenge area, where the teacher creates a problem for the week and, using the materials provided, the students work to solve the problem. A science learning center can be the place where students can play teacher-prepared or commercially prepared science games. Alternatively, the center can become the place where scientific literacy is promoted. Place in the center trade books related to the center topic for students to peruse.

Whatever you decide the focus of your science learning center should be, a few simple rules must be upheld to ensure its success. The guidelines for a science learning center are set out in Table 11.4.

Figures 11.2 and 11.3 provide examples of some typical science learning centers. Centers should be found in an area of the classroom where they are least likely to interfere with normal classroom operations. The information that is provided on classroom safety in Chapter 10 should guide you in the placement of the science learning center.

A pegboard or a felt board can be designed so that it will stand on its own atop a table or desk and can easily be stored when necessary. Pockets made from cloth or heavy cardboard serve as areas to hold activity cards, instructions, or small materials needed for the activity. Any material that is sturdy enough to withstand student wear, without being so heavy that it topples over, will serve as the backdrop for your science learning center. Appropriate pictures or diagrams should be displayed on this board. If the activity requires a more formal means of record keeping, place record sheets or assessment

1. Obtain light-bulb record books

Process Skill: Recording data

Each student will receive a light-bulb record book. The outer covers are made from yellow cardboard. Several sheets of white paper for students to record their data are stapled between the covers.

2. Page 1 of record book

Process Skill: Observing

On the table is a box with a bulb sticking out of the top. A switch protrudes from one side. A card near the box states:

Make as many observations as possible. Write the word OBSERVATIONS on the top of page 1 in the light bulb record book. Record your observation on that page.

3. Record book

Process Skill: Predicting

A card that is numbered with a 3 and has a drawing of the box with the bulb will be at the center with the following directions:

Label the next blank page in your record book PREDICTIONS. Predict what is inside the box causing the bulb to light. List and/or draw your predictions on that page.

4. Record book, battery, bulb, wire

Process Skill: Manipulating materials

Card numbered 4 near a battery, bulb, and wire, asks the students to do the following:

Label the next blank page of your record book MANIPULATING MATERIALS. Take the battery, bulb, and wire from the table. Using only those three pieces of material, get the bulb to light. Record in the record book drawings of ways you manipulated the materials—whether the bulb lit or not.

5. Record book, battery, bulb, wire, bulb holder, switch

Process Skill: Manipulating materials

At the next station the above materials will be laying near card number 5. The students will be asked to do the following:

Label the next blank page of your record book MANIPULATING MATERIALS. Take the battery, bulb, wire, bulb holder, and switch from the table. Get the bulb to light as you did at station 4. This time wire it so that the switch will turn the bulb on and off. Record in the record book drawings of ways you manipulated the materials—whether the bulb lit or not.

6. Record book, box, battery, bulb, bulb holder, wire, switch

Process Skill: Interpreting data, inferring, formulating models

The above materials will be found at station 6. The students will be asked to do the following:

Label the next blank page of your record book INTERPRETING DATA, INFERRING, FORMULATING MODELS. Using the materials given and your results from activities 4 and 5, try to create a box like the one you observed at stations 2 and 3. When finished go back to your prediction page in the record book. Was your prediction correct?

FIGURE 11.1 ● Process-Oriented Science Learning Center Lesson

sheets in a pocket on the board. Figure 11.4 provides an example of a typical science learning center backdrop.

Bulletin Boards and Other Displays

An activity-based science classroom should include a science bulletin board and a science display area. Lettering used for the bulletin board should be no smaller than

TABLE 11.4 ● Science Learning Center Guidelines

1. The purpose and objectives for the activity are made clear; the students understand what they are supposed to do at each center. The activity is designed so that it enhances the students' understanding of a concept rather than serving to frustrate and confuse.

2. All students have an opportunity to work at the center before the activity is changed.

3. Activities at the center do not interfere with other lessons going on in the classroom. Activities that require darkness, loud noises, or excessive amounts of physical activity are not appropriate for a learning center. The center is in an area where the teacher can readily observe the children in action.

4. At least one 2-foot-by-4-foot table or work area of equivalent size is dedicated to this center. If the activity requires additional space, adequate floor space will be allocated. If audiovisual materials are to be used, electrical outlets are close by.

5. Consumable materials at the centers are replenished frequently.

6. When water is required for an activity, the center is located close to a water source. If this is not possible, care is taken so that children running to sinks or water fountains are not interfering with students engaged in other classroom tasks.

4 inches high. Plan the topic to be addressed, and focus on one concept. Don't use too many words. Try to find visuals that will enhance the students' understanding of the concept, but avoid using too much material. If display colors, sizes, and shapes change too frequently, the intended message may get lost.

Science displays should be designed to appeal to the students' natural curiosity. They can be theme oriented and designed by the teacher or a collection of unrelated items provided by the students. For a theme highlighting mammals, the display table could contain pelts of various mammals for the students to touch and to compare and antlers or horns for the students to use to determine the animal they came from and the animal's age. There may be footprints of various mammals with a challenge to the students to determine which animal left the print. Books or pictures of various mammals would be left at the table.

FIGURE 11.2 ● Science Learning Center

- Outlets should be available when needed.
- Bulletin board contains pertinent science information.
- Center is located near the door to gain access to water from fountain in hall since no water is available in this classroom.

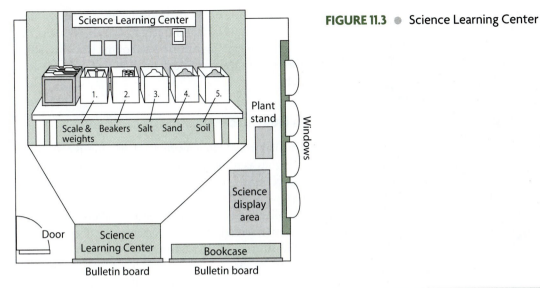

FIGURE 11.3 ● Science Learning Center

In a hodgepodge approach, the display area may be a catchall for the various science-related items children bring in that they would like to share. Items on the display table should be ones the students are allowed to touch: household items, such as an old radio or clock that can be taken apart to examine the inner works, or unusual rocks or plant parts that may serve to pique a student's curiosity. An item that requires special care, such as a geode or a parent's rock collection that a student brings in, may be better suited for teacher-supervised display.

Which is better: large-group instruction or small science learning centers? No matter what the mode of instruction is, science learning will be facilitated when careful

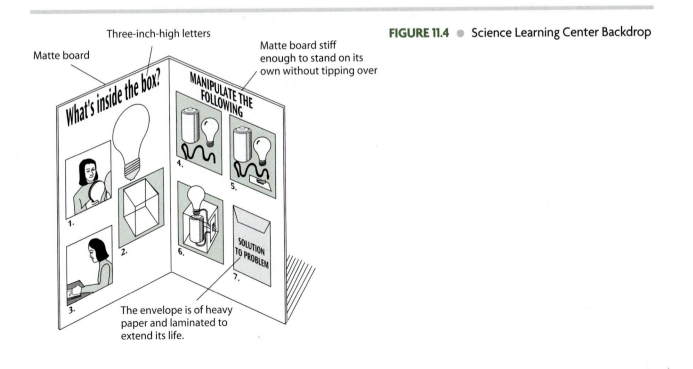

FIGURE 11.4 ● Science Learning Center Backdrop

Community resources stimulate children's interests in science and its practical value.

thought is given to the physical arrangement of the classroom. Allowing the students to travel freely to learning centers implies that certain behaviors are expected of the students. Using instruction time to teach cooperative roles will facilitate class exploration.

Human Resources

A readily available and often overlooked resource is colleagues. Using colleagues as resource people for instructional guidance and assistance enables us to broaden educational activities and to foster cooperation.

Your colleagues—other classroom teachers, the principal, the school nurse, the resource teacher, the librarian—are all potential sources of assistance. The experienced teacher who is willing to share activities, materials, and support is a natural aide. Teachers in another school or grade level may be able to suggest teaching activities and loan equipment or share materials. Upper-grade-level students are also sources of help because they may be available to provide a demonstration or to serve as a teaching assistant or tutor.

Community volunteers can provide enriching services. Communities may contain engineers, professors, sewage treatment personnel, medical professionals, computer specialists, and mechanics who are interested in education. In addition, parents may offer suggestions. Corporations and institutions may have an educational officer who can assist by providing names of employees who are willing to volunteer their time and talent to assist within the schools. Consider contacting retirement groups; chambers of commerce; local women's clubs; local, state, or national agencies; or even the Yellow Pages. Their members are experienced and may have time to volunteer.

A volunteer can enable you to devote more time to planning, diagnosing the individual needs of students, and prescribing learning activities for these needs. Volunteers may offer other benefits. They extend the number of people available to help the teacher and often bring skills that professional educators do not have, so the educational process maximizes opportunities for all students. Perhaps most important are the positive effects that volunteering can have on the volunteers themselves, and the public relations value is certainly important (Hager-Shoeny & Galbreath, 1982).

Table 11.5 lists vocations that volunteers might have. Look to individuals such as these to help with your school program.

Not all volunteers feel confident to make a presentation to a classroom on their particular area of interest. They may prefer, instead, to be involved in one or more of the following ways:

- Demonstrating scientific concepts,
- Serving as a mentor,
- Tutoring,
- Providing science fair project assistance,
- Providing career choice assistance,
- Reviewing school safety equipment,
- Assisting in science competition instruction,
- Demonstrating societal and technological applications of content,
- Furnishing specialized equipment,

TABLE 11.5 ● Science Classroom Volunteers

Area of Science	Volunteer
Animals	Zoologist, entomologist, microbiologist, zookeeper, veterinarian, beekeeper, marine biologist, paleontologist, cytologist, animal trainer, physician, forest ranger, physiologist, chemist, ecologist, neurobiologist, wildlife manager, farmer, rancher, geneticist, anatomist, mammalogist, limnologist, nurse, dietitian, x-ray technician, pharmacologist, forensic specialist, pharmacist
Plants	Botanist, paleobotanist, agronomist, horticulturist, farmer, forest manager, chemist, ecologist, geneticist, paleontologist, nutritionist, landscape architect, soil pathologist, soil scientist conservation officer, park ranger, agricultural extension agent
Weather	Meteorologist, ecologist, agronomist, TV weather forecaster, airport flight controller, geologist, oceanographer, climatologist, fisherman, boat captain, farmer, pilot, environmentalist, soil and water conservation agent
Physical and chemical properties	Chemist, biochemist, pharmacologist, architect, inventor, mechanic, carpenter, molecular biologist, physicist, ecologist, musical instrument maker, musician, toxicologist, metallurgist, geologist, photographer, builder, police lab forensic criminologist, materials scientist, technician, water company technician, engineers: chemical, textile, industrial, gemologist, acoustical, optical, mechanical, civil, nuclear, agricultural, ceramic, cosmetics developer, building inspector, potter
Electricity	Physicist, geologist, computer hardware/software designer, electrician, radar technician, amateur radio operator, designer, industrial engineer, electrical engineer, telephone system technician, thermal engineer, mechanical engineer, electronic engineer, electrical inspector, inventor, radio/TV engineer
Earth and space science	Astronomer, geologist, paleontologist, pilot, astronaut, geographer, cartographer, ecologist, physicist, biologist, chemist, surveyor, geotechnical tester, aerial photographer, volcanologist, seismologist, oceanographer, soil scientist, aeronautical engineer, aviation engineer, construction engineer, civil engineer
Behavioral and social science	Animal psychologist, clinical psychologist, marketing professional, business manager, psychiatrist, sociologist, anthropologist, city planner, applied economist, school psychologist, historian, archaeologist, geographer, pollster, market research analyst, demographer, statistician

Source: North Carolina Museum of Life and Science, *Science in the Classroom,* as cited by Triangle Coalition for Science and Technology Education, *A Guide for Planning a Volunteer Program for Science, Mathematics, and Technology Education* (College Park, MD: Triangle Coalition, 1992), p. 59.

- Assisting in speakers' bureaus,
- Spearheading public awareness campaigns,
- Encouraging projects for girls and minorities,
- Arranging field trips,
- Maintaining equipment, and
- Assisting with special demonstrations.

The tips in Table 11.6 may help volunteers to feel comfortable in their roles. Volunteers may not always be aware of the relevance of their knowledge and skills for elementary students; explain the benefits the students will receive from their assistance. The following advice was adapted from a list of suggestions for volunteers prepared by the Lane County Juvenile Department in Eugene, Oregon (Hager-Schoeny & Galbreath, 1982):

Increase interaction and discovery by directly involving children in demonstrations available from community volunteers.

TABLE 11.6 ● Tips for Teachers Working with Volunteers

1. Take time to talk with the volunteer outside the class-room, explaining class procedures, schedules, expectations, and objectives.

2. Prepare the volunteer with specifics about the assignment, where materials can be found, and what the learning objectives are.

3. Make the volunteer comfortable by explaining the obvious support facilities: where to place personal items, find a rest room, and get a cup of coffee.

4. Keep channels of communication open with the volunteer. Exchange a home number if appropriate and convenient. Plan and follow the schedule developed for the volunteer. Inform the volunteer of a schedule change as soon as possible. Keep in mind that volunteers have additional responsibilities and cannot be expected to wait for an assignment or materials preparation and that their responsibilities may prevent them from fulfilling their commitment. You will need to be understanding if this occurs.

5. Keep a special folder for regular volunteers with current assignments.

6. Inform volunteers about the students' level of ability, special problems, and students who need assistance.

7. Encourage your volunteer to sign in and to wear a name tag. Other faculty members and administrators will want to acknowledge a volunteer in the building.

8. Let every volunteer know how much you and the class appreciate the help. A thank-you note goes a long way toward making the experience a rewarding one for a volunteer.

9. Evaluate the volunteer encounter. Consider the specific request, the background of the volunteer, and the constraints of the situation.

Source: Project Technology Engineering Applications of Mathematics and Science, Yakima Valley/Tri-Cities MESA, *Tips for Teachers Working with Volunteers,* as cited by Triangle Coalition for Science and Technology Education, *A Guide for Planning a Volunteer Program for Science, Mathematics, and Technology Education* (College Park, MD: Triangle Coalition, 1992), p. 54.

- Invite volunteers to serve as partners.
- Clearly define the differences in the tasks and roles of employees and volunteers.
- Screen volunteers and accept only the ones who can contribute. Check references and interview each candidate as you would a prospective employee.
- Require a specific commitment of time and resources from volunteers.
- Provide an orientation program to acquaint volunteers with their functions.
- Provide supervision.
- Make assignments based on the volunteers' skills, knowledge, interests, capacity to learn, time available, and resources.

chapter summary

The rich history of experimental innovation in science education provides us with several dependable lessons about what works, what helps children. The alphabet-soup programs illustrate the benefits of inquiry-based experiences: children's achievement, attitudes, and skills improved over traditional text-based programs with teacher-centered instruction. Even so, textbooks remain the most used form of curriculum in elementary and middle school science.

Researchers do not suggest that texts be completely abandoned in favor of nontext, hands-on programs. However, researchers and scholars warn of the inherent shortcomings of texts and the extraordinary interests of publishers to obtain adoptions in key states. This chapter offers practical recommendations for selecting, enhancing, and using science texts if that is your choice or only curriculum option.

Best practices have emerged from the research and extensive experiences gained from classroom use. These best practices are identified, and web-based and print resources that measure up are described. Bulletin boards and classroom displays can be effective tools for making these best practice materials visible to learners. Practical suggestions are offered. Communities also may abound in high-quality physical or human resources that can strengthen the science program and learning opportunities for children. The chapter concludes with tips for where to look for supplemental human resources and offers practical tips for preparing volunteers and visitors in order to effect a good match for your students' needs.

reflect and respond

1. Why do you think most teachers have historically reverted to teacher-centered instruction and authoritarian treatment of science through extensive uses of textbooks even though they may know about more effective alternatives?

2. What characteristics do you think a science textbook must have in order to address all of the National Science Education Standards? What do you consider to be the most important of these characteristics? Why?

3. Why do you think something as simple as resequencing the topics of a textbook is related to increased student science achievement?

4. What signs do you think indicate that a textbook should be avoided or considered?

5. Why do you think that reading enhancements typically found in textbooks (such as bold print for special words) could interfere with the goals of scientific literacy? Do you believe that the goals of scientific literacy run counter to the goals of general literacy? Why?

6. What do you think an effective science program would need to look like to satisfy the expectations of a best practice? How do you think you might be able to defend your viewpoint to a parent, teacher, or school administrator who might hold an opposing view?

7. Examine several different science textbooks or print resources for a selected grade level. What evidence do you find that shows inclusion of the criteria for effective programs?

8. Carefully study the course of study or curriculum guide for a school science program. Compare the program against the list of supported beliefs about effective school science programs. How does the program compare to the list?

9. Use the ideas from this chapter to develop your own form for reviewing science textbooks or trade books. Try your form and ask two other persons to do the same. How well did your reviews of the same material agree? What revisions may be necessary in your form? Why?

Where the Classroom Comes to Life

Explore—Video Homework Exercise. Go to MyEducationLab at www.myeducationlab .com and select the topic "Classroom and Community Resources," then watch the videos "Latino and Chicano Educational Materials" and "Science Resources," and respond to the questions below.

1. How are resources different from the science textbook? What criteria must a resource meet to be judged a high-quality resource?

NSES

TS-A

TS-D

TS-F

2. Select a lesson plan that you have recently developed. Did you use a resource other than the textbook to develop the lesson? If so, what kinds of resources did you use? What criteria did you use to determine whether the resource provides safe, standards-based lessons or information for you to use with your students?

3. Could you find a science trade book to help introduce the concept from the last science lesson plan you created? Identify at least one trade book that could be used with your lesson.

4. Is there a large population of non-English-speaking children in your classroom? Create a list of trade books that are available in more than one language. How could you use these in your science classroom?

5. How can you use the non-English-language trade books to engage children in your science lesson?

Enrich—Video Homework Exercise. Go to MyEducationLab and select the topic "Classroom and Community Resources," then watch the videos "Using Centers1" and "Using Centers2," and respond to the questions below.

NSES

TS-D

PR-D

1. How can science centers accommodate students with special needs?

2. How can you use a science center to encourage student inquiry?

3. If you had to create a science center, what would you put into your center and why?

Expand—Weblink Exercise

Science Literacy. Go to MyEducationLab Resources section and select "Weblinks," then click on the links for "Science Text Central", "Textbook Selection and Respect for Diversity in the US," and "Lawrence Hall of Science" for additional information on how to select the various resources, including texts, supplementary books, curricular materials, and web-based materials. Why is it important for teachers to know how to evaluate these resources?

NSES

TS-F

PD-A

PD-C

part two

Learning Cycle
Inquiry Lessons
for Teaching Science

Lessons and Activities to Meet the NSE Standards for Elementary and Middle School Science

The next three sections contain examples of commercial and public domain hands-on materials that have been *modified* to meet the content standards for elementary and middle school science. Section I is devoted to life science lessons, Section II includes physical science lessons, and Section III contains earth and space science lessons. Our intention is to show the techniques for modification, planning, and methods of teaching. The lessons and activities are a resource for ideas and an exemplar of modification techniques.

More than 150 life, physical, and earth and space science activities are found within 60 lessons designed to fit the science learning cycle format suggested in the text. A clearly written engaging question and concept statement can be found at the beginning of each lesson. Any concepts that are important to the lesson expansion are also identified in the beginning of the lesson.

The student outcomes or objectives are included in the evaluation phase of each lesson. Those of you who expect to see objectives or learner outcomes listed first in an activity are encouraged to look carefully at the evaluation phase of each lesson before starting the exploration phase.

Grade levels are suggested in the beginning of each lesson. Each teacher best knows his or her students' limitations. If, upon reading the lesson, you find the activities too difficult or too easy for your students, then by all means find a lesson that is more suitable for your students' ability levels.

You will not find a time limit on the lessons. Lessons using a science learning cycle format may take one class period or several class meetings. One lesson may represent a unit or just one piece of that unit. The length of time for each lesson will depend on the ability level of your students and the amount of detail for each activity. Generally, the lessons are organized so that the exploration and expansion phases take one or two class meetings and the explanation phase takes one class meeting. Questions designed to meet the goals of science in personal and social perspectives, science and technology, science as inquiry, and the history and the nature of science from the National Science Education Standards may be asked at any time during the lesson. Just because they are listed after the expansion phase does not mean that you have to wait until after expansion to ask them. The evaluation phase may also be given in parts, during or after the exploration phase, as part of the explanation phase, and during or after the expansion phase.

These lessons are designed to give your students a chance to explore a science concept thoroughly. Collect materials and try each activity before you present it to your students to make sure everything works according to the plan, to make you aware of any potential problem areas, to ensure that you have foreseen all safety requirements, and to give you an opportunity to correct problems before the activity is presented to the students.

Make sure that each student is aware of any safety precautions before engaging in the science activity. If certain skills are required before the students can engage in an activity, then spend the time to teach those skills before starting the new activity. Advance work will ensure the success of a lesson presented in a science learning cycle.

Specific National Science Education Standards developed within each lesson are identified in the Appendix in this text and can be found at the NSES website (http://www.nap.edu/readingroom/books/nses/html/6s.html).

Life Science Lessons

Lesson Name	NSE Content Standards for Life Science	Grade Level	Activities
Plants			
Plant Parts and Needs	Characteristics of Organisms	K–4	Plant Dig • Eggshell Planters • Food Storage
Osmosis and Capillary Action	Regulation and Behavior	5–8	Colored Carnations • Three-Way Split
Plant Photosynthesis	Population and Ecosystems	5–8	Radish Growth: Light versus Dark in a Bag • Radish Growth: Light versus Dark in Soil
Starch Exploration	Diversity and Adaptations	5–8	Microscopic Starch • Beans and Starch Grains
Animals			
Colors of Wildlife	Organisms and Environments	K–4	Animal Similarities and Differences • Create a Rainbow Animal
Bird Life	Life Cycles of Organisms	K–2	What Comes First: the Bird or the Egg? • The Developing Chick (or Duck)
Wildlife and Domesticated Animals	Organisms and Environments	K–4	Animal Needs • Domestic versus Wild Charades
A Bug's Life	Life Cycles of Organisms	3–4	Ordering Life Cycle Stages • Growing Mealworms
Crickets: Basic Needs of an Organism	Regulation and Behavior	5–8	Cricket Needs • Cricket Behavior
Animal Adaptations	Diversity and Adaptation	5–8	Mitten and Tweezer Beaks • Fish Adaptations
Owl Pellets	Populations and Ecosystems	5–8	Owl Pellet Dissection • Owl Research or Field Trip
Environment			
Humans and Trash	Organisms and Environment	K–4	Trash and Animals • Classroom Landfill and Recycling
Useful Waste	Populations and Ecosystems	5–8	Rating Garbage • Litter-Eating Critter • Making Paper
Litter in Our Waterways	Populations and Ecosystems	5–8	Sink-or-Float Litter • Plastic Food
Human			
Sense of Taste	Characteristics of Organisms	K–4	Buds and Tasters • Supertasters
Skeleton	Characteristics of Organisms	1–4	Bones Assembly Line • Newsprint Bone Bodies
Temperature Receptors on Skin	Structure and Function	5–8	Soaking Hands • Hot/Cold Receptor Mapping
Building Microscope Skills	Structure and Function	5–8	Microscope Use and Crystal Comparisons • Charcoal Crystals
Sex-Linked Genes	Reproduction and Heredity	5–6	Family Traits • Sex-Linked Traits
Passing of Traits	Reproduction and Heredity	7–8	What Traits Do You Share? • Inherited or Environmentally Altered?

Plant Parts and Needs

Grade Level ● K–4

Discipline ● Life Science

Engaging Question

What are the basic parts of a plant?

Materials Needed

For Exploration

large paper or large plastic bags	resource books on plants	crayons
spoons for digging, or a spade or shovel	poster paint	markers
white paper	art paper	

For Expansion

eggshells (halves or larger)	water
potting soil	sunlight or artificial light
mung beans	colored markers

Safety Precautions: Always have the proper adult:student ratio when taking the students away from the school campus. Make sure that the students are buddied up and that they are able to cross streets safely and know enough not to talk to strangers while walking to the dig site or while on the site.

Make sure all students can identify any poisonous plants at the dig site, such as poison ivy or poison oak. If large amounts of poisonous plants are in the area, it may be better to choose a different site.

Demonstrate to the students a safe method for digging up the plants, and make sure they practice what was demonstrated. Remind the students never to put anything in their mouths unless the teacher gives prior approval. Do not eat the plants!

Exploration

What will the students do?

Take the students on a walking field trip to an area near the school where plants can be dug up without harming the environment. Identify the plants the students may dig up, and then allow them time to dig, making sure they get most of the root systems. Instruct the students to put their plants in bags and bring them back to school. Back in class, ask the students to choose one of their plants and spread it out on a piece of white paper. Ask them to use the materials provided to draw pictures of their plants.

Plant Dig

Explanation

Concept: The basic parts of a plant are roots, stems, and leaves.

Once the students have drawn their pictures, provide them with resource books that identify other plants. Ask the students the following questions:

- How are these plants different from the plant in front of you?
- How are they the same?
- What do all of our plants have in common?
- Continue with this line of questioning until the students understand that the basic parts of a plant are roots, stems, and leaves. You may choose to use a sentence starter such as: The part of the plant anchoring it to the soil is called the _____ (root). The part of the plant growing up from the ground is call the _____ (stem). The part of the plant growing off of the stem, and used most often to identify the plant is called the _____ (leaf).
- Ask the students to return to the drawings they created of their plants. Ask them to label the roots, stems, and leaves in their drawings. At this time the teacher may provide the students with the common names for their plants, or ask the students if they already know what they dug up, or ask them to look through the resource books to identify their plants.

Expansion

Eggshell Planters

PROCESS SKILLS USED
▶ Observing
▶ Gathering data
▶ Recording data
▶ Interpreting data
▶ Manipulating materials

How will the idea be expanded?

Help the students collect eggshells (halves or larger). Ask the students to draw two eyes and a nose on their eggshells with colored markers. Provide potting soil so that the students can fill the shells with soil and sprinkle mung beans on top. Have them put a little more soil on top of the seeds. Sprinkle a small amount of water on the soil. Place the filled shells near the window. Challenge the students to observe the shells each day. When they discover bean sprouts appearing, have them draw a smile on the shell to complete the face.

Once the beans are well grown, ask the students to pull one of the sprouts out. Can you identify its root, stem, and leaves? Ask the students to describe what they did to help the plant grow from the bean seed to the sprout. What things were necessary for plant growth? Make a list on the board. Review with them why the items they identified are necessary for plant growth. Discuss the fact that leaves are necessary to plants because they are the place in the plant where food is created. The water and minerals are taken from the soil through the roots and brought up to the leaves. Gases from the air enter the plant through the leaf, and with the help of sunlight the leaves make food for the plant.

What additional ideas can be used for expansion?

Food Storage

The teacher can share with the students ways in which plants store food and what humans do with this knowledge. For instance, when food is stored, such as in nuts and seeds, the leaves drop off because they are no longer needed. Also, food is stored in various parts of plants. Provide the students with actual fruits, vegetables, and seeds (or pictures of them) to classify. Make a bulletin board

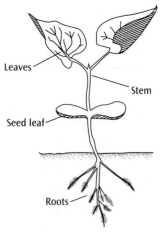

Leaves

Stem

Seed leaf

Roots

of drawings done by students of roots, stems, leaves, flowers, fruits, and seeds eaten by humans. Hang the pictures near the appropriate term. Some possibilities are roots (beets, carrots, radishes, sweet potatoes), stems (asparagus, celery, green onions), underground stems (onions, potatoes), leaves (lettuce, spinach, cabbage), flowers (artichokes, broccoli, cauliflower), fruits (apples, pears, tomatoes, peaches, plums, apricots), seeds (nuts, peas, beans).

Science in Personal and Social Perspectives

- What would your life be like without plants? Why do you need to take care of plants?
- How might taking care of plants help you to develop responsibility?
- Ask the students if any of their parents or grandparents have a garden or grow plants indoors. Discuss the special care these plants need. Discuss how large fields of plants can be watered.

Science and Technology

- Why do plants sometimes need to be fertilized?
- Do all plants have to be in soil in order to grow? Hydroponic farming does not use soil. Can you think of what it uses instead of soil to grow plants?

Science as Inquiry

- Why do you need to know what plants need to grow?
- Why is research done on growing plants?
- What must we do to keep the plants healthy?
- During what part of a plant's life cycle can it grow without sunlight? Why?

History and Nature of Science

- Discuss with the students jobs or professions that involve caring for plants, such as gardening, working as a forest ranger, selling vegetables in a grocery store, or working in a nursery or flower shop.
- Growing and caring for plants takes a lot of work; some of the people who do this are agronomists, horticulturists, florists, botanists, and nutritionists.
- Ask the students to have their parents help them discover what Luther Burbank and Gregor Mendel did to help us understand plant growth better.

Evaluation

Upon completing the activities, the students will be able to:
- identify the root, stem, and leaf on a complete plant;
- name the four things most plants need to live;
- when given potting soil, sunflower seeds, water, and a cup, demonstrate the steps necessary to grow and care for a plant; and
- when given a beet, spinach, and a piece of asparagus, identify which is a root, which a stem, and which a leaf.

Osmosis and Capillary Action

Grade Level ● 5–8
Discipline ● Life Science

CONCEPTS TO BE CONSTRUCTED

▶ Fluid is drawn up the stem of a plant by osmosis and capillary action.

▶ Fiber membranes run throughout a flower from the roots to the petals.

SCIENCE ATTITUDES TO NURTURE

▶ Curiosity
▶ Perseverance

Colored Carnations

PROCESS SKILLS USED

▶ Observing
▶ Predicting
▶ Reasoning
▶ Inferring
▶ Recording data

Engaging Question

How does water move through a plant?

Materials Needed

For Exploration (per student group)

   2 to 3 white, long-stem carnations   water
   food coloring   knife or sharp blade
   2 clear cups or glass beakers

Safety Precautions: Remind students to take care not to drop glass or beakers, which would increase the likelihood of cuts, and to use caution if using the knife or sharp blade.

Exploration

What will the students do?

Separate the class into groups of four to six students. Give each group two carnations and two beakers or clear cups. Fill the cups or beakers with water. Dissolve one color of food coloring in one cup and a different color in the other. Dark colors like red or blue work well. Take one of the carnations and cut a fresh end on the stem (this may be done by the teacher with students in each group assisting). After this cut, split the stem in half, starting a cut with the knife and further splitting it along the fibers without breaking them. Place each half of the stem in each beaker and observe the white flower. Record your observations over three-minute time periods for a total 30 minutes.

Explanation

Concept: Fluid is drawn up the stem of a plant by osmosis and capillary action.

Ask the students questions such as the following to help invent this concept:

• What did you observe during the first 3 minutes of this experiment?
• How long did it take before you observed any changes in your flower?
• What were these changes? Why do you think they happened?

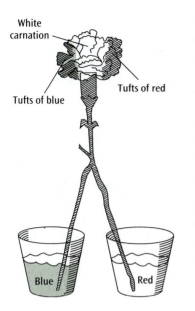

White carnation

Tufts of blue

Tufts of red

Blue

Red

The stems of green plants support the plants and hold up the leaves and flowers. Some plants, like this carnation, have thin, green stems. Other plants, such as trees, have thick wooden stems. The trunk of an oak tree is its stem. It holds heavy branches and thousands of leaves. Water and food move up and down the plant through the stem. Water moves through special tubes in the stem. The water goes from the roots to the leaves and other parts of the plant. Other tubes carry food from the leaves to the roots and other plant parts. The colored water in our experiment is drawn up the stem of the carnation by osmosis and capillary action. The water molecules diffuse through the fiber membranes from a lesser to a larger concentration of plant sap (osmosis). The fibers are so tiny that the adhesive force of the water molecules to the fiber walls becomes very great. This capillary force in combination with the osmotic pressure pulls the water up the flower.

Ask the students to summarize their understanding of capillary action by completing this sentence starter:

Capillary action is the process whereby _____.

Expansion

PROCESS SKILLS WILL BE USED
► Communicating
► Problem solving
► Experimenting
► Recording data

How will the idea be expanded?

When the stem is split three ways, it is very likely that the flower will be three colored. Ask the students to design an experiment to demonstrate this. This will show that the fibers must somehow run all the way from the stem to the petals of the flower. Encourage the students to experiment with how many ways they can get the stem to split to create as multicolored a flower as possible.

Three-Way Split

Ask the students to think about the following: What would happen if the stem were cut irregularly, such as diagonally? What if a cut was made that was jagged and cut across the fibers? How many other types of plants can be used to demonstrate this same phenomenon? Demonstrate this.

Science in Personal and Social Perspectives

- If you wanted to give someone a bouquet of carnations to celebrate the Fourth of July and could find only white ones, what could you do to some of them to get red and blue ones too? Do you think the same thing is done by florists?
- If you were to receive a bouquet of flowers and you wanted them to stay fresh for a long time, what should you do for them, and why?

Science and Technology

- How has knowledge of capillary action been used to create more efficient car engines?
- Artificial hearts and other organs are continuously being developed. How will osmosis and capillary action of blood affect the function of these artificial organs?

Science as Inquiry

- What force is pulling the colored solution up the stem of the carnation in this activity?
- What if the flower were placed in *clear* water? Would the liquid still be drawn up the stem? How could you tell?
- Could a plant live without a stem? Why or why not?

History and Nature of Science

- Can you name some people who work with plants?
- Why do you think it might be important for a farmer to understand plant growth? A florist? A grocer?
- Would you like to work in any of these occupations? Why or why not?
- How did the tradition of giving flowers on special occasions get started? Can you trace the history of this tradition? Can you trace the history of when flowers were artificially colored?

Evaluation

Upon completing the activities, the students will be able to:

- explain the purpose of splitting the stem in two during this lesson;
- demonstrate their knowledge of capillary action by explaining the process using a piece of celery, food coloring, a beaker, and water; and
- observe several plants in various stages of watering (underwatered, overwatered, just right) and explain why the plant looks as it does.

Plant Photosynthesis

Grade Level ● 5–8
Discipline ● Life Science

Engaging Question

How do plants feed themselves?

Materials Needed

For Each Student Group

Radish seeds	1 piece of aluminum foil
2 zipper storage bags (large size)	paper towels
2 paper towels	metric ruler

⚠️ *Safety Precautions:* Remind students not to put anything in their mouth and to avoid eating leaves or seeds of plants. Do not play with plastic bags and keep them away from the face.

Exploration

PROCESS SKILLS USED

▶ Predicting
▶ Observing
▶ Inferring
▶ Controlling variables
▶ Experimenting
▶ Reducing experimental error
▶ Analyzing

What will the students do?

Provide each group of students with some radish seeds, 2 zipper storage bags, 2 paper towels, and 1 piece of aluminum foil. Challenge the students to design a way in which they could use these materials to compare the growth of radish seeds. Explain to them that the variable to be manipulated in this experiment is light. All other factors must remain constant. The students must write up the method they plan to use; do not be concerned if the students change too many variables. This will be a valuable lesson to them, as they will soon discover by their experimental results. Once they have designed and written up their experimental methods, including predictions of potential outcomes, give them time to act on their design. Check their uncovered bags each day. When leaves begin to grow in the uncovered bag, uncover the covered bag and compare the two environments.

Radish Growth: Light versus Dark in a Bag

Explanation

Concept: Photosynthesis is a process in which chlorophyll-bearing plant cells, using light energy, produce carbohydrates and oxygen from carbon dioxide and water. Simply put, it is a way in which green plants use the sun's energy to make their own food.

Uncovered bag
(radish begins growing)

Covered bag
(with aluminum foil)

Have the students share the data they collected. Ask the following questions:

- Where did you place your bags in the room?
- Were they both put in the same place?
- Why is it important to make sure the bags were in the same area?
- What about the number of seeds you used? Was that kept constant?
- Is it important to keep the number of seeds the same? Why or why not?
- What happened inside both of your bags? Was it as you predicted?
- If so, can you explain why? If not, why not?
- Did the seeds sprout leaves in both the covered and uncovered environments? What color were they?
- Which environment appears more successful?
- What gives your skin color? (Pigment.) Do plants have pigment?
- Where did the green leaves come from? Does anyone know the name of the pigment that gives plants their green color? (Chlorophyll.)
- Do you think, based on your experimental results, you can determine what the chlorophyll does for the plant? (It makes food for the plant.)
- Complete this sentence: The process whereby the chlorophyll makes use of light energy to make food for the plant is called _____ (Photosynthesis).

Expansion

Radish Growth: Light versus Dark in Soil

PROCESS SKILLS USED
▶ Experimenting
▶ Hypothesizing
▶ Predicting
▶ Observing
▶ Analyzing
▶ Controlling variables
▶ Inferring
▶ Recording data

How will the idea be expanded?

Challenge the students to design another experiment, this time planting the seeds in soil instead of bags. Once again make light the manipulated variable. Predict the outcome, plan and record the methods, and act on your design. Once the seeds in the light begin to sprout, compare these results to the bag experiment. Were your predictions accurate? Why do you think you obtained the results you did? Did photosynthesis occur in the covered pot? The uncovered pot? Why? Continue to grow the plants and measure and record the results for one month.

Science in Personal and Social Perspectives

- How do plants help people survive on this planet?
- What would your life be like without plants?

Science and Technology

- Because they need land to live and grow things on, some people in Brazil are cutting down the tropical rain forests. Should this concern you? Why or why not? Do you think there is a technological solution to the problem of vanishing rain forests? Share your ideas.
- Of what advantage has hydroponic farming been to the people of the world?

- New concepts for further inquiry include growth rates, leaf shapes, deciduous versus coniferous, and so on.
- Can photosynthesis occur if a plant does not contain chlorophyll?
- Does photosynthesis take place in plants that grow on the ocean floor?

History and Nature of Science

- What impact has the farming industry had on our daily lives? On the lives of people throughout the world today and in the past 100 years?
- Who was Gregor Mendel (1822–1884)? How did his knowledge of photosynthesis open up an entirely new field of genetics?
- Can anyone become a landscape architect? What kind of background knowledge does a person in this field need?

Evaluation

Upon completing the activities, the students will be able to:

- when provided with two examples of the same plant, one grown in a shady environment and the other in a sunny one, identify which was grown where;
- observe plants growing around the classroom and accurately predict what will happen to the leaves if a small piece of paper is clipped over part of a leaf for one week; and
- read a problem about a science exploration and accurately determine which variable should be manipulated and which should be controlled.

Starch Exploration

Grade Level ● 5–8
Discipline ● Life Science

**CONCEPTS TO BE
CONSTRUCTED**

▶ Starches have a structure that
is unique for each type of
vegetable.

▶ Starch grain, hilum, slide
preparation, and microscope
use are concepts to be
expanded.

**SCIENCE ATTITUDES TO
NURTURE**

▶ Curiosity

▶ Perseverance

▶ Cooperation with others

Microscopic Starch

Engaging Question

Are all starches the same?

Materials Needed

For Each Student Group

microscope	rice that was soaked in water
5 slides	for at least 4 hours
1 scalpel	kidney beans
cover slips	corn kernels
tapioca	potatoes

Safety Precautions: Although the starches are edible, the students should be
discouraged from tasting them. Caution should be used around electrical outlets for
the electric microscopes. The bulb for the microscope will get hot. Students should be
reminded of safety techniques when using the scalpel.

Exploration

**PROCESS SKILLS WILL BE
USED?**

▶ Observing

▶ Predicting

▶ Comparing

▶ Manipulating materials

▶ Recording data

What will the students do?

The students will prepare slides of each of the given vegetables by using the scalpel to gently scrape a newly cut surface
on the vegetable. A very small speck of a single vegetable
should be placed on each slide with a drop of water. A cover
slip should be applied. The students should make predictions before observing the different starch grains. Will all of
them look alike, since they are all starches? What do you
think? Record this prediction. The students should observe each prepared slide under
the microscope and draw their observations of the starch from each vegetable.

Explanation

Concept: Starches have a structure that is unique for each type of vegetable.

Key questions to ask the students to help them come to these conclusions are:

- What did you observe as you looked at the potato grains?
- How were they different from the corn or rice?
- What did the bean and tapioca starch look like?
- Ask the students to compare their drawings to actual pictures of the various grains.
  Were you able to observe the detail these pictures show?
- Can you differentiate between parts of the grain?
- Ask the students to complete this concluding statement: While potatoes, rice, and
  beans are all considered starches, they differ in their _____ (structure).

What additional information will help develop the concept?

The students should find countless oval, ellipsoidal, or even triangular-shaped, almost transparent bodies that look like miniature oyster shells when they observe the potato starch grains. Since the grains are not flat, it may help if the students slowly rotate the fine adjustment on the microscope back and forth to get all the parts in focus. Usually, on the narrower end, the students will find a tiny dark spot that is not in the center of the grain. This is called the *hilum,* the oldest part of the starch grain, around which the remainder of the shell has grown layer by layer until fully formed. If you focus up and down at this point, you will find concentric lines or rings called *striations,* which indicate the layers where the grain has grown larger and larger.

Corn starch is different from potato. The grains may have an irregular globular shape or a very distinct polygonal shape. The shape will vary depending on the part of the kernel the students take their samples from—the horny or the floury portion. Corn starch has a central hilum that is usually a point but sometimes shows two, three, or four radiating clefts.

Rice starch grains are very small and many sided. They may be square, triangular, or pentagonal in shape. The hilum is not distinct, but in some grains a central portion appears brighter. This difference may be due to the drying of the grain. Ovoid or spherical shapes are usually due to a number of grains being compacted together.

Bean starch grains are usually ellipsoidal or kidney shaped. They have an irregular branching cleft running out from the center that appears black because of enclosed air.

Tapioca grains are usually circular or loaf shaped, depending on whether they sit on their flat surfaces or on their sides. The hilum is centrally located, usually coming to a point or small cleft. When students view the flattened surface, the hilum may appear triangular.

Corn starch

Rice starch

Bean starch

Tapioca starch

Expansion

Beans and Starch Grains

How will the idea be expanded?

- The students may brainstorm a list of other starch-containing foods. Obtain these foods, prepare slides, and check students' predictions by looking for evidence of starch grains. Are they similar to any of the grains previously identified? Are they different? What kind of starch do you think this food contains?
- The students may obtain several different kinds of beans. Pose a question: "Will all beans contain the same kind of starch grains, no matter the type of bean?" Allow the students to design an experiment to answer that question.

Science in Personal and Social Perspectives

- Do you think the differences in the starch grain will affect your ability to digest that starch? Why or why not?
- Are there any other kinds of plants that contain starch grains that humans do not eat? What are these? Why do you think we do not eat them?
- Why are starches important in a person's diet?

Science and Technology

- Why does the United States send starchy foods to underdeveloped countries? What kinds of conditions are necessary to grow starch-containing foods? Can modern technology do anything to help these underdeveloped nations to grow starches on their own?

- What kinds of products have modern industries created that make use of starches? How have these helped modern society? How have these hindered modern society?

Science as Inquiry

- Are all starch grains, no matter the plant they come from, the same? Will starch grains from many different varieties of potatoes look the same? Why or why not?
- What is the name of the oldest part of the starch grain? Does finding this structure under the microscope help in identifying the type of plant the starch grain came from?
- Did the process skills the students had to engage in to do these activities (predicting, manipulating materials, forming hypotheses, solving problems, recording data, making careful observations) enhance their overall academic growth?

History and Nature of Science

- Why do you think a person responsible for creating frozen dinners should understand that different vegetables have different starch structures?
- What kinds of jobs entail making careful observations and accurately recording what was observed?
- Do you think an insurance adjuster could benefit by learning the skills you utilized while participating in this lesson?

Evaluation

Upon completing the activities, the students will be able to:

- prepare a slide of starch grains;
- accurately draw starch grains observed under a microscope;
- identify with 80 percent accuracy the various starch grains and their sources; and
- explain in writing or orally why certain starches can be digested by humans while other starches cannot.

Colors of Wildlife

Grade Level • K–4

Discipline • Life Science

NATIONAL SCIENCE EDUCATION CONTENT STANDARDS–LIFE SCIENCE—GRADES K–4

Organisms and Environments

▶ An organism's patterns of behavior are related to the nature of that organism's environment, including the kinds and numbers of other organisms present, the availability of food and resources, and the physical characteristics of the environment. When the environment changes, some plants and animals survive and reproduce, and others die or move to new locations.

Engaging Question

Are animals all the same color? Why or why not?

Materials Needed

For the Entire Class

Magazines that have a wide variety of animal pictures, such as *National Geographic, Ranger Rick, National and International Wildlife,* and *Audubon.* Try to have magazines that can be cut up.

Construction paper, crayons or markers, scissors, glue, felt, cotton balls, natural materials from outdoors (acorns, leaves, grass); an appropriate storybook with a wide variety of different-colored animals in it will also help introduce the topic. Richard Buckley and Eric Carle's *The Greedy Python* (New York: Scholastic Books, 1992) is a good selection.

Safety Precautions: Remind students not to poke each other with the scissors and to use scissors only while seated.

CONCEPTS TO BE CONSTRUCTED

▶ Wildlife occurs in a wide variety of colors.
▶ Camouflage allows an organism to blend in or hide in its environment.

SCIENCE ATTITUDES TO NURTURE

▶ Curiosity
▶ A desire for reliable sources of information

Exploration

PROCESS SKILLS USED

▶ Observing
▶ Comparing
▶ Generalizing

What will the students do?

Introduce the lesson by reading the students a book such as *The Greedy Python.* Encourage the students to make note of the color of the python and of all the other animals it comes across. You will return to the ideas provided by the story later.

After the story and brief discussion about it, provide each student group with several wildlife magazines to look at. Ask the students to find pictures of animals, make observations about the animals, and compare the animals to one another. Create two lists on the board. Title one list *similarities;* the other *differences.* Ask the students to share their observations about the animals they found by providing information about the similarities and differences of the animals. Ask each student to cut out three different animals.

Animal Similarities and Differences

Explanation

Concept: Wildlife occurs in a wide variety of colors.

Refer back to the story you read. For instance, if *The Greedy Python* was used, you might ask these questions to help invent the concept:

• What animals did you see in the book?
• What colors were they?
• Why do you think the python was so successful in eating all the animals?
• Could a green python hide easily in a jungle?
• Hold up a variety of different-colored pieces of construction paper. Ask the students to identify the colors. Then ask the students to raise their hands if they cut out animals that match the color of the paper you are holding. Assist them to complete this statement about animals: Animals appear in a _____ (variety) of colors.

- Let the students help in gluing the animals on to the construction paper that matches the animal's color. Hang these animal pages around the room.
- Ask the student farthest from each picture if it is difficult to identify the animal on the page, that is, a red animal on a red piece of paper. Ask why he or she thinks it is difficult.
- How would this coloration help the animal survive in the wild? Draw the students to the conclusion that camouflage allows an organism to blend in or hide in its environment.

Expansion

Create a Rainbow Animal

PROCESS SKILLS USED
▶ Observing
▶ Manipulating materials
▶ Generalizing
▶ Comparing
▶ Communicating

How will the idea be expanded?

Use the materials from the material list to have the students create their own animal. The animals may be real, or students can make them up. Encourage the generalization that wild animals appear in a wide variety of colors and that the animals' colors and markings help them to survive. Encourage the students to look for rainbow animals—those that have three or more distinct colors on their bodies. Ask the students to share their creations with one another. Get them to communicate to one another how their animal can hide in its environment.

Science in Personal and Social Perspectives

- Where would you find _____? (Insert an animal name.)
- Do you think it is as important for a pet to blend in with its surroundings as it is for wild animals? Why or why not?
- Do we need to protect the environment where some animals live? Why or why not?
- What are some things society can do to protect animal environments?

Science and Technology

- Hunters used to wear only clothing that blended into the environment when they hunted. Today we see hunters wearing bright orange vests and bright orange hats. Why do you think the design of their clothing changed?

Science as Inquiry

- Where could you learn more about a particular animal?
- What are some ways in which color helps animals to survive?
- Besides color, what other kinds of things can animals use for camouflage?

History and Nature of Science

- Can you think of any jobs in which people work with or study animals?
- Can you think of any jobs in which people work with aquatic animals?
- Can you think of any animals that work? (Police dogs, seeing-eye dogs, sled dogs, horses, pigeons, animals that help on a farm.) How are these animals trained?

Evaluation

Upon completing the activities, the students will be able to:

- construct an animal using a variety of colors when given materials;
- explain how a cartoon animal relates to a real animal; and
- make a graph of animals that have one, two, or more colors.

Bird Life

Grade Level ● K–2

Discipline ● Life Science

NATIONAL SCIENCE EDUCATION CONTENT STANDARDS–LIFE SCIENCE— GRADES K-2

Life Cycles of Organisms

► Plants and animals have life cycles that include being born, developing into adults, reproducing, and eventually dying. The details of this life cycle are different for different organisms.

Engaging Question

What is a life cycle?

Materials Needed

For Exploration

reproducible pictures of birds at various stages of their life cycle, that is, egg, one to two days old, two weeks old, month old, adult. Enough copies to supply student groups of four or five students per group with a set.

computer software such as *Birds and How They Grow* or a video that shows birds as they develop in the nest

poster paper

crayons or markers

glue

For Expansion

access to an incubator with developing chicken or duck eggs and the ability to make daily observations

journal or computer-generated log to record observations

🛈 *Safety Precautions:* Stress the importance to students of respecting the developing bird and not banging on the sides of the incubator or creating excessive noise while making observations.

CONCEPTS TO BE CONSTRUCTED

► Wildlife occurs in a wide variety of colors.

► Camouflage allows an organism to blend in or hide in its environment.

SCIENCE ATTITUDES TO NURTURE

► Curiosity

► Cooperation with others

Exploration

PROCESS SKILLS USED

► Observing

► Comparing

► Predicting

What will students do?

Provide each student group with a stack of bird development pages. Have the students work in teams to color the various pictures of the bird in different stages of its life cycle. After they complete that task, ask them to lay out each of the pictures in front of the team. Ask them to describe what is different in each picture. (The children should be identifying differences such as that in one picture it was an egg and in the next it is a chick with little to no feathers, and then in the next it has a feathers but mostly soft fluffy ones, then in the adult picture it has a full set of feathers.)

If the students are capable of writing, ask them to record these differences on the poster paper under a heading titled "Differences." Ask them to then describe anything the pictures may have in common. (The children should be able to identify that once past the egg stage, each of the chickens has two legs, wings, a beak, etc.) Record those on the poster paper under the heading "Same." Then ask the students to decide as a group what picture comes first, then second, then third, and so on. Ask the students to arrange the pictures in order on a sheet of poster paper.

Which Comes First: The Bird or the Egg?

Explanation

Concept: Animals have a life cycle that includes being born, developing into an adult, reproducing, and eventually dying.

Ask the student teams to share items from their list labeled "Differences." Did each of the student teams come up with similar lists? Ask them to explain any observations that did not show up on all of the student team "Differences" lists.

Then ask the student teams to share items from their list labeled "Same." Did each of the student teams come up with similar lists? Ask them to explain any observations that did not show up on all of the student team "Same" lists.

Hang up the team posters with the ordered pictures in the front of the room. Ask the students to look at the posters and check for similar or different orders. Have them share their observations. If differences exist among the posters, ask them to predict why some teams pasted the pictures in one order and other teams in another.

Some sample questions to ask the students as they make their observations are:

- How are the birds in the various pictures similar? How are they different?
- Why do you think this team put the picture of the egg first? Or the picture of the adult bird, or the small bird?
- Which picture represents the bird before it is hatched?
- Which picture shows the bird just after it has hatched?
- Which picture shows the bird as an adult?

After the students respond to your questions, explain to them that these pictures represent various stages in the bird's life. Ask them to think about their own life. Do they remember seeing pictures of themselves as babies? Have they changed since they were babies? Just as they have changed, the pictures that they placed in order show how the bird will change as it gets older. You can use one of the posters to add labels to the pictures such as: egg, one day old, two weeks old, one month old, and adult. Give the student teams an opportunity to rearrange their posters in the order from egg to adult if theirs was out of order.

Ask the students to complete this sentence starter: A life cycle is a process that starts with _____ (being born), developing into an _____ (adult), then making more of you or _____ (reproducing) and then eventually _____ (dying).

Expansion of the Idea

**The Developing Chick
(or Duck)**

PROCESS SKILLS USED

▶ Observing

▶ Predicting

▶ Recording data

▶ Drawing conclusions

How will the idea be expanded?

This expansion activity can take place in your classroom if you have access to the materials and space permits or if your school has one central area for containing live animals that is more conducive to this type of activity. Do not do this activity if you do not feel comfortable growing live chicks or ducks or if your building does not have the facilities to accommodate growing birds. You may want to do this activity in conjunction with a teacher from a higher grade level so that older students could be responsible for making sure the needs of the birds are met as they hatch.

Another possibility is finding a website that has a live camera trained on an incubator with developing chicks or ducks. Several schools throughout the United States have made this service available. Search the Internet for such a site. This activity is often done during the spring of the year.

Still another possibility is for the teacher to create a "virtual bird" via a computer graphics program. "Grow" the bird over a period of days. Provide the students with its weight and height to enter into a database. Ask them to make predictions about changes in the bird's height and weight, amount of feather cover, beak size, and so forth over time.

Once you have established a source for observations, have your students engage in the following activity:

- Visit the incubator site the day the eggs are placed in the incubator. Have them record their observations in a journal. Start with "day 1" and continue beyond hatching. If space and time permit, allow the students to make observations throughout the rest of the year.

- Assign student teams different times during the day to go to the incubator to record their observations on a daily basis. Remind them not to tap on the incubator or to disturb the eggs in any way.

Throughout the time that the students are making their observations, bring the students together as a class on a weekly basis to discuss what they have observed. Have them make predictions about what they could expect to see happen next. If all of the eggs do not hatch, be prepared to discuss why. Offer possible reasons such as improper development, lack of essential needs such as heat to foster egg development, or even the possibility that the egg was not fertilized. If some of the chicks die, be prepared to have a conversation about this as a natural part of a life cycle. You will have to judge whether all of your students at this grade level are prepared for this.

Another possible activity to expand on the concept of animals having a life cycle that includes being born, developing into an adult, reproducing, and eventually dying—without going through the expense and time needed to hatch live chicks or ducks—is to show a variety of videotapes that take students through the life cycle of different animals. Conversations about the videotape should lead students to conclude that the details of a life cycle are different for different animals.

Science in Personal and Social Perspectives

- Could someone have expected you to stay the same as when you were born? Why is this a silly idea?
- If you live in a tiny house or apartment and you have an opportunity to get a puppy, would you choose one who had a mother that was a large dog? What do you know about the life cycle of a dog that might lead you to believe this is not a good idea?

Science and Technology

- How can an incubator help us hatch an egg if a mother bird is not around?
- If you don't see an animal in every stage of its life cycle, how do you know it went through different stages? What evidence do we use to prove that it did? Think about the evidence we used in our class activities to answer this question.

Science as Inquiry

- The observations and predictions the students make about the developing bird and conclusions that they draw provide them with early science inquiry skills. Gathering and organizing data extend their inquiry skills.

History and Nature of Science

- What do you think your doctor needs to know about the human life cycle to help you as you grow? Invite a pediatrician into your class to share ideas with your students.
- Visit a pet store. Have the students prepare questions to ask the shopkeepers about what they know about the life cycles of the different pets in their store and how that information helps them keep their pets healthy.

Evaluation

Upon completing the activities, the students will be able to:

- describe what a life cycle is and use it in the context of the life of a bird and the life of a human;
- order pictures in the proper sequence for the life cycle of an animal other than a bird or human; and
- label the stages of growth of a given animal from birth to adult.

▶ An organism's patterns of behavior are related to the nature of that organism's environment, including the kinds and numbers of other organisms present, the availability of food and resources, and the physical characteristics of the environment. When the environment changes, some plants and animals survive and reproduce, and others die or move to new locations.

CONCEPTS TO BE CONSTRUCTED

▶ Wildlife includes animals that are not tamed or domesticated.

▶ The concepts of endangered animals, extinct animals, threatened animals, and safe animals are important concepts to be expanded.

SCIENCE ATTITUDES TO NURTURE

▶ Curiosity

▶ Cooperation with others

▶ Openness to changing their minds when evidence for change is given

▶ Openness to questions about their own ideas

Animal Needs

Wildlife and Domesticated Animals

Grade Level ● K–4
Discipline ● Life Science

Engaging Question

What is wild?

Materials Needed

For Exploration

Pictures of both wild and domesticated animals, attribute blocks

⚠ *Safety Precautions:* Tell students not to throw attribute blocks and to use care when acting out animals in the expansion activity so as to not hit another student.

Exploration

PROCESS SKILLS WILL BE USED

▶ Observing

▶ Hypothesizing

▶ Inferring

▶ Categorizing

▶ Recording data

What will the students do?

Using attribute blocks, ask the students to place these blocks into two different groups. This activity will ensure that the students understand the concept of grouping. Next, ask the students to look around the room at the pictures hanging up. What do you observe in the pictures? (Animals.) Divide the class into groups of four to six. Provide them with pictures of both wild and domesticated animals (at least as many pictures as there are students in a group). Each student in the group will pick up an animal and record characteristics of the animal that make it different from any other. Some prompting questions could be: Where do they live? How do they get their food? Are they dependent on humans for their survival? Once each child in the group has listed the characteristics of the animal he or she chose, ask the students to decide how they could put their animals into two different groups. Once they make that decision, then divide the animals.

Explanation

Concept: Wildlife includes animals that are not tamed or domesticated.

Ask the students questions such as the following to help invent this concept:

- How did your group decide to divide your animals?
- What characteristics of your animals led you to this decision?
- How do the animals in one of your groups get their food?
- How do the animals in your other group get their food?

- Do either of your groupings separate the animals into whether they rely on humans for their survival?
- On the basis of the students' responses to the questions above, ask them to complete these statements: Animals that do not rely on humans for survival and that are neither tame or owned are called _____ (wild). Animals that rely on humans for their survival are called _____ (domesticated).

Expansion

Domestic versus Wild Charades

How will the idea be expanded?

PROCESS SKILLS WILL BE USED
▶ Observing
▶ Classifying
▶ Analyzing
▶ Inferring
▶ Communicating

Ask the students to choose an animal, and without telling anyone else in the class, write down the name of that animal. The students may choose one from a picture in the room or think of one on their own. Divide the class in half, and collect their listed animals in two groups. Explain to the students how the game of charades is played. Have students from one half of the class pick from a pile of animals that came from the other half of the room and vice versa. Ask the students to look at the name of the animal on the card, and without saying what is written on the card, act out the behaviors of that animal for the students on your side of the room to guess. Write the words *domestic* and *wild* on the board. Once the students guess which animal was acted out, ask the student who just acted out the animal to decide whether that animal should be listed as domestic or wild. Make sure all of the students agree on the listing before acting out the next animal.

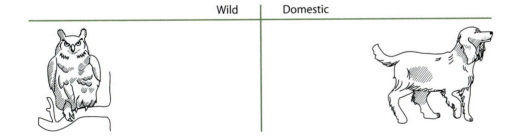

Wild	Domestic

Science in Personal and Social Perspectives

- Name some domesticated animals that we could find in your neighborhood. What would the neighborhood be like if these animals were wild?
- What do you think life would be like if any of the wild animals we acted out no longer existed; that is, if they became extinct?
- What do you think would happen if you tried to tame a wild animal?
- Why is a wildlife preserve important to our society?
- Can the study of wildlife give us any ideas about how people behave? If so, how? If not, why not?

Science and Technology

- Propose a method to change an animal from wild to domestic.

Science as Inquiry

- What important facts must we remember when dealing with wildlife?
- What things are important to remember when taking care of pets?
- What is the difference between a wild and a domesticated animal?

History and Nature of Science

- What type of job requires knowledge of wildlife or requires someone to work with wild animals?
- Interview a zookeeper. What special skills does someone in this line of work need?
- What kind of jobs would have to be created if wildlife started taking over our community?
- Choose a domesticated animal. Search throughout history to determine when it first became domesticated and why.

Evaluation

Upon completing the activities, the students will be able to:

- give two examples of a wild animal;
- give two examples of a domestic animal; and
- list the characteristics of a wild and a domestic animal; and
- draw a picture of an animal and identify it as wild or domestic by drawing an appropriate habitat for it.

A Bug's Life

Grade Level ● 3–4

Discipline ● Life Science

Engaging Question

Are the life cycles of *all* animals the same?

Materials Needed

For Exploration

a set of reproducible images of a black beetle's life cycle from egg, larva (the mealworm), pupa, and adult (the black beetle)

a set of reproducible images of a dog's life cycle from birth to adult

a set of reproducible images of a butterfly's life cycle from egg larva (the caterpillar), pupa, and adult (the butterfly)

For Expansion

mealworms to raise as part of the expansion activity; available at a pet shop or bait store

materials to raise the mealworm in, such as a large container with a lid and food like bran, flour, dried bread, cracker crumbs and oatmeal; a slice of apple or carrot will be needed to provide humidity

journal or computer-generated logs to record observations and other data student teams identify as important to collect

⚠ *Safety Precautions:* Tell students that care should be used in handling the mealworms and to avoid placing hands in their mouth after working with the insects. Remind them to wash their hands immediately after handling any insects.

▶ Plants and animals have life cycles that include being born, developing into adults, reproducing, and eventually dying. The details of this life cycle are different for different organisms.

▶ Plants and animals closely resemble their parents.

CONCEPTS TO BE CONSTRUCTED

▶ Animals have a life cycle that includes being born, developing into an adult, reproducing, and eventually dying. The details of a life cycle are different for different animals.

▶ Plants and animals closely resemble their parents.

SCIENCE ATTITUDES TO NURTURE

▶ Curiosity

▶ Cooperation with others

▶ Openness to questions about their own ideas

Exploration

PROCESS SKILLS USED

▶ Observing

▶ Comparing

▶ Drawing conclusions

▶ Recording data

▶ Making hypotheses

What will students do?

Have the students work in teams of two or three. First, give the student teams the pictures that represent the life cycle of a black beetle. Do not give them in order from birth to adult. Just ask the student teams to arrange them in that order, if indeed the students think they all belong together. Time how long it takes the teams to put these in order. Stop this activity once each team has recorded how long it took them to come to an agreement as to the proper placement.

Then without explanation ask the students to set those pictures aside. Now provide them with the pictures that represent the life cycle of the butterfly. Once again, do not give the pictures to the students in any kind of order. Again ask the student teams to arrange them in order from birth to adult if, indeed, they think all of the pictures belong together. Again time how long it takes for the student teams to put these in order from birth to adult.

Ordering Life Cycle Stages

Do this same activity a third time, making use of the pictures that represent the life cycle of a dog.

Which took the longest: arranging the life cycle of the black beetle, the butterfly, or the dog? Ask the students to discuss within their groups possible reasons for the time differences.

Explanation

Concept: Animals have a life cycle that includes being born, developing into an adult, reproducing, and eventually dying. The details of a life cycle are different for different animals.

Ask the students as a class to share their reasons for why it may have taken them longer to order one animal's life cycle than another. Ask questions such as:

- Did each of these animals start its life cycle in a similar form?
- At what stage or stages of the life cycle do these animals look different?
- Why was it easier to arrange the life cycle of one animal than another?

The students will be sharing responses such as the animals they are more familiar with are easier to arrange in order from birth to adult. Animals that have basically the same form from birth to adult are easier to arrange. After the students discuss their observations, ask them to summarize what they have learned by completing this statement: The life cycles of bugs are similar to dogs in that they _____ (include being born, developing into an adult, reproducing, and dying). The life cycles of bugs are different from dogs in that _____ (as they move from being born to an adult their bodies change in that what they start out as and what they look like as an adult are totally different).

Expansion of the Idea

Growing Mealworms

PROCESS SKILLS USED
▶ Observing
▶ Predicting
▶ Recording data
▶ Drawing conclusions

How will the idea be expanded?

Provide each student team with the materials you assembled for the expansion phase of this activity. Give the students ample time to make observations of the mealworm. Ask them to recall the exploration activity and to predict what the mealworm will look like as it becomes an adult. Once their observations of the mealworm are complete, guide them in constructing a growth chamber for their mealworms. This is done by placing in a large container with a lid (such as a 2-pound coffee can or a plastic shoe storage container with lid) the food mixture of bran, flour, dried bread, cracker crumbs, and oatmeal. By placing an apple slice or carrot in the container, humidity will be added to the environment. Place several mealworms into the container, and store it in a warm area (between 75° and 80° F). Have students record the number of mealworms placed into the container. Light is not needed for growth, so a warm, dark cabinet or storage area in the classroom will be an ideal growth area. Students should check the container every few days, adding more food and apple or carrot.

Ask the students to collect information on changes in the mealworm over time. Have any mealworms begun to change body form? What do they now look like? How many mealworms are now in the container? Are there other stages in the black beetle's life cycle present? Count and record how many of each.

Since a mealworm will stay in the larval stage for about six months, chances are that the container may eventually contain a form of the black beetle in each stage of its life cycle. It will depend upon the ages of the mealworms when obtained from the supplier. Ideally, you would like to find that within the growth chambers, there are black beetles as larvae, pupae, and adults within a few weeks.

Ask the students to explain why their mealworm counts changed. What happened to those mealworms? Do all of the adults look alike? Could you tell one adult from another? Is that an easy thing to do? Ask the students to find within their growth chamber an example of the black beetle in each stage of the beetle's life cycle. Help them to conclude that each larval mealworm ended up looking like its parent, and that each generation of black beetles that follows will look just like their parents in the adult stage of their life cycle.

Science in Personal and Social Perspectives

- How does having an understanding of the life cycle of an insect help protect your home from being overrun with insects?
- What "bug" problems do you commonly face? During what stage of the bug's life cycle does that bug "bug" you?

Science and Technology

- What kinds of things have cities done to control insect populations like flies or mosquitoes? At what stage of their life cycle are they easier to control?
- Do you think it is a good idea to use chemicals to control insect populations? Why or why not? What kind of an impact will continued use of chemicals have on future insect populations?

Science as Inquiry

- Design an experiment to determine at which stage in an insect's life cycle it feeds and at which stage it reproduces. Use the mealworms and black beetles to carry out your planned experiments. Be sure to apply proper scientific methods such as controlling variables, making consistent observations, and accurately recording data for later analysis.

History and Nature of Science

- In the late 19th century, growers in California brought the ladybug over from Australia to help battle tiny insects that threatened orange groves. The ladybugs fed on the smaller insects to control their population. Today there are several beneficial insects used by gardeners. These include ladybugs, mealworms, parasitic nematodes, parasitic wasps, praying mantises, green lacewings, and predatory mites. Identify at what stage of the insects' life cycle they are most beneficial. Using an electronic resource such as a website or CD-ROM, find pictures of these insects in the most beneficial stage of their life cycle and prepare a multimedia presentation that describes how they benefit gardeners.

Evaluation

Upon completing the activities, the students will be able to:

- describe the life cycle stages of an insect and explain how these differ from the life cycle stages of a mammal;
- accurately predict what the offspring will look like when given a picture of an early stage in the life cycle of a given organism (Do the things you learned about animals and their life cycles hold true for plants? Why or why not?); and
- design an experiment to show how plants go through a life cycle and demonstrate that each new plant will look like its parent.

Crickets: Basic Needs of an Organism

Grade Level ● 5–8
Discipline ● Life Science

NATIONAL SCIENCE EDUCATION CONTENT STANDARDS–LIFE SCIENCE— GRADES 5–8
Regulation and Behavior

▶ All organisms must be able to obtain and use resources, grow, reproduce, and maintain stable internal conditions while living in a constantly changing external environment.

CONCEPTS TO BE CONSTRUCTED

▶ All organisms, no matter the size, have a basic need for food, water, shelter, and space in a suitable arrangement.

▶ Living organisms respond to stimuli from their environment. Animals in captivity must be able to adapt to their environments in order to survive.

SCIENCE ATTITUDES TO NURTURE

▶ Curiosity

▶ Cooperation with others

Engaging Question

What are the basic needs of all living things?

Materials Needed

For Each Group of Students

1 terrarium
1 plastic pint container with
   screen top
1 hand lens

1 piece of black construction paper
seeds (6 each of clover, grass,
   wheat, radish, and bean)

For the Entire Class

Eric Carle's *The Very Quiet Cricket* (New York: Philomel Books, 1990); 4 plastic bags, each containing eighteen crickets; felt pen, paper clips, tape or staples, chart paper.

🛈 *Safety Precautions:* Remind the students to wash their hands after handling the crickets, and not to eat the seeds or put them in their mouth and not to poke each other with the staples or paper clips.

Exploration

Cricket Needs

PROCESS SKILLS USED

▶ Observing
▶ Recording data
▶ Experimenting
▶ Drawing conclusions

What will the students do?

Begin the lesson by doing something that students of this age level would never expect. Read very animatedly *The Very Quiet Cricket* by Eric Carle. Although not age appropriate, the story is very effective in getting students to think about the task to come. Divide the class into research groups of four. Allow library time for the students to find answers to the following questions: What is necessary for the survival of a cricket? Are their needs similar to human needs? What requirements do they have for food, water, and shelter? Can many crickets live in a small space? How many can live comfortably together?

Explanation

Concept: All organisms, no matter the size, have a basic need for food, water, shelter, and space in a suitable arrangement.

Ask the student groups to report on the results of their inquiries. Through their reporting, continue to question them to clarify the results of their research efforts. Questions for clarification may include:

- What did you discover about the crickets' eating habits?
- What kind of habitat does a cricket survive in best?
- Does a cricket need water?

Help the students to draw the conclusion that all organisms, no matter the size, have a basic need for food, water, shelter, and space in a suitable arrangement by asking them to complete this sentence starter: An animal's habitat will provide it with its basic needs of _____ (food, water, shelter, and space in a suitable arrangement).

Expansion

PROCESS SKILLS WILL BE USED

▶ Observing
▶ Communicating
▶ Problem solving
▶ Formulating models
▶ Classifying
▶ Questioning
▶ Hypothesizing

How will the idea be expanded?

Set up a terrarium with a few crickets living in it. Encourage the students to make observations about the crickets in the terrarium as they are collecting their data. Assign each of the different research groups from the exploration phase of this lesson one of the following tasks so that they will understand the behavior of a cricket:

Cricket Behavior

- Take a cricket from the terrarium. Place it on a smooth surface and then on a rough surface. Watch the cricket for three to five minutes on each surface. Record your observations. Which surface causes the greater obstacle to movement? Why do you think this is so? Try manipulating the environment in other ways: hot versus cold surface or light versus dark conditions. Return the cricket to the terrarium.
- Obtain a shoebox. Cut a hole on one side about the size of a small flashlight. Cut a hole on the other side just big enough for your eye to peep inside. Take a cricket from the terrarium. Place the cricket in the dark end of the shoebox (opposite end from the flashlight hole), and put on the lid. Cover the flashlight hole with your hand in an effort to make the box as dark as possible inside. Watch the cricket's behavior for five minutes. Record your observations. Now place a small flashlight in the hole and turn it on. Observe the cricket for another five minutes. Record your observations. Were there any differences in the cricket's behavior when the light was on versus when it was off? If so, why do you think this occurred? Return the cricket to the terrarium.
- Take a cricket from the terrarium and place it in a shoebox. As a group, decide on three different kinds of food you think a cricket might like to eat. Place the three types in front of the cricket. Make sure you keep accurate records about the amount of food placed in the box. It may be important to weigh each food choice. Put the lid back on the box. Place the box in a dark, quiet place in the classroom. Ask the group members to make predictions about which food type they think the cricket will choose. Make and record observations every thirty minutes for one school day. Did the cricket choose the food you predicted? Why or why not? Do you think more than one cricket should be used in this experiment? Why or why not? Return the cricket to the terrarium.

Ask each of the different research groups to report on its findings. Encourage all the students to communicate to one another exactly what they did, why they did it, and what they discovered as a result. Help them in their discussion to come to the following conclusions: Living organisms respond to stimuli from their environment. Animals in captivity must be able to adapt to their environment in order to survive.

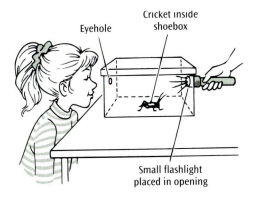

Eyehole

Cricket inside shoebox

Small flashlight placed in opening

Science in Personal and Social Perspectives

- What legends exist about crickets? How and why have these been handed down through generations?
- What could you do for an animal if it has lost its mother? How could you help it survive without removing it from its environment?
- Why would it be important for you to know how to care for an animal in a situation like that?

Science and Technology

- Do you think fluctuations in cricket populations could tell us something about what people are doing to their environment? How would you design an experiment to determine what humans are doing to their environment?
- Do you think it is important that humans understand something about other animals no matter what their size? Why or why not?

Science as Inquiry

- Why does a terrarium need to have soil in it?
- Can a cricket drink water out of a bowl? Why does a cricket rub its wings?
- What are the basic needs of a cricket?

History and Nature of Science

- What kinds of occupations deal with a variety of animal species? (Game wardens, zookeepers, wildlife officers.)
- What would it be like if there were no one who understood the basic needs of certain animals? Was there ever a time in history when our lack of understanding affected the life of an animal? Provide an example.
- What does an entomologist do?

Evaluation

Upon completing the activities, the students will be able to:

- design and build their own terrarium for a cricket, making sure that it is designed to meet all of the cricket's basic needs;
- pick one animal and determine its basic needs for food, shelter, water, and space;
- pick a domesticated animal such as a chicken, dog, or hamster and describe the adaptations necessary for that animal to survive in the wild; and
- participate in a discussion of how humans would have to adapt in order to survive in the wild.

Animal Adaptations

Grade Level ● 5–8
Discipline ● Life Science

Engaging Question

What is so good about an adaptation?

Materials Needed

For Exploration

Enough tweezers and mittens so that each student in the class has one or the other of these. Numerous pipe cleaners, paper wads, and strips of construction paper to serve as "food" for the birds. Place pictures of various kinds of birds with different feeding habits all around the classroom.

For Expansion

Pictures of various kinds of fish placed around the room. The fish should demonstrate such differences in coloration as light-colored belly, dark upper side, mottling, vertical stripes, or horizontal stripes. Differences in body shape could be flat bellied, torpedo shaped, horizontal disc, vertical disc, or hump-backed. The mouth shapes may be an elongated upper jaw, duckbill jaws, an elongated lower jaw, an extremely large jaw, or a sucker-shaped jaw. A fish tank with fish that live at different levels of the tank would also serve to emphasize the secondary concept. Art materials such as crayons, markers, scissors, scrap material, construction paper, chalk, old buttons, yarn, pieces of felt, and so on are also needed.

Safety Precautions: Remind the students to walk, not run, while participating in the bird-feeding activity. Use caution with scissors in the expansion activity.

► Biological evolution accounts for the diversity of species developed through gradual processes over many generations. Species acquire many of their unique characteristics through biological adaptation, which involves the selection of naturally occurring variations in populations. Biological adaptations include changes in structures, behaviors, or physiology that enhance survival and reproductive success in a particular environment.

CONCEPTS TO BE CONSTRUCTED

► The shape of a bird's beak determines the type of food it will eat. This is one form of adaptation.

► Many animals have developed specialized adaptations in order to survive their environments. Fish utilize adaptive coloration, body shape, and mouth placement to help them survive in different aquatic environments.

SCIENCE ATTITUDES TO NURTURE

► Skepticism

► A desire to be shown alternative points of view or have them proven

Mitten and Tweezer Beaks

Exploration

PROCESS SKILLS USED
► Observing
► Inferring
► Experimenting
► Analyzing

What will the students do?

Distribute the pipe cleaners, paper wads, and paper strips throughout the room. Place some on the floor and some of them in harder-to-get-to places. Each student will choose the type of "beak" (mitten or tweezers) that he or she wants to use. The students will explore a bird's eating habit by trying to pick up the different types of food using the beak they chose.

Explanation

Concept: The shape of a bird's beak determines the type of food it will eat. This is one form of adaptation.

Ask the students questions such as the following to help invent this concept:

• Choose two students that used different kinds of beaks (i.e., mitten and tweezer). Why was it easier for _____ (student's name) to pick up the paper strips than _____ (a different student's name)?

- What kind of beak did each have?
- Do you see any pictures of birds in this room with a beak that would work like the tweezers? Can you think of any others?
- What do you think they use these beaks for?
- What types of food can a bird with a beak like a pair of mittens eat?
- Why do you think some birds eat one kind of food and others a different type? Do you think it would be to a bird's advantage if it could eat a different kind of food than that for another type of bird? For instance, a robin will eat worms, but it won't eat nectar like a hummingbird, yet you can find both of them living in the same area.
- Ask the students to complete this summary statement: Many varieties of birds can survive in one area because they eat different kinds of food. Their ability to eat different foods has to do with the shape of the _____ (beak). Having a different beak shape is an example of an _____ (adaptation).

Expansion

Fish Adaptations

PROCESS SKILLS USED
▶ Hypothesizing
▶ Observing
▶ Questioning
▶ Classifying
▶ Analyzing
▶ Inferring
▶ Manipulating materials
▶ Communicating

How will the idea be expanded?

The students will look at pictures of different types of fish and try to categorize them in three different ways: coloration, mouth shape, and body shape. A discussion should ensue on how these three classifications are important adaptations to ensure the fish's survival in its environment. After the discussion, the teacher should assign each student or group of students a particular combination of adaptations from each of the three groups, such as mottled coloration, torpedo body shape, and sucker-shaped jaw. Ask the students to use the art materials that you provided to create fish with those three types of adaptations. Ask them to create environments in which fish with those adaptations could survive. Have the students share their creations.

Science in Personal and Social Perspectives

- What are some ways in which people have adapted to their environment?
- What are some ways in which we share our environment with the birds? Fish?
- What has society done to improve the lives of animals in their habitat?

Science and Technology

- If you were to make a hummingbird feeder, would it be useful to know the type of beak this bird has? Why?
- What are some disadvantages of taking an animal out of its natural habitat?

- Could an animal adapt quickly enough to survive in a new environment? Why or why not?
- Choose an animal. Outline all of the problems that would need to be overcome for that animal to survive in a different habitat.

Science as Inquiry

- Can an animal's inability to adapt to rapid changes in its environment lead to its extinction? What other events may lead to the extinction of an animal?
- Is there any one species of bird that has a beak that allows it to winter in an area with a relatively cold climate? What advantage does this beak shape have over any other?
- If you were to buy a fish from a pet store and wanted one that would clean the food off the gravel in the bottom of your fish tank, what kind of a mouth shape would it have?

History and Nature of Science

- How important is it for a zookeeper to understand the special feeding adaptations many animals have developed? Why?
- If you were working at a nature center and were responsible for creating an aquarium that made use of fish found at a local lake, what would you need to know about the local fish to make your display enjoyable for center visitors?

Evaluation

Upon completing the activities, the students will be able to:
- identify bird beak adaptations and explain how these contribute to the survival of the bird;
- design an ideal habitat for an animal of their choice, emphasizing that animal's special adaptations for survival in its environment; and
- explain why several species of fish can live together in one lake without competing with one another for food.

NATIONAL SCIENCE
EDUCATION CONTENT
STANDARDS–LIFE SCIENCE—
GRADES 5–8

Populations and Ecosystems

▶ Populations of organisms can be categorized by the function they serve in an ecosystem. Plants and some microorganisms are producers—they make their own food. All animals, including humans, are consumers, which obtain food by eating other organisms.

▶ Decomposers, primarily bacteria and fungi, are consumers that use waste materials and dead organisms for food. Food webs identify the relationships among producers, consumers, and decomposers in an ecosystem.

CONCEPTS TO BE CONSTRUCTED

▶ The owl coughs up, or regurgitates, owl pellets which contain the undigested parts of animals eaten by the owl, such as hair and bones.

▶ Digestion and eating habits are important concepts to be expanded.

SCIENCE ATTITUDES TO NURTURE

▶ Curiosity

▶ Willingness to withhold judgment until all evidence is presented

Owl Pellets

Grade Level ● 5–8
Discipline ● Life Science

Engaging Question

What is an owl pellet?

Materials Needed

For Each Student Group

One owl pellet, which may be obtained through a local division of your state department of natural resources or wildlife. Sterilized pellets can be ordered through a supplier. One dissecting kit, glue, handouts of the skeleton of a vole, mouse, or rat.

⚠ Safety Precautions: Remind the students to use caution when handling the sharp dissecting tools.

Exploration

PROCESS SKILLS USED

▶ Observing

▶ Predicting

▶ Inferring

▶ Hypothesizing

What will the students do?

Provide each pair of students with an owl pellet and a dissecting kit. Ask the students what they think the pellet is. How was it created? What do they think they will find as they carefully pick the matted hair away from the owl pellets? After student predictions are shared, instruct the students to keep everything they find as they pick away carefully at the pellets. Try to reconstruct a skeleton of a rodent, using the picture as a guide.

Explanation

Owl Pellet Dissection

Concept: The owl coughs up, or regurgitates, owl pellets, which contain the undigested parts of animals eaten by the owl, such as hair and bones.

Ask the students questions such as the following to help invent this concept:

• What kind of rodent do you think your owl ate?
• Did you find the remains of more than one kind of rodent?
• What do these findings tell you about the type of food an owl eats?
• What is an owl capable of digesting?
• On the basis of your dissection of the owl pellet, tell me what an owl pellet is. An owl pellet is _____ (coughed up or regurgitated by the owl. It contains the undigested parts of the animals eaten by the owl).

PROCESS SKILLS USED

▶ Observing
▶ Communicating
▶ Problem solving
▶ Formulating models
▶ Recording data

How will the idea be expanded?

Owl Research or Field Trip

- Take the students on a field trip to an area where owls are known to nest. Look carefully on the ground around the area. What do you expect to find to indicate to you that owls may be in the area? How are pellets different from owl scats?
- Invite a wildlife specialist to bring an owl to visit your classroom to discuss its characteristics and habitat. Ask your class to prepare in advance sound questions to ask the visitor about the owl.
- Assign each student team to write a report about a different species of owl. This report should include such things as where it is found and its life span, habitat, and food preferences.

Science in Personal and Social Perspectives

- What might happen to owls if humans disrupt their habitats?
- What are some ways that owls are adapted to their environment?
- How are we adapted to our environment?
- What has technology done to improve the lives of animals in their habitats? What could society do?

Science and Technology

- What are some disadvantages of taking an animal out of its natural habitat and placing it in another environment?
- If you came across some bones of an animal, how could you go about identifying which animal they came from?

Science as Inquiry

- What special needs does an owl have in order to survive in any habitat?
- Why were the bones and hair of the rodents not digested by the owls?

History and Nature of Science

- What kinds of professions are dedicated to ensuring animal safety? What kinds of careers endanger animals?
- In this activity you found the bones of a rodent and reconstructed them to determine which rodent it was. Do any other careers expect you to take evidence and reconstruct it to find answers? Which ones?

Evaluation

Upon completing the activities, the students will be able to:

- construct a food chain, placing the owl at the highest level;
- dissect an owl pellet and use the bones found to reconstruct the skeleton of a rodent; and
- speculate on how information provided through owl pellet dissection can assist people in raising the survival rate of many owl species.

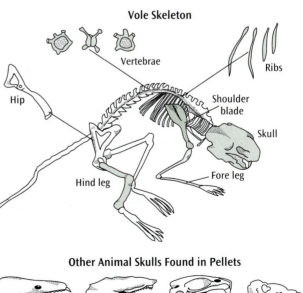

Vole Skeleton

Vertebrae

Ribs

Hip

Shoulder blade

Skull

Hind leg

Fore leg

Other Animal Skulls Found in Pellets

Shrew · Mole · Rat · Sparrow

▶ Humans depend on their natural
and constructed environments.
Humans change environments in
ways that can be either beneficial
or detrimental for themselves and
other organisms.

**CONCEPTS TO BE
CONSTRUCTED**

▶ Human-made trash affects all
living matter.

▶ Recycling can decrease the
amount of waste humans
create.

**SCIENCE ATTITUDES TO
NURTURE**

▶ A desire for reliable sources of
information

▶ Curiosity

**Trash and
Animals**

Humans and Trash

Grade Level ● **K–4**

Discipline ● **Life Science**

Engaging Question

What *harm* does my trash cause?

Materials Needed

For Exploration

Selected (clean) trash, drawing paper, crayons, glue, stapler. Enough of these materials
should be collected so that each child in the class can actively participate in the lesson.
One large box filled with a piece of trash for each child, five or six medium-sized boxes
that can be labeled for glass, paper, plastic, aluminum, and so on.

Safety Precautions: Remind the students to use caution when handling trash,
not to put fingers in mouth, and to wash hands thoroughly after handling trash.

Exploration

PROCESS SKILLS USED

▶ Questioning

▶ Inferring

▶ Predicting

▶ Hypothesizing

▶ Communicating

▶ Manipulating materials

What will the students do?

Before doing this lesson with the class, collect enough trash
so that each child in the class may have several pieces to
choose from. Be sure that any trash that is chosen is free of
rough edges, broken glass, or sharp points so that the children will not be harmed during the lesson. Wash out any
plastic bags and cans used as trash.

Ask each student to think of an animal and draw a picture of it.

Supply the students with a large selection of trash. Ask the students to choose one
piece that particularly intrigues them. Ask the students to draw a picture of how that
piece of trash would hurt their animal if the animal came across that piece of trash while
outside. Ask the students to attach the piece of litter to their picture. Each student
should be allowed to share the picture with the class, explaining how his or her animal
was harmed by the piece of trash he or she chose. Encourage the students to act out how
the animals moved both before and after the trash affected them.

Explanation

Concept: Human-made trash affects all living matter.

Ask the students questions such as the following to help invent this concept:

- What is wrong with leaving our garbage just anywhere?
- How do you think trash can hurt animals besides the ways each of you just
  shared? The teacher can give such examples as: How many of you have been

fishing? What happens when your line gets stuck? Just as it tangles up in the weeds, if you simply cut the line and leave it in the water, it can get tangled on ducks' necks, legs, and beaks. It can keep them from walking, flying, and swimming. Sometimes it may become wrapped around their beak, and they starve to death.

- Hold up a plastic ring from a six-pack of pop cans. Could this hurt an animal? If so, how? Explain how fish or birds can get tangled up in it. Check the local wildlife office for pictures of tragedies like these. Show the students how to break up the plastic rings before they place them in the garbage. Explain that even though they put the ring in the garbage, eventually that garbage bag will break down and that plastic ring will be left to cause possible harm to some animal. If they cut it up before placing it in the trash, there is less of a chance of its harming an animal.
- In what ways do people get rid of their trash? Do you think the ways in which we get rid of our trash harms animals?
- How do you think our trash harms plants?
- What can you conclude about human-made trash? Complete this sentence: All human-made trash affects _____ (all living things).
- What do you think we can do to get rid of trash? (Pick up trash alongside the road, reduce our use of materials in excessive packaging, recycle, and so on.)

Expansion

PROCESS SKILLS WILL BE USED

▶ Observing
▶ Communicating
▶ Problem solving
▶ Formulating models
▶ Classifying
▶ Questioning
▶ Hypothesizing

How will the idea be expanded?

Refer back to the explanation phase of this lesson. Remind the students of the conversation they had in which you asked about the ways in which people get rid of their trash. Perhaps some students mentioned that their garbage is hauled away by a service. Ask them to think about where that trash goes after hauling. Introduce the term *landfill* (the place where trash gets hauled to be buried in the ground) if they are not already familiar with it. Ask them to suggest alternatives to taking trash to a landfill. As they make suggestions, list them on the board.

Classroom Landfill and Recycling

After the students have created a list, show them a large box in the front of the room labeled *landfill*. (Note: The teacher should have filled this box with a piece of trash for every child in the class.) Have each child pick out one item. Ask them if they think it can be recycled. If so, they should place it in the appropriately labeled medium-sized box. Sum up this activity by getting the children to surmise that recycling can decrease the amount of waste created by people.

Science in Personal and Social Perspectives

- What can you do to help eliminate excessive trash?
- Do you know what to do with recyclable materials where you live? If not, why not ask your parents to help you work on recycling some of your trash?
- What are some ways businesses can cut down on their trash?
- How can companies that make different products help the environment?
- Do you think businesses have a responsibility to reduce the amount of trash they create? Why or why not?

Science and Technology

- Do you think twice about buying a toy that is not only boxed but also wrapped in paper and then in plastic? Do you think the practice of excessive packaging affects our environment?
- Create a map of what happens to a toy's packaging from the time the toy is packaged until the packaging no longer exists.

Science as Inquiry

- What kinds of household items can be recycled?
- How does trash harm animals?
- How does trash harm plants?
- It has sometimes been said that one person's trash is another person's treasure. After doing these activities, how true do you think that statement is?

History and Nature of Science

- Who is responsible for making sure that animals are not harmed by human trash?
- Who is responsible for making sure that plants are not harmed by human trash?
- Do you think you could make a career out of collecting recycled trash? Can people make money from recycling?

Evaluation

Upon completing the activities, the students will be able to:

- separate recyclables into appropriate groups;
- state three ways in which trash harms animals; and
- draw pictures of our environment before trash was recycled and after it was recycled. The students will be able to explain the difference between the two drawings.

Useful Waste

Grade Level ● 5–8

Discipline ● Life Science

NATIONAL SCIENCE EDUCATION CONTENT STANDARDS–LIFE SCIENCE— GRADES 5–8

Populations and Ecosystems

▶ The number of organisms an ecosystem can support depends on the resources available. Lack of resources and other factors, such as predation and climate, limit the growth of populations in specific niches in the ecosystem.

Engaging Question

Is one man's trash another man's treasure?

Materials Needed

For Exploration

aluminum food can	plastic soda bottle	rope
bottle cap	metal can	bug-spray can
glass bottle	cigarette butt	orange peel
newspaper		

For Expansion

art supplies—crayons, markers, scissors, construction paper, glue	old piece of screen
food blender	rolling pin
strips of scrap paper	water

Safety Precautions: Remind students to be careful of the sharp edges and glass, and to exercise care when carrying and using the scissors and blender.

CONCEPTS TO BE CONSTRUCTED

▶ A great majority of human-made waste can be recycled or reused.

▶ Recycle, reuse, water, litter, useful and nonreusable waste, landfill, and hazardous waste are important concepts to expand.

SCIENCE ATTITUDES TO NURTURE

▶ Curiosity

Exploration

PROCESS SKILLS USED

▶ Observing
▶ Questioning
▶ Hypothesizing
▶ Predicting
▶ Reasoning
▶ Recording data

What will the students do?

Separate the class into groups of four to six students. Give each group the materials listed above for exploration concealed in a brown grocery bag. Ask the students to remove the items from the bag, make observations, and rate or arrange the items in order from the most usable to the least usable. The students' reasoning behind their rating scheme should be recorded.

Rating Garbage

Explanation

Concept: A great majority of human-made waste can be recycled or reused.

Ask the students questions such as the following to help invent this concept:

- What did you find in your bags?
- How did you rank these items from most usable to least usable?
- Why did you put _____ (name item) as the most usable?
- Why did you put _____ (name item) as the least usable?

- Refuse is often regarded as useless waste and ends up in landfills and pollutes our environment. Although not all human-made materials can be recycled, they can be reused in a number of ways not originally intended. Why is it important for us to recycle and reuse?
- What is the difference between recycling and reusing?
- What can you do to see that materials such as those found in your bags are recycled or, if possible, reused?
- So what do you think it means when someone says "One man's trash is another man's treasure"?

PROCESS SKILLS USED

▶ Communicating
▶ Problem solving
▶ Interpreting data
▶ Classifying
▶ Making assumptions
▶ Drawing conclusions
▶ Manipulating materials

Litter-Eating Critter

Making Paper

How will the idea be expanded?

Ask the groups of students to decide what kind of litter-eating creature they could create using the materials found in their grocery bags and the art supplies you make available. After they create plans for their creatures, allow them sufficient time to make and explain to the class just how their litter-eating creatures function.

Hold up the insecticide can to introduce hazardous wastes that are found in the home. Ask the students whether they can think of any household items that cannot be disposed of in a regular fashion. Some examples of items that are dangerous and need to be disposed of properly are paint thinners, paints, and motor oils. Ask the students if they are aware why these items cannot be dumped in regular landfills. Explain in detail the impact these items have on the environment.

Encourage the students to learn how to recycle paper by doing the following activity with them: Collect different types of paper scraps, and using a blender, cut the paper into very small pieces. Mix the fine paper to a pulp mixture with water. Pour the mixture out of the blender, and roll it flat. This can be done on an old piece of screen using a rolling pin. Place an old towel over the pulp as you roll it flat to help squeeze out some of the excess water. Allow the new piece of paper to dry before use.

Science in Personal and Social Perspectives

- Do you think you have a responsibility to future generations to reduce the amount of waste you create? Why or why not? Do you think your parents and grandparents thought about the amount of waste they generated in the past and how it would affect the quality of your life?
- How can reducing, reusing, and recycling our resources help to ensure that future generations will have a lifestyle comparable to or better than ours?

Science and Technology

- How does a landfill function? Who is responsible for selecting a site for the landfill? How long can we continue dumping our waste into the same landfill?

- What technological advances have decreased the amount of waste we put into our landfills? What technological advances have added to the problem of overflowing landfills?
- What things can you do to reduce litter in your home? What plans do you have for reducing, reusing, and recycling waste materials you generate?

Science as Inquiry

- How can a product be recycled or reused?
- Can all waste products be recycled? If not, is there anything else that can be done with a waste product first before you throw it away?
- Should cost factors prohibit you from recycling waste products? Why or why not?

History and Nature of Science

- How many different jobs are involved in the recycling of any product?
- Aside from using natural resources, what other sources can manufacturers go to in order to obtain materials to create their products?

Evaluation

Upon completing the activities, the students will be able to:
- differentiate between litter and waste in terms of definitions and usefulness;
- rank a pile of materials according to which are the most to least recyclable and which are the most to least reusable;
- identify and collect from home one clean waste item, one clean recyclable item, and one clean reusable item; and
- start a recycling project for the entire school.

Litter in Our Waterways

Grade Level ● 5–8
Discipline ● Life Science

CONCEPTS TO BE CONSTRUCTED

▶ Irresponsible actions by people are causing the earth's waterways to become littered. This upsets the ecological balance of the waterway.

▶ Beaches, floating, lakes, litter, oceans, recycling, and rivers are important concepts to expand.

SCIENCE ATTITUDES TO NURTURE

▶ Avoidance of broad generalizations when evidence is limited

Sink-or-Float Litter

Engaging Question

Should I worry about litter in the river if I can't see it?

Materials Needed

For Exploration

aquarium
plastic six-pack holder
empty aluminum/tin food can
empty plastic 2-liter soda bottle
metal bottle cap

water to fill aquarium three-fourths full
empty aluminum soda can
empty glass soda bottle
metal can opener

Safety Precautions: Remind students to be careful of the sharp edges and glass and to keep hands away from the aquarium.

Exploration

PROCESS SKILLS USED

▶ Observing
▶ Questioning
▶ Hypothesizing
▶ Predicting
▶ Experimenting
▶ Recording data

What will the students do?

● Display the seven litter items specified in the materials list above. Ask the students to predict which items will sink when placed in the water. Record their predictions. Allow student volunteers to place each item in the water (one at a time) and observe what happens. Record the results and compare with the initial predictions made by the students.

● Ask the students if they think any of the items that floated could sink eventually. After soliciting several answers, point out that some empty containers may fill with water and sink. The time they take to sink may vary based on certain conditions, such as rough water or human manipulation.

● Ask the students to generate a list of litter they think may be underwater in lakes and rivers. Ask the students how they think it got there.

Explanation

Concept: Irresponsible actions by people are causing the earth's waterways to become littered. This upsets the ecological balance of the water.

Ask the students questions, such as the following, to help invent this concept:

● What types of litter sank to the bottom of the aquarium? What types of litter floated on top?

● Do you think that those that floated may eventually sink?

- What do you think happens to the litter after it sinks?
- How do you think this affects water life, such as aquatic plants and animals?
- What do you think will happen to an aquatic animal if it eats a piece of litter, such as a plastic bag?
- Litter that floats is easily mistaken for food by many aquatic animals. It is not uncommon for sea turtles to mistake plastic bags for jellyfish and eat them. When this happens, the sea turtle thinks it is full because the plastic bag is stuck in its stomach. It eventually starves to death. Ducks and some fish get their beaks or bodies tangled in six-pack rings. This prevents them from eating, and they starve to death.
- Litter that sinks is not always considered a nuisance. Some sunken ships become places for coral reefs to grow upon.
- How do you think litter such as this could end up in a lake or river? Help the students to make a summary statement about the actions of irresponsible people when it comes to littering our waterways. Ask them to now answer the inquiry question—Should I worry about litter in the river if I can't see it?

Expansion

PROCESS SKILLS USED

▶ Communicating

▶ Problem solving

▶ Interpreting data

▶ Classifying

▶ Making assumptions

▶ Drawing conclusions

How will the idea be expanded?

Plastic Food

Ask the students to collect and save every piece of plastic waste used in their homes for one week, clean the waste, and bring it to school. Divide the class into groups of four to six. Ask them to pool their plastic collection. Ask the students to classify the waste according to how an aquatic animal might look at that plastic as a source of food. The categories might be *definitely, somewhat likely,* and *unlikely*. List some animals that would go for the "food" in each of the categories. Share these divisions with the class. Once they have discussed their divisions, ask the students to divide the plastic waste according to whether an animal could get tangled up in it. Again, discuss the classification scheme the students developed and why. Ask the students as a summary activity to state one positive thing they could do to prevent further pollution of a waterway.

Science in Personal and Social Perspectives

- Does litter affect your everyday life? If so, how?
- What could you do to cut down on litter?
- Why should someone who lives far from a major waterway be concerned with litter in our waters?
- Do you and your family recycle? If so, what and how?
- Who in our community should be responsible for cleaning up our waters?
- What are some projects in your neighborhood that deal with litter control?
- What are some different litter control agencies operating in your community?

Science and Technology

- Contact a local hospital. Determine how its medical waste is disposed of. Do you think its disposal methods will keep that waste out of our waterways? Why or why not?

Science as Inquiry

- Are pollutants that float in a waterway just as dangerous as pollutants that sink? Why or why not?
- Are people in danger if they play on beaches near polluted water? Why or why not?
- Can a sunken ship ever be beneficial to aquatic organisms?

History and Nature of Science

- Are there any special precautions one must take if his or her job is to clean up a waterway?
- How could an oceanographer use his or her knowledge of ocean currents to help the Coast Guard to identify businesses or cruise ship lines that pollute the waterways?
- Do health care workers have a responsibility to the rest of us to know exactly where their garbage will be disposed? How can they prevent it from ending up in the nation's waterways?

Evaluation

Upon completing the activities, the students will be able to:

- explain how plastic bags could cause the death of a sea turtle;
- give an example of a piece of plastic litter that can be harmful to aquatic life and propose a solution about how this product could be eliminated from the environment without harming wildlife; and
- write a letter of concern to a product manufacturer that they believe uses excessive amounts of plastic packaging on its products.

Sense of Taste

Grade Level ● K–4

Discipline ● Life Science

NATIONAL SCIENCE EDUCATION CONTENT STANDARDS–LIFE SCIENCE— GRADES K-4

Characteristics for Organisms

▶ The behavior of individual organisms is influenced by internal cues (such as hunger) and by external cues (such as a change in the environment). Humans and other organisms have senses that help them detect internal and external cues.

Engaging Question

What is a taste bud?

Materials Needed

For Each Pair of Students

lemon juice	4 paper cups	blue food coloring
cocoa powder	wax paper	10 cotton-tipped swabs
brown sugar	magnifying glass	hole puncher
salt		

Preparation

For each pair of students, label four cups A, B, C, and D. Fill three of the paper cups with water. Dissolve the salt in cup A, the cocoa in cup B, and the brown sugar in cup C (corn syrup may be used instead of brown sugar). Pour some lemon juice in cup D. Create an outline of a tongue on a sheet of paper, and duplicate it for each pair of students.

🛈 *Safety Precautions:* Before distributing the cotton-tipped swabs, remind the students that they are to be used carefully and cautiously to avoid eye injury. Also, to avoid contamination of the unknowns and to inhibit the spread of germs, students should be reminded not to put used cotton-tipped swabs back into the cups after they place them on their tongue.

CONCEPTS TO BE CONSTRUCTED

▶ A person can taste sweet, sour, salty, and bitter in every single area of the tongue that has taste buds.

▶ People with more taste buds taste things more strongly than those with fewer taste buds.

SCIENCE ATTITUDES TO NURTURE

▶ Cooperation with others

▶ Curiosity

Exploration

PROCESS SKILLS USED

▶ Observing

▶ Predicting

▶ Experimenting

▶ Evaluating

▶ Generalizing

▶ Inferring

▶ Recording data

What will the students do?

Ask the students to choose partners, or assign partners yourself. Each set of partners should be provided with four paper cups labeled A through D, each filled with a different liquid. Ask the students to make predictions as to what kinds of tastes they think they have and where on the tongue they think they will taste them. Once predictions are recorded, have one student dip a clean cotton swab into the paper cup labeled A, then touch the cotton swab to the tip of his or her partner's tongue. He or she will then touch the back and the sides of the tongue. Record how your partner thought liquid A tasted. Was it as predicted? Mark on the tongue map the places on the tongue where liquid A was tasted. Repeat this procedure for liquids B and C. Do the same for each partner. Remember that a *clean swab* should be used for each cup and by each student.

Buds and Tasters

Concept: A person can taste sweet, sour, salty, and bitter on every area of the tongue that has taste buds.

Ask the students questions such as the following to help invent this concept:

- How did your partner think each liquid tasted?
- Did you agree with your partner?
- Did you find any special places on the tongue where these tastes could be detected? Why or why not? Have the students share their findings. They should conclude that there is no single area on the tongue where each of these tastes can be detected more so than another. Your tongue is the organ that gives you your sense of taste. If you observe it closely starting at the tip, you will notice thousands of tiny bumps that make you tongue look rough. The tiny bumps are called *filiform papillae.* They are responsible for grabbing onto your food as you chew. The roundish *buttons* you find interspersed within the filiform papillae are called *fungiform papillae.* Anywhere from five to seven taste buds can be found on each fungiform papilla. The *taste buds* are made up of a bundle of cells, each containing special sensors or receptors that can pick out the four basic tastes of sweet, sour, bitter, and salty. The *circumvallate papillae,* found on the back of your tongue, are larger than the other papillae. Found within deep furrows of the circumvallate papillae are taste buds that also can detect the four basic tastes.
- Chewing grinds up your food. It also wets the food by mixing it with saliva, the liquid made by small organs in your mouth. When your food is well mixed with saliva, your taste buds can pick up messages about its flavor. Nerves take these messages to taste centers in each side of your brain. Your brain then decides what you are tasting.
- Your senses of taste and smell work closely together. The taste of many foods is really a mixture of taste and smell. Food often seems to have no taste when you have a cold. The cold stops up your nose and dulls your sense of smell. When you cannot smell the food, a part of its taste seem to be missing.
- Ask the students to complete this statement: Taste buds for sweet, sour, salty, and bitter can be found _____ (all over or in every part of) the tongue.

Expansion

Supertasters

PROCESS SKILLS USED
▶ Observing
▶ Problem solving
▶ Recording data
▶ Inferring

How will the idea be expanded?

Ask the students to go back with their partners to perform the following task:

- Cut a piece of wax paper 1 inch square. Punch a hole using the paper puncher in the middle of the 1-inch-square piece of wax paper.
- Place the piece of wax paper on the tip of your partner's tongue just slightly off center. Be sure the tongue is slightly wet so the paper will stick.
- Using a cotton-tipped swab, dab blue food coloring where the hole is. Be careful not to use too much coloring. For accurate data collection, you want just the dot of tongue exposed to be dyed.
- Use the magnifying glass to count the number of larger, raised dots that did not turn blue. These will be the *fungiform papillae.*
- Take the number of fungiform papillae you discover and multiply by six. This will give you an estimate of the number of taste buds your partner has.
- Repeat this procedure for the other partner.

Were you able to find the same number of fungiform papillae on your partner as your partner found on you? Did everyone have the same number of taste buds?

You will discover that the fewer the raised dots, the less likely the person tasted the four basics tastes all over his or her tongue. Some people are *supertasters* because they have a large number of fungiform papillae, whereas those with just a few are considered *nontasters*.

Science in Personal and Social Perspectives

- Where on the tongue did your partner taste the sweet liquid, the sour, salty, and bitter? Was it the same place as yours?
- Why do you think many adults tolerate flavorings such as hot pepper sauce that a baby cannot?

Science and Technology

- Do you think that people from countries other than your own have different amounts of taste buds on their tongue? How do you explain that many cultures tolerate food that is much spicier than typical "American" fare? Does the number of taste buds have anything to do with it? How might you design an experiment to determine the answers to these questions?

Science as Inquiry

- How do the filiform papillae differ from the fungiform papillae or the circumvallate papillae?
- What do the fungiform papillae and the circumvallate papillae have in common?
- Where on the tongue can the circumvallate papillae be found?

History and Nature of Science

- Ask the students to generate a list of spices used in cooking. Assign each student a spice. From which country does it originate? How does it grow? How is it harvested? How important is that spice to the society of the country in which in grows? When was it first used as a spice?
- Do you think someone with permanent damage to his or her nose resulting in the loss of the sense of smell would have a promising career as a professional chef? Why or why not?

Evaluation

Upon completing the activities, the students will be able to:

- list the four major tastes that can be picked out by receptors on the tongue;
- design a method for separating the class into nontasters, regular tasters, and supertasters; and
- describe the role of the filiform papillae, fungiform papillae, and the circumvallate papillae.

Skeleton

Grade Level ● 1–4

Discipline ● **Life Science**

NATIONAL SCIENCE EDUCATION CONTENT STANDARDS–LIFE SCIENCE— GRADES 1–4

Characteristics for Organisms

▶ Each plant or animal has different structures that serve different functions in growth, survival, and reproduction. For example, humans have distinct body structures for walking, holding, seeing, and talking.

CONCEPTS TO BE CONSTRUCTED

▶ The internal support system for muscles in mammals is the bones. All the bones arranged together make up the skeleton.

▶ Joints help skeletons to move.

SCIENCE ATTITUDES TO NURTURE

▶ Curiosity

Bones Assembly Line

Engaging Question

What does my skeleton do for me?

Materials Needed

For Each Student

One large sheet of newsprint, markers, crayons, several brass paper fasteners, a packet of paper bones that when put together will create a replica of a human skeleton.

Safety Precautions: Explain to the students how to use the brass fasteners. Remind them that they could cause hurt if they poke themselves or others with the pointed edge.

Exploration

PROCESS SKILLS USED

▶ Observing

▶ Questioning

▶ Manipulating materials

▶ Analyzing

What will the students do?

Introduce the lesson by reading two poems from *A Light in the Attic,* by Shel Silverstein. The poems are "Day After Halloween" and "It's Hot!" Begin a discussion with the students about the ideas behind the poems. Ask questions such as "What would it be like if we didn't have a skeleton? Why do we need bones in our bodies?"

Give each child several brass fasteners and a packet containing paper bones cut into the different major bones of the body using the figure on page 392. Ask the students to empty the packets and to manipulate the materials in any way they wish in an effort to determine what they can create with all the bones. Encourage them to use the brass fasteners to assemble the bones. Walk around the room asking questions such as "What do you think all of these different parts make up? Do you think you know where all the parts go? What could the brass fasteners represent in a real body that helps us to move? How do the bones in our body connect for real?"

Explanation

Concept: The internal support system for muscles in mammals is the bones. All the bones arranged together make up the skeleton.

Using a picture of a skeleton and a life-size skeleton, ask the children if they know the nonscientific names of the bones. Write these on the board. If students offer the

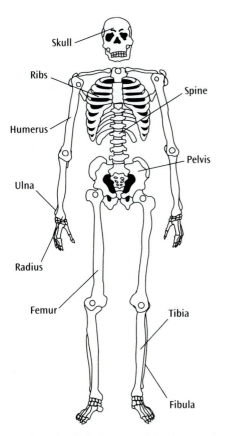

Skull

Ribs

Spine

Humerus

Pelvis

Ulna

Radius

Femur

Tibia

Fibula

scientific names, list those as well; compare them to the common name, e.g. scapula for collar bone. Show a picture of the muscle system of the human body. Explain to the students how the bones help give the muscles support.

Walk around the classroom very stiffly. Encourage some or all of the students to do the same. Really play it up. Tell them they cannot bend their elbows or knees. Remind the students that they used brass fasteners to connect the bones in their skeleton.

- Ask the students if they think brass fasteners are used in our bodies. Of course not; what do we have? (Joints.)
- Ask the children to demonstrate what would happen to them when they are standing up if they did not have bones in their body. The students should drop to the floor.
- Ask the students to complete this sentence about our skeleton: Our skeleton supports our _____ (muscles).

Expansion

PROCESS SKILLS WILL BE USED

▶ Observing
▶ Classifying
▶ Recording
▶ Manipulating materials

How will the idea be expanded?

Pair up the students and provide each child with a large sheet of newsprint and a pencil. Ask the students to spread the paper out on the floor. The paired children should take turns. One child should lie flat on the paper with his or her face down. The other child should outline the body. Let each child switch roles. After they have created their outlines, have each child fill in the outline with the bones of the body.

Newsprint Bone Bodies

Science in Personal and Social Perspectives

- Do you think it is good to know what is inside our body? Why?
- How do joints help us move?
- Could you do the same activities you do on a daily basis if you didn't have a skeleton?

Science and Technology

- What do you think scientists do with bones found in nature?
- Do you think bones found by scientists tell them anything about the organism and the environment it lived in?
- How do you think we see our bones inside our body? What is that picture called?

Science as Inquiry

- How do bones connect together?
- Why do you think it is good to understand how our bodies move?
- Why do you think we have two bones in our forearms and lower legs?

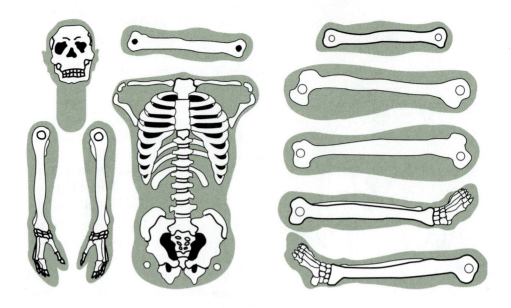

History and Nature of Science

- What is the name of the person who shows you pictures of your bones inside you?
- If you had some back problems and you wanted your spine readjusted, what type of professional would you go to?
- What would you call a person who went to different locations to dig up buried bones and artifacts?
- What does a doctor do if you have a broken bone? How do you think the first doctors figured out how to mend broken bones?

Evaluation

Upon completing the activities, the students will be able to:

- assemble a paper skeleton;
- identify at least five bones in the body with common names;
- understand why we need joints in our bodies and explain what they do; and
- play Hokey-Pokey Skeleton; that is, do the Hokey-Pokey, but use the common names of bones rather than body parts.

Temperature Receptors on Skin

Grade Level ● 5–8
Discipline ● Life Science

Structure and Function

Engaging Question

What is it about skin that allows me to feel changes in temperature?

Materials Needed

For Each Student Group

a source of hot and cold water
3 bowls
6 nails

2 fine-tipped pens, each a different color
paper towels

🛈 *Safety Precautions:* Ask students not to poke each other with the nails and to use care around the water: If it is knocked over, be sure to clean it up immediately. Make sure hot water is not so hot that it will scald.

▶ Specialized cells perform specialized functions in multicellular organisms. Groups of specialized cells cooperate to form a tissue, such as a muscle. Different tissues are in turn grouped together to form larger functional units, called organs. Each type of cell, tissue, and organ has a distinct structure and set of functions that serve the organism as a whole.

CONCEPTS TO BE CONSTRUCTED

▶ Skin has spots, called receptors, for feeling temperatures that are hotter or colder than body temperatures.

▶ Water can feel hot and cold to our bodies at the same time.

SCIENCE ATTITUDES TO NURTURE

▶ Curiosity
▶ Perseverance

Exploration

PROCESS SKILLS USED

▶ Observing
▶ Questioning
▶ Designing an experiment
▶ Recording data
▶ Predicting
▶ Generalizing

Soaking Hands

What will the students do?

Divide the students into cooperative working groups of four. Ask the materials manager to obtain three small bowls. Fill one with hot water, one with cold water, and the third with warm water. The groups' mission is to find out how hands feel when placed in water of different temperatures. Encourage the groups to design an experiment to solve this problem. Ask them to record their data. Their experimental designs may look something like this: Each student in the group will take turns placing one hand in hot water and the other in cold. Hands should be left for several minutes in the water. Remove hands from those bowls and immediately immerse them in the warm water. Students should be able to describe what happens next. There may be some variations to this plan. Teachers may find that some groups first put both hands in cold and then in hot. They all should be able to help invent the concept, no matter the experimental design.

Explanation

Concept: Skin has spots, called receptors, for feeling temperatures that are hotter or colder than body temperatures.

To help invent this concept, ask each of the student groups to report on the experiment they designed. Ask the following questions:

- What did you do? What results did you get?
- Did the water feel hot and cold at the same time? If so, how can that be?
- Do the results have to do with the temperature of the water your hand was in first or just the temperature of your hand?
- Lead the students to conclude that the temperature of the water their hand was in first will determine how hot or cold their hand felt. Share with them that on their skin are receptors that sense temperatures different from normal body temperature.
- Ask them to now respond to the inquiry question: What is it about skin that allows me to feel changes in temperature?

Hot/Cold Receptor Mapping

PROCESS SKILLS WILL BE USED
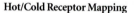
- ▶ Observing
- ▶ Classifying
- ▶ Recording
- ▶ Predicting

How will the idea be expanded?

Ask each student to use one of the pens provided to the groups to draw a square on the back of his or her hand. Place one nail in the bowl of cold water and another in the bowl of hot water. Ask the group members to pair up. Ask one student from each pair to take the nail from the cold water and touch the tip of the nail to any spot in the square of his or her partner's hand. If it feels cold, mark that spot with the pen (marking all the cold ones in the same color). Now switch so that each partner has cold receptors marked. Other student pairs in each cooperative group can be doing the same thing with the hot water and a nail. Be sure to use a different color pen for hot spots. Now exchange bowls and make marks for the opposite water type. Are you surprised at where you find the hot and cold receptors?

Science in Personal and Social Perspectives

- People say that to test bathwater, you should use your elbow, or to test a baby's bottle, you should use your wrist. Why do you think they chose those particular body parts?
- How would you test your bathwater: with your hand or your toes? Why?

Science and Technology

- On a hot summer day, it is nice to enter an air-conditioned building. After you've been in the building for an hour, you might begin to think the air-conditioning has been shut off. Why do you think you feel this way?
- How has technology allowed us to exist comfortably in the winter and the summer? Can you design a way to keep cool during hot weather without using an air-conditioner or fan?

- Could you find a way to pick up a snowball and not feel the cold?
- Which part of your hand is most sensitive to hot things?
- What is a receptor?

History and Nature of Science

- Why do people who work in meat lockers wear gloves?
- Do you think it is important for someone who is involved in child care to make sure that his or her heat receptors are not damaged? Why or why not?
- In 1853, Georg Meissner described a corpuscle that became known as *Meissner's corpuscle*. What is this, and what did Meissner do to discover it?

Evaluation

Upon completing the activities, the students will be able to:

- identify the different hot and cold receptors on each hand;
- explain how water can feel hot and cold at the same time;
- identify the child with the cold hands when looking at a picture of children involved in building a snow fort (the one without gloves); and
- view a picture of working firefighters with and without fire coats and identify which ones will feel hot. Why is this not the same as pictures of children in the winter with and without coats?

**CONCEPTS TO BE
CONSTRUCTED**

► A microscope is used to identify objects not visible to the naked eye.

► Identifying a compound by its characteristic crystal shape and slide preparation is an important concept to expand.

**SCIENCE ATTITUDES TO
NURTURE**

► Curiosity

► Perseverance

Building Microscope Skills

Grade Level ● 5–8
Discipline ● Life Science

Engaging Question

What is the advantage of using a microscope?

Materials Needed

For Exploration

noniodized salt	water	microscope
iodized salt	eye droppers	scale
sugar	cups	graduated cylinder
alum	slides	pictures of crystals
borax	slide covers	

For Expansion

water	laundry bluing
noniodized salt	household ammonia

⊙ *Safety Precautions:* Ask students to avoid placing hands near eyes or mouth while working with materials to prepare slides. When using an electric microscope, be sure to use proper safety measures near electrical outlets. The microscope lamp may be hot to touch. Apply the usual safety standards when working with such chemicals as bluing and ammonia.

Exploration

Microscope Use and
Crystal Comparisons

PROCESS SKILLS USED

► Observing

► Classifying

► Recording data

► Diagramming

► Comparing

► Manipulating instruments

What will the students do?

Measure out 5 grams of each solid. Dissolve each in a separate cup containing 25 ml of water. Be sure to label the cup with the name of the material dissolved in the water. As the solution is forming, label a slide for each solute. Place a drop of each solution on its assigned slide. Allow the water to evaporate. Carefully place the cover slip over the remaining crystals on the slide. Focus each slide under the microscope, and record your observations for each at low power. Focus under a higher power, and again record observations.

Explanation

Concept: A microscope is used to identify objects not visible to the naked eye.

Key questions to ask students to help them come to this conclusion are:

• What shapes did you observe on the slide?

• How does it compare to a drawing of the crystal shape?

- Can you share a diagram of those shapes with the class? How are these shapes similar? How are they different?
- How did the microscope help you to observe the crystal?
- What advantage do you see in using a microscope over just using your eye? The students should be able to conclude that a microscope can be used to identify objects not visible to the naked eye.

Expansion

How will the idea be expanded?

- Use the results of the previous crystal comparison activity to graph the crystal shapes versus the number of substances that have that particular shape.

Charcoal Crystals

- The students should be encouraged to brainstorm a list of other possible substances that contain crystals. Observe these under the microscope.
- The students will grow a crystal garden in a Styrofoam egg carton by first placing pieces of charcoal into the egg sockets. In a separate container, mix the following substances:

6 tablespoons of water   6 tablespoons of laundry bluing
6 tablespoons of noniodized salt   2 teaspoons of household ammonia

Once this solution is prepared, the students should carefully pour it over the pieces of charcoal in the egg container. The students can then place these in an area in the classroom where they will not be hit or bumped. The crystals will grow for several days. If the students want colored crystals, they may place a few drops of food coloring on the charcoal after the solution is poured on them. The students may wish to make each egg socket a different color. Once the crystals have grown, the students may safely carry them home in their egg cartons. If the crystals do get bumped in transit, sometimes they can be revived by putting a little water on them.

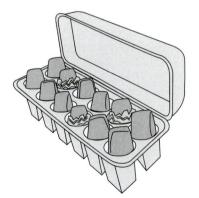

Science in Personal and Social Perspectives

- While rummaging through your kitchen for a salt shaker, you come across a container you think will work. After placing the salt into the container, you find that no salt comes out of the holes when you shake the container. Why do you think this happened? Will the size of the salt crystals determine the size of the holes that should be on top of a shaker?
- Do you think there are any other areas of your life in which the skills you learned in this lesson can be applied? If so, where?
- How do you think your increased knowledge of crystal shapes will help you become a better consumer? Would you buy ice cream that contained frost crystals? Why or why not?

Science and Technology

- Knowing that salt or sugar can be placed in solution allowed past generations to preserve foods more easily, thus ensuring their survival. How have our present-day technologies expanded on these early ideas?

- Think about the frozen food industry. How does it make use of their knowledge of crystal formation?

Science as Inquiry

- What scientific concepts did you discover while participating in these activities?
- What problem-solving techniques did you employ?
- What procedures were used with the microscope?

History and Nature of Science

- How important is it for a gemologist to understand the differences between crystal shapes? Why?
- In addition to knowledge about crystals, what other kinds of skills would a geologist need? A gemologist? A hospital laboratory technician?
- Anton van Leeuwenhoek is credited with creating one of the earliest microscopes. What kinds of discoveries was he able to make with his primitive microscope?

Evaluation

Upon completing these activities, the students will be able to:

- demonstrate proper slide preparation techniques;
- prepare a slide of a crystal and focus it under a microscope;
- identify on a diagram the basic crystal shapes; and
- state why different compounds may have different crystal shapes.

Sex-Linked Genes

Grade Level ● 5–6

Discipline ● Life Science

NATIONAL SCIENCE EDUCATION CONTENT STANDARDS–LIFE SCIENCE—GRADES 5–8

Reproduction and Heredity

► Each organism requires a set of instructions for specifying its traits. Heredity is the passage of these instructions from one generation to another.

► Hereditary information is contained in genes, located in the chromosomes of each cell. Each gene carries a single unit of information. An inherited trait of an individual can be determined by one or by many genes, and a single gene can influence more than one trait. A human cell contains many thousands of different genes.

Engaging Question

Whom do I get my genetic traits from?

Materials Needed

For Exploration

pictures of several generations of a family in which the resemblance over the generations is easy to see and pictures of family members in which the relationship is not so obvious

or arrange to have a family come into your class or have a video of a family showing multiple generations

or have students bring in family pictures of themselves and a sibling or adult family member or bring in a picture of a family

poster paper or chalkboard to collect class observations

For Expansion

50 drinking straws (this is for a class of 25 @ 2 per student)

0.5-cm × 2-cm strips of light and dark blue construction paper (37 total)

0.5-cm × 2-cm strips of light and dark green construction paper (37 total)

0.5-cm × 2-cm strips of light and dark red construction paper (13 total)

⊘ Safety Precautions: None needed.

CONCEPTS TO BE CONSTRUCTED

► Traits are passed from parent to offspring.

► Sex-linked traits are carried through sex chromosomes. Heredity information is contained in genes, located on the chromosomes of each cell.

SCIENCE ATTITUDES TO NURTURE

► Curiosity

► Tolerance for others opinions

Family Traits

Exploration

PROCESS SKILLS USED

► Observing

► Comparing

► Recording data

► Making hypotheses

What will students do?

If you have enough pictures of various families throughout the generations, the students can work in groups of four to six; if you have a small number of pictures or videotape of a family, then work together as a class. Either way, ask the students to look at the family members closely for similarities. If the students are having trouble or look confused, encourage them to look for similar traits such as hair or eye color, freckles, skin coloration, height, etc. Ask students to record the things they find that the family members have in common. Tell them to be prepared to share their observations and to draw some conclusions about their observations and those of the class.

Explanation

Concept: Traits are passed from parent to offspring.

If the students worked as separate teams, ask the student teams to share with the class the pictures they used to make their observations. If they made their observations from videotape, this will not be necessary. As the students share their observations, record commonly recurring ideas for all to see. For example, if one group talks about all family members having green eyes and another group talks about all family members having brown eyes, then record "eye color" for all to see. Continue with the sharing until all students or student groups have had an opportunity to share their observations and until you have a list of observations that includes a variety of traits (skin, eye, and hair color; body shape and height).

Ask the students leading questions to invent the concept of a trait, such as:

- Did all the siblings in the picture have the same color of eyes? Or hair?
- Did you see much resemblance between the mother and her daughter? Or between the parent and the child?
- Share with the students that the list of observations they made are of characteristics we get passed on to us from our parents. Those characteristics are called *traits*. These traits are given direction by genes that are carried on our chromosomes. We inherit or receive the genes from one or both of our parents. For instance, some of you may have found that a child looked just like one of the parents in the pictures. Others of you may have found that the child looked like a combination of both parents. Thus, traits are passed from parent to offspring. What a person looks like on the outside is called the person's *phenotype*. The inherited traits that make a person look like that (what's on the inside) is called the person's *genotype*.
- Ask the students to answer the inquiry question: Whom do I get my genetic traits from?

Expansion

PROCESS SKILLS WILL BE USED

▶ Observing
▶ Predicting
▶ Recording data
▶ Drawing conclusions

What preactivity preparation is necessary?

Before the activity, the teacher should cut the straws into 10- and 7-cm lengths. These will be representing X and Y chromosomes, respectively. To demonstrate the naturally occurring distribution, you will need three times as many 10-cm lengths (X chromosomes) as 7-cm lengths (Y chromosomes). For a class of 25 students, you need 37 long and 13 shorter-length straws. To the long straws, tape a strip of light- or dark-blue paper near one end; then tape a strip of light- or dark-green paper a few centimeters below the blue paper. (See diagram.) Tape a red strip to the short straws at the same distance from one end as you taped the blue strip to the long straws. (See diagram.)

Prepare the rest of the straws in the same manner, alternating the light- and dark-colored bands.

Use the following key: Long straws = X chromosomes; short straws = Y chromosomes; blue strips = color blindness gene (dark blue, the trait is not present; light blue, the trait is present); green strips = baldness gene (dark green, the trait is not present; light green, the trait is present); red strips = hairy ears gene (dark red, the trait is not present; light red, the trait is present).

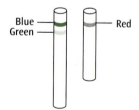

Blue ——
Green ——
—— Red

Sex-Linked Traits

How will the idea be expanded?

Give two straws to each student so that they receive either two long straws or a long and a short straw. They cannot receive two short straws, as you are modeling how sex chromosomes are inherited. Remind them of the earlier exploration activity. Explain to them that each straw represents one of the sex chromosomes they inherited from their parents; a long straw represents an X chromosome, and a short straw represents a Y chromosome. Two X chromosomes (long straws) mean that you will be female; an X and a Y chromosome (1 short, 1 long straw) mean that you will be male.

Share the key to the colored bands. Have the students determine their gender and what traits they will inherit. Ask them to identify their phenotype (what they will look like on the outside) and their genotype (what traits their genes carry). For example, if they have one long straw (representing an X chromosome) and one short straw (representing a Y chromosome), they have a male phenotype and XY genotype. If the long straw has a dark blue band and a light green band and the short straw has a dark red band, then the phenotype is a colorblind male. In another example, if a student has two long straws with a dark blue band on one straw and a light blue band on the other and a light green band on both straws, then the phenotype is a colorblind female with an XX genotype.

Have the students trade a straw with another student (just don't let them end up with two short straws). Again have them identify the phenotype and genotype. Ask them what conclusions they can draw about the three traits: color blindness, baldness, and hairy ears. Use your questioning skills to get students to reflect on the observations they shared about the phenotypes and genotypes.

The students should be led to conclude that color blindness, specifically affecting green color vision, and baldness (premature baldness at the crown of the head) are recessive traits that are carried only by the X chromosome. The gene for hairy ears is a recessive trait that is carried on the Y chromosome; thus, girls don't get hairy ears. If the recessive gene for hairy ears is present, it is with increasing age that it is expressed more prominently in men carrying this trait. These traits are sex linked. Thus, the concept developed is that sex-linked traits are carried through sex chromosomes, and heredity information is contained in genes, located in the chromosomes of each cell.

Science in Personal and Social Perspectives

- Have you ever known a family in which all of the siblings look almost exactly alike or in which a child looked as if he or she were cloned from one of the parents? Can you now explain how this is possible?
- Do you think personality traits can be inherited as well? Explain your answer.

Science and Technology

- Understanding how traits are inherited has led many couples to seek genetic counseling before having children. What do you think one could learn from genetic counseling?
- There are many products on the market designed to prevent hair loss. Do you think these are useful to someone who has inherited the sex-linked gene for baldness? Why or why not?

Science as Inquiry

- What is the difference between someone's genotype and his or her phenotype? How can these be determined?
- If you had a grandfather on your mother's side who was bald, will you be bald when you get older? What would your genotype have to be to show up bald if you were a female?

- Gregor Mendel is known as the "father of genetics." What observations did Mendel make that led to this branch of science? Describe his experiments.
- Genetic engineering is one of the fastest-growing career fields. Research the skills needed to be a genetic engineer and what industries would require the services of someone trained as a genetic engineer.

Evaluation

Upon completing the activities, the students will be able to:

- describe a trait and explain what it means to inherit that trait;
- when given a particular phenotype, predict the possible genotype for the given traits;
- look at the phenotypes of a given couple and predict the phenotypes of their male and female offspring; and
- research information on sex-linked genes and identify other phenotypes that result because of a sex-linked gene other than those discovered in the expansion activity.

Passing of Traits

Grade Level ● 7–8

Discipline ● Life Science

Engaging Question

Are personality traits inherited?

Materials Needed

digital cameras to loan students to take home to take pictures of family members that possess similar traits or students should bring in family pictures of themselves and a sibling or adult family member or bring a picture of a family in which similar traits are obvious

poster paper
index cards (Each student should have as many index cards as there are students in the class.)

Safety Precautions: None needed.

► Every organism requires a set of instructions for specifying its traits. Heredity is the passage of these instructions from one generation to another.

► Hereditary information is contained in genes, located in the chromosomes of each cell. Each gene carries a single unit of information. An inherited trait of an individual can be determined by one or by many genes, and a single gene can influence more than one trait. A human cell contains many thousands of different genes.

► The characteristics of an organism can be described in terms of a combination of traits. Some traits are inherited and others result from interactions with the environment.

Exploration

PROCESS SKILLS USED

► Observing
► Comparing
► Recording data
► Making hypotheses

What will students do?

Have students use digital cameras to take close-up pictures of one another. Then allow them to take the cameras home to take a picture of a family member or members with whom they share similar traits. The students should return the cameras to the class, download the pictures they took, and print them. If a digital camera is not available, students should bring in a recent photo of themselves and pictures of family members (this can be aunt, uncle, grandmother, etc. Be sure you are sensitive to the feelings of adopted students or students in step or foster families).

Ask the students to tape or glue the photos on the poster paper. Below the photos create a list of physical traits that the people in the photos share. Display the photo posters around the room.

Provide each student with a stack of index cards. Have students use one card for each poster they observe. On the card, they will write the name of the student who prepared the poster and then list some observable traits of that student as shown by the poster. Once students have listed the traits, instruct them to leave the index cards on the appropriate student's desk. In the end, each student should have a stack of index cards with descriptions of traits that other students observed in his or her poster.

CONCEPTS TO BE CONSTRUCTED

► Traits are passed from parent to offspring.
► The characteristics of an organism can be described in terms of a combination of traits. Some traits are inherited, and others can be the result of interactions with the environment.

SCIENCE ATTITUDES TO NURTURE

► Curiosity
► Tolerance for others opinions
► Avoidance of broad generalizations when evidence is limited

Explanation

Concept: Traits are passed from parent to offspring.

Using your questioning skills, encourage students to reflect on the observations their peers made about their poster. Ask questions such as:

What Traits Do You Share?

- Were the observations your peers made about inherited traits similar to the ones you observed?
- Were you surprised that your peers noticed a trait that you did not see at first? If so, what were some of those?

The students should be making suggestions about traits such as the shape of the lips, nose, chin, cheekbones, eyebrows, eyes, coloring of hair and skin, height, dimples, freckles, and smile.

Encourage them to conclude that some traits are easily observable and that these traits are passed from parent to offspring.

Inherited or Environmentally Altered?

PROCESS SKILLS USED
- ► Observing
- ► Predicting
- ► Recording data
- ► Drawing conclusions

How will the idea be expanded?

Have the students reuse the index cards by passing them back to the student who filled them out. Ask the students to move around the room again, looking at each student's poster. This time ask them to list on the reverse side of the appropriate card any personality traits that they may know about that student. Once completed, have the cards returned to the students to whom they apply. Ask each student to take a new index card and to complete a "personality trait" list for himself or herself as well. Not all students will feel comfortable sharing the results of this activity aloud; instead, ask them to create a data chart that lists the type of personality trait in one column and the number of times someone in the class identified that trait for them in the other. Without naming the personality trait (to eliminate student embarrassment) or by using yourself as an example, ask the students to think about the top three personality traits on their list. Ask them to determine where they think they got that trait from. Is there someone in their family who exhibits the same trait? Does more than one person in their family exhibit that same personality trait? Do you exhibit traits that are a combination of traits from your parents? The characteristics of an organism can be described in terms of a combination of traits.

Ask the students to think about these questions: Do you think this trait is inherited, or was it learned by living in the family environment? How far back can you trace this personality trait in your family? To your grandparents? Your great-grandparents? Your great-great-grandparents?

Personality traits may be inherited just like a laugh or the sound of one's voice. However, some personality traits can be acquired through years of living in a certain environment. The same can happen to physical characteristics. Certain traits are inherited, but changes in the gene environment can occur during cell reproduction to alter the phenotype expressed. Thus, some traits are inherited and others result from interactions with the environment.

Science in Personal and Social Perspectives

- What would be the advantage of thoroughly reviewing the observable traits found within your family tree? Would it be as easy to trace personality traits?
- What observable traits do you have that you think you inherited from your male parent? From your female parent? What observable traits do you have that you believe are a combination of both parents?

Science and Technology

- How have some couples turned to technology to alter the outcome of some observable traits in their offspring?
- Can genetic engineering change the personality traits of an offspring?

Science as Inquiry

- Choose a famous family such as that of a president, a king or queen, or a known actor. Research the family lineage to identify any inherited traits carried through the generations.
- If you were born with red hair and each of your siblings had brown hair, but you knew of a deceased great uncle with red hair on your father's side of the family, explain how that red-hair gene showed up as your phenotype.

History and Nature of Science

- Gregor Mendel is known as the "father of genetics" because of his extensive experiments with pea plants. What other organisms have scientists turned to as a means of adding to the ever-increasing body of knowledge in the field of genetics? Share at least two organisms and the work done with those to explain a genetics concept.
- How would one use the concept that some traits are inherited and others result from interactions with the environment to explain why some people have the ability to play a musical instrument and other people in the same family don't have that ability?

Evaluation

Upon completing the activities, the students will be able to:

- describe a trait and explain what it means to inherit that trait;
- determine how a particular trait such as curly black hair can be found on a child from a family in which siblings all have straight black hair and the parents have straight black hair; and
- explain why when identical twins are raised apart they could exhibit identical personality traits.

Physical Science Lessons

Lesson Name	NSE Content Standards For Physical Science	Grade Level	Activities
Waves: Sound and Light			
Sound versus Noise	Position and Motion of Objects	K–4	School Sound Search • Magazine Sound Search
High versus Low and Soft versus Loud Sounds	Position and Motion of Objects	2–4	Megaphones and Vibrating Straws • Bell Ringers
Vibrations Causing Sound	Position and Motion of Objects	2–4	Sound Makers • Waxed-Paper Kazoo
Loudness and Pitch	Position and Motion of Objects	2–4	Soda Bottle Orchestra • Cigar Box Strings • Fish Line Harps • Homemade Music
Sound Movement as Waves	Position and Motion of Objects	2–4	Vibrating Fork • Striking Rod • Clapping Blocks • Sound Producers? • Tapping Tank • Paper Cup Telephone
Sound Waves	Transformations of Energy	5–8	Soup Can Reflectors • Slinky Waves • Sound Waves and the Ear
Energy Changes in Sound Production	Transformations of Energy	5–8	Noise and Sound Identification • Sound Movement • Sound Game: "What Is Sound?"
Matter			
States of Matter	Properties of Objects and Materials	3–4	Plastic Bag Chemistry • Marble Matter
Changing Matter	Properties of Matter	5–8	Physical and Chemical Paper Change • Polymer-Rubber Balls
Identification of an Unknown	Properties of Matter	5–8	Physical Properties of an Unknown • Chemical Properties of an Unknown
Using the Scientific Method to Solve Problems	Properties of Matter	5–8	Exploring with Efferdent Tablets • Exploring with Cornstarch
Heat Energy	Properties of Objects and Materials	1–4	Liquid Birthday • Liquids to Solids
Physics			
Structure Strength	Motion and Forces	5–8	Simple Construction • Triangle Construction
Mirrors and Reflection	Transformations of Energy	5–8	Mirrors and Reflectors • What Is a Mirror?
The Slinky Potential	Transformations of Energy	7–8	Energy Conversions with a Slinky • Energy Transfer—Having a Ball!
Toys in Space	Motion and Forces	5–8	Toy Behavior in Zero Gravity • Toys and Newton
Simple Machines: The Lever	Motion and Forces	5–8	Lever Creations • Spoons and Nuts • Lever Scavenger Hunt

Sound versus Noise

Grade Level ● K–4

Discipline ● Physical Science

NATIONAL SCIENCE
EDUCATION CONTENT
STANDARDS–PHYSICAL
SCIENCE—GRADES K-4

Position and Motion of Objects

▶ Vibrating objects produce sound. The pitch of the sound can be varied by changing the rate of vibration.

Engaging Question

When does sound become noise?

Materials Needed

For the Discrepant Event, the teacher will need:
  1 whistle

Exploration—conducted in four student groups, each student will need:
  1 notebook or journal for recording data

Expansion—conducted in groups of three to four students per group, each group will need:
  Magazines for cutting up
  1 tape recorder with blank audiotape and/or computer with recording capabilities
  1 computer with Internet access
  1 large piece of poster paper

**CONCEPTS TO
BE CONSTRUCTED**

▶ Sound can be considered useful or simply noise.
▶ Sound can be pleasant or unpleasant.

🛈 *Safety Precautions:* The students should be reminded of the importance of walking, not running, as they move through the school to find a place to listen to different sounds. They should use care when carrying pencils or pens to record their observations and to exercise caution when using the scissors in the expansion activity.

Discrepant Event: While the students are working quietly at their desks, make sure no students are looking, and then take out a whistle and blow it loudly. Ask the children what they first thought when they heard the whistle. Record some of their thoughts on the board. Tell the students that you will get back to the list they generated after they do the following activity. Then lead the students through the exploration phase of the lesson.

Exploration

PROCESS SKILLS USED

▶ Observing
▶ Classifying
▶ Predicting
▶ Describing
▶ Recording data
▶ Communicating

What will the students do?

Divide the class into four groups. Send each group to different parts of the school building, such as the janitors' workroom, the playground, the gym, the music room, and their own classroom. Ask them to go to these areas quietly. Have them sit quietly in their areas for 3 minutes, creating a list all of the sounds they hear while in those areas. Return to the classroom. Instruct the students to work with the people in their group to decide if there is any way they

School Sound
Search

could group the sounds. When all of the groups have analyzed their lists, share the categories of sounds with the rest of the class. Ask the students if any of the groups came up with categories their group never thought of.

Explanation

Concept: Sound can be considered useful or simply noise.

Place on the chalkboard or a whiteboard in separate columns the terms *useful, noise, pleasant,* and *unpleasant.* Ask the students whether any of these terms fit the feelings they had when you blew the whistle unexpectedly. Do any of these terms fit the categories you placed your sounds under? If so, which of your sounds would go under the different headings? Encourage members of the group to write their sounds under the appropriate headings. Do all sounds fall *only* into one classification? Where do fire alarms and whistles fall? Sounds can be harmful. We need ear protection from some sounds. Ask the students to summarize their findings as shown in the table on the board by completing these statements: Sounds can be useful when _____. Sounds can be considered just noise when _____. Or you can ask the students to answer the inquiry question: When does sound become noise?

Expansion

Magazine Sound Search

PROCESS SKILLS USED
▶ Observing
▶ Classifying
▶ Communicating
▶ Inferring
▶ Manipulating materials
▶ Interpreting data

How will the idea be expanded?

The children will work in groups, looking through magazines, cutting out possible sources of sound. Each group will create an audiotape, mimicking the sounds that the different items they collected make. Each group will place its pictures on a poster, then play its tape to the other groups. The members of the other groups will guess which item the sound goes with and then determine if it is useful or noise, pleasant or unpleasant, or any combination of these. They must be able to explain why they would classify the item that way. If your classroom has computers with access to the Internet, you can change this into a web-based search of objects that make noise instead of a magazine search. The students could cut and past the objects found into presentation software, recording their sounds on the computer and adding them to their presentation.

Science in Personal and Social Perspectives

- When listening to a portable CD player or MP3 player with earbuds on, is it wise to have the volume so loud that those around you can hear it?
- If you were asked to create a sound that would serve as a warning for some devastating disaster like a tornado, what would this sound be like? How would you categorize it? How unique would it have to be?

Science and Technology

- Why was it necessary for the Occupational Safety and Health Administration (OSHA) to set standards for an acceptable noise level in work areas?

- Many airports near major cities were built in areas that have long been considered migratory routes for some animals and mating habitats for others. The constant roar of jet engines affects the behavior of these animals. What have people done to eliminate some noise hazards brought upon these creatures? What must we continue to do?

Science as Inquiry

- How would you classify the sound best suited for quiet study time?
- Can sounds be classified into more than one category?

History and Nature of Science

- Which type of work do you think would be most affected by noise pollution? Least affected? Which type of work would you choose? Why?
- Do you think it is important for a music critic to distinguish between a useful sound or noise? A pleasant or unpleasant sound?

Evaluation

Upon completing the activities, the students will be able to:

- listen to an audiotape of various sounds and classify them according to useful/noise and pleasant/unpleasant; and
- take one of the assigned categories—useful/pleasant; useful/unpleasant; noise/pleasant; noise/unpleasant—and, over a week, find some music that they think fits into their assigned category and explain why they believe it does. Encourage the students to get their families involved in their search. If they cannot find some music that fits their category, they can create their own sound.

High versus Low and Soft versus Loud Sounds

Grade Level ● **2–4**
Discipline ● **Physical Science**

NATIONAL SCIENCE EDUCATION CONTENT STANDARDS–PHYSICAL SCIENCE—GRADES K–4

Position and Motion of Objects

▶ Vibrating objects produce sound. The pitch of the sound can be varied by changing the rate of vibration.

CONCEPTS TO BE CONSTRUCTED

▶ Sounds vary in loudness and pitch.

▶ Loudness is determined by the strength of the vibration. Pitch is determined by the length of the vibrating object. Magnification of sound is achieved by megaphones and speakers.

Engaging Question

What can I do to make a sound, sound louder or sound higher?

Materials Needed

For the Discrepant Event, the teacher will need:
   1 large and 1 small bell

Exploration—conducted whole class, each student will need:
   1 piece of paper at least 8-inch × 8-inch square and tape for the paper
   1 plastic straw
   Scissors to cut the straw

Expansion—conducted in groups of three or four students per group, each group will need:
   4 different-sized bells
   A journal or paper to record predictions and observations

Safety Precautions: Remind students to be careful when using the scissors and to remember basic scissors safety. Also, be careful when placing the straws into your mouth, and during the expansion activity, do not ring a bell in anyone's ear.

Discrepant Event: Find a time when the students are working quietly in their seats. Take a large and a small bell, and ring them at the same time. Ask the students, "Did I get your attention? Did you hear just one noise or two? Did one sound softer than the other? Higher than the other?" Tell them that today's activities will help to clarify their responses.

Exploration

Megaphones and Vibrating Straws

PROCESS SKILLS USED

▶ Observing
▶ Communicating
▶ Inferring
▶ Predicting

What will the students do?

Ask half the students to shout "hello" to you from their seats. Now ask them to cup their hands around their mouths and shout "hello" again. Ask those who did not yell whether they noticed a difference in the sound produced. Now let the other half try it. Give the children pieces of paper, and have them roll them into cones. Tape the sides together to maintain the cone shapes. Use the scissors to cut away about 1 inch of the pointed end of each cone. Once again, have half the class shout "hello," and then shout again, holding the cut ends of the cones by their mouths. Once again, ask the listeners whether they noticed a difference in the sound produced each time. Allow the other half to test their cones too.

Give the students one straw each. Ask them to cut a little piece off both sides of one end so that what remains looks like an inverted V. Ask them to predict what will happen when they blow into the cut end of the straw. What do they need to do to get the cut V-shaped pieces to vibrate? As they hold the straws in their mouths, they should continue to blow into the straws and start cutting off pieces at the ends of the straws. What is happening to the sound as the straw gets shorter?

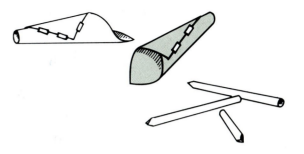

Explanation

Concept: Sounds vary in loudness and pitch.

Ask the students the following questions about their exploration activities:

- When did the "hellos" sound the loudest? Was it when you used nothing, your hand, or your school-made megaphone?
- What does a megaphone do? It magnifies sound. It increases the strength of the vibration, thus making the sound louder.
- What happened to the sound produced by the straw as you cut it?
- Was the loudness of the sound the same? What property of sound changed? The pitch got higher. *Pitch* is determined by the length of the vibrating object.
- Summarize this activity by asking the children to respond to the inquiry question: What would you do to make a sound, sound louder? What would you do to make a sound, sound higher?

Expansion

PROCESS SKILLS USED

▶ Predicting
▶ Designing an experiment
▶ Communicating
▶ Controlling variables
▶ Experimenting
▶ Observing
▶ Recording data
▶ Hypothesizing
▶ Inferring

How will the idea be expanded?

Divide the students into groups. Give each group at least four different-sized bells. Before ringing each bell, ask the students to create a prediction sheet identifying the loudness and pitch of the bell. Have each group design a way that will most fairly and accurately ring the bells. Emphasize the importance of keeping all other variables constant when comparing the four bells, such as having the same person ring the bells for each trial or having each person in the group ring each bell to determine whether the person doing the ringing affects the loudness or pitch. After filling out their prediction sheet and designing a way to ring the bells without letting their predictions prejudice them, they should ring the bells. Record your results. Did your results match your predictions? Is there any way in which you can alter the bell to magnify the sound coming from it?

Bell Ringers

Science in Personal and Social Perspectives

- What harm can the earbuds on headsets have on your eardrums? What does the magnification of sound do to your eardrums?
- Would the magnification of sound be useful at a baseball or football game? Why or why not? Would everyone at these games appreciate sound being magnified?

Science and Technology

- How has knowledge of loudness, pitch, and magnification led to the creation of devices that are important for crowd control? For large group communication? For the production of music?
- Why do you think a baseball stadium needs to be designed differently from a concert hall? In which would you want the sound to be louder? To be magnified?

Science as Inquiry

- What does it take to control the loudness of the sound created by a piano?
- How could you change the pitch of a guitar?

History and Nature of Science

- In what careers would you need to understand that loud sounds could set objects vibrating, which could cause structures to collapse? (Safety engineers, contractors, civil engineers, hotel/motel managers, high-rise office building workers)
- How can a cheerleader save his or her voice by knowing about sound, loudness, pitch, and magnification?

Evaluation

Upon completing the activities, the students will be able to:

- infer, when given a set of pictures (large bell, small bell, siren, whistle), which would create a loud or soft sound and then explain their response, using terms such as *pitch* and *vibration;*
- infer, when given another set of pictures (long and short guitar strings, large bell, small bell, man's voice, child's voice), which would create a high or low sound; and
- give at least three ways in which one could magnify one's voice.

Vibrations Causing Sound

Grade Level ● **2–4**

Discipline ● **Physical Science**

Engaging Question

What causes sound?

Materials Needed

For the Discrepant Event, the teacher will need:

    1 recording device with prerecorded classroom sounds

Exploration—conducted in groups of three to four students per group, each group will need:

    2–3 rubber bands of varying thicknesses
    At least a 12-inch length of string
    1 plastic kitchen fork
    1 metal pan filled with water
    1 tuning fork with a rubber mallet

Expansion—conducted whole class, each student will need:

    1 plastic comb
    1 piece of waxed paper large enough to cover the comb

Safety Precautions: Remind students of the importance of using the rubber bands as instructed. Any other use may result in injury to eyes or faces. Exercise caution when carrying the kitchen forks during the exploration activity.

Discrepant Event: Ask the students to listen carefully as you play the tape recording of classroom sounds. Try to guess what these familiar sounds are. Can you give any descriptive terms to remember them by?

CONCEPTS TO BE CONSTRUCTED

► Vibrations are caused by the movement of air molecules due to a disturbance.
► There are many ways to produce sounds. You may not be able to see all vibrations.

Exploration

PROCESS SKILLS USED

► Observing
► Communicating
► Recording data
► Experimenting
► Predicting
► Inferring

What will the students do?

- Have the students place their hands on their throats and make sounds. Record what it feels like.
- In groups, ask the students to stretch and pluck rubber bands and strings. Record their observations.
- Have the students place the handle end of a kitchen fork between their teeth. Quickly flick the other end of the fork. What do their teeth feel like?
- In groups, ask the students to tap pans of water and observe.

Sound Makers

- In groups, have the students tap tuning forks with rubber mallets and observe. Ask them to predict what will happen if they strike a tuning fork and quickly thrust it into a pan of water. Have them check their predictions.

Explanation

Concept: Vibrations are caused by the movement of air molecules due to a disturbance.

To invent the concept, ask the students the following questions about their exploration activities:

- What did it feel like when you placed your hands on your throat and made sounds? Did your hands begin to tingle?
- What happened to the rubber bands when you stretched them out and plucked them?
- How did your teeth feel when you flicked the kitchen fork?
- What path did the water create when the pan was gently tapped?
- Did the tuning fork tickle your hand when you struck it with the rubber mallet?
- What happened when you thrust the tuning fork into the water? Was it as you predicted?
- As the students are sharing their responses, record key terms they use to describe their observations. They may use terms such as they felt movement or it tickled or tingled. Elicit the idea that sound is produced by movement. If no one says "vibrate," introduce this term now. Ask the students to reflect on what was vibrating; in each case they might say their throat, the rubber band, the fork, etc. Ask them to think about what surrounded each of those objects: air. Summarize by asking for their ideas on the inquiry question: What causes sound?

Expansion

Waxed-Paper Kazoo

PROCESS SKILLS USED
▶ Inferring
▶ Experimenting
▶ Hypothesizing
▶ Communicating

How will the idea be expanded?

Have each student make a comb-and-waxed-paper kazoo by folding a piece of waxed paper over the teeth of a comb. Instruct the children to place their lips on the wax paper and to hum a tune. How is the sound being produced? What is vibrating?

Science in Personal and Social Perspectives

- How is sound made? Can you avoid sound?
- Do sounds affect the way you feel and act?
- Would you want to attend a concert or go to a movie where the sound kept echoing off the walls? Why or why not?

Science and Technology

- The quality of speakers and sound systems relies heavily on sound vibrations; how has modern technology eliminated a lot of excess vibrations?
- How important a role does the design of a room play in carrying sound vibrations?
- How did an understanding of sound vibrations help in the creation of the microphone, the phonograph, the telephone, underwater depth sounding, and ultrasound? How have these inventions changed the world?

- Knowing that sound is produced by a vibrating object, do you think you can make a bell ring under water? Try it.
- Some birds, such as loons, can dive under water for their food and stay down for an extended period of time. Do you think they call to one another while they are under the water? Can they hear each other? What could you do to determine whether your answer is correct?

History and Nature of Science

- Who was John William Strutt, also known as Baron Rayleigh? What role did he play in helping us to understand how sound behaves? (For second grade, the teacher could give a brief biography of Baron Rayleigh. He was born in England in 1842. While many people before him expressed opinions about the nature of sound— Pythagoras, Galileo, Mersenne, Chladni ["the founder of modern acoustics"], Colladon and Sturm, and von Helmholtz—Baron Rayleigh was the first to put it all together in a book titled *Theory of Sound,* which he published in 1877. A second edition was published in 1894. In 1904, Rayleigh won the Nobel Prize for physics, mainly for his work that led to the discovery of argon and other inert gases. Baron Rayleigh died in 1919.)
- Sound production is important in entertainment. Develop a list of entertainment careers that utilize sound.

Evaluation

Upon completing the activities, the students will be able to:

- predict from a given set of objects which will vibrate and produce sound (Nerf ball, drum, taut rubber band, loose rubber band, ruler, feather); and
- spend one week in which they will be expected to test various wall surfaces to determine which ones allow for maximum and for minimum sound vibrations. They will share their findings with the class and, based on these findings, accurately predict which type of wall surface would be best for a movie theater or a concert hall.

Loudness and Pitch

Grade Level ● 2–4
Discipline ● Physical Science

Position and Motion of Objects

▶ Vibrating objects produce sound. The pitch of the sound can be varied by changing the rate of vibration.

CONCEPTS TO BE CONSTRUCTED

▶ Sounds vary in loudness and pitch.

▶ Size and strength of vibration will affect loudness and pitch.

Engaging Question

If I change the loudness of a sound, do I change the pitch?

Materials Needed

For the Discrepant Event, the teacher will need:

    1 glass
    1 large nail to tap on the glass
    Water to eventually fill the glass

Exploration—conducted in four student groups that will rotate through four different stations:

All students will need:

    A journal or paper to record data as they rotate through the stations

Station 1 will need:

    6–8 glass soda bottles
    6–8 glasses
    2 large nails to tap on bottles and glasses
    Water source to fill bottles and glasses with varying levels of water

Station 2 will need:

    Rubber bands of varying widths and lengths
    1 cigar box or sturdy shoe box

Station 3 will need:

    8 different lengths of fish line
    16 eye hooks
    A foot long, 1-inch × 8-inch board

Station 4 will need:

    A guitar or a piano with the guts exposed

Expansion—conducted whole class, you will need:
    The glasses or bottles from previous activity
    A song that is familiar to whole class to be played on glasses or bottles

Safety Precautions: Remind students that care should be taken when handling any of the glass containers used in many of the activities and to protect eyes against flying rubber bands by wearing goggles!

Discrepant Event: Ask the students to predict what will happen to the sound as you tap an empty glass with a nail and gradually add water as you tap. Once all predictions have been given, begin to tap the glass and fill it as you do so. Did the sound behave as you predicted? What happened to the sound as more water filled the glass? Do you have any ideas why this happened?

Soda Bottle Orchestra

What will the students do?

Divide the class into four groups. Have each group rotate through the following activities:

Soda bottles, glasses, water, nails: Set up a center with glasses and bottles filled with water at varying levels. Have children explore sound variation with water levels in both glasses and bottles. Ask them to record their observations, taking special note of the relationship between the sound produced and the amount of water in the different containers.

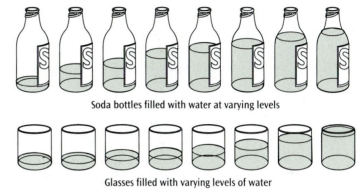

Soda bottles filled with water at varying levels

Glasses filled with varying levels of water

Rubber bands of varying widths and lengths, open cigar box or shoe box: Stretch the different-sized rubber bands over the open cigar box. Pluck the rubber bands. What kinds of sounds do they make? Record the sounds made by the different-sized rubber bands.

Make a fish line harp by cutting at least eight different lengths of fish line. String each line through two eye hooks that are screwed into a foot-long piece of board (a 1 × 8 will do) the same distance apart as the string length. (The teacher can make this harp ahead of time.) Pluck the strings. What do you observe about the relationship between the string length and the sound produced? Is there a relationship between the sound produced and the tightness of the string?

Cigar Box Strings

Strum a guitar, or play a piano in which the guts are exposed. If you are using a guitar, what relationship do you observe between the size of the guitar string and the sound it produces? For the piano, what relationship do you observe between the size of the piano string and the sound it produces?

Fish Line Harps

Concept: Sounds vary in loudness and pitch.

Ask the students to reflect on their exploration activities by responding to the following questions:

• What did you observe when you tapped the various glasses and bottles?
• What happened to the sound if you used a lot of force to strike the nail to the container? In which containers were the sounds higher?
• How were you able to make the rubber band sound loud when plucked?
• What types of sounds were produced with very skinny, tightly stretched rubber bands? Very fat, loosely stretched ones?

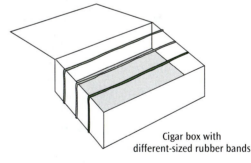

Cigar box with different-sized rubber bands

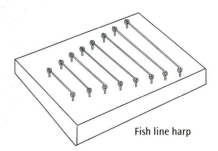

Fish line harp

- When you played the harp, which length string gave you the highest sound? The lowest? Did you try loosening the strings? What happened to the sounds when the strings were loose?
- When you played the guitar or piano, what did you do to create a very loud sound? How were you able to get a very high sound? A low sound?
- Summarize all the answers by asking the students to complete these sentence starters: The strength of the vibration determines the _____ (loudness) of the sound. When you change the length of the vibrating object, you change the _____ (pitch).

Expansion

Homemade Music

PROCESS SKILLS USED
▶ Predicting
▶ Communicating
▶ Experimenting
▶ Interpreting data

How will the idea be expanded?

On the basis of your conclusions from the previous activities, choose a song familiar to everyone in your group and try to play that simple melody on the glasses, the bottles, or any of the other instruments. Each group will take a turn performing for the other groups.

Science in Personal and Social Perspectives

- The ability to produce music enriches the lives of children and can lead to a lifetime skill. The ability to control sound enhances self-concept.
- How could you use sound to help you determine how much soda you have left in a can? Or how much milk is left in a carton? Or how much laundry detergent is left in its container? Or if a new bottle of perfume or aftershave is totally full?

Science and Technology

- Many video games use sound to heighten the suspense and action of the play. Do you think these games would be as popular if all sound were eliminated?
- What effect does the loudness and pitch of music have on moviegoers? Would scary movies be as effective without the sound effects?
- How has the computer industry made use of the loudness and pitch of sounds in personal computers?

Science as Inquiry

- What properties affect the pitch of a sound? The loudness of a sound? Can you create an instrument with high pitch and soft sound? With low pitch and loud sound?

History and Nature of Science

- Children enjoy music for listening and movement and may look to a future as an entertainer. Ask the students to trace the history of an instrument. Who designed it? How does it produce sound?
- Where do you think someone with a background in music production, sound engineering, or the creation of musical instruments could use his or her talents?

Evaluation

Upon completing these activities, the students will be able to:

- predict whether a high or low pitch will be produced by looking at pictures of various-sized strings or columns of water;
- predict loudness and softness of sound when given pictures of thick or thin strings of the same length;
- create a high-pitched sound when given a straw; and
- create a low pitch with a soda bottle.

Sound Movement as Waves

Grade Level ● 2–4
Discipline ● Physical Science

NATIONAL SCIENCE
EDUCATION CONTENT
STANDARDS–PHYSICAL
SCIENCE—GRADES K–4
Position and Motion of Objects

▶ Vibrating objects produce sound.
The pitch of the sound can be
varied by changing the rate of
vibration.

Engaging Question

Can sound move through everything?

**CONCEPTS TO
BE CONSTRUCTED**

▶ Sounds move in the form of
waves through air, water, wood,
and other solids.

▶ Sound waves must strike your
eardrum for you to hear sound;
sound waves weaken with
distance.

Materials Needed

For the Discrepant Event, the teacher will need:

> The students seated as desks or tables

Exploration—conducted in five student groups that will rotate through five different
stations:

All students will need:

> A journal or paper to record data as they rotate through the stations

Station 1 will need:

> 1 12-inch length of string tied to the handle end of a metal fork

Station 2 will need:

> 1 metal rod

Station 3 will need:

> 2 wooden blocks, which can easily be made by cutting a 2-inch × 4-inch board in
>   4-inch pieces
> 1 meter stick

Station 4 will need:

> Piece of cloth
> Cotton balls
> Feathers
> Cork
> Nerf ball

Station 5 will need:

> A tank of water such as a fish tank

Expansion—conducted per student pair, each pair will need:

> 2 paper cups
> 2 paper clips
> 1 length of string at least 2-feet long
> 2 metal food cans
> 1 length of fishing line to make a can phone

⚠ *Safety Precautions:* Remind students that care should be taken when handling
the kitchen fork and tuning forks; keep them away from your own eyes and those of
your friends. Be careful where you place your fingers as you bang the two wood blocks
together; avoid crushing them between the blocks.

Discrepant Event: Ask the students to listen as they tap the sides of their desks. Now ask them to lay their ears on their desktops while tapping the sides of the desks with the same force as before. Have them describe the sounds they hear. Are there any differences? If so, why?

Exploration

PROCESS SKILLS USED

▶ Observing
▶ Recording data
▶ Predicting
▶ Inferring
▶ Describing
▶ Communicating
▶ Measuring
▶ Defining operationally

What will the students do?

Divide the class into five groups. Have each group record its observations while rotating throughout the following activity centers.

Vibrating Fork　　Tie about a 12-inch length of string to the handle end of a fork. Allow it to bang on the side of a desk or a wall as you set it in swinging motion. Write a description of the sound it creates. Can you manipulate the string or fork in any way to change the pitch or loudness of the sound? Can you feel the vibrating fork through the string?

Striking Rod　　Hold the metal rod and strike it against a wall, a book, a desk, a variety of surfaces. Is sound produced? Which striking surface will make the rod sound the loudest? The softest? Why do you think this is so?

Clapping Blocks　　Take turns with members of your group clapping the two wood blocks together. Use the meter stick to measure the distance at which the clapping blocks sound the loudest. How far can you move away from the clapping blocks and still hear them?

Sound Producers?　　Using the cloth, cotton, feathers, cork, and Nerf ball, try to produce a sound. Is it possible to create a sound if you simply drop the items on your desk? What if you strike them with your hand? Are these items capable of producing sound? Why or why not?

Tapping Tank　　Place your ear to one end of the filled fish tank. Have another student gently tap the glass on the other side of the tank. Can you hear this sound? If so, did the sound travel through the glass or through the water? This time place your ear so that it is directly above the tank. Have a friend gently drop a quarter into the fish tank when you are not looking. Could you hear when the quarter hit the bottom of the tank?

Explanation

Concept: Sounds move in the form of waves through air, water, wood, and other solids.

Ask the students to reflect on their exploration activities to answer the following questions:

- Were you able to make the fork sing? How did you do this?
- Did the hand that was holding the string feel anything as the fork sang?
- What about the metal rod? How did you get it to sound the loudest? Could you see the rod moving as it made sound?
- What about the wood blocks? Were they very loud? How did your hands feel as you banged the blocks together?
- What about the cloth, cotton, feathers, cork, and Nerf ball? Were you able to get them to make a sound when they were dropped? Why or why not? Do these items

behave like the fork, metal rod, or wood blocks? What can those items do that the cloth items cannot? (Help students realize that objects that vibrate will set the air in motion to create a sound.)

- Could you hear sound through the water? When was it the easiest to detect?
- Why is it important that your ear be facing the source of the sound? Sound waves must strike your eardrum for you to hear sound.
- On the basis of your observations from our class activities, how would you answer our engaging question: "Can sound move through everything?" The students should conclude that sound cannot move through everything. Sounds move in waves through air, water, wood, and other solids.

Expansion

How will the idea be expanded?

Provide each student with two paper cups and any length of string (minimum two feet). Instruct the students to poke a small hole in the end of each of their paper cups and thread the string through the holes. Tie the end of the string to a paper clip to prevent the string from slipping out of the cup. Ask the students to work in pairs trying out their paper cup telephones. Experiment with loose versus tight string and long versus short string. Compare results. Touch the string as they talk to dampen the sound. Ask each pair to try using the metal can–fishing line telephone. Ask whether there is any difference between this phone and the one they made. Which telephone sets up more vibrations? What can student's say about how sound travels?

Paper Cup Telephone

Science in Personal and Social Perspectives

- Where in your house would be the best place to set your stereo speakers: on a metal table or a cloth-covered bench? Or would neither of these be good? Can you suggest a good place?
- Why do you think most homes have doorbells? How are these better than just yelling for our friends?
- Do you think it is fair for people who are fishing to use a fish echolocator to determine where the fish are before they begin fishing?
- Do you think it is ethical for someone to use knowledge of sound to eavesdrop on other people for such purposes as collecting military intelligence, listening in on criminals, or listening to other people's conversations?

Science and Technology

- What materials would you use and how would you go about building a soundproof room? Can you create a plan that would be easy to follow that takes all variables into account in building this room? Work with your parents to create a working model of your design.

Science as Inquiry

- A knowledge of the conductivity of sound helps to develop further concepts of controlling sound loudness, quality, and usefulness.
- Do you think you could design a can phone that lets three or more people use it at once? Try it. Draw a diagram of your design.

History and Nature of Science

- How have marine biologists used their knowledge of sound to study the humpbacked whale? Why should we be concerned about the singing behavior of the humpbacked whale?
- Why would a pilot be concerned with how sound travels? If you had been a pilot of the supersonic Concorde, would you have had a problem trying to get permission to land your plane in Columbus, Ohio? If so, why?
- How did Alexander Graham Bell apply his understanding of sound? Identify one of his inventions, and describe how it works.

Evaluation

Upon completing the activities, the students will be able to:

- rank-order a given set of materials from good to poor conductors of sound: air, wood, metal rod, cotton string, wire, water, cotton balls; and
- take an object that is capable of creating sound when struck and alter it so that when it is struck, the loudness of the sound is decreased.

Sound Waves

Grade Level ● 5–8

Discipline ● Physical Science

▶ Light interacts with matter by transmission (including refraction), absorption, or scattering (including reflection)

And Position and Motion of Objects from K-4

▶ Vibrating objects produce sound. The pitch of the sound can be varied by changing the rate of vibration.

Engaging Question

What is a sound wave?

Materials Needed

For the Discrepant Event, the teacher will need:

    1 soup can with both ends open
    1 balloon
    1 strong rubber band
    1 rectangular mirror smaller than the opening of the soup can
    1 flashlight

Exploration—conducted in groups of three or four students per group, each group will need:

    1 soup can reflector like the one used in the discrepant event
    1 flashlight
    1 Slinky
    Journal or paper to record observations

Expansion—conducted in groups of three or four students per group, each group will need:

    1 Slinky
    1 plastic ruler
    1 diagram of the inner ear

CONCEPTS TO BE CONSTRUCTED

▶ Sound travels in waves. Waves consist of areas of compression and rarefaction. Waves move through the air.

▶ Sound waves cause vibrations as they hit the eardrum, causing us to hear sounds.

Safety Precautions: Be sure that all rough edges are filed off soup cans before providing the cans to student groups. Make sure there are no sharp edges on the mirrors; file them if necessary. Encourage the students to use caution near edges of mirror and soup can.

Discrepant Event: Stretch a piece of the balloon over one end of the soup can. Secure it tightly with the rubber band. Glue a small piece of mirror on the balloon membrane, slightly off center. Shine a flashlight onto the mirror so that its reflection shows up on the chalkboard. Ask the students to observe the mirror's reflection on the board. Ask one student to come up and speak into the open end of the can. What happens to the mirror's reflection on the chalkboard when someone speaks into the can?

Exploration

PROCESS SKILLS USED

▶ Observing
▶ Experimenting
▶ Predicting
▶ Hypothesizing
▶ Inferring

What will the students do?

Divide the students into groups depending on class size. Have one soup can reflector for each group. Provide each group with a flashlight. Ask the students to predict and then record what happens to the soup can reflectors as

Soup Can Reflectors

they vary the loudness of the sound. What do you think is causing the mirror's reflection to move? Think of this as you begin to play with a Slinky. Stretch and shake the Slinky, and record what the Slinky looks like as you do this. A diagram may be useful at this point. Try to label where the Slinky looks mashed together and where it looks thin on your diagram.

Explanation

Concept: Sound travels in waves. Waves consist of areas of compression and rarefaction. Waves move through the air.

- What do you think caused the mirror to move? Can you actually see the balloon moving as someone speaks into the open end of the can? Speaking into the can set the balloon membrane vibrating.
- Can you feel the vibration of the balloon if you lightly touch it as someone speaks into the open end? What type of pattern does the moving mirror make on the board? How is this pattern similar to the movement of the Slinky?
- What would be a good name to describe the path sound travels in? (Waves.) Ask for a volunteer to share his or her drawing of Slinky movement with the class. Reproduce this drawing for all to see.
- As you moved the Slinky, were you able to detect areas where the Slinky was mashed together? Were you able to detect areas where it was more spread out?
- Share with the students that these Slinky movements are similar to sound waves. Areas where sound waves are mashed together are called *compression;* areas that are spread out are called *rarefaction.* Ask the students to complete this statement that answers the inquiry question: Sound travels in the form of _____ (waves). A wave has a _____ (high) and _____ (low) area. At times, the waves are mashed together or _____ (compressed); at other times, the waves are spread out.

Expansion

PROCESS SKILLS USED

▶ Observing
▶ Manipulating materials
▶ Inferring
▶ Predicting
▶ Communicating

Slinky Waves

Sound Waves and the Ear

How will the idea be expanded?

Ask the students to take turns laying their heads on their desks while another student stretches the Slinky out on top of the desk and releases it rapidly, or have another student hold a ruler over the edge of the desk and strike it quickly. Ask the student with his or her head on the desk what this felt like. What did the student's ear detect?

Provide the students with diagrams of the inner ear. Ask them to label what they believe is the path that sound takes as it reaches our ears. Use the ear model to trace this path for the students. Allow them to check their labeled predictions with the model you are tracing. Remind them that sound waves vary in strength. As the sound waves hit the eardrum, they cause it to vibrate in rhythm with them, causing sound messages to the brain. The human ear can interpret sound waves with frequencies ranging between 16 and nearly 20,000 vibrations per second. Vibrations above 20,000 are termed *ultrasonic.*

Science in Personal and Social Perspectives

- Why is it important that you never put anything in your ear smaller than your elbow? What kind of ear-cleaning products do you think are the safest to use?
- Have you ever tried to talk to your friends while you are under water swimming? Is it easy to understand someone talking under water? Why or why not?
- Interview people in different lines of work who use earplugs, such as factory workers, road construction crews, or building contractors. What types of earplugs do they use? How well do they think their earplugs work?
- Is it a good idea to wear headphones while riding your bicycle? Why or why not?

Science and Technology

- How effective are earplugs in preventing potentially damaging sounds from reaching your eardrum?
- Write to the manufacturers of the various earplugs. What materials do they use to make their earplugs? Is any one material better than another? What is the most widely used brand of earplugs? (A teacher can assign this question as homework or as another expansion activity for the class to investigate.)

Science as Inquiry

- At a track meet, why do you think you see the spark and smoke from the starter's gun before you hear the sound made by the gun? Can you explain this phenomenon in terms of sound waves?
- If someone in the room was speaking to you and you could detect only faint, muffled sounds, what might be the probable cause for your loss of hearing? How is sound supposed to travel from your ear canal to your brain?

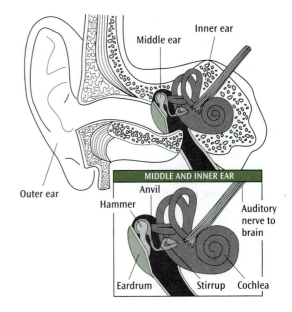

History and Nature of Science

- What do you think would happen to you if you had a job working at an airport loading cargo onto planes and you did not wear protective headphones?
- Why would a piano tuner need to be aware of compression and rarefaction of sound waves? How could he or she apply this knowledge in his or her work?
- Interview a local audiologist. What does his or her job entail? What kind of knowledge is needed to perform the job? Ask if the audiologist could share with you any cases in which a person's job affected his or her hearing. Share the interview with the class.

Evaluation

Upon completing the activities, the students will be able to:

- identify areas of rarefaction and compression on a diagram of sound waves; and
- trace the path of the sound waves from their source through the ear when given a worksheet with a diagram of the ear. The students should be able to label the ear canal, eardrum, bones of the middle ear, and nerve to the brain.

NATIONAL SCIENCE
EDUCATION CONTENT
STANDARDS–PHYSICAL
SCIENCE—GRADES 5-8

Transformations of Energy

▶ Energy exists in many forms, including heat, light, chemical, nuclear, mechanical, and electrical.
Energy can be transformed from
one form to another.

Energy Changes in Sound Production

Grade Level ● 5–8
Discipline ● Physical Science

CONCEPTS TO BE CONSTRUCTED

▶ Sounds are produced by
vibrations.

▶ A vibrating object has an
energy source. Moving energy
is referred to as *kinetic*.
Vibrations that cause sound can
be produced by hitting,
plucking, stroking, or blowing
an object.

Engaging Question

Do energy changes make sound?

Materials Needed

Exploration—conducted whole class, you will need:

Journal or paper to record observations

Various percussion instruments, such as drums, cymbals, and xylophones

Materials to make noises, such as pots and pot lids

Expansion—conducted in groups of three or four students per group, each group
will need:

1 soup can with both ends open

1 balloon

1 strong rubber band

1 rectangular mirror smaller than the opening of the soup can

1 flashlight

For Homework Assignment

12 used soft drink cans

Tape to seal top of cans

Materials to put into cans to make noise: dried rice, beans, peas, marbles, BBs, gravel,
sand, bits of Styrofoam, puffed rice, and any other small objects.

Safety Precautions: Remind the students to exercise caution when making
sounds with the instruments. They should be reminded not to hold the instruments
up to a friend's or their own ear when the sound is loud or piercing. During the expansion activity, they must use care when handling the mirrors and watch for sharp edges
on the cans.

Exploration

**Noise and Sound
Identification**

PROCESS SKILLS USED

▶ Observing

▶ Recording data

▶ Predicting

▶ Hypothesizing

▶ Experimenting

What will the students do?

Activity 1. Ask the students to close their eyes, sit perfectly
still, and not speak. Tell them to listen carefully to all the
noises they can hear, even the slightest sounds that they normally ignore. After a few minutes ask them to open their
eyes and write descriptions of every noise they heard and, if
possible, identify what they believe is the source of those
sounds. Students should describe noises in terms ordinarily used for sounds, such as
high, low, loud, soft, hissing, rumbling, piercing, musical.

Activity 2. Tell the students that they are going to play a listening game. Ask the students to
close their eyes while the teacher makes a sound and then try to guess what the sound was.

The first one to guess what the sound was will make the next sound. Make sure everyone gets a turn.

Activity 3. Present various percussion instruments to the class, such as drums of various sizes, cymbals, pots, pot lids, and xylophones (toy ones work as well). Ask the students to guess how you can get each one to produce a sound. Ask the students to predict what causes each one to make a sound. Allow the students to experiment with the various instruments, asking them to take note of how sound is produced on each instrument. Ask the students to describe what it feels like. After students have done this, have them strike the instrument again and then hold it tightly. Ask them if the sound stopped. Why did it stop?

Explanation

Concept: Sounds are produced by vibrations.

Activity 1. Ask the students to go back to the first list they made. Make two columns on the board, one labeled *descriptive words* and the other *sound sources*. Ask the students to help fill in the chart from the lists they created. The class will be referring to this list after they discuss the other two activities.

Activity 2. Ask each student: What type of sound did you make for everyone to guess? How was the sound made? What energy source did you use to make it? Add these sounds to the list already on the board; include a third column, *how made*, to the chart.

Activity 3. When you hit your instrument, what did you set up? How did you get the sound to stop on your percussion instrument? Go over the list on the board from each of the activities. As the students share that they had to strike the object in some way (e.g., hitting, plucking, stroking, and blowing) to set it in motion, share with them that this energy of motion is called kinetic energy. As they went from no motion of the object to motion, they changed energy from one form to another. Energy causes movement. All of these actions use energy to create vibrations. Vibrations are the source of sound. Ask them how they would now respond to the inquiry question: Do energy changes make sound? The moving energy is called kinetic energy.

Expansion

PROCESS SKILLS USED
▶ Experimenting
▶ Predicting
▶ Inferring

How will the idea be expanded?

Divide the class into groups. Have each group stretch a piece cut from a balloon over one end of a soup can, using a rubber band to hold it tightly in place. Glue a small piece of mirror slightly off center. Darken the classroom, and hold the can at an angle to the blackboard. Using a flashlight, shine the beam so that it strikes the mirror and reflects on the board. Ask the group to predict what will happen to the mirror's reflection on the board as someone speaks into the open end of the can. Ask someone in the group to talk into the open end of the can. Ask the other members of the group to take note of what happens to the mirror's reflection as the person speaks into the can. Do your observations

Sound Movement

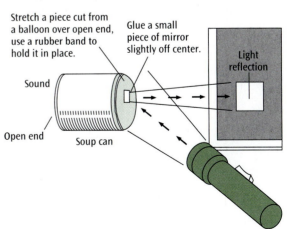

Stretch a piece cut from a balloon over open end, use a rubber band to hold it in place.

Glue a small piece of mirror slightly off center.

Light reflection

Sound

Open end   Soup can

match your predictions? What do you think causes the changes in the reflection? What source of energy causes the balloon to vibrate?

What is the home assignment?

This assignment may be done alone or with other family members.

Sound Game: "What Is Sound?"

1. Go home and sit down in your bedroom or the room of your choice, close your eyes, and be very quiet for three minutes. Listen carefully. Do you hear anything? Write down the sounds you hear and describe them.

2. If you heard new sounds, what were they, and why do you think you haven't heard them before?

3. How did the quiet make you feel? (To show how the quiet made you feel, you may write a descriptive paragraph, write a poem, or draw a picture.)

How well can you match sounds?

Students will construct a game for younger students. After the students have made the game, they will take it to a primary class and supervise the younger students playing it.

Preparation

Place small objects in a pair of cans, and then seal the cans with tape. Be sure the students cannot see in the cans and that the cans are prepared in pairs with approximately the same amount of material in each set of cans.

Procedure

1. Shake the cans and listen to the noise they make.
2. Can you hear the different sounds they make?
3. Do any of the cans make the same sound?
4. If you find cans that sound alike, put them next to each other.
5. Have a friend listen to the cans and find out whether he or she agrees.
6. You may want to make more cans with different sounds to determine how well your friends can tell the difference.
7. Does the speed at which you shake the can affect the sound?

Science in Personal and Social Perspectives

- What would your life be like without sound?
- What are some sounds that you hear around you, and how are they made?
- How have people made use of their knowledge that a vibrating body will produce a sound? What types of signals have we created because of this? (Fire alarms, smoke detectors, burglar alarms, foghorns.)
- When you wake up in the middle of the night and hear creaking stairs, knowing what you now know about sound, how can you explain away any fears that you might have?

Science and Technology

- How do vibrating strings allow us to create a violin, a guitar, or a bass fiddle? Why is it that some of the sounds created by these instruments sound soothing to some, while others may think of these same sounds as simply obnoxious noise?
- How do we record and transmit the sounds we make or the sounds that are made around us? Choose something that records sound or something that sound is recorded on. Draw a diagram explaining how it works.

- Explain how it is possible to create a percussion instrument. Make one, and describe how it works. Use terms such as *vibration* and *energy* in your explanation.
- Why do you think you enjoy certain types of music? Survey people of different ages as to their choices in music. Create a pie chart or bar graph to describe your results. Would you have predicted these results?

History and Nature of Science

- Why do you think it is important that a car mechanic is able to distinguish one sound from another? How does his or her job depend on recognizing engine sounds?
- Why do you think Beethoven was able to continue his musical career after he became deaf? Do you think it is possible for deaf people to "feel" sounds?
- What other occupations can you think of in which reliance on sound is essential?

Evaluation

Upon completing the activities, the students will be able to:

- describe sources of sound, explaining how a vibration is set up and the energy source for that vibration;
- report on their home assignment "What Is Sound?" and share with the class their poems, paragraphs, or drawings about the sounds they observed; and
- work successfully with the younger students when they play the "What Is Sound?" game they made, helping the younger students invent the concept of vibration.

States of Matter

Grade Level ● 3–4
Discipline ● Physical Science

NATIONAL SCIENCE EDUCATION CONTENT STANDARDS–PHYSICAL SCIENCE—GRADES K-4

Properties of Objects and Materials

▶ Materials have different states—solid, liquid, and gas. Some common materials such as water can be changed from one state to another by heating or cooling.

CONCEPTS TO BE CONSTRUCTED

▶ Anything that occupies space and has mass is called *matter*. Matter can be found in a solid, liquid, or gaseous state.

▶ Matter is made up of atoms which are joined together as molecules. Matter can undergo a physical or a chemical change.

Engaging Question

What is matter?

Materials Needed

Exploration—conducted in groups of three or four students per group, each group will need:

    A journal or paper to record observations
    2 plastic zipper storage bags, one labeled A and the other labeled B
    1 teaspoon of sodium bicarbonate, placed in bag A, which is then zipped closed
    1 teaspoon of calcium chloride (sold as ice melter during winter months), placed in bag B, which is then zipped closed
    1 magnifying glass
    1 small medicine cup with 10 ml of water in each

Expansion—conducted whole class, you will need:

    3 clear cups or plastic beakers
    Enough marbles to fill a cup
    Sand
    Water
    Graduated cylinder
    Scale

🛈 *Safety Precautions:* Remind students that safety goggles must be worn at all times. Since this is a guided discovery lesson, they are to listen to the teacher at all times before they begin to manipulate the materials—this is for their safety! Tell students not to taste anything during these activities.

Exploration

PROCESS SKILLS USED

▶ Manipulating materials
▶ Collecting and recording data
▶ Communicating
▶ Observing
▶ Hypothesizing
▶ Predicting inferring

What will the students do?

Because you are using unknown chemicals, it is best to lead the students through a guided discovery. First ask the students to think about common household products they are familiar with that might look like a white powder. Write that list on the board and even bring in the objects they suggest. Have them there so that *all* students have something to draw upon when they are asked to make predictions later in this opening activity. Do the same with clear liquids.

Provide the students with a clear plastic zipper storage bag labeled A. Ask them to make and record their observations on the unknown in bag A and to make a prediction as to what they think the unknown powders may be. Once the students have had sufficient time to make those observations, ask them to set bag A aside. Now guide the students through the same process with unknown B. (Stress the importance of keeping bags sealed and not tasting the unknown substances. Encourage the students to make observations about the shape of the unknown white powders). Now ask the students to first make a prediction as to what they think will happen if they combine unknown A with unknown B. Ask the students to open bag A, taking care not to touch or eat the substance, and pour it into bag B; then seal the bag. Ask the students to record their observations once the two unknown powders are combined. Did they behave as predicted?

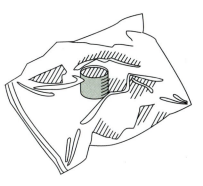

Plastic Bag Chemistry

Set aside the bag of the combined unknowns A and B and provide the students with a small clear cup of an unknown liquid C. Again, ask the students to make and record as many observations about unknown C as possible and to make a prediction as to what unknown C could be. Remind them about safety when making observations of unknowns (eliminate the sense of taste as it is an unknown and gently waft the fumes of the unknown toward their nose, do not place the cup directly under the nose to smell).

Once they have completed recording their observations about unknown C, ask the students to make a prediction about what they think will happen if they combine unknown C with unknowns A and B. After they record their predictions, allow them to combine unknown C with the bag containing unknown A and B. Remind them to immediately seal the bag once C is combined with unknowns A and B.

Encourage them to observe the bag, making careful observations (not only looking at the bag but also holding it to feel for any changes in temperature) and perhaps even drawing what they observed.

Explanation

Concept: Anything that occupies space and has mass is called *matter*.

By working with the unknown white powders, students can make observations in which they realize that the unknown substances are in a *solid* state of matter. By observing the unknown *liquid* and the mystery solution, also in a *liquid* state, they can see they are using another state of matter. Upon mixing the *solid* with a *liquid*, they can see the bag expanding, thus observing the third state of matter, a *gas*. Careful use of questions will also get the students to realize that *solids* always retain their shape, no matter the container. *Liquids* take up the shape of the container, and a *gas* will take up as much space as you give it.

Ask the students the following questions to help get to the ideas stated above:

- You drew pictures of the unknown white powders in bag A and in bag B. When you mixed them together, did they change their shape? (Work on the children's understanding of the concept of a solid, which does not change in shape. Physical change can be observed if they crush the solids; what was created is a *heterogeneous mixture*—a combination of two or more substances each distinct from the other.) If so, how? Why?

- Share your predictions as to what unknowns A, B, and C were. On what did you base your predictions? (Based predictions on common white powders they were familiar with). If time permits, an entire expansion activity can be done in which the students are given what one of the unknowns (A or B) is and they use a variety of known powders to see whether they get a similar reaction. Otherwise, at this point, you should share with the students the identity of the unknowns.

- What shape was the liquid in when it was inside the cup? What about when you poured it out? Why? (Work on the concept of liquids taking the shape of their container and only within the limit of the volume that the sample occupies.)
- What happened when you mixed the solids with the liquids? What did you observe? (Listing all of their observations will allow you to expand on specific secondary concepts you want the students to understand, such as physical versus chemical change.)
- Why did your bag get bigger? What took up that space in the bag? If you used a bigger plastic bag, would it be blown all the way up, too? If so, why? (Work on the concept of a gas taking the shape of its container.)
- Ask the students to now respond to the inquiry question: What is matter?

If you use this activity for older students, you could also introduce the students to chemical nomenclature. Provide students with the chemical formulas for the unknowns involved in the activity (older students may help derive these formulas and help balance the equation).

1) $NaHCO_3 + CaCl_2 + H_2O \longrightarrow NaCl\,(aq) + HCl\,(aq) + CaCO_3 + H_2O$
unknown A unknown B unknown C sodium hydrochloric calcium water
chloride acid carbonate

2) $CaCO_3 + H_2O \longrightarrow H_2CO_3 + CaO$
calcium water breaks carbonic calcium
carbonate down into acid oxide

3) $H_2CO_3 \longrightarrow H^+ + HCO^-_3 \longrightarrow$
carbonic breaks hydrogen calcium breaks
acid down into ion oxide down into

4) $CO_2(g) + H_2O$
carbon water
dioxide

as a gas that fills the bag

Expansion

Marble Matter

PROCESS SKILLS USED
▶ Measuring
▶ Predicting
▶ Hypothesizing
▶ Observing
▶ Recording data

How will the idea be expanded?

Again, this activity can be performed as a guided discovery or a class demonstration. Provide each student group with three clear cups or plastic beakers, marbles, sand, and some water. Ask the students to weigh a cup, then fill the cup with marbles. Record the weight of the cup and the number of marbles. Ask questions such as the following: How many marbles did you put in the cup? Do you think you can put in any more marbles? Did the marbles take the shape of the cup? (Work here to make sure the students understand that the marbles did not change their shape.) What was the weight of the cup? What state of matter are the marbles?

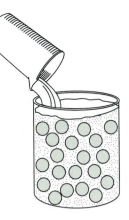

Ask the students to weigh another cup. Have them fill the cup with sand and then weigh it. Have them place a mark on the cup indicating the top of the sand. Use the same line of questioning for the marbles.

Now ask the students whether they think both cups are full. Ask the students if they think they can pour any of the sand into the cup filled with marbles. Solicit responses. React to responses: I thought you told me the cup with the marbles in it was full; how can you possibly put anything else into this cup?

Have the students pour some sand into the cup of marbles. Mark the new level of sand on the sand cup. What happens? Were you able to add sand into an already-filled cup of marbles? Why? What is the weight of your new mixture? What is the weight of the sand remaining in the cup? Subtract this remaining weight of sand from the original weight of sand. How much sand did you lose? Subtract the original weight of the marbles from the new weight of the marble and sand mixture. Is this amount gained equal to the amount lost from the sand cup? (Reinforce the concept of matter—anything that occupies space and has mass; concept of states of matter—two different solids. Secondary concept—physical change, matter was not created or destroyed, it still has the same weight; nothing was lost, just placed in different containers.)

Weigh a third cup and fill it with water. Have the students weigh this cup. Ask the students whether they think it is possible to put water into an already-filled cup of sand and marbles. Why or why not? What state of matter is the water? What do you know about liquids? (For older students, instead of weighing the water in a cup, introduce them to a graduated cylinder; have them measure out so many milliliters of water and record the volume of water in milliliters that they pour into the marble-sand cup.)

Was your prediction correct? What happened when you tried to add water to the marble-sand cup? Why could the container that was already filled with marbles still hold more sand and water?

Do you think we could have started with the water, then the sand and marbles? Why? What does this tell you about the sizes of molecules of different materials or substances? (The concept of solids versus liquids leads into a discussion of the size of particles. Smaller-size particles can slip between the larger ones. Make an analogy to molecules. Introduction of this new term may lead into a new unit on atoms and molecules.)

Science in Personal and Social Perspectives

- Which would you rather take a bath in: water mixed with sand or water mixed with bubble bath beads? Why?
- What would happen if you burned a dollar bill? Could you tape it back together and still have a dollar?

Science and Technology

- How has knowledge of chemical changes allowed the food industry to create cake mixes that can be made in a microwave rather than a regular oven?
- Getting matter to change its shape has allowed us to create many large buildings, such as the Sears Tower in Chicago. How is this so?

Science as Inquiry

- The students engage in manipulative skills during the activities.
- For understanding the concept of physical versus chemical change, ask the students to explain why they can heat snow and get water or why they can mix flour, eggs, water, baking soda, and sugar together, heat the mixture, and taste not these separate ingredients but a cake.
- Why can't you put a round peg in a square hole?

History and Nature of Science

- Using a list of all of the concepts discovered in the activities, ask the students to survey their parents and other adults to find out whether they make use of any of these concepts in their work. Where do they see them utilized? Are these people in typical scientific careers? Can anyone use these science concepts?
- Early scientists called *alchemists* thought they could turn simple elements into gold. Did everyone believe them at that time? Why or why not? Do you believe them? Why or why not?

Evaluation

Upon completing the activities, the students will be able to:

- demonstrate a physical change when given a piece of paper;
- provide examples of solid matter, liquid matter, and gas; and
- demonstrate how to capture a gas.

Changing Matter

Grade Level ● 5–8

Discipline ● Physical Science

Properties of Matter

Engaging Question

Do chemical changes result in useless matter?

Materials Needed

Exploration—conducted whole class, you will need:

1 compact disc (CD), 1 plastic baby bottle, 1 pan with nonstick suface, 1 pair of nylons, 1 football helmet

1 piece of paper per student

Expansion—conducted whole class, for each student you will need:

1 clear plastic cup containing 30 ml of white glue (e.g., Elmer's)

2–3 drops of food coloring (any color)

Popsicle sticks

1 cup with 30 ml of liquid starch for half the class

1 cup with 30 ml of a saturated borate solution for half the class (solution made by combining half cup of water with 1 cup of borax, such as 20 Mule Team Borax sold in the soap aisle at grocery store)

Paper towels for cleanup

1 lunch-size zipper storage bag for storing rubber balls

🛈 *Safety Precautions and/or Procedures:* During the exploration phase, when the paper is burned, the teacher should make sure there is adequate ventilation in the classroom. The teacher should also be sure the matches are kept away from the students and use care when an open flame is present: Sleeves must be pushed up, hair pulled back, and eyes protected. During the expansion phase, the students should be discouraged from putting their hands in their mouths. Be sure that they wash their hands as soon as they are finished with the activity.

▶ Substances react chemically in characteristic ways with other substances to form new substances (compounds) with different characteristic properties. In chemical reactions the total mass is conserved. Substances are often placed in categories or groups if they react in similar ways, for example, metals.

CONCEPTS TO BE CONSTRUCTED:

▶ An alteration of the composition or the properties of matter is called a *chemical change*. An alteration of the shape of matter without a change in its chemical composition is called a *physical change*.

▶ Small, single units of matter are called *monomers*. A substance that will speed up a chemical reaction without being affected itself is called a *catalyst*. A bond linking the chains of atoms in a polymer is a *cross-linker*. A compound formed by adding many small molecules together in the presence of a catalyst or by the condensation of many smaller molecules through the elimination of water or alcohol is a *polymer*.

Exploration

PROCESS SKILLS USED

▶ Observing

▶ Predicting

▶ Inferring

What will the students do?

Introduction: The teacher will allow the children to examine the following items: compact discs, baby bottles, nonstick pan, nylons, and a football helmet. As the students view the items, tell the students that you would like them to think about each item, and that by the time they finish the activities, they should be able to tell you what all the items have in common.

Student Activity: Give each student a piece of paper. Ask each of them to make his or her paper look different in some way. Then ask them to share what they did to make it look different.

Physical and Chemical Paper Change

Explanation

Concept: An alteration of the composition or the properties of matter is called a *chemical change*. An alteration of the shape of matter without changing its chemical composition is called a *physical change*.

Ask such questions as "What did you do to make the paper look different?" If they tore it up, ask, "If I taped it back together, would I still have a piece of paper? By changing its shape, did I do anything to change the molecules that came together to make that piece of paper?" Be sure to allow the students time to share their comments with one another. Explain that a change in shape with no loss of molecules is called a *physical change*.

If students suggest burning the paper, ask whether they think they will still be able to use the paper once you change it by burning it. Then burn it over the aluminum pie pan. Is the paper still in a usable form? If not, why not? Explain that the paper underwent a *chemical change*. When it burned, carbon atoms were lost. Do all chemical changes result in useless matter? Think about how you might respond to this question as we go through the next guided activity.

Expansion

Polymer-Rubber Balls

PROCESS SKILLS USED

▶ Observing

▶ Measuring

▶ Recording data

▶ Predicting

▶ Inferring

How will the idea be expanded?

1. Ask the students to use the graduated cylinders to measure out 30 ml of glue. Pour it into the clear cup. Choose a color from the food coloring, and mix it with your glue (use Popsicle sticks for stirring). Do you still have glue in front of you? What kind of change did the glue undergo?

2. What do you think will happen if you mix the colored glue with the liquid you have in front of you? (The teacher should place the liquid starch in front of half of the class and a borate solution in front of the other half.) Please make some predictions, and share them with one another on each side of the room. What do you think will happen when you mix the glue with the unknown liquid in front of you? Make your predictions and record them.

3. Ask the students to measure out 30 ml of either the starch or the borate solution. Encourage the students to make predictions about how much of the solution they will need to bring about a change in the glue. Since they do not know for certain how much starch or borate solution they will need, encourage the students to add one of these slowly, stirring all the time, until they see a change. Record how much starch or borate solution was necessary to bring about a change in the glue. Record any new observations you may have made about the colored glue.

4. Did you create anything new, or can you still tell the glue from the starch or borate solution? Can you pick up this new piece of matter? (Encourage the students to do so—the more they manipulate it in their hands, the more the water will come out, and eventually they will have created their own rubber ball.) What do you think you can do with it? What kind of change do you think you created by combining the glue with the starch or the borate solution? Why do you say this?

Go back to the original question: Do all chemical changes result in the creation of useless matter? How many of you think you created a new form of matter that is useful? What did you do differently from your classmates? What do you think you can do with your newly created piece of matter? How useful is it? As a teacher, you may encourage the students from the different sides of the room to compare their newly created rubber balls. Do they bounce the same? Roll the same? Feel the same? Two different catalysts were used to create this special kind of chemical change, which is called a *polymerization reaction*. After they finish, the students may place their balls in a zipper storage bag, where they will stay fresh for a few weeks.

Do you think that other inventions could have been discovered just by people mixing things together in the lab and making careful observations about how much and of what materials they mixed together?

Teflon, used to coat pans, is one of these accidental chemical combinations that was discovered in a lab when scientists weren't looking for it. Chemists realized that it was possible to get small pieces of matter to link up chemically when a catalyst was used to force the reaction to occur. Sometimes these smaller pieces of matter, called *monomers*, add together in one long chain to create *polymers*. Saran Wrap, Lucite, Plexiglas, and Teflon are polymers that are formed by this additive process. Polymers can also be formed by bringing monomers together, removing water or alcohol through a condensation reaction, and forcing the monomers to link together. This is what happened to form nylon, and this is what happened here to create a new form of matter—rubber balls! In addition to these synthetic polymers, there are naturally occurring polymers such as silk, cellulose, and rubber.

Go back to some of the first items that you showed to the students: the football helmet, the baby bottle, the CD, the nylons, and the nonstick pan. Encourage the students to think about the activities they just participated in as they try to answer the very first question you asked: What do all of these things have in common?

They were all created by a chemical change in which small pieces of matter, called monomers, were linked together to form polymers. These polymer reactions created new kinds of matter that have proven to be very useful.

Science in Personal and Social Perspectives

- Suppose you're tired of the color of your bedroom and you want to change the color of your walls. Will your room undergo a physical change or a chemical change?
- Can you name any products that were created because of a polymerization reaction that have directly affected your life?
- There is much controversy over the use of Teflon bullets. Police unions bitterly oppose their use. Why do you think this product, formed from a polymerization reaction, is of serious concern to our society?
- Knowledge of chemical changes has led to the invention of many products that have greatly changed society. Can you think of any products that were created as the result of a chemical change?

Science and Technology

- A technological advancement for many parents is the disposable diaper. Describe the materials that are used to make a disposable diaper. How has this technological advancement created more problems for society? Suggest possible solutions.

Science as Inquiry

- Can you demonstrate the difference between a physical change and a chemical change?
- Explain how a polymer can be created. How is this a unique type of chemical change?

- Can you name some monomers or polymers that are found in nature? How about some synthetic ones?

History and Nature of Science

- Do you think a cement finisher or a beautician needs to understand how a chemical change can occur? Why or why not?
- Are physical or chemical changes common in the type of work your parents do? Identify one of the changes, and explain where it occurs.
- Interview a female over age sixty. Ask her to describe what nylon stockings were like when she was twenty. How and why did they change?

Evaluation

Upon completion of the activities, the students will be able to:

- appreciate the need to think about a problem first, and then use clear, concise language to communicate the action taken on the problem;
- demonstrate the differences between physical and chemical changes;
- make predictions based on previous experiences;
- utilize the scientific method to solve a newly designed problem;
- explain how certain chemical reactions, such as polymer formation, can result in the creation of useful materials; and
- explain what a football helmet, a compact disc, a nonstick pan, a baby bottle, and a pair of nylons have in common.

Identification of an Unknown

Grade Level ● 5–8

Discipline ● **Physical Science**

▶ Substances have characteristic properties such as density, boiling point, and solubility, which are independent of the amount of the sample. A mixture of substances can often be separated into the original substances by using one or more of these characteristic properties.

Engaging Question

Can I rely solely on physical properties to identify an unknown?

Materials Needed

Exploration—conducted in groups of three or four students per group, each group will need:

> 1 pair of goggles for each student
> 5 clear plastic medicine cups, labeled 1–5
> In each cup, add 2 tablespoons of one of the unknown powders. Suggested powders to use are granulated sugar, table salt, baking soda, cornstarch, and plaster of Paris. Be sure to secretly record the cup number for each powder.
> 5 toothpicks
> 1 piece of black construction paper
> 1 hand lens per group member

Expansion—conducted in groups of three or four students per group, each group will need:

> Same materials each team used during the exploration phase
> 50 ml of water to start with (have more available if needed) and an eye dropper
> 5 small cups and 10 ml of iodine with eye dropper
> 5 small cups and 20 ml of vinegar with eye dropper
> Paper towels for cleanup

Expansion—step 4 done as a teacher demonstration, you will need:

> Heat source, such as a small candle in a lump of clay sitting in a pan of aluminum foil filled with wet sand, or an alcohol burner.
> 5 small pieces of aluminum foil, each fashioned into a small dish
> 1 clothespin to use as a handle to hold the foil, dish over the flame
> Water nearby to douse the open flame

Safety Precautions: Remind students of the following: Never taste any of the unknown substances unless the teacher gives permission. Goggles must be worn at all times! Wash hands between testing different unknowns and immediately after the lab is completed. Remove all combustible material from the area of the flame during the heat tests during expansion. Roll up sleeves and tie back hair when using an open flame.

Physical Properties of an Unknown

PROCESS SKILLS USED
▶ Observing
▶ Manipulating materials
▶ Inferring
▶ Collecting and recording data
▶ Communicating

What will the students do?

Start the lesson by asking the students the following: Have you ever thought about some of the common substances we use in our homes? For instance, how many of you can name some common white powder substances we may use in our homes? (List these on the board. If the ones that are used as secret powders are not suggested, make suggestions that will help the students think about those possibilities.) What are they used for? How do we know that what it says on the container is really what is inside? The following activity will provide you with skills to help identify unknown substances.

Give each student group five small cups numbered 1–5 and containing five different secret powders. The students will also receive five toothpicks to use as stirring sticks, some black construction paper to dump their powders on, and a hand lens. Ask the students to try to determine what the unknowns are, based on their observations of physical characteristics. The following questions should serve as a guide to encourage the students to focus on physical properties: How are the powders alike? How are they different? Do they feel the same? Does any powder have an odor? Are they the same shade of white? Can you list three properties of each powder? Can you list more than three? Using the hand lens, can you discover anything new about the powders? Are all the powders really powders? Can you describe the particles that make up each powder? Do you think a powder can be identified by the shape of its particles? Describe which properties of the powders seem to be the same and which seem to be different. Which properties are helpful in describing a particular powder?

Concept: Physical properties alone are not always sufficient characteristics to identify an unknown.

Ask the students to share answers to questions that were asked during the exploration phase. Refer back to the original list of common white powders from home. Ask the students to match up the unknowns to knowns on the basis of physical characteristics they observed. Salt and sugar are made of cube-shaped particles, but salt is much more uniform and less broken. Cornstarch, baking soda, and plaster of Paris are similar in appearance, and it is hard to distinguish one from another simply on the basis of physical characteristics.

Chemical Properties of an Unknown

How will the idea be expanded?

Discussion before the activity: Ask students whether they know why canaries were used in coalmines years ago, what good it is to know the pH of pool water, and why a gas

PROCESS SKILLS USED

▶ Designing an experiment

▶ Observing

▶ Measuring

▶ Predicting

▶ Hypothesizing

▶ Recording data

▶ Evaluating

▶ Controlling variables

▶ Interpreting data

▶ Reducing experimental error

gauge in a car is useful. Once you obtain answers to these questions, ask what these three questions have in common. Work at getting to the idea that all of these are indicators of some sort: Canaries indicate the quality of the air, pH indicates the acidity or alkalinity of water, and a gas gauge indicates the amount of gas in the car.

Indicators can be used to conduct tests on the secret powders to assist in a more accurate determination of the unknown. These indicators may bring about a physical or chemical change in the secret powder. (Be sure the students already know the difference between a physical change—one in which a change of shape can occur but the chemical composition of the original material is not altered, such as freezing of water or shredding paper—and a chemical change—a change in the composition of the original material in which molecules are lost and cannot be put back into the material to return it to its original composition, such as burning sugar or mixing vinegar and baking soda.)

During a discussion of the indicators, ask the students the following, to see whether they can determine how the indicators can be used in determining the identity of the secret powders: What do you think might happen when water (or iodine, vinegar, or heat added) is mixed with the secret powder? How might you go about doing this without contaminating your secret powder sample? Why is it important to avoid contamination?

Action: Observe the reactions of the five secret powders when acted on by the water, iodine, vinegar, and heat. Reaffirm the notion of contamination at this point. Have the students use separate eye droppers for the water, iodine, and vinegar. Be sure they use different toothpicks and clean containers to mix the unknown with the indicator. The students should record their results.

1. *Water:* What happens to each powder when you put a few drops of water on it? Did each powder mix with the water? Did any of the powders disappear? Did you put the same amount of powder in each cup? Is this important? What will happen if you add 20 drops of water? 50? 80? Does additional water affect the powders? Did any powders disappear? Where did they go? Did the powder leave the cup?

   As students work with the water, they will discover that sugar, baking soda, and salt are soluble in water. By comparing the number of drops needed to dissolve these powders, some students may conclude that sugar is more soluble in water than baking soda and that salt is the least soluble of the three. Both cornstarch and plaster of Paris are insoluble in water. Plaster of Paris will harden if permitted to stand for a short period of time. After hardening, plaster of Paris cannot be changed back into its original state. The concepts of solubility and evaporation, as well as the differences among solution, suspension, and mixture, can be highlighted through this portion of the activity if necessary.

2. *Iodine:* Place small amounts of secret powders in five separate cups. Add a few drops of iodine. Do all the powders react to iodine in the same way? How can iodine be used to distinguish one powder from another? Take a cracker and a piece of potato; how do these react with the iodine? Was this reaction similar to any of the secret powders' reactions? What do the cracker and potato have in common?

   The cup containing cornstarch will show a striking blue-black color when iodine is added. A deep blue or blue-black color on contact with iodine is the standard test for the presence of starch. The starchier the food, the more obvious and deep the blue color will be.

3. *Vinegar:* Place small amounts of secret powders in five separate cups. Add a few drops of vinegar. What happens when you put a few drops of vinegar on each

powder? Did any powder react more than others? Do you think that powders that dissolved in water will also dissolve in vinegar? Which powder do you think will take the least amount of vinegar to dissolve? The most? How can you find out? How can vinegar be used to distinguish baking soda from the other powders? If you place vinegar on an unknown substance and it bubbles, can you be sure that the substance is baking soda? Could it be another substance?

Baking powder fizzes actively when vinegar is added, while other powders fizz only slightly or not at all. Other powders can be tested with vinegar. A solution of powdered milk is curdled by vinegar.

4. *Heat:* In the interest of safety, this part may be done as a teacher demonstration for the whole class. Support a small candle in a lump of clay. This will supply sufficient heat to test the effects of heat on the powders. Fashion the aluminum foil into a small dish to be used to heat the secret powders. Use the clothespin as a handle for your aluminum dish when holding the dish over the flame. Be sure to make a separate dish for each powder.

Remove any combustible items from the area where the candle will be used. Roll up loose sleeves and tie back long hair while working with the burning candle. It is extremely important to use dry powder when performing this activity, to prevent spattering. Never use powders that have been mixed with any liquid. Place a small amount of powder in the dish and heat it.

Did any of the powders change when heated? Was an odor given off during heating? Do all the powders look the same after cooling? Compare them with samples of powders that were not heated. Were any new substances formed by heating?

When heated, baking soda and plaster of Paris seem to remain unchanged, while salt snaps and crackles. Starch turns brown and smells like burned toast. Sugar melts, bubbles, smokes, smells like caramel, turns brown, turns black, and finally hardens. The heat test, then, is a good way to detect sugar, since sugar is the only one of the secret powders to melt and turn shiny black when heated. The same reaction occurs to sugar even when it is mixed with any of the other powders.

After using the indicators, ask the students to share their results to help determine the identity of the unknown powders. Which powder turned black when iodine was added? Can you name the powder or powders that are soluble in water? Which liquid added to which powder caused bubbles? How can a hand lens help you to identify a powder? Is a hand lens helpful in identifying all substances?

Science in Personal and Social Perspectives

- Based on what you now know about physical and chemical properties of matter, explain why it is important to wash your hands before you eat any food. Do you think dirt on your hands could contaminate your food?
- Has this activity changed your mind on decisions you make about whether you like a certain food? Were you just using physical properties to judge the food in the past?
- How has this activity changed your mind on whether or not you want a certain person as your friend? Did you judge the person solely on his or her physical properties?

Science and Technology

- Do you think an automobile manufacturer could be competitive if it based a car's performance ability on results from one test? Why or why not? Encourage interested students to research the performance tests that cars undergo.
- Which properties of coal or oil make them a useful form of energy for our power plants: physical or chemical?

- Students engage in manipulative skills during the activities.
- You are given one of the five powders. When tested with vinegar, it bubbles. Can you identify the powder? Can you be sure of its identity?
- You are given one of the five powders. It dissolves in water. Can you identify the powder? Are additional tests needed? Can you eliminate any powders?

History and Nature of Science

- Can you think of any jobs in which avoiding contamination of materials is important?
- What care should be taken when mixing unknown substances with known substances? What good is knowing possible reactions? In what careers might this knowledge be necessary?

Cornstarch: The cornstarch can be used to demonstrate how dust explosions occur in coal mines or grain elevators. Cornstarch can also be used to explain how bread becomes toast.

Baking soda: The reaction of baking soda and vinegar results in the release of carbon dioxide gas. This gas can be used as a fire extinguisher. Most dry-powder extinguishers utilize baking soda; it can also be used to smother fires.

Plaster of Paris: This is nothing more than hydrated calcium sulfate. When mixed into a paste with water, it sets quickly and expands. It is because of this property that it is used as a fine casting material.

Salt: Salt can be used to lower the freezing point of water; examples are road salts and salt used in ice cream makers.

Sugar: Its numerous uses in foods are obvious, but also our knowledge of the chemical composition of sugar and the food calories it provides have led people to discover sweeteners that work like sugar but with fewer calories.

Evaluation

Upon completing the activities, the students will be able to:

- when given five unknown powders, demonstrate the steps necessary to identify them by using physical properties;
- demonstrate how water, iodine, vinegar, and heat can be used to identify an unknown powder; and
- explain the advantages of an indicator test over reliance on merely physical properties to identify an unknown.

▶ Substances have characteristic properties such as density, boiling point, and solubility, which are independent of the amount of the sample. A mixture of substances can often be separated into the original substances by using one or more of these characteristic properties.

▶ Substances react chemically in characteristic ways with other substances to form new substances (compounds) with different characteristic properties. In chemical reactions the total mass is conserved. Substances are often placed in categories or groups if they react in similar ways, for example, metals.

**CONCEPTS TO
BE CONSTRUCTED**

▶ Problems should be thought out before action is taken to solve them. The *scientific method* is a useful tool in problem solving.

▶ Matter can be combined in many ways. It can become a mixture, a solution, a suspension, or a colloid.

Using the Scientific Method to Solve Problems

Grade Level ● 5–8
Discipline ● Physical Science

Engaging Question

Why is it important to follow a set procedure to solve a problem?

Materials Needed

Exploration—conducted whole class as teacher introduction:

> 50 ml of 91 percent rubbing alcohol (sold over store counter)
> 2 Efferdent tablets
> 2 cups of cornstarch
> Plastic bin, such as dishwashing container or plastic shoe container
> Water

Exploration—conducted in groups of three to four students per group, each group will need:

> 1 pair of goggles for each student
> Paper towels for each group

For half the class to solve for the unknown liquid from the teacher introduction with the Efferdent tablets:

> Efferdent tablets
> Possible unknown liquids to test, such as a clear soft drink, vinegar, alcohol, and water

For half the class to solve for the unknown powder from the teacher introduction using cornstarch and water:

> 1 plastic bin
> A container of water (at least 100 ml)
> Possible unknown white powders such as flour, baking soda, and cornstarch

Expansion—conducted in groups of three or four students per group, each group will need:

> Same materials each team used during the exploration phase
> 1 balloon per student

The teacher may also want to obtain any other clear liquids or unknown white powders the students decide to use in the experiments they design.

🚦 *Safety Precautions:* Goggles should be worn by teacher and students during all activities.

Advance Teacher Preparation

For clear liquid: Pour about 50 ml of alcohol as close to 100 percent pure as possible into a container. Typical rubbing alcohol is 70 percent; the water content will cause the Efferdent to dissolve slowly. Therefore, 91 percent rubbing alcohol, also available over the counter, will be more effective.

For white powder: Add 2 cups of cornstarch to a large container or plastic bin (dish-washing containers work well). Slowly add water until a gooey consistency is reached. This material will pour or drip slowly but will not splatter when struck with a quick blow. This is a non-Newtonian fluid. Rather than a solution or mixture, it is called a *colloid:* The starch is suspended in the water.

Exploration

PROCESS SKILLS USED

▶ Problem solving
▶ Communicating
▶ Inferring
▶ Designing an experiment
▶ Recording data
▶ Measuring
▶ Observing
▶ Defining operationally
▶ Synthesizing and analyzing information

What will the students do?

Teacher Introduction: Ask the students to imagine traveling through space. All of a sudden, the spaceship crash-lands. Tell them, "You have no idea where you landed. You do find several objects on the planet. Your hope is that manipulating these objects will give you some clues about the place where you have landed." Show them a container with a clear liquid in it. This is one of the things found at the landing site. Other items that were found were several packages of Effer-dent tablets, used on earth to clean dentures. Ask them what they think will happen if you drop two tablets into the clear liquid. Encourage a variety of predictions. Now drop the tablets into the liquid. Did you predict accurately? What do you think this liquid could be? In a few moments, you will be given a chance to experiment to determine what it is and whether there is a way to get the Efferdent to dissolve in it.

Exploring with Efferdent Tablets

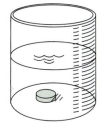

Explain to the students that in addition to the clear liquid and Efferdent tablets, they found some white powder and mixed it with water from their spaceship. Show them the mixture you created. Tell them, "You were trying to figure out what the powder was, especially because it didn't get all gooey like the paste you use at school. Some of you will need to design an experiment to determine what this white powder is."

Student Activity: Now assign the students on one side of the room to solve for one of the unknowns (what the clear liquid is—7-Up or vinegar, for example) and the students on the other side to solve for the other unknown (what the white powder is—flour or baking soda, for example). Encourage use of the scientific method to solve for the unknowns. Use the following guide questions to help plan student experiments: What do you think the problem is? How will you go about solving the problem? What materials do you think you will need? What will you do with those materials to help solve your problem? Do you think it will be important to keep accurate records of the information you collect while doing the experiment you designed?

Explanation

Concept: Problems should be thought out before action is taken to solve them. The *scientific method* is a useful tool in problem solving.

Ask the students to share with you the methods they used to go about solving their problem. Key questions to get them to share are: Do you think it is important to plan before you act? Why? What steps did you use in designing your experiment? Share your data.

This methodical way of problem solving is called the *scientific method.* The steps to be followed are:

1. State the problem.

2. Generate predictions or hypotheses to help solve the problem.

3. Design an experiment to help solve the problem.

4. Create a list of materials needed to solve the problem.

5. Gather the materials and act on the experimental design.

6. Collect and record the data.

7. Draw conclusions and share them with peers.

Expansion

Exploring with Cornstarch

PROCESS SKILLS USED

► Problem solving

► Communicating

► Inferring

► Designing an experiment

► Recording data

► Measuring

► Observing

► Defining operationally

► Synthesizing and analyzing information

How will the idea be expanded?

Trade what you wrote down to solve for your unknown with the students on the other side of the room. Could they replicate your experiment? If not, what changes do you think you need to make to the method you followed? Make those changes based on the *scientific method.* Does it become easier for the students on the other side of the room to replicate your experiment with those changes in place? Now ask them where they think they landed. The students should reason that since they found objects on earth that behaved in ways they weren't familiar with, perhaps they could still be on earth.

Once the students from each side of the room have discovered what the unknowns were, the students may want to play with the ooze formed with the cornstarch and water. Demonstrate to the students the balloon method for carrying their ooze in space. Use a plastic 1- or 2-liter soda bottle to make a funnel. Remove the cap and cut off the top of the bottle about 2 to 3 inches from the neck. Invert this, place a balloon over the bottle opening, pour the ooze into the funnel, and milk it into the attached balloon. Knot the balloon. Stretch the balloon into various shapes. What happens? Why can you do this?

Science in Personal and Social Perspectives

- Do you think you can use the scientific method to help you solve personal problems you have?
- How would you go about explaining an important event that happened in your life to a friend? Will the story have the same impact if you leave out important details?
- Do you think it is as important to be able to communicate accurately your feelings about some issue as it is to be able to give directions for performing a particular task?

Science and Technology

- How important do you think it is to have motor oil that is the right weight in your car's engine? Can these differences in the oil's weight be affected if dirt particles are dissolved in the oil? Will dirt particles dissolve in the oil, or will they create a colloid?

- Can solutions be created when the materials involved are at temperatures close to freezing? Do you think this knowledge will be important as we try to create space stations hundreds of miles from earth?

Science as Inquiry

- What are the differences among solutions, mixtures, suspensions, and colloids?
- What steps are involved in the scientific method?

History and Nature of Science

- If you were an auto mechanic, would knowledge of solutions be beneficial? What kinds of solutions does an auto mechanic work with?
- What other careers rely on knowledge of the differences among solutions, suspensions, colloids, and mixtures? Name three and state why.

Evaluation

Upon completing the activities, the students will be able to:

- take a given problem and design an experiment to solve it, using the steps in the scientific method;
- demonstrate examples of mixtures, solutions, suspensions, and colloids; and
- upon looking at a diagram of a mixture, solution, suspension, or colloid, identify each combination of matter.

Heat Energy

Grade Level ● 1–4

Discipline ● Physical Science

Liquid Birthday

Engaging Question

How can matter change from a solid to a liquid, or a liquid to a solid?

Materials Needed

Exploration—conducted whole class, you will need:

10 small birthday candles
1 hot plate
1 double-boiler pan to melt candles

Expansion—conducted whole class, you will need:

1 square piece of aluminum foil (around four-inch square) for each student
1 spoon to place a small amount of hot wax on the foil

Safety Precautions: Tell the students not to move too close to the hot plate and not to touch the hot melted wax. Be sure to use a hot plate that has adjustable settings and a visible on/off light. Melt wax slowly. To avoid fires, melt in a double boiler.

Exploration

PROCESS SKILLS USED

▶ Classifying
▶ Observing
▶ Inferring
▶ Generalizing
▶ Communicating

What will the students do?

Allow the students to handle the birthday candles. Ask them to determine whether they are a liquid or a solid. Collect their responses. Once there is consensus as to their solid state, ask for suggestions on how the solid candle could be turned into a liquid. During this discussion, if no student suggests it, suggest using the hot plate to melt the candles. Place the candles in the double boiler over the hot plate, set at a low setting, and melt them. Ask the students to make observations as heat energy is added to the candles.

Explanation

Concept: Adding heat energy can change solids to liquids or liquids to gases.

To help the students create this concept, ask the following questions:

• If you place your hand close to the pan (do not touch it!), does it sense that the pan is hot?
• What happens to the candles as the heat energy moves from the hot plate to the pan? Can you explain why this is happening?
• What is a common way in which birthday candles are melted?
• What other types of things in your home release heat energy?
• As the hot plate releases heat energy to the saucepan, it is transferred to the candles, causing them to melt. What can you do to change the candles back into solids?

- Is heat energy added when an ice cube melts? How could you use heat energy to get water to turn to steam?
- Ask the students to complete the following summary statements: By adding ____ _____ (heat energy) to a solid, I can change it to a liquid. By adding ____ _____ (heat energy) to a liquid, I can change it to a gas.

Expansion

Liquids to Solids

PROCESS SKILLS USED
▶ Inferring
▶ Questioning
▶ Observing
▶ Communicating

How will the idea be expanded?

Ask the students to make predictions about what will happen to the candles once the double boiler is taken off the hot plate. Give each child a piece of aluminum foil and a drop of the liquid wax. Ask the students to make observations of their wax. Divide the class in half. Ask half the class to determine ways in which they can turn the liquid wax back to a solid in the shortest time possible. Ask the other half to determine ways to keep their drops in the liquid state. In which case do you need to add heat energy? Where is heat energy removed?

Science in Personal and Social Perspectives

- Imagine you are riding in a car on a long trip through Florida in July. During the long ride, you spend time coloring and drawing pictures. You leave your crayons on the car seat when you stop to eat lunch. What do you think you will find when you return to the car after lunch? Why?
- Where in your home would be a good place to store candles? Why? Would you store them in the attic? If so, why? If not, why not?

Science and Technology

- Why do you think it is important to understand why heat energy can melt a solid? Describe how this concept is applied in manufacturing glass objects, such as vases and mirrors.
- The oil that is used in a car engine is in a liquid state, yet when cool, it is very thick. What do you think will happen to it as the car engine continues to run? Will this affect the design of an engine?

Science as Inquiry

- What does it take to change a solid object into a liquid state?
- Can objects change their state of matter without gaining or losing heat energy?

History and Nature of Science

- Aside from automobile engineers, are there other careers in which people must understand that the addition or subtraction of heat energy will change an object's state of matter?
- How do you think a hairdresser utilizes the concept identified in these activities? If you were having your hair done by a hairdresser, would you feel more comfortable if this person understood something about heat energy?

Evaluation

Upon completing the activities, the students will be able to:

- demonstrate how heat energy can be added to a rubber band without using fire or a hot plate; and
- demonstrate how heat energy can be removed from an ice cube, draw a picture of it, and write three sentences describing how this is done.

Structure Strength

Grade Level ● 5–8
Discipline ● Physical Science

► If more than one force acts on an object, then the force can reinforce or cancel one another, depending on their direction and magnitude. Unbalanced forces will cause changes in the speed and/or direction of an object's motion.

CONCEPTS TO BE CONSTRUCTED:

► The strength of a structure depends on the arrangement of the materials used in construction.

► A variety of materials can be used to create a structure. A triangular arrangement of materials provides a more stable structure than a square.

Engaging Question

Is it the materials or the way in which they are arranged that give a structure its strength?

Materials Needed

Exploration—conducted in five student groups, each group will need:

Clay
Straight pins such as dissecting pins
Glue and/or tape

Each group will use one of the five building materials:

Straws
Toothpicks
Popsicle sticks
Toilet paper or paper towel tubes
Newspaper tightly rolled into tubes

Expansion—conducted whole class:

Students will use the structures they created during the exploration phase.

ⓘ *Safety Precautions:* Remind students to use care in handling the pins to attach straws together, not to stand on chairs when building tall structures, to ask the teacher for help, and not to throw any of the building materials.

Exploration

Simple Construction

PROCESS SKILLS USED

► Observing
► Predicting
► Manipulating materials
► Hypothesizing
► Inferring

What will the students do?

Divide the class into five working groups. Provide one group with straws, another with toothpicks, another with Popsicle sticks, the fourth with toilet paper or paper towel tubes, and the fifth with sheets of newspaper rolled slightly longer than the paper towel tubes but just about the same diameter. Allow each group access to clay, pins, glue, or string to attach the building materials together.

Ask the students to make observations about the materials provided. Ask them to make predictions about how the materials could be used. Encourage the students to think beyond the usual uses for the materials. Allow them to manipulate the materials and to put them together in as many ways as possible. Ask the students to draw pictures of the different creations. Ask them to identify which of their creations remained standing the longest.

Concept: The strength of a structure depends on the arrangement of the materials used in construction. A variety of materials can be used to create a structure.

Key questions to ask to help identify these concepts are:

- What kinds of things did you create with these materials?
- Did anyone create a structure that remained standing?
- What did that structure look like?
- What kinds of materials did you use?
- How long did your structure remain standing?
- Why do you think one structure stood longer than another?
- Do you think you could use the same materials yet make your structure stronger? How do you think you could do that?

Expansion

PROCESS SKILLS USED

▶ Observing
▶ Predicting
▶ Manipulating materials
▶ Hypothesizing
▶ Inferring

How will the idea be expanded?

Let's look at what each team has created. Your challenge at this point is to answer the inquiry question: Is it the materials or the way in which they are arranged that give a structure its strength? Give the students time to revisit their original creations and make any changes necessary to derive an answer. Ask them to share their answers. Share with them structures that are sturdier when they are arranged in a triangular shape, versus those left as squares. Lead the students to complete this statement: The strength of a structure depends on the _____ (arrangement) of the materials used in construction.

Triangle Construction

Science in Personal and Social Perspectives

- Take a field trip with an adult family member to the attic or basement of your house or that of a friend. What kinds of support systems are found in the house? What materials were used? In what arrangements are those support systems placed?
- Think of some common objects found around your house that you typically use once and throw away. Do you think you could use them to create a structure? How long do you think a structure would last if it was built out of the material you have in mind?

Science and Technology

- Can you name three famous buildings that are known for the uniqueness of their structure?
- Why do you think that certain areas in the United States have strict laws about the types of structures that can be built there?

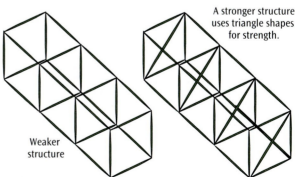

A stronger structure uses triangle shapes for strength.

Weaker structure

- Can you make a house out of a deck of cards? How is it possible? Why is it possible?
- Do you think you can support a two-pound weight in a structure made out of old newspapers? How will you manipulate the newspapers to make this possible? Try it.

History and Nature of Science

- Choose one of the following occupations and explain how important knowledge of structural arrangement and strength is to that occupation: mechanical engineer, civil engineer, architect, contractor.
- Do you think a paper carrier or someone working in a fast-food restaurant would use the ideas you discovered through these activities in his or her work? How?

Evaluation

Upon completing the activities, the students will be able to:

- work in cooperative groups of four and use drinking straws and clay to build a bridge that spans across the classroom. The strength of the structure built will be tested by using metal washers;
- view two toothpick structures and determine which of the two has the greater strength and be able to explain why (create them according to the accompanying picture); and
- draw a picture of a structure that could survive in an area where strong winds occur often. Write a narrative explaining what the structure is and why it was so designed.

Mirrors and Reflection

Grade Level ● 5–8

Discipline ● Physical Science

NATIONAL SCIENCE EDUCATION CONTENT STANDARDS–PHYSICAL SCIENCE—GRADES 5–8

Transformations of Energy

▶ Light interacts with matter by transmission (including refraction), absorption, or scattering (including reflection).

Engaging Question

What is a mirror?

Materials Needed

Exploration—conducted in groups of three or four students per group, each group will need:

    A mirror at least 3 inches square

    1 metal spoon

    1 4-inch square of aluminum foil

    1 4-inch square piece of clear plastic

    1 piece of black paper

    1 piece white paper

    1 pencil

    1 piece of Mylar paper

Expansion—conducted in groups of three or four students per group, each group will need:

    Same materials used during the exploration phase

Safety Precautions: Be sure that rough edges on mirrors are filed or taped. Demonstrate to the students the proper handling of mirrors and Mylar paper: Hold them by the edges to avoid fingerprints. Stress the importance of sharing.

> **CONCEPTS TO BE CONSTRUCTED**
>
> ▶ An object must be shiny, smooth, and reflect light to be called a *mirror*. Light bouncing off a shiny surface is called *reflection*.
>
> ▶ Mirrors with a bowl-shaped surface are called *concave*; those that are rounded outward are called *convex*.

Exploration

> **PROCESS SKILLS USED**
>
> ▶ Observing
> ▶ Predicting
> ▶ Making assumptions
> ▶ Brainstorming
> ▶ Recording data

What will the students do?

Allow the students to observe various materials and predict whether they will be able to see themselves. Ask the students to brainstorm ideas of when and where they have seen mirrorlike materials such as the ones they are working with. Manipulate the materials to determine whether they can see images of objects in them. Ask the students to describe their observations. Encourage the students to think about the position of that object in the mirrorlike materials versus what it looks like when they look at it directly. Ask the students to predict what their name will look like after they write it on the paper and look at it in each of the materials. Instruct the students to write their name and view it in the mirror and each of the other materials. Can you see it in all of the objects? Does it look the same as it is written? Why or why not? Can you write it so that you can read it correctly when you look in the mirror?

Mirrors and Reflectors

Concept: An object must be shiny, smooth, and reflect light to be called a *mirror.* Light bouncing off a shiny surface is called *reflection.*

Assist the students in creating these concepts by doing the following: Refer back to the list that they brainstormed during the exploration phase. If terms such as *smooth, reflect, light,* and *shiny* are not listed, add them to the list. Ask the students to help explain the meaning of those terms. Can an object be considered a mirror without light? Does the surface of the object need to be shiny? Can surfaces that are rough or bumpy give images as clear as shiny, smooth surfaces? A mirror is _____ (any shiny, smooth object that can reflect light).

Expansion

What Is a Mirror?

PROCESS SKILLS USED
▶ Observing
▶ Predicting
▶ Manipulating materials
▶ Classifying
▶ Inferring

How will the idea be expanded?

Using the same materials from the exploration activity, ask the students to classify them into groups of things that are shiny, things that are smooth, and things that reflect light. Were you able to classify all of the materials? Could some of the materials fall into more than one group? Which materials were shiny and smooth and reflected light? Can you call these objects mirrors?

Can the spoon be considered a mirror? Describe the images seen inside the spoon. Where have you seen mirrors like these before? Have you ever been to a grocery store and seen these kinds of mirrors? What purpose do these mirrors serve? Mirrors with a bowl-shaped surface are called *concave;* those that are rounded outward are called *convex.*

Science in Personal and Social Perspectives

- Mirrors are used quite a bit in our everyday lives. When and where have you seen mirrors? What are their purposes?
- How often do you use a mirror? Describe the mirrors that you use and what you use them for.

Science and Technology

- How do different people use mirrors? What can be learned by looking in a mirror?
- How do scientists use mirrors? Have you ever used a microscope that uses mirrors? Did you ever see a telescope that makes use of mirrors?
- Can you list at least three machines that make use of mirrors? Draw a working diagram of one of them.

Science as Inquiry

- Why is a light source needed for an object to be considered a mirror?

- Which type of mirror would you use if you wanted objects to appear larger than they actually are: concave or convex?
- Why do words appear to be written backward when viewed in a mirror?

History and Nature of Science

- What careers are linked to the use of mirrors? Do your parents use mirrors in their work?
- Would some careers be more difficult without mirrors? Think of your school bus driver.
- The German chemist Justus von Liebig was instrumental in creating the mirror that we currently use. Trace the history of the mirror, describing the role von Liebig played.

Evaluation

Upon completing the activities, the students will be able to:

- write their names upside down and backward on a piece of paper to illustrate their knowledge of what a mirror can do;
- describe the three properties of a mirror or mirrorlike object and use them in sentences; and
- classify materials into *shiny, smooth,* and *reflects light* categories.

The Slinky Potential

Grade Level ● 7–8
Discipline ● Physical Science

CONCEPTS TO BE CONSTRUCTED

► Energy is a property of many substances and is associated with mechanical motion. Stored energy is called potential energy. Energy of motion is called kinetic energy.

► Energy can be transformed from one form to another. Momentum is described as the mass of an object times the velocity of the object. Momentum is always conserved.

Engaging Question

Why *do* Slinkies slink?

Materials Needed

Exploration—conducted in groups of three or four students per group, each group will need:

    1 Slinky or equivalent toy

    Access to a flight of stairs that are wide enough for the Slinky to fit but not so wide that the top of the Slinky ends up falling over itself onto the same step

    Paper or journal to record observations

Expansion—conducted whole class teacher demonstration:

    A golf ball and a Ping-Pong ball

    Access to a hard floor surface near a wall that can be used to mark height of bounced balls

    Masking tape to mark ball height on the wall

🛈 *Safety Precautions:* Caution students about acceptable behavior while working with the Slinky on the stairs. Ask the students to watch one another as they descend the stairs with the Slinky to avoid falling.

    As a precaution students should wear goggles when dropping the golf and Ping-Pong balls, as they cannot control the height and angle of the rebound when the balls are dropped simultaneously.

Exploration

Energy Conversions with a Slinky

PROCESS SKILLS USED

► Manipulating materials
► Communicating
► Observing
► Inferring

What will students do?

Have the students, working in teams, go to designated areas within the school building where they have access to a flight of stairs. Remind them of safety measures while working on the steps. Ask them to predict what will happen to the Slinky when it is placed on the top step of a flight of stairs and they push the top half of the Slinky toward the edge of the step. Ask them to predict how many stairs the Slinky will descend before it stops. Do you think it will make it to the bottom of the stairs? Give them an opportunity to have at least three trials with the descending Slinky.

Explanation

Concept: Energy is a property of many substances and is associated with mechanical motion. Stored energy is called *potential energy*. Energy of motion is called *kinetic energy*.

Ask the students to describe the motion of the Slinky as it descended the steps. Ask them to explain the conditions necessary for a successful journey from the top to the bottom of the steps. What variables must they adjust so the Slinky can move down the entire flight of stairs?

The students should begin to talk of the Slinky uncoiling and coiling as it moved down the steps. Ask them what they think "pulled" the Slinky down. They should be talking about the force of gravity pulling on the end of the Slinky as it moved down the steps.

Explain to them that the Slinky had energy stored in it as it was sitting on the top of the step. This is known as *potential energy*. By pushing the top of the Slinky to get it started down the stairs you imparted some of your own energy to the Slinky. Once gravity takes over, that stored or potential energy is converted to kinetic energy as the coils pull the trailing end of the Slinky down. This energy has now given the trailing end of the Slinky momentum. It is that momentum that causes the end to move up and past the high point of the arc as the Slinky falls over on itself. Gravity then takes over and continues to pull the Slinky down. Again this process is repeated as the Slinky moves down the stairs, transforming gravitational energy and the potential energy of the spring into kinetic energy until it reaches the bottom of the stairs. With this explanation, ask your students at what point in the Slinky's descent does it have its greatest kinetic energy? (When it falls from one step to the next.) At what point is the potential energy the greatest? (When it is poised ready to fall from one step to the next.)

Can you make the Slinky walk back up the steps? Why or why not? (You can't do this because you'd have to create potential energy from nothing. This would be against the law of conservation of energy, which states that energy cannot be created nor destroyed.) In this lesson the students should conclude that energy can be transformed from one form to another. This will be reinforced in the expansion activity.

Now that we have had this discussion about how the Slinky behaves, who can answer our inquiry question: Why *do* Slinkies slink? (Students should demonstrate through their responses that they understand the differences between potential and kinetic energy.)

Expansion

PROCESS SKILLS USED
▶ Observing
▶ Predicting
▶ Identifying
▶ Controlling variables

How will the idea be expanded?

Hold a Ping-Pong ball and a golf ball up in front of the class. Ask the students to predict how high they think the Ping-Pong ball will bounce if you drop it from chest height onto a hard floor. Ask them to predict how high they think the golf ball will bounce if you drop it from chest height onto a hard floor. Collect all predictions, and then drop each ball one at a time. Ask some students to mark a spot on the wall behind you with tape at the height of the ascent with the first bounce for each ball. How accurate were their predictions? They should have discovered

Energy Transfer—Having a Ball!

that when dropped separately from the same height, the balls will bounce to approximately the same height.

Now ask the students to predict what will happen when you drop both balls at the same time with the Ping-Pong ball positioned on top of the golf ball. Record these predictions. *Note:* Be sure to practice this before you do it in front of your students so that when the balls are released simultaneously, the Ping-Pong ball will shoot straight up, 10 to 15 feet.

Now drop the balls so that the Ping-Pong ball is positioned over the golf ball. Ask the students again to mark the height of the bounce for each ball. Did the balls respond as predicted? What do you think happened? At what point did the balls have potential energy? When was that converted to kinetic?

Ask the students where the energy came from to cause the Ping-Pong ball to bounce so high? (It came from the golf ball.) What happened to the golf ball if it transferred some of its energy into the Ping-Pong ball? (It bounced lower than it did before.) Repeat this activity or allow the student teams to repeat this activity so they come to understand that particular scientific phenomena become laws when they hold up with repeated testing. In this case, they will be justifying the law of conservation of momentum.

In this activity, energy is transferred from the golf ball to the Ping-Pong ball. This demonstrates how momentum is conserved. Momentum is described by the formula M (momentum) $= m$ (mass) $\times v$ (velocity). When dropped separately, each ball gained momentum based on the mass of the ball.

A sidebar conversation may need to occur about how friction plays into this experiment. The classroom is not an ideal setting because it can not demonstrate a perfectly elastic collision. There is some loss of kinetic energy with each bounce due to friction. If friction from the air were not present, the ball would bounce at the same height with each bounce.

When the Ping-Pong ball was dropped directly over the golf ball, momentum had to be conserved. For that to happen, the mass of the golf ball times the velocity of the golf ball had to equal the mass of the Ping-Pong ball times the velocity of the Ping-Pong ball ($m_{gb} \times v_{gb} = m_{ppb} \times v_{ppb}$). Since the golf ball has greater mass than the Ping-Pong ball, to make the equation equal, the velocity of the Ping-Pong ball had to increase proportionally. Thus, what they observed was the transfer of energy from the golf ball to the Ping-Pong ball to maintain the law of conservation of momentum.

Science in Personal and Social Perspectives

- How can you apply the concept that energy can be transferred while playing a game of baseball?
- Why is it important to wear a helmet when roller blading or skateboarding? Where is energy transferred from if you are moving along on your skateboard, not wearing a helmet, and you hit the pavement?

Science and Technology

- What role do air bags in automobiles play if a car stops suddenly? How has the knowledge that energy can be transformed from one form to another been applied in air bag technology?
- Explore the different materials that are used to make bike safety helmets. Which material absorbs energy transformation most efficiently? What kind of a rating scale do helmet manufacturers use?

Science as Inquiry

- Collect balls of various sizes and masses. Predict which ball will allow the Ping-Pong ball to bounce higher when it is used instead of the golf ball in the expansion activity. Support your predictions and justify your outcomes by applying the concept of momentum to the mass and velocity of the balls using the formula $M = m \times v$.

History and Nature of Science

- Explore the possible professions that apply the concept of energy transformations to their work end product.
- In recent years, the number of accidents on amusement park rides has increased. Using the concepts you learned in these activities, create a job description for a person who is responsible for inspecting amusement park rides.

Evaluation

Upon completing the activities, the students will be able to:

- explain the difference between potential and kinetic energy and demonstrate this using a toy such as a Slinky or a top or a Frisbee;
- accurately predict which ball will have greater velocity when dropped simultaneously and vertically in the following order: a basketball under a Ping-Pong ball, a basketball under a volleyball, and a small rubber ball under a Ping-Pong ball; and
- create a campaign for increased use of safety helmets while skateboarding, demonstrating the concept that energy can be transformed from one form to another.

Toys in Space

Grade Level ● 5–8
Discipline ● Physical Science

▶ An object that is not being subjected to a force will continue to move at a constant speed and in a straight line.

CONCEPTS TO BE CONSTRUCTED

▶ Things that behave one way on earth will behave differently in space due to zero-gravity conditions.

▶ An astronaut will experience weightlessness while traveling through space. Toys can be used to explain a variety of scientific principles.

Toy Behavior in Zero Gravity

Engaging Question

Can I play with my yo-yo in outer space?

Materials Needed

Exploration—conducted whole class, you will need:

　1 or more Wheel-o, yo-yo, paddle ball, ball and jacks, self-propelling car, magnetic marbles, spinning top, wind-up toy such as a flip mouse, gyroscope

Expansion—conducted whole class, you will need:

　Same toys as above
　Toys in Space video available through NASA, Lewis Research Center, Cleveland, OH

🛈 *Safety Precautions:* Teacher and students should wear goggles to be sure that no eye injuries occur.

Exploration

PROCESS SKILLS USED

▶ Observing
▶ Predicting
▶ Manipulating materials
▶ Hypothesizing
▶ Inferring

What will the students do?

Provide the students with the toys from the materials list. Ask them to play with the toys and make observations about how they function. After adequate time has been spent playing with the toys, ask the students to make predictions as to how they think the toys would function in zero gravity. Encourage the students to make as many predictions as possible.

Explanation

Concept: Things that behave one way on earth will behave differently in space due to zero-gravity conditions.

To assist the students in developing this concept, ask them the following questions: How do the toys work in the classroom? Can you demonstrate them for me? How does gravity behave on earth? What does it do to objects on earth? If there were no gravity on earth, how do you think these toys would behave? Have you ever seen movies of astronauts as they travel in space? How do they look? If you were an astronaut, could you play with your yo-yo in outer space? Think about how you can respond to this as we move to the next activity.

Expansion

How will the idea be expanded?

Show the NASA videotape *Toys in Space*. Discuss afterward the discrepancies between the students' predictions and what really happened. An astronaut will experience

PROCESS SKILLS USED
▶ Observing
▶ Predicting
▶ Manipulating materials
▶ Hypothesizing
▶ Inferring

weightlessness while traveling through space. So, can you play with your yo-yo in space? Of course, you can—but does your yo-yo respond the same as it does on earth?

Toys can be used to explain a variety of scientific principles. If the students really show an interest in the behavior of the toys under zero-gravity conditions, you may want to introduce the students to some of Newton's laws, which govern the behavior of these toys on earth. If you want the students to really understand Newton's laws, take care to plan additional activities that engage the students in science processes to enhance their understanding of these laws. The laws are as follows:

Toys and Newton

1. *Law of inertia:* Every body continues in its state of rest or of uniform motion in a straight line, except insofar as it is compelled by forces to change that state.

2. Force equals mass times acceleration.

3. The force exerted by an object A on another object B is equal in magnitude and opposite in direction to the force exerted by object B on object A.

Science in Personal and Social Perspectives

- How do you decide what kinds of toys to play with? Did you ever think that you could use them to help explain science concepts?
- Why do you think you or your friends choose particular toys to play with? Is it important that you play with the same things as your friends? Why or why not?
- Can you choose one of your toys and explain how or why it works? Ask your friends to help you decide which science concept is applied to explain why your toy works.

Science and Technology

- Toys are actually like models of particular systems. Why do you think it would be easier to make a toy model of some invention first? What advantage would that give to certain industries?

Science as Inquiry

- Is it possible for toys on earth to behave the same way when under zero-gravity conditions? Is it possible for toys in space to behave the same way when on earth?
- Describe two different scientific concepts that can be explained by using a bicycle.

History and Nature of Science

- Do you think a Wheel-o could have been invented if the creator did not understand something about magnetism?
- If you were to become a toy designer, would knowledge of science concepts be useful in your career?

Evaluation

Upon completing the activities, the students will be able to:

- describe one scientific concept that can be explained with the use of a roller skate; and
- create a toy using materials of their choice that can be fun and explain a scientific concept; and
- design a toy that can still function in the absence of gravity and write a few sentences to describe it.

Simple Machines: The Lever

Grade Level ● 5–8
Discipline ● Physical Science

► If more than one force acts on an object, then the forces can reinforce or cancel one another, depending on their direction and magnitude. Unbalanced forces will cause changes in the speed and/or direction of an object's motion.

CONCEPTS TO BE CONSTRUCTED

► A lever is a rigid bar that pivots around a point that is used to move an object at a second point by a force applied at a third point. The pivot point is the *fulcrum,* the object moved is the *load,* and the place where the force is applied is the *effort.*

► There are three kinds of levers. A *first-class lever* is a fulcrum between effort and load; the effort moves in the opposite direction of the load, as in a seesaw or a balance. A *second-class lever* is a load between the fulcrum and the effort; effort is applied in the same direction as the load should be moved, as in a wheelbarrow or a bottle opener. A *third-class lever* is an effort between the fulcrum and the load, which magnifies the distance moved by the load but reduces its force, as in a hammer, a catapult, or a fishing rod. Additional terms that may be introduced in this lesson are *resistance, friction, work,* and *machine.*

Engaging Question

How can one person do the work of ten?

Materials Needed

For the Discrepant Event, the teacher will need:

> Several small pieces of sand paper
> Squirt bottle filled with water
> Several marbles or glass beads
> Squirt bottle filled with cooking oil
> Container of hand lotion
> Paper towel or wipes

Exploration—conducted in groups of three or four students per group, each group will need:

> Goggles for each group member
> 1 board at least 18 inches long and 1/4 inch wide
> 1 fulcrum, proportional in size to the board, for an 18-inch board a triangular piece cut out of a 2 × 4 will work well
> Any proportionally sized objects to be used as a load, such as blocks of wood or books.

Expansion—conducted in groups of three or four students per group, each group will need:

> Goggles for each group member
> 2 plastic spoons
> 1 rubber band
> Some peanuts

Safety Precautions: Remind students that safety goggles must be worn at all times. Discourage students from sending the load material flying across the room. Warn them of the potential danger to themselves and other students.

Discrepant Event

PROCESS SKILLS USED

► Observing
► Hypothesizing
► Inferring
► Drawing conclusions

What will the teacher and students do?

Do not show the students what you are giving them. Ask them to close their eyes and to put out their hands, and place a small amount of one of the following in their hands: sandpaper, nothing, water, hand lotion, cooking oil, two or three marbles or beads. Tell them to be sure not to let anyone else see what they have. Once everyone has received one of the items, ask the class to rub their hands together (all at the same time) with the objects still in their hands. After the students have had time to do this and to comment on what just happened, then ask questions such as: What did your hands feel like? Who had the hardest time rubbing his or her hands together? The easiest? Why? Did your hands change temperature? What do you think caused your hands to get hot/cold/no change? Why was it easy for some and not for others? What do you think is prohibiting you from sliding or rolling the objects in your hands? (Resistance.) What is this resistance to movement called? (Friction.) What did you need to do to overcome friction? (Exert some energy—effort.) By using effort to move your hands over a distance, you have done work. What do we call an object that will do the work for us? (A machine.)

Exploration

PROCESS SKILLS USED

▶ Manipulating materials
▶ Collecting and recording data
▶ Communicating
▶ Observing
▶ Hypothesizing
▶ Predicting
▶ Inferring

What will the students do?

Instructions: Use a long board and a triangular-shaped block in as many combinations as you think possible to move the weighted object (blocks, books, metal pieces). Draw the methods you tried. Discuss possible solutions with your peers. Try to record the results of those as well.

Lever Creations

Explanation

Concept: A lever is a rigid bar that pivots around a point, which is used to move an object at a second point by a force applied at a third point.

Have the students draw the results of their manipulations on the board. With help from the class, identify on their drawings the pivot point, the object being moved, and the place where they had to apply a force to get the object to move. Solicit class ideas as to names for these points. Identify the pivot point as the *fulcrum,* the object moved as the *load,* and the place where force was applied as the *effort.*

Key questions to ask: Did these inventions make it easier for you to do work? What do we call objects that make our work easier? What has the machine we invented allowed us to do? What do you think we call it? Why? Once the concept *lever* has been invented, ask the students whether they can see any differences in the placement of the three points on any of their diagrams. If necessary, supply diagrams that show different placements of the points. Key questions: Is there any advantage to changing the position of the three points? What happens to the direction of the effort and load in each of the diagrams? Can you see some practical uses for the different positions of the points? As you go through the different arrangements of the points, identify the three classes of levers: A *first-class lever* is a fulcrum between effort and load; the effort moves in the opposite direction of the load, as in a seesaw or a balance. A *second-class lever* is a load between the fulcrum and the effort; effort is applied in the same direction as the load should be moved, as in a wheelbarrow or a bottle opener. A *third-class lever* is an effort between the fulcrum and the load, which magnifies the distance moved by the load but reduces its force, as in a hammer, a catapult, or a fishing rod. Now that we've discussed your inventions tell me: How can one person do the work of ten?

Spoons and Nuts

How will the idea be expanded?

Instructions: Given two plastic spoons, a rubber band, and some peanuts, design and demonstrate a first-, second-, and third-class lever. Share your inventions with the class.

Home extension

Lever Scavenger Hunt

What will the students do?

Have the students ask an adult to go with them on a lever scavenger hunt. Make a list of all of the places where levers are being used in some form or another. How many of these are combination levers? How many are compound levers of the first, second, or third class? Bring these lists back to school to share with the class.

Science in Personal and Social Perspectives

- Where in your home did you find a lever being used? Did any of these places surprise you? Were any of these uses a case where two of the lever types were used in combination? (Nail clippers, piano) Did you find any compound levers? (Scissors, pliers, nutcracker, tweezers)
  - When you need to cut a piece of paper, why is it easier to use scissors than a knife? What advantage does using a pair of scissors have over using a knife for cutting?
  - Which simple machine makes it possible for people to play a piano?

Science and Technology

- Why would it be difficult for you to wear your ice skates in the house but not your roller skates? How have industries used this information to overcome friction?
- How do you think the invention of the parking meter has affected your city? How about cities such as Chicago or New York?

Science as Inquiry

- Students will be able to explain the function of the fulcrum, load, and effort; various combinations of these points can create a first-, second-, or third-class lever. They will be able to explain how machines help us to do work and to overcome friction.

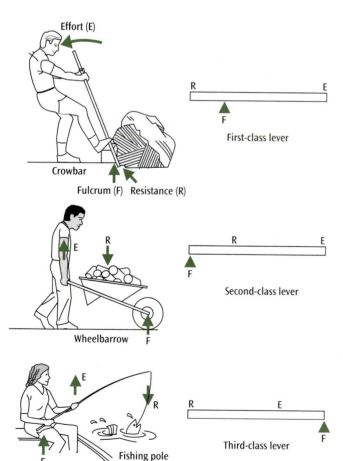

Effort (E)

Crowbar

Fulcrum (F)   Resistance (R)

R ▲ E

F

First-class lever

Wheelbarrow

R ▲ E

F

Second-class lever

Fishing pole

R   E

F

Third-class lever

- This activity lays the foundation for new concepts to be identified in new lessons, such as the relationship between effort and work, mechanical advantage, other types of simple machines, and so on.

History and Nature of Science

- Archimedes of Syracuse was perhaps the greatest of the Greek mathematicians and scientists. He lived from 287 to 212 B.C. He is credited with inventing the catapult, which the Greeks used during the Second Punic War against the Roman army. It is said that Archimedes was slain during this war while he was studying mathematical figures, which he habitually drew in the dust. What do you think he meant when he said, "Give me a fulcrum on which to rest, and I will move the earth"?
- Who needs to know about levers? Which careers rely on the use and/or knowledge of levers? (Manufacturers of playground equipment, laborers, dock workers, piano makers, typewriter manufacturers, parking meter repair persons)

Evaluation

Upon completing the activities, the students will be able to:

- classify the following items as a first-, second-, or third-class lever: hammer, nutcracker, seesaw, wheelbarrow, balance, bottle opener, fishing rod;
- identify the fulcrum, the effort, and the load on each item, when given a hammer, wheelbarrow, and nail extractor; and
- predict the direction of the load when effort is applied with each of the following: fishing rod, balance, bottle opener.

Earth and Space Science Lessons

Lesson Name	NSE Content Standards For Earth & Space Science	Grade Level	Activities
Astronomy			
The Solar System and the Universe	Objects in the Sky	K–3	Rhythm Activity • Postcard Writing
The Expanding Universe	Earth in the Solar System	5–8	Expanding Balloon/Universe • Build a Solar System Salad
Constellations	Earth in the Solar System	5–8	Connect the Stars • Evening Field Trip • Create a Constellation
Geology			
Earth Layers	Properties of Earth Materials	K–4	Clay Earth Layers • Clay Continents
Fossils	Properties of Earth Materials	2–4	Fossil Observations • Plaster Molds and Casts
Rock Types	Structure of the Earth System	5–8	Rock Categorization • Rock Collection Field Trip
Cooling Crystals	Structure of the Earth System	5–8	PDB Crystal Formation • Rock Type versus Crystal Formation
Weathering	Structure of the Earth System	5–8	Freezing Bottle • Weathering Field Trip • Rock Identification • Chemical Weathering • Mechanical Weathering
Crustal Plate Movement	Earth's History	5–8	Moving Plates • Mapping Volcanoes and Earthquakes • Oatmeal and Cracker Plate Tectonics
Aging Human/ Aging Earth	Earth's History	7–8	Living Human—Living Earth • The Rock Record
Meteorology			
Rain Formation	Objects in the Sky	K–4	Rain in a Jar • Water Drop Attraction
Dew Formation	Objects in the Sky	K–4	Soda Bottle Condensation • Thermometer Reading and Dew Point
Radiant Energy	Objects in the Sky	2–4	Temperature and Colored Surfaces • Temperature: Sun versus Shade • Magnifiers: Capture the Sun • Sun Tea
Weather Forecasting	Structure of the Earth System	K–4	Weather Log Creation • Weather Map Symbols • Weather Data Collection
Air Mass Movement	Structure of the Earth System	5–8	Coriolis Effect: Globe • Coriolis Effect: Top • Air Movement: Dry Ice • Oil and Water Fronts • Create a Rain Gauge • Air Masses and Parachutes
Air Pressure	Structure of the Earth System	5–8	Balloon Balance • Paper Blowing • Newspaper Strength
Solar Heating	Earth in the Solar System	5–8	Temperature versus Surface Color • Optimum Thermometer Placement
Air Movement and Surface Temperature	Structure of the Earth System	5–8	Convection Current and Surface Temperature in an Observation Box • Paper Bag Balance
Uneven Heating of the Earth	Structure of the Earth System	5–8	Tower of Water • Aneroid Barometer • Uneven Heating and Air Pressure • Air Pressure versus Water Temperature • Air Temperature versus Movement of Air • Heat Transfer on a Wire • Heat Movement Through Air • Heat Transfer Through Metal • Movement of Smoke over Hot and Cold Surfaces: Clouds • Movement of Smoke over Hot and Cold Surfaces: Wind Patterns

The Solar System and the Universe

Grade Level ● K–3

Discipline ● Earth and Space Science

Engaging Question

Would you vacation on Mars?

Materials Needed

For Exploration

books on planets, such as Jeff Davidson, *Voyage to the Planets* (Worthington, OH: Willowisp Press, 1990) and Joanna Cole, *The Magic School Bus Lost in Space* (New York: Scholastic, 1988)

For Expansion

postcard outline, poster paper, paints, and markers, resource books on the planets

Safety Precautions: The students should be reminded to sit and listen without poking or hitting one another. During the expansion activity, they should clean up any paint spills immediately, and they should not put markers or paint brushes in their mouths.

Exploration

PROCESS SKILLS USED

▶ Observing

▶ Questioning

What will the students do?

- You should read books such as *Voyage to the Planets* or *The Magic School Bus Lost in Space* to the students. Ask them to recall questions as you are sharing the book with them.
- Teach the students the following chant, clapping the beat. Allow them to fill in the planet of their choice once they get the rhythm down:

Rhythm Activity

A—B—CDE, How many planets can there be?
F—G—HIJ, There are eight we know of today.
K—L—MNO, To which one would you like to go?
P—Q—RST, I'd like to visit Mercury.
U—V—WXY, I've been watching it in the sky.
Z—Z—ZZZ, Know anyone who'll come with me?

Explanation

Concept: The earth is part of the solar system.

Ask the students to recall the names of the planets from the stories and chanting activity. Share with them that it has been found through observations of the nighttime sky and satellite observations that the earth is just one of eight planets that move around the sun.

Explain that the status of Pluto as a planet has changed. Each of the planets has unique characteristics because of its distance from the sun. Ask them if they would like to vacation on Mars or any of the other planets? In the next activity we will discuss your make-believe trip.

Expansion

Postcard Writing

PROCESS SKILLS USED
▶ Inferring
▶ Observing
▶ Questioning

How will the idea be expanded?

Once the students know the chant and sing it with all eight planets' names, ask them to choose one of the eight as a place they'd like to go on vacation. Break the students into eight planet vacation groups. Provide the student teams with grade-level-appropriate resource books on the planets. Ask them to plan a drawing of their planet as close to reality as possible, and then work as a cooperative group to create one drawing of that planet. Draw a sun on your mural paper. Ask the different groups to come up to the mural and place their planet in its appropriate order from the sun.

Give students a copy of the postcard outline. Ask them to write postcards to family members, describing their trips to the planets they drew. Teach them how to address a postcard. Ask them to design an appropriate stamp for the planet they visited. When all of these are completed, tape the postcards near the planet of origin.

Questions that help invent additional concepts

- Is the earth all alone in space? (No, there are seven other planets.)
- What else is found in the earth's neighborhood? (Planets, moons, dust, meteors)
- How do we know there are other planets in our neighborhood? Has anyone ever seen them? (We can see them in the sky; they look like stars. We have satellites that have gone close to them and sent back pictures to the earth.)
- What is unique about your planet? (Answers will vary.)
- How close to the sun is your planet? (Answers will vary.)

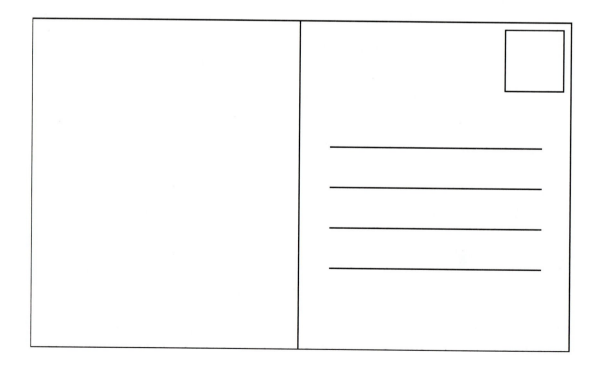

- Are all the planets the same size? (No. Go into detail about their planets.)
- Do you think you could live on your vacation planet as easily as you can on the earth? Why or why not?

Students will apply knowledge they learned about their planets to answer these questions.

Science in Personal and Social Perspectives

- Do you think if the earth were as close to the sun as Mercury, you could still live on it? Why or why not?
- If someone told you that he or she could take you on a plane ride to the planet Mars, would you believe it? Why or why not?

Science and Technology

- Do you think people can invent a way so that it will be possible to live on any of the other planets? How do you think we can do this?

Science as Inquiry

- Students will be able to name the eight planets, list their order from the sun, and discuss one characteristic of each after completing and participating in the above activities.

History and Nature of Science

- Do you think that a person who is responsible for monitoring the air quality of the planet earth can learn anything from understanding what the atmosphere is like on the planet Jupiter?
- How important is it that space scientists know the positions of the planets before launching satellites or rockets into space? What kinds of skills do space scientists need in order to do their jobs?

Evaluation

Upon completing the activities, the students will be able to:

- answer the questions included in the expansion phase of this lesson, as well as the new outcomes questions;
- draw lines from the picture of a planet to a group of words that briefly describe the planet. The picture question below is an example of the kind of question that could be made for this assessment:

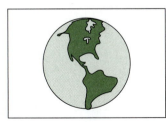

Water and oxygen present

- create a planet mobile (this can be done as a home extension) out of the following materials: wire coat hanger, paint, tape and/or glue, papier-maché or balls of different sizes, string, and cardboard, paper, or newspaper.

The Expanding Universe

Grade Level ● 5–8

Discipline ● Earth and Space Science

NATIONAL SCIENCE EDUCA-
TION CONTENT STANDARDS–
EARTH AND SPACE SCIENCE—
GRADES 5–8

Earth in the Solar System

▶ The earth is the third planet
from the sun in a system that
includes the moon, the sun, seven
other planets and their moons,
and smaller objects, such as asteroids and comets.

**CONCEPTS TO BE
CONSTRUCTED**

▶ Our universe appears to be
expanding: Distances between
parts of the universe are vast.

▶ Planets orbit the sun. The
planets are very small and very
far away from the sun.

**SCIENCE ATTITUDES
TO NURTURE**

▶ Openness to changing their
minds when evidence for
change is given

▶ Openness to questions about
their own ideas

**Expanding Balloon/
Universe**

Engaging Question

How far is far when discussing distances between planets?

Materials Needed

For Exploration

round balloons (one for each student), wide-tip felt markers (black and red)

For Expansion

1 fresh pea	the school track	1 small walnut
1 large walnut	1 dried pea	1 smaller bean
1 8-inch head of cabbage	1 bean	1 grapefruit
1 big orange	1 9-inch head of cabbage	a bicycle

Safety Precautions: Advise students to use extreme caution while blowing up the
balloon. Do not allow children to chew on the balloon.

Exploration

PROCESS SKILLS USED

▶ Observing

▶ Predicting

▶ Hypothesizing

▶ Inferring

What will the students do?

Instruct each student to

1. inflate a round balloon partially, pinching the neck closed
   with thumb and forefinger;
2. make specks with a wide-tip felt marker all over the surface
   of the balloon, noting their positions and letting them dry;
3. blow more air into the balloon and look at it, again noting
   the position of the specks.

Explanation

Concept: Our universe appears to be expanding. Distances between parts of the universe
are vast.

Help the students invent the concept by asking them such questions as:

- What has happened to the distance between the specks? (It has increased, expanded.)
- What do you think will happen to the specks if you continue to add air to the balloon? (They will continue to move away from one another.)
- Imagine that the balloon is space and one of the specks is the neighborhood the earth is found in. Put a red mark on one of the specks to represent the earth's neighborhood. Blow up the balloon some more while watching the red speck. What do you think you could say about space if you were on this red speck? (The earth is very far from other parts of the universe.)

Expansion

PROCESS SKILLS USED
▶ Observing
▶ Communicating
▶ Formulating models
▶ Recording data

How will the idea be expanded?

Have students observe the fixings for a solar system salad (see materials needed). They should decide which of the items correspond to the eight planets and the earth's moon. The students should check with one another to come to some consensus. Then they will discuss decisions with the teacher.

Build a Solar System Salad

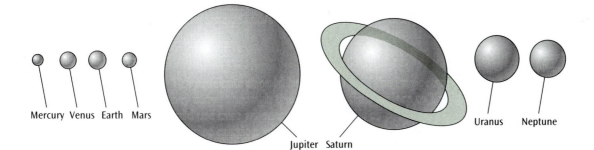

Mercury Venus Earth Mars

Jupiter Saturn

Uranus Neptune

After a discussion on relative sizes, take the salad items out to the school track. While bicycling around the track, drop off the planets to show their relative distance from each other. Allow all the students to participate. Some may be lap counters; others should do the riding. To make it really effective, each student should ride the bicycle. As the children grow tired, the vast distances between the planets will be apparent to them. Each lap represents 211,265 miles in space.

Mercury: $^2/_5$ lap   *Jupiter:* 5 $^1/_2$ laps
Venus: $^3/_4$ lap   *Saturn:* 9 $^1/_2$ laps
Earth: 1 lap   *Uranus:* 19 $^1/_2$ laps
Mars: 1 $^1/_2$ laps   *Neptune:* 30 laps

What questions can help invent additional concepts?

- Which of the salad fixings did you have a hard time assigning a planet to?
- Did you find it necessary to look in some reference books to help you decide which item represents which planet?

Mercury: Fresh pea   *Jupiter:* 9-inch cabbage
Venus: Walnut   *Saturn:* 8-inch cabbage
Earth: Larger walnut   *Uranus:* Grapefruit
Moon: Dried pea   *Neptune:* Big orange
Mars: Bean

- How did your legs feel after you dropped off the solar system salad fixings?
- Imagine you are out in space dropping those items off at the different planets. What would be the total distance you would have traveled? (*Hint:* What is the distance from the sun to Uranus?)
- If the center of the football field represents the sun, what can you say about the planets with respect to the sun? What do the planets do?

Science in Personal and Social Perspectives

- Do you think it will ever be possible for you to travel to the other planets? Would you like to do this? Why or why not? What do you think you would need to pack for your trip?
- Would you purchase a ticket today to spend some time in a space station? Do you think you will live long enough to use the ticket?

Science and Technology

- Do you think space stations will solve the problems of pollution and overpopulation on earth?
- Do you think the vastness of space will allow us to ship our garbage out into space and never be affected by it on the earth? How do you think this will be possible?

Science as Inquiry

- The students will be able to explain the concept of the expanding universe and discuss the implications that has for life as we presently know it on the earth.
- Why is it possible to view planets in the nighttime sky? Do all of the planets always maintain the same orbital paths?

History and Nature of Science

- If it was your job to create a satellite that would move through outer space, sending back to the earth information about other planets, what kinds of knowledge do you think you would need to have? What would be the qualifications for your job? Pretend you need to employ someone to fill such a job. Write a job description and give it a title. Does the race or sex of the person applying matter?

Evaluation

Upon completing the activities, the students will be able to:

- complete the activities above;
- write a few sentences after they participate in the bicycle activity about how they felt when they finished and what they think about the distances between the planets. Ask the students to share their feelings with one another. How tired they became and how much they want to share with others what they did will provide an effective measure of success; and
- when provided with ten different kinds of vegetables for a solar salad, use these new items to arrange the members of the solar system. Also ask them to decide how far they would have to be from one another if 1 inch equals 1 million miles.

Constellations

Grade Level ● 5–8

Discipline ● Earth and Space Science

NATIONAL SCIENCE EDUCATION CONTENT STANDARDS— EARTH AND SPACE SCIENCE— GRADES 5–8

Earth in the Solar System

▶ The earth is the third planet from the sun in a system that includes the moon, the sun, seven other planets and their moons, and smaller objects, such as asteroids and comets.

Engaging Question

What star patterns do you see in the sky?

Materials Needed

For Exploration

construction paper
1 pen or pencil per student

overhead projector
4 or 5 flashlights

Safety Precautions: Remind students to be careful not to poke themselves or others with the pen or pencil.

CONCEPTS TO BE CONSTRUCTED

▶ Constellations are groups of stars.

▶ Big Dipper, Little Dipper, Polaris or North Star, Cassiopeia, Perseus, and the Pleiades found in Taurus are concepts to be expanded.

SCIENCE ATTITUDES TO NURTURE

▶ Refusal to believe in superstitions or to accept claims without proof

▶ Openness to changing their minds when evidence for change is given

▶ Openness to questions about their own ideas

Exploration

PROCESS SKILLS USED

▶ Observing
▶ Predicting
▶ Hypothesizing
▶ Inferring

What will the students do?

The students will view a dot-to-dot pattern presented to them and predict what the pattern will look like once the dots are connected. This pattern is made on the chalkboard by using an overhead projector and black construction paper with holes punched in it for dots as the transparency. Place several different patterns on the overhead. Have the students take turns connecting the dots on the chalkboard.

Connect the Stars

Explanation

Concept: Constellations are groups of stars found in the sky. Ask the students questions such as the following to help invent this concept: What do you think these patterns represent? Do you recall seeing these same patterns anywhere? Review each of the patterns again and ask once again if anyone recalls seeing these patterns anywhere.

Patterns represent star constellations. Star constellations are made up of a group of stars and are given a name traditionally based on the pattern they make in the sky. These constellations were named by people in the past and usually have a story or legend attached to them.

Once again, project the patterns up on the board, again connecting the dots. This time go through the names of the constellations presented, and give a brief history of how they got their names. Some easy constellations to showcase are the Big Dipper, the Little Dipper, Cassiopeia, Perseus, and the Pleiades found in Taurus.

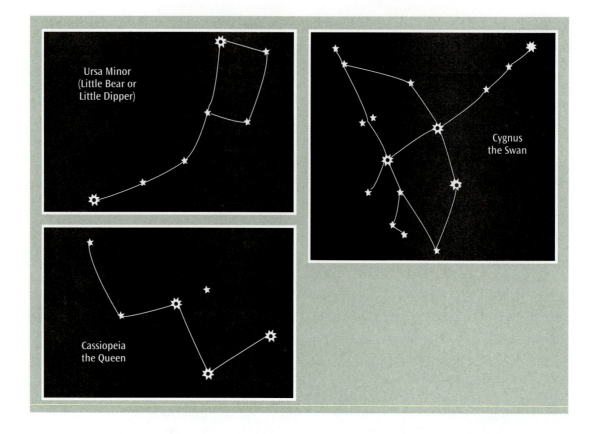

Ursa Minor
(Little Bear or
Little Dipper)

Cygnus
the Swan

Cassiopeia
the Queen

Identify the North Star—Polaris—for the students. Explain how all the other constellations in the Northern Hemisphere appear to revolve around this star. Thus, at different times of the year only certain star patterns are visible in the nighttime sky in the Northern Hemisphere. We call these star patterns _____ (constellations).

Evening Field Trip

PROCESS SKILLS USED
▶ Observing
▶ Communicating
▶ Formulating models
▶ Recording data

Create a Constellation

How will the idea be expanded?

- Take the students on an evening field trip to an area where electric lights are minimal. Be sure you pick a clear night. Ask everyone to bring a blanket and lie on the grass. Try to identify as many constellations as possible.
- Ask the students to create a constellation of their own and name it, much as the ancient Greeks and Indians did as they observed stars in the nighttime sky. Have them write reports about how their constellations got their names. Share the reports orally with the class.

Science in Personal and Social Perspectives

- How can star constellations help you if you get lost at night?
- How can you develop watching stars into a hobby?

Science and Technology

- What kind of equipment can you use to improve your view of the stars?
- How has astronomy equipment been perfected since the time of Galileo's first telescope?

- How can we use our knowledge of constellations to find a particular star in the sky?
- Why do all stars in the Northern Hemisphere appear to revolve around Polaris? Is this our closest star?

History and Nature of Science

- How are constellations used by astronomers who study other phenomena in the sky?
- Is there any difference between an astronomer and an astrologer? Do they both use their knowledge of constellations in some form? If so, how?

Evaluation

Upon completing the activities, the students will be able to:

- identify Polaris, the North Star;
- identify the Big and Little Dippers in the northern sky; and
- explain how at least two different constellations got their names;
- identify the star closest to the earth.

Earth Layers

Grade Level ● K–4

Discipline ● Earth and Space Science

Properties of Earth Materials

▶ Earth materials are solid rocks and soils, liquid water, and the gases of the atmosphere. The varied materials have different physical and chemical properties, which make them useful in different ways.

CONCEPTS TO BE CONSTRUCTED

▶ The earth is made up of three layers: the *core*, *mantle*, and *crust*. The differences in the layers are caused by the amount of heat and pressure upon them and the material found within each.

▶ Large land masses found on the crust of the earth are called *continents*. Large bodies of water on the crust are called *oceans*.

SCIENCE ATTITUDES TO NURTURE:

▶ Curiosity

▶ Cooperation with others

Clay Earth Layers

PROCESS SKILLS USED

▶ Observing

▶ Manipulating materials

▶ Predicting

Engaging Question

Why does the earth have layers?

Materials Needed

For Exploration (One Per Student)

2-inch diameter ball of red, yellow, and gray clay; plastic knife; white construction paper; 3 crayons of red, yellow, and gray

For Exploration (for Entire Class)

Green and blue clay, green crayon, globe of the earth, tennis ball, soccer ball. Maps of ocean floors are useful but optional.

🛈 *Safety Precautions:* Remind students to be careful not to poke themselves or others with the plastic knife. Be sure to wash hands after using the clay. Remind them not to eat the clay.

Exploration

What will the students do?

Guide the students through this portion of the lesson by first asking them to pick up the red clay and work it into a ball.

1. Flatten out the yellow clay and wrap it around the red ball of clay.
2. Flatten out gray clay and then wrap it around the yellow-covered ball of clay.
3. Using their plastic knives carefully, cut the clay ball in half.
4. Draw on construction paper what the sliced-open clay ball looks like.

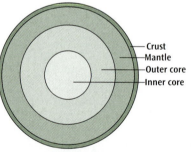

Explanation

Concept: The earth is made up of three layers: the *core*, *mantle*, and *crust*. The differences in the layers are caused by the amount of heat and pressure upon them and the material found within each.

Tell the students that you would like them to think of the clay ball as a *model* or representation of the earth. Since the students are most familiar with things found on the surface of the earth, ask them to give you suggestions of things they find there. If possible, draw pictures of their suggestions or write the names on the board. Ask whether anyone has an idea for another name to call the earth's surface. You might make an analogy to a pie that has a different material on the inside than outside. What do you call the outer covering of the pie? *Crust*—this same name is given to the outer surface of the earth. Ask the students to label the gray layer on their diagram the *crust*.

Now ask the students to look past the outer covering and focus on the yellow layer. The yellow clay represents the mantle. This layer of the earth is in a slightly liquid form. It is under enough pressure to heat the rock and melt it. Ask the students to label the yellow layer on their diagram the *mantle.* Share with them that this is where the magma comes from during volcanic activity. When there are cracks in the crust, the magma gets pushed up from the mantle through the weight of the earth's crust.

Continue with questions to get the children to think about what the very middle of something is usually referred to. Get the students to think about what they call the center of an apple. The red ball represents the *core.* Because the core is under such great pressure it is very hot, leaving the outer core in a solid state and the inner core in a semi-liquid state. Ask the students to label the red layer on their diagram the *core.*

Ask the students to reflect on what they now know about the characteristics of the earth's layers to answer this question: Why does the earth have layers?

Expansion

PROCESS SKILLS USED
- ▶ Manipulating materials
- ▶ Observing
- ▶ Hypothesizing
- ▶ Inferring

How will the idea be expanded?

Hold up the tennis ball. Ask the students how they think the tennis ball is like the earth. Encourage them to use the terms *crust, mantle,* and *core.* Hold up a soccer ball. Ask the students how the soccer ball is like the earth. Hold up the globe. Tell them that this represents what the earth would look like if they were up in the sky looking down. Ask the students to observe the globe carefully. After they look at the globe, ask the students if they think the soccer ball or the tennis ball is more like the earth's surface. Engage the students in a conversation about how the soccer ball is not one solid piece but many pieces sewn together. The crust of the earth does not look like one solid piece but like many pieces separated by water. The pieces appear to fit together. Ask the students for suggested names for the land masses and the bodies of water. If none is given, tell the students that the land masses are called *continents* and the bodies of water are called *oceans.* If maps of the ocean floor are available, share them with the students. Be sure to point out that the crust still exists below the ocean water.

Clay Continents

Provide the students with some green and blue clay. Ask them to put their two halves of clay back together again, gently sealing the gray clay so that they have one ball of clay again. Ask the students to use the green clay to place some land masses or continents on their earth. Ask them to add blue clay between the continents to represent the oceans. Then ask them to use their green and blue crayons to draw the continents and oceans on their drawings and to label them.

Science in Personal and Social Perspectives

- It has been found that the movement of the semiliquid material in the mantle of the earth causes the crust to move. When the crust moves, earthquakes occur. Have earthquakes ever occurred where you live? What should be done to protect people during earthquakes?
- What continent do you live on?

Science and Technology

- How has knowledge about continent movement changed the way we construct buildings?
- Can earthquakes be detected? How?
- Do you think if technology could come up with a way to drain the oceans that would be better for life on the earth? Why or why not?

Science as Inquiry

- Which layer of the earth is very hot yet still in a solid state?
- The land masses on the surface of the earth appear to fit together, yet many are far apart. Do you think they were once together? If so, why?
- Is there crust under the oceans? How do we know this?

History and Nature of Science

- A seismologist would need to understand that the earth is in layers. Why do you think this is true? What do you think a seismologist does?
- Should oceanographers be concerned about the earth's layers?
- Many oil companies get their oil out of the North Sea. Do you think these companies used their knowledge of the earth's layers to find their drilling sites? Why or why not?

Evaluation

Upon completing the activities, the students will be able to:

- draw a diagram of a cross section of the earth and label the continents, oceans, crust, mantle, and core;
- identify from a diagram the different layers of the earth;
- explain how the earth can be compared to a soccer ball; and
- point out continents and oceans on a globe.

Fossils

Grade Level ● 2–4
Discipline ● Earth and Space Science

NATIONAL SCIENCE EDUCA-
TION CONTENT STANDARDS-
EARTH AND SPACE SCIENCE—
GRADES 2–4
Properties of Earth Materials

▶ Fossils provide evidence about
the plants and animals that lived
long ago and the nature of the environment at that time.

Engaging Question

What is a fossil?

Materials Needed

For Exploration

A variety of fossil samples for class observations, construction paper, and crayons or markers.

For Expansion

seashells (1 or 2 per student)	plaster of Paris
leaves or plants	water
1 aluminum pie tin per student	1 plastic spoon per student
petroleum jelly	paper towels
2 paper cups per student	old newspapers

Note: Plastic samples of seashells, readily available through science equipment suppliers, may be preferred over actual seashells. Young children will find these easier to work with.

⓵ *Safety Precautions:* Students should be reminded not to eat the plaster. Take care to avoid water spills. Should they occur, wipe them up immediately.

Exploration

PROCESS SKILLS USED

▶ Observing
▶ Brainstorming
▶ Predicting
▶ Hypothesizing
▶ Communicating

What will the students do?

Pass the fossil samples around to the students without telling them what they are looking at. Ask the students to make careful observations about these unknown objects and to share their observations with the class. Encourage the students to think about what these things could possibly be. Is it a plant or an animal? Is it an image of a plant or an animal, or a piece of the real thing? Do you think it is still on the earth? How do you think this could have been formed? Allow the students sufficient time to brainstorm with one another ideas on the fossils' possible origins. Ask the students to draw the unknown object and to color it the way they think it would look if the actual object (plant or animal) were right in front of them. If the students are capable of writing sentences, ask them to write three or four sentences below their pictures describing how they think the image in the rock was formed.

**CONCEPTS TO BE
CONSTRUCTED**

▶ A record of an ancient animal
or plant found in sedimentary
rocks is called a *fossil*.

▶ *Fossils* provide clues to ancient
environments. Evidence that
humans were present during
primitive times is called an
artifact. A hollow space left in
sedimentary rock when a plant
or animal body decays is called
a *mold*. When sediments fill
the hollow space and harden,
the hardened sediments
formed in the shape of the
plant or animal are called *casts*.

**SCIENCE ATTITUDES
TO BE NURTURED**

▶ Curiosity
▶ Tolerating other opinions,
explanations, or points of view
▶ Avoidance of broad
generalizations when evidence
is limited

Fossil Observations

Explanation

Concept: A record of an ancient animal or plant found in sedimentary rock is called a *fossil*.

Help the students invent the concept by asking them to share with the class the drawings they created. Some questions to ask the students to help invent the concept are:

- Why did you choose those colors for your drawing?
- Depending on the unknown you observed, was it easy or difficult for you to decide what this would look like if it were right in front of you? Why?
- How do you think this was formed?
- Will you please share with us your ideas?

Through this line of questioning, the process of fossilization can be brought out. When an animal or plant dies, it is covered with mud, rocks, sand, and so on. Pressure is applied over many years, so the layers turn to stone, leaving an imprint of the plant or animal. The records of ancient animals and plants found in sedimentary rocks are called fossils. Additional source books or films on fossils may be shared with the class at this time. Also share examples of local fossils.

Expansion

Plaster Molds and Casts

PROCESS SKILLS USED
▶ Observing
▶ Manipulating materials
▶ Predicting

How will the idea be expanded?

Ask the students to bring in seashells or leaves to use in making an image, or provide these or plastic models for them. Ask the students to use the old newspapers to cover their desktops. Give each student a pie tin. Provide enough petroleum jelly that the students can spread a thin-to-medium film over the bottom and sides of the pie tin. Remind them that the entire inside of the tin is to be covered with jelly. Once they have chosen the item they want to make an image of, instruct the students to cover the shell or plant with a thin layer of petroleum jelly.

Step 1. Pour plaster into a pie dish.

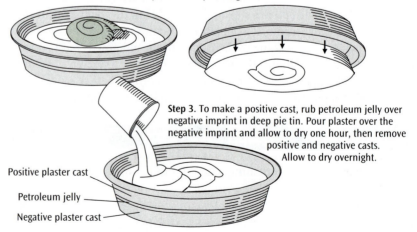

Step 2. Push shell into plaster. After drying an hour, carefully remove shell and allow plaster to dry overnight.

Step 3. To make a positive cast, rub petroleum jelly over negative imprint in deep pie tin. Pour plaster over the negative imprint and allow to dry one hour, then remove positive and negative casts. Allow to dry overnight.

Positive plaster cast
Petroleum jelly
Negative plaster cast

Place the shell or plant in the bottom of the pie tin so that the flattest side rests on the bottom of the pan.

In one of the cups for each student, place enough dry plaster of Paris so that when mixed it will be enough to cover the bottom of the pie tin with about 15 mm ($^1/_2$ inch) of plaster. In the second cup place enough water so that each student will have created the proper consistency of plaster once he or she mixes (using the plastic spoon) the dry powder with the water. Once the students have mixed their plaster, instruct them to pour it carefully over the shell or plant into the pie tin. Allow about 1 hour for the plaster to harden. Remember: As the plaster dries it will become quite warm and then cool. Wait until it has cooled before removing it from the tin.

Once the plaster has hardened, turn the pie tin upside down over the paper-covered desk and tap the tin lightly to remove the plaster cast. The plaster will still be quite wet at this time; students need to be reminded to use care as they remove their shells or plants from the plaster. Once the shells or plants are removed, set the plaster casts in a safe place to cure fully (dry out and harden). This should take at least a day. Once the casts are cured, the students will have what is known as a *negative imprint* or *mold* of a plant or animal. If desired, a *positive imprint* or *cast* can now be created by spreading additional petroleum jelly over the surface of the negative imprint and placing it back into a deeper petroleum-jelly-lined pie tin. On top of the first cast pour additional plaster. After it has hardened (about 1 hour) carefully turn the tin upside down and remove the old and new plaster casts. Since the surface of the old cast was thoroughly covered with petroleum jelly, the two casts should readily come apart with a knife blade. The new cast formed from the negative imprint is called a positive imprint. After this has had a chance to harden thoroughly (about one day), the students may want to paint or color with markers their newly formed fossils.

Science in Personal and Social Perspectives

- Why do you want to know about fossils? Has our study of fossils given you any ideas about what life was like in the past?
- Do you think you could have lived during the time when dinosaurs roamed the land? Why or why not?

Science and Technology

- How can fossils tell us what ancient environments were like?
- Evidence left by early people is called an artifact. Some examples are arrowheads, ancient beads, and animal skins used as clothing. Why do you think we don't call them fossils?

Science as Inquiry

- Why can fossils be found only in sedimentary rocks?
- Can you find fossils where you live? Where do you think you would go to look for fossils?

History and Nature of Science

- Paleontologists (fossil experts) study and learn from fossils. If you were a paleontologist, what kind of information would you share with others on the imprints you just made?

- How is an archeologist's job different from a paleontologist's? An excellent book for this topic is Gloria and Esther Goldreich, *What Can She Be? A Geologist* (New York: Lothrop, Lee and Shepard, 1976).
- Describe how the Leakeys (Louis, Mary, and son Richard) used fossil evidence to determine the changes in human body form throughout history.

Evaluation

Upon completing the activities, the students will be able to:

- demonstrate how a fossil can be formed by using sand, water, and a seashell;
- pick out the fossils when given several items to choose from, such as a seashell, a leaf, a sedimentary rock with a shell imprint or leaf imprint on it, a geode, or an igneous rock such as obsidian; and
- tell or write in their own words what a fossil is and what information it can provide humans.

Rock Types

Grade Level ● 5–8

Discipline ● Earth and Space Science

NATIONAL SCIENCE EDUCATION CONTENT STANDARDS— EARTH AND SPACE SCIENCE— GRADES 5–8

Structure of the Earth System

► Changes in the solid earth can be described as the "rock cycle." Old rocks at the earth's surface weather, forming sediments that are buried, then compacted, heated, and often recrystallized into new rock. Eventually, those new rocks may be brought to the surface by the forces that drive plate motions, and the rock cycle continues.

Engaging Question

Are all rocks made the same?

Materials Needed

For Exploration (for Each Cooperative Group of Students)

several samples of igneous rocks, sedimentary rocks, metamorphic rocks, 1 jar, 2 sheets of construction paper, sand, mud, and pebbles

For Expansion (for Each Student)

goggles, hammer and chisel, collection bag, 3 empty egg cartons, old newspapers, and a marker

Safety Precautions: Remind students to handle rock samples carefully. No throwing rocks! If you choose to take the students outside to collect rock samples, be sure proper safety procedures are followed. Pair up the students and make sure they know the boundaries for rock sample collection.

Exploration

PROCESS SKILLS USED

► Observing
► Classifying
► Inferring

What will the students do?

Divide the class into cooperative learning groups of three or four students. Provide each group with sand, numerous rock types, and pebbles. Ask the students to categorize the rocks. What's different about them? How are they alike? After the students have shared the results of their categorizing, ask them to set those samples aside in the categories they identified.

Give each cooperative group a jar and ask them to put rocks, sand, mud, and water into it. Put a lid on the jar and shake it for a few moments. Ask the students to draw a picture of what the jar looks like after the materials have settled.

CONCEPTS TO BE CONSTRUCTED

► Rocks may be classified into three groups: *igneous*, *sedimentary*, and *metamorphic*, depending on how they are formed.

► *Igneous* means "fire formed." Cooled magma and lava create igneous rocks such as granite and obsidian. *Sedimentary* rocks are formed in water by layers of sediments building up from weathered igneous, metamorphic, and other sedimentary rocks or decaying organic matter; examples are limestone and sandstone. *Metamorphic* rocks are very hard rocks that may be formed from igneous or sedimentary rocks under extreme heat and pressure; marble and gneiss are examples.

SCIENCE ATTITUDES TO BE NURTURED

► Open-mindedness
► Perseverance
► Curiosity

Explanation

Concept: Rocks may be classified into three groups: igneous, sedimentary, and metamorphic, depending on how they were formed.

Ask the students to fold a sheet of construction paper into three parts. Now go back to the different piles of rocks the students first categorized. Ask them what kinds of differences they noted. Explain that rocks come in all shapes, colors, and sizes. However, they weren't all made the same way. Use the example of lava from a volcano. What happens to the lava when it dries? It becomes a hard rock called *igneous*, meaning "fire formed." Cooled magma and lava create igneous rocks like granite and obsidian. In the first part

Rock Categorization

of the construction paper, draw or describe how igneous rock is formed. Provide the students with various samples of igneous rocks to observe.

Refer back to the shaken jar. What does it currently look like? Steer the students toward looking at the layers of materials. Did your group classify any of the rock samples based on whether you could see layers? What do you think rocks formed from the buildup of materials in layers are called? *Sedimentary* rocks are formed in water by layers of sediments building up from weathered igneous, metamorphic, and other sedimentary rocks, or decaying organic matter. Limestone and sandstone are sedimentary. In the second part of the construction paper, draw or describe how sedimentary rocks are formed. Provide the students with various samples of sedimentary rocks to observe.

Ask the students whether they think they classified any rocks that have not yet been described. Have the students share those rocks with the rest of the class. Make sure they do not fit under igneous or sedimentary categories. Explain to the students that the igneous or sedimentary rocks can be put under extreme heat and pressure inside the earth, which changes the look of the rock. These are called *metamorphic* rocks; examples are marble and gneiss. Metamorphic rocks are very hard. In the third part of the construction paper, draw or describe how metamorphic rocks are formed. Provide the students with various samples of metamorphic rocks to observe.

Summarize how rocks are formed by completing these statements: Rocks formed "from fire" are called _____ (igneous); rocks when placed under heat and pressure change into _____ (metamorphic) rocks; and rocks formed from the buildup of materials in layers are called _____ (sedimentary).

Expansion

Rock Collection Field Trip

PROCESS SKILLS USED

▶ Observing

▶ Classifying

▶ Collecting

▶ Comparing

▶ Communicating

How will the idea be expanded?

This expansion activity may be done as a home extension activity or as a class field trip. Identify a site where students will be permitted to collect rock samples. Either take them as a class or provide instructions to parents to take the students to the collection site. Be sure the students are given instruction on how to use the hammer and chisel to extract rock samples from the bedrock. Encourage the students to break their samples into pieces small enough to fit into the egg carton depressions. Remind the students to think about the different colors and textures that different kinds of rocks have. Classify the collection into igneous, sedimentary, and metamorphic, and designate one egg carton for each rock type. After a sufficient amount of time has passed (one or two months), ask the students to bring their collections to school to share with the class.

Science in Personal and Social Perspectives

- If you were going to build a home along the ocean, would you want the underlying rock to be igneous, sedimentary, or metamorphic? Why?
- Have you ever washed your hands with a pumice-based soap? Have you ever used a pumice stone to smooth away rough skin? Where do you think pumice comes from?

Science and Technology

- Which type of rock is best used for building purposes?
- Would you trust a bridge made of sedimentary rocks? Do you think it would last as long as a bridge made with igneous rocks? What about a bridge made of metamorphic rock?
- Which type of rock would be a wise choice to build a dam with?

Science as Inquiry

- Where in the world would I easily find an igneous rock? A sedimentary rock? A metamorphic rock?
- Can an igneous rock be formed from a sedimentary one? Can a sedimentary rock be formed from a metamorphic or igneous rock?
- What kind of rock is the local bedrock?

History and Nature of Science

- Would a civil engineer responsible for placing a bridge across the Mississippi River between Illinois and Missouri need to understand the type of bedrock found in the area before plans for the bridge could be made? Why or why not?
- As a construction worker you decide to build your own home. You want to make it out of stone. Which kind of rock type would you use, and why? Is it important that a construction worker or even a home owner know the differences among igneous, sedimentary, and metamorphic rocks?

Evaluation

Upon completing the activities, the students will be able to:

- look at six different rocks and identify whether they are igneous, sedimentary, or metamorphic;
- identify different areas of the world where the three different rock types can be found; and
- reflect, and then write a description of an igneous rock formed when lava cooled outside the earth.

Structure of the Earth System

▶ Changes in the solid earth can be described as the "rock cycle." Old rocks at the earth's surface weather, forming sediments that are buried, then compacted, heated, and often recrystallized into new rock. Eventually, those new rocks may be brought to the surface by the forces that drive plate motions, and the rock cycle continues.

CONCEPTS TO BE CONSTRUCTED

▶ The rate at which a crystal cools affects the size of the crystal.

▶ Crystals can be seen in many rocks.

SCIENCE ATTITUDES TO BE NURTURED

▶ A positive approach to failure

▶ Perseverance

Cooling Crystals

Grade Level ● 5–8

Discipline ● Earth and Space Science

Engaging Question

Why do some rocks, made of the same materials, have different names?

Materials Needed

For Exploration (for Each Group)

3 glass caster cups
3 small test tubes (10 ml)
test tube holder
paradichlorobenzine (PDB) flakes
(found in supermarkets, hardware
stores, pharmacies)

1 hand lens per student
grease pencil
crushed ice
two 500-ml beakers
one 150-ml beaker
tongs

For Exploration (for Entire Class)

hot plates, paper towels

For Expansion

samples of the igneous rocks rhyolite, granite, and obsidian; 1 hand lens per student

Safety Precautions: Remind students that extreme care should be used near the hot plate and in handling the hot water and PDB, and also that goggles should be worn at all times. Be sure the room is well ventilated when melting the PDB.

Exploration

PDB Crystal Formation

PROCESS SKILLS USED

▶ Observing

▶ Predicting

▶ Manipulating materials

▶ Recording data

▶ Drawing conclusions

What will the students do?

Ask the students to fill one of the 500-ml beakers with 300 ml of water. Place a caster cup in the beaker. Boil the water on the hot plate. Fill the other 500-ml beaker with crushed ice. Place the second caster cup in the beaker. Leave the third caster cup at room temperature.

Carefully observe some PDB flakes. Record those observations. Fill each of the three small test tubes with PDB flakes. Half-fill the 150-ml beaker with water. Place the three test tubes in the beaker. Place the beaker with the test tubes on the hot plate. Heat the beaker gently until the PDB melts.

Using the tongs, carefully remove the caster cup from the boiling water. Dry the cup and label it *A*. Using the test tube holder, remove one test tube and pour the PDB into this caster cup. Time how long it takes for the PDB to completely become a solid. Record the time. Record your observations of the PDB flakes for cup A.

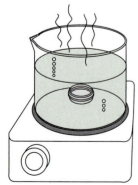

Caster cup in boiling water
on hot plate

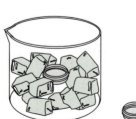

Caster cup
in ice

Caster cup at
room temperature

Remove the second caster cup from the beaker with ice. Dry the cup quickly and completely. Label it *B*. Pour the second test tube of PDB into this cup. Time how long it takes for the PDB to turn completely solid. Record the time. Record your observations of the PDB flakes for cup B.

Pour the third test tube of PDB into the cup at room temperature. Label it *C*. Again, time how long it takes for this PDB to solidify completely. Record the time. Record your observations of the PDB flakes for cup C.

Explanation

Concept: The rate at which a crystal cools affects the size of the crystal.

How does the rate of cooling affect the size of crystals? Record the cooling times for samples A, B, and C on the board. Look at the contents of each caster cup with the magnifying glass. Draw the contents of each caster cup on your paper. When the PDB was placed into the test tubes, there was no difference between tubes. Once it was placed into cups A, B, and C, a change occurred. How are they different? What caused this difference? What conclusions can you draw? The students should conclude that the rate at which a crystal cools affects the size of the crystal formed.

Expansion

How will the idea be expanded?

PROCESS SKILLS USED
- ▶ Observing
- ▶ Recording data
- ▶ Generalizing
- ▶ Formulating models

Ask the students to observe the crystals in the samples of granite, rhyolite, and obsidian with a magnifying glass. Draw the crystals in each sample on your paper. Compare the crystals in the caster cups to the samples of granite, rhyolite, and obsidian. Which PDB crystals are most similar to the crystals in the rock samples? (Cup A, granite; cup B, obsidian; cup C, rhyolite.)

Rock Type versus Crystal Formation

Granite, rhyolite, and obsidian are igneous rocks essentially made of the same material. Explain why they look different. Where would igneous rocks have a chance to cool slowly? Where would igneous rock cool rapidly? If you saw a rock that contained large interlocking crystals, what would you say about the way it formed? The more slowly a crystal cools, the larger the crystals are. Granite cooled slowly, and crystals were able to form. Rhyolite cooled more rapidly than granite, but more slowly than obsidian. Igneous rocks cool slowly deep in the earth. They cool rapidly on the surface. Large interlocking crystals form slowly inside the earth. So how do you respond to the inquiry question: Why *do* some rocks, made of the same materials, have different names?

Science in Personal and Social Perspectives

- What kinds of crystals do you eat regularly? (Salt and sugar)
- How does the size of a crystal determine its quality? Do you think your knowledge of how crystals form will assist you in determining the quality of precious rocks and gems?

Science and Technology

- The strength and quality of rocks are important for construction. What is the best type of rock for long-lasting buildings?
- How has the scarcity of quality gems on the market affected your life, your community, or the world?

Science as Inquiry

- What kinds of rocks are found in the area where you live? Can you classify them according to their crystal structure?
- Can crystals be found in sedimentary rocks? Why or why not?

History and Nature of Science

- What kinds of careers would use information on crystal formation? (Some possibilities include geologist, geophysicist, volcanologist, jeweler, sculptor, and geographer.)
- Choose one of the career suggestions from the question above and research the skills necessary to enter that career. Provide an oral report to the class.

Evaluation

Upon completing the activities, the students will be able to:

- identify where a crystal cooled (on the earth's surface or inside the earth) and at what rate when given drawings of crystals of different shapes and sizes;
- examine samples of igneous rocks and explain why they have different-sized crystals; and
- explain how the prices of precious jewels are affected by crystal formation.

Weathering

Grade Level ● 5–8

Discipline ● Earth and Space Science

▶ Soil consists of weathered rocks and decomposed organic material from dead plants, animals, and bacteria. Soils are often found in layers, with each having a different chemical composition and texture.

Engaging Question

If rocks are so hard, what causes them to break apart?

Materials Needed

For Discrepant Event
> soda bottle and cap, water, freezer

For Exploration
> field site to collect data, stereomicroscope, hammer

For Expansion
> dilute hydrochloric acid (HCl); igneous, sedimentary, and metamorphic rock samples

ⓘ *Safety Precautions:* Review with the students ahead of time the rules that should be followed for everyone's safety during the field trip. Visit the field site before the students do to guard against any possible hazards at the site.

The day before you begin this lesson, take a glass soda bottle and ask a student to fill it with water all the way to the top. Cap the bottle so that no water can escape. Now ask the students what they think will happen to this bottle if you place it in the freezer for a day. Record their predictions on the board, where they will remain untouched until the next day. Twenty-four hours later, remove the bottle from the freezer. If the bottle was totally filled before freezing, it should now be cracked, as the ice expanded upon freezing. Ask the students what they observe. Did it behave according to their predictions? Why did this happen? What happens to water when it freezes? On your observations, do you think water could do this to other items besides glass? Think about this as we engage in today's activity.

CONCEPTS TO BE CONSTRUCTED

▶ Weathering is the name given to the various mechanical and chemical processes that break down rock.

▶ Erosion, soil formation, and rock formation occur at different rates depending upon the type of rock: igneous, sedimentary, or metamorphic.

SCIENCE ATTITUDES TO NURTURE

▶ Open-mindedness

▶ A desire for reliable sources of information

Freezing Bottle

Exploration

PROCESS SKILLS USED

▶ Observing

▶ Hypothesizing

▶ Predicting

▶ Measuring

▶ Using spatial relationships

▶ Recording data

What will the students do?

Tell the students that they are going on a field trip around the school grounds to answer the following question: If rocks are so hard, what causes them to break apart? An old road or empty prairie or field will be an ideal site. Remind the students about appropriate care of a collection site. Remind them to take care as they travel through the site and to try not to destroy any animal homes or wildflowers or plant growth. Ask the students to look for rocks that appear to be broken apart. They are to record a description of the area in which they find them, taking care to note the soil conditions (wet, dry, sandy, clay), an estimate of the original size of the rock, a physical description of the rock (color, shininess, hardness, porosity), and a prediction based on their findings as to what they think caused the rock to break apart. A small sample of the rock should be collected for further study in the classroom. Upon returning to the classroom, the students will make a composite chart of their field

Weathering Field Trip

observations. Headings for this chart could include *collection site, soil conditions, rock size, physical properties* (color, luster, hardness, pore size), *possible cause for breakage.*

Explanation

Concept: *Weathering* is the name given to the various mechanical and chemical processes that break down rock.

Draw the students' attention to the composite chart in the front of the room. To guide the students in inventing the concept of weathering, ask such questions as: In looking at this chart, are there any we can group together? Do any of them sound as if the different groups of investigators were looking at the same rocks?

Ask the students to bring up the sample rocks whose descriptions sound similar. Do you think these are the same rocks?

Once double sightings have been eliminated, begin to focus on the chart again, this time asking, Is there any one area where broken rocks were found more often than any other? Or is there any one soil condition where broken rocks are found more often than any other?

If this is the case, then ask the students if they think this soil condition contributed to the presence of broken rocks. If it is a very wet area, then you can relate this back to the discrepant event: how the freezing and thawing of water will contribute to the cracking of the rocks. If this is a dry area, ask the students if they made note of any vegetation growing in the area. They may have found the broken rocks due to roots growing through the surface of the rock. It may be a very dry area where wind blows through rather rapidly, causing the rocks to break up.

On the basis of the results of our field study, if rocks are so hard, what causes them to break apart? Solicit ideas from the students. Share with them that the name of this process that causes the breaking up of rock due to running water, wind, rain, or roots is called *weathering.*

What happens to the rock pieces as they are carried by the rain, wind, or running water? What term can we use to describe the carrying away of this weathered material? (Erosion) Ask the students if they observed the soil where they found the rock. Was it similar in composition to the rock itself? Engage the students in a discussion of how the weathering of rocks assists in soil formation.

Expansion

Rock Identification

PROCESS SKILLS USED
- ► Observing
- ► Classifying
- ► Experimenting
- ► Predicting
- ► Inferring
- ► Interpreting data
- ► Recording data
- ► Communicating

How will the idea be expanded?

If your students collected rock samples that fell into one type (all igneous, or all sedimentary, or all metamorphic), then in addition to their samples, provide them with rock samples from the missing rock groups. Ask the students to try to group the rock samples according to the characteristics from the composite chart from the first activity. Suggest to them that based on hardness, porosity, and composition, they should be able to group their rock samples into three different groups.

Once they have their samples in three groups, the students can perform the following experiments to determine possible sources of weathering.

Chemical Weathering   *Acid Test.* Take one sample from each rock group. Predict what will happen to the rock when you drop three drops of dilute HCl on it. Do you think each rock will react the same way? Which one do you think will weather the most? In nature, what type of weathering could we consider this to be? (This is known as *chemical weathering.*)

Rust/Oxidation. Do you notice any color changes in your rock? Are there what appear to be rust spots on the rock? What do you think causes this?

Water. Cover the three different rock samples with water, and place them in a freezer for a day. Do the rocks crumble easily in your hands? If you strike them with a hammer lightly, do they fall apart? Are the insides still wet? Which rock type was most susceptible to the freezing water? Since the water simply froze and broke the rock apart, this is known as *mechanical weathering.*

Roots. In what area did you find this rock? Are there still traces of plant matter on the rock? Did you see any roots pushing up right through the surface of the rock? Do the roots cause chemical or mechanical weathering? Overall, which rocks are most easily weathered and which are most difficult to weather? Can you guess how each of these rock groups was originally formed based on your weathering observations? Lead a discussion on rock formations: igneous, sedimentary, and metamorphic. Detailed discussions will be provided in a separate lesson for each rock type.

Science in Personal and Social Perspectives

- Why does one need to use special fishing lures if a river or lake is muddy or murky due to erosion?
- What would you suspect was happening if the water in your favorite fishing stream looked clean, yet the number of fish began to dwindle? You have noticed that some of the rocks along the bank are beginning to crumble and wash downstream. What could you do to verify your suspicions? Whom would you talk to about this problem?

Science and Technology

- What role does strip-mining of coal or clear-cutting of timber play in allowing the forces of weather to affect erosion?
- How has an increased understanding of the forces of weathering and erosion caused us to change our farming practices since the Dust Bowl days of the 1930s?

Science as Inquiry

- How does weathering differ from erosion? What factors contribute to soil formation? What processes have occurred to create the different rock types? Can you name the three different rock types?
- In which rock formation would you most likely place a building like the Sears Tower? Why? Which rock type would you be least likely to use to build a house? Why?

History and Nature of Science

- Why would a civil engineer need to understand the processes of weathering and erosion?
- Do you think a contractor or cement finisher would find knowledge of weathering, erosion, soil, and rock types useful in his or her work?
- Research the great pyramids of Egypt. How were they built? What are they made of? When were they built? Would they still exist if they were first built in Chicago?

Evaluation

Upon completing the activities, the students will be able to:

- draw a diagram showing the relationships among rock types, soil types, weathering, and erosion;
- when given a weathered rock sample and a description of where the sample was found, suggest the most probable source for its weathering;
- list at least four agents of erosion; and
- discriminate between constructive and destructive geologic forces.

Crustal Plate Movement

Grade Level ● 5–8
Discipline ● Earth and Space Science

Engaging Question

Is the earth's surface one solid piece?

Materials Needed

For Exploration (for Each Group of 4 to 6 Students)

4 wood blocks
1 liter of water
a heat lamp or 150- to -200-watt bulb
   and socket

plastic shoebox (heavy plastic type,
   which will not melt under lightbulb)
food coloring
stacks of books to raise box above lamp

For Expansion

maps of the world showing the crustal plate boundaries, a list of places famous for volcanic eruptions, a list of sites of recent earthquakes

🛈 *Safety Precautions:* The students should be reminded to use care with the heat source. Don't place the heat source too close to the plastic box or books. Use care around water and electricity. Wipe up any water spills immediately. Do not touch heat source with wet hands.

Exploration

PROCESS SKILLS USED

▶ Experimenting

▶ Observing

▶ Predicting

▶ Inferring

What will the students do?

Each student group should place its plastic box on two stacks of books. The box should be high enough so that a heat source (lamp) will fit beneath. Pour water into the box. Place the four small wood blocks in the box. All the blocks should touch, forming a square. Place the heat source beneath the box directly under the center of the blocks. Turn the light on and place a drop of food coloring in the water where the four blocks meet. Observe the blocks for about five to ten minutes. What happens to each of the four wood blocks? What happens to the food coloring?

Explanation

Concept: The theory of plate tectonics states that the crust of the earth is not one solid piece, but rather several separate plates that are in motion on top of molten material.

Ask the students to share their observations on the movement of the four wood blocks and the food coloring. Why do you think this happened? If you were to relate this activity to the earth's crust, what do you think the blocks represent? (Early land masses that separated millions of years ago.) What would the water represent? (The molten layer of the earth called the *mantle.*) What happened to the temperature of the water over time? (It warmed up.) What happened to the food coloring? (It slowly moved along the surface as the water continued to warm.) Through questioning along this line, help the students to conclude that the theory of plate tectonics states that the crust of the earth is not one solid piece but rather several separate plates that are in motion on top of molten material.

Expansion

PROCESS SKILLS USED
▶ Observing
▶ Predicting
▶ Making conclusions

How will the idea be expanded?

Pair up the students. Provide each pair with a world map indicating the boundaries for the crustal plates. The students should be free to mark on the maps you provide. Provide the students with a recent list of volcanic and earthquake activity. Ask them to plot on the map the places where the most recent earthquakes and volcanoes have occurred. You may give them a list of volcanic and earthquake activity for the past fifty years to plot. Ask the students to share some observations they have made about the relationship between earthquakes and volcanoes from this exercise. The students should conclude that most earthquake and volcanic activity occurs where two or more crustal plates come together.

Mapping Volcanoes and Earthquakes

Science in Personal and Social Perspectives

- Would you choose to live along a crustal plate boundary? If you did, how might it affect your life?
- Do you think the government should help pay to repair homes for people who chose to build their homes on a known crustal boundary?

Science and Technology

- Are you aware of any other theories about formation or movement of the earth's crust? What part do you think technology has played in theory change and advanced knowledge about different phenomena?
- How do we use our knowledge about movement of the earth's crust when we construct buildings in areas where crustal plates are known to move?

Science as Inquiry

- Is there still movement of the earth's crust? How do we know?
- A lot of volcanic activity occurs in the Hawaiian Islands. Are they on the edge of a crustal plate? If not, what is causing the volcanic activity? Research the formation of these volcanic islands.

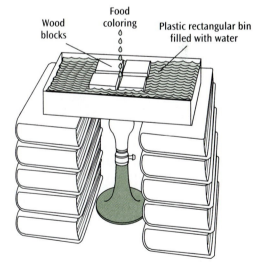
Food coloring
Wood blocks
Plastic rectangular bin filled with water

- Explain how a solid crust can move. What does the mantle layer of the earth have to do with this movement?

History and Nature of Science

- Who is Charles Lyell? What career changes led him to many geological discoveries?
- Would a seismologist be concerned with crustal plate movement? Why?
- Why would a civil engineer be concerned with the location of crustal plate boundaries? What does a civil engineer do?

Evaluation

On completing the activities, the students will be able to:

Oatmeal and Cracker Plate Tectonics

- demonstrate the theory of plate tectonics by using a bowl of oatmeal and some soda crackers;
- identify the area known as the Ring of Fire on a world map and explain what it is; and
- briefly explain the theory of plate tectonics.

Aging Human/Aging Earth

Grade Level ● 7–8

Discipline ● Earth and Space Science

NATIONAL SCIENCE EDUCATION CONTENT STANDARDS– EARTH AND SPACE SCIENCE— GRADES 7-8

Earth History

▶ The earth processes we see today, including erosion, movement of lithospheric plates, and changes in atmospheric composition, are similar to those that occurred in the past. The earth's history is also influenced by occasional catastrophes, such as the impact of an asteroid or comet.

Engaging Question

Are the processes that shaped the earth in the past still occurring today?

CONCEPT TO BE CONSTRUCTED

▶ The earth's processes that we see today, including erosion, movement or crustal plates, and changes in atmospheric composition, are similar to processes that occurred in the past. The earth's history is also influenced by occasional catastrophes such as the impact of an asteroid or comet.

Materials Needed

For Exploration

pictures of the earth, including views from space and close-up pictures of various biomes

pictures of the other planets and the earth's moon

journal or notebook to record data

access to older community members

audio or videotape recorder

For Expansion

geologic maps of your state and the region where your school is located. These are maps that show the ages of the various rock layers identifying the periods and epochs, and the depth of each layer from the surface.

geologic time scale

access to reference materials on the geology of the local region, or access to geologists who live/work in the region

SCIENCE ATTITUDES TO NURTURE

▶ A desire for reliable sources of information

▶ Tolerance of other opinions, explanations, or points of view

▶ Openness to changing their minds when evidence for change is given and openness to questions about their own ideas

⚠ *Safety Precautions:* During the exploration activity the students should work in pairs and never go into an interview without a formal introduction by a trusted adult.

Exploration

PROCESS SKILLS USED

▶ Observing
▶ Inferring
▶ Predicting
▶ Communicating
▶ Comparing and contrasting
▶ Formulating hypotheses
▶ Using space-time relationships

What will students do?

Introduction. The teacher should hang pictures of the earth around the classroom—scenes from the major biomes such as pictures of forests, mountains, or deserts. An old calendar may be a good source for such scenes. Also hang pictures of the other planets and the moon around the classroom. Ask the students to look around the room at all of the pictures. After students have had time to view the pictures, ask them why they think scientists call the earth a "living planet." Solicit their responses. To get them started, use guiding questions, such as: What do you think is evidence of living things? Do you see any evidence of that in any of the pictures found around the classroom?

Living Humans—Living Earth

Encourage them to think about changes in the surface of the earth; recall for them events in recent years, such as the earthquake in Iran, volcanoes in Mexico, and the numerous hurricanes that strike from the Atlantic Ocean. All of these are evidence that the earth's surface is constantly changing shape, wearing down one area and building up another. The forests and grasslands are evidence that on the earth, the sun's energy is being used to grow new life.

Ask them to ponder this question: How is your body like the earth? Solicit student ideas. These may include things like our bodies have mountains and valleys—high and low spots; we are covered with a thin crust—our skin; and we make use of the sun's energy to get food to help us grow as well. Like the earth, changes have happened to our bodies over time. We've grown since we were babies, we've acquired some cuts and bruises, but even with that our bodies have repaired themselves. This is much as the earth does after a catastrophe like a forest fire or flood.

Conclude with this statement: Just as there are changes in our living bodies over time, so too has the living earth changed.

Student Activity. Assign the students to "interview teams." Explain to them that their task is to identify and interview a person in their community who can share information on changes in the physical environment of the community over time. Stress that the purpose of the interview is to capture stories on changes in the ecology of the region—not social changes. Remind the students of the introductory discussion's conclusion: Just as there are changes in our living bodies over time, so too has the living earth changed. Ask them to use this conclusion to shape their interview questions. For instance, the students could ask the interviewee to recall something he or she liked to do outdoors when young, such as swimming in a certain pond or walking across a frozen creek in the dead of winter. The students could then ask if a young person could still do that today. Is the pond still there? Has the creek been widened or does water still flow there?

Provide the students with audiotape or videotape recorders for the interviews. Teach them skills in setting up an interview, the proper etiquette in calling the person they want to interview, introducing themselves, showing respect and courtesy to the person speaking, and so on. For safety's sake stress to the students the importance of performing the interview as a team. Never go into the person's home without at least another student or a parent present while they conduct the interview. If at all possible, invite the person to the school for the interview.

Ask the students to prepare a multimedia presentation on the ecological changes that they discovered through their interviews. Ask them to speculate on causes for the identified changes and to pick at least one change and research the exact reason for that change. For example, if a person said, "As youngsters we used to swim across the Mississippi River," and your students know that this is not possible today because the spot the person talked about is now much wider than it was then, the students should do some research to find out why the river is much wider today. Encourage them to bring in pictures and/or video of the sites in the past and present.

Explanation

Concept: The earth's processes we see today, including erosion, movement of crustal plates, and changes in atmospheric composition, are similar to those processes that occurred in the past.

Hold a public forum for the students to present their findings. Invite the people who were interviewed, parents, and the community to hear the students' presentations. A public forum presentation will provide a real-world context for the students' work and demonstrate the importance of good communication skills, both spoken and written. As the students share their findings, ask them to classify the causes for the ecological changes as "human-made" or due to "nature." Discuss how both may occur or how humans may speed up natural causes like erosion. Now that we have looked at geologic events of the past and changes in our local geology today, how would you complete this sentence: Processes that shape the earth today, such as volcanoes, earthquakes, and erosion, are the _____ (same) processes that were shaping the earth in the past.

How will the idea be expanded?

PROCESS SKILLS USED
▶ Observing
▶ Inferring
▶ Hypothesizing
▶ Interpreting data

Provide the students with a series of maps showing the rock record for your region and for your state. These are typically available through your state department of natural resources, geology division. The major geologic eras, periods, and epochs should be marked on the maps, as well as the relative thickness of the layers represented. Also provide the students with a geologic calendar, which provides the names and duration for all of the geologic eras, periods, and epochs. If the students have never worked with a geologic calendar, review the components, explaining the differences between eras, periods, and epochs.

Using the maps, ask the students to compare the rock record of the local region to the geologic calendar. Are all of the epochs present in your region? What epoch is missing in your region? How does your region compare with the rest of your state? Are there differences in the thickness of the rock layers? Are the same layers missing throughout the state as are missing in your local region? Ask the students to reflect on their findings from the interview activity. Knowing what and why geologic changes happened in recent times from the interviews with the local people, can you project how some of the rock layers may be absent from the rock record?

Ask the students to determine where in their local rock record did humans first appear on the planet? How far below the surface is that rock layer? When did the dinosaurs first appear on the planet? How far below the surface is that event in your local rock record? What about animals like a horse or a mastodon? When did they first appear on the earth? How far below the surface is that event in your local rock record? Why aren't all of these animals still found on the earth today? Would a process like erosion or even an earthquake wipe out the dinosaurs? What do you think happened in the earth's history to eliminate some animal species? Can we tell this from the rock record?

Use the reference materials on the geology of the local region to provide some answers to these questions. Invite a local geologist or even a paleontologist or a paleobotanist to come in and talk to the class about the local geologic record, explaining the geologic processes that have occurred in their state and region. Conclude this activity by having the students share answers to the questions posed, to restate the primary concept that processes that occurred in the past still occur today, and that the earth's history is also influenced by occasional catastrophes such as the impact of an asteroid or comet.

Science in Personal and Social Perspectives

- While we cannot always control the impact that nature has on our local ecology, we can control human impact. Identify one local ecological change caused by humans and propose solutions to minimize such impact in the future.
- The rock layers below the surface were formed by natural processes that occurred, in some cases hundreds of thousands of years ago. Engage in a debate about the pros and cons of extracting rock below the surface just because we own the land above the surface.

Science and Technology

- Humans have applied various technologies to extract rock from the earth. Some mining operations take place at the surface, typically called surface or strip mining. Mining below the ground makes use of a "longwaller." Research these two types of technology, describing how they each work, determining which has less impact on the local environment, and defending your response.
- To map the ocean floor, sonar is used. What is this device? Can it be used to provide a rock record of the layers of the ocean floor also? If not, how do we determine what the rock record is below the ocean floor?

Science as Inquiry

- Review the local rock record. What kinds of rock can be found within the first two hundred feet below the surface? Propose a way to verify that the map of the local rock record is correct. Describe in detail what you would need to do to investigate the validity of the map.

History and Nature of Science

- Would a paleobotanist be a good source of information on changes in our local ecology? Why? What does a paleobotanist do?
- Some scientists believe that by studying the gases that surround a planet like Jupiter today, we can have insight into the ancient atmosphere that surrounded the earth. Why would we want to know more about the earth's early atmosphere? What can we learn about our own planet from studying the gases that surround other planets?

Evaluation

Upon completing the activities, the students will be able to:

- discuss the age of the earth's crust at different locations (i.e., ocean floor, different continents) by describing where it is older in other places, and using that information to explain how the earth's crust has changed over the last billion years;
- explain why even though the earth's history is very long and the time of human life on earth is incredibly short, we have permanently altered our environment. A student will be able to discuss the implications of the environmental crisis as it exists in the context of the earth's history;
- when provided with a rock record history of two different areas, explain the differences between the two records; and
- explain the difference between a geologic era, period, and epoch.

Rain Formation

Grade Level ● K–4

Discipline ● Earth and Space Science

Objects in the Sky

▶ The sun, moon, stars, clouds, birds, and airplanes all have properties, locations, and movements that can be observed and described.

▶ The sun provides the light and heat necessary to maintain the temperature of the earth.

Engaging Question

Why does it rain?

Materials Needed

Exploration—conducted in groups of four to six students per group, each group will need:

> 1 glass jar with lid, about the size of a large mayonnaise jar
> Hot-to-boiling water, enough to fill jar $1/4$ full
> Ice cubes, enough to fit on inverted lid from jar

Expansion—conducted in pairs, each pair will need:

> 1 clear plastic lid such as that from a coffee can
> 1 eyedropper
> 1 pencil
> 1 cup of water
> Paper towels

🛈 *Safety Precautions:* The students should be reminded to avoid bumping the tables once the exploration activity is set up. If the hot water spills out, it could hurt the children. If the glass jar breaks, it could cut someone.

CONCEPT TO BE CONSTRUCTED

▶ Raindrops form as water vapor condenses and falls from the sky.

The process whereby water leaves the earth's surface, moves into the air, collects in clouds, and falls back to the earth's surface is known as the *water cycle*. Water leaves the earth's surface as vapor and moves into the air in a process called *evaporation*. Once in the air the water vapor gets cold and changes back to a liquid state forming clouds in a process called *condensation*. Once the water falls from the clouds back to the earth this is called *precipitation*.

Exploration

PROCESS SKILLS USED

▶ Observing

▶ Predicting

▶ Recording data

Rain in a Jar

What will the students do?

Set groups of four to six students around a table. In the middle of the table place a one-quart jar with enough hot-to-nearly-boiling water to cover the bottom of the jar. Once each team has a jar like this with which to make close observations, the teacher should ask the students to make predictions about what will happen when they cover the jar with the lid turned upside down, holding three or four ice cubes. After the students have recorded their predictions and shared them with the class, instruct someone from each group to place the lid carefully over the jar and place the ice cubes on top of the inverted lid. Ask the students to watch the jar for four or five minutes. Ask them: What did you observe? Was it as you predicted? Record these observations.

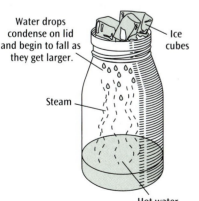

Water drops condense on lid and begin to fall as they get larger.

Ice cubes

Steam

Hot water

Concept: Raindrops form as water vapor condenses and falls from the sky.

The students should have observed that water drops collected on the inside of the lid. As time progressed, more water drops formed. As the drops became bigger, it got to the point at which the lid could no longer hold the drops, and the drops began to fall back into the jar. Ask the students the following questions to help them conclude that rain-drops form as water vapor condenses and falls from the sky.

1. What observations did you record? Where do you think the drops of water on the lid came from? (From the *condensation* of water vapor inside the jar. The hot water in the jar *evaporated* and changed into a *gas*—water vapor. When the water vapor hit the cool lid, it *condensed* and changed back to a *liquid.*)

2. What happened to the drops of water as they collected on the lid? (They got bigger as more water vapor *condensed* and collected on the jar lid.)

3. At what point did the water drops start to fall from the jar lid? (As they collected on the lid, they grew bigger and soon pulled together with other drops. Their weight pulled them down.)

4. What do you call water drops that fall from the sky? (Rain.) Ask the student teams to create a drawing of an area with land and a lake and sky with some clouds in it. Ask them to use this drawing to trace a drop of water from the lake to the sky and back again.

5. How does this demonstrate why it rains?

Expansion

Water Drop Attraction

PROCESS SKILLS USED
▶ Observing
▶ Inferring
▶ Measuring

How will the idea be expanded?

Pair up the students. Provide each pair with a plastic coffee can lid or the like, an eyedropper, a cup of water, and some paper towels. Ask the student pairs to do the following: One student should hold the plastic lid bottom-side-up. The other student should fill the eyedropper with water and squeeze as many separate drops of water on the lid as possible. The child holding the lid should then quickly turn the lid over. Hold the lid at least eight to ten inches over the tabletop, directly over some paper towels. Ask the student not holding the lid to use the point of a pencil to move the tiny drops together as the lid is held upside down. What happens when you do this? Ask the students to switch roles, allowing one to hold the lid and flip it and the other to use the eyedropper and pencil. Did the same thing occur?

The water molecules appear to attract one another. As you pull them together, it seems as if they readily jump to one another. As they grow bigger, they eventually are overcome by gravity and fall from the lid. Water may fall like this from the sky, not just in the form of rain. The teacher may solicit ideas from the students on other forms in which water falls from the sky (snow, sleet, hail). Explain to the students that all of these are called *precipitation.*

Science in Personal and Social Perspectives

- Why do you think it rains more in certain places than in others?
- Read the poem "Little Raindrops" by Aunt Effie (Jane Euphemia Browne) to the class. After reading it, ask the students whether they think they are affected by emotional changes with changes in the weather.

Science and Technology

- Why do you think meteorologists study rain patterns? Do these patterns affect where people will build cities?
- Why do scientists *seed* rain clouds in dry areas? Do you think farmers in these areas want to be able to make it rain when water is scarce? Why?

Science as Inquiry

- What do you call it when water turns into water vapor? (Evaporation)
- When water vapor collects on an object to form water droplets, what is it called? (Condensation)
- What do you call water that falls from the sky? (Precipitation)
- What do we call the process by which water evaporates, condenses, and falls from the sky? (The water cycle)

History and Nature of Science

- How important do you think it is for a farmer to understand the water cycle?
- If you were a botanist working in the desert, why would you be curious about how a cactus grows?
- When you watch a local weather forecast, does the meteorologist help explain where the next rainfall will come from?

Evaluation

Upon completing the activities, the students will be able to:

- show how they can make rain when given a jar of hot water, a pie tin, and some ice cubes;
- explain where evaporation, condensation, and precipitation are occurring in the jar demonstration they set up; and
- draw a picture of something they think they would not have in their lives if it did not rain. Ask them to explain the reasoning behind choosing that object.

Dew Formation

Grade Level ● **K–4**

Discipline ● **Earth and Space Science**

NATIONAL SCIENCE EDUCATION CONTENT STANDARDS– EARTH AND SPACE SCIENCE— GRADES K–4

Objects in the Sky

▶ The sun, moon, stars, clouds, birds, and airplanes all have properties, locations, and movements that can be observed and described.

▶ The sun provides the light and heat necessary to maintain the temperature of the earth.

CONCEPT TO BE CONSTRUCTED

▶ Cold surfaces collect more water drops than warm surfaces do.

▶ Dew, frost, temperature measurement with a thermometer, dew point

Engaging Question

Why do my shoes get wet if I walk through the grass on a cool, dry summer morning?

Materials Needed

Exploration—conducted in groups of four to six students per group, each group will need:

    1 timer or a clock with a minute hand
    1 glass soda bottle
    1 container large enough for the bottle to fit in
    Ice cubes and water to fill container
    Paper towels

Expansion—conducted in pairs, each pair will need:

    1 thermometer
    1 glass filled with ice, then add water to fill
    Paper towels

Safety Precautions: The students should be reminded to use care when handling the bottles. Wipe up any water spills so that students do not slip on wet surfaces.

Exploration

Soda Bottle Condensation

PROCESS SKILLS USED

▶ Observing

▶ Predicting

▶ Measuring

▶ Inferring

▶ Recording data

What will the students do?

Set groups of four to six children around a table. In the middle of the table, place a container large enough to hold a soda bottle. In this container, place four or five ice cubes and enough water so that once the bottle is placed in the container, it will be covered with cold water up to its neck. Give one child in the group a glass soda bottle. Remind the other students that they each will get a turn. If enough bottles are available, each child may be given one at this time. Ask the children to wrap their hands around the bottle for two minutes to try to get it very warm. When the two minutes are up, ask the students to exhale inside the bottle. What did you observe? Record those observations.

Then ask the students to make predictions about what will happen after they put the bottle into the container of ice water for two minutes, take it out, quickly wipe it off, and again exhale into the bottle. After they have recorded their predictions and shared them with the class, the students should take turns putting their bottles

into the ice water container, taking them out, wiping off the excess water, and then exhaling inside them. What did you observe? Was it as you predicted? Record these observations.

Concept: Cold surfaces collect more water drops than warm surfaces.

Ask the students to reflect on their observations by asking the following:

- What observations did you record when you exhaled on the warmed bottle?
- What observations did you record when you exhaled on the cooled bottle?
- Was there a difference between the two? Why do you think this happened?
- When the students exhaled into their warmed bottles, they may have observed some condensation, but very little. Their warm breath and the warmed bottle did not differ greatly in temperature. Therefore, water vapor did not condense readily. When the students exhaled into the cooled bottles, the difference in temperature between their breath and the bottles was enough to make water drops collect on the cold bottles. The students will be able to conclude that cold surfaces collect more water drops than warm surfaces when you ask them questions about what they did.
- Now ask them to respond to the inquiry question: Why do your shoes get wet when you walk through the grass on a cool, dry summer morning? Remind them to think about the summer air temperature compared to the ground temperature. (The cool grass allowed water vapor to come out of the warm air and condense on the grass.) Do you know what we call the water you find on grass in the morning? (Dew) When it's a very cold morning, this dew appears to be frozen. What name do we give it then? (Frost)

Expansion

PROCESS SKILLS USED
▶ Observing
▶ Measuring
▶ Comparing
▶ Recording data

How will the idea be expanded?

Pair up the students. Give each pair a thermometer. Practice reading the thermometer. Be sure each student knows how this is done. As the students work in pairs, ask them to fill a glass with ice and add enough water to cover the ice. Record the temperature their thermometer is reading. Place the thermometer in the glass. Watch the outside of the glass and record the temperature at which water begins to form on the outside of the glass. Explain to the students that for this particular day, with this particular amount of moisture in the air, the temperature they just recorded would be called the *dew point* for the day. When the air reaches that temperature, then *dew* will begin to form on the grass outside.

Thermometer Reading and Dew Point

Science in Personal and Social Perspectives

- Other than the noise involved, why do you think it is not a good idea to mow grass very early on a summer morning?
- Explain how your feet could get wet when you run through the grass in the spring.
- Why does frost form on car windows in the winter?

Science and Technology

- Do you think auto manufacturers are concerned with dew formation when they build new cars? Do you think the auto manufacturers think carefully about the kind of paint they put on new cars because they know that dew may form on them? What would happen to a car if dew formed on it day after day and there was no protective paint on the car? Would the same thing happen to your bicycle?

- How does a rear window defogger/deicer eliminate frost on the car window?

Science as Inquiry

- What do you call it when water turns into water vapor? (Evaporation)
- When water vapor collects on an object to form water droplets, what is it called? (Condensation)
- When water collects on a cold surface, what may form? (Dew or frost)
- What is a *dew point*?

History and Nature of Science

- Why would a landscaper be concerned about dew/frost formation? Have you ever seen plants wrapped in cloth or covered in plastic bags? Why do you think landscapers or home owners do this?
- Do you think a person in the lawn care business should pay attention to weather forecasts that give the dew point? Do you think it could be used to help the person decide when to start work in the morning?

Evaluation

Upon completing the activities, the students will be able to:

- use a bottle and a bowl of ice water to demonstrate how dew can form;
- demonstrate how to determine dew point using a glass, ice cubes, and a thermometer; and
- explain why their shoes get wet when they run through grass on a sunny summer morning.

Radiant Energy

Grade Level ● 2–4

Discipline ● Earth and Space Science

NATIONAL SCIENCE EDUCATION CONTENT STANDARDS–EARTH AND SPACE— GRADES 2–4

Objects in the Sky

▶ The sun, moon, stars, clouds, birds, and airplanes all have properties, locations, and movements that can be observed and described.

▶ The sun provides the light and heat necessary to maintain the temperature of the earth.

Engaging Question

What kind of energy do we get from the sun?

Materials Needed

Exploration—conducted in groups of four to six students per group, each group will need:

For Activity 1

2 pie pans
Sand to fill the pie pans
2 coins
2 black plastic garbage bags

For Activity 2

2 glass jars or 2 beakers
Water, enough to fill each jar
1 thermometer
Shady spot and sunny spot to place jars
Paper or journal to record data and graph results

For Activity 3, may be done by teacher as a class demonstration

1 magnifying glass
1 piece of paper
Sunny day

Expansion—for whole class, you will need:

1 thermometer
1 large glass container filled with water
3–6 tea bags, consistent with the size of the container

Safety Precautions: Before starting the activities, go over the following safety rules:

- The students should call the teacher if the thermometer is dropped and broken and should avoid touching broken glass or the liquid inside the thermometer.
- Activity 3 should be done only by a teacher or other adult.
- Avoid playing with the magnifying glass or placing a hand between the paper and magnifying glass.
- Do not let children stare at or touch the point of light during Activity 3.

> **CONCEPT TO BE CONSTRUCTED**
>
> ▶ The sun produces energy in the form of heat, referred to as *radiant energy*.
>
> ▶ The sun's heat energy can be used to perform work.

Temperature and Colored Surfaces

PROCESS SKILLS USED
► Predicting
► Observing
► Hypothesizing
► Measuring
► Recording and analyzing data
► Graphing

What will the students do?

Activity 1. Ask the children to fill the pie pans with sand. Put one pan of sand, one coin, and one garbage bag in direct sunlight. Put the other pan, coin, and bag in shade. Predict what the differences will be between the objects in the sun and those in the shade. After a while, have the children feel and compare the objects. How did the objects that were in the sun feel? What about the ones that were in the shade? Why do the things that were in the sun feel warm? Why do they feel cool if they were in the shade?

Temperature: Sun versus Shade

Activity 2. On the second day, have the students fill two jars with water. Record their starting temperatures. Place one of the jars in the sun and one in the shade. Predict how much temperature change will take place in both as time progresses. Have students record the temperatures of the two jars every half hour for a total of three hours. Take a final temperature reading. Graph the results with a bar graph using different colors for the sunny and shady sites.

Magnifiers: Capture the Sun

Activity 3. (Do this on day 2 while waiting for the results of Activity 2). On a sunny day, hold the magnifying glass over a piece of paper until the light comes to a point. Hold it there for a few seconds. What happens to the paper? What made the hole in the paper? What does this tell you about what the sun does for us? What can the sun do to your skin and eyes?

Explanation

Concept: The sun produces energy in the form of heat, referred to as *radiant energy.*

What does your graph tell you about a sunny environment versus a shady one? Why do you think there were such temperature differences at the two sites? What does the sun do for the earth? The sun provides us with *radiant energy.* Would the strength of radiant energy change if the earth were closer to the sun? What if the earth were farther from the sun? What would life be like in either case?

Expansion

Sun Tea

PROCESS SKILLS USED
► Predicting
► Observing
► Inferring
► Hypothesizing

How will the idea be expanded?

Fill a large jar with water and add six tea bags. Record the temperature inside the jar. Predict what will happen to the water after a few hours. (Suggest to the students that they might want to think about more than just a temperature change.) Decide where you would place the jar if you wanted to make tea. Place the jar in that spot. Throughout the day, check the jar and record the changes. Ask: "What do you think is happening inside the jar? How did the water change into tea? What part did the sun play in this process? What other ways can the sun's heat be harnessed to help things work?"

Science in Personal and Social Perspectives

• Why is the sun important to us?
• What are some of the things we need to be aware of when we are in the sun?

Science and Technology

- What are some ways in which people use solar energy? (Solar batteries, skylights, heating water to warm rooms, and so on)
- Are these beneficial? If so, in what ways?
- Why might we need to explore ways to use solar energy in the future?
- Why do clothing manufacturers create lighter-colored clothing for the summer months? Would a manufacturer make more money selling black or white T-shirts in the summer?

Science as Inquiry

- Why are people more careful about being exposed to the sun during the summer than during the winter?
- New concepts to be identified for invention in new lessons include global warming, the ozone layer, and the greenhouse effect.

History and Nature of Science

- What are some careers in which people can work with solar energy?
- Why would it be important for a botanist, a florist, or a gardener to understand how the sun heats the earth?

Evaluation

Upon completing the activities, the students will be able to:

- while blindfolded, tell which objects were in the sun and which were in shade, and give reasons for the answers;
- create a collage showing the many uses of solar energy; and
- draw pictures showing ways they can protect themselves from the damaging effects of the sun.

▶ Weather changes from day to day and over the seasons. Weather can be described by measurable quantities, such as temperature, wind direction and speed, and precipitation.

Weather Forecasting

Grade Level ● K–4

Discipline ● Earth and Space Science

CONCEPT TO BE CONSTRUCTED

▶ Weather data can be collected and reported.
When collecting weather data it is important to control as many variables as possible; therefore, your weather instruments need to be accurate. Weather data can be recorded using symbols instead of words. The different cloud types are associated with different kinds of weather.

Engaging Question

How do symbols help us to collect and report the weather?

Materials Needed

Exploration—conducted in groups of four to six students per group, each group will need:
Various weather collection instruments, such as barometer, thermometer, sling psychrometer, wind vane, rain gauge, anemometer, clinometer, nephoscope, and cloud charts
The students should have prior experience with the weather equipment as they were learning about individual weather phenomena such as air pressure, humidity, temperature, air masses, and fronts.

Expansion—conducted by six teams, for each team you will need:
Weather collection instruments from the exploration phase
Collection of weather maps from newspapers

⚠ *Safety Precautions:* Remind students to use care with weather instruments when collecting data; when outdoors, obey school rules, avoid talking to strangers, and exercise caution if inclement weather prohibits data collection.

Exploration

PROCESS SKILLS USED

▶ Brainstorming
▶ Observing
▶ Formulating models
▶ Predicting
▶ Measuring
▶ Questioning

Teacher introduction: How many of you have nicknames? When you write letters or e-mails or your name in school, do you sign them with your full name or your nickname? Which is easier for you to write?

Try to picture in your mind a McDonald's or a KFC restaurant. Imagine that you are in the parking lot or are riding down the road and you spot one of these places. What image comes to mind first? How many of you remembered a shape or a symbol for the restaurant first?

Can you think of any other things in your life, such as toys, games, or bicycles, for which you might remember the symbol for the manufacturer rather than the actual name of the company?

For which stores, restaurants, toys, or games do you find the symbol easiest to remember? How often do you use the item or frequent the store? Do you find that the more you use the item or frequent the store, the easier it is to remember the symbol?

Now imagine you're a meteorologist and you collect weather data every day for years. Just like you and your nickname or McDonald's and its golden arches, would it help the meteorologist to have symbols to record data with instead of words? Why or why not?

What will the students do?

Challenge the students to prepare a weather log or a data chart that they will use to collect weather information. Encourage them to keep in mind the previous discussion. Allow the students to break into their own groups. This will help when the students eventually collect weather information on weekends.

Try to give as little input as possible. Give the students time to brainstorm all the factors that may be important to forecast weather. Have the instruments available for them to look over as they try to think of what they need to create a good weather forecast.

Encourage the students to use their designed chart for 1 week. At the start of the next week, ask the student groups to share the information they obtained. As a class, determine the group that was the most accurate in predicting daily weather.

Explanation

Concept: Weather data can be collected and reported.

Controlling variables is important in making reliable weather observations. Each separate weather measurement is a variable that cannot be controlled. Ask the students the following questions to help them invent the concept:

- Did the weather factors that you chose to observe give you enough information to forecast the weather?
- Could you have been more accurate had you collected other types of data?
- Which factors could increase error in your data?
- Did you try to control any human factors that might have made your readings faulty?
- Can you simplify the way in which you recorded your data?

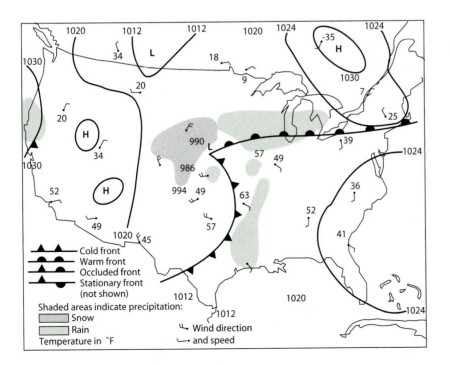

Weather Map Symbols

PROCESS SKILLS USED
▶ Observing
▶ Interpreting data
▶ Inferring
▶ Creating models
▶ Making conclusions

How will the idea be expanded?

Symbols can be used to designate some weather observations. Collect a supply of weather maps from as many different newspapers as possible. Once you have a number of maps that vary in sophistication, distribute them to your students and ask whether the students can interpret them. Create a list on the board of all of the different symbols they observe on the maps. Encourage the students to speculate about what each symbol represents. After exploring the various symbols found on the maps, break the class up into six groups. Assign each group one of the following tasks:

1. Draw a station model diagram that shows wind direction and speed, type of high cloud, type of middle cloud, sea-level pressure, pressure change, type of low cloud, dew point, sky cover, present state of weather, air temperature.
2. Create a chart that shows the weather map symbols for highs, lows, fronts, isobars, and air masses.
3. Create a chart titled "Present State of the Weather" that shows and briefly describes the symbols for precipitation.
4. Create a chart titled "Sky Cover" that shows the symbols for the different fractions of cloud coverage.
5. Create a chart titled "Major Cloud Types" that shows the symbols for and names of the major cloud types.
6. Create a chart titled "Wind Scale" that lists the speed and shows the symbols for the wind.

Weather Data Collection

As the student groups report on the symbols they discovered to represent the various weather phenomena, ask them to decide how they could use some of this information to make recording weather information easier. How can you use this information to predict weather?

Science in Personal and Social Perspectives

• What changes have you experienced in the amount of attention you pay to weather forecasts now that you have had a chance to collect weather information yourself?
• Do you think you can create a family weather station at your house without spending a large amount of money on expensive weather equipment? What types of weather instruments could you create?

Science and Technology

• In the summer of 1990, a sudden flood wiped out the town of Shadyside, Ohio. Could an improved weather radar system have helped to save lives? Could it have prevented the sudden flood?

Science as Inquiry

• Create graphs for each of the weather factors collected over the one-week time period. Study your graphs. Do you see any great fluctuations in any of the readings over time? If so, with which weather factor?
• Was there ever a dramatic rise or decrease in the barometric pressure?
• Did you examine your graphs to see if any other factor changed dramatically when the barometer did? If you did find some changes, with what other factors?

- What kind of pressure system was over the area when the barometer changed dramatically?
- What conclusions can you draw about the relationships among different weather factors?

History and Nature of Science

- Survey local radio and television stations. Where do they get their weather forecast information from? Is there a resident meteorologist who prepares the forecast? If so, find out whether you can interview that person. Prepare some key questions you would like to have answered in the light of the experiences you have just had collecting your own weather data.

Evaluation

Upon completing these activities, the students will be able to demonstrate the use of symbols for collecting and reporting weather data by completing the following tasks:

- Ask the students to look at the data they collected from the exploration phase of this lesson and consider the following questions: Is there a weather factor that you did not consider collecting that you would add now? Would it be important to be consistent in your data collection? In other words, did you consider things such as making sure you collect your information at the same time every day, or that at least two people in the group are responsible for reading the instruments to check for accuracy?
- Revise your weather log to include all the factors necessary to make a sound weather forecast. You may ask the teacher for sample weather logs or suggestions on what data to collect. Be sure the variables that can be controlled are controlled!
- Once you have revised your log, show it to the teacher. If it is judged complete, then collect weather data for a month.

Some teachers may have their students so proficient on the various weather instruments that it becomes second nature to them. Collect weather data every day for the entire school year. Your class may want to give a daily weather report to the school on the intercom each day.

Structure of the Earth System

► Global patterns of atmospheric movement influence local weather. Oceans have a major effect on climate, because water in the oceans holds a large amount of heat.

CONCEPT TO BE CONSTRUCTED

► When moving air masses of different temperature and different moisture content come in contact, it results in precipitation and other identifiable weather phenomena.

Lines of temperature differences between two air masses are called *fronts*. A *warm front* is caused by a relatively warm mass of air advancing over a mass of relatively cold air. A *cold front* is caused by a mass of relatively cold air displacing relatively warm air.

Air Mass Movement

Grade Level ● 5–8
Discipline ● Earth and Space Science

Engaging Question

How do air masses affect our weather?

Materials Needed

Exploration—conducted in groups of four to six students per group, each group will need:

Station A

    1 globe of the earth
    1 eyedropper
    1 cup filled with colored water
    Journal or paper to record data

Station B

    1 small child's toy top
    1 piece of paper cut the size of the flat top side of the top
    1 marker

Station C (for safety reasons, this may be done as a teacher demonstration)

    1 pair of goggles
    Dry ice
    Gloves to handle dry ice
    1 container of water
    1 thermometer
    1 piece of heavy string
    Matches

Expansion—conducted in groups of four to six students per group, each group will need:

    1 small juice bottle with cap
    Cooking oil, about $1/4$ cup
    Cold water, about $1/4$ cup
    Red and blue food coloring

Safety Precautions: Use extreme caution when handling the dry ice. If the students are immature, the teacher or another adult may need to handle the dry ice for that part of the experiment. Heavy-duty safety gloves should be made available for anyone handling the dry ice. Goggles should be worn. Care should be taken when handling any of the instruments. Exercise care with glass containers.

What will the students do?

Station A. Spin the globe quickly so that it moves in a west-to-east direction. Pretending that you are on the globe at the North Pole, use the medicine dropper to start some colored water rolling in a stream south toward the equator. Carefully record your observations, being sure to include the movement of the water both north and south of the equator.

Coriolis Effect: Globe

Station B. Obtain a small flat-sided top. On a piece of paper, draw a circle the size of the top. Push this down over the handle of the top and center it on the top. As you spin the top in a counterclockwise direction (from west to east) with one hand, hold a marker in your other hand and try to draw a straight line on the paper attached to the top. Record what happens when you do this.

Coriolis Effect: Top

Station C. Break a piece of dry ice with a hammer, and place a few small pieces into a container of water. Be sure to use caution when working with the dry ice (gloves and goggles). Observe the air around the container over a period of time. Measure the temperature of the air mass (1) just above the container, (2) about 1 meter above the container, and (3) near the base of the container. Record these readings.

Air Movement: Dry Ice

Light one end of a piece of string, and then blow out the flame. The end should begin to smoke. Give the smoking string to the students, and have them wave it around the container. Ask them to record their observations of the movement of the smoke.

Explanation

Concept at Stations A and B: Air masses, low-pressure areas, and fronts move generally from west to east.

- At Station A, in what direction did the stream turn in the Northern Hemisphere? In the Southern Hemisphere?
- What effect do you think the land masses with their mountain ranges will have on the moving air?
- At Station B, what happened when you tried to draw a straight line on the paper from the center to the edge of the top?
- Because of the earth's rotation, the motion of a body as seen from the earth appears to deflect to the right in the Northern Hemisphere. This fictitious deflecting force is also called the *Coriolis effect.* How do you think the Coriolis effect can help explain the results you obtained when trying to draw a straight line on the paper on the spinning top?

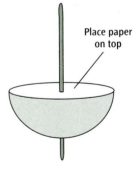

Place paper on top

Concept at Station C: When moving air masses of different temperature and different moisture content come into contact, it results in precipitation and other identifiable weather phenomena.

- Where was the air mass the highest?
- What happened to the air as it cooled?
- What were your temperature readings around the container? If there were differences, why do you think they occurred?
- What happened when you waved some smoking string in the air around the container? In what direction did the air flow around the container?
- What kind of precipitation do you think could occur if warm air were blown over the cold air flowing from the container?
- From what you have discovered through your explorations at Stations A, B, and C, how do you think air masses affect our weather?

Oil and Water Fronts

PROCESS SKILLS USED
► Manipulating materials
► Formulating models
► Hypothesizing
► Inferring

How will the idea be expanded?

Fill a bottle halfway with cooking oil. Add some red food coloring, cap the bottle, and shake well. This will represent a warm air mass. In a separate container, add blue food coloring to cold water. What do you think will happen as you pour the cold water into the bottle of oil? Slowly pour the water into the bottle.

The following concepts can be demonstrated with this arrangement of materials:

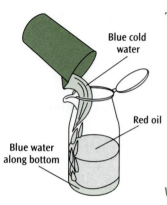

Blue cold water

Red oil

Blue water along bottom

- Lines of temperature differences between two air masses are called *fronts*.
- A *warm front* is caused by a relatively warm mass of air advancing over a mass of relatively cold air.
- A *cold front* is caused by a mass of relatively cold air displacing relatively warm air.
- Advancing cold fronts lift warm air. Advancing warm fronts result in the warm air being lifted.
- Fronts do not all move at the same speed or in the same direction.
- The amount of moisture in the air controls the kind of weather along the front.

What questions can help students invent expansion concepts?

- What happened when you poured the cold water into the oil? Did it behave as you predicted? Which liquid is denser? How do you know?
- Place the screw cap on the bottle. Slowly turn the bottle on its side. How does the heavier liquid move, and what is its final position?
- If a cold air mass moves toward a warm air mass, would the leading edge of the cold air mass be at the ground level or above the ground? Why? (Remember that the blue water represents the cold air mass, and the red oil is the warm air mass.)
- If a warm air mass moves toward a cold air mass, would the leading edge of the warm air mass be at the ground or above the ground? Why?
- How would you describe a stationary front? What factors affect its formation?

Science in Personal and Social Perspectives

- If you were planning a picnic for Saturday and you heard on a Thursday weather forecast that a warm front would be moving into the region on Friday evening, would you switch the day of your picnic to Sunday? Why or why not?

Science and Technology

- What effect do extremes in precipitation have upon area populations (not just human)?
- How do you think knowledge of such weather phenomena as air masses, fronts, and precipitation have assisted in the invention of the material Gore-tex, which is now used in running clothes, tents, tarpaulins, and so on? How has this invention allowed us to enjoy our environment more, no matter what the weather conditions?

Science as Inquiry

- What kind of pressure system do you think would bring your area a large amount of precipitation? A small amount? Create your own rain gauge to measure precipitation by following the steps below.

Create a Rain Gauge

Use the following materials to create your own rain gauge: large straight-sided jar, long narrow jar or large test tube, meter stick, metric ruler, and masking tape. Place a ruler vertically in the large jar and pour in water until it reaches the 10-mm mark on the ruler. Pour this water into the narrow jar, to which you have attached a strip of masking tape. Place the masking tape at the exact level of the water. This represents 10 mm in the jar. Repeat this procedure for levels of 20 mm, 30 mm, and so on.

Place the large jar outside, away from any obstruction, to collect rain. Why is that important? The top of the jar should be about 30.5 cm above the ground. To read the amount of rain, empty it into the measuring jar at the same time each day. Keep a daily record in a chart form.

Do you think you can determine how much snow you would have had if you had 50 mm of rain collected in your gauge? What if you have 50 mm of snow? How much rain would that be? The student can do two things here: (1) Obtain a tall, straight-sided container, such as an empty juice can. Carefully fill it with loose snow, but do not pack the snow in the can. Heat the snow until it is completely melted. Use the rain gauge to measure the amount of water. If you know the length of the can, you can compare the amount of snow to rain. (2) The student could guesstimate the amount of rain the snow is equal to by knowing that the ratio of snow to rain is usually 10 to 1. A wet, heavy snow may have a ratio as low as 6 to 1, while in dry, fluffy, new-fallen snow, the ratio may be as high as 30 to 1.

History and Nature of Science

- How is it possible for airplanes to fly in the eye of the storm during a hurricane? What kind of information do pilots need to understand about air masses in order to do this?
- Create a list of all of the types of jobs that can be affected when air masses of different temperatures and moisture contents come in contact. Are any of those jobs in areas in which you would like to work?

Evaluation

The following parachute activity, as well as the questions covering personal development, science, technology, society, academic growth, and career awareness could be used to assess the students' knowledge of the relationships among air masses, fronts, and precipitation.

Air Masses and Parachutes

Parachute Materials

12-inch square sheet of tissue paper
8 glue-backed hole reinforcers
4 strings, 10 inches in length each

washer for weight
paper person (for decorative purposes only)

Punch a hole in each corner of the tissue with a pencil point. Place a hole reinforcer on each side of the hole. Tie the four strings to each hole. Tie the loose ends of the strings together around the washer. Be sure the strings end up being of equal length. Decorate with a paper person attached to the washer. You may find that a small hole in the very center of the tissue will help the parachute to open more quickly.

Fold up your chute, and throw it into the air. Have a partner time from the moment you release it until the moment it begins to descend. Time its descent.

- How does the parachute depend on air pressure?
- What if your parachute came from several hundred meters above the earth's surface? Would it fall any differently?
- Would the parachute fall differently if a cold front were in the area? What about a warm front?
- What if a warm front were just moving into the area, replacing a cold front. Would it be safe to parachute during that time? Why or why not?

Air Pressure

Grade Level ● 5–8

Discipline ● Earth and Space Science

NATIONAL SCIENCE EDUCA-
TION CONTENT STANDARDS–
EARTH AND SPACE SCIENCE—
GRADES 5–8

Structure of the Earth System

▶ The atmosphere is a mixture of nitrogen, oxygen, and trace gases that include water vapor. The atmosphere has different properties at different elevations.

▶ Global patterns of atmospheric movement influence local weather. Oceans have a major effect on climate, because water in the oceans holds a large amount of heat.

CONCEPT TO BE CONSTRUCTED

▶ Air has weight.

▶ Air can exert pressure. Temperature and air movement are factors that influence air pressure.

Engaging Question

What factors influence air pressure?

Materials Needed

Exploration—conducted in groups of four to six students per group, each group will need:

> Modeling clay
> 1 pencil
> 1 meter stick
> 3 balloons
> String
> Journal or paper for recording data

Explanation—for teacher as a demonstration, you will need:

> 1 beach ball
> 1 scale

Expansion—conducted in groups of four to six students per group, each group will need:

> 2 books at least $1/2$ –1 inch thick
> 1 sheet of typing paper
> Journal or paper for recording data
> 1 straw for each student in group
> Balance system from the exploration phase, replacing balloons with two small paper lunch bags
> 1 small lamp as a heat source

Expansion—for demonstrations, you will need:

> 1 long strip of thin wood, roughly the thickness and length of a meter stick
> 1 sheet of newspaper
> 1 narrow strip of paper taped to a pencil

🛈 *Safety Precautions:* The students should take care that when blowing during the activities, they don't hyperventilate and get dizzy. Have a paper bag available for any hyperventilating student to breathe into slowly. This will balance the oxygen–carbon dioxide ratio and return the student to normal.

What will the students do?

Provide the students with modeling clay, pencil, yardstick, three balloons, and a string. Ask them to manipulate these materials so that they can create a balance as in the diagram.

Suspend and balance two uninflated balloons. Ask the students to record their observations. Then ask them to predict what would happen to this balanced system if they were to replace one of the uninflated balloons with an inflated balloon. Record their predictions. Now replace one of the uninflated balloons with an inflated balloon. Record students' observations. Do they match the predictions?

Balloon Balance

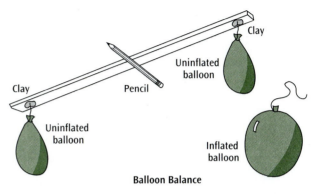

Clay

Uninflated balloon

Clay

Pencil

Uninflated balloon

Inflated balloon

Balloon Balance

Explanation

Concept: Air has weight.

What kinds of data did you collect? Did you obtain results as you predicted? Hold up an uninflated beach ball. Ask the students to help you weigh it. Now ask one of the students to blow it up. Ask for their predictions as to whether it now weighs the same. How is this demonstration similar to the balance you just created? What happened with the balance when you replaced the uninflated balloon with an inflated balloon? Weigh it. Does it weigh the same? Why or why not? (Air has weight.)

Expansion

How will the idea be expanded?

Ask the students to place two books (at least a quarter- to a half-inch thick) 3 inches apart on a desktop. Place a sheet of $8^1/_2$-inch by 11-inch paper across the book lengthwise. Have the students predict if they can blow the paper off the books by blowing into the space between the books. Record your predictions, then try it! Repeat the experiment, this time using a straw placed just under the edge of the paper to blow between the books.

What happened to the paper when you blew without the straw? With the straw? Were you able to blow the paper off the books either time? Did the paper move at all? If so, how? This activity demonstrates that air has pressure. Air moving fast, such as the air you blew out between the books and underneath the paper, creates a lower pressure than the

Paper Blowing

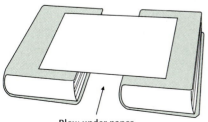

Blow under paper

pressure above the books. Thus you see a slight dip in the paper. When you use a straw to blow through, the straw creates a narrow, high-speed path of low pressure between the books. Now the pressure underneath the paper bridge is much lower than the pressure above the paper; thus, you observe a big dip in the paper bridge. This dip is caused by the higher air pressure on top of the paper. Thus, air exerts pressure, and the speed of the moving air will effect the air pressure.

Newspaper Strength   A good teacher demonstration is to take a yardstick or some other relatively long, thin piece of wood and place it on a table top. Smooth out a large piece of newspaper over the wood. Leave about six to eight inches of wood sticking out one side. Make sure there are no air spaces between the newspaper and the table top. Ask the students whether they think you can hit this stick and make the paper go flying. Once you take several predictions, hit the stick. What happened? The stick broke, and the paper remained on the tabletop. Why? Because on every square inch of that paper, air is exerting a pressure of 14.7 pounds per square inch. A full sheet of newspaper is typically 27 inches by 23 inches, or 621 square inches. If there are 14.7 pounds of pressure exerted on every square inch of the newspaper, that means that there are 621 square inches times 14.7 pounds per square inch, or 9,128.7 pounds of pressure being exerted by the air on that paper. You would have to hit the stick with a force equal to that amount to get the paper to move!

Science in Personal and Social Perspectives

- What does air pressure have to do with a smooth ride on your bike or in a car?
- What happens when your bike gets a flat tire? What does this do to the air pressure in the tire?

Science and Technology

- In the second activity, you found that faster-moving air causes lower air pressure. How do you think this fact has influenced the design of airplanes?
- Ask a student to demonstrate lift by taping a narrow strip of paper to a pencil. Hold the pencil by your mouth, and blow over the strip of paper. What happens to it? How do you think this movement is similar to air blowing over the wing of an airplane?

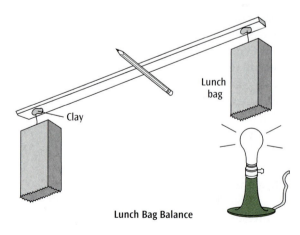

Lunch Bag Balance

Science as Inquiry

- Does all air have the same weight? Ask the students to replace their uninflated balloons in the balanced system with two paper lunch bags. Get the system to balance. Now place a lit lamp several inches below one of the bags. What happened to that balanced system? Which weighs more: cold or hot air?
- What kind of air pressure do you think would be associated with a cold front? A warm front?

- Ask the students to share information with one another on Daniel Bernoulli (1700–1782). He was a Swiss doctor, mathematician, biologist, physiologist, physicist, astronomer, and oceanographer. Can you think of any people today who are as well versed in as many areas as Daniel Bernoulli was? Do you think it is more difficult to be an expert in all of these areas today? Why?
- Invite a pilot to speak to your class. Ask him or her to explain how knowledge of air pressure helps the pilot to control an airplane.

Evaluation

Upon completing these activities, the students will be able to:

- predict and then explain why two balloons suspended on equal-length strings about 3 inches apart come closer together when the students blow between them; they will be able to demonstrate this phenomenon;
- look at a picture of an unbalanced system, in which one balloon is inflated and the other is uninflated, and explain why this system is unbalanced; and
- demonstrate that a Ping-Pong ball can hover over the end of a drinking straw; they will also be able to explain why this happens and be able to share and explain this phenomenon to children in a primary grade.

Solar Heating

Grade Level ● 5–8

Discipline ● Earth and Space Science

CONCEPT TO BE CONSTRUCTED

▶ The earth's surfaces are heated unevenly.

▶ Uneven heating creates wind and makes the water cycle occur. The sun is the source of energy that determines the weather on the earth.

Engaging Question

Are all surfaces of the earth equally heated?

Materials Needed

Exploration—conducted in groups of four to six students per group, each group will need:

> 3 paper cups, cut down so that they are about 5 centimeters deep
> 3 small thermometers
> Dark-colored soil, light-colored sand, and water—enough to fill shortened cup with one of each
> 1 lamp for heating cups

Explanation—for the whole class, you will need:

> Satellite photos of the earth

Expansion—conducted in pairs, for each pair you will need:

> 1 thermometer
> Journal or paper for recording data

⚠ *Safety Precautions:* The students should be careful when using the lamp and around electricity.

Exploration

Temperature versus Surface Color

PROCESS SKILLS USED

▶ Observing
▶ Predicting
▶ Comparing
▶ Questioning
▶ Describing
▶ Manipulating materials
▶ Recording data

What will the students do?

Ask the students to cut paper cups down so that they are about only five centimeters deep. Fill one with dark-colored soil, one with light-colored sand, and the third with water. Instruct the students to place a thermometer into each cup, covering the bulb with about 0.5 centimeter of soil, sand, or water. Record the temperature of each. Place a lit lamp so its bulb is about fifteen centimeters from the tops of the cups. After five minutes, record the temperature of each cup. Identify which cup gained heat the fastest, and record this information. Remove the lamp from the cups. Predict which cup you think will lose heat the fastest. Record your prediction. Leave the cups untouched, and after ten minutes, record the temperature of each cup. Which lost heat the fastest? Record the data. Did you predict correctly?

Dark soil   Light sand   Water

Explanation

Concept: The earth's surfaces are heated unevenly.

What kinds of data did you collect? Did you obtain results as you predicted? How do you think this activity helps explain the uneven heating of the earth's surfaces?

Look at satellite pictures of the earth. Describe the different surfaces. Why do dark-colored surfaces absorb more heat energy from the sun? What do lighter-colored surfaces do that would prevent as much absorption of the sun's energy as dark surfaces? (The lighter surfaces reflect more of the sun's energy, whereas dark land absorbs it. Also, dark land loses its heat faster than water.)

Expansion

PROCESS SKILLS USED

▶ Observing
▶ Predicting
▶ Comparing
▶ Manipulating materials
▶ Recording data
▶ Hypothesizing

How will the idea be expanded?

Optimum Thermometer Placement

Ask the students where they think they should place a thermometer to measure the air temperature every day. Ask the students to predict and then record air temperature taken on blacktop, grass, in the shade of a tree, a sandy area, and a gravel area. Take these readings at ground level and at 1 meter from the ground. Does this make a difference? Will the time of day make a difference? Have the students record the temperature at these various sites during different times of the school day. Which site and time give the most accurate reading for actual air temperature? Once the class decides this, then at that site and time, daily temperature readings can be taken for a weather log for the class. The students can also practice taking temperature readings in degrees Celsius and Fahrenheit. How do these findings reinforce your answer to the inquiry question "Are all surfaces of the earth equally heated?"

Science in Personal and Social Perspectives

• What are ways of staying cool on a hot day or warm on a cold day?
• Why are swimming pools, ponds, lakes, or oceans good places to cool off?
• What kinds of clothes will help to keep you cool in summer? What kinds will keep you warm in winter? How and why?

Science and Technology

• How do we attempt to control the temperature in our homes? What kinds of heating and cooling systems do we utilize?
• What alternative sources of energy, aside from fossil fuels, should we continue to develop? How efficient do you think these are or will be?

Science as Inquiry

• Aside from unequal heating of the different-colored surfaces of the earth, temperature is also determined by many other factors. Discuss how the following could affect air

temperature: cloud cover, time of day, time of year, wind, latitude, altitude, and oceans or other large bodies of water.
- At what temperature in degrees Celsius does water freeze? Boil? At what temperature in degrees Fahrenheit does water freeze? Boil?

History and Nature of Science

- Who helps supply energy to keep our homes cool in summer and warm in winter (coal miner, lumberjack, oil-field worker, power plant operator, heating–ventilation–air conditioning personnel, and so on)? Choose one of these jobs, and identify how the workers supply energy. What raw material do they make use of?

Evaluation

Upon completing these activities, the students will be able to:

- fill three identical-sized cans with tap water. Insert a thermometer through a cover made out of the bottom of a Styrofoam cup. One can should be painted dull black, one left shiny metal, and the last painted shiny white. Ask the students to predict what will happen to the temperature of the water when the cans are placed in direct sunlight or equally distanced from a 150- to 300-watt lightbulb. The students should be able to record the temperature of the water in the cans at 1-minute intervals. They should be able to write a short report of their observations;
- record the temperature of the cans in Celsius and Fahrenheit; and
- choose an optimal location outdoors to record daily temperature observations.

Air Movement and Surface Temperature

Grade Level ● 5–8
Discipline ● Earth and Space Science

NATIONAL SCIENCE EDUCATION CONTENT STANDARDS–EARTH AND SPACE SCIENCE— GRADES 5–8
Structure of the Earth System

► Global patterns of atmospheric movement influence local weather. Oceans have a major effect on climate, because water in the oceans holds a large amount of heat.

Engaging Question

Does the temperature at the earth's surface affect the movement of air masses?

Materials Needed

Exploration—conducted as a whole class, you will need:

Make an Observation Box
   1 cardboard box (about the size of a grapefruit box or a one that holds a ream of paper)
   Clear plastic food wrap
   Clear tape
   1 plastic straw

CONCEPTS TO BE CONSTRUCTED

► Air moves downward over cold surfaces and upward over warm surfaces.

► A volume of warm air has less mass than an equal volume of cool air; particles of warm air are farther apart than particles of cool air. Cold air, being heavier than warm air, sinks, pushing warm air upward.

Remove the top of the box. If you are using something like a grapefruit box, as you cut off the lid, leave a 3-cm edge for strength. Turn the box over so that the box is resting on the lid. Cut a window in the side that is now considered on top, leaving half the top intact. Cut out one side, again leaving a 3-cm edge for strength. Tape clear plastic food wrap to the side and the half-window on top. In one end of the box, cut a small hole that is just large enough to insert a plastic straw. See the figure for assistance in construction.

   1 35-ml syringe
   1 plastic straw cut into three even pieces
   Heavy cotton string cut into three 4-cm pieces
   Scissors
   Matches
   Ice water
   Hot water
   Aluminum pan
   Metric ruler

Expansion—conducted as a whole class, you will need:
   1 ³/₄-inch dowel rod 3 feet long with a hole slightly larger than ¹/₄ -inch drilled exactly in center
   1 ¹/₄-inch dowel rod 1 foot long to be placed through the hole of the larger dowel
   1 paper clip to be used as a sliding balance
   2 small paper lunch bags
   2 thumbtacks of equal size and weight
   1 lamp as a source of heat

Safety Precautions: Use caution around open flame.

Remove 1/2 of box bottom.
Cover with food wrap;
tape airtight.

Leave 3-cm edges
for strength.

Plastic straw

Create a window on one
side of the box; cover with
plastic wrap, and tape airtight.

Cut off box top;
leave 3-cm edge for strength.

Convection Current and Surface Temperature in an Observation Box

PROCESS SKILLS USED
▶ Observing
▶ Experimenting
▶ Formulating models
▶ Questioning
▶ Communicating
▶ Inferring

What will the students do?

Take a piece of string and fold it in half. Place the folded end into one of the pieces of straw, allowing about 0.5 cm to hang out the end. Be sure it fits snugly in the end. Do this for each piece of straw.

Slip the open end of the prepared straw onto the syringe. Light the string. Collect smoke in the cylinder by slowly pulling out the plunger. Remove the straw and lay it aside where it will not burn anything. You may need more smoke later.

Place a pan of ice water inside the observation box. Be sure the straw is in place through the end of the box but not hanging over the pan. Let the pan sit for 3 or 4 minutes. After the wait, insert the smoke-filled syringe into the straw of the observation box. Gently force the smoke through the straw into the box. Carefully observe what happens to the smoke as it moves over the pan of ice water.

Complete the procedure using a pan of hot water instead. Once again, make careful observations of the smoke as it moves over the hot water.

Explanation

Concept: Air moves downward over colder surfaces and upward over warm surfaces.

- What path did the smoke take as it moved over the cold surface? (It spread out slowly over the pan, staying close to the pan's surface.)
- What path did the smoke take as it moved over the hot surface? (It slowly spread out and upward.)
- Do you think a force is acting on the smoke as it moves above the warm or cold surfaces? (A force is something that causes a change in shape or a change in motion of a body. It is easy to see the change in shape; this also shows the change in motion.)

Expansion

Paper Bag Balance

How will the idea be expanded?

Set up the dowel rod balance as in the figure. Fasten the two paper bags to the balance rod using the thumbtacks. Balance the rod using the sliding paper clip. Hold the rod stationary. Put the lighted bulb just below the open end of the bag on one side. Keep the bulb under the bag for thirty seconds. Then gently let go of the bar. Observe the bag for several minutes.

What questions can help invent additional concepts?

- What happened to the bag on the side near the bulb?
- How do you know this?
- Was the temperature of the bag away from the bulb colder or warmer than the bag near the bulb?
- What happened when you gently released the balance?
- From your observations, which has the greater mass? Is it the bag of warm air or the bag of cool air?

- The bags in this activity have the same volume. Which do you think has more gas particles? Why?
- What do you think this activity demonstrates about what happens to a substance when heated?

Warm air has less mass than an equal amount of cool air: Particles of warm air are farther apart than particles of cool air. Cold air, being heavier than warm air, sinks, pushing warm air upward.

Science in Personal and Social Perspectives

- How would the absence of wind affect your life? Do you think life would be changed in any way if there never was a wind?
- How does the presence of wind affect you personally? How do you think strong winds would affect you if you lived in a coastal city?

Science and Technology

- How has wind power become a source of energy in some regions of the world? How has this harnessing of the wind changed the lives of people living there?
- How has knowledge of air mass saved lives? In what circumstances?

Science as Inquiry

- The students will develop process skills needed to identify moving air as wind and to determine that air has mass.
- The students will be able to explain the movement of air over surfaces of varying temperatures and apply this knowledge to explain why wind occurs.

History and Nature of Science

- How will knowledge of wind behavior assist a pilot in flight? What kind of training must a pilot undergo in order to understand how wind behaves? Can just anyone become a pilot? What skills do you think are necessary to become a successful pilot?
- Read a book on Amelia Earhart. What do you think happened to her when she vanished in her plane over the Pacific Ocean?
- Can you list any other occupations in which knowledge of wind and its behavior is necessary?

Evaluation

Upon completing the activities, the students will be able to:

- answer all of the questions included in this lesson;
- demonstrate the movement of smoke over cold air and warm air to a group of younger students or parents and be able to explain the concept behind the movement; and
- demonstrate that cold air sinks and warm air rises when given a thermometer, a pan of ice water, and a fan.

Uneven Heating of the Earth

Grade Level ● **5–8**
Discipline ● **Earth and Space Science**

Engaging Question

Is there a relationship between how the different earth surfaces are heated and air pressure?

Materials Needed

Exploration—conducted as a whole-class demonstration, you will need:

    1 long clear tube, open on both ends but with caps available
    Tub of water

Exploration—conducted in groups of three or four students per group, each group will need:

    1 balloon
    2 baby food jars
    5 rubber bands that will fit snugly over baby food jars
    1 straw with one end cut to make a point
    Tape
    Tongue depressor
    Marking pen

Expansion—conducted in five groups so that each group rotates through five stations:

Station Air Pressure
    2 clear glasses, 1 filled with cold and the other with hot water—glasses must be identical
    1 index card
    2 different colors of food coloring

Station Air Temperature
    1 index card with a spiraling line drawn on the card
    Scissors and tape
    Thread
    Heat source such as a burning candle

Station Heat Transfer
    1 candle or source of wax
    1 heat source to melt wax
    1 length of wire at least 6 inches long

Station Heat Movement
    1 lamp without a shade
    1 glass beaker large enough to fit over the lamp bulb

2 can lids—be sure any rough edges are smoothed
1 candle or source of wax
1 heat source to melt wax
2 thumbtacks
1 candle

Safety Precautions: The students should take care when using any glass containers. To avoid burns, exercise extreme caution when using the hot water. Also, when using the lamp, remember that the bulb can get hot. When using the candle, be watchful of the open flame. Be sure all sleeves are rolled up, all hair is pulled back, and no shirts are dangling into the flame.

Exploration

PROCESS SKILLS USED

▶ Observing
▶ Measuring
▶ Questioning
▶ Recording data
▶ Predicting
▶ Formulating models

What will the students do?

The following two activities could be done ahead of time to introduce the concept of air pressure. Once the students understand this concept, then the third activity can be performed to teach the main concept.

Tower of Water

Close one end of a long, clear tube with a stopper or cap. Stand this in a tub of water. Fill the tube with water. Seal the top end of the tube with the stopper or cap. Remove the seal at the bottom, keeping the opening of the tube under water. What happens to the water in the tube? Why? What do you think will happen if you remove the stopper from the top of the tube? Try it! Was your prediction correct? Why does all of this happen?

Aneroid Barometer

Cut the open end off a balloon. Obtain a large-size baby food jar and extend the balloon over the mouth of the jar. Make sure the balloon is stretched taut. While you hold it, have your partner fasten it in place with a rubber band. Be sure to make a tight seal. Use the second rubber band to make sure the seal is tight. Why do you think a tight seal is important? Draw a sketch of your jar. Show what the balloon seal would look like if the pressure inside the jar were greater than the pressure outside of the jar. Cut one end of the straw at an angle to make it pointed. Gently place a 3-cm strip of tape on the uncut end. Place this on the center of the balloon-covered jar. Be sure it sits securely in the center. Attach a tongue depressor to the smaller jar at the top and the bottom of the jar, using two rubber bands at each location (a total of four). Place the two jars side by side on a level support so that the pointed straw is in front of the tongue depressor. Label the point where it hits 0 to show the starting position.

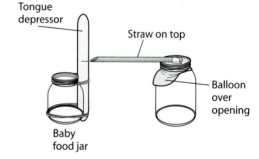

Tongue depressor

Straw on top

Balloon over opening

Baby food jar

What questions can be used for student activities?

- What do you think will happen to the pointer as the air pressure outside the jar increases?
- What will happen when the air pressure outside decreases?
- Try increasing the air pressure within the jar by placing your hands over the balloon jar for about 10 minutes. What happens to the pointer?

- Try decreasing the air pressure within the jar by placing the balloon jar in a pan of ice water. What happens to the pointer?

Uneven Heating and Air Pressure

Make use of the barometers created in the second activity or provide the students with commercially made aneroid barometers. After the students have had a chance to observe how their barometers work, divide the class into three groups. In the very beginning of the school day, instruct one third of the students to place their barometer in the same safe place in the playground in the sun on the blacktop or gravel; one third in the same safe place in the playground in the shade on the grass near a tree; one third in the same area of the classroom. Instruct each group to place a thermometer in their area also. Ask the students to take readings from their barometers and thermometers throughout the course of the school day. Instruct the students to note any changes that occur in the area where they placed the barometer, such as the amount of sunlight, changing shade conditions, or wind picking up or dying down. Remind the students about the importance of keeping a careful record of their observations.

Explanation

Concept: Uneven heating of the earth affects air pressure.

If the students have made careful observations and recorded their data accurately, you should be able to create a class chart of data collected at the three sites. Ask the students from each of the groups to examine their data as a group first. If their data for the different time readings are not all the same, ask them to average the readings for that time period. These averages could be placed on the chart.

Through careful questioning and calling attention to the group data, the students may find that the barometric readings as well as thermometer readings were different at each of the sites. Ask them whether they see some sort of relationship between the temperature at the site and what was happening with the barometer. What happened to the barometric reading as your temperature increased? As it decreased? Were the barometer readings any different in the shade than in the sun or the classroom? Why or why not?

The earth is heated unevenly because of varying types and colors of surfaces found on the earth. What was the color of the site where you placed your barometer and thermometer? Which color site had the warmest temperatures? The coolest? Were the barometer readings different for these sites? What conclusions can you draw about uneven heating of the earth and air pressure?

Expansion

PROCESS SKILLS USED
▶ Observing
▶ Hypothesizing
▶ Predicting
▶ Communicating

Air Pressure versus Water Temperature

How will the idea be expanded?

Concept: Uneven heating of the earth gives rise to wind patterns that move locally and around the globe.

Set up stations around the classroom so that the children can practice the following:

Fill two clear glasses with water. Place an index card on the top of one. Holding the card in place, invert the cup and place it on top of the other cup. Remove the card. Obtain some very hot water. Put food coloring in it. Use this water to fill one of the clear glasses from your practice session above. Do the same with cold water and a different color of food coloring. Place a card over one glass. Be sure to wear an oven mitt to hold the hot glass. Try inverting the cold over hot and hot over cold. What happens in each set of cups? Why?

Draw a spiraling line on an index card. Cut out this snake, and tape a thread to the center of it. Blow on the snake from the bottom. What happens to the snake? What do you think will happen if you suspend it above a burning candle? Try it! Why is this snake moving?

Air Temperature versus Movement of Air

Light a candle, and allow the melting wax to harden at different spots on a wire. Hold one end of the wire in a candle flame. What do you think will happen to the wax drops on the wire? Does something happen to all of the drops at the same time? How is heat transferred from one end of the wire to the next?

Heat Transfer on a Wire

Remove the shade from a lamp, and plug it in. Place your hand carefully near the side of the bulb, keeping the light off. Turn on the lamp. Did you notice a change in the temperature of your hand? Place a cool beaker around the lit bulb. Can you feel the heat from the bulb?

Heat Movement Through Air

Cover one side of a large tin can lid with candle soot. Fix a tack to the opposite side with candle wax. Fix a tack to the side of a clean tin can lid. Support each lid in a clay mound so the tacks are directly opposite the candle flame, a small but equal distance away. Which tack do you think will fall first and why? Did it occur as you predicted?

Heat Transfer Through Metal

As the students rotate through the five stations, set up a sixth demonstration area so that the small groups can observe the teacher perform the following activity.

Make an observation box before beginning the demonstration. The following materials will be needed: one card-board box (about 30 cm × 30 cm × 50 cm), clear plastic food wrap, plastic tape, one plastic straw.

Remove the top of the box. Leave a 3-cm edge for strength. Turn the box over. Cut a window in the new top, leaving half of the top intact. Cut out one side, again leaving a 3-cm edge for strength. Tape clear plastic food wrap to the side and to the half-window on top. In one end of the box, cut a small hole that is just large enough to insert a plastic straw. See the figure for assistance in construction.

Additional Materials

1 35-ml syringe	matches
1 plastic straw (cut into 3 even pieces)	ice water
heavy cotton string (three 4-cm pieces)	aluminum pan
scissors	metric ruler

Teacher Demonstration

Movement of Smoke over Hot and Cold Surfaces: Clouds

1. Take a piece of string, and fold it in half. Place the folded end into one of the pieces of straw, allowing about 0.5 cm to hang out the end. Be sure it fits snugly in the end. Do this for each piece of straw.

2. Slip the open end of the prepared straw onto the syringe. Light the string. Collect smoke in the cylinder by slowly drawing out the plunger. Remove the straw and lay it aside where it won't burn anything. You may need more smoke later.

3. Place a pan of ice water inside the observation box. Be sure the straw is in place through the end of the box but not hanging over the pan. Let the pan sit for three or four minutes. After the wait, insert the smoke-filled syringe into the straw of the observation box. Gently force the smoke through the straw into the box. Carefully observe what happens to the smoke as it moves over the pan of ice water.

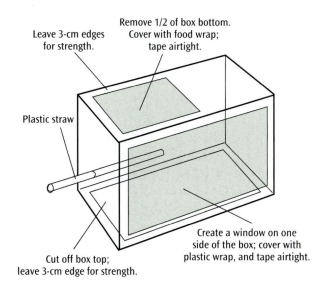

Leave 3-cm edges for strength.

Remove 1/2 of box bottom. Cover with food wrap; tape airtight.

Plastic straw

Create a window on one side of the box; cover with plastic wrap, and tape airtight.

Cut off box top; leave 3-cm edge for strength.

4. Complete the procedure using a pan of hot water instead. Once again ask the students to make careful observations of the smoke as it moves over the hot water.

Additional Activity/Demonstration Materials Needed

observation/convection box	tape	scissors
drinking straws	index cards	empty soda bottle
straight pins	clay	small fan
paper clips		

Movement of Smoke over Hot and Cold Surfaces: Wind Patterns

Remove the pan of water used in the activity above, and replace it with a candle. Cut a 10-cm hole in the observation box in the lid directly above the candle so that the observation box now looks like the figure. Light the candle, and place it inside the box directly under the hole. Once again, inject air through the straw to keep the wick smoking. Observe the behavior of the smoke in the box. Which direction is the smoke in the straw coming from: horizontal or vertical? Place a pan of ice cubes directly below the smoking wick, and leave the burning candle in place. What happens to the smoke as it moves over the pan and on toward the candle?

Concept: Uneven heating of the earth gives rise to wind patterns that move locally and around the globe. *Convection* is hot air rising above cold. *Conduction* is heat transferred through surface of objects. *Radiation* is heat energy that travels in waves.

What questions can be used for student activities?

- What three types of heating did you experience in the above activities?
- When warm air rises over cold air, what type of current does this represent?
- If you had a choice of the type of heating for your home, would you choose one that made use of conduction, convection currents, or radiation? Which do you think is the most efficient? The least efficient?
- How can a toaster be used to demonstrate the three different types of heating?

What questions can the teacher use for the demonstration?

- What path did the smoke take as it moved over the cold surface? (It spreads out slowly over the pan, staying close to the pan's surface.)
- What path did the smoke take as it moved over the hot surface? (It slowly spread out and upward.)
- What path did the smoke take as it moved over the ice and on toward the candle? (It stayed close to the pan's surface and then rose up over the candle.)
- Do you think a force is acting on the smoke as it moves above the warm or cold surfaces? (A force is something that causes a change in shape or a change in motion of a body. It is easy to see the change in shape; this also shows the change in motion.)
- What name could you give this change of motion? Why do you think it occurs? (Wind is caused by the uneven heating within the observation box. The teacher should elaborate on this concept of local and global winds.)

Science in Personal and Social Perspectives

- Do you think you could run a mile in Denver, Colorado, as easily as you could in Chicago, Illinois? Why or why not?

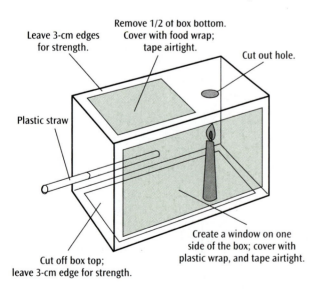

Leave 3-cm edges for strength.

Remove 1/2 of box bottom. Cover with food wrap; tape airtight.

Cut out hole.

Plastic straw

Create a window on one side of the box; cover with plastic wrap, and tape airtight.

Cut off box top; leave 3-cm edge for strength.

- On a hot summer day, can you feel a difference in your comfort level when you are wearing a dark-colored shirt compared to a light-colored shirt? Why?
- Why do you think you have to bake a boxed cake mix at a different temperature when you are in a place at a high altitude compared to a place closer to sea level?

Science and Technology

- What causes winds?
- Why is a desert climate different from a forest climate?

History and Nature of Science

- Who was Bernoulli, and how did his work explain the concept of air pressure?

Evaluation

Upon completing these activities, the students will be able to:

- compare cloud patterns of different areas when given satellite photographs;
- look at an aerial map of a coastal state and be able to predict where most of the clouds will form;
- demonstrate the ability to read a barometer;
- explain the difference in barometric readings over land and sea;
- explain why you would expect the air to be warmer in the daytime over land than sea; and
- engage in a reflective discussion on the cause of wind and its importance.

appendix

National Science Education Standards: Content Standards for K–4 and 5–8

K–4 Physical Science Standards

Content Standard B—K–4:

All students should develop an understanding of:
- Properties of objects and materials
- Position and motion of objects
- Light, heat, electricity, and magnetism

Properties of Objects and Materials Concepts

- Objects have many observable properties, including size, weight, shape, color, temperature, and the ability to react with other substances. These properties can be measured using tools such as rulers, balances, and thermometers.
- Objects are made of one or more materials, such as paper, wood, and metal. Objects can be described by the properties of the materials from which they are made, and these properties can be used to separate or sort a group of objects or materials.
- Materials have different states—solid, liquid, and gas. Some common materials such as water can be changed from one state to another by heating or cooling.

Position and Motion of Objects Concepts

- The position of an object can be described by locating it relative to another object or the background.
- An object's motion can be described by indicating the change in its position over time.
- The position and motion of objects can be changed by pushing or pulling and the size of the change is related to the strength of the push or pull.
- Vibrating objects produce sound. The pitch of the sound can be varied by changing the rate of vibration.

Light, Heat, Electricity, and Magnetism Concepts

- Light travels in a straight line unless it strikes an object. Light can be reflected by a mirror, refracted by a lens, or absorbed by the object.
- Heat can be produced in many ways, such as burning, rubbing, and mixing chemicals. The heat can move from one object to another by conduction.
- Electricity in circuits can produce light, heat, sound, and magnetic effects. Electrical circuits require a complete loop through which the electrical current can pass.
- Magnets attract and repel each other and certain kinds of metals.

K–4 Life Science Standards

Content Standard C—K–4:

All students should develop an understanding of:
- The characteristics of organisms
- Life cycles of organisms
- Organisms and environments

Characteristics of Organisms Concepts

- Organisms have basic needs, which for animals are air, water, and food. Plants require air, water, and light. Organisms can only survive in environments in which they can meet their needs. The world has many different environments, and distinct environments support the life of different types of organisms.
- Each plant or animal has different structures which serve different functions in growth, survival, and reproduction. For example, humans have distinct structures of the body for walking, holding, seeing, and talking.
- The behavior of individual organisms is influenced by internal cues such as hunger and by external cues such as an environmental change. Humans and other organisms have senses that help them detect internal and external cues.

Life Cycles of Organisms Concepts

- Plants and animals have life cycles that include being born, developing into adults, reproducing, and eventually dying. The details of this life cycle are different for different organisms.
- Plants and animals closely resemble their parents.
- Many characteristics of an organism are inherited from the parents of the organism, but other characteristics result from an individual's interactions with the environment. Inherited characteristics include the color of flowers and the number of limbs of an animal. Other features, such as the ability to play a musical instrument, are learned through interactions with the environment.

Organisms and Their Environments Concepts

- All animals depend on plants. Some animals eat plants for food. Other animals eat animals that eat the plants.
- An organism's patterns of behavior are related to the nature of that organism's environment, including the kinds and numbers of other organisms present, the availability of food and resources, and the physical characteristics of the environment. When the environment changes, some plants and animals survive and reproduce, and others die or move to new locations.

National Resource Council. (1996). Science content standards, *National Science Education Standards*. Washington, D.C.: National Academy of Sciences, pp. 123–160.

- All organisms cause changes in the environment where they live. Some of these changes are detrimental to themselves or other organisms, whereas others are beneficial.
- Humans depend on both their natural and their constructed environment. Humans change environments in ways that can either be beneficial or detrimental for other organisms, including the humans themselves.

K–4 Earth and Space Science Standards

Content Standard D—K–4:

All students should develop an understanding of:
- Properties of Earth materials
- Objects in the sky

Properties of Earth Materials Concepts

- Earth materials are solid rocks and soils, liquid water, and the gases of the atmosphere. These varied materials have different physical and chemical properties. These properties make them useful, for example, as building materials, as sources of fuel, or for growing the plants we use as food. Earth materials provide many of the resources humans use.
- Soils have properties of color and texture, capacity to retain water, and ability to support the growth of many kinds of plants, including those in our food supply. Other Earth materials are used to construct buildings, make plastics, and provide fuel for generating electricity, and operating cars and trucks.
- The surface of the Earth changes. Some changes are due to slow processes, such as erosion and weathering and some changes are due to rapid processes such as landslides, volcanoes, and earthquakes.
- Fossils provide evidence about the plants and animals that lived long ago and nature of the environment at that time.

Objects in the Sky Concepts

- The sun, moon, stars, clouds, birds, and airplanes all have properties, locations, and movements that can be described and that may change.
- Objects in the sky have patterns of movement. The sun, for example, appears to move across the sky in the same way every day, but its path changes slowly over the seasons. The moon moves across the sky on a daily basis much like the sun. The shape of the moon seems to change from day to day in a cycle that lasts about a month.
- The sun provides the light and heat necessary to maintain the temperature of the Earth.
- Weather can change from day to day and over the season. Weather can be described by measurable quantities, such as temperature, wind direction and speed, precipitation, and humidity.

5–8 Physical Science Standards

Content Standard B—5–8:

All students should develop an understanding of:
- Properties and changes of properties in matter
- Motions and forces
- Transformations of energy

Properties and Changes of Properties in Matter Concepts

- Substances have characteristic properties such as density, boiling point, and solubility, which are independent of the amount of the sample. A mixture of substances can often be separated into the original substances by using one or more of these characteristic properties.
- Substances react chemically in characteristic ways with other substances to form new substances (compounds) with different characteristic properties. In chemical reactions the total mass is conserved. Substances are often placed in categories or groups if they react in similar ways, for example, metals.
- Chemical elements do not break down by normal laboratory reactions such as heating, electric current, or reaction with acids. There are more than 100 known elements which combine in a multitude of ways to produce compounds, which account for the living and nonliving substances that we encounter.

Motions and Forces Concepts

- The motion of an object can be described by its position, direction of motion, and speed.
- An object that is not being subjected to a force will continue to move at a constant speed and in a straight line.
- If more than one force acts on an object, then the forces can reinforce or cancel one another, depending on their direction and magnitude. Unbalanced forces will cause changes in the speed and/or direction of an object's motion.

Transformations of Energy Concepts

- Energy exists in many forms, including heat, light, chemical, nuclear, mechanical, and electrical. Energy can be transformed from one form to another.
- Heat energy moves in predictable ways, flowing from warmer objects to cooler ones until both objects are at the same temperature.
- Light interacts with matter by transmission (including refraction), absorption, or scattering (including reflection).
- In most chemical reactions, energy is released or added to the system in the form of heat, light, electrical, or mechanical energy.
- Electrical circuits provide a means of converting electrical energy into heat, light, sound, chemical, or other forms of energy.
- The sun is a major source of energy for changes on the Earth's surface.

5–8 Life Science Standards

Content Standard C—5–8:

All students should develop an understanding of:
- Structure and function in living organisms
- Reproduction and heredity
- Regulation and behavior
- Populations and ecosystems
- Diversity and adaptions of organisms

Structure and Function in Living Systems Concepts

- Living systems at all levels of organization demonstrate complementary structure and function. Important levels of organization for structure and function include cells, organs, organ systems, whole organisms, and ecosystems.
- All organisms are composed of cells—the fundamental unit of life. Most organisms are single cells; other organisms, including humans, are multicellular.
- Cells carry on the many functions needed to sustain life. They grow and divide, producing more cells.
- Specialized cells perform specialized functions in multicellular organisms. Groups of specialized cells cooperate to form a tissue, such as a muscle. Different tissues are in turn grouped together to form larger functional units, called organs. Each type of cell, tissue, and organ has a distinct structure and set of functions that serve the organism as a whole. The human organism has systems for digestion, respiration, reproduction, circulation, excretion, movement, control and coordination, and for protection from disease.
- Disease represents a breakdown in structures or functions of an organism. Some diseases are the result of intrinsic failures of the system. Others are the result of infection by other organisms.

Reproduction and Heredity Concepts

- Reproduction is a characteristic of all living systems; since no individual organism lives forever, it is essential to the continuation of species. Some organisms reproduce asexually. Other organisms reproduce sexually.
- In many species, including humans, females produce eggs and males produce sperm. An egg and sperm unite to begin the development of a new individual. This new individual has an equal contribution of information from its mother (via the egg) and its father (via the sperm). Sexually produced offspring are never identical to either of their parents.
- Each organism requires a set of instructions for specifying its traits. Heredity is the passage of these instructions from one generation to another.
- Hereditary information is contained in genes, located in the chromosomes of each cell. Each gene carries a single unit of information, and an inherited trait of an individual can be determined by either one or many genes. A human cell contains many thousands of different genes.
- The characteristics of an organism can be described in terms of a combination of traits. Some traits are inherited and others result from interactions with the environment.

Regulation and Behavior Concepts

- All organisms must be able to obtain and use resources, grow, reproduce, and maintain a relatively stable internal environment while living in a constantly changing external environment.
- Regulation of an organism's internal environment involves sensing external changes in the environment and changing physiological activities to keep within the range required to survive.
- Behavior is one kind of response an organism may make to an internal or environmental stimulus. A behavioral response requires coordination and communication at many levels, including cells, organ systems, and whole organisms. Behavioral response is a set of actions determined in part by heredity and in part from past experience.
- An organism's behavior has evolved through adaptation to its environment. How organisms move, obtain food, reproduce, and respond to danger, all are based on the organism's evolutionary history.

Populations and Ecosystems Concepts

- Populations consist of all individuals of a species that occur together at a given place. All of the populations living together and the physical factors with which they interact compose an ecosystem.
- Populations of organisms can be categorized by the function they serve in an ecosystem. Plants and some microorganisms are producers—they make their own food. All animals, including humans, are consumers, which obtain food by eating other organisms. Decomposers, primarily bacteria and fungi, are consumers that use waste materials and dead organisms for food. Food webs identify the relationships among producers, consumers, and decomposers in an ecosystem.
- For ecosystems, the major source of energy is sunlight. Energy entering ecosystems as sunlight is converted by producers into stored chemical energy through photosynthesis. It then passes from organism to organism in food webs.
- The number of organisms an ecosystem can support depends on the resources available and abiotic factors such as quantity of light and water, range of temperatures, and the soil composition. Given adequate biotic and abiotic resources and no disease or predators, populations, including humans, increase at very rapid (exponential) rates. Limitations of resources and other factors such as predation and climate limit the growth of population in specific niches in the ecosystem.

Diversity and Adaptations of Organisms Concepts

- There are millions of species of animals, plants, and microorganisms living today that differ from those that lived in the remote past. Each species lives in a specific and fairly uniform environment.
- Although different species look very different, the unity among organisms becomes apparent from an analysis of internal structures, the similarity of their chemical processes, and the evidence of common ancestry.
- Biological evolution accounts for a diversity of species developed through gradual processes over many generations. Species acquire many of their unique characteristics through biological adaptation, which involves the selection of naturally occurring variations in populations. Biological adaptations include changes in structures, behaviors, or physiology that enhance reproductive success in a particular environment.
- Extinction of a species occurs when the environment changes and the adaptive characteristics of a species do not enable it to survive in competition with its neighbors. Fossils indicate that many organisms that lived long ago are now extinct. Extinction of species is common. Most of the species that have lived on the Earth no longer exist.

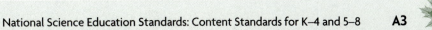

5–8 Earth and Space Science Standards

Content Standard D—5–8:

All students should develop an understanding of:

- Structure of the Earth's system
- Earth's history
- Earth in the solar system

Structure of the Earth's System Concepts

- The solid Earth is layered with a thin brittle crust, hot convecting mantle, and dense metallic core.
- Crustal plates on the scale of continents and oceans constantly move at rates of centimeters per year in response to movements in the mantle. Major geological events, such as earthquakes, volcanoes, and mountain building, result from these plate motions.
- Land forms are the result of a combination of constructive and destructive forces. Constructive forces include crustal deformation, volcanoes, and deposition of sediment, while destructive forces include weathering and erosion.
- Changes in the solid Earth can be described as the rock cycle. Old rocks weather at the Earth's surface, forming sediments that are buried, then compacted, heated, and often recrystallized into new rock. Eventually, these new rocks may be brought to the surface by the forces that drive plate motions, and the rock cycle continues.
- Soil consists of weathered rocks, decomposed organic material from dead plants, animals, and bacteria. Soils are often found in layers, with each having a different chemical composition and texture.
- Water, which covers the majority of the Earth's surface, circulates through the crust, oceans, and atmosphere in what is known as the water cycle. Water evaporates from the Earth's surface, rises and cools as it moves to higher elevations, condenses as rain or snow, and falls to the surface where it collects in lakes, oceans, soil, and in rocks underground.
- Water is a solvent. As it passes through the water cycle it dissolves minerals and gases and carries them to the oceans.
- The atmosphere is a mixture of oxygen, nitrogen, and trace gases that include water vapor. The atmosphere has different properties at different elevations.

- Clouds, formed by the condensation of water vapor, affect weather and climate. Some do so by reflecting much of the sunlight that reaches Earth from the sun, while others hold heat energy emitted from the Earth's surface.
- Global patterns of atmospheric movement influence local weather. Oceans have a major effect on climate, because water in the oceans holds a large amount of heat.
- Living organisms have played many roles in the Earth system, including affecting the composition of the atmosphere and contributing to the weathering of rocks.

Earth's History Concepts

- The Earth's processes we see today, including erosion, movement of crustal plates, and changes in atmospheric composition, are similar to those that occurred in the past. Earth's history is also influenced by occasional catastrophes, such as the impact of an asteroid or comet.
- Fossils provide important evidence of how life and environmental conditions have changed.

Earth in the Solar System Concepts

- The Earth is the third planet from the sun in a system that includes the moon, the sun, eight other planets and their moons, and smaller objects such as asteroids and comets. The sun, an average star, is the central and largest body in the solar system.
- Most objects in the solar system are in regular and predictable motion. These motions explain such phenomena as the day, the year, phase of the moon, and eclipses.
- Gravity is the force that keeps planets in orbit around the sun and governs the rest of the motion in the solar system. Gravity alone holds us to the Earth's surface and explains the phenomena of the tides.
- The sun is the major source of energy for phenomena on the Earth's surface, such as growth of plants, winds, ocean currents, and the water cycle. Seasons result from variations in the amount of the sun's energy hitting the surface, due to the tilt of the Earth's rotation axis.

Adeniyi, E. O. (1985). Misconceptions of selected ecological concepts held by some Nigerian students. *Journal of Biological Education, 19* (4), 311–316.

Alexakos, Konstantinos. (2001, March). Inclusive classrooms. *Science and Children,* 40–43.

Alfke, D. (1974, April). Asking operational questions. *Science and Children,* 18–19.

Altermatt, E. R., Jovanovic, J., & Perry, M. (1998). Bias or responsivity? Sex and achievement-level effects on teachers' classroom questioning practices. *Journal of Educational Psychology, 90* (3), 515–527.

American Institute of Physics. (2002). *Science & engineering indicators: S&E workforce demographics.* FYI Number 126: November 20, 2002. [Online: http://www.aip.org/fyi/2002/126.html]

American National Standards Institute. (2000). ANSI Z87.1 2000, New York, NY, 10018. www.ansi.org

Antonouris, G. (1989). Multicultural science. *School Science Review, 70* (252), 97–100.

Appleton, K. (1993). Using theory to guide practice: Teaching science from a constructivist perspective. *School Science and Mathematics, 93* (5), 269–274.

Arbor Scientific Company (ASC). (1996). *Arbor Scientific—Innovation in science education.* Ann Arbor, MI: Arbor Scientific.

Arena, P. (1996). The role of relevance in the acquisition of science process skills. *Australian Science Teachers Journal, 42* (4), 34–38.

Arnold, D. S., Atwood, R. K., & Rogers, U. M. (1973). An investigation of the relationships among question level, response level, and lapse time. *School Science and Mathematics, 73,* 591–595.

Assistive Technology Act (P.L. 103–218). (1998). U.S. Government Documents. (http://www.resna.org/taproject/library/laws/ata98sum.html, retrieved November 11, 2007).

Ausubel, D. P. (1963). *Psychology of meaningful verbal learning.* New York: Grune and Stratton.

———. (1968). *Educational psychology: A cognitive view.* New York: Holt, Rinehart and Winston.

Baker, D. (1988). *Research matters to the science teacher teaching for gender differences.* National Association of Research in Science Teaching.

Baker, L. (1991). Metacognition, reading, and science education. In C. M. Santa & D. E. Alvermann (Eds.), *Science learning: Processes and applications.* Newark, DE: International Reading Association.

Bannasch, S. & Tinker, R. (Winter, 2002). Probeware takes a seat in the classroom. *The Concord Consortium, 6* (1). [Online: www.concord.org/newsletter/2002winter/probeware.html].

Barman, C. R. (1996). How do students *really* view science and scientists? *Science and Children, 34* (1), 30–33.

———. (1997). Students' views of scientists and science: Results from a national study. *Science and Children, 35* (1), 18–23.

Barman, C. R., & Ostlund, K. L. (1996). A protocol to investigate students' perceptions about scientists and relevancy of science to students' daily lives. *Science Education International, 4* (4), 16–21.

Barnes, C. P. (1978). *Questioning strategies to develop critical thinking skills.* (ERIC Document No. 169486)

Beaton, A. E., Mullis, I. V. S., Martin, M. O., Gonzales, E. J., Kelly, D. L., & Smith, T. A. (1996). *Mathematics achievement in the middle school years: IEA's third international mathematics and science study (TIMSS).* Chestnut Hill, MA: Boston College.

Begley, S. (1996, February 19). Your child's brain. *Newsweek,* 55–62.

Bell, Beverly. (2007). Classroom assessment of science learning. In S. K. Abell & N. G. Lederman (Eds.), *Handbook of research on science education.* Mahwah, NJ: Lawrence Erlbaum Associates.

Bennett, W. J. (1986). *What works.* Washington, DC: U.S. Department of Education.

Berger, C. F., Lu, C. R., Belzer, S. J., & Voss, B. E. (1994). *Research on the uses of technology in science education.* In D. L. Gabel (Ed.), *Handbook of research on science teaching and learning* (pp. 466–490). New York: Macmillan.

Bergman, A. B. (1993, February). Performance assessment for early childhood: What could be more natural? *Science and Children,* 20–22.

Biddulph, F., & Osborne, R. (1984, February). Children's questions and science teaching: An alternative approach. *Learning in science project* (Working Paper No. 117). Hamilton, New Zealand: Waikato University, February. (ERIC Reproduction Document No. ED 252400)

Biddulph, F., Symington, D., & Osborn, R. (1986). The place of children's questions in primary science education. *Research in Science and Technological Education, 4* (1) 77–78.

Biehle, J., Motz, L., & West, S. (1999). *NSTA guide to school science facilities.* Arlington, VA: National Science Teachers Association.

Birnie, H. H., & Ryan, A. (1984, April). Inquiry/discovery revisited. *Science and Children,* 31.

Bloom, B. (1984). The search for methods of group instruction as effective as one-to-one tutoring. *Educational Leadership, 41* (8), 4–17.

Bloom, B. J. (1984). The 2 sigma problem: The search for methods of group instruction as effective as one-to-one tutoring. *Educational Researcher, 13,* 4–16.

Bloom, B. S. (1956). *Taxonomy of educational objectives: The classification of educational goals, Handbook I: Cognitive domain.* New York: Longmans, Green.

Blosser, P. E. (1985). Using questions in science classrooms. In R. Doran (Ed.), *Research matters to the science teacher, 2.* (ERIC Document No. 273490)

———. (1993). *Using cooperative learning in science education.* Columbus, OH: ERIC Clearinghouse for Science, Mathematics, and Environmental Education. (ERIC Reproduction Document No. ED 351207)

Bredderman, T. (1982, September). Activity science—The evidence shows it matters. *Science and Children,* pp. 39–41.

———. (1984). The influence of activity-based elementary science programs on classroom practices: A quantitative synthesis. *Journal of Research in Science Teaching, 21* (3), 290–303.

Brennan, J. (1970). An investigation of factors related to safety in the high school science program. Ed.D. dissertation, University of Denver, Denver, CO. (ERIC Document No. ED 085179)

Brown, D. R. (1979). Helping handicapped youngsters learn science by doing. In M. B. Rowe (Ed.), *What research says to the science teacher* (Vol. 2, p. 85), Washington, DC: National Science Teachers Association.

Brown, I. D. (1986). Topic 4: Teacher questioning techniques. *Staff development project—Science Grades K–6.* Jackson, MS: Mississippi Association for Teacher Education. (ERIC Document No. ED 285726)

Bruer, J. T. (1998). Brain science, brain fiction. *Educational Leadership, 56* (3), 14–18.

Bruner, J. S. (1961). The act of discovery. *Harvard Educational Review, 31,* 21–32.

———. (1962). *The process of education.* Cambridge, MA: Harvard University Press.

Budiansky, S. (2001, February). The trouble with textbooks. *Prism.* [Online: www.project2061.org/research/articles /asee.htm]

Bybee, R. W., Ferrini-Mundy, J., & Loucks-Horsley, S. (1997). National standards and school science and mathematics. *School Science and Mathematics, 97* (7), 325–334.

Bybee, R., & Hendricks, P. W. (1972). Teaching science concepts to preschool deaf children to aid language development. *Science Education, 56* (3), 303–310.

Carlsen, W. S. (2007). Language and science learning. In S. K. Abell and N. G. Lederman (Eds.), *Handbook of research on science education.* Mahwah, NJ: Lawrence Erlbaum Associates.

Chaillé, C., & Britain, L. (1991). *The young child as scientist.* New York: HarperCollins.

Chappius, J. (2005). Helping students understand assessment. *Educational Leadership, 63* (3), 39–43.

Checkley, K. (1997). The first seven and the eighth. *Educational Leadership, 55* (1), 8–13.

Cheney, M. S., & Roy, K. R. (1999). Inclusive safety solutions: What every teacher should know about special education and laboratory safety legislation. *The Science Teacher, 66* (6), 48–51.

Chin, C. (2007). Teacher questioning in science classrooms: Approaches that stimulate productive thinking. *Journal of Research in Science Teaching, 44* (6), 815–843.

Chivers, G. (1986). Intervention strategies to increase the proportion of girls and women studying and pursuing careers in technological fields: A West European review. *Journal of Engineering Education, 11* (3), 248.

CHRIS: Hazardous Chemical Data. (1989). U.S. Department of Transportation, Superintendent of Documents. Washington, DC: U.S. Government Printing Office.

Cleeland, L. (1984). Vistibular disorders—Learning problems and dyslexia. *Hearing Instruments, 35,* 8: 9F.

Coble, C. R., Levey, B., & Matthies, F. (1985). *Science for learning disabled students.* (ERIC Document No. 258803)

Cole, J. T., Kitano, M. K., & Brown, L. M. (1981). Concept analysis: A model for teaching basic science concepts to intellectually handicapped students. In M. E. Corrick, Jr. (Ed.), *Teaching handicapped students science: A resource book K–12 teachers* (pp. 51–53). Washington, DC: National Education Association.

Colgan, C. (2002). Lab accidents: An unintended consequence of hands-on science. *School Board News, 22* (14), 8.

College Board. (1987). *Get into the equation: Math and science, parents and children.* (ERIC Document No. 295785)

Comer, C. C., Davis, B., Fulton, B., Gerlovich, J., Sinclair, L., Summerlin, L., West, B., Winegarner, M., & Wineberg, S. (2001). *Science & safety: Making a connection.* Council of State Science Supervisors, American Chemical Society, Eisenhower National Clearing House, National Aeronautics and Space Administration, National Institutes of Health.

Committee on Undergraduate Science Education. (1997). *Science teaching reconsidered: A handbook.* Washington, DC: National Academy Press.

Cooper, H. H. (1979). Pygmalion grows up: A model for teacher expectation, communication, and performance influence. *Review of Education Research, 49,* 389–410.

Council of State Science Supervisors. (1999). *Science and safety: It's elementary!* [Online: Available: http://csss.emc.org.]

Craven, John A. III, & Hogan, T. (2001, September). Assessing student participation in the classroom. *Science Scope,* 36–40.

Cremin, L. A. (1976). *Public education.* New York: Basic Books.

Czerniak, C. M., & Haney, J. J. (1998). The effect of collaborative concept mapping on elementary preservice teachers' anxiety, efficacy, and achievement in physical science. *Journal of Science Teacher Education, 9* (4), 303–320.

D'Arcangelo, M. (1998). The brains behind the brain. *Educational Leadership, 56* (3), 20–25.

Dalton, B., Morocco, C. C., Tivnan, T., & Rawson Mead, P. L. (1997) Supported inquiry science: Teaching for conceptual change in urban and suburban science classrooms. *Journal of Learning Disabilities, 30* (6), 670–684.

Damian, C. (2002). The power of convergent learning. In *ENC Focus, 9,* 2. Columbus, OH: U.S. Department of Education, Eisenhower National Clearinghouse.

Dean, R. A., Dean, M. M., & Motz, L. L. (1997). *Safety in the elementary science classroom.* National Science Teachers Association, Arlington, VA. Booklet stock number PB 30, ISBN 0-87355-117-6.

Decker, L. E. (1981). *Foundation of community education.* Charlottesville, VA: Mid-Atlantic Center for Community Education.

Demers, C. (2000, October). Beyond paper and pencil assessments. *Science and Children,* 24–29, 60.

Denkla, M., Kantrowitz, B., & Wingert, P. (1989, April 17). How kids learn. *Newsweek,* 53–54.

Dewey, J. (1916). *Democracy and education.* New York: Macmillan.

———. (1937). *Experience and education.* New York: Collier Books.

Dillion, G. (1977). Mimeograph. In D. L. Hager-Schoeny et al., *Community involvement for classroom teachers* (2nd ed., p. 27). Charlottesville, VA: Community Collaborators.

Dillon, J. T. (1988). The remedial status of student questioning. *Journal of Curriculum Studies. 20* (3), 197–210.

Dillion, S. (2007). Focus on 2 R's cuts time for the rest, report says. *New York Times,* July 25, 2007. http://www.nytimes.com/2007/07/25/ education/25child.html?ex=1187150400&en=fb445900851a8ae8&ei=5070

District of Columbia v. Howell, 607 A.2d 501, 503 (D.C. App. 1992)

Dixon, N. (1996). Developing children's questioning skills through the use of a "Question Board." *Primary Science Review 44,* October, 8–10.

Donovan, M. S., & Bransford, J. D. (Eds.). (2005). Pulling threads. In *How students learn science in the classroom.* Washington, DC: National Academies Press.

Doolittle, P. (1997). Vygotsky's zone of proximal development as a theoretical foundation for cooperative learning. *Journal on Excellence in College Teaching, 8*(1), 83–103.

Downs, G., & Gerlovich, J. (1983). *Science safety for elementary teachers.* Ames, IA: Iowa State University Press.

Driver, R. (1983). *The pupil as scientist?* Milton Keynes, England: Open University Press.

———. (1994). *Making sense of science.* London: Routledge.

Driver, R. (1996). *Young people's images of science.* Bristol, PA: Open University Press.

Driver, R. (1997). Can we believe our eyes? In Annenberg/CPB (Ed.), *Minds of our own videotape program one.* Math and Science Collection, P.O. Box 2345, South Burlington, VT, 05407–2345.

Driver, R., Guensne, E., & Tiberghien, A. (1985). *Children's ideas in science.* Milton Keynes, England: Open University Press.

Duckworth, E., in Kantrowitz, B., & Wingert, P. (1989, April 17). How kids learn. *Newsweek,* p. 55.

Dunn, R., & Dunn, K. (1975). Finding the best fit—learning styles, teaching styles. *NAASP Bulletin, 59,* 37–49.

Ebrahim, A. (2004). The effects of traditional learning and learning cycle inquiry learning strategy on students' science achievement and attitudes toward science. Unpublished doctoral dissertation, Ohio University, Athens, OH.

Ediger, M. (1994). *Technology in the elementary curriculum.* U.S. Department of Education (ERIC Reproduction Document No. ED 401882)

Education Week (1999, October 7). Science group finds middle school textbooks inadequate.

Educational Testing Service. (1989). *A world of differences: An international assessment of mathematics and science.* Princeton, NJ: Center for the Assessment of Educational Progress.

———. (1992). *National assessment of educational progress.* Washington, DC: U.S. Department of Education.

Eggen, P., & Kauchak, D. (1992). *Educational psychology: Classroom connections.* New York: Macmillan.

Elfner, L. E. (1988). *Exemplars: Women in science, engineering, and mathematics.* Columbus, OH: Ohio Academy of Science.

Elliott, D. L., & Carter, K. (1986). *Scientific illiteracy in elementary science textbook programs.* Paper presented at the Annual Meeting of the American Educational Research Association, San Francisco, April, 1986. (ERIC Document No. 269257)

Elstgeest, J. (1985). The right question at the right time. In W. Harlen (Ed.), *Primary science: Taking the plunge.* London: Heinemann Educational Books.

enGauge. (2007). *Scientific literacy: 21st century skills.* North Central Regional Educational Laborabory. [Online: http://www.ncrel.org/ engauge/skills/scilit.htm]

Fathman, A. K., Quinn, M. E., & Kessler, C. (1992). *Teaching science to English learners, grades 4–8.* Washington, DC: National Clearinghouse for Bilingual Education. (ERIC Document Reproduction Service No. ED 349844)

Fields, S. (1989, April). The scientific teaching method. *Science and Children,* 15.

Finson, K. (2002). Drawing a scientist: What we do and do not know after fifty years of drawings. *School Science and Mathematics,* 102, November.

Flick, L. B. (1989). Will the real scientist please stand up! *Science Scope, 13* (3), 6–7.

———. (1995). *Complex instruction in complex classrooms: A synthesis of research on inquiry teaching methods and explicit teaching strategies.* Paper presented at the National Association for Research in Science Teaching, San Francisco (April 1995). (ERIC Reproduction Document No. ED 383563)

FOSS (1990). *Full option science system.* Berkeley, CA: Lawrence Hall of Science.

Foster, G. W., & Heiting, W. A. (1994). Embedded assessment. *Science and Children, 32* (2), 30–33.

Gallagher, J. J., & Aschner, M. J. (1963). A preliminary report on analyses of classroom interaction. *Merrill-Palmer Quarterly, 9,* 183–195.

Gambrell, L. B. (1983). The occurrence of think-time during reading comprehension. *Journal of Educational Research, 75,* 144–148.

Gardner, H. (1983) *Frames of mind: The theory of multiple intelligences.* New York: Basic Books.

Garthwait, A., & Verrill, J. (2003, May). E-Portfolios: Documenting student progress. *Science and Children,* 22–27.

George, R., & Kaplan, D. (1998). A structural model of parent and teacher influences on science attitudes of eighth graders: Evidence from NELS: 88. *Science Education, 82,* 93–109.

Gerlovich, J. A. (1996). Was I supposed to know that?: Teacher understanding of science safety issues. *Science Education International, 6* (3), 33–39.

Gerlovich, J. A. (1997). Safety standards: An examination of what teachers know and should know about science safety. *The Science Teacher, 64* (3), 46–49.

Gerlovich, J. A. (1999). Policies based science safety programs: A must. *Spectrum—Special Edition, 25* (3), 21–23.

Gerlovich, J. A., et al. (2003). *Total science safety system CD* (Kentucky Edition). Waukee, IA: JaKel, Inc.

Gerlovich, J. A. (2004). Science safety in middle schools: Issues and solutions. *Middle Matters, 13* (2), 1–3.

Gerlovich, J. A., Adams, S., Davis, B., & Parsa, R. (2003). Alabama science safety: A 2001 status report. *Alabama Science Teachers Association—ASTA Journal, 25* (1), 7–9.

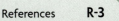

Gerlovich, J. A., McElroy, D., Parsa, R., & Wazlaw, B. (2005). National science safety indexing project: A beginning. *The Science Teacher, 72* (6) 43–46.

Gerlovich, J. A., & Gilchrist, J. (2001). Inner city physical science takes flight. *Iowa Educational Leadership 4* (1), 10–16.

Gerlovich, J. A., & Hartman, K. (1990). *Science safety: A diskette for elementary educators.* Waukee, IA: JaKel.

———. 1998. *The total science safety system: Elementary, 4th edition* [computer software], Waukee, IA: JaKel, Inc.

Gerlovich, J. A., & Parsa, R. (2002). Surveying science safety: NSTA analyzes safety in the classroom. *The Science Teacher, 69* (7), 52–55.

Gerlovich, J. A., & Woodland, J. (2001). Nebraska secondary science teacher safety project: A 2000 status report. *The Nebraska Science Teacher, 1* (1), 4–11.

Gerlovich, J. A., Hartman, K., & Gerard, T. (1992). *The total science safety system for grades 7–14.* Waukee, IA: JaKel.

Gerlovich, J. A., Jordan, L., Parsa, R. (2004). The 2003 status of science safety in Tennessee secondary schools. *Journal of the Tennessee Academy of Science, 79* (4), 83–91.

Gerlovich, J. A., McElroy, D. et al. (2004). Unpublished study completed for the Kentucky Department of Education.

Gerlovich, J. A., McElroy, D., Kennon, T., & Ross, A. (2007). The status of science safety in Arkansas secondary schools. *Arkansas Science Teachers Journal.*

Gerlovich, J. A., Parsa, R., & Wilson, E. (1998). Safety issues and Iowa science teachers. *Journal of the Iowa Academy of Science, 105* (4), 152–157.

Gerlovich, J. A., Parsa, R., Frana, B., Drew, V., & Stiner, T. (2002). Science safety status in Iowa schools. *Journal of the Iowa Academy of Science, 109* (3-4), 61–66.

Gerlovich, J. A., Whitsett, Lee, & Parsa, R. (2001). Surveying safety: How researchers addressed safety in science classrooms in Wisconsin. *The Science Teacher, 64* (4), 31–35.

Gerlovich, J. A., & McElroy, D. (2007). *National Edition—Total Science Safety System CD-ROM.* Waukee, IA: Jakel, Inc.

Glencoe Science Professional Series. (1994). *Alternative assessment in the science classroom.* (ERIC Reproduction Document No. ED 370778)

Goldhammer, A., & Isenberg, S. (1984). *Operation: Frog* [Educational software]. New York: Scholastic.

Goleman, D. (1995). *Emotional Intelligence.* New York: Bantam Books.

Good, R. G. (1977). *How children learn science.* New York: Macmillan.

Good, R. G., Wandersee, J. H., & St. Julien, J. (1993). Cautionary notes on the appeal of the new "ism" (constructivism) in science education. In K. Tobin (Ed.), *The practice of constructivism in science education* (pp. 71–87). Washington, DC: AAAS Press.

Gorodetsky, M., Fisher, K. M., & Wyman, B. (1994). Generating connections and learning with Semnet, a tool for constructing knowledge networks. *Journal of Science Education and Technology, 3* (3), 137–144.

Graesser, A. C., & Person, N. K. (1994). Question asking during tutoring. *American Educational Research Journal, 31,* 104–137.

Greenfield, S. (1995). *Journey to the centers of the mind.* New York: W.H. Freeman.

Guerra, C. J. (1988, March). Pulling science out of a hat. *Science and Children,* 23–24.

Guskey, T. R. (2005). Mapping the road to proficiency. *Educational Leadership, 63* (3), 32–38.

Habecker, J. E. (1976). *An analysis of reading questions in basal reading series based on Bloom's taxonomy.* Unpublished doctoral dissertation, University of Pennsylvania, Philadelphia.

Hager-Schoeny, D. L., & Galbreath, D. (1982). *Utilizing community resources in the classroom: An in-service reference collection.* Charlottesville, VA: University of Virginia, Mid-Atlantic Center for Community Education.

Hallahan, D. P., & Kauffman, J. M. (2000). *Exceptional learners.* Boston: Allyn and Bacon.

Halloran, J. D. (1970). *Attitude formation and change.* Great Britain: Leicester University Press.

Hammrich, P. L. (1997, January). Yes, daughter, you can. *Science and Children, 34,* 21–24.

Hamrick, L., & Harty, H. (1987). Influence of resequencing general science content on the science achievement, attitude toward science, and interest in science of sixth grade students. *Journal of Research in Science Teaching, 24* (1), 16.

Haney, J. (1998, September). Concept mapping in the science classroom: Linking theory into practice. *The Agora, 8,* 1–7.

Hannaford, C. (1995). *Smart moves.* Arlington, VA: Great Ocean Publishing Co.

Hargie, O. D. (1978). The importance of teacher questions in the classroom. *Educational Research, 20,* 99–102.

Harlen, W. (1992). *The teaching of science.* London: David Fulton Publishers.

———. (1993). *Teaching and learning primary science.* London: Paul Chapman Publishing.

Harms, N. (1981). VIII. Project synthesis: Summary and implications for teachers. In N. C. Harms & R. E. Yager (Eds.), *What research says to the science teacher* (Vol. 3). Washington, DC: National Science Teachers Association.

Harris, R. (1981). An audio-tactile approach to science education for visually impaired students. In M. E. Corrick, Jr. (Ed.), *Teaching handicapped students science.* Washington, DC: National Education Association.

Hart, D. (1994). *Authentic assessment: Handbook for educators.* New York: Addison-Wesley.

Haury, D. L. (1993, March). *Teaching science through inquiry.* Columbus, OH: Clearinghouse for Science, Mathematics, and Environmental Education (EDO-SE-93-4).

Hazen, R. M., & Trefil, J. (1992). *Science matters: Achieving science literacy.* New York: Doubleday.

Healy, J. (1994). *Your child's growing mind.* New York: Doubleday.

Hein, G. E., & Price, S. (1994). *Active assessment for active science: A guide for elementary school teachers.* Portsmouth, NH: Heinemann.

Holdren, J. (1994). The Limits of Thematic Instruction. In *Common Knowledge* (Vol. 7, No. 4). Core Knowledge Foundation, Charlottesville, VA 22902.

Holliday, W. G. (2002, January). Selecting a science textbook. *Science Scope,* 16–20.

Holt, J. (1971). *How children learn.* London: Penguin Press, p. 52.

Hood, K., & Gerlovich, J. (2007). Preservice teacher goes from ick to wow! *Science & Children, 44* (6), 42–44.

Horton, P. (1988). Class size and lab safety in Florida. *Florida Science Teacher, 3* (3) 4–6.

Hovey, A. (2005). *Critical issue: Science education in the era of No Child Left Behind—history, benchmarks, and standards.* North Central Regional Laboratory. [Online: http://www.ncrel.org/sdrs/areas/issues/content/cntareas/science/sc600.htm]

Howard, P. (1994). *Owner's manual for the brain.* Austin, TX: Leornian Press.

Humphreys, A., Post, T., & Ellis, A. (1981). *Interdisciplinary methods: A thematic approach.* Santa Monica, CA: Goodyear Publishing Company.

Humrich, E. (1988). *Sex differences in the second IEA science study: U.S. results in an international context.* Paper presented at the annual meeting of the National Association for Research in Science Teaching. (ERIC Document No. ED 292649)

Hunkins, F. P. (1970). Analysis and evaluation questions: Their effects upon critical thinking. *Educational Leadership, 27,* pp. 697–705.

Hurd, P. D. (1986, January). Perspectives for the reform of science education. *Phi Delta Kappan,* pp. 353–358.

Hurd, S. (2003). Using Journaling to Motivate Science Learning. *Masters Project submitted to the Faculty at Ohio University, Athens, Ohio.*

Iatridis, M. (1981, October). Teaching science to preschoolers. *Science and Children.*

Iowa Code Annotated, Sections 656.1 to 686. End, Volume 51–53, West Group, 1998, plus 2001, Cumulative Annual Pocket Part (laws through 2000 regular session).

Iwasyk, M. (1997, September). Kids questioning kids: "Experts" sharing. *Science and Children,* 42–46.

Jarrett, D. (1997). *Inquiry strategies for science and mathematics learning: It's just good teaching.* Northwest Regional Educational Laboratory. (ERIC Reproduction Document No. ED 413188)

Jegede, O. J., Alaiyemola, F. F., & Okebukola, P. A. O. (1990). The effect of concept mapping on students' anxiety and achievement in biology. *Journal for Research in Science Teaching, 27* (10), 951–960.

Jelly, S. (1985). Helping children raise questions—and answering them. In W. Harlen (Ed.), *Primary science: Taking the plunge* (p. 54). London: Heinemann.

Jendron, J. (2007). *The power of assistive technology: University of South Carolina Assistive Technology Project.* Retrieved from the ConnSense Bulletin. [Online: http://www.connsensebulletin.com/jendron.html]

Jensen, E. (1998). *Teaching with the brain in mind.* Alexandria, VA: Association for Supervision and Curriculum Development.

Johnson, F. (1997). New standards show too many students know too little science. *NSTA Reports, 9* (3), 1, 12.

Johnson, R. T., & Johnson, D. W. (1991). So what's new about cooperative learning in science? *Cooperative Learning, 11* (3), 2–3.

Jones, G. M., Mullis, I. V. S., Raisen, S. A., Weiss, I. R., & Weston, E. A. (1992). *The 1990 science report card, NAEP's assessment of fourth, eighth, and twelfth graders.* Washington, DC: U.S. Department of Education.

Jones, M. G., & Wheatley, J. (1988). Factors influencing the entry of women into science and related fields. *Science Education, 72,* 127–142.

Jones, R. M. (1985, May). Teaming up. *Science and Children,* 21.

Jonsson, P. (2003). Lab safety: Beyond goggles. *The Christian Science Monitor,* January 28, 2003.

Kahle, J. B. (1990). Why girls don't know. In M. B. Rowe (Ed.), *What research says to the science teacher. Vol. 6: The process of knowing.* Washington, DC: National Science Teachers Association.

Kahle, J. B., & Lakes, M. K. (1983). The myth of equality in science classrooms. *Journal of Research in Science Teaching, 20* (2), 131–140.

Kahle, J. B., & Rennie, L. J. (1993). Ameliorating gender differences in attitudes about science: A cross-national study. *Journal of Science Education and Technology, 2* (1), 321–333.

Kahn, S. (2003). Including all students in hands-on learning. *enc Focus 10* (2), 14–17.

Kamen, M. (1996). A teacher's implementation of authentic assessment in an elementary science classroom. *Journal of Research in Science, 33* (8), 859–877.

Katz, L., in Kantrowitz, B., & Wingert, P. (1989, April 17). How kids learn. *Newsweek,* p. 55.

Kinnear, J. (1994). *What science education really says about communication of science concepts* (Report No. CS508-657). Sydney, Australia: Annual Meeting of the International Communication Association. (ERIC Document Reproduction Service No. ED 372455)

Kinoshita, J. (1999, January/February). Replenishing the brain's neurons. *Brainworks: The Neuroscience Newsletter, 9,* 1–2.

Kirch, S. A., Bargerhuff, M. E., Cowan, H., & Wheatly, M. (2007). Reflections of educators in pursuit of inclusive science classrooms. *Journal of Science Teacher Education, 18,* 663–692.

Kirk, M., Matthews, C. E., & Kurtts, S. (2001, December). The trouble with textbooks. *The Science Teacher,* 42–45.

Knezek, D. (2007). *NETS-S Refresh Flier* [Online: http://cnets.iste.org/students/NESBRO_ISTE_PDF_proof.pdf]

Knuth, R. (1995). *Engaging learning through technology.* Paper presented at the IVLA/IAECT Conference, Chicago, October.

Koch, J. (2007). A gender inclusive approach to science education. In D. Sadker & E. S. Silber (Eds.), *Gender in the classroom: Foundations, skills, methods, and strategies across the curriculum.* Mahwah, NJ: Lawrence Erlbaum Associates, Publishers.

Koran, J. J., & Koran, J. L. (1973). *Validating a teacher behavior by student performance* (Report No. FSDE-730-063). Tallahassee, FL: Florida State Department of Education.

Kotulak, R. (1993). Research discovers secrets of how brain learns to talk. *Chicago Tribune,* April 13, section 1, pp. 1–4.

———. (1996). *Inside the brain.* Kansas City, MO: Andrews and McMeel.

Kroot, N. E. (1976). *An analysis of the responses of four, six, and eight year old children to four kinds of questions.* Unpublished doctoral dissertation, Indiana University, Bloomington.

Krueger, A., & Sutton, J. (Eds.). (2001). *EDThoughts: What we know about science teaching and learning.* Aurora, CO: Midcontinent Research for Education and Learning.

Kuhn, T. S. (1970). *The structure of scientific revolutions.* (1st edition published in 1962). Chicago: University of Chicago Press.

Kwan, T., & Texley, J. (2002). *Exploring safely: A guide for elementary teachers.* National Science Teachers Association.

Lake, K. (2001). Integrated curriculum. *School improvement research series (NWREL).* (http://www.nwrel.org/scpd/sirs/8/c016.html, retrieved October 15, 2007).

Landmark College (2006). *Assistive technology for the classroom.* [Online: http://www.landmarkcollege.org/institute/assistive_technology/index.html]

Langrehr, J. (1993). Getting thinking into science questions. *Australian Science Teacher Journal, 39* (4), 36.

Leahy, S., Lyon, C., Thompson, M., & Wiliam, D. (2005). Classroom assessment: Minute by minute, day by day. *Educational Leadership, 63* (3), 19–24.

Lederman, N. G., & Niess, M. L. (1998). 5 apples + 4 oranges = ? (Editorial). *School Science and Mathematics, 98* (6), 281–284.

Lee, M. H., & Sandra K. Abell, S. K. (2007). Assessing for science learning. *Science and Children, 44* (7), 66–67.

Lee, O., & Paik, S.-H. (2000). Conceptions of science achievement in major reform documents. *School Science and Mathematics, 1* (1), 16–26.

Levin, T., & Long, R. (1981). *Effective instruction.* Washington, DC: Association for Supervision and Curriculum Development.

Levine, D. U., & Ornstein, A. C. (1983). Sex differences in ability and achievement. *Journal of Research and Development in Education, 16* (2), 62–66.

Lind, K. (1999). Science in early childhood: Developing and acquiring fundamental concepts and skills. In AAAS (Ed.), *Dialogue on early childhood science, mathematics, and technology education* (pp. 73–83). Washington, DC: American Association for the Advancement of Science.

Linn, E. (1994). Science and equity: Why it's important. *Mathematics & Science Education, 4,* (1), 1, 4.

Los Angeles Unified School District. (1977). Title IV-D: Effects of teacher expectation on student learning project. In *The Reflector.* Los Angeles: Unified School District Office of Instruction.

Loucks-Horsley, S. (Ed.). (1990). *Elementary school science for the '90s.* Andover, MA: The Network.

Lowery, F. J. (1997). *NSTA pathways to the science standards.* National Science Teachers Association.

Macomber, R. D. (1961). Chemistry accidents in high school. *Journal of Chemical Education, 38* (7), 367–368.

Madrazo, G. M., Jr. (1997, March). Using trade books to teach and learn science. *Science and Children,* 20–21.

Marbach-Ad, G., & Sololove, P. G. (2000, November). Good science begins with good questions: Answering the need for high-level questions in science. *Journal of College Science Teaching, 30* (3), 192–195.

Marek, E. A., & Cavallo, A. M. L. (1997). *The learning cycle: Elementary science and beyond.* Portsmouth, NH: Heinemann.

Martin, R., Wood, G., & Stevens, E. (1988). *An introduction to teaching: A question of commitment.* Boston: Allyn and Bacon.

Martin, R. E. (1984). *The credibility principle and teacher attitudes toward science.* New York: Peter Lang.

Marx, R. W., Blumenfeld, P. C., Krajcik, J. S., & Soloway, E. (1997). Enacting project-based science. *The Elementary School Journal, 97* (4), 341–358.

Matthews, M. R. (1998). In defense of modest goals when teaching about the nature of science. *Journal of Research in Science Teaching, 35* (2), 161–174.

McComas, W. F. & Wang, H.-C. A. (1998). Blended science: The rewards and challenges of integrating the science disciplines for instruction. *School Science and Mathematics.*

McCracken, M. (1986). *Turnabout children.* Boston: Little, Brown.

McDonough, T. (2001). Thematic instruction. On Purpose Associates website. [Online: www.funderstanding.com/thematic_instruction.cfm]

McIntyre, M. (1984). *Early childhood and science.* Washington, DC: National Science Teachers Association.

McKinney, W. J. (1997). *The educational use of computer based science simulations: Some lessons from the philosophy of science.* Boston: Kluwer Academic Publishers.

McLane. K. (1998, Fall). Integrating technology into the standard curriculum: Extending learning opportunities for students with disabilities. *Research Connections in Special Education,* p. 3.

McLeod, R. J. (1979, October). Selecting a textbook for good science teaching. *Science and Children,* 14–15.

Mechling, K. R., & Oliver, D. L. (1983a). *Characteristics of a good elementary science program, handbook III.* Washington, DC: National Science Teachers Association.

———. (1983b). *Science teaches basic skills, handbook 1.* Washington, DC: National Science Teachers Association.

———. (1983c). Activities not textbooks: What research says about science programs. *Principal, 43.*

Meyer, K. (1998). Reflections on being female in school science. *Journal of Research in Science Teaching, 35*(4), 473–474.

Meyer, L. A., Greer, E. A., & Crummey, L. (1986). *Elementary science textbooks: Their contents, text characteristics, and comprehensibility* (Technical Report No. 386). Champaign, IL: University of Illinois. (ERIC Document No. 278947)

Mid-continent Research for Education and Learning. (2001). In what ways can integrating curriculum enhance learning? In A. Krueger & J. Sutton (Eds.). *EDThoughts: What we know about science teaching and learning.* Aurora, CO: Mid-continent Research for Education and Learning, pp. 56–57.

Moreno, N. P. (2007). Teaching the nature of science: Five crucial themes. *NSTA Reports, 18* (5), 9–10.

Morgan, N., & Saxton, J. (1991). *Teaching, questioning & learning.* New York: Routledge.

Morris, C. (2007). *Lev Semyonovich Vygotsky's zone of proximal development.* (updated April 16, 2007) http://www.igs.net/~cmorris/zpd.html retrieved July 6, 2007.

Mullins, I. V. S., & Jenkins, L. B. (1988). *The science report card: Elements of risk and recovery.* Princeton, NJ: Educational Testing Service.

Mullis, I. V. S., Martin, M. O., Beaton, A. E., Gonzalez, E. J., Kelly, D. L., & Smith, T. A. (1997). *Mathematics achievement in the primary school years: IEA's third international mathematics and science study (TIMSS).* Chestnut Hill, MA: Center for the Study of Testing, Evaluation, and Educational Policy, Boston College.

Munson, B. H. (1994). Ecological misconceptions. *Journal of Environmental Education, 24* (4), 30–34.

Murphy, N. (1994). Helping preservice teachers master authentic assessment for the learning cycle model. In L. E. Schafer

(Ed.), *Behind the methods class door: Educating elementary and middle school science teachers.* Columbus, OH: ERIC Clearinghouse for Science, Mathematics and Environmental Education.

National Association of Biology Teachers. (1990). *NABT guidelines for the use of live animals.* Position Statement of NABT, January 1990.

National Center for Education Statistics. (2006). *The nation's report card: Science 2005.* U.S. Department of Education. [Online: http:// nces.ed.gov/pubsearch/pubsinfo .asp?pubid=2006466]

National Center for Educational Statistics. (2003). Homepage for the National Assessment of Educational Progress (NAEP). 2003. [Online: www.nces.ed.gov/nationsreportcard/]

National Center for Educational Statistics. (2006). Highlights from the TIMMS 1999 video study of eighth-grade science teaching. [Online: http://nces.ed.gov/pubsearch.]

National Center for Educational Statistics. (2003). Homepage for the National Assessment of Educational Progress. [Online: http:// www.nces.ed.gov/nationsreportcard]

National Council of Mathematics. (1991). *Principles and standards for school mathematics.* (http://standards.nctm .org/document/appendix/numb.htm, retrieved October 15, 2007).

National Curriculum Council. (1989). *Science: Non-statutory guidance.* London: NCC.

National Education Goals Panel. (1997). *The national education goals report: Summary.* Washington, DC: Author.

National Geographic Society. (2007). *National Geographic Explorer.* [Online: http://magma.nationalgeographic.com /ngexplorer/]

National Park Service. U.S. Department of the Interior. (2007). *LearnNPS.* [Online: http://www.nps.gov/learn/home.htm]

National Research Council (2000). *Inquiry and the National Science Education Standards: A guide for teaching and learning.* Washington, DC: National Academy Press.

National Research Council. (1992). *National Science Education Standards: A sampler.* Washington, DC: Author.

———. (1996) *National Science Education Standards.* Washington, DC: National Academy Press.

———. (1997). *Every child a scientist: Achieving scientific literacy for all.* Washington, DC: National Academy Press.

National Science Board Commission on Precollege Education in Mathematics, Science, and Technology. (1983). *A revised and intensified science and technology curriculum for grades K–12 is urgently needed for our future.* (ERIC Document No. 239 847)

National Science Teachers Association. (1982). *Science-technology-society: Science education for the 1980's: Position statement.* Washington, DC: Author.

———. (1983). *Conditions for good science teaching in secondary schools.* Washington, DC: Author.

———. (1993). *Position Statement on Laboratory Science.* Arlington, VA: National Science Teachers Association.

———. (2000, July). *NSTA position statement: Multicultural science education.* Washington, DC: Author. (www.nsta.org /159&psid=21, retrieved August 2, 2003).

———. *NSTA Handbook, 1996–97.* Arlington, VA: Author.

NationMaster. (2007). *Education statistics: Scientific literacy by county.* [Online: http://www.nationmaster.com/graph /edu_sci_lit-education-scientific-literacy]. (retrieved July 29, 2007)

NCREL: North Central Regional Educational Laboratory. (2003). *Thematic or integrated instruction.* September 17, 2003, [Online: www.ncrel.org/areas/issues/students/atrisk /at71k12.htm]. All rights reserved. Reprinted with permission.

Nickerson, R. S. (1995). Can technology help teach for understanding? In D. N. Perkins, J. L. Schwartz, M. M. West, & M. S. Wiske (Eds.), *Software goes to school—teaching for understanding new technologies.* New York: Oxford University Press.

Niguidula, D. (2005). Documenting learning with digital portfolios. *Educational Leadership, 63* (3), 44–47.

North Carolina Museum of Life and Science. (1992). Science in the classroom. In Triangle Coalition for Science and Technology Education, *A guide for planning a volunteer program for science, mathematics, and technology education* (p. 59). College Park, MD: Triangle Coalition.

North Central Regional Education Laboratory. (2005). *Critical issue: Technology: A catalyst for teaching and learning in the classroom.* [Online: http://www.ncrel.org/sdrs/areas/issues /methods/technlgy/te600.htm]

Novak, J. D. (1979). *A theory of education.* Ithaca, NY: Cornell University Press.

———. (1991, October). Clarify with concept maps. *Science Teacher, 45.*

Novak, J. D. (1990). Concept mapping: A useful tool for science education. *Journal of Research in Science Teaching, 27* (10), 937–949

Novak, J., & Gowin, D. B. (1986). *Learning how to learn.* New York: Cambridge University Press.

NWREL: Northwest Regional Education Laboratory. *Integrated curriculum* by K. Lake. November 3, 2003. [Online: www.nwrel.org/scpd/sirs/8/col6.html]

O'Brien, G. E., & Lewis, S. P. (1999). Connecting to resources on the internet. *Science and Children, 36* (8), 42–45.

O'Sullivan, C. Y., Reese, C. M., & Mazzeo, J. (1997). *NAEP 1996 science report card for the nation and the states.* Washington, DC: National Center for Education Statistics.

Occupational Safety and Health Administration. (1991). *Rules and Regulations* (FR Doc. 91-288886). (*Federal Register* 569235).

Osborne, R., & Freyberg, P. (1990). *Learning in science: The implications of children's science.* In S. Loucks-Horsley (Ed.), *Elementary school science for the '90s* (p. 49). Andover, MA: The Network.

Oskamp, S. (1977). *Attitudes and opinions.* Englewood Cliffs, NJ: Prentice-Hall.

Ostlund, K. L. (1992, March). Sizing up social skills. *Science Scope,* 31–33.

Padilla, M., Muth, D., & Lund Padilla, R. (1991). Science and reading: Many process skills in common. In C. M. Santa & D. E. Alvermann (Eds.), *Science learning: Processes and applications* (pp. 14–19). Newark, DE: International Reading Association.

Pearlman, S., & Pericak-Spector, K. (1992, October). Expect the unexpected question. *Science and Children,* 36–37.

Pert, C. (1997). *Molecules of emotion.* New York: Charles Scribner's Sons.

Peterson, P., & Knapp, P. (1993). Inventing and reinventing ideas: Constructivist teaching and learning in mathematics. In G. Cawletti (Ed.), *Challenges and achievements of American education.* Alexandria, VA: Association for Supervision and Curriculum Development.

Petty, R. E., & Cacioppa, J. T. (1981). *Attitudes and persuasion: Classic and contemporary approaches.* Dubuque, IA: William C. Brown.

Philips, W. C. (1991). Earth science misconceptions. *Science Teacher, 58* (2), 21–23.

Piaget, J. (1954). *The construction of reality in the child.* New York: Basic Books.

Piburn, M., & Enyeart, M. (1985). *A comparison of the reasoning ability of gifted and mainstreamed science students.* (ERIC Document No. 255 379)

Pollina, A. (1995). Gender balance: Lessons from girls in science and mathematics. *Educational Leadership, 53* (1), 30–33.

Prather, J. P. (1991, April). *Speculative philosophical analysis of priorities for research in science education.* Research report presented at the 64th Annual Meeting of the National Association for Research in Science Teaching, Fontana, WI.

Price, S., & Hein, G. E. (1994, October). Scoring active assessments. *Science and Children,* pp. 26–29.

Project 2061. *Science for all Americans online.* Chapter 1: The nature of science. [Online: http://www.project2061.org /publications/sfaa/online/chap1.htm]

Project Learning Tree. (2006). *The national project learning tree educational guides.* 1111 19th St., NW Suite 780, Washington, DC., 20036. American Forest Foundation.

Project Learning Tree. (1993). *Pollution search: PreK–8 activity guide* Washington, D.C.: American Forest Foundation.

Project Technology Engineering Application of Mathematics and Science. (1992). Tips for teachers working with volunteers. In *Triangle Coalition for Science and Technology Education: A guide for planning a volunteer program for science, mathematics, and technology education.* College Park, MD: Triangle Coalition.

Puckett-Cliatt, M J., & Shaw, J. M. (1985, November–December). Open questions, open answers. *Science and Children,* 14–16.

Raizen, S. A., & Kaser, J. S. (1989, May). Assessing science learning in elementary school: Why, what and how? *Phi Delta Kappan,* 718–722.

Rakow, S. J. (1986). *Teaching science as inquiry.* Bloomington, IN: Phi Delta Kappa.

———. (1989, November–December). Safety supplement. *Science Scope.*

———. (1989). You spoke and we listened. *Science Scope 13* (3), S3.

Raloff, J. (2001). Errant texts: Why some schools may not want to go by the book. *Science News, 159* (11). [Online: www .project2061.org/research/articles/scinews.htm]

Reichel, A. G. (1994). Performance assessment: Five practical approaches. *Science and Children, 32* (2), 21–25.

Reichert, B. (1989, November–December). What did he say? Science in the multilingual classroom. *Science Scope,* 10–11.

Renner, J. W., & Marek, E. A. (1988). *The learning cycle and elementary school science teaching.* Portsmouth, NH: Heinemann.

Rennie, L., & Parker, L. (1986). *A comparison of mixed-sex and single-sex grouping in year 5 science lessons.* Paper presented at the Annual Meeting of the American Educational Research Association, San Francisco. (ERIC Document No. ED 273 443)

Rice, D. C. (2002, March). Using trade books in teaching elementary science: Facts and fallacies. *The Reading Teacher, 55* (6), 552–563.

Rice, J. R. (1983, January). A special science fair: LD children learn what they can do. *Science and Children,* 15–16.

Riley, J. P. (1986). The effects of teachers wait-time and knowledge comprehension questioning on science achievement. *Journal of Research in Science Teaching, 23* (4), 335–342.

Risner, G. P. (1987). *Cognitive levels of questioning demonstrated by test items that accompany selected fifth-grade science textbooks.* (ERIC Document No. 291752)

Risner, G. P., Skeel, D. J., & Nicholson, J. L. (1992, September). A closer look at textbooks. *Science and Children,* 42–45, 73.

Roberts, R. M. (1989). *Serendipity: Accidental discoveries in science.* New York: Wiley.

Rodriguez, I., & Bethel, L. J. (1983). An inquiry approach to science and language teaching. *Journal of Research in Science Teaching, 20* (4), 291–296.

Rogers, D. L., Martin, R. E., Jr., & Kousaleos, S. (1988). Encouraging science through playful discovery. *Day Care and Early Education, 16* (1), 21.

Rop, C. (1998, December–January). Breaking the gender barrier in the physical sciences. *Educational Leadership, 55,* 58–60.

Rosenshine, B. (1976). Classroom instruction. In W. L. Gage (Ed.), *The psychology of teaching methods.* Chicago: University of Chicago Press.

———. (1979). Content, time, and direct instruction. In P. L. Peterson & H. C. Walberg (Eds.), *Research on teaching: Concepts, findings, and implications.* Berkeley, CA: McCutcheon.

Ross, M. E. (1997). Scientists at play. *Science and Children, 34* (8), 35–38.

Rothkopf, E. Z. (1972). Variable adjunct question schedules, interperson interaction, and incidental learning from written material. *Journal of Educational Psychology, 63,* 87–92.

Rowe, M. B. (1970). Wait-time and rewards as instructional variables: Influence on inquiry and sense of fate control. *New Science in the Inner City.* New York: Teachers College, Columbia University.

———. (1973). *Teaching science as continuous inquiry.* New York: McGraw-Hill.

———. (1974). Wait-time and rewards as instructional variables, their influence on language, logic, and fate control: Part I—Wait time. *Journal of Research in Science Teaching, 13* (2), 81–94; Part II—Rewards. *Journal of Research in Science Teaching, 13* (4), 291–308.

Rutherford, F. J., & Ahlgren, A. (1988). Rethinking the science curriculum. In R. S. Brandt (Ed.), *Content of the curriculum.* Alexandria, VA: Association for Supervision and Curriculum Development.

———. (1990). *Science for all Americans.* New York: Oxford University Press.

Ryan, J, Esq. (2001). *Science classroom safety and the law: A handbook for teachers.* Batavia, IL: Flinn Scientific, Inc.

Sabar, N. (1979). Science, curriculum, and society: Trends in science curriculum. *Science Education, 63* (2), 257–269.

Sadker, D., & Silber, E. S. (Eds.) (2007). *Gender in the classroom: Foundations, skills, methods, and strategies across the curriculum.* Mahwah, NJ: Lawrence Erlbaum Associates.

Sadker, D., Sadker, M., & Thomas, D. (1981). Sex equity and special education. *Pointer, 26* (1), 33.

Sargent-Welch Scientific Co. (2006). *Equipment catalogue.* Skokie, IL: Author.

Schlichter, C. L. (1983, February). The answer is in the question. *Science and Children,* 10.

Schrock, K. (2007). *Kathy Schrock's guide for educators: Critical evaluation information.* [Online: http://school.discovery.com/schrockguide/eval.html]

Schwartz, J. L. (1985). *Sir Isaac Newton's Games* [Educational software]. Pleasantville, NY: Sunburst Communications.

———. (1995). Shuttling between the particular and the general: Reflections on the role of conjecture and hypothesis in the generation of knowledge in science and mathematics. In D. N. Perkins, J. L. Schwartz, M. M. West, & M. S. Wiske (Eds.), *Software goes to school: Teaching for understanding new technologies* (pp. 7–22). New York: Oxford University Press.

Scruggs, T. E., & Mastropieri, M. A. (2007). Science learning in special education: The case for constructed versus instructed learning. *Exceptionality, 15* (2), 57–74.

Scruggs, T. E., Mastropieri, M. A., Bakken, J. P., & Grigham, F. J. (1993). Reading versus doing: The relative effects of textbook-based and inquiry-oriented approaches to science learning in special education classrooms. *The Journal of Special Education, 27* (1), 1–15.

Sexton, C. M. (2006). Using technology in science teaching: How technology can help with analysis and synthesis of data. Keynote at the 6th International Educational Technology Conference held in Famagusta, Cyprus, May 2006.

Shakeshaft, C. (1995). Reforming science education. *Theory Into Practice 34* (1), 74–79.

Shapiro, B. (1994). *What children bring to light: A constructivist perspective on children's learning in science.* New York: Teachers College Press.

Shavelson, R. J., & Baxter, G. P. (1992, May). What we've learned about assessing hands-on science. *Educational Leadership,* 20–25.

Shaw, K. L., & Etchberger, M. L. (1993). Transitioning into constructivism: A vignette of a fifth grade teacher. In K. Tobin (Ed.), *The practice of constructivism in science education* (pp. 259–266). Washington, DC: AAAS Press.

Shaw, K. L., & Jakubowski, E. H. (1991). Teachers changing for changing times. *Focus on Learning Problems in Mathematics, 13* (4), 13–20.

Shepardson, D. P., & Pizzini, E. L. (1991, November). Questioning levels of junior high school science textbooks and their implications for learning textual information. *Science Education, 5* (6), 673–682.

———. (1992). Gender bias in female elementary teachers' perceptions of the scientific ability of students. *Science Education, 76* (2), 147–153.

Shrigley, R. L. (1987, May). Discrepant events: Why they fascinate students. *Science and Children,* 25.

Shymansky, J. A., Hedges, L., & Woodworth, G. (1990). A reassessment of the effects of inquiry-based science curricula of the 60's on student performance. *Journal of Research on Science Teaching, 27* (2), 127–144.

Shymansky, J. A., Kyle, W. C., Jr., & Allport, J. M. (1982, November–December). How effective were the hands-on programs of yesterday? *Science and Children,* 14–15.

Silver, H., Strong, R., & Perini, M. (1997). Integrating learning styles and multiple intelligences. *Educational Leadership, 55* (1), 22–27.

Sinclair, L., Gerlovich, J., & Parsa, R. (2003). South Carolina statewide science safety project. *Journal of the South Carolina Academy of Science, 1* (1); 19–27.

Slavin, R. L. (1995). *Cooperative learning.* Boston: Allyn and Bacon.

Smith, D. D., & Luckasson, R. (1992). *Introduction to special education.* Boston: Allyn and Bacon.

Smith, P. G. (1995, September). Reveling in rubrics. *Science Scope,* 34–36.

Snow, R. E., Corno, L., & Jackson, D. (1996). Individual differences in affective and cognitive functions. In D. C. Berlinger & R. C. Calfee (Eds.), *Handbook of Educational Psychology* (pp. 243–310). New York: Macmillan.

Solomon, J. (1997, September–October). Is how we teach science more important than what we teach? *Primary Science Review, 49,* 3–5.

Sousa, D. A. (1996). Are we teaching high school science backward? *National Association of Secondary School Principals' Bulletin, 80* (522), 9–15.

Spady, W. G. (1994). Choosing outcomes of significance. *Educational Leadership, 51* (6), 18–22.

Sprenger, M. (1999). *Learning and memory: The brain in action.* Alexandria, VA: Association for Supervision and Curriculum Development.

Stallings, C., Gerlovich, J., & Parsa, R. (2001). Science safety: A status report in North Carolina schools. *The Science Reflector, 30* (3), 11–12, 17.

Starr, M. L., & Krajcik, J. S. (1990). Concept maps as a heuristic for science curriculum development: Toward improvement in process and product. *Journal of Research in Science Teaching, 27* (10), 987–1000.

State of Iowa. (1988). *School code of Iowa.* Des Moines, IA: Author.

Staver, J. R., & Bay, M. (1987). Analysis of the project synthesis goal cluster orientation and inquiry emphasis of elementary science textbooks. *Journal of Research in Science Teaching, 23* (7), 629–643.

Stefanich, G. P. (1985). *Addressing orthopedic handicaps in the science classroom.* (Educational Resource Document No. 258 802)

Stern, L., & Roseman, J. E. (2001, October). Textbook alignment. *The Science Teacher,* 52–56.

Stone, C. L. (1982). *A meta-analysis of advance-organizer studies.* Paper presented at the Annual Meeting of the American Educational Research Association, New York. (ERIC Document No. 220476)

Styer, S. (1984, March). Books that ask the right questions. *Science and Children,* 40–42.

Suchman, J. R. (1962). *The elementary school training program in scientific inquiry.* Report to the U.S. Office of Education, Project Title VII. Urbana: University of Illinois.

———. (1971). Motivation inherent in the pursuit of meaning: Or the desire to inquire. In H. I. Day, D. E. Berlyne, & D. E. Hunt (Eds.), *Intrinsic motivation: A new direction in education.* Toronto: Holt, Rinehart, & Winston.

Sumrall, W. J. (1995). Reasons for the perceived images of scientists by race and gender of students in grades 1–7. *School Science and Mathematics, 95* (2), 83–90.

Taba, H., Levine, S., & Elsey, F. F. (1964). *Thinking in elementary school children* (U.S. Office of Education Cooperative Research Project No. 1574). San Francisco: San Francisco State College.

Technology-related assistance for individuals with disabilities Act of 1988 (P.L. 100–407). (November 13, 1988). U.S. Government Documents (http://www.resna.org/taproject /library/laws/ata98sum.html, retrieved November 11, 2007).

Tinker, R. ProbeSight: What are probes? *The Concord Consortium.* September 14, 2003. [Online: http://probesight .concord.org/what/body_index.htm]

Tobin, K. (1984). Effects of extended wait-time on discourse characteristics and achievement in middle school grades. *Journal of Research in Science Teaching, 21* (8), 779–791.

Tobin, K. G., & Capie, W. (1982). *Wait-time and learning in science. AETS Outstanding Paper for 1981.* (ERIC Document No. ED 221353)

Tobin, K., Tippins, D. J., & Gallard, A. J. (1994). Research on instructional strategies for teaching science. In D. L. Gabel (Ed.), *Handbook on research on science teaching.* New York: Macmillan.

Tom Snyder Productions. (2005a). *Rainforest researchers.* (http://www .tomsnyder.com/products/product.asp?SKU =RAIRAI&Subject= Science), retrieved September 10, 2007).

Tom Snyder Productions. (2005b). *The great ocean rescue.* (http:// www.tomsnyder.com/products/product.asp?SKU =GREOCD& Subject=Science, retrieved October 1, 2007).

Treagust, D. F., Jacobowitz, R., Gallagher, J. J., and Parker, J. (2003, March). Embedded assessment in your teaching. *Science Scope,* 36–39.

Triangle Coalition for Science and Technology Education. (1991). *A guide for building an alliance for science, mathematics and technology education.* College Park, MD: Author.

———. (1992). *A guide for planning a volunteer program for science, mathematics and technology education.* College Park, MD: Author.

U.S. Department of Education. (2002). *Twenty-fourth annual report to Congress on the implementation of the individuals with disabilities education act.* Washington, DC: U.S. Government Printing Office.

U.S. Department of Labor, Occupational Safety and Health Administration. (1990). 29 CFR Part 1910, Occupational Exposures to Hazardous Chemicals in Laboratories. *Federal Register.* Washington, DC: U.S. Government Printing Office.

———. (1991). 29 CFR Part 1910.1030, Occupational exposure to bloodborne pathogens; Subpart Z, bloodborne pathogens: Standard summary applicable to schools. *Federal Register.* Washington, DC: U.S. Government Printing Office.

U.S. Office of Education. (1977, December 29). Education of handicapped children: Assistance to the states: Procedures for evaluating specific learning disabilities. *Federal Register, Part III.* Washington, DC: U.S. Government Printing Office.

Vadero, D. (2007). Collecting evidence. *Technology Counts: A Digital Decade, 26* (30), 30, 32–33.

Valdez, P. (2007). Students learn best by teaching. *Science Scope, 30* (7), 70–73.

Valentino, C. (1985). *Question of the week.* Palo Alto, CA: Dale Seymore Publications.

Van Horn, J., Nourot, P. M., Scales, B., Alward, K. R. (1993). *Play at the center of the curriculum.* Columbus, OH: Merrill.

Van Tassell, M. A. (2001) Student inquiry in science: Asking questions, building foundations and making connections. In G. Wells (Ed.). *Action, talk & text: Learning and teaching through inquiry.* New York: Teachers College Press.

van Zee, E. H., Kurose, A., Simpson, D., & Wild, J. (2001). Student and teacher questioning during conversations about science. *Journal of Research in Science Teaching, 38* (2), 159–190.

Victor, E. (1985). *Science for the elementary school.* New York: Macmillan.

Vogt, M. E. (1995). *Cross curricular thematic instruction,* [Online: www.eduplace.com/rdg/res/vogt.html]

Von Glaserfeld, E. (1993). Questions and answers about radical constructivism. In K. Tobin (Ed.), *The practice of constructivism in science education* (pp. 23–38). Washington, DC: AAAS Press.

Vygotsky, L. S. (1978). *Mind and society: The development of higher mental processes.* Cambridge, MA: Harvard University Press.

Wadsworth, B. J. (1996). *Piaget's theory of cognitive and affective development.* White Plains, NY: Longman Publishers.

Wagner, K. (1998). Unpublished report. Columbus, OH: Ohio Department of Education.

Watson, S. B. (1992, February). Cooperative methods. *Science and Children,* 30–31.

Weinburgh, M. (1995). Gender differences in student attitudes toward science: A meta-analysis of the literature from 1970 to 1991. *Journal of Research in Science Teaching, 32* (4), 387–398.

Weiss, I. R., Pasley, J. D., Smith, P. S., Banilower, E. R., & Heck, D. J. (2003). *Looking inside the classroom: A study of K–12 mathematics and science education in the United States.* Chapel Hill, NC: Horizon Research.

West, S. S., Westerlund, J. F., Nelson, N. C., & Stephenson, A. L. (2001). *Conditions that affect safety in the science classroom: Results from a statewide safety survey.* Austin, TX: Texas Association of Curriculum Development.

West, S. S., Westerlund, J. F., Stephenson, A. L., & Nelson, N. C. (2002). *Conditions that affect secondary science safety: Results from 2001 Texas survey.* Austin, TX: Texas Education Agency. Available at http://bluebonnet.bio.swt.edu.

Western Regional Environmental Education Council. (1992). *Project WILD and Aquatic Project WILD.* Golden, CO: Author.

———. (1994). *Project Learning Tree.* Golden, CO: Author

———. (1995). *Project WET.* Golden, CO: Author.

Wheeler, G., & Sherman, T. F. (1983). Readability formulas revisited. *Science and Children, 20* (7), 38–40.

Wilen, W. (1986). *Questioning skills for teachers.* Washington, DC: National Education Association.

Willert, M. K., & Kamii, C. (1985, May). Reading in kindergarten: Direct vs. indirect teaching. *Young Children, 3.*

Williams, C. K., & Kamii, C. (1986, November). How do children learn by handling objects? *Young Children, 26.*

Williams, I. W. (1984). Chemistry. In A. Craft & G. Bardell (Eds.), *Curriculum opportunities in a multicultural society* (pp. 133–146). New York: Harper & Row.

Williams-Norton, M., Reisdorf, M., & Spees, S. (1990, March). Home is where the science is. *Science and Children,* 13–15.

Willis, S. (1995a, Summer). Reinventing science education. *Curriculum Update.* Alexandria, VA: ASCD.

———. (1995b, Summer). Reinventing science education: Reformers promote hands-on, inquiry-based learning. *Curriculum Update.* Alexandria, VA: ASCD.

Wilson, L. D., & Blank, R. K. (1999). *Improving mathematics education using results from NAEP and TIMSS.* Washington, DC: Council of Chief State School Officers.

Windram, M. P. (1988, March). Getting at reading through science inquiries. *Roeper Review,* 150–152.

Wiser, M. (1995). Use of history of science to understand and remedy students' misconceptions about heat and temperature. In D. N. Perkins, J. L. Schwartz, M. M. West, & M. S. Wiske (Eds.), *Software goes to school—teaching for understanding new technologies* (pp. 23–28). New York: Oxford University Press.

Wolfe, P., & Brandt, R. (1998). What do we know from brain research? *Educational Leadership, 56* (3), 8–13.

Wolfinger, D. M. (1984). *Teaching science in the elementary school.* Boston: Little, Brown.

Wright, D. (1980). A report on the implications for the science community of three NSF-supported studies of the state of precollege science education. In H. A. Smith (Ed.), *What are the needs in precollege science, mathematics, and social science education? Views from the field.* Washington, DC: National Science Foundation.

Yager, R. (1991, September). The constructivist learning model. *Science Teacher,* 52–57.

Yager, R. E. (1984). The major crisis in science education. *School Science and Mathematics, 84* (3), 196.

Yager, R. E., & Penick, J. E. (1987, October). New concerns for affective outcomes in science. *Educational Leadership,* 93.

Young, J. S. (1970). A survey of safety in high school chemistry laboratories in Illinois. *Journal of Chemical Education 47* (12), A828–838.

Zimmerman, B. J., & Pike, E. O. (1972). Effects of modeling and reinforcement on the acquisition and generalization of question-asking behavior. *Child Development, 43,* 892–907.

index